THE LETTERS AND FRIENDSHIPS OF
SIR CECIL SPRING RICE

Works by Sir Cecil Spring Rice

THE STORY OF VALEH AND HADIJEH
Translated from the Persian by MIRZA MAHOMED
and C. SPRING RICE.
(*Duckworth*, 1903. 4°)

SONGS FROM THE BOOK OF JAFFIR

POEMS

CECIL SPRING RICE.   *Aged 35*

Photo: M. B. Brady, Washington, U.S.A.

THE LETTERS
AND FRIENDSHIPS

of

SIR CECIL SPRING RICE

A RECORD

Edited by
STEPHEN GWYNN

VOLUME I

LONDON
CONSTABLE & CO LTD
1929

PUBLISHED BY

Constable & Company Limited
London W.C. 2

·

BOMBAY
CALCUTTA   MADRAS
LEIPZIG

Oxford University
Press

·

TORONTO

The Macmillan Company
of Canada, Limited

PRINTED IN GREAT BRITAIN BY ROBERT MACLEHOSE AND CO. LTD.
THE UNIVERSITY PRESS, GLASGOW.

PREFATORY

No attempt has been made to collect exhaustively the letters written by Sir Cecil Spring Rice to his acquaintances and friends. The materials available were too ample.

There were, first, in print, the little Memoir of him written by Sir Valentine Chirol and published by Murray in 1919, and Mr. Bernard Holland's preface to the volume of Spring Rice's Poems collected by him and published by Longmans in 1920. Next, in manuscript, there was the huge mass of correspondence, private and official, addressed to him, of which he had preserved a surprising amount. There were the copies of many of his official dispatches which he had retained—especially after he took to the use of a typewriter.

But in the main this book has been built up about a few correspondences maintained over a long period. For the first half of his life the letters to his own family were the main source, supplemented by those to his Eton tutor, Mr. Luxmoore. This source, however copious, fails after the death of his elder brother, Stephen, in 1902, and virtually dries up after his own marriage, in 1905.

The most continuous series of letters is that to Ronald Munro Ferguson, now Lord Novar, which begins in 1886 and lasts till his death. Many letters to Lady Novar are included in this heading. Next comes that to Sir Valentine Chirol, which began in 1895, and also continued to the end. Out of either of these latter groups a complete history of Spring Rice's life for the period covered could be constructed.

Then there are the letters to his American friends, of whom Roosevelt was the earliest of all and the most important ; but the correspondence with Senator and Mrs. Lodge is spread over the years from 1887 onwards. So, but much more intermittently, is that with Henry Adams. To these could have been added the long series addressed to Mrs. Cameron, but her papers have been deposited in an American library. On the other hand, though no worthy portrait of Mrs. Lodge is available, Helleu's sketch preserves for readers the image of one of the American hostesses to whom Spring Rice gave so much affection in return for so much kindness and good comradeship.

In selecting from the letters addressed to him it has been necessary to consider space. But those from Roosevelt throw so much light on the nature and beliefs and interests of the man whom Spring Rice thought probably the foremost of his time that a considerable proportion of these have been included. A number of short letters from Lord Grey of Fallodon are also printed to illustrate the relations between Spring Rice and the chief whom he valued most.

Thanks are due to all who have allowed the use of letters— above all to Mrs. Roosevelt, and very greatly also to the representatives of Henry Adams.

Lord Novar and Sir Valentine Chirol have gone far beyond permitting the use of letters : they have been at pains to help in all ways. Without seeking to render them in any degree responsible, it may be said that the work owes much to their constant encouragement ; and even more to the revising eye of a friend who prefers to be unnamed.

Indeed the editor has throughout experienced more courtesy and kindness than can be acknowledged ; but he has accepted it as proof of how many admire and love the memory of the man whose personality these letters preserve.

CONTENTS

LIST OF ILLUSTRATIONS

VOLUME ONE

CHAPTER I

FROM SCHOOL TO THE FOREIGN OFFICE

THIS book must open with something which may seem more proper for a preface, yet cannot easily be detached from the main narrative. Sir Cecil Spring Rice, whose Life and Letters are here brought before the public, had spent thirty years in the service of the British Foreign Office when he found himself promoted to the post which he had always desired and for which his career had specially fitted him. Yet neither he nor anyone else foresaw the full scope of his charge. As British Ambassador at Washington during the Great War he held the most important embassy of which there is record, with one exception. Count Bernstorff, pitted against him on behalf of Germany, played the opposing hand in that momentous game.

With such stakes on the board, and they mounted constantly as the struggle continued, neither of the players could escape a fury of criticism. Certainly Sir Cecil Spring Rice did not, and the matters in dispute must be considered later. But one matter is not in dispute. Count Bernstorff did not win. When America came into the war on the side of the Allies, the British Ambassador's diplomatic mission was accomplished.

Doubtless—indeed there is positive evidence of the fact—if he had lived longer his services would have been honourably recognised ; but as it fell out, after his object had been attained, he was relieved of his post with some abruptness and lack of consideration ; and having spent the last ounce of his strength during those years of strain, he died suddenly before any action could be taken to mitigate an apparent slight. All this made it the more desirable that the story of his work should be fully set out, and the man most fit to perform this duty was willing to undertake it namely, his friend Sir Valentine Chirol. But when the project was proposed, essential documents were still withheld by authority. Time went on, other persons concerned in those high transactions gave their account of what had passed, and the British Ambassador's name was not spared : so, in fairness to his memory, leave was given to publish at last his version of the events. But unhappily time had not stood still with Sir Valentine Chirol who no longer felt equal to such a labour as was involved, and it was entrusted to me—partly because I was in some far-out degree Cecil Spring Rice's kinsman, though we never met.

This matters the less because Spring Rice, like all born letter-writers, revealed himself fully in his letters. Not even Sir Valentine Chirol could add much by any characterisation to what is already so fully displayed.

But it is a serious undertaking for an amateur to handle the correspondence of an expert ; and only this consoles me, that my very ignorance of diplomatic history may be of some assistance : for in selecting from Spring Rice's huge mass of correspondence I have chosen those letters which expounded international politics in simple language—an art in which he excelled. And, recalling how he touched the diplomatic world at critical and widely scattered centres, it seems to me possible that this book may serve for a survey of diplomatic history through thirty momentous years, seen through the eyes of one most skilled observer.

What those years brought to pass comes briefly to this : the overthrow of the balance of power which had been precariously maintained for more than a century in Europe, and the establishment of a new equilibrium over a far wider area of the earth's inhabited surface. Yet at the opening of 1887, when Spring Rice began his first term of foreign service at Washington, who could have guessed that the overthrow of Russia's predominance in Europe would come from Japan ? or that Germany's amazing effort to acquire an even greater ascendancy would be finally defeated by America's intervention ?

When Spring Rice first knew the United States, it was a power without either army or navy and had never attempted to exercise influence beyond the bounds of its own continent : when he first knew Japan, few believed that the European weapons which this Oriental power had adopted would enable her to cope even with China. When he took up his first post in Europe, at Berlin in 1895, he was thought fantastic for believing that Germany's new naval programme pointed to a serious challenge of England on the seas.

In so far as any shaping of this book has been technically possible, its first object has been to trace a career in which a character reveals itself. Yet perhaps readers will find behind this a deeper unity in the slow setting of the stage for a foreseen tragedy—in the gradual mustering of forces for a struggle, of whose imminence Sir Cecil Spring Rice preached like one crying in the wilderness, until at last, the storm burst, and he had no longer to prophesy but must strain every fibre to a supreme effort of resistance.

That was no hour for charm ; yet it is curious to speculate what it was worth to England at that grim juncture that her Ambassador, thirty years before, as a young attaché, should by his social qualities have won close friendship among the best Americans—for some of whom England was still the traditional enemy ; and indeed should have so linked himself up, and been linked, with them that he counted as a fully accepted member of the most brilliant group in American society.

The title which has been given to this book is justified by the fact that Cecil Spring Rice had a genius for friendships. Very few men have maintained intimacies formed at varying stages in life so long and so affectionately across long separations. It was characteristic of him that his friendships were not only with men and women but with households : when he gave his affection it covered the whole life of a home. That was nowhere truer than in the case of the most notable of all his attachments. But when a chance companionship of travel made Spring Rice and Theodore Roosevelt friends, it meant more than his admission to the intimacy of a remarkable group. It meant that the ablest and most powerful American of his generation could henceforth call to his aid for any common purpose one of the best brains in the British diplomatic service : it meant also that the two men worked together, in an association, loose and voluntary yet profoundly sympathetic, for a common ideal—the preservation in vigour and prosperity of the English-speaking peoples throughout the world. These pages trace the life of a British civil servant who loved his own country with passion, yet who was almost as much at home among the best Americans as with his own people. In the last year that he had to live, he saw the younger nation take her place beside the elder in a world war ; it was the end for which he had striven and he rejoiced in it. How far he had helped to accomplish it must be considered later ; but beyond dispute he had been, increasingly through his career, a link between the two branches of the English-speaking race. Perhaps this was the more possible because he was not in the strictly limited sense an Englishman. He had the special pliancy and adaptability which has enabled many notable Irishmen to be easily at home outside the boundaries within which they were brought up.

Genealogy makes a dull prelude : but some men, and Sir Cecil Spring Rice was one of them, cannot be understood without knowledge of their parentage and upbringing.

His forbears, coming from Wales to Ireland in early Tudor times and changing their name Rhys into Rice, acquired land in Kerry, where the conquering Norman had blended very closely with the Gael. Also, like many others of the " old English," to use a term that was current in Stuart times, they adhered to the old religion. Such families, after years of tribulation under Cromwell, had their months of triumph under James II., and Sir Stephen Rice rose then to be Chief Baron of the Irish Exchequer. Then came the Boyne, and Protestant ascendancy. Sir Stephen was one of the more fortunate Catholics whose property was saved from confiscation by the Treaty of Limerick, and he was able to withdraw to it and end his days peaceably if obscurely. In the eighteenth century his successors saved their position by a change of creed and became a part of the Protestant landed gentry who owned and ruled Ireland. One of them married Mary Fitzgerald, daughter to the fourteenth Knight of Kerry, of the oldest Norman blood in Ireland : and since Fitzgeralds had intermarried not only with Butlers of Ormond but with O'Briens of Thomond, half the houses, native and foreign, that had borne rule in Munster were mixed in this strain. The son of this marriage, Stephen Edward Rice, married Alice Spring, whose family owned land on the border of Kerry and Limerick ; and the name was now changed to Spring Rice.[1] Their son, Thomas Spring Rice, entered political life as Member for Limerick, rose to ministerial rank and finally became Chancellor of the Exchequer in Lord Melbourne's administration from 1835-9. After this he retired upon a peerage of the United Kingdom as Lord Monteagle of Brandon, with a permanent post as Comptroller of the Exchequer. Three of his sons entered the English Civil Service. The eldest became Deputy Chairman of the Board of Customs, another was Registrar of the Court of Bankruptcy ; the second, Charles Spring Rice, entered the Foreign Office and had risen to be Assistant Under-Secretary when premature death closed his career. He left eight children, of whom Cecil Spring Rice was the third child and the second son.

The particular Irish landlord stock from which Cecil Spring Rice came bred by no means the traditional hardriding, fox-hunting, convivial country gentry, whose sons have constantly distinguished themselves in war and not seldom in administration. The Spring Rices were able methodical people, diligent officials, with a high sense of duty ; and their tastes were for the more cultured pleasures. In counting what Ireland meant to Cecil Spring Rice, one must reckon his association with a group of high literary distinction. The de Veres, of whom Aubrey de Vere is the best known, though his father and brother, the elder and the younger Sir Stephen de Vere, had perhaps more poetic talent than he, were kinsfolk and neighbours of the Spring Rices in County Limerick. The first Lord Monteagle's daughter (Cecil Spring Rice's aunt) married Sir Henry Taylor, whose repute as a poet stood very high in the last century : and Cecil Spring Rice grew up acquainted with him as well as with Aubrey de Vere. These were links with the past—friends and followers of Wordsworth, contemporaries and friends of Tennyson. His first cousin, the second Lord Monteagle, only some ten years his senior, married Miss Elizabeth Butcher, daughter of the Bishop of Meath. Professor Henry Butcher (Andrew Lang's collaborator), his brother " J. G." now Lord Danesfort, and their group of sisters, whose names will sparkle through all social memoirs of the 'eighties and 'nineties, were thus brought into the kin or clan.

Yet in so far as Cecil Spring Rice knew these people, he knew them out of Ireland. Ireland was in his blood : but Ireland counted for very little in his upbringing. It was never his home. Charles Spring Rice, a Civil Servant with his work in London, died in 1870 when Cecil Spring Rice was only eleven years old. The young family were left to grow up under the care of their mother.

She was by birth Elizabeth Marshall, daughter of William Marshall, M.P., owner of Hallsteads and Patterdale, on Ullswater—and also of Old Church, a smaller house near Hallsteads. The Marshalls, York-

---

[1] It is spoken as two syllables of one word with accent on the second.

shire manufacturers, had retired from their business and settled down
all over the Lake country, and Old Church and Patterdale and Hallsteads were home to Cecil Spring Rice and to all his brothers and
sisters.   Ullswater was the background to which his thought always
reverted.   He was a great lover of beautiful nature and studied it in
an experience that ranged all round the world : but tarn and beck
and fell and trees waving over lake water are never out of his mind,
even if he is describing Persia or Japan.

Also in the Lake Country there were associations, marked as nowhere else in the world, between the beauty made with words and the
beauty of nature.   Wordsworth was only a few years dead when
Cecil Spring Rice was born ; he was a familiar figure to many who
became the boy's intimates.   Ruskin, still living at Brantwood, was
known to the clan of them.   And the old lady who presided at Hallsteads could remember Walter Scott walking into their dining-room.

Another thing which that upbringing gave him was the taste for
outdoor exercise.   The Marshall clan were not sportsmen, as the
word is used, but they had the cult of long mountain tramps.   Cecil
Spring Rice was delicate and rather frail as a boy, but active, and he
acquired at Ullswater the bent which made it hard for him in all
times and places to see a mountain without wanting to go up it.
There is no better school for physical training.

Throughout life, till death severed the tie, Cecil Spring Rice's chief
mentor and closest comrade was his brother Stephen who, after the
father's death, took on his fifteen year old shoulders much of a
father's responsibility.   The elder shepherded the younger to the
gates of the University.   There came their first parting : but it made
no break, and the younger, a Balliol undergraduate, wrote to the
elder who had just won his fellowship at Trinity, Cambridge :

" Just before I received your letter I had been thinking of
the old bachelor room in Patterdale where we used to sleep,
and how you used to tell me about geology, after we had gone
to bed.   You gave me interests then which I hope I shall never
lose—and the more I see of men here, the more I think that I
have the great advantage over most that no one ever took the
smallest trouble about teaching them more than the routine
work.   Some one did with me."

Yet it was not only the elder brother who educated this impression-
able boy, and encouraged him to push study always far beyond the
mere routine work.   It was the atmosphere of the whole family
circle.   " I suppose he learns a great deal in the holidays," wrote the
wise tutor to whom Cecil Spring Rice was first attached when he went
to Eton.   " School, however, must furnish the criticism," the letter
added ; and it did.   But no other school in England was so little
likely to check the free development of a willing mind as that to
which first the elder and then the younger brother won admission on
the most privileged footing.

Mr. Spring Rice had sent his eldest son to Lee's preparatory school at Brighton, noted for turning out scholarship winners, and in 1868 Stephen Spring Rice was elected to the foundation at Eton, about which a few words of explanation may be given for American readers.

Eton has roughly about a thousand boys, more than nine-tenths of whom are " Oppidans," living in separate houses kept by masters of the school. Each house has from thirty-five to forty boys, and although the school meets without distinction of houses in work and play, a boy's interests and friendships are naturally formed in the house to which he belongs. Elected Scholars, however, of whom there are always seventy, live together in " College," which is a separate house, distinct from the school : and consequently they are in close contact with nearly double the number of Etonians. But it is more important that these Etonians are the picked brains of the school. No one can be an Oppidan unless his parents can pay a very large sum yearly. No one can be a Colleger unless he wins in an open competition one of the ten or twelve places offered yearly, which entitle a boy to board and education free of cost. But Collegers as well as Oppidans have the advantages which come from association with the young of highly-placed families. No Eton boy is likely to be embarrassed in the presence of a duke ; he has rubbed shoulders with embryo dukes at the " wall game " ; and every Eton boy has the chance of forming acquaintances which may be of material use in after life. There probably never was a British Government which did not include Etonians :—certainly the Labour Ministry of 1924 does not furnish an exception. But here is Cecil Spring Rice's own comment, written to his Eton tutor on December 6, 1900, from Teheran, where he was then in charge of the Legation :

" I start for Cairo when Hardinge arrives. Isn't it queer our meeting out here in this out-of-the-way place, and my going out to meet him on the road in state and handing over the Legation and doing generally the faithful vassal ? Who could have thought of our meeting so at Eton ? And there is Curzon now in India, to whom I write officially every month." [1]

These contacts were all part of Cecil Spring Rice's equipment ; even before leaving school he had full opportunity of studying persons who would be ultimately—and indeed before long—of consequence. Such acquaintances might have been skilfully used to his personal advantage ; but this aptitude he never acquired. He got from Eton his full share of that ease of manner which no other school is so successful in imparting : but his gratitude, which was deep, went out for things that lay deep. Eton affords training for character even more than other English public schools, if only because the control is

[1] Sir A. H. Hardinge had just been appointed Minister to Persia. Lord Curzon was Governor-General of India. Both had been contemporaries of Spring Rice at Eton and later at Balliol.

less strict, and life there, for the elder boys, comes very close to that of an undergraduate at Oxford or Cambridge. There is no place where a boy can be more idle : personal ambition or a sense of duty makes the stimulus to work : compulsion is of the slightest. Apart from, and beyond all this, Eton offered to Etonians, along with the inheritance of a great tradition, heirlooms that only Winchester can rival. Lying on the Thames, at the foot of the rise which is crowned by Windsor Castle, its central buildings have the mellow beauty of one of the riverside colleges at Oxford or Cambridge : the rich woodlands about the water-meadows, and the slow-flowing river, build up among them pictures of what is most essentially and characteristically England : and from the first all this meant much to the imaginative and observant small boy of twelve, who entered Eton in August 1871.

There are two sides to the education given in any school and the less important comes, as a rule from the professed teachers : but Eton, being a rich foundation, gets the pick of the profession and a King's Scholar has the chance of instruction from minds more than usually fit to give it. Each scholar is assigned to a special tutor for private study and supervision outside his routine of class work, and Cecil Spring Rice fell into the wise hands of Mr. W. M. Johnson, who wrote to Mrs. Spring Rice at the end of the boy's first term :

Dec. 18, 1871.

" He is evidently frail in body but has borne the roughing and the hard fagging very cheerfully.

He has a very gracious manner and expresses more gratitude for ordinary civilities than any boy of my acquaintance and is very obliging and takes a kindly view of his schoolfellows. He has not so much hard sense as courtesy, and at times he seems likely to fall away into something like silliness.

His pace in work is not very good for so intelligent a boy and I think it likely that he will be beaten by some boys of coarser minds in competitive examinations.

He seems eager for knowledge and rushes to a book readily when released from a temporary task.

He will have told you much more about his school than I can and I can trust him for giving a true and kindly account of it. The taking care of him this autumn has been more of a real job than I generally get and has been at once interesting and comforting ; he is a really good pupil and worthy of more attention than we can give him."

This letter is signed by William Johnson ; but the writer is better known under the name which he took later—William Johnson Cory. His volume, *Ionica*, had been published before Cecil Spring Rice was born ; but the fame of these poems, two or three of which are now to be found in scores of anthologies, came later ; he was known in 1872 only as a singularly successful Eton master.

In another report, six months later, this tutor speaks of " his peculiar gentleness and tenderness of manner which he shows to his schoolfellows without any pride or reserve. They evidently think him rather too unlike themselves but they all admit he is very obliging and disinterested."

But this was quickly followed by an intimation that the tutor was resigning his post at Eton and parting from " as good a pupil as I have ever had. . . . Our intercourse has been long enough to make an indelible and delightful impression on me." Mr. Johnson recommended as a successor Mr. Luxmoore," who is of all the masters I have known the most highminded, original and devoted to duty, though not at all suited for general popularity."

The wise old man had seen well. This brilliant and rather wayward boy was soon linked to Mr. Luxmoore by all the impulses of a most affectionate and constant nature. In letters from far off out-posts of British diplomacy, Cecil Spring Rice was to prove his lasting memory of readings and talks at school. It shows in references back to the Greek classics, love of which never left him : but even more than this, in the simple homeward turning for counsel or for encouragement to one who, as the years went on, took more and more a parent's place.

That is not how a man looks back to the teacher who simply ground him sharp for the hour of examinations. Yet Mr. Luxmoore's duty in the school period was rather to hold in than encourage his pupil's love for literature and intellectual curiosity, which ranged far outside the allotted lines of study.—On the other hand, this vagrancy was fostered by a remarkable man, who was also a remarkable educator.

Oscar Browning, one of the most variously read men of his day, was then an Eton master, and he delighted to make friends with the pick of the school. Early in 1874 he was writing to Cecil Spring Rice—and also as the letters show, to George Nathaniel Curzon— accounts of the travel in which he spent his vacations. The first of them, dated April 1874, from Ajaccio, gives a description of Corsica, and of the Bonaparte family—and so, by way of Prosper Merimée and his novel *Colomba*, branches off into a brilliant discussion on modern literature. Nothing could be more stimulating or flattering for a boy of fifteen than to receive such an epistle. Others follow from Spezzia and from Florence. In August, Browning is in Lapland, and again writing to both lads, and trying to make them write to each other. At Eton his house was open to them on Sunday evenings and A. C. Benson in his *Memories and Friends* has left a sketch of these gatherings : [1]

" The ' Sunday evenings ' were a very civilised affair, and much valued by boys of artistic and literary tastes. The music was in the drawing-room, and on the other side of the lobby, O. B.'s

---

[1] The authorities of Magdalene College, Cambridge, who own the copyright of A. C. Benson's work, have kindly sanctioned the insertion of this and of the long extract which follows on p. 13.

fine and comfortable library was thrown open. I, a boy of twelve, used to ensconce myself in a big chair, choose a book, and survey the scene. One would see boys like Lord Curzon, J. K. Stephen, the present Lord Portsmouth, and Alfred Lyttelton conducting a political or literary argument with much force and frankness. Cecil Spring Rice or George Wyndham would sit absorbed in a book. O. B., then a small, light-stepping, bustling figure, with a handsome profile and curly black locks, would flit about, join laughingly in an argument, be appealed to by another boy for a book on a particular subject, utter oracles. He would take a volume out of one's hands, ask one a question about it, indicate another book for future reading.

" Many boys of this date," he adds, " owe their intellectual interests to O. B."

But it appears from the correspondence that at Christmas 1876, when " O. B." was in London, proposing to take Curzon and Cecil Spring Rice to Irving's *Hamlet*, Cecil Spring Rice's elder brother had a word to say.

The relation between the two lads was singular in its quality. Stephen Spring Rice was forced into maturity by the charges which fell upon him at his father's death, and he was almost a father to the clever boy, not quite three years younger than himself, whose cleverness was so different from his own. The elder lad's intelligence was not only brilliant but many-sided ; many of their contemporaries thought him the more remarkable of the two. Yet there were in him none of the queer twists which made the world so deflecting to his younger brother, whose mind was full of windows opening out in every direction.

By the time that Cecil Spring Rice had attracted Oscar Browning's attention, Stephen had left Eton for Cambridge, as a Scholar of Trinity : but the two kept closely in touch, and evidently the Cambridge undergraduate wrote in fierce denunciation of dilettante study.

" I don't know," Oscar Browning wrote, " from which portion of Stephen's mind (you must admit a very various and versatile one) it comes that he is so terribly afraid of my influence upon you. However, by all means take his advice, though I don't agree with his arguments or his conclusions. To me thought is the reality, action the shadow, and the whole of this world seems to me constantly on the point of rolling away in an unsubstantial nothing, the mere reflection of some energy and power which we know not and never can know. . . . I should have thought that you had plenty of specimens of models of limited industry before your eyes and could quite sufficiently understand what they come to. . . ."

Cecil Spring Rice's reply can be inferred from Oscar Browning's
next letter.

" Do not, my dearest Cecil, think such letters priggish . . .
and do continue to write to me what you think. What life
would be to me without H. Sidgwick, Jebb, Gerald Balfour,
Cornish, you and Curzon I do not like to think, and whilst such
spirits are abroad, it matters very little whether we live or die."

Now, for two schoolboys to find themselves placed in the same
category with three or four men of distinction already widely recognized, is not judicious : and Stephen Spring Rice was probably quite
right in his protests. Such an intimacy bred an atmosphere of the
forcing house. But the friendship continued, till in 1876 Oscar
Browning was dismissed by the headmaster, Hornby, from his post
at Eton—to the fury of Cecil Spring Rice, who wrote to his brother :
" As you say, things are past a joke here. If the Head does do as he
likes it will be very bad indeed, for the only hope is in unselfishness
in a few to spread thence to the mass. And this, by enforcing rivalry
on unwilling fellows by continual examinations (2 a half)—never
encouraging any extra diligence in literary matters (don't think I
should ever put that before school duties : but school duties pure and
simple become hardening above all other causes) ; and by expelling
O. B. simply for holding liberal views—he does his best to destroy.
Any unselfish diligence I mean." [1]

Elsewhere his letters show that " extra diligence " included the
reading of Darwin's *Origin of Species* as well as a good deal of philosophy. They show also that he concerned himself about theology ;
and one at least of his friends discussed with him the inability to
pray. Similar symptoms can be observed in almost any clever lad's
development ; but it is noticeable that Cecil Spring Rice's chief
confidant on these matters was his mother. She, no doubt, got most
of his intimacy and affection, but his sisters had a great share. The
family was grouped in pairs, brother and sister, and Cecil's special
sister was Margaret (or Daisy), next below him in age. But Evelyn,
a still younger sister, was always much in the pictures of them that
never left his mind : and to the sisters he wrote chiefly about his
amusements—the other side of school life.

For although slight, he was active, and at the end of his school
career, disappointment over an examination was set off by a good
place in the school hundred yards. He played football, as everybody
does at Eton, and was enough interested in the game to go on with it
at Oxford. In summer there was the choice to make between " wet
bob " and " dry bob "—rowing or cricket : and Eton made him not
only a lover of lakes and rivers but a skilled waterman. Though he
never followed any form of athletics with the whole-hearted concentration necessary to success, he showed the common desire for athletic

---

[1] This letter is quoted in Westham's *Life of Oscar Browning*.

distinctions, being very amenable to influences and glad to do whatever his friends were doing.   But chiefly and above all, here and in all
places, his liking was for congenial companionship.   He liked popularity and it came easily to him.

There was only one limitation to his pleasure in the pursuit of it.
Coarseness of speech always offended him, and some indulgence in it
is a common symptom of adolescence—as he found among some of
those he liked best.

> " Individually they are very jolly," he wrote to his brother
> (who from Cambridge had admonished him against ' un-
> socialism ') . . . " but collectively they strew the ground with
> curses and strange oaths as they roll along and their conversa-
> tion is awful.   Stephen collectively is awful but individually he
> is very jolly.   Particularly to go on a walk with."

" Individually " in this case completely got the better of " col-
lectively " : J. K. Stephen, most brilliant of all in Cecil Spring Rice's
group of King's Scholars, became his closest school friend.   One of
the chief bonds was a devotion which they shared to the knack of
light verse.   In those days the ideal of every clever young scholar
was to imitate Calverley's *Verses and Translations*, and none of them
all succeeded so well as " J. K. S.", whose *Lapsus Calami* take rank
with the best in this kind.   Cecil Spring Rice as a schoolboy was not
far behind his friend.

Naturally the school journal got hold of these two clever young
Collegers.   A long letter to his mother (expounding, it may be noted,
his views on spiritualism) breaks off with this enquiry :

> " Have the *Etonians* come ?   I am lying among thorns till
> you tell me.   I won't tell you what is mine until you send your
> guesses.   Do you think the paper is *very* bad ?   I hope not.
> But you musn't expect much of such a very boyish paper.   You
> see none of the contributors are more than 18, and very few
> have had the smallest practice in writing.   I know the editors
> and it is very curious to see what fellows write, and what !
> Some whom one would least expect produce perfectly amazingly
> unnatural productions."

Not improbably these reflections apply to G. N. Curzon, then one
of the editors, who was principally responsible in 1877 for a more
ambitious venture.

To EVELYN.

> " . . . There is, I believe some day to be published a new
> edition of selections from the *Etonian*.   I don't know whether
> it will be a success or even what it will be like—I suppose
> nothing very wonderful.   Only there was a horrid little boy
> here who described a day of his stupid life at Eton and got

praised everywhere and everywhen since, and this affair is to
be published by the same man, and I suppose is pretty sure not
to meet with the same success. . . . "

There appeared accordingly *Out of School at Eton* : *By some Present
Etonians*, a volume of fifty pages, published by Sampson Low—containing a preface and fifty-seven miscellaneous items. A dozen of
them are attributed in the marked copy to C. A. S. R.—the other
contributors being C. (Curzon), M. T. T. (Tatham) and J. K. S.

All of Cecil Spring Rice's attempts were in verse, with one notable
exception, " The Tale of a Top," which is a story of selfishness,
ironically shown : and for the work of a beginner it has astonishing
power.   The verses are most varied : unlike J. K. S., who is always
in the lighter vein, C. A. S. R. tried a ballad in the border style, a
translation from Pindar into very good Swinburnese, and, in " The
Friar and the Fairy," an elaborate piece of fantasy. Among the rest,
here is " A Valentine," which would be hard to beat for airy charm :

A VALENTINE.

I'm the boat that you have lost,
    Floating down the river,
I'm the boat that you have lost,
    Which you've lost for ever.
I have floated miles away,
Floated, floated many a day,
    Floated down the river,
Past the rapids white with spray,
Past the reaches calm and gray,
I have floated many a day,
    And shall float for ever.

Down the beck I hurried fast,
Down the little beck I pass'd
    Down into the river ;
So I reach'd the sea at last,
    Where I float for ever ;
Storm and rain and tempest-toss'd,
Warp'd by sun and wind and frost,
Floating bottom-uppermost,
I'm the boat that you have lost,
    Which you've lost for ever.

Here for ever shall I float,
Here in waters most remote
    From my own dear river,
Here for ever shall I float,
Most unhappy little boat,
    Float and float for ever ;

> If you don't, whate'er the cost,
> Answer by return of post,
> You'll be haunted by the ghost
> Of the boat that you have lost,
> Lost perhaps for ever.

Another of the poems was an essay in satire—which all Etonians recognised as a portrait of a senior boy.

> " The World, the Flesh, the Devil once
> Agreed to patronise a dunce."

' My gift is trousers,' lisped the World ; the Flesh gave indolence ; but the Devil's was more subtle.

> " For him the most reserved shall prate,
> For him each foible of the great,
> Each grosser thought and mean delight,
> Each silly love and petty spite,
> Whatever's vile and mean and low,
> Shall in his presence stronger grow.
> Sin's faithful friend and virtue's foil,
> Round every heart 'tis his to coil ; . . .
> This gift, this power seems best to me,
> This heaven-corrupting courtesy."

A. C. Benson, two years younger than Cecil Spring Rice (but sixteen is a young man and fourteen a child), tells how this easy and daring handling of literature completed the fascination already exercised over him by the Colleger whose room was opposite to him in the New Buildings on the Upper Passage :

" He was not a tall boy, and still in jackets, with a big Eton collar, but he moved quickly and lightly with a decidedly abstracted air ; I can see him skimming fleetly into school, in tall hat and long-sleeved cloth gown (the official costume of Collegers), the sleeves flirting out behind him. His clothes well-worn but fitting him gracefully ; a strong muscular development, and every inch of it under control—he was a very promising football player, of remarkable speed and agility. I can even remember how his shapely hands, instead of bulging out awkwardly at the wrist, seemed to continue with a certain delicacy the lines of his strong arms. He was pale in those days, with what might almost be called *morbidezza* of complexion, and his hands unusually white. And then his features—the face stands out on the darkness as I write, pale, smooth-browed, the eyes at once fearless and gentle, the nose finely shaped, short upper lip, and the small lower lip, generally somewhat parted from the upper with a downward curl that gave a touch of fastidiousness, almost of scorn, to his expression, with a finely moulded chin. He wore his hair long, it tumbled over his brows, and he used to throw it back with an impatient gesture of the hand.   My father had a number of Arundel pictures, and often turned them over with us at home ;   there was certainly an Italian touch about Spring-Rice's face in those days, both of outline and colouring, and I used again and again, in looking at the Arundels, to see something that reminded me of him in the face of a singing angel, or a Tuscan youth absorbed in his own pleasant solitary thoughts.

" For a year or more I felt for Spring-Rice that speechless and adoring sense of hero-worship which is a natural and even inspiring stage in most imaginative boys.

" But here is the curious thing, that though it was almost a species of devotion to watch my hero far-off, to meet him going to and fro, to sit near him, to hear him speak—he had a low, rapid, slightly husky utterance, the words very precisely enunciated, which I thought sate finely upon him, especially when in excited moments it rose into a more impassioned and clearer strain—though to see and hear him thus would communicate a thrill of pleasure to a whole day, I never attempted to attract his attention, or make his acquaintance, and never even exchanged a word with him during those years.   It was very unadventurous, but it did not seem to be a thing to be hoped for, and much less schemed for.   I told him long after with what a degree of admiration and worship I had surrounded him ;   we laughed over it, and he was forced to confess that he was wholly unaware of my existence, except as a rather tousled inoffensive boy who had a room opposite him.

" But then the unexpected happened.   My tutor had taken me to Henley in 1877 ;   and after a morning in the hot sun, running with the Eton Eight, lunching heavily in a drag, I was seized with a headache so insupportable that I decided upon instant flight.   I went over the glaring river bridge and down the little street by the river, found a special just starting, and ensconced myself in a corner of a carriage—my tutor had given me a return ticket—only thankful to escape out of the glare of the sun.   I was alone in the carriage, and just as the train started, the door was opened, and Cecil Spring-Rice stepped lightly into the carriage.   He came and sate down opposite me, smiled and nodded, and said, ' We mustn't let anyone suspect that we escaped—the heat is dreadful ! '   We talked on, and in two minutes he was telling me an Irish ghost story, how arrived at I forget, of which I can remember every smallest incident, and still more his absorbed look as he spoke, and the quick little gestures of his hands.   We walked down to College together :   my headache had disappeared, and I was in the seventh heaven of delight.   Now, I thought, I shall see and talk to him occasionally.   But it was not to be.   He never spoke to me again for the rest of his time at Eton, and the only difference it made was that we nodded when we met.

" But I did often hear him talk to others ;   and his talk was of a very singular type for a boy.   He was neither emotional nor sentimental.   He was petulant and argumentative, and had a sharp, rather trenchant tongue, with a good deal of personal satire at his command.

" He was liked ; but he was certainly feared. He was not in those days in the least gregarious. He deeply disliked any touch of coarseness or loudness or stupidity ; and I should say that his humour was then of a distinctly derisive order. But he was felt to have a high standard, not that of a priggish moralist but that of a guarded and reserved nature, who felt deeply the sense of beauty in nature, literature and art, and had no desire to speak lightly or easily of things that were to him sacred and inviolable.

" Yet I remember once in later years how in his company I attended a little meeting of boys who formed an Essay Society at Eton, and discussed a paper read by one of the members. He was asked to speak, and spoke, I recollect well, with great lightness and humour, but with a serious background to all he said, and how easily and gracefully he seemed to include his hearers in a circle of sympathy and unaffected goodwill."

That was Spring Rice, seen from a distance by an admiring junior. His contemporaries would scarcely have stressed so much the aloofness—though there was in him always something of the solitary. On the other hand, he was always easily companionable, and he had one hall-mark of that quality. Throughout life he was known affectionately by a nickname which began in these years. Letters to him from J. K. S. in schooldays begin with " Dear Spring Rice " ; they pass on to " Dear Cecil " : but here and there in them comes the name by which he was to be known all through the diplomatic service, and in many capitals. He was " Dear Springy " to J. K. S. as he was to Sir Edward Grey, to Theodore Roosevelt, and to scores of other correspondents—women as well as men : though Mrs. Cabot Lodge, one of his closest friends, always wrote to him " Dear Mr. Springy."

As to these early displays of talent with his pen, rhyming for amusement continued to be one of his pastimes through life ; it was almost tragically a distraction in the final years of stress ; but he never cared to push his accomplishment, as J. K. S. did, into an art. On the other hand, the literature of devotion charmed him from very early days, and shortly after his first appearance in this schoolboy publication he sent an essay on Thomas à Kempis to a magazine which surprisingly sent him " a little cheque for a guinea. It was stamped and crossed and all kinds of things," he wrote to his mother, " and I thought I hadn't lived in vain."

All this meant some diffusion of the effort which a prize-winner must put out. The highest distinction at Eton is the Newcastle Scholarship, to be held at Oxford or Cambridge. In the spring of each year all the leading boys at Eton compete to be among " the select " from whom the Newcastle scholar is eventually chosen ; and Cecil Spring Rice, to his tutor's disappointment, failed to be included. This emphasised the advice already given by Mr. Luxmoore—that he should depart from the family tradition and go to Oxford. Henry

Butcher, another Cambridge man, but at this time an Oxford tutor, confirmed the view that the Oxford schools, in which more scope was given for the power of writing, and less weight placed on exact knowledge, would suit the young man better : and also, that since he inclined to enter the Civil Service, the Oxford training would give a better equipment for the particular type of examination to which competitors were subjected.

" I think if Cecil is to earn his own start in life, it would be wrong to forego Oxford," Mr. Luxmoore wrote to Mrs. Spring Rice. " In point of education, I think it better for him, and though I set the social discipline and strengthening of Trinity higher than that of Oxford, I think Cecil may quite be trusted to take care of himself and to get the best.

" The only thing is that he thinks Stephen will feel his falling off from the Cambridge tradition.   I must trust to you to see that there is no disappointment which would at all hinder their accord.   I value family ties educationally very high, and I would put a great deal in the other scale if I thought Stephen would feel it as want of loyalty : otherwise I am clear."

But Stephen, then a foundation scholar of Trinity, did not raise the question of loyalty.   He confined himself to letting his younger brother know exactly what one University, from its high places, thought of the other : and he overdid it, as this letter to Mrs. Spring Rice shows.

" Stephen came down to tell me all kind of wicked things about Oxford.   It is sad to think that such a large distinguished place could be so utterly demoralized, if one may judge from Stephen's testimony.   2500 undergraduates and all doomed to enervating influences and certain degeneracy !   It is a wonder the educational reforms were not more sweeping and that such a wicked place is yet allowed to cumber the ground. Seriously, I don't see that Oxford is sure to do me harm because it suits the bent of one's mind.   I don't care myself one way or the other, but if I was more entirely unprejudiced even than I am, such an array of witnesses against a place, and warning fingers held up, is almost a sufficient inducement to go there. . . . I don't care one way or the other ; it is my tutor's business, I should say, who knows me better than anyone but you, and you can't tell about examinations and so on.   He stands in a parent's place in an educational point of view, and if anyone has the right of saving me the trouble of making up my mind, he has.   I am very much pleased at that trouble being taken from me."

The end of it all was that he won an open exhibition at Balliol, ranking below a scholarship in value and prestige : but a Balliol exhibition, at all events in Jowett's time, counted above an open scholarship in any other college. A note from one of the Fellows of the college says :

"Your essay was almost the best—and your history the best of the lot. One man showed more knowledge but then his style was very inferior."

How wide his schoolboy reading had extended may be judged from a note from W. Wayte, congratulating him on the Balliol success, which goes on to ask to see the paper on Mazzini which Spring Rice had read to the Eton Essay Society.

Perhaps in this account too little has been made of the athletic side. Rowing counted for much, both here and at Oxford. There is no trace, however, in him of that sense of personal responsibility which English school life often exaggerates ; he did not feel that either the athletic reputation of his House or its discipline rested on his shoulders. Yet the thought of Eton and the love for Eton never left him ; Eton, next to his home in Ullswater, embodied England for him ; and twenty years after he left Eton, he wrote to the man who for him embodied its spirit :

CONSTANTINOPLE,
Nov. 15, 1898.

" MY DEAR TUTOR,

Indeed I was delighted to hear from you. I think of you and your garden as almost the pleasantest thing I have to think about : Old Church comes first, but next to that the corner of Eton where you live.

I wish I had been at the dinner [1] and yet I am rather glad I wasn't. No doubt it is a good thing that the rich and noble should send their sons to a beautiful place where they can live happy and active lives. But as you say, if the governors come from the upper classes and the upper classes go to Eton, we haven't so much more credit in educating governors than the P. & O. steamers : they mostly go to India by them. Still, it is tremendously important as things are now, that the upper classes who are to rule us, should be under good influences at Eton and I should think there can be no doubt about that. . . . But the question still remains—what are the influences besides courage, truth and gentlemanly feeling ? Are they taught to love power, wealth and ostentation—the glory, not the thing ? Do they admire their country because it is large or because it is great ? . . .

Suppose it is true, as I daresay it is, that the history of England in the next fifty years could be divined in the Eton pupil rooms ! It is rather a fearful thought. How are our

---

[1] Of Old Etonians.

future rulers ? Are they physically healthy and mentally vigorous—above all, have they courage of body and mind ? I see in the papers that there are reports from many schools showing that the boys are below par in body at any rate. This is a very dreadful thing to think about. Rome finished, as we all know, from internal and not external reasons. The cause of their fall was in the Romans, not the barbarians. How are our young Romans ? "

In the chapel at Eton many of the old stalls are visibly identified with the memory of some Etonian whom the school desires to commemorate. One of these bears the name and arms of Sir Cecil Spring Rice. Yet he is more intimately remembered when the school sings from its hymn book his verses which express, perhaps better than anything which has been written by any other man, the spirit and the teaching that Eton would desire to impart—the religion of the English public school. They belong to the end not the beginning, and their place is in the last chapter of this book, as the last word of his life. But the end grew harmoniously out of beginnings which Eton helped to make.

In short, Eton, through its many contacts, was in Cecil Spring Rice's career a richly varied preparation for a richly varied life : and no money could have given him more advantages either for pleasure or profit. One of the best lessons was that of living with people, many of whom had lavish means, and yet keeping a nice frugality. In this there could have been no better mentor than his brother : and assuredly no other school could have given so full opportunity for learning it.

Another phase in education began before Cecil Spring Rice went up to Balliol : he spent his last Christmas vacation from school in a first visit to Germany, with Mr. Luxmoore for guide and companion. Cologne, its cathedral and its museum, especially the Dürer prints, delighted him ; drawing was an accomplishment for which he had almost as much natural aptitude as for verse. But the chief joy of that journey came from music. At Leipzig they heard Brahms play his own music.

" He played the piano and afterwards came up to a box near us and we (and all the rest) levelled our glasses at him. He had a round, strong face, nice-looking—confound the word."

There was skating also ; and many little things to notice.

" The little carts drawn by dogs—a new aspect of the canine, I didn't expect. Their grave and orderly behaviour is quite impressive to look at : then suddenly a free friend comes up and claims to be treated as a dog and a brother, and the old Adam reasserts itself and one breathes free. Before it was a little super-canine."

Truly, a great many windows were open in this schoolboy mind.

Oxford enchanted him, as was natural.   Very soon he was writing to his mother : " I don't think I could ever get tired of this place. The river, the colleges, and the trees in the garden—I wish you could see it.   But it is to be lived in, not shown over."

The years which Cecil Spring Rice spent at Balliol may be summed up by saying that he contrived to enjoy himself to the top of his bent, and none the less to take two first classes, in classical moderations in his second year, and at the close of the fourth in the final school of *literae humaniores*.[1]   He rowed also in the college boat and won the college mile :   and enhanced the reputation for wit—especially for satirical verse—which he had brought from Eton.

Also, in spite of his versatility in competition with other young men in athletics, in literary amusements and in the solid work of the schools, he contrived to see a great deal more of women's society than was usual in that period at Oxford.   This was made easy for him by his friendship with Henry Butcher, then a tutor of University College. Mrs. Butcher, daughter of Archbishop Trench, the poet and essayist, had beauty to match her husband's, and a grave charm : and their house in Norham Road was constantly frequented by Butcher's three sisters, then all unmarried, of whom only the eldest, Lady Prothero, is still alive.   More picturesque and delightful personalities never lit up any group and they were the close friends of the Spring Rice sisters. Naturally, Oxford was at their feet.   Also, the Butchers had made alliance with Miss Rhoda Broughton, a popular novelist, and a very witty, sharp-tongued woman :   Cecil Spring Rice became welcome at her home also.   Fifteen years later Mrs. Cameron, one of the leading ladies in the society of Washington, where he had become accepted as an intimate, was on her travels in England while he was in Tokio, and wrote to him that she had met Rhoda Broughton.   " She said that you were the most delightful undergraduate ever known, and I believed her."

As to Balliol itself, E. C. Selwyn, an Eton contemporary wrote from Olympian heights at Cambridge :

> " Of course, I am one of those who cannot honestly congratulate you on your choice of a university, however well they may think of Balliol for picking you up along with a handful of very rough diamonds from the mangers of Manchester and the smugdom of Scotland."

The 'handful' included W. P. Ker, afterwards Professor, and the finest and most learned critic of literature in his day : H. C. Beeching, even more distinguished in letters than in the church where he became Dean of Norwich : and J. W. Mackail, scholar and poet.   Also of Spring Rice's own year were G. N. Curzon and St. Loe Strachey,

[1] This in the main meant ancient history and philosophy, with a special stress on Aristotle's *Ethics* and Plato's *Republic*.

afterwards editor of the *Spectator*.   Sir Edward Grey was a couple of years his junior and at this stage barely an acquaintance : the same is true of J. A. Spender, editor of the *Westminster Gazette*.   St. John Brodrick (Lord Midleton) and Lord Selborne were contemporaries and acquaintances at Oxford, but not of his college.   Clinton Dawkins, a year junior, became his close friend.   But the most intimate alliance of this time was with Thomas Farrer (now Lord Farrer), who later married Evelyn Spring Rice.

Over and above his friendship with other undergraduates was the tie formed between him and R. L. Nettleship, then a tutor of Balliol. This shy and serious don, tongue-tied and hesitant before his classes, ranked with the foremost brains of that day in Oxford, and when he found sympathy he was capable of sudden expansion.   Contemporaries remember how overpowering was Cecil Spring Rice's admiration for this delicate, sensitive, yet bold intelligence.

Selections from his correspondence of this period shall begin with two letters to his brother, then reading for his finals at Cambridge.

BALLIOL,
To STEPHEN.   Feb. 17, 1878.

   " Don't answer me.   I only write to console you for your many calamities.   Another Tripos ! woe on woe—I do pity you, as far as I can.   I have done no work this term and I have almost forgotten what it is like. . . .

   Of course, men ask one out a great deal : every Freshman I know complains bitterly of it, there is no time for anything but eating.   I don't mind it, but am resigned at the prospect of my popularity decreasing.   Men here are very pleasant as a rule : not a bit party-ish with a few exceptions : those are certainly rampant. . . . It's not nearly such a change as I expected. Lowry, and Tatham are here and I knew hardly anyone at Eton, so I don't feel leaving it so much.   But Jem Stephen and Burrows are a loss : and Stephen goes to Cambridge, worse luck.   So that stop is permanent. . . . "

But J. K. S. and his brothers remained intimates through constant meetings in London for many years.

Balliol was then dominated to an extraordinary degree by the personality of its Master.   Benjamin Jowett was not only a writer, a scholar and a wit, but deliberately a moulder of men for the work of Empire.   Cecil Spring Rice never took kindly to his handling ; but the correspondence is full of the Master's doings and sayings—recounted for the most part in a spirit of criticism.

To STEPHEN.   Thursday, March 14, 1878.
   " Do you know him ?   He is the most splendid institution here, if it was only for the way he stimulates the imagination of undergraduates in the fabrication of stories about him.   There

was a secret society of undergraduates here who met every Saturday and invented authentic anecdotes of 'the Jowler.' I invented one, which was told me with great gusto the other day as coming from a very trustworthy source. He is really very pleasant indeed if conversation is started for him : he won't start talking of himself, and he does unobtrusive kind things that no one could without a very good heart. But he is fearfully commonsensical. The only prudent man in Oxford, they say. Poor man, he suffers agonies from the Ritualistic canons —but he keeps up his acquaintance with them : goes out a duty walk once a term with Liddon and preaches in the evening on making friends with the mammon of unrighteousness."

The only subject which recurs with equal frequency is rowing : and for the uninitiated it may be explained that " Torpid " means the beginner's boat. These race in the spring term, the " eights " proper racing in the summer term : both sets of races being conducted in the fashion described in this letter to his sister Margaret (or Daisy).[1]

" . . . Balliol has been bumped again : which that you may understand, hear and digest inwardly. Every college has a boat ; and these on certain days in the year race in the following extraordinary fashion. They are arranged in order of last year's merit on the river, by the banks, with a space of fifteen yards between each boat. Then a gun fires and they are pushed out ; then another gun fires and they start, rushing after each other. If one that is in front of another be slower than the succeeding one, it is caught up and ' bumped ' and has to change places with the ' bumper ' next day : and so on for a week. Balliol has so far succeeded in getting bumped every day, which is very unpleasant for Balliolites and goes to the heart. The partizans of each boat rush along the bank and shout : and if they find a man shouting for the wrong college they cool his ardour in the river. . . . "

A letter to another sister, Agnes, combines the two subjects. (The beginning in rhyme was characteristic not only of his letters but of his talk.)

ETONIAN CLUB, OXFORD.
(Undated.)

" I grieve, I lament, I sorrow and cry, a remarkably penitent sinner am I, but my time is so very much taken up. I have to go down to row on the river every day from 3 to 5—or from 2.30 to 5.30, I can never tell. And then all the morning I work

---

[1] Now Mrs. Birch Reynardson.

—and my rooms are on the ground floor and in the evenings men come in from hall just to see how I am getting on, you know—I and my biscuits. The river is the most disagreeable. That is vile. I have to go out in an eight first, working as hard as possible in rather a lazy boat with a persecutor in the stern to swear at one—which he always does in as ungrateful a way as possible, just when one is doing most work. Besides, it is rather detestable to lose one's identity and become ' bow ' or ' two ' or ' three '; one might as well be in the army. And then the idea of it—to become as like a machine as possible—its awfully degrading. The much-souled human being, I have observed in myself, cannot approximate himself to the machine and is therefore a bad oar. All this going on for weeks and weeks for the pleasure of bumping once or being bumped a dozen times and wearing a pink coat and a cap on the back of one's head. . . .

The Master preached a very fine sermon in the 'Varsity Church. An old one, I was told, preached eight years ago. Always the same, of course, no religion good and no religious man bad. He made everyone laugh on one occasion. It was rather surprising hearing an old man in a church telling a crowded congregation that he would illustrate his point by an amusing story. He was very historical and very inaccurate too, I believe—illustrating his point by the history of the Jesuits who, he said, left the world behind them once, and were now left behind by the world. He described an ideal churchman who should have been constantly orthodox ' from the robber council of Chalcedon to the tumultuous assembly of Nicæa and who would have had to anathematize himself two or three times at least. . . . ' ”

OXFORD UNIVERSITY BOAT CLUB.

To MR. LUXMOORE.

“ . . . I am in a very miserable state, so you will please console me and be as comforting as possible. I haven't yet secured my 2nd in mods and now I have to row in our torpid : which is a vile bad one ; the bow came in two and I had to take his place untrained. I like the honour but I have the blisters ; and when one has work to do undone, and skin coming to pieces, and a fragmentary back, a scarlet coat is but a small consolation. That is the guerdon of our toil. It's very absurd but even in this centre of light a red coat seems as sweet as erst the blue.[1] Unfortunately, my work is in a very bad state ; and what will become of me I don't know. I picture to myself the Master

[1] Permitted to those who rowed for Eton.

greeting me on the fatal day. ' Got a third, Mr. Spring Rice ?
I didn't think you would come out so high. Allow me to
congratulate you, Mr. Spring Rice. Good morning.' And
then, as a kind of P.S., ' And don't be inaccurate, Mr. Spring
Rice.' I should have nothing to do but take to my bed. It
would be a capital position to take him in. He would have to
come and find me ashy pale, and quivering for consolation. And
he would come up and read me that interesting chapter in his
Plato in which he treats of the immortality of the soul : ' an
exceedingly interesting question, though it has no direct bearing
on practical life.' And if I had only Canon Liddon in the background struggling between politeness and orthodoxy, I should
die happy. . . .

Life here gets very uneventful. The only thing that makes
one day different from another—(except fish and porritch on
alternate mornings) is our debating society and the sermons.
I have heard three of the last from our Master. Doesn't he
seem to begin at the wrong end ? ' The Mosaic books are not
wholly unhistorical.' ' Purity is better than orthodoxy, wise
persons than sectarians.' ' The Gospel facts may or may not
be accurate but there is no doubt that honesty is the best
policy.' Moses and Job and Solomon and Christ lived and died
that their lives might suggest to Dr. Jowett sundry platitudes
and truisms, and if the facts are not exactly and correctly stated,
why, they make a very edifying allegory : in which Dr. Jowett's
young friends may live and move and have their commonplace
being. ' Swollen with wind and the rank mist they draw.'
Fancy Oliver Cromwell told to take the *Pilgrim's Progress*
instead of the Bible to fight for: ' it was equally true and
considerably more edifying.' I do not love thee, Dr. Jowett :
which is very ungrateful for he has been very kind to me ; and
has devoted his whole life to doing young men good—especially
young women."

ETONIAN CLUB, OXFORD.
(Undated.)

Letter to AGNES.

" . . . Our boat goes worse every day. The races begin on
Thursday and I hate all my fellow Torpidees. We all hate each
other and we are all quite right. I went to lunch with the
Butchers to-day. They were in very good spirits and talked
about Miss Broughton with whom Mrs. B. has struck up a great
friendship.

She does seem very amusing, certaily, and I hope to meet
her soon. My days are so very monotonous now I have nothing

to write about except that Paton has given me a beautiful little Dante as large as a lozenge and that the Master has asked me to dinner. I look forward to that rather ; he always has amusing people to stay with him. You know they come on a Saturday and go away on the Monday, and spend the Sunday in walking up and down Oxford with our Master, who smiles and nods his old white head up and down like a venerable cherub.

We were debating Darwinism last night. A large majority voted in its favour which would have been more satisfying had anyone shown any knowledge whatever of the subject. People certainly do look funny getting up to speak of necessity (we all have to once a term) and forgetting unfortunately what they have to say : with a furtive look at their notes and a convulsive clutch of the back of their chairs. I will write to Daisy and the Mother soon. Give them my love, please."

The set in which Cecil Rice lived at Balliol included several people very quick with their pens : and it was H. C. Beeching who set the fashion for a whole sheaf of pasquinades by his verses on the Master :

> " First come I, My name is Jowett,
>   There's no knowledge but I know it.
>   I am Master of this College.
>   What I don't know isn't knowledge."

This is the text as found in the *Masque of Balliol*, under which name these flying things were brought together in a broadsheet. One of them has attained, if not immortality, at least a fame which is likely to last as long as that of the victim to whose coat it was pinned—namely the couplet :

> " My name is George Nathaniel Curzon,
>   I am a most superior person."

It is now admitted that the inventor of this terribly happy rhyme was Professor Mackail ; but many attributed it to Spring Rice—and especially Lord Curzon did so, with some resentment, for he considered that it had done him a mischief, and that the hurt came from one who was his friend. There was perhaps some justification for Lord Curzon's wrath. These pasquinades were concocted more or less jointly and Spring Rice had his finger in the pie : it is possible that he may have invented another couplet which does not appear in the printed version but which was well known :

> " My cheek is pink, my hair is sleek,
>   I dine at Blenheim once a week."

There is, anyhow, no doubt that from the first Curzon seemed to Spring Rice (as indeed to most other people) a too consciously " superior person," and throughout their long knowledge of each other we find Spring Rice's perception of Curzon's real merit struggling with a still keener sense of his flamboyancy.

The *Masque* contains another quotation which should be quoted here :

> " Can story telling be a vice
> When you've an uncle like Sp—— R——e ? [1]
> My versatility is such
> None likes me little, or knows me much."

This also is Professor Mackail's and suggests that from the first Cecil Spring Rice could say a great deal and yet disclose little of himself. He was elusive—and family tradition preserves a few lines in which he suggested this quality.

> " I am an Irishman, you see ;
> That is what expresses me.
> I am changing as the weather,
> You must take me altogether,
> Hopeless of distinguishing
> Which is Rice and which is Spring."

The only fugitive verse of his Oxford period which had a wide popularity for some generations of undergraduates does not appear in the Balliol broadsheet—that being only devoted to members of the College.   But in those days when Liddell was Dean of Christ Church and walked the streets of Oxford, (" the Broad " and " the High "), like a tall quarto, beside his wife, who had the proportions of a post-war *Who's Who*, everyone knew these lines :

> " I am the Dean and this is Mrs. Liddell.
> She plays the first and I the second fiddle.
> She is the Broad, I am the High,
> *We* are the University."

Many years later, in 1900, Mr. Tuckwell, author of *Reminiscences of Oxford*, republished some of these pasquinades, and the names he affixed to them were those of Beeching, Mackail and Spring Rice—at a time when it was not convenient for any of the three to be convicted of chaffing dignitaries in print.   The page of the book was cancelled.

Waifs and Strays, another Balliol collection of more serious versifying, contained also several numbers by Spring Rice : and in short, he must have spent a good deal of time in rhyming—though his facility was astonishing.   Also, when F. R. Benson, then at Christ Church, organised a performance of the *Agamemnon* and set the first example of reproducing Attic drama in its own language, Cecil Spring Rice was in the cast.   A letter to his sister keeps a startling image of the actor, who was also a reputed athlete.

[1] This is said to refer to his habit of quoting a mythical uncle as the authority for surprising incidents which he related.

"Do you get on with Miss Benson ? Her cousin here is getting too too : very much too, I think : as far as a yellow waistcoat, green satin trousers (to judge by appearances) and hair enough to stuff a chair with. The play continues : he goes up and down to London managing. The other day when he got to Didcot, he said the train was close : got out at ten o'clock (it's about twelve miles off) and arrived at Oxford by twelve, having run—tall hat, yellow waistcoat and all."

It would not have been surprising if a scholar with so many talents for amusing himself had failed in the final schools, and he himself was in despair. But when in July 1887 the class list appeared with his name in Class I. there came a jubilant postcard from J. K. S. " Did I not always tell you so ? " Probably that power of general appreciation which with him replaced minute scholarship accounted for his success.

There followed a period of fluctuation. Unlike his brother, who had a course clearly mapped out and from a Fellowship at Trinity had gone on to a Clerkship in the Treasury, Cecil Spring Rice had never looked much beyond the needs of the moment. It had been always generally understood that he should aim for the Foreign Office in which his father had served ; and immediately after his degree examination he went for some time to study French at Tours. Returning in the autumn, he presented himself for an All Souls Fellowship and, by the account which he received through Nettleship, plainly did not do well. " They thought you didn't know much (which was natural) and that you talked a good deal, which was not unnatural." But the rest was consolation—and exhortation to try elsewhere.

What Cecil Spring Rice actually did was to go abroad, first to Paris, where he saw the machinery of government.—The Senate was " like the Union at its worst, only people shook their fists in each others faces and paid not the smallest respect to the President."

From France he went on to Dresden where in January he was homesick and much depressed because he had received news that an examination was to be held of candidates for the Home Civil Service— and the notice was too short for him to prepare himself. " I should certainly like to get this unpleasant period of doing nothing over," he wrote.

There was no certainty that a competition for clerkships in the Foreign Office would be held before he had passed the age limit for entrants, and by April 1882 Nettleship was remonstrating with him for having abandoned all thoughts of the Civil Service. His friend and kinsman, Farrer, said, " Why not take to literature ? " The suggestion was met with jeers.

"I think a literary life, being the only one for which an examination is not necessary, would very well suit my peculiar bent. The only difficulty is setting up shop. I think after serious deliberation sandwich men is the best plan. Stephen would object to have a board over 113a,[1] I am afraid."

But he mentioned the suggestion to his brother without comment. In fact, it would have been for him the easiest way to success. Everything in his education had fitted him for it, and already he was showing in his letters from Dresden that quickness of observation and versatility of interest which would have made him at least an admirable journalist. Both his brother and Farrer were deep students of Bradshaw, and he sent them both many details about the German railways ; he saw student duels and detailed their very odd procedure : he picked up sidelights on the German police. Wherever he went through life, the habit of noting such things stayed with him, and the prompting to put them on paper was a real form of the need for self expression. But of the strong driving force which makes it impossible for some men to be anything but writers, there is no trace in him ; and the gifts of his pen found far better scope in recording the experiences of a diplomatist than those of a literary man.

Yet for the moment he was unsettled and the unsettlement made him unhappy. When the results of the Home Civil competition were announced, he wrote to his brother :

" I am not sure what I shall do with myself, as there is to be no F.O. examination and I couldn't expect the mother to send me into diplomacy. I might be a don which would be dignified, or a master which would be lucrative, or a parson which would be neither. However, I don't care a hang just at present. . . . "

J. K. S. also heard by letter of his uncertainty and protested.

" I am really rather perturbed at your statement about the F.O. Please don't go and be-don yourself without reflection, and only because you will like pelf, and people to spend Sunday with you. Look round the spacious orb and find some occupation to rekindle the constant enthusiasm which flamed in you when a youth."

Yet it is more than likely he would have drifted into teaching, as the easiest way out of his difficulties, but for his elder brother's steady pressure. Fortunately, a competition for Foreign Office clerkships was announced, to be held in September ; he came back to England, read for a few weeks in preparation, and headed the list of competitors. His appointment was announced in the *Times* of October 12, 1882. One of his contemporaries at Eton and Balliol, Arthur Hardinge,[2] who had already entered the Foreign Office, wrote joyfully :

" As I told you, and as everybody but yourself felt certain

[1] 113a Queen's Gate, then the family home.
[2] Sir A. H. Hardinge, afterwards Ambassador at Madrid.

would be the case, you were easily first, Fairholme [1] coming out second, Mallet [2] third, and Anstruther fourth.   I am delighted to think that you will come here shortly."

[1] G. F. Fairholme, C.M.G., retired from the Foreign Office 1903.
[2] Sir Bernard Mallet, K.C.B., transferred to Treasury, 1885.   Registrar-General, 1909-20.

CHAPTER II

EARLY OFFICIAL LIFE

At the time when Cecil Spring Rice entered the Foreign Office, there was a division of duties between the diplomatic staff, serving abroad, and the clerks in Downing Street, permanently attached to their post there. It was for this latter branch of the service, in which his father had spent his official life, that Cecil Spring Rice entered, though within a few years he drifted rather than made his way into the diplomatic side. But in 1882 he looked forward to a life in London differing only from that of other civil servants by its special duties.

Almost immediately after he had secured his appointment the death of his mother left the household without its accustomed head. The home in Queen's Gate was kept on ; Stephen Spring Rice controlled all the funds ; family resources were treated as a family purse and for several years the younger brother accepted this control in the simplest spirit ; dozens of his letters show how he accounted to his elder, in a general way, for his expenditure, and drew through him to meet them, till the elder married and set up his own abode. But from the first Cecil Spring Rice made contribution to the needs of his younger brothers and sisters, increasing according to his means. These young people were bound together by a touching loyalty of affection ; and never a shade of disagreement arose from the attitude of semi-dependence which the younger man accepted towards his elder by four years, who was also his most intimate friend.

There is very little record of these years in the correspondence, because the brothers and sisters were all living together. A few letters to his Balliol friend Tom (now Lord) Farrer, who later married Evelyn Spring Rice, are full of light-hearted chaff—largely about railways, for this friend's favourite study was time-tables, and there are Greek verses addressed to him as βραδσανιόμωρον. At other times the intersprinkled ornaments are not in Greek. For instance :

" I asked you to dine last week and you didn't answer. And the world being very evil and the times waxing very late, I suppose if I wrote and asked you again to come any blessed or cursed day this blessed or cursed week, you would not write or speak. However, come—as the post said to the snail :

Come, come, darling, come,
I am deaf and you are dumb :

29

> Come, come, dash it all,
> I can stand and you can crawl.
> The post is I : the snail is Tom,
> Then come, come, darling, come."

There was a deal of gaiety and going out ; a letter from J. K. S. speaks of " a dance which lacked lustre since your agile limbs and Stephen's nimble tongue " were absent. But first and last, Cecil Spring Rice was a hard and serious worker. In the autumn of 1883 he used his leave to go to Italy and get a colloquial use of the language. Letters from Genoa to Stephen show him already at the business in which he was to excel—making swift notes of whatever revealed the life, social, economic and political, of the people among whom he found himself. For instance, on November 8, 1883 :

" . . . A new cotton mill was opened at Venice amid tre-mendous ovations. The local member spoke of the old aspect of the beach of Venice—the deserted sands and solitary wind—of the glories of Saint Mark and then of his decay—and finally drank to the health of the new Venice in the name of Italy and civilisation. Another, not to be outdone, said that he could already see in his mind's eye a factory rising on every island and lighters in every lagoon (Bene ! Benone !) All the nobility here are taking to banking or business—and they intend to make Genoa cut out Marseilles."

Then comes reference to a little-remembered episode in diplomacy.

" I hope that we shall put off going to war with France till I get back, as I don't know what the railways will do in that case. What a fool everyone is made out to be. I never heard of anything like a Prime Minister publishing a telegram he knows to be false, about a man with whom he was at the moment negotiating—and then making his own paper confess the imposture. And then complaining that these barbarians are entirely ignorant of the procedure of civilised diplomacy !

The incident which nearly brought France and England to war in 1883 arose out of the operations in Madagascar. Tamatave was bombarded by a French fleet and occupied on June 13. The British consul, then seriously ill, was ordered to quit his house within twenty-four hours and died before the time was over. On the 16th a British missionary was arrested. On July 17 M. Challemel-Lacour, Minister for Foreign Affairs, declared in the Chamber his certainty that Ad-miral Pierre " had not ignored the consideration mutually incumbent upon two great civilised nations." But eventually an apologetic despatch was written and £1000 as damages were paid to the arrested missionary.

At this time relations with France were greatly strained, owing to

the aggressive colonial policy by which M. Ferry's government sought
to divert the national mind from dreams of a *revanche* on the Rhine.
Bismarck, well pleased, was secretly urging these oversea adventures
in Cochin China, Tunis and the Congo.

Lord Granville, then Foreign Minister, was not only pacific but a
lover of France : yet the friction was acutely felt in Egyptian affairs,
which from 1882 onwards became the chief anxiety of the Foreign
Office.   These came under the Eastern Department, to which Spring
Rice had been assigned ; and he felt more than the normal share of
interest which already centred upon one romantic personage.   This
man—General Gordon—figures largely in two letters written to Mr.
Luxmoore at Eton.   But these, in the first instance, describe Spring
Rice's first tutor, William Johnson, who on leaving Eton in 1872 had
assumed the name of Cory.   He had lived for some time in Madeira,
married there, and in 1882 returned a widower with an only son, to
live the rest of his life at Hampstead.

F.O., Jan. 29, 1884.

" DEAR TUTOR,

   I saw Cory the other day, being determined not to miss
him.   It was Sunday and I started early and walked up.   I
arrived at that infernal house of his about twelve, and came just
in time to see him standing at the top of those high steps with
his little son whom he was helping to get down.   He saw someone had come but had no idea who.   I told him who I was and
he asked me if you were coming, and I said that you were away.
He looked very blind and old as he came down the steps, but
walked along very actively when on the level.   He said he
would show me the beauties of rustic Hampstead.   He had been
out every day for six months and had not come to the end of it.

He asked me what I was doing.   I told him, and I was then
questioned about the examinations I had to undergo, and we
talked a little about his old pupils.   Every now and then he
stopped to ask the boy what was the name of this or that tree :
which the boy generally knew.

We talked about Egypt.   He said he had no faith in Gordon.
' They have so many sane men who could do it, why trust it to
a madman ? '   He talked of Dilke a good deal and said he hoped
he would live and get strong because he was a good Whig.

At dinner Cory went on talking of the blue books, which he
said he read right through.   ' The business of Government is
the finest and most interesting in the world.'   He seemed to
have a good deal to do with various statesmen and described
them very graphically.   I should think he got information too,
not at most people's disposal.

I left him soon afterwards, promising to send him blue books.
By the way, I asked him what he thought of ' Inglesant ' :   he

said it was '*mouldy*.'   'Democracy' was a beautiful book : and
he couldn't praise Howells too highly.   I left at three : he took
me to the door ; and I haven't seen him since.   When I got back,
it seemed as if Hampstead was a long way off S. Kensington."

F.O., February.   (Undated.)

" I thought you would be glad to hear about Cory.   You see
much of what he said is come true.   I was rather interested
yesterday to hear from a man that Col. Stewart has written a
letter describing Gordon's proceedings.   I suppose his account
must be true but it seems strange.   It appears that he was with
the King of the Belgians when our Govt. sent for him : that he
had no money and had to go to ask the King to let him off
(' You see,' he said, ' my Queen wants me to go to Egypt,') and
that he borrowed twenty pounds to get back.   When he came
to England he was asked by a friend if he had any money to
take him ? He had forgotten all about that, and seemed very
much surprised when he was told that the Government would
pay his journey.   When he got to Cairo, Baring asked him to
dinner ; and in the evening he got up and said it was time for
him to go.   Baring went down with him to the door, where his
servant met him.   He took off his evening coat and put on a
grey one, being otherwise in dress clothes and white tie, etc.
' Take that back,' he said to the servant, ' or you may sell it if
you like.   I shan't want it again.'   Then he took a small black
bag.   ' Is that right ?   1000 cigarettes ?'   ' Yes,' said the
servant.   ' Then I'm ready,' said Gordon, and went off.   The
train was waiting and he started then and there, after a brief
delay at the station caused by the ' Sultan's son ' whom he
brought with him, and who refused to go without the proper
decorations, which had to be procured.   Baring thought
Gordon was mad, but he got a letter the next day to say that he
had gone so suddenly because he knew there was a plot to
murder him.   The Sultan's son was a great nuisance on the
way.   As they got further from Cairo he got more and more
royal in his demeanour, till, on the steamboat, he stalked into
the best cabin and sat there in state, refusing to move.   Gordon
heard of this, and went into the cabin.   His Majesty asked him
what he meant by entering unannounced into the royal
presence ?   Gordon pointed to the royal robes—which consisted
of a combination of all the known European uniforms with an
Arab element pervading it—and said that he had come to tell
him to change his clothes.   The Sultan protested.   Gordon was
inflexible.   The Sultan requested him at least to go.   Gordon
refused to move, and the Sultan had at last to undress his royal

person in Gordon's presence, and put on his old dirty Arab clothes which he had worn at Cairo before he had become great.

'You will now,' said Gordon, 'remove to the small cabin. I myself will sleep on deck : and my servant shall take your place. Go,' and His Majesty went.

On the way across the desert they met an old Arab friend of Gordon's who was of great use to them though he was nearly blind. Gordon gave him a hundred pound note. He had great difficulty in explaining its use : the Arab expostulating that he could see no use in paper for a blind man. Gordon said that it was an order on a great house of business in England. The Arab said, " Thank you : here all merchants are rogues. But perhaps in England it is different," and took it. All the the way across the desert he talked of what he would do in Khartoum. He seemed to think of nothing else. I was rather amused at an economist I heard the other day, who when he was told of Gordon burning the Govt. Bills expressed his horror, as an economist should : but added, ' I wish someone would burn my bills, though, at my tradesmen's.'

Two days ago I met Sir H. Robinson, who, of course had very much to do with Gordon in S. Africa. He had a very strong objection to him and said, ' When I heard he had been appointed, I said that I knew the Govt. had chosen a man for their servant who would prove their master : and a mad one too.' He said that he had been sent to deal with an awful brute among the natives who was brought to face him with great difficulty. As soon as he saw him, however, Gordon fell upon his neck and called him a brother in Christ ; which was quite contrary to official precedent. Robinson added that there was no one so undecided in word or so decided in action : that he would telegraph one thing in the morning, another thing in the evening, and a third thing on the next day. The only other person I have met who knew him was Sir Bartle Frere, who said that he was impossible to deal with ; ' Tell him a thing's for his interest, he'll do the opposite ; tell him it's his duty and nothing will keep him from doing it, and doing it the shortest way.' I also heard that when he arrived at Souakim in his first visit to the Soudan he found Arabi in command. He went round the prisons and hospitals and found them as they always are under the Egyptian Govt. He sent for Arabi and gave him his choice of three days in prison, three days in the hospital, or back to Cairo. Arabi chose the latter. He used to be called ' Back-to-Cairo Pasha ' by the Arabs, as that was the only order he ever gave to an Egyptian official. Robinson said that Gordon was with him when the invitation came from the King of the

Belgians to go to the Congo. Robinson told him it was a vile climate, that the natives were savages, that it was folly to accept. Gordon said that was precisely the reason he accepted : because he would have killed himself long ago if religion had allowed it— that ' his life was a burden and a weariness to him.'

I suppose he is the strangest man we have ever produced. Lord Wolseley told a man who said he was mad, that the remark reminded him of a story he had once heard of Pitt when he wanted the King to employ Wolfe in Canada. The King said he was young. Pitt said time would cure that. The King said he was of no family. Pitt said he couldn't help it. Then the King said, ' He is mad.' Pitt said, ' If he is mad I wish he would bite some of Your Majesty's other Generals.'

I heard last night that the money for his journey was actually borrowed on Lord Hartington's security at the Athenaeum and the Reform, as Gordon announced his intention of starting by the mail, it then being 5 o'clock and the banks shut. Doesn't it seem strange ? I also heard from the same source that the reason he can't get on with English people is that he can't get over an aversion to anyone who works for money. He doesn't separate it into another art, like Plato. I wish he did. The man who told me this said at the end, ' He is without the three strongest passions which make men good or bad—the love of money, the love of fame, and the love of women.'

What a curious state of things ! Everyone is looking into each other's faces and asking what is the last news and what will be the next. There is a poor fellow in the Turkish Dept. whose brother has just landed at Souakim and who expects to decipher a telegram every moment with bad news in it.''

Baker Pasha—sometime Colonel Valentine Baker—an officer with a brilliant military record, who forfeited his commission in the British army and then distinguished himself for Turkey in the war against Russia, was now serving in the Khedive's army. He was despatched in December 1883 to Souakim on the Red Sea with about 3000 gendarmerie. Gordon had been sent to conduct the evacuation of Khartoum ; Baker's task was to withdraw inland garrisons from the Eastern Soudan into Souakim. In attempting the relief of Tokar, one of the posts, he and his force were overwhelmed by the Dervishes. A purely British force was then sent out under General Graham which defeated Osman Digna's army at El Teb on March 13. But Gordon was already beleaguered in Khartoum, and in autumn an expedition for his relief was prepared under the command of Lord Wolseley. A passing note shows that already Cecil Spring Rice had the disposition to think far ahead, and with imaginative insight.

September 20, 1884.

To STEPHEN.

" . . . What's the betting Wolseley gets up the Nile ? And if he doesn't—And if he does—How about Gordon ? It's funny that a man whom it took one journalist to send should take our only general, two thousand camels, a thousand boats, and ten thousand men to bring back again. However, the years and the months will show ! "

There is no more on this subject ; but the tragedy when it came left its mark. Writing to his brother in 1896, when Kitchener's first move towards the Soudan was announced, he cried out with a kind of horror :

" Who has been consulted ? What influence has been brought to bear ? . . . Excuse a somewhat excited view . . . but as I was in the private secretary's room at the time of Khartoum, I cannot quite get it out of my head."

The Foreign Secretary of these years appears to have left on the young man only an impression of his charm. Spring Rice had personal relations with his chief and went down to stay at Walmer Castle—Lord Granville's residence as Warden of the Cinque Ports. He was then acting as private secretary, and there is a letter, dated April 1885, from one of his most serious-minded friends, Bernard Holland.

" I hear you have been serving your Earl and Master in Kent. I have been meditating on you of late from an admirer's point of view. I think you are a good deal better than most people, because you serve the Idea as well as the Earl, but I wish you would correct an acidity in your judgment of other people (except those who are enemies of the public good)."

The exception was specially designed for Mr. Gladstone, whom Bernard Holland proceeded to consign to the bottomless pit. He thought, however, that age would probably correct the acidity. Cecil Spring Rice's tongue was always an edged weapon, though perhaps, as years went on, it was directed more specially against those whom he considered " enemies " of the " idea," which he certainly never ceased to serve.

His immediate contemporaries and colleagues in the service seem to have regarded him chiefly in these years (if their letters are a guide) as " the wicked wit of the F.O." They clamour for " another anecdote soon, if you have a minute to spare " ; and there was much demand for his other accomplishment of caricature, with which he was prone at this time to adorn official note paper. For instance, Sir Drummond Wolff had been sent out by Lord Salisbury on a special mission in 1885 to negotiate an agreement with Turkey for the evacuation of Egypt within two years. This afforded a subject, and Lord Vaux of Harrowden wrote from Constantinople :

" Your sketch of Wolf and the Turk was much appreciated and we are waiting for a favourable opportunity to show it to the Great Man himself—of course, suppressing your name—and after that it is to be preserved in the Archives of the Agency."

It will be remembered that Mr. Gladstone's Ministry was defeated on the Budget, in June 1885, and resigned office : but since a Redistribution Bill had been passed in 1884 by agreement between parties, a stopgap Tory Government was formed, to carry on until a new register should be completed and a general election held in the newly formed constituencies. This took place in December and the Liberals gained a large majority. When the new Parliament assembled in January 1886, Lord Salisbury's Government was defeated on the address and Mr. Gladstone formed a new Ministry in which Lord Rosebery became Foreign Secretary.

Cecil Spring Rice was now selected for the post of précis writer to the Minister—that is, virtually, assistant private secretary. Lord Rosebery at the same time chose for his parliamentary private secretary a young Scottish landlord, an ex-Guardsman, who in 1884 had been elected Member for Ross and Cromarty and in 1886 (after redistribution) sat for the Leith Burghs. In that way Ronald Munro Ferguson (now Lord Novar) came into close association with Cecil Spring Rice, and from the first the two young men found each other extremely good company. This book will show how the friendship lasted.

The position also involved for Spring Rice some direct contact with home politics, which were then at an exciting and critical period.

In the previous Parliament, Mr. Gladstone's Ministry had been alternately fighting Irish Nationalists and giving in to them. The first stage in the agrarian revolution had been passed ; tenants had acquired a right to their holdings so long as they paid a rent which a court fixed. This broke the power of the landlords and ruined many of them : but it did not appease the Irish demand for Home Rule. Under the new electoral law in 1884 the franchise in Ireland was greatly widened, and as a result the Nationalists captured virtually all seats in Leinster, Munster and Connaught provinces and about half of those in Ulster. Mr. Gladstone yielded to this demonstration and suddenly declared for Home Rule—splitting the Liberal party, from which the Duke of Devonshire, Bright, Chamberlain and some eighty others seceded, taking the name of Liberal Unionists. The first Home Rule Bill, introduced on April 18, was defeated on the second reading on June 8, 1886. Mr. Gladstone decided to dissolve Parliament, a fresh General Election was held in July, and the combined forces of Conservatives and Liberal Unionists gained a large

P.S. I sent the copy of the deed to
      the wrong house at St Ives —
      Could you
      enquire?
      or have you
received it?

Dear Edward

      I am
      unable to
contain my
feelings as you
see. My

name is
            yrs affecte

                  Cecil Arthur Spring
Clerk in the F.O.   Rice

LETTER TO MR. EDWARD O'BRIEN, PROBABLY IN 1885, WHEN THE LIBERALS WERE
DEFEATED AND THE FIGURE OF LORD SALISBURY ROSE LIKE A CLOUD.

majority. Mr. Gladstone resigned and Lord Salisbury took office again, having the Irish revolution and Parnell still to deal with.

The Irish question bulked so large at that time as to colour all politics. By birth Cecil Spring Rice belonged to the Irish landlord class ; his friends, English as well as Irish, were for the most part fiercely opposed to all that Parnell stood for, and took the same view of Mr. Gladstone as did Bernard Holland. But by tradition and by temperament the Spring Rices were Liberals, and his cousin, Lord Monteagle, the head of their house, had one of the fairest minds that was ever allied to a high sense of personal duty. Cecil Spring Rice knew little of Ireland at first hand : he had visited it occasionally ; his centre there had been not so much Mount Trenchard as Valencia, the Knight of Kerry's home ; for Julie Fitzgerald, who afterwards married his brother Stephen, had long been a close friend of his sisters and of himself. The Irish people with whom he was in touch were Irish of the landlord class, but Irish people who loved Ireland more than their class, and had, so far as was possible in a time of revolution, dispassionate and candid intelligences. Traditionally, they were Liberals, and Arthur Hardinge wrote to Spring Rice in February 1885 : " I am sure that, like most intelligent men, you must in your heart have given up this most impotent and most mischievous party. It can only be family pride which makes you still profess to belong to them." But Spring Rice held to his allegiance, and this made it easier for him to be on intimate terms with a young Member of Parliament who was committed to support the Home Rule position. As regards their chief, the Foreign Secretary was officially somewhat detached from Irish affairs ; but he could not be aloof from the conflict, which raged not only between parties but between the factions of the broken party. Lord Rosebery, however, never was much of a party man, and on that account all the more attractive. Cecil Spring Rice's official service under him as précis writer only lasted seven or eight months, but it left a mark. He was fascinated, as was natural, by that brilliant and versatile intelligence. There was in him much of the instinctive hero-worshipper, and Lord Rosebery was perhaps his first hero—and Munro Ferguson's as well.

However, they worshipped gaily. Here are letters from one secretary to the other secretary, collecting information for " Our Lord," as they called him. The first is written four days after the defeat of the Home Rule Bill. Ferguson was then in Scotland with Lord Rosebery.

To FERGUSON.   FOREIGN OFFICE,
                                            June 11, 1886.

" MY DEAR CHERUB,

I have no news for you and if I had I wouldn't do anything to satisfy your debased taste—only I write to get a note out of you, as I suppose you'll stay on in Scotland. A man at Oxford has discovered that there is a place on the top of our

heads where an eye once was. Its rudiments are clearly dis-
cernible and latterly a beast has been found in New Zealand
with the eye developed. This is perfectly true and shows that
we were once fonder of looking up to heaven than we are now.
I saw a man last night who was a chapel friend of Chamberlain's [1]
and much deplored his perversion. He said their common
Minister had complained that we had brought him (Chamberlain) up to believe in one God, and now that it had become
himself. But he said he would return to the fold when he had
learned his lesson. He said Chamberlain sympathised with the
South at the beginning of the American Civil War and only
changed sides towards the end. He seemed a sort of lobbyist
like other great people [2] and had been interviewing Manning—
who said, ' I am an Imperialist, and in this faith will die.'
Manning showed a good deal of anxiety about the prospects of
the Church in Ireland, and indeed no wonder. The Duke of
Norfolk could not appear at a Catholic education meeting
because the Irish said they would hoot him off the platform.
The Church only wants an excuse to go over. This man was a
tall, fat, heavy-eyed person who dropped an occasional ' h '
and spoke as if every sentence ought to have begun, ' My Lords
and Gentlemen.' He advocated Mr. G.'s scheme as being
absolutely perfect and explained the talk about Ireland in
London in this way :

' When I was last here all the world was talking of Egypt.
I am a merchant and have much to do with Egypt. Things
are neither better nor worse—in principle—now than then.
We pay as much and get as little. Does anyone talk of Egypt
now ? Not a word. It's all Ireland. The fact is, people only
want a peg to hang abuse of Mr. Gladstone on, or an excuse for
turning Tory, which they've been in their hearts for years.

' If this Irish question were really serious, we know that
Ireland would be a crown colony in five minutes—or a separate
nation—one or the other. It's only a two-penny halfpenny
question, really—and so we keep it dangling on. And there are
fifty thousand voters in Birmingham who think as I do. Are
we going to destroy our system of party Govt. for that ? God
bless you—no.'

At which moment he upset my glass. Afterwards he described
an interview between Morley and Bright which ended by
Bright asking Morley if he justified the Dublin murders !
Morley said, ' No, I explain them.' Bright said, ' Then I think

[1] Joseph Chamberlain was originally a Unitarian.
[2] The duties of a parliamentary private secretary involve much interviewing, and in another letter Ferguson is addressed as "My Dear Lobbyist."

I had better go to bed,' and went. This was a year ago at Chamberlain's.''

June 19, 1886.

'' I don't like Mr. G.'s last speech as it doesn't seem to take advantage of the enthusiastic side of the question. His speeches on the way up were better. I don't see why Almighty God should have been dragged in by the ears (if he has any) either. Our Lord's speech was much better.

Bryce wants him to speak in the E. end, but he says he's had enough of speaking and that his boxes [1] are the real thing and the speaking very poor froth. Also he says he doesn't know anything about the subject. I'm sorry for this.

Surely you could make it a question not of detailed knowledge but principle and sentiment. The desire for Home Rule is sentimental and must be met by sentiment. The strength of the adversaries lies naturally enough in detailed objections. If you enter into these, you are fighting with assegais when you might be using Martini Henrys. It's chivalrous but not good tactics. The argument which is the strength of the American Irish should be now our strength too : ask yourself what makes these cooks and housemaids subscribe their wages to an Irish parliamentary fund, and when you have understood the feeling, try and make others see it too—and that would be using a stronger argument than all the objections of detail. However, I am going off—not my head, but to the Durdans.''

June 23, 1886.

'' The *Spectator* is interesting on Lord R. Have you seen it ?

He was in the best form at the Durdans, especially with Lady Dalhousie, whom he chaffed in his most amusing way about the contrast between herself and the Secretary for Scotland in point of view of work. He also made a most beautiful sketch of the speech he would have delivered on the occasion of the Queen's jubilee—how she was born in happy innocence, etc., etc., and wooed and wed the husband of her choice. We all screamed with laughter, especially Sanderson,[2] whose spectacles came off into his soup.''

The Home Rule Government resigned on July 21, and Lord Salisbury formed an administration in which Lord Iddesleigh (Sir Stafford Northcote) was Foreign Secretary. No Liberal Unionists took

---

[1] Despatch boxes—work of the office proper.

[2] Sir Thomas (afterwards Lord) Sanderson, permanent head of the Foreign Office then and for many years. The spectacles were so integral a part of his personality that the Office always knew him as '' Lamps.''

office ; they professed to look forward to the reunion of the Liberal Party.

Parliament met on August 7 and continued to sit through that month. On July 1st, 1886, Spring Rice wrote to Ferguson, who was then electioneering in his constituency :

" I went out a sail on Sunday and being becalmed on Monday didn't arrive till Tuesday (with the milk, as H. L.[1] said)—at five in the morning. The next day, coming to the office, I saw a box for me. I opened it and saw in red ink :

> ' Situation of précis-writer vacant.
> No yachtsman need apply. R.'

You may imagine my feelings and H. L.'s amusement at them.

The ' political hermaphrodite ' is good. You might compare them to the Chinese torture of making a man sit on a razor so that he is gradually slit up the middle—into Tory or Liberal. Randolph and Parnell are going it. I hope you won't blackguard your opponent more than is absolutely necessary, because, even if you hit him, some of the dirt sticks to your own hands.

Ld. R.'s bell rings.—' Will you write to Mr. Munro Ferguson of Novar and ask him to transmit forthwith for my information the full report of Sir A. Orr Ewing's address, as well as to inform me whether the expression " political hermaphrodite " is his own. The last statement to be on oath.'

I have given the message.
Yours ever,
C. A. S. R."

Evidently Lord Rosebery suspected that his official précis writer was furnishing platform material to the parliamentary private secretary—a conjecture which had good grounds. Here is a letter written on July 6 (after the first election results had come in) which contains more than mere ingenious terms of reproach for Liberal Unionists.

" Thanks very much for your letter. We are now gone coons. Do not, however, give us the additional misery of knowing that you are a gone coon too. You must certainly win and win in a magnificent canter.

I wish I could think of anything remotely interesting from the political point of view. It seems to me now that the Tories, having been engaged in various and intricate incantations for some time past, have at last succeeded in calling up the spirit of coercion, and now that he's come they will find it hard to get rid of him. Seriously, things are very bad. I don't

---

[1] Henry Austin Leigh, official private secretary to the Minister.

know if worse than if a Gladstonian majority were to come to pass, but still very very beastly for everyone.

Remember this little fact. That the American war—the most bullying folly we ever committed—was loudly applauded by the feeling of the richer and the more educated classes—see Lecky for that—and that Dr. Johnson, the greatest swell of the literary world wrote a pamphlet in support of it.

Remember also what I quoted before. The magic of property in land changes sand into gold—the magic of property in institutions turns thieves into honest men.

The best of all possible seats in the best of all possible counties ! "

FOREIGN OFFICE,
July 21, 1886.

" DEAR FERGUSON,
The chief says, ' Invite Ferguson to the Durdans from Saturday to Monday next.'

So I do and I have no doubt you will go.

He also says, ' Tell Ferguson I am profoundly hurt at his not writing to me, and that he ought to express repentance.' I have no doubt you will.

Harcourt met Hartington at Londonderry House. Hartington said, ' Are you come here to remind us that the house belonged to the founder of the Union ? (Lord Castlereagh). ' Yes,' said Harcourt, ' and to add that he cut his own throat.'

Yesterday Mr. G. went to the ball at Grosvenor House. He was received warmly by the Duke, but backs were largely turned, especially female ones. Lady Spencer was ostentatiously cut by—Lady Ardilaun. Poor Lady Spencer !

Batoum is in a curious state and when you come back you will find subjects of interest here, but perhaps I had better not write a letter about things a drunken man should not know. And you will, I suppose, be in that state on Friday evening.

Goodbye and give us news and good news of Leith."

Friday was to be the declaration of the Leith polling : and however the result was celebrated, the news was good : the Government went out, but Ferguson kept his seat. More jottings of the time follow.

FOREIGN OFFICE,
August 13, 1886.

" DEAR FERGUSON,
I was rather amused at a conversation I had with the Duchess of Marlborough about Lord Randolph. It appears he has most *affection* for our Lord among contemporary poli-

ticians and most *sympathy* with Chamberlain. Dilke he never liked. He is never angry, so she said, about abuse of himself and he is never angry when abusing others. She was very much hurt when I hinted that I had heard his wife wrote his address. ' No,' she said, ' he has no particular political adviser except his mother.' She said Lord Salisbury was a child about everything but foreign politics and that he had to be advised about the smallest things.

I also talked to our only General (Wolseley) who was very great on the Russian plan for the invasion of India communicated by Nicolson.[1] He gave 1889 as the year of Armageddon. He had heard Morier was in favour of an understanding with Russia but said that he could not for a moment regard such an understanding as anything more than a truce in which to prepare for war. He said he thanked God Lord Rosebery wasn't a ' vestryman like most of our ministers.'

I dined with Currie [2] last night where diplomats from various parts of the world met. Sir J. D. Hay [3] was splendid. He is a little, upright man with very dark face and very white moustaches, spry and bright-eyed with a clear voice. He looked quite big as he sat : when he got up, his smallness was quite a surprise. He described presenting his credentials. You ride up with all your retinue to a great closed gate. Trumpets sound : the gate unbolts and opens and the Sultan appears in jewels and gold—with his umbrella over his head—on horseback. (You know the horse is a Moor's throne.) You dismount, take his hand : and His Shereefian Majesty, descendant of Fatima, daughter of the prophet (probably also the son of a black slave from Khartoum) begins to—bark—as shyness has such an effect on him that he can't speak plainly. The Foreign Minister explains that he is blessing your grandmother with the usual compliments—but I am marking time and must really stop.''

Spring Rice, deprived of his précis-writership by Lord Rosebery's resignation, applied for leave and spent it on visiting his younger brother Gerald who had then settled in Canada. He alludes to his departure in a letter, in which, as in a great many others, he amused

[1] General (then Colonel) M. H. Nicolson, a distinguished soldier and linguist who served much on the Afghan border.

[2] Sir Philip H. W. (afterwards Lord) Currie, was then senior clerk in charge of the Eastern Dept. at the Foreign Office ; later he was ambassador at Constantinople and at Rome.

[3] Sir John Drummond Hay, Britain's diplomatic representative in Morocco from 1847 to 1886.

himself by making suggestions for his politician friend to work into speeches. This one shows where he stood on the Irish question.

Foreign Office,
August 14, 1886.

" Dear Ferguson,

You might hammer away at the Markis.

His Lordship says, ' Strong in the verdict of a united country to which we have appealed we take our stand, etc., etc., nothing will move us.' But what would a member of the Irish party say ? because we must take them into account now.

' You say, my Lord, you are strong in the verdict of a united country—that is a few thousand votes have changed sides. Have we no united country ? What does the Conservative victory in England look like when compared to ours in Ireland ? If you intend to stand firm in the name of popular feeling, we shall stand firm too—for what is the popular feeling you rely on compared to ours ? As long as you appeal to national prejudice and national tradition and to the weight of numbers, the arguments which have weight with you will have tenfold weight with us. For the national pride of the nation which oppresses another has never prevailed in the end against the national hatred of the nation which is oppressed. One is fitful, uncertain, the luxury of wealth and ease : the other is perpetual and untiring in good fortune or in bad.

The Irishman clothes himself with hate as with a garment and he'll only take it off for the sunshine.

That is the style of the Limerick trumpet which was once our daily delight.

However, in sober Scotch you might point out that the way to conquer this *national* feeling is by merging it in an *imperial* feeling—just as England and Scotland, by Act of Parliament, became Great Britain. But the ' United Kingdom of Great Britain and Ireland, the Empire of India, the Australian and Canadian colonies, etc.,' will some day be blended, with or without Acts of Parliament, in Greater Britain. It is the only way.

The argument that Ireland, while kept down by coercion, might be conciliated by improvements by Act of Parliament seems like the old work-house policy which first made a man a slave and then made him a beggar. Also it's very expensive. One's throat takes a long time quenching when you drink at another man's expense. You give a man a drink and ask if it doesn't make him another man, and he answers, ' Yes, and the other man is mighty thirsty, too.' "

This habit of " devilling " for his friend lasted with Spring Rice up to the time as long as the friend remained a candidate for Parliament. " He wrote the speeches and I delivered them," says Lord Novar ; who says also that " Springy " had a great deal to do with making and keeping him a Home Ruler, he himself having no strong feeling on the question.

It is more to the present purpose that Lord Novar remembers those months in the secretaries' room as among the pleasantest of his life. These young men had friendly access to their chief and it is not hard to believe Lord Novar that Lord Rosebery was the best of all talkers then living. Apart from that, they were exceedingly well able to amuse each other. " Springy's " gift of caricature was a source of joy, and official labours did not deny him time to indulge it. When Lord Iddesleigh on Lord Rosebery's resignation became Foreign Secretary, his head figured largely ; and it is recorded that, having done what no previous Minister had been known to do and undertaken a tour of the office, he found the mantelpiece in Mr. Spring Rice's room decorated with a portrait of himself—not designed for his eye.

Mr. Francis Villiers—son of a former Secretary for Foreign Affairs whom the Foreign Office then always called " the great Lord Clarendon"—was chief official private secretary to Lord Rosebery, and the younger men found him a friendly superior : indeed, his friendship with Spring Rice grew close and lasting. At the time, according to Lord Novar, he contemplated with some disapproval, the irregular ways of Lord Rosebery's précis writer. " Springy's table—and he had a very big table—was always two feet deep in papers," says Lord Novar, " and, there was Springy with his hair standing on end." But, like many other workers who apparently live in a litter, he could always find the paper he wanted. As to his hair, nature dealt with that by premature baldness.

His handwriting also, as many notes in the correspondence show, was a cause of scandal. In those days the Foreign Office, still innocent of typewriters, placed great importance on a fine round script. Spring Rice's hand, first and last, had no official appearance ; there were traces of the Oxford type in it, but it was not typically the scholar's ; it lacked the clean finish, just as his spelling never had the born scholar's instinctive rightness. On the whole it was a legible hand, but few of his letters are without some word that must be guessed from the context. It is a delicate and sensitive writing, varying from day to day, according to health or mood, but free from the downward droop of the lines which marks a discouraged nature. It is indeed the writing of a poet rather than of a man of affairs—or even of a man of letters : though long use made an improvement and Mr. Villiers would have had less reason to find fault with what he wrote at fifty than at twenty-four.

One more letter of his gossip from the Foreign Office may close the period of his service within doors. For the rest of his life, though he had yet no guess of it, he was to be continually employed abroad, in the other branch.

FOREIGN OFFICE,
August 17, 1886.

" I met d'Aubigny last night at Currie's. He told me he had known the King of Bavaria well as an attaché and described an attempt made to give him a taste for female society by the direction of the Bavarian Cabinet. An actress was deputed (after due inspection from competent authorities) to give him lessons in elocution. In the course of her third lesson she went nearer and nearer to the king, " et lui effleure le genou. Le roi se lève, et avec un geste terrible la consigne à la porte. Les nouvelles se repandent. Le corps diplomatique en était très ému, je vous assure, etc., etc."

Cross is to be Lord Cross of Furness. Lord Salisbury (who is the first Prime Minister since Pitt who has dined at Clapham —I saw the house) confided this fact with shouts of laughter to Philip Currie at dinner.

Philip, who knows Lord Salisbury well, says the better you know him, the more he takes fun out of every subject except the Christian religion as by law established in England. But his health is really very bad indeed and it is very doubtful if he can stand much strain or work even when he can take it laughing."

Spring Rice's visit to his brother Gerald at Pense in the North-West Territory was a success. Weather had gone wrong, the crops had been a failure, but he enjoyed being with the farm hands.

" You couldn't have jollier companions : the only thing I don't like is sleeping in a bed with someone else, and I got out of that by sleeping on the floor in the kitchen."

They spent ten days out camping and hunting : their meat was stolen by an Indian woman's dog ; they had to depend on their guns ; and once were " pretty well done for," lacking water till they came on some half breeds and his French was useful, and they camped alltogether

" They come over here to trade furs for pipes and baccy. I do their portraits. They sit and grin and simper and bring the pictures home to their wives."

Returning in November he reported enthusiasm in America for Mr. Gladstone and strong feeling against Lord Randolph Churchill. This he had gathered " by talking to any extent in the train and the steamer."—In the course of this talking he had made the beginnings of a friendship whose importance no man then could have guessed.

Theodore Roosevelt, having been defeated for the mayoralty of New York, sailed next morning for England in company with his

Dear Lobbirol

    Lord Rosebery says

    "Did the Master write to
Schadhorst?"

      I have never seen him & can
only do his portrait by implication.

    You see his hands

        Yrs ever

          C A S R

LETTER TO MR. FERGUSON SHOWING MR. CHAMBERLAIN UNDER THE WHIP
OF MR. SCHNADHORST, ORGANISER OF THE "CAUCUS."

sister, Mrs. Cowles. Spring Rice had been told they would be on board, and that he should introduce himself, which he did. His note to his brother says :

" I came over with Roosevelt, who has been standing for the mayoralty of New York against H. George and who is supposed to be the boss Republican young man. He is going to be married and then to be in England in February so that you will see him, I hope."

Here, for a curiosity, is the first letter written by Roosevelt to Spring Rice : the beginning of a correspondence which if printed in full would fill volumes.

BROWN'S HOTEL,
Nov. 16.

" MY DEAR MR. RICE,

 Thank you very heartily for your courtesy, which I assure you I appreciate. I will dine with you with pleasure at the Savile Club on Wednesday. Friday I go out to Buxton's. I shall see you this evening at 7.30.

Always truly yours,
T. ROOSEVELT."

The acquaintance must have ripened fast into friendship, for on December 2 of that year Cecil Spring Rice acted as best man when Theodore Roosevelt married Miss Edith Kermit Carow at St. George's, Hanover Square. " Characteristically, he had me married in bright orange gloves," Roosevelt wrote long after, " which I accepted with a calm wholly unwarranted."—Mrs. Cowles adds a note : " Dear Springy was so delightful and like himself when I went to put on Edith's veil. I warned Theodore to start immediately for the church as it was a foggy day, and they were intensely occupied in a discussion over the population of an island in the Southern Pacific."

The two men were almost exactly of an age : Roosevelt just on twenty-eight, Spring Rice just short of it. But the senior by four months was by many years the elder mind, more mature through experience. At twenty Theodore Roosevelt, breaking away from all the traditions of his class and upbringing, entered American politics and was elected a Republican member of Assembly in the State of New York. He had only just left Harvard and on his twenty-second birthday he married his first wife, Miss Lee. In April 1882, while Cecil Spring Rice was still uncertain what career to follow, Roosevelt was demanding in the New York Assembly the impeachment of a judge for corruption, and forced the appointment of a committee to investigate. By the age of twenty-three he was recognised as an independent power and secured re-election in spite of the popular reaction which brought a Democrat, Grover Cleveland, into office as Governor of New York by a huge majority in the autumn of 1882.

He was elected for a third term in 1883, still fighting a lone hand as reformer. Early in 1884 he lost within two days his mother and his wife. Later in that year, a political crisis helped to age this man of twenty-five. A Presidential election was impending, and the progressive elements in the Republican party, Roosevelt included, fought fiercely to oppose the choice of James G. Blaine, a Republican candidate. But the Convention at Chicago carried Blaine—and split the Republicans. A large body seceded and became Independents—who rapidly were fixed with the name of mugwumps. Roosevelt refused to join the movement : he thought Blaine personally a bad candidate, but he was not prepared to destroy the Republican party on that issue : and acting in concert with Cabot Lodge, who had joined him in the opposition to Blaine, he accepted the party's decision and worked hard for Blaine's success.

Cleveland was elected—the first Democrat to hold the Presidency since the Civil War. Roosevelt withdrew from public life and for nearly two years lived on the Elkhorn Ranch in the " Bad Lands," and established himself as a comrade among the cowboys of the Little Missouri. He was on his ranch in 1888 when he learnt that a body of Independents had nominated him as candidate for the Mayoralty of New York—the Democratic candidate being Hewitt, while Henry George was put up by the " United Labour Party." Hewitt, a man of high character, who had the backing of Tammany, won : George ran second : Roosevelt was third, but he had regained the confidence of the Republican independents.

He had already written copiously. His *History of the Naval War of 1812* was published in 1882 and his volume on Thomas Hart Benton in the " American Statesmen " series in 1886 : and several of his papers on ranch life and hunting had appeared.

This combination of the student with the political reformer and the pioneer was exactly to the taste of Cecil Spring Rice, who loved literature, cared exceedingly for " The Idea " in politics, and throughout his life looked up to the man of resolute courage. He had found the man on whom more and more his faculty of hero-worship spent itself, in a new course of life which opened in December 1886—in a certain sense at his request, but without his having any idea where the opening would lead him. He applied to his official superiors to be allowed an exchange of duty with one of the secretaries of Legation at Washington—for that capital was not then dignified with an Embassy. Arthur Hardinge wrote to him a comment which compares oddly in the later developments.

" I hope you may get your exchange, though why choose Washington which is out of all politics ? Of course it is interesting in a way, and West is a charming chief. But still it seems so off the line."

Why he chose it, why he suddenly thought of this variation in his way of life, the letter gives no indication. Possibly, for the family tie was very strong, he wished for the chance to be within reach of his emigrated brother. Possibly the suggestion came from Roosevelt : still more possibly both causes operated. At all events, the exchange was only contemplated as a temporary affair ; he had as yet no thought of going into the other branch of the service. He wrote to Ferguson :

> " . . . I am going to Washington, if Villiers allows, for six months or a year as a change.
>
> Did I tell you about my acquaintance, Roosevelt ? He has been married—I had to be his best man as he knew nobody in London. I wore my frock coat. . . . He is in Italy. When he comes back, you must be civil to him as he is one of the most amusing people one can meet, and his wife is charming. You must also try and induce our Lord to be kind to him.

The frock coat is mentioned here as something of an unusual concession to ceremony. Spring Rice, according to testimony, did not take much care how he should be clothed. Arthur Hardinge, replying to a letter which had described the marriage of some friend of them both, makes this comment :

> " It was so like him to be disgracefully dressed on his wedding day, and it was just the sort of thing (don't be angry with me) that you would have done yourself, only that you would have probably been very late into the bargain."

There are indeed strange legends about the clothes in which Cecil Spring Rice did actually get married.

He was throughout life, in spite of his official training, untidy and casual. Another friend of his remembers him, having risen early in the morning to meet her and her husband, guests of honour, and presenting to the world the back view of a collar with his name written largely and legibly across it. But no one denied his charm ; and to the young men who about this time were leaving the universities he was known as one of the most admired and quoted among those who had begun to take their places in the world. They keep a memory of his natural but entirely modest ease with important seniors, presences that froze others like huge icebergs ; they remember how skilfully he could keep up the bowling after dinner to some formidable batsman, such as Mr. Joseph Chamberlain.

One of these observers notes that " Springy " was in a measure distrusted by some of his official chiefs as " too clever and fly-away " : he did not conform to the type of the perfect clerk who could " put all you wanted about any subject on half a sheet of letter paper." But such half-sheets contain nothing that has been gained by entering into other people's minds. The perfect official of this type has no imagination, no desire to get into other people's minds : whereas " there was Springy, watching you all the time like a cat through his twinkling eyes from behind his pince-nez."

CHAPTER III

FIRST YEARS AT WASHINGTON

BEFORE the letters and extracts which make the substance of the next three chapters are read, it is well to bear in mind what were Cecil Spring Rice's relations with the United States and with their people. He came to Washington, a young man fastidiously brought up, but above all imbued with that supreme disgust for political corruption which has put vitriol into the ink of so many writers : he saw much that revolted him and did not spare his satire. If American testimony of the period is to be taken into account, his scorn is not surprising. Again, he was a devoted lover of the country which he served, and the society in which he found himself was impregnated with a traditional hatred for Great Britain. That again repelled him, as was natural, because the common speech, and the common blood, made it seem unnatural. Yet at the end of his work, and as it proved, at the end of his life, he could write with all sincerity, in a farewell letter to one of the most prominent Americans :

" Looking back on my many years spent in Washington . . . the memory is one of a bright vista of friends. Whatever may be said of the relations, politically speaking, of England and America, one thing is absolutely certain—in no country can we Englishmen make such friendships."

He might well say it. He came to America having only two friends in advance—though Theodore Roosevelt was no common man to have for a friend, and Roosevelt's sister was also a pillar of strength. But even so it was notable that within a couple of years he had become an accredited member of perhaps the most distinguished group of men and women that America could then show. It is best depicted in that queer and attractive autobiography which is called *The Education of Henry Adams* : a single sentence from this indicates that two brilliant women were its controlling powers.

" Senator Cameron of Pennsylvania had married in 1880 a young niece of Senator John Sherman of Ohio, thus making an alliance of dynastic importance in politics, and in society a reign of sixteen years, during which Mrs. Cameron and Mrs.

Lodge led a career, without precedent and without succession, as the dispensers of sunshine over Washington."

From 1887 to 1895 Washington was Spring Rice's place of abode, with two periods of absence during which the tie was maintained by many correspondences, both with men and women. Later on, again and again in far-off places we find him turning back to the thought of homes in America almost as if they were his own. On the other hand Henry Adams, recalling the life of those years, sets the young Englishman in the group as one of its outstanding figures.

" Whatever one's preferences in politics might be, one's house was bound to the Republican interest when sandwiched between Senator Cameron, John Hay and Cabot Lodge, with Theodore Roosevelt equally at home in them all, and Cecil Spring Rice to unite them by impartial variety."

Of the men, Adams himself and his close intimate, John Hay, were the most characteristic figures : their houses almost side by side made one of the material pivots. Mrs. Hay, and the swarm of his wife's nieces who surrounded Henry Adams, came in, as did Senator Lodge and Senator Cameron, by right of alliance. Roosevelt, when he was in Washington, was scarcely less an essential personage of the circle than Adams and Hay ; but he was often a grass widower at Washington and at these times Cecil Spring Rice used to come and keep house with him. Mrs. Roosevelt, though she was familiar in the Washington group, evidently associated herself in Spring Rice's imagination with her home at Sagamore Hill on Oyster Bay in Long Island, and this was outside the Washington radius. But, in 1887 Roosevelt was still living on his ranch, and had no part in Washington life.

Life there was town life, but in a town not very much bigger than Oxford—some 150,000 people—it was a society where an old resident knew by sight everyone who kept a carriage. The standard of living was determined by the average expenditure of Congressmen who received a thousand a year—ministers having fifteen hundred. Few people were rich, and the way of existence was simple. Mr. Secretary Bayard always prepared his own terrapin on the table in a chafing dish, and a well-known Senator made a ceremony of carving his Rhode Island Turkey. The Roosevelts when they came into residence occupied a very small house in a back street and asked their friends in to high tea, or a steak and a glass of claret.

Another household in Washington where Spring Rice was always welcome was that of Mrs. Cowles, Roosevelt's sister and confidante, a woman of talent that matched her brother's. Lord Novar, writing of the intimacy in which he found his friend established here, says : " You might have thought they had been brought up together when I joined their circle "—only a year later.

MRS. CAMERON

From an etching by Paul Helleu

As for the group or coterie, its associations were in the main Republican, but not severely exclusive : at least one Democratic household belonged to the circle, that of Mr. Endicott, Cleveland's Secretary for War, whose daughter became Mrs. Joseph Chamberlain ; and in this family Cecil Spring Rice was speedily at home. Others, not definitely political, were of the set ; for instance, Mr. and Mrs. Winthrop Chanler ; and from the time when Miss Mary Leiter—afterwards Lady Curzon—appeared in Washington, she was more than welcome everywhere.

The ultimate test of admission to the coterie was at the threshold of 1603 H Street, the house of Henry Adams. In his view, a modern salon should be organised to keep people out, not to draw them in ; and he acted on his theory. This remarkable man, after his wife's death, never went into society ; society had to come to him. In a town of diplomats and officials, he called on no one, and never left a card—not even on ambassadors. They like the rest had to be introduced by those permitted to stand sponsors, and such introductions were eagerly sought after. His household was conducted on simple and regular lines, by a negro major-domo and a negress housekeeper. At breakfast—for he lived in the continental fashion—covers were laid for six ; at dinner for four ; intimates came when they pleased and at the midday meal there was often a search for chairs. Nobody had a better established footing in this hospitable house than " Springy."

But above all the young man was made welcome by the two presiding ladies in their houses at Washington, and not only there. Every year in the hot weather the British Ambassador moved up to Manchester on the Massachusetts shore north of Boston, where a cold current sets in ; and some of the staff always followed him. Near by, at Nahant, Senator Lodge had his home ; and at Beverley Senator and Mrs. Cameron used to take a seaside house. These households were happy extensions of the Washington group, almost as homelike as Old Church or Hallsteads on his adored Ullswater.

Cecil Spring Rice was throughout his life a lover of society, but of society that included women. He was no clubman. Few men have made more lasting friendships with other men, and it was a man's job to live on terms of intimacy with Roosevelt. But Spring Rice had also a singular gift for friendship, and lasting friendship, with women and it was never more happily employed than in these years. He was more than commonly sensitive to beauty and those who knew him remember how he would sometimes come back from a function depressed, moping, and not fit to speak to, till some of his friends, forcing him to confession, would draw out the declaration, " They were all such ugly people there."—This was the last charge that could be brought against the ladies who specially adopted him. John Hay says in one of his letters, written years later, " Mrs. Cameron is more beautiful than ever, which was superfluous " ; and by all testimony Mrs. Lodge whom Spring Rice reverently worshipped was a radiant

vision in youth and kept even into her years of grandmotherhood
that grace of line and movement which is the habit of beauty.

These ladies were attracted to the young man by his wit, his
knowledge and his charm, and his gift for equal companionship; but
it is plain also that his perfect incompetence to take care of himself in
small but vital matters was an appeal that they could not resist.
And so while he instructed them to read Plato's *Republic*, and to
think accurately, with detailed information, about the relation of
states and the duties of citizenship, or delighted them with stories of
Irish banshees, they taught him to bring his socks and linen to be
revised and corrected, and in general endeavoured that he should
when necessary be properly dressed on parade—a result which, by
consent of testimony, was always difficult to accomplish. His profession made it almost necessary that he should be well dressed on
occasion and his lithe active figure helped out his natural *chic*. But
part of his nature was a dislike to ceremony, and though never
slovenly, he was untidy to excess. It is agreed by those who knew
him in America, and by others who met him later in life, that the
ladies who took his wardrobe in hand had their work cut out. He
submitted with meekness, and, at all events in these early years, with
shyness ; for with all his exuberance of talk he was timid, and with
those whom he liked, almost deprecatory ; and they liked him the
better for it.

Also, since he neither knew nor cared what he ate and lacked the
most rudimentary knowledge how to care for his not very robust
health, Mrs. Lodge and Mrs. Cameron fetched him out to their homes
to be dieted and cossetted. Moreover, being in essential matters
much more grown-up than this diplomat, they elder-sistered him,
Mrs. Lodge in particular took in hand from the first to curb the
sharpness of his tongue and told him plainly that he must say fewer
of the biting things that came so quick to the tip of it. This is said
to have worked a perceptible amendment, though even to the end of
his days, and, as British Ambassador in war-time, he could not always
resist such temptation.

One thing should be noted that endeared him to these American
women of the world. He had no austerity and loved gossip, and was
as ready as anyone to retail stories on the themes that have provided
so much of the world's amusement ; and at times, in his correspondence with men one finds him indulging in the picturesqueness of
some Rabelaisian phrase—though these always sounded odd in
his mouth. But it is remembered of him by the survivor of those
hostesses to whom he owed so much, and gave so much, that never
once was his talk with her other than she would have chosen for
her daughter to hear.

Yet in these earlier years, there was always an estranging element.
These people loved him, he loved them, but they hated his country :
Senator Lodge, for instance, notably. At last in 1898 the events of
the Spanish American War brought a marked change, which spread

and developed, until in the last period of Spring Rice's career he found himself England's representative at Washington in the European War, and Senator Lodge championing in the Senate the cause of the Allies before America had yet declared for them and against Germany.

Roosevelt counted for much in that transformation, as he counted for much in all the development of modern America : and as this book goes on, it will be seen how Cecil Spring Rice found himself the trusted counsellor, not only of his own Government, but of the President of the United States, on matters of world politics.   It will be seen also that among all the men whom he met and watched, he ranked none higher than this American—none perhaps so high.

All this should be remembered by those who read his sketches of American life and of the American people.   It should be remembered also that what seemed to him disgraceful in America irked him because it disgraced a nation of his own blood.   Americans were never to him really foreigners.   Had they been, he would have judged them by a less exacting standard.

When Cecil Spring Rice joined the British Legation at Washington the Minister was Sir Lionel Sackville-West (afterwards Lord Sackville).   President Cleveland had been two years at the White House, and his Secretary of State was Mr. Bayard ; but Republicans had a majority in the Senate.   The period since the war of North and South was shorter than that which separates us in 1929 from the struggle in South Africa.   Two of the men with whom Spring Rice became most intimate, John Hay and Henry Adams, were only twenty years his seniors ; but Hay had been Lincoln's Secretary through the war, and Adams was with his father at the Embassy in London, staving off a conflict between Great Britain and the North.

Irish questions were scarcely less to the fore at Washington than in London.   Mr. Arthur Balfour, as Chief Secretary in Lord Salisbury's Government, was drastically coercionist, and the Parnellites had powerful support in America.   Spring Rice described the situation to his brother Stephen in a letter dated March 9, 1887.

" Feeling here was, I think, pretty well expressed by Blaine's son.   He thought the Home Rule Bill must necessarily come to smash and that it justly did—as from a commercial and military point of view a separate Govt., possibly independent, would be very dangerous, especially to the American trade.   But that some sort of way by which, like the Southern States, Ireland should be left to work out her own salvation should be devised, he regarded as very necessary.   He seemed to think that it would not be very difficult either, and didn't regard the question as very important.   Perhaps, he said, it is more awkward to us than to you.

There are some curious questions arising.   Notably in the

relation of the Pope to the Irish and Socialists.　There is great
fear of the spread of the Catholics.　The only thing is that, as a
good many are rich, the Pope will not be able to take openly the
socialistic side."

Ireland apart, there was chronic friction between England and
America on the claims of American vessels to fish in Canadian waters.
In 1885, American boats were seized by the Canadian authorities on
a charge of poaching, and their catch and nets were confiscated.
The matter had come before Lord Rosebery and his private secretaries,
who were now planning to renew their companionship in America.

March 18, 1887.

To FERGUSON.

"It's a grand thing if you really are coming out here.　We
should have a splendid time.　I am going up to New York and
I shall meet Roosevelt there who is the great hunter of the
West.　He would be only too glad to take you to his ranch
and then on all over his Rocky Mountain district.　You will
come back with heads enough to provide horns for all the
c——ds[1] in Scotland.　I will carry your gun and cook.　In
April I shall go off to Virginia and will tell you what that is
like.　If you come in the summer, you won't see any political
people, as they don't collect here till December.　They are
splendid fellows to talk if you get hold of them, and you could
fill buckets full of information in a few days.　I won't trouble
you with any shop.　I passed a cart load out to our beloved
chief, which I wouldn't have done if I hadn't believed that it
really is worth while to put a certain amount of pressure on
public opinion in order to get a settlement over and done before
the next fishing season begins.　Do you remember in our
golden days, how, when the business began and the papers were
teeming with seizures, a letter arrived from West, looking very
pregnant in a big envelope ?　And how it turned out to contain
merely an extract from a newspaper on the subject of the Irish
vote and the influence of the Home Rule Question on the
relations of the two countries.　I remember our Lord lifting his
eyebrows and holding out the document at arms-length and
saying, ' This is a satisfactory elucidation of this important
question and shows conclusively the advantage of a well-
informed diplomatic agent.'

The diplomatic agent in question " [West] " is a curious
person.　His conversation is just like his correspondence—when

---

[1] This ancient and most respectable word is so written in the MS. :
Spring Rice was almost absurdly fastidious, even on paper.

it exists at all.   At first sight you would think he was about as
bad a man as you could have here.   But I can't think he is at
all a bad man.   The Americans thoroughly understand him
and tell him all sorts of things they don't to anyone else.   They
have a common taste for whiskey, poker and business, and a
common hatred for female society.   He never humbugs anyone,
and never makes any bones over asking for what he wants, and
he always gets it.   To our Government unfortunately he is so
hopelessly reserved that unless he is directly asked for anything
he never gives anything at all.

Bayard is just the other way.   He is very intellectual and
cultured :   he has a most captivating manner and striking
appearance.   And they all hate him.   That sort of thing
doesn't go down among a lot of politicians and business men
like the Senators.   They don't like to call him their superior
and so say he is a pompous ass.   I like him tremendously and
as I had said I was précis writer to Lord Rosebery (which on
enquiry turned out to be true) he was very jolly to me and
I see him pretty often.   We have made friends also over
Wordsworth, who is my love.

The worst of it is that it is pretty evident that, as a free trader
openly professing his conviction, everything he does is viewed
with the greatest suspicion.   Of course, the quarrel is purely
one of protection and tariff.   Perhaps the absurdity of cutting
off their own noses to spite their faces may make itself felt in
time, but in order to let this work we should avoid any possibility of an armed encounter.   The possibility is even probable.

Only one thing besides.   The worst of the system of government advocated by Maine as the only system of popular government possible is that its conservatism and stability are founded
on the mutually opposed working of four independent powers—
the Government, the Senate, the House, and the Supreme
Court.   It is like a word-padlock, and unless all the rings are
arranged the right way, it won't open.   That is all very well if
you want anything maintained.   But it isn't if you want anything done.   In Foreign policy it makes intercourse with the
Secretary of State simply a farce.   He has no power and he
knows he has none.   Even with a Secretary of State of the same
party as the Senate, the same thing occurred.   With the two
parties opposed in politics, the thing becomes hopeless.   The
only chance is to let circumstances work so as to give a good
object lesson to the interests represented and the Senate.
West is very good in that way.   He knows lots of the Senators
and works on them very well.

I believe he is going to London (although he seems to wish

not to have it known and so you needn't say so) and if he does,
I hope you'll make his acquaintance and get our Lord to work on
his feelings and squeeze something out of him.   You would
probably get more out of his daughter who is very bright and
keen.   If she could be quoted here by London-going Americans
as having been well received in London, it would do her and our
poor Legation here a great deal of good.   People here say this
pretty strongly ; I mean the English faction in Washington and
New York.   I wish you could get Lady Rosebery to take this
up, as it is absurd how well everyone here seems to know everything that goes on in London.   Lord Rosebery seems as well
known here as in England."

Mr. Bayard was very definitely friendly to England in general and
to Cecil Spring Rice in particular, as letters from him prove. The
first, written in May 1887, conveyed thanks to " your aunt, Lady
Taylor," for an autograph of " her distinguished husband," the poet,
who had died in 1886. "It will greatly enrich my copy of his writings,
and the channel through which it comes will always give it increased
value."   To these phrases of old-world courtesy was added the gift
of " a stick with an association. . . . cut for me at Mount Vernon
and grown on the soil that contains the ashes of Washington."
The second, on July 10, 1887, rendered thanks for a copy of Seeley's
Expansion of England, and for "the Fourth of July sonnet, with
which " Mr. Bayard wrote " you have enriched and adorned it." [1]

"Long may the roots and fibres of the 'generous tree'
retain their vitality on both sides of the Atlantic.   There is,
and I suppose we must expect there always will be, a great deal
to make those anxious who cherish the 'generous tree,' and
seasons of despondency will come—but a touch of friendly
hands does much to reassure those

> who speak the tongue
> That Shakespeare spoke—the faith and morals hold
> Which Milton held."

The third letter promised remonstrance through the American
Minister at Rome and the Italian Minister at Washington against the
proposed disturbance of the grave of Keats, and thanks Spring Rice
for a copy of Sir Henry Taylor's correspondence, " which from you,
who were of Sir Henry's kindred, gives a flavour of his personality
to it."
One feels a sort of fragrance like lavender over these interchanges
between the old-world statesman and the young diplomat.   Wherever
there were true lovers of poetry, Spring Rice was at home ; but this

---

[1] Apparently of his own writing, but it is not among his published verses.

man loved like himself the poetry of his own countryside and even of his own clan.

Quite other impressions of America, however, are given by his letters to his brother.

March 22, 1887.

To STEPHEN.

" . . . My appointment is up in June. Unless it is extended which is not very likely. . . .

With some difficulty I have established a reputation as *homme sérieux* and now can talk to an old man without being considered mad. Adams, son of the Minister [1] and joint author of *Democracy*, is rather an interesting sort of cynic, and I had a real jolly evening with him last night talking over England and America. The feeling about politicians is very bitter, certainly, and there is good reason for it. Owing to there being no provision whatever for election expenses, these have to be raised from the party leaders. The effect is that not only are the party leaders directly interested, but the election officials are in the pay, not of the Govt. but of the candidates. At the last N. York election one-fifth of the whole body of the electors were so employed. . . .

Society here is much quieter than it was. But the papers accuse the French secretary of having received large sums of money from the wife of a Senator with whom he was flirting. They say the Senator discovered the missing sum and traced it to the Secretary. He then petitioned Bayard to ask for his recall. Bayard has denied it and the papers reprint the story with further details of the sum and the banker's name. Jolly, isn't it ? There is not a word of truth in it and the story has been told three times at the same season of the year of three different persons who were going on leave. . . . "

March 25, 1887.

" There is nothing new here except the news that the extradition treaty negotiated by Lord Rosebery and Phelps [2] seems to have busted.

The Irish don't seem so much excited over the debates " [*i.e.* at Westminster] " as one would think. Perhaps it is that one

---

[1] Henry Adams was son of John Quincy Adams who was American Minister in London during the American Civil War ; and grandson of John Quincy Adams, sixth President of the United States. His novel, *Democracy*, published in 1880, contained bitter things indeed about politicians in Washington. The secret of its authorship was known to very few in 1887. Spring Rice had been misled, for there was no collaboration. Ultimately Adams allowed his name to appear on the Tauchnitz edition in 1907.

[2] American Minister in London.

gets accustomed to the tone of the press which is eminently
anti-English.

Cousin Allan Rice has just had a trial, from which it appears
that he stood for a division of New York, that the democrats
were in a majority of 8000 : that he was a Republican, and that
Henry George transferred all his Irish to the Republican side
for Rice.   That in consequence he was in a clear majority of
2000.   That then a certain machine leader came to him and
wanted him to bet 100 to 1 that he would not be successful :
that Rice refused : and that in consequence at the last moment
this man transferred all his clan bodily to the Democratic side
and Rice lost by 460.

That is a curious story of an election, isn't it ?

I go to New York to-day for a week to meet Theodore Roosevelt, who is to return with his bride.

I am getting to like this much more as I get to know more
about it.   The doings of the ' criminal classes,' as they call the
diplomatic corps, are also amusing, and if it doesn't last too
long, a novel experience.   But I am not fitted for diplomatic
life.   Everyone who writes to me asks whether I am made very
unhappy by the fascinating American girl.   They are much
like the English, as seen in our native South Kensington,
especially the smart American."

689 MADISON AVENUE,
March 29, 1887.

To FERGUSON.

" ... About your coming here.   It would be perfectly
splendid and you must.   I can guarantee you every sort of
introduction to every sort of person.   You had better make
friends with the Americans now over in England. . . . Elliot
Roosevelt, brother to Theodore, is going over with a very
charming wife.   He has an enormous acquaintance here and
will put you up to all sorts of tips for the sport in the West.   I
expect what Mrs. Elliot Roosevelt (who is very pretty) would
like is a help on in the way of invitations. . . . They are the
best born and best bred sort of Americans.

Senator Hale of Maine has a very beautiful place in his own
State and if I can find out his address in London I will send him
a letter to you.   All he would expect would be an introduction
to the House of Commons—nothing else.   I am troubling you
about these things because I am sure you would like to have
done your good turns before you receive them.

Theodore Roosevelt is going West to look after his ranch
because he has suffered losses in cattle and men, two of whom

(the latter) went out horse stealing, were surrounded at night, driven out of their dug-out by fire and hanged. He regrets their loss as he says they were the only honest people he ever had. That is, they robbed other people.

My dear Ferguson, it would be grand if you would come out here. Mind you settle the Fisheries first. I am very sorry to hear the Chief doesn't approve of my being here ; but I can't say I regret it, as I have been reading pretty hard and have made acquaintances and learnt things which will help me much, if I ever get to thinking over what is to become of our race."

" *Our* race," it will be noted.

WASHINGTON,
April 5, 1887.

To DAISY.

" . . . I have just come back from New York where I had a week chiefly spent in seeing Theodore Roosevelt. . . . The editor of the *N. Y. Tribune*[1] sent an invitation to me and Roosevelt to breakfast, and we two and Cabot Lodge, a member of Congress and a Republican literary man, went together at 10. You can have no idea of the magnificence of the house. There was nothing vulgar about it, but its splendour was astonishing. The Hall is all yellowish marble carved (and carved very well), varied with American oak inlaid with ivory. Then there is a cross passage or gallery with a vaulted roof of stamped leather as far as I can make out. The rooms were all inlaid wood and stamped leather, with huge Italian mantel-pieces of marble exactly copied from originals in Italy. The owner was a tall refined-looking man who received us cordially and made us welcome to the dining-room, where we sat and began to talk politics. It was the first real piece of political wire-pulling I had come across and it was a curious thing to watch. The question was whether Blaine was or was not to be nominated for the next Republican election as Republican candidate. I am getting quite excited over it and shall have a great interest when I get back.

I also was introduced to a club called the Century Club where all the learned men go. They are exactly like English literary men, and the club is like a glorified Savile."

April 22, 1887.

To FERGUSON.

" George Curzon seems no end of a boss : please extinguish him as soon as you can. I wish there were better pups among

---

[1] Whitelaw Reid, special ambassador for Queen Victoria's Diamond Jubilee ; ambassador to the Court of St. James', 1905-12.

the Liberals, although, if I were you, I shouldn't mind being the best-bred one of your age.   I see the old one " [Mr. G.] " wants a return of all the meetings and speakers of importance on the Irish side.   I'll get you any particulars you like : please ask for any papers or tips which you might care to quote.   Of course, the speakers (who are very often not Irish) are very violent.   But then, as they all say : ' The Irish voters insist on it : the English and German don't mind it.'   As to the sub-scriptions, a politician said to me that he had never stood for any position without receiving a deputation from the local branch of the league, stating that they were open-minded Irishmen without political prejudice, and that they would be glad to know if the honourable gentleman would subscribe to the cause of suffering Ireland.   In fact, it is one of the most well-known and regular expenses of an election and is returned as such to the ' machine managers ' in the formal report made by the candidate.   If you want to know the exact nature of the sympathy shown, ask people what was said in England in the first half of this century about Spain, Poland and Italy.   Of course, they sympathise with any people who are opposed by somebody else.   We do it ourselves.   Also, the nature of the feeling has been quite revolutionized by the old man joining the Irish : now, they think here that it is not a national but a party question, and their sympathy is increased or diminished accordingly.

The history of the South since 1870 has been curious.   You know that after the war they were obliged to rule the South by ' carpet baggers '—men sent down from New York to stand for the political appointments and elected by the black voters. This first period was marked by the most awful murders and excesses of different descriptions, and in 1870 it was determined to recur to the old system.   Since then the South has worked out its own salvation and lately there has been a great talk about the ' white man of the New South '—' United America ' and all sorts of manifestations of brotherly love.   Together with that there is an enormous commercial boom, and the money of the North is flowing down South on the most magnificent scale.

The change is rather a wonderful one and seems to astonish even Americans.   It's rather odd to dine with a man who was a middy on board the ' Alabama,' and see opposite to one a Northern General.   No one seems to think anything of that now.   And yet the difference in character between the North and the South must be very great.   Yet managing their own business seems to cure their differences, now that the question

of relative strength is settled beyond doubt.   It can't be in
doubt between England and Ireland."

May 13, 1887.

" I dined the other day in an old country house once belonging to a great Southern family whose last descendant died in the
poorhouse a week ago.   The house is taken and refitted by
the Secretary of the Navy.[1]   After dinner we drank some old
Madeira which had come from the cellars of a ruined Southerner
into Dan Webster's hands and thence to its present owner.
Dan Webster's grand-daughter took over enough and to spare
of it.   After dinner we sang ' Marching through Georgia,' and
swore ' We'd hang Jeff Davis on a sour apple tree.'   One of the
guests was a Southern General who didn't join in dancing
because his leg had been shot off in the war.   He did in the
singing, though.   He wasn't the only Southerner there.

The country round here is more beautiful than words can
describe.   It is all broken country with rivers and waterfalls
and any amount of trees.   The dogwood and lilac are all out
now.   I take morning rides and delight my soul.   Why can't
you come in a week and join me ?   I wish you weren't a
legislator."

April 22, 1887.
To DAISY.

" . . . I went out walking to the Country Club, which is a house
about four miles out where people ride and walk to and have
tea.   Near it is the country house of the Secretary of the
Navy.   The Secretary keeps open house, or rather open
cottage, and everyone who goes there has anything to
eat, drink or smoke that they can wish.   He is a clever
lawyer who has married an enormously rich (and fat) lady with
whose money he is gaining popularity and influence.   They are
both perfectly kind and the reverse of snobbish.   I must say I
have seen nothing like that here.   The richest people live in the
quietest way and only spend money in entertainments and
flowers—not in huge houses and gorgeous carriages.

We had a great Irish meeting here when General Sheridan
who is one of the possible candidates for the Presidency, said
that America would send, not only arms and money but men too,
to Ireland in case of a war.   This was largely applauded as you
may imagine.   It's so funny the way the papers are continually
abusing us, if you contrast it with the kindness shown by
individual Americans to English people."

[1] Mr. Whitney.

May 20.

To FERGUSON.

" During a debate in the Senate on the subject of the Nicaraguan canal, the house sitting with closed doors, a Senator entered hurriedly with a telegram announcing the explosions at Westminster. Bayard, the present Secretary of State, got up and made a vehement speech denouncing the attempt and suggesting a public vote of condemnation. This was carried with one dissentient (who was drunk). Since then the whole press has been opposed in the most remarkable way to Bayard : every opportunity of slighting him is taken and he is and will be the victim of a mysterious persecutor. Irish influence in politics here will probably increase indefinitely till some overt act (probably in the interest of Rome) will draw upon itself the combined resistance of the non-Irish."

May 23.

" I was rather distressed at your account of our Lord's feelings about my staying on here. I don't want to particularly, in fact, I don't want to at all, but I didn't wish to make any fuss one way or the other and just let things go as the fates choose. The result is that I shall be here till December in all probability. You know that there is very little experience of Foreign politics to be got here—in fact, none ; but the economic questions, etc., are very interesting indeed, and I shouldn't have another such opportunity. I shouldn't think there was any country where the labour question is so important, and it may be both raised and solved here before very long."

May 26, 1887.

" The rich are beginning to show their sense of responsibility by endowing schools and hospitals. But as regards the poorer classes, they regard them as fools for not being richer, and don't show them much sympathy. The consequence is that the feeling of the poor is something awfully bitter in the big towns. You would be rather astonished if you read the reports of Father McGlynn's meetings in favour of the anti-Poverty Society. A New York ' Machine Politician ' told me that there was only one class of men who couldn't be bribed, and that was the poorest. ' You could get Jay Gould but you couldn't get that man ' (pointing to a car driver), ' he's a follower of Henry George.' As far as the rich are concerned, by this state of things their life becomes intolerably dull. They are separated from the poor by so deep a gulf that they have no influence as politicians or as employers of labour or as landlords. As the chief enjoyment derived from money seems to be power. they have to go to Wall Street to find a field for ambition. They can't be rich enough. And with all this they are intolerably dull. The young men, if born rich, become drunkards. Perhaps this is exaggerated, but all the same nobody can deny that it is the dullest country in the world to be rich in, and the bitterest perhaps to be poor in. Of course, this is likely enough to be changed as soon as the danger is perceived, which it is getting to be already. Therefore, to point a moral, I would, if I were you, keep up as close a connection with Raith and Novar [1] as you can, whether it means loss of ready money or not.

As soon as I can I will write about the Irish here. The Legation has nothing to do with Secret Service and so I can't say anything about the darker side. Blaine is arriving in London on the 17th. He knows Lord Rosebery, but I doubt whether he will care to see any English politicians, as he has been quite lately intriguing with Pat Ford and others of a similar disposition. But he is well worth while knowing, I am told. His present object is to catch the Irish vote which was only partially won at the last election. The Irish vote is enormously and increasingly powerful here—it would astonish you to see how much. At any rate it would do no harm to conciliate him and make him reasonable. He is coming with two daughters, one of them very clever and amusing.

June 2, 1887.

" I am just starting for a visit to Theodore Roosevelt at his country place. His ranch having busted mainly in consequence of the last winter, he has parted with most of his horses and says he is now camping in the ruins of past glory. I think I shall have great fun.

Father McGlynn and Henry George have been preaching to the inhabitants of New York that their condition is infinitely more wretched than the Irish tenants who live under the ' most equitable land-law in the world.' More evictions, they say, take place in New York than in the whole country of Ireland. Ten times as many nearly. I shall perhaps see the Labour Union procession in honour of ' Editor O'Brien ' [2] as they call him. Some of the New York papers are against him, but not many since the riot. I notice an intense unwillingness to say anything hostile to the Irish. This, of course, comes

---

[1] Ferguson's properties in Scotland.

[2] William O'Brien, M.P., who had come to the States from Canada, after stormy episodes when he denounced Lord Lansdowne, then Governor-General of the Dominion.

from the fact that a very large number of newspaper writers are Irish, and that the papers themselves depend so largely upon the bar-room and liquor-saloon which again are almost wholly Irish."

June 17.

" I don't see, however, that it would be at all easy to satisfy American feeling on the subject of Ireland. It is not only the Irish vote. That was perhaps at its maximum strength some ten years ago, and though increased in numbers it has not increased relatively. There is, also, besides the necessity of considering this vote, the fact that England stands to the Americans exactly as France for so many years stood to us—as the only foreign nation with which they come in contact. Consequently, both in Maine and Kentucky, where there are next to no Irish, but only settlers of characters much like the old Cumberland and Yorkshire farmers, England is the country with whom America has had its two European wars and which sympathised with the South. Senator Ingalls, who made that violent speech in the Senate against England, was from Kentucky and has practically no Irish in his constituency. So there is a large amount of absolutely unreasonable hostility which time and a judicious treatment of political questions will soften down ; and all this finds expression in a virtuous indignation at the wrongs of Ireland, in the same way as whenever Russia becomes unpleasant to us, we used to be in the habit of pointing out that the oppressor of Poland was without the pale of civilisation.

This country itself is a pretty good instance of the solution of the great question of centralization and decentralization. Now this is based on a constitution to which all the leaders of different states were parties, and in which the supreme man of that time took no personal share, as far as can be shown, except as mediator. This sort of question has been decided here by a constitutional enactment and it seems to me that some such compromise between parties, issuing from the declared inability of the present parliamentary system to cope with it, is the only possible means of solution. If Washington had propounded a constitution without consulting any of the other leaders and insisted on carrying out his will or resigning, there would never have been a constitution at all. We shall have to wait till out of mere weariness all parties consent to a conference before any satisfactory solution is obtained. It must be constitutional ; more than laws—and its sanction must be war, if violated.

I am tired out by a night journey, as I have just come back

from Long Island, where I have been staying with Theodore
Roosevelt whom I like better every day I see him."

WASHINGTON,
June 24, 1887.

To STEPHEN.

" . . . We are as full of the Jubilee here as you are there. The
papers have on the whole been very friendly—quite surprisingly so. The only contretemps has been in Boston where
the Irish party objected to the use of Faneuil Hall for the
celebration. They first went to the Mayor (an Irishman) who
went to bed and sent word to say he had nothing to do with
granting the Hall. Then they called a meeting of the Aldermen, which body consists of six Americans, one Englishman
and seven Irish. The result was a drawn vote. Then a mob
collected and tried to bash the celebrations on the head and did
bully one man out of his shirt for suggesting to them the
sacredness of liberty and toleration. On which the police (all
Irishmen) attacked the mob and cleared their countrymen off
the streets in the space of four minutes.

The Democratic Mayor of New York attended the celebration amid wild enthusiasm. The flags were hoisted in honour
of the day. Great cursing among the Irish, but it has not done
them any harm.

I enclose a pretty story (quite true) anent the execution by a
band of 300 orderly citizens of one of the chief magistrates of a
Kentucky town who was elected by terrorism and executed (by
shooting) when his rule got too intolerable."

June 30, 1887.

" The great heat is passed over and it is grown fairly tolerable
especially in the evenings, which are beautiful. The town is
almost wholly deserted, being inhabited mainly by blacks now.
A few people stay on, living most of the day in a partially dressed
state and seeing each other in the evenings. We mostly meet
in a house where there is a very spacious balcony looking out on
to a garden full of fireflies. Now that the moon is bright, it is
very pleasant there and we listen to endless nigger songs sung
in two parts with banjo accompaniment (not the ones you hear
in England but the real old plantation songs which are very
attractive). Sometimes a Southerner will call and tell us
Rabbit stories—*i.e.* Uncle Remus.

I met a very charming man the other day—Secretary Lamar
—once appointed by the Confederates to represent their

Government in St. Petersburg. His great friend here is Adams, son of the Minister in London at the time of the war. It was in London that they first met, sitting next each other during the debate on Roebuck's motion for the recognition of the South. Since they have been in Washington they have been constantly together till the death of Adams' wife, with whom he wrote *Democracy*. It seemed so fearful to Lamar (she was poisoned by an overdose of chloral) that he has never dared enter the house since and as Adams never leaves it they have not met.

The Adams family are as odd as can be. Two Presidents, a Minister to England, and then the present brood. They are all clever, but they all make a sort of profession of eccentricity. One of them wrote a book, of which a review appeared so bitter and strong that he wrote to the Editor to ask who had done it ? He was told, his brother.—Two of them were arguing. One said, ' It seems to me I am the only one of the family who inherits anything of our grandfather's manners.' ' But you dissipated your inheritance young,' answered the other.

I like the one here, who since his wife died has no friends and no absorbing interest and takes an amused view of life, tempered by an attachment to Japanese art. He lives in a beautiful house and works at a history of ten years, 1800-1810. He has a friend who lives with him, the librarian of the State Dept., who corresponds with Aubrey de Vere. Unfortunately for me he has gone away. Lamar, however, stops.

It is amusing in the high Govt. and opposition circles to hear of the hatred for Blaine. They are much amused at his reception in London. If he accepts the invitations he gets from the rich and the great, he will offend the Irish. If he refuses them he will offend the capitalists. Those are his two backers. The news now is that he intends to be Secretary of State and to run Harrison for President."

July 1, 1887.

To FERGUSON.

" We are in the middle of a conference on Samoa [1] about which you know or remember as much as I do. Your coming here will be most welcome (of course, to me) but also, as you will find, to all sorts of very jolly and interesting people. The worst of it will be that they will not all be in the same place. I said I would go and stay with John Hay at Cleveland. I wish

[1] The Samoan Conference—concerning the protectorate of the islands, to which Germany had forcibly asserted a claim—was conducted between the British and German Ministers and the Secretary of State, Mr. Bayard. It reached no conclusion.

you would look him up in London and then it would be easier to take you too, tho' I know he would be only too glad. . . .

What sport it will be having you here. I wonder if you will really come. I am half afraid you will be disappointed, and avenge it on me.

The Labour Party are pretty strong and the feeling is gaining ground more and more that they will run a candidate of their own. They have recently had a great battle over the ' American ' question—whether their flag is to be the stars and stripes or the red flag. They think the stars and stripes will do for them and have forbidden the other. They are certainly in earnest, though their troubles are many. They have been beaten in all their strikes, or all the most important ones. They have been beaten in Chicago and Cincinnati, where they are strongest and where they nearly won. There is a great revolt going on against the system of the Knights of Labour, subordinating all unions to the central power absolutely. But for all that, each defeat only seems to encourage them to try again and they are growing more reasonable and more capable of independent political action.''

July 12, 1887.

To STEPHEN.

" I went to the Conference as protocolist, which was rather fun. The Secretary of State sits at the table head ; the German to his right and West to the left. The Secretary clears his throat and makes a speech in senatorial style—very eloquent and rather long. The shorthand writer takes it down. He and the German Secretary and I sit at the table foot. Then the German says (in English) he will read a written statement. Of course, wholly irrelevant to Bayard's speech. Then West reads a written statement. Then Bayard asks questions but is too deaf to hear the answers, and resumes his speech where he left it off. Then another irrelevant written statement. Then a remark from the German that if an agreement is come to, his Govt. would be glad to see it in the following form, which is read ; but as the American view happens to be wholly different, the exordium ' Agreement between the U.S., Germany and Gt. Britain ' sounds odd. Then we all get hungry and yawn. Then the sitting is adjourned and we telegraph home. This has been going on for some days. I have done their portraits. I was detected doing the Secretary of State's. Fortunately he is a great friend of mine through Uncle Henry (Taylor) for whose works he has an enormous admiration.''

July 8, 1887.

To STEPHEN.

" I don't know whether you are interested in U.S. Finance. It is in a very odd state at present, as you may see from the reports. Imports largely exceed exports. The money in the Treasury is accumulating fast. There is no way of getting rid of it unless the Government goes into the open market and buys up the bonds not yet ' ripened,' thus raising their price. The effect of the want of cash (theirs all concentrated in the Govt. hands) is odd. First of all there is great speculation in land, then there is a constant liability to panics. Jay Gould is, of course, the moving spirit. That gentleman came to Washington in order to present a piece of property to Mount Vernon, so he said. He stayed one night in a hotel opposite the Treasury. The next day a great corner in coffees came to grief. The next a great corner in wheat in Chicago suddenly broke. The next day an enormous bank in Cincinnati followed. The next, the sudden fall in Gould's Manhattan stock brought a panic in Wall Street such as had not been known for years. That day Field, Gould's rival, transferred to him at a heavy loss almost all his stock. The next day the Secretary of the Treasury anticipated $9,000,000 due two months hence for interest, and the market recovered. If that had been done before ? Isn't this a great country ? . . ."

July 15, 1887.

" . . . There is a great battle going on between Gould and his one remaining rival, Garrett of the Baltimore and Ohio. Betting is on Gould, who will no doubt ruin Garrett, his enemy, having just made five million out of his old friend and ally, Field. The Vanderbilts, since their father's death, do not gamble. While he was alive they lost six million in two months when he was travelling in Europe. They paid the losses in U.S. stock which he had deposited. He came back to find it lost. Since then they have not meddled with the stockmarket. The Astors invest in real estate in New York. Gould will no doubt be the richest man in the world if justice doesn't overtake him. Money will be very tight in autumn here, and there may be very possibly a small panic owing to the great sums in the Treasury. This I should think was certain. . . ."

July 19, 1887.

To FERGUSON.

" . . . I am stopping now with Whitney, a New York wire-puller and Secretary to the Navy. Other members of the Cabinet turn up and their talk is very interesting. One of the odd things about this country is that most people can speak, but that so little is thought of speaking. This man, the most prominent citizen of New York, whose influence with that of one or two others elected Cleveland, has never or hardly ever made a public speech. He talks of speaking as one of the 'intellectual means' of securing an election. The 'material means' and the 'personal means' are of much greater importance. This reduces politics to a level which you may sneer at, if so inclined. Yet the system resulted in the election of the most honest politician, because he was the most honest. And yet you hear so little and read so little (except in the Mugwump papers) which would lead you to suppose honesty was the best policy here. I firmly believe that there is very little real internal corruption. The wire-pulling and underground organisations imply an enormous amount of it, just as the conduct of a business transaction by the sharp speculators in corn here implies a large amount of trickery : and yet it results in good corn being sold to the people who want it, and on the whole, being sold cheap.

There is a good deal of difficulty with the next election because they are determined not to levy taxes on Government employees for party purposes : and the railway people have lost hope of bribing officials with gifts to party funds. The result is that in this election the Democrats may very well be beaten for want of funds. Blaine will not lack in that particular. . . .

The Knights of Labour are breaking up. The plan was to make a great association, divided into lodges according to trades. If one trade struck, the others, even if they had no complaint, were to strike too, if by so doing they could help the original strikers. It was a great self-denying organization. However, it was found that the workmen did not possess sufficient power of self-denial : also that, as the society did not embrace all the operatives, strikers were easily replaced by the employers and the strikes resulted in the defeat of the strikers and the substitution of non-union hands. Revolt followed revolt and the Knights are now in a very poor position."

July 26, 1887.

" . . . I hope you will meet John Hay ; if not, I shall in any case take you to see him either at Cleveland, Ohio or in Washington, as he is a brick. Your sister ought certainly to come, but if she wants to have a fine time she should be in New York for the winter. An English girl is a great object of interest. Perhaps from her rarity here.

Blaine's triumphal progress is exciting the greatest interest here. Blaine's and Buffalo Bill's. It seems really as if the cordial social reception given to Americans in England had a most mollifying effect. They don't quite realise it and express the greatest surprise.

I am now staying (in rather a lordly fashion) with the Secretary to the Navy and the Secretary of War who live outside the town. The kindness of the former (who saw I looked ill and carried me off in his carriage) surpasses anything I ever dreamed of. I wish I could return half the kindness I have received here ! So will you think when you come."

American hosts thought, however, that he earned his welcome. Roosevelt wrote :

SAGAMORE HILL,
July 5, 1887.

" DEAR CECIL,
. . . We have all been speaking of how we wished you were here, especially during the last few days, when we have had various other guests to compare with you ; and, in perfect seriousness, we have all concluded that though we like them for a little while, it is you alone whom we would wish to stay just as long as you could. We would have awfully good fun if you were here now—among other things I have marked out a first-class rifle range."

July 29, 1887.

To STEPHEN,
. . . I am still staying at the ' Whitney Farm ' as it is called here. The air is several degrees cooler and life very cheerful. There is a sort of cabinet meeting there, as the Secretary of War, of the Navy, and of the Treasury are staying. Mrs. Cleveland came last night ; as the President, whose country place is next, was working too hard to speak to her, and she ' thought she'd drop in.' She is a tall, very pretty and direct person. She also turned out to be very amusing. She had just been a tour in the North with the President. She said she had to get accustomed to people saying they were discontented with her looks—which she said was natural, as one eyelid was bitten and was as big as an egg and she had to have it bandaged. ' Which was a great pity,' she said, ' as, of course, the President was there for his talking and I for my looks. And the President had a sore throat.'

She said she had a great trouble on her mind. The President had gone on the loose and bought himself an orange tawny linen suit. He now threatened to wear it. She had used every artifice in her power to prevent it. ' What would he look like in it, think ? ' (The President is 5 feet high and 4 feet wide : he has no neck and six chins.) At last he found it so hot that he had said he *must* wear it. So she had told him he would certainly lose the Irish vote if he wore a yellow suit, and this argument prevailed. All this she told in a slight Northern accent, exceedingly quietly in voice and manner. It appears that the Cabinet are blossoming since the hot weather. The Southern Secretary finds it pleases his constituents to wear a home-made pair of pants—two, that is—one red and one blue. I asked him if they were cool ! ' Very cool in winter,' he said. Another time he was asked why he wore the red one ? He said to get rid of the blue. Mrs. Cleveland told an anecdote about an American who had come with the Queen of Hawaii. Someone mistook him for a native and began slowly and distinctly (as to one more conversant with Hawaiian) to ask, ' Are—you—mar-ried ? ' The Colonel answered shortly and at once, ' Thank God, no.'

I spend most of my evenings in a Nicaraguan hammock out of doors. I sit there till 10 or 11 and then go to bed. I am up by seven and read till 9. That time I have to myself, as no one else gets up early and I have read through Ellwood's Life of himself, Cavendish's *Life of Wolsey*, and Coleridge's *Table Talk*. The first two are so wonderfully good that they spoil one for other books for some time after."

August 9, 1887.

To FERGUSON.

" First of all about business. I will meet you at Montreal on your arrival—shall be there on September 10. . . . We can then go to Ottawa. . . . In October I have to be back in Washington. You had better go across to Vancouver then to Portland, Oregon, or San Francisco by steamer, and back to Chicago, where I will get letters for you. I should like to go that way but I don't think my brother would like it much—I mean my leaving him so soon.

The session begins here the first Monday in December. You ought to be back by then in Washington. Theodore Roosevelt wants you to go to his ranch in the West in October. I would, if I were you ; it is a most exciting life and not at all like Westminster, so that you will get health by it. Bring plenty of flannel shirts—not white but rather dark, for a reason I had better not explain. November, you might be about in New York."

Then comes a description of purely fashionable life for which
Spring Rice had no taste or even tolerance, in America or anywhere
else.　But this letter, from which a few unfair sentences have been
omitted, illustrates the temptation to say scathing things for which
Mrs. Lodge reproved him ; and the correspondence of later years
shows that her reproof had its effect.　He said plenty of hard things
later, but never without meaning them seriously.

Sept. 6, 1887.

To DAISY.

" I have not behaved over well about writing, which is the
natural consequence of roaming about.　I am now in a beautiful
place, rather like Coniston.　But I must describe my wander-
ings.　I was at last released at Washington and, leaving the
Minister and my successor together, I went to Newport, of
which you must have heard—the finest watering place in the
world.　It is very old and was one of the first colonies.　At the
bottom of the town lies the old fishing village and harbour,
filled now with all sorts of beautiful yachts.　Away out on the
point are two long rows of cottages—built of wood with double
coach-houses and wonderful lawns.　There is a walk from
garden to garden by the rocks on which the Atlantic breaks.
Two or three of the cottages are fine houses ; the rest are small
but infinitely luxurious.　The inhabitants are the richest men
and the most beautiful women in the world.　Their life is everything that riches and beauty ought to entail.　It begins at 11,
when all society meets at a place called the Casino, where a
band plays and where a rare lawn tennis player appears every
now and then.　But the chief occupation then and afterwards
is talking.　They all suffer from a ' determination of words to
the mouth ' which is surprising to the Briton.　One sees there
in a horse-shoe cloister crowds of these beautiful and gorgeous
creatures (all of whom one soon learns to know by sight) sitting
and talking with heroes in white flannel (put on for ornament,
not for tennis), white straw hats, and instead of a waistcoat a
wondrous coloured sash round the waist.　There one sees
beauties fresh from the smiles of the Prince of Wales and consequently tremendously fêted.　(The P. of W.'s smiles are
called by the newspapers ' trans-Atlantic reputation.')　There
is also a pretty and graceful Miss Wilson who is the beloved of
the phoenix of our diplomatic [1] service—a brother of Lady de
Grey's.　Her sister married a rich man and has yachts and

[1] Miss Wilson married her phoenix, " Mungo " Herbert, who became
Ambassador at Washington but, as will be read later, died early—and
deeply regretted by Spring Rice.

diamonds.   Then there is a beautiful and quiet lady married to
an Irishman who, unfortunately, is little better than Irishmen
should be.   Having spent all her money, he asked her father
for more, saying it was spent on dresses and dinners.   On
enquiry it turned out to be spent on gambling.   So he sent for
his daughter and she lives now in America.   Her ambition, I
was told, had always been to marry a handsome man who should
take her into London Society.   Her wish was granted.   One
of the strangest people there was a pretty young woman of
20, married to a German Jew.   His one thought (besides getting
money for her to spend) was to see her happy.   He let a beautiful country house to strangers and took her to Newport where
he lived at nights, going up and down to New York constantly.
Once I was told she was seen putting his hair straight up.   She
asked him if he liked it.   He said, ' Yes.'   She said, ' Don't say
yes, it spoils all the fun.   Say no.'   She was always giving
dinners and forgetting to appear herself—leaving him to play
host.   One day she went out to a party and sat in an open
carriage in a pouring storm.   She wouldn't have it closed ' for
the fun.'   The next day she fell ill.   Soon there was straw laid
down and every one was told she was dying.   At a ball there
was at the Casino I heard ever so many people say how sorry
they were.   Her husband wasn't told by the doctor for fear
he should go mad.   He was there kissing her hair and feet and
had to be taken away.   Someone told me she saw him sitting
at the stair foot with her dog (which was very melancholy at
not seeing her) in his arms.   Now she is slowly getting better
but all her strength is gone—partly from excitement and carelessness in past years.

The people who are interesting to write about are not those
whose history is the most cheerful.   There are ever so many of
the last.   For instance, the whole Vanderbilt family.   The
husbands are devoted and the wives good.   One of them told
me last night that she lived in the old Vanderbilt house in New
York and was so pestered with beggars that no one was ever
admitted without a card, and she had always to look out of the
window before she ventured to cross the pavement to her
carriage.   She is charitable enough and has 250 old women
whom she looks after and gives concerts to.   One morning she
was in bed and someone brought a card to her—a name she
knew very well.   She told the servant to show the lady up.
She came and it was someone else—an awful-looking woman
in widow's weeds who sat down by her side, fixed her with
her eyes, told her she was in her power and demanded
jewels.   Fortunately there was an alarm by her bedside.   She

sounded it and the servants rushed in and carried off the woman howling.

Many things might I recount of fair Newport : but I have no more time. I left after a fortnight and went to a place called Nahant where I had friends. There is a peninsula running into the Atlantic and joined by a narrow road to the shore. At the extreme end of it is the house I stayed in surrounded on three sides by water with splendid rocks. There were some jolly children and I lived very quietly there playing lawn tennis and riding on the beach (which is about three miles off) and bathing off the rocks. All that coast is broken into promontories and islands and deeply wooded. There are pleasure houses all the way along ; built very picturesquely in the Queen Anne style of wood with stone foundations. My host was Cabot Lodge, the grandson of an Englishman, but a very anti-English member of Congress. He had written several books which I have read—one a life of Hamilton, which is very good indeed. His wife is pretty and very pleasant. I hope they will come to England some day. . . ."

In this household Spring Rice came to be almost a member of the family, and here, as elsewhere, he earned his welcome as much by devotion to the children as in any other way. Telling stories was among the gifts he had cultivated first in in his own home as assiduously as making up rhymes ; and in the Lodge and the Roosevelt households, a series of sagas grew up which were regularly called for. A letter from Roosevelt, written to Lady Spring Rice after his death, paints this side of him.

" He was dear with our children ; he wrote the most fascinating child's verses—I think we remember Elephant Johnny and the Crocodile long before ever you had heard of them. His tender heart was wrung whenever any of our children were sick. His tastes were so simple that he always fitted right into our very domestic life. Whether we went riding or rowing or walking, or took all the children on a picnic or for a play in the old barn, he gave a zest to the enjoyment of all of us."

On August 30 the appointment of an International Commission to discuss the Fisheries question was announced, and Mr. Chamberlain—leader in the Commons of the Liberal Unionists, who were then in alliance but not in coalition with the Tory Government—undertook to act as First Commissioner for the British. This news confronted Cecil Spring Rice when he returned from his tour in Canada, where he had joined Ferguson. He found it startling, because Mr. Chamberlain, who up to 1885 had acted in support of the Irish party on the agrarian question and in opposition to coercion, was now almost the fiercest of their antagonists.—It will be seen that Spring Rice soon changed his tone about Mr. Chamberlain's mission.

Oct. 28, 1887.

To STEPHEN.

" . . . What does the Govt. mean by sending Jo. here. They might as well send Judas Iscariot as Ambassador to Heaven as Chamberlain to America ; and he pegs away as if his name wasn't enough to drive them mad here, but he must needs rub it in as deeply as possible.

Herschell has been and is gone. He is singularly unhappy about the political situation in England. One feels almost inclined to envy this country where the only question of foreign policy relates to mackerel and seals, and the only question of democratic policy is whether one set of men or another shall have the right of appointing consuls and postmasters. But ours is certainly more dramatic."

Nov. 4, 1887.

" . . . We are all in the expectation of J. C.'s arrival. Why did Lord Salisbury send him ? What an idea—worthy of Canning himself. But I imagine there is a very deep-rooted feeling that the Irish must not go too far here. They made an ' eviction ' campaign in one of the Territories against an alien land company. The President put his foot down hard and said the law must be enforced. They try the boycott. It is declared illegal and they are heavily prosecuted. They try dynamite and they are hanged, or will be on the 12th instant.

You see, I mix up the Irish and the Socialists, who are quite distinct ; but in the conversation, though not the press writing, of Americans, the Irish agitation is looked at from two points of view ; one as anti-English, in which case it is naturally applauded ; the other as anti-law, in which case it is looked upon as a dangerous sort of conflagration which should be restricted to the dear neighbour's property.

The upshot is that if they try to make the U.S. pay money in the form of ships, forts, embargoes, and the like, to feed fat a sentimental grudge against England, the ' great foot of the United States ' will be firmly planted.

This town is getting gradually full again and diplomats and statesmen are flocking in. I have been too busy to join in the corresponding frivolities and have spent most of my evenings reading an intensely interesting history of Jefferson's administration by the son of Minister Adams.[1] The author is here and

[1] Henry Adams.

I often go and see him. He found his wife dead on the floor one day and the next was the first day since they had been married that they were separated. Since then he has regarded life with a frivolity which rather shocks people who don't know him well; but I can quite understand that there are griefs so great that after them one is independent of joy and sorrow or the respect of men.

I went the other evening to Bayard, who has just got a collection of photos of historical English and Scotch characters. Among them Bonny Dundee, the flower of them all.

Afterwards he broke out in the most passionate harangue in the name of unity and peace in this Conference. It was curious to think of this in the mouth of a man whom our newspapers would call a Yankee sharper—and will be calling so soon.

The woods are divine now. All the browns and golds and reds in the world are banked up along our stream, rock and creek are fading away in the evening in a golden mist. It is the Indian summer now."

Nov. 11, 1887.

" Chamberlain is at N.Y. where he is being entertained by the Chamber of Commerce. He seems in no hurry to proceed to Washington.

He had difficulty with the reporters but finally decided to let them all come at a certain date : then he sat in the middle of the room and twenty or thirty sat round and cross-questioned him. He is not much loved here. And he is a curious choice to have made but I daresay it will be all right."

Nov. 23, 1887.

" . . . Chamberlain has arrived and is in high spirits—very popular and conciliatory and getting on capitally with everyone, women, children and politicians. He is not very hopeful, nor is anyone, but it is a good thing to try. He had an interview with the reporters which did him credit and was a success. He had all fifty with cigars and spirits and *carte blanche* as to questions. His readiness was very much admired.

The Canadians are very good fellows and I hope to see a good deal of them. The U.S. Commissioners are amusing. One a New England Republican, strong and determined ; the other a Western Democrat, full of stories more or less amusing, and both very willing to be pleased with everything."

Dec. 2, 1887.

" Chamberlain is making himself very popular here. He is always on the smile and especially kind to ladies. He has won the hearts of his enemies so far as his pleasantness is concerned, and he has a fine way of talking, short and frank, which is new and surprising to the Americans. The Conference has been sitting for some time but how much longer it will sit is a mystery. A great dinner was given by the American Commissioners to the English, and the table was loaded with orchids in honour of the illustrious Joseph. . . . ''

Dec. 20, 1887.

'' Jo. is gone awa' across the border to spread his conquests further. I don't know what the Canadians will think of him. Rather small beer, they intend : so did the Washingtonians : but the event undeceived them. He has been frank and out-spoken to the last degree, but as far as I can make out has offended nobody really.

It has been great sport watching his proceedings. He has taken to dancing : is an accomplished flirt : and the representa-tives' wives make it very rough for their husbands if they are not civil to him.''

Some miscellaneous jottings about American society may be brought together here. At the end of November Ferguson was being introduced to Washington. Spring Rice reports to his brother on November 29 :

'' We saw the famous General Sheridan ; a very jolly little man who has passed most of his life on the frontier with Indians, and who has a most charming and delightful wife who goes with him on all his tours and never leaves him : and, now that he has got gouty, doesn't dance any more. He was standing by Bismarck's side during Sedan and the great man talked to him all the time. He said he thought his power with his soldiers was caused by his never failing to come among them if there was a sudden attack anywhere ; and also by his habit of profane swearing, which he learnt among the Indians. He was the first employer of Buffalo Bill in the West and liked him very much—chiefly because he was such a gentleman.

The press here says what a country England must be ! ' Hates Mr. Gladstone and loves Buffalo Bill and W. L. Sulli-van ! '' [the famous prize-fighter].

Again to his sister Evelyn on December 2 :

'' I have been going round to all the sights because Mrs. Dugdale and Miss Ferguson are here, and I have shown them

the Capitol, Mrs. Cleveland and the President.   Seeing the latter
on public reception days is done thus :

You go into the open door of the White House and sit in a
big drawing room with a ghastly picture of Lincoln opposite
Mrs. Washington, as if they were married.   The room is fine.
About a hundred men, women and children appear, sitting
about.   Then the door opens and the fat short President
appears.   You form a line and move past as hard as you can,
shaking hands.   The children get their heads patted.   He told
Mrs. Dugdale that it was cold weather for the time of year.
We agreed, like people on the stage, all at once."

Dec. 15.
To DAISY.
" . . . I have had my term here prolonged for three or four
months.   That means coming back in May or June.

I am writing a Christmas letter and I hope you will pass it as
merrily as with all these absences you can.   I shall spend it
among people whom you don't know, but whom I am as
friendly with as one can be with people one has only known a
year.   I have become quite fond of Washington and feel almost
at home there now ; so that I don't mind staying on at all,
though, of course, I get homesick at times.

I have just written a long letter to Bernard and Agnes [1] which
I hope they will get in time, telling them as much as I had time
for about my friends and acquaintances here.   Mrs. Dugdale
and Miss Ferguson, sister to my friend, were here.   Mrs. D.
was splendid in her enthusiasm and her questions.   She asked
a man who had lost father, brother, property, and an arm in
the war whether he had been much interested in it.   He stated
the above mentioned reasons for being so.   ' Did you know
General Lee ? '   ' I was with him two years and surrendered
under him at the end.'   ' Were you ever in camp ? '   ' For
two years I never slept in a house but once.'   ' Are you glad the
slaves are free ? '   ' If I were free myself, I should be.'
The man was the original of Carrington [2] in *Democracy*.
The original of Victoria Dare is now a poor invalid—pale,
struggling with disease and married to a man who adores her so
deeply that you can tell when she is ill by his face.   The
diplomat was a Greek, in the service of Turkey.   He received

[1] His youngest brother and eldest sister.
[2] Carrington was Mr. James Lowndes : Victoria Dare was Miss Emily
Beale ; the diplomat, Aristarchi Bey ; and Mrs. Lightfoot Lee was Mrs.
Lawrence.

orders to return to Constantinople.   A friend told him it was that he might be executed.   So he remained in Paris, where he now is.

I saw Mrs. Lightfoot Lee here who lives near Philadelphia, in the country ;   a clever, interesting-looking widow.

The putative author, Henry Adams, whose wife died suddenly, is a great friend of mine.   He is queer to the last degree ; cynical, vindictive, but with a constant interest in people, faithful to his friends and passionately fond of his mother and of all little children ever born ;   even puppies.   He lives in a Japanese house full of strange trophies from Japan and a precious idol given him by the Japanese Minister.   He has no cards and never goes out.   A friend of Aubrey de Vere's lives with him :   an ideal librarian :   small and dark :   always arranging books and living all day in the library of the State Department like a spider in a web watching all the books that fly through the world and digesting them slowly.   Next door is the house of John Hay, the poet, who drops in to talk and chat and argue and compare notes : the best story-teller I have ever heard, and such a good sort, too.   My other friends of the sober kind are the Secretary of State, Bayard, who is very like dear Uncle Taylor, and a Boston family, Endicott, Secretary of War—who are of a real New England Puritan stock whose ancestors hung Quakers in irons at Salem. . . . ''

Passing to the more political comment, we find him writing on November 7 to Ferguson, who was then at New York :

Whitelaw   Reid . . . is   at   present   bound   to   Blaine,   in whose interests he is subsidising the Labour Party.   He is very clever and agreeable and quite likely to be amenable to the gentle influences of society, in his political relations.   But he is not a very trustworthy authority on any subject.   I must say, though, I like having a talk with him as well as with any-one here.   You will find New York speaking of itself as the capital.   After all, New York is not anything of the kind, and that is one of the commonest mistakes into which foreigners fall.

To his brother, who was an expert on finance, and a strong Free Trader, he wrote in some detail about the issue which was then becoming dominant, whether the heavy tariffs, which had been imposed to raise revenue in the decades of financial stress after the Civil War, should be retained for purposes of protection.

Dec. 2.

" . . . Recent elections have certainly strengthened Cleveland's position, as they have shown that he has control of

New York, which is the pivot state.   It is a good thing for us,
as Cleveland is friendly and a free trader.   He is an honest man
and drives all his dishonest supporters perfectly wild.   Their
discontent, however, only makes them howl under the lash but
draw the chariot just as well."

But in a few days the note changes.   Cleveland sent a message to
Congress pointing out that there was a large surplus in the Treasury
and proposing to reduce the superfluous yield of taxation by lessening
the duties on imports.   Spring Rice wrote :

To STEPHEN.

"The President's message is a very great surprise.   The
Democrats are split ; one section being protectionist.   It was
thought that the Speaker would concert with the leader of that
section, Randall, to arrange a basis of common action.   Instead
of this, the President announces a programme which is certain
to be rejected by his own party in the house.   Its object is
solely to secure a platform for the next election ; it has no
meaning in the present Congress.   The Republicans are now
certain (so they say) of success, as they have long tried to bind
the Democrats down to free trade and now they have a good
cry for the election.

On the other hand there is the advantage of an honest chief
of an honest party pledging himself in an intelligible manner to
a simple, straightforward course of action.   That makes good
fighting.

I should, however, very much doubt the immediate policy of
the action.   The Republicans have a scheme which is simple and
good for reducing the surplus by abolishing the internal tobacco
excise and the sugar duties.   That is likely to be more popular."

He adds on December 20 :

"About Cleveland's message.   The result will be *nil* as far
as the policy of the message is concerned for this session.

Some of the President's friends say that he is really tired of
office : that he is longing to retire with his wife from all the
bother of work and publicity—and that having spent some
time lately in earnest thought and reading over the question
he has come to a conclusion, and means, come what may, to
state it frankly.   It is quite in keeping with his character,
which is as honest and independent as any man living."

At the end of the year he was expected back in London, for his
brother Stephen was about to marry Julie Fitzgerald, daughter of the
Knight of Kerry, to whom all the elder group of the Spring Rice

brothers and sisters had long been devotedly attached. But on December 9 he wrote :

" DEAR STEPHEN,
You will think me an unnatural brother but I am not going to be present at your wedding. You may believe it isn't from absence of feeling. Thornton, with whom my exchange is, asked for a prolongation for three months and I didn't see that I had a strong enough reason to refuse, as he has to be with his parents till they are settled. The proceedings of Congress just met and the effects of the Fisheries negotiation, successful or otherwise, will certainly give plenty of occupation. My dear boy, don't think it is from heartlessness, as I should come if I possibly could."

To his future sister-in-law he sent this letter :

WASHINGTON,
Dec. 15, 1887.

" MY DEAR JULIE,
Will you be at Valencia ? I hope so, as I want this letter to reach you in time for the New Year, to wish you all the happiness possible to a Fitzgerald who changes her name for—the better, of course.

I am sending you to London on approval a dressing case which if you don't like you will send away or change. It is beautiful (according to the owner's account) and has a long history which I won't repeat—and I hope you will like it, and use it, though not for rouge, of which I disapprove.

Please give my love to all who are at Valencia and don't forget Charles.[1] I have now seen in reality the smoke of the great city of New York which he took me up the mountain to see.

I wonder if you will answer me and what you will say when you do. But by this time I suppose you are steeled to writing such letters. I am coming back in June and will therefore be obliged to miss your great event. I am writing in a very unbecoming tone but I am really very sorry, indeed. You will be surprised to hear it, but I have a great affection for Stephen, and a more absolute trust in him than for any other person in the world.—Now I will go and call on Sir Thomas Grattan Esmonde,[2] and then hang myself, for I have earned my long rest."

[1] Charles was the Knight of Kerry's butler, a household institution.

[2] Sir Thomas Grattan Esmonde, now a Senator of the Irish Free State, and Mr. T. P. O'Connor were members of Parnell's party, then on one of the periodic missions to the United States, to collect funds and organise support for the Home Rule cause.

Dec. 15, 1887.

To STEPHEN,

"I am very sorry about my remaining here. However, it would be a pity, as things are now, as the Commission are returning in January and I should like to see this game out before I go. But if it is a disappointment to you, I am very, very sorry about it. It does certainly seem a long time since I was in London. As to the rumours of our friend Stead, that Chamberlain was prevented from yielding by Tupper,[1] the story is a vile lie as there was no thought of yielding in Chamberlain's mind.

He continues his course of popularity and is become a great element in this society. Everyone admires his wonderful cleverness and readiness of tongue. He has two great advantages. First he has not the slow reserve associated here with the character of an official Englishman ; he is frank and open to the last degree. Then he has so much self-control. He can utter a short sentence and argue with quick returns ; he doesn't preach and he doesn't wrangle. That gives him a great advantage as they have not much social practice here as to men's society. The men are business men or politicians or club men ; society men have practice of women's society but seldom of men's.

The reception to Esmonde and O'Connor was a very hearty one. The President of the Senate presided and reminded his audience of the sack of Washington by a ' brutal and cowardly British soldiery,' with other amenities of the same kind. Several other Senators were present. On the whole the language was not unfriendly to England and Chamberlain was not mentioned by name, or as far as I can make out, alluded to.

It has made Chamberlain perfectly furious, however, and he uses the strongest language about the impertinence of the whole proceeding. . . ."

Feb. 10, 1888.

". . . Chamberlain's impressions of Washington are briefly these.

That if you want to be rich and then richer, this country is the best to live in. That if you want real life and not the means of living, England is the place. Dullness he finds rampant everywhere ! Dullness in Society—in politics—*ad libitum*. A general and hopeless stagnation without any moment of emotion to relieve it. He uses his tongue with great

---

[1] Sir Thomas Tupper, the leading Canadian member of the Commission.

freedom in this sense and surprises people with his frankness.
They don't mind and as a rule concur as to its truth.

He is very bitter about what he calls the strong brogue with
which all the newspapers talk, and indeed he is so justly.   As to
Ireland, he talks a great deal, arguing with ferocity and direct-
ness, sometimes pitted against a whole tableful of men.   I think
he is acknowledged to get the best of it.   He is always remind-
ing them of the blood and money spent for the Union, and asking
them why they don't sympathise with his own struggle in that
direction.   They answer with a reference to the sympathies of
England in the time of America's struggle.   He says Gladstone's
sympathies were against them ; his own were with them ; but
now Gladstone has been forgiven for opposing the Union of
their country because he is now for destroying the Union of his
own.   And so on and so on—which is interesting to hear and to
watch.   I would write to you more about the splash he has
made in our great pond, only I couldn't describe it fully. . . .

Our treaty is really progressing but it is sure to be squashed
in the Senate, not because the Senate disapproves of it, but
because they disapprove of the present Government.

The balance of power in that august body is held by a drunken
porter from Virginia who spent the vacation in jail.   He constantly violates every rule of order and decency but he turns
the vote and is accordingly honoured and worshipped.

I spend all my days in this way.   Read till 10.   Breakfast.
Go to Legation till 3.   Call on Officials' wives till 6.30 dinner.
Official receptions.   Converse with Chamberlain till 1 or 2.
Bed.

Now, these teas are wondrous things.   You call at a house on
the lady's day, together with a monstrous horde of persons
from the uttermost parts of America.   The lady says she is
glad to see you and then asks your name.   She then passes
you on to another lady in a low dress who takes you to have
tea at a table served by a young lady of her acquaintance from
Buffalo or Little Rock, Arkansas.   These ladies are very often
pretty and charming ; always rather amusing.   I asked the
one from Little Rock if it was a large town ?   She said, ' Oh
yes, there were two germans there ' (*i.e.* Cotillon clubs, by
which she measured the size of cities).   I asked her afterwards
if it was true that ladies in the States were often engaged to
three men at a time.   She said she was herself ; that was why
she didn't want to go back.

Chamberlain shares my hatred of the Diplomatic body,
who seem to me the most odious set of men I have ever seen
in my life.   They give one some amusement by their various

ways of pronouncing the English language, but by few other means. . . ."

The Fisheries Commission agreed on the draft of a Treaty, which on Febuary 15 was signed and made public. But the terms were much criticised in Canada, and in New England, the chief American fishing centre. An opposition was worked up in the Senate where the Republican majority finally threw out the Treaty.

Feb. 16, 1888.

To STEPHEN.

" The Conference is finished and Chamberlain will stay for merchant shipping and copyright [1]—then away to take his blessed seat on the Conservative benches and on the Liberal party. He gets on swimmingly with greater and greater success ; except that his view of America is not very pleasing to the ordinary politician, as he always says that it is no place where a politician has any possible position. This he maintains with great persistence.

A new man is coming out here, a certain Arthur[2] Herbert, who will no doubt be a great success.

An Embassy from the Kingdom of Corea has arrived. They wear red tall hats, the brims uppermost, but are guileless and pleasing. They were asked what they thought of the American girl, after a big reception, and answered with the pertinent question, ' Why they wear all their clothes on the floor ? ' . . . "

Feb. 24, 1888.

" I am still here, waiting for Herbert to arrive, when I shall go up North if I can. The weather is as beautiful as it can be—bright and warm. Chamberlain goes back in a week and will make two speeches (please God, pleasant ones and not anti-Irish) before he goes.

My friends John Hay and Henry Adams have gone down south where they hope to have a pleasant warm season without politics. It seems to me that it makes little difference whether politics are important as with us or perfectly unimportant, as here—the excitement about them is equally great and they are just as absorbing.

I have been spending a good deal of time out in the country where there is a house [3] now untenanted by its owners to which I go and read in the afternoon. It is the only possible way of

---

[1] Bills relating to these international matters were still before Congress. The question of securing copyright to British authors in America was under discussion during the whole of Spring Rice's residence in Washington as secretary to the Embassy.

[2] See above, p. 74.   [3] Mr Whitney's.

being fairly quiet, and very pleasant it is too.   Only the last time I went, I found a New York democratic convention which had been invited to dine out there by the owner and came in for it rather unexpectedly. . . . "

                                                              March 6, 1888.
To FERGUSON,
     " I ought to have written to you before and I hope you will forgive me but while Chamberlain was here I didn't wish to be led into the temptation of gossiping.

He and his secretaries had a very amusing time here in all respects but as to the Treaty, it is as good as non-existent. It has no chance of passing the Senate and the best hope is that consideration will be postponed.

.   .   .   .

I heard an exciting scene in the Senate.   Ingalls (acting President of the Senate), champion of the Republican Party, and of the American nation, bloody-shirter and tail twister, got up and said that ' Grover Cleveland had proved that no origin was so low, or antecedents so base as to disqualify a man from being Democratic candidate for President.'   Also he called General Hancock, who won Gettysburg, a traitor, and General McClellan a coward.   The speech was answered by a Kentuckian veteran in the Southern war—one Blackburn, who made as good a reply as I have ever heard.   He said that he saw Sheridan blushing in his seat at the small part he himself had taken in the war in comparison with that taken by the Senator from Kansas—and what was that part ?   In 1861 he had served as state senator ; in 1862 the same ; in 1863 his spirit stirred him to take an active part in the great struggle and he served as Judge Advocate for the Kansas Volunteers.   When Hancock was bleeding on Cemetery heights and McClellan com- manding the army of the Potomac, he was safely in the rear prosecuting Kansas Jayhawkers for rifling henroosts.—The blow has been a heavy one for the bloody-shirters ; and to us, who are accustomed to hear Ingalls boasting that there are few Americans who do not regret Waterloo, it is a great blessing to see that he is as little generous to his own countrymen. . . . "

Letters to Stephen follow : one marks the birth of a new word

                                                              March 6.
     " The ' Trusts ' are exciting a good deal of feeling.   You know what they are—monopolies on a large scale when an industry is protected.   The States are pitching into them sharply."

March 16, 1888.

To STEPHEN.

" . . . Joe has left a very pleasing impression. Nobody knows whether or no he left an engaged man. I think it very probable, but though I know the family [1] here better than anyone else, I have never heard a word breathed of any engagement. But it would be odd if there were none. The family is the oldest in the county, being descended from the first—the very first—Governor of Massachussets. They have provided many other Governors to the State, and members of the Cabinet to the Union. The present man is Secretary of War— a lawyer and a gentleman. The lady is very English—no accent, quiet, pretty, very dignified and staid for 21 years and perfectly true and straight. He is very fortunate in his choice.

The surplus question here is still on the books. In spite of the message, the Democratic wing voted for a large reduction of internal revenue in Committee. You understand here that the Committees have charge of a bill which they elaborate and decide by vote. The minority introduce a minority bill. The two go before Committee of the whole House. An amendment is finally moved by the chairman of the original Committee, entirely altering the whole. This is, of course, a compromise brought out in the debate. The bill is then voted or vetoed.

You see the despotic power of the small standing committees which take evidence, etc., just like a department with clerks and other fixings—and give orders to the Treasury whose Secretary reports to them just as if they were the real executive. The confusion is immense and results in an almost absolute deadlock, as the existence of the Government is never dependent on a vote of the house.

There is great dissatisfaction with Cleveland (which takes the form in Republican circles of accusing him of beating his wife). But I can't think the Republicans will really win. The Treaty is a new blow and I doubt whether the administration will be able to get even a postponement. Rejection will imply the retaliatory bill, which is what the Republicans want. Brutes. There is nowhere in the world, I should think, such a base system of politics and politicians. I see it more and more clearly every day. The constitution, which confines politics to a small and petty range, has the natural effect on politicians.

[1] Mr. Chamberlain's engagement to Miss Endicott was made public shortly after this.

They can never hope to effect a great and wide-spreading change. All they can do is to change the governors, not the government. The battle is mainly for places on which the real seriousness of politics depends.

The reverse of the medal is better. There is little danger of any real attack on the conditions of labour and property. The country is happy and doesn't care what goes on in Washington. The *Tribune* prints on the first page a letter from Smalley about the successor to the Duke of Rutland. Inside in small type is a brief abstract of a great speech on the tariff by the leading Republican Senator."

March 30, 1888.

" No news of importance. I have been to New York and stayed there a week with the Roosevelts. I had a very amusing time mainly with them and Allen Rice.

I saw Cooper, late Mayor of New York. He said very earnestly, alluding to the Local Government Bill[1] : ' We tried government by boards in New York sixty years ago. The result is that we found it impossible. The only power left now to the Aldermen here is giving franchise to apple stalls. We found that the only way universal suffrage could be made compatible with good government was by getting a vote, not for a ticket, but a *man* ; people were interested in that and we could get a good man to stand. Into his hands we confided the *whole* responsibility.' You know the history of the New York ring which has been repeated in every city similarly governed. I hope in consequence the Local Government Bill is not a Government by elective boards, as it is a recognised failure in this country.

The Treaty[2] has a better chance in the Senate than is supposed. But it doesn't do to be too hopeful. I think that politics in this country are just as vile and low as anything connected with human baseness can be, and the opinion grows stronger and stronger. I saw the really powerful men in New York— the leaders of the leaders—who send men to Congress, tell them how to vote—choose Senators and cancel them, and are hardly ever mentioned in the papers. Their power is just like the power of a good business man who knows how to spend money judiciously."

---

[1] That carried by Mr. Ritchie, which established county, borough, and district councils.

[2] An Extradition Treaty to include dynamiting amongst extraditable offences. The Senate's committee decided for it, but it was opposed, and shelved.

April 27, 1888.

To STEPHEN.

" This letter refers to the brother [1] of a great friend of mine here, Henry Adams, who has been particularly kind to me. If he calls on you, could you get him introductions to theologians in Cambridge, especially Lightfoot, if possible ?

I have been in New York for a day or two with the despatch bag and seeing West's family off. I saw a good many people there, chiefly journalists. An odd thing about New York is the very great difficulty of meeting people together. There is one lady only who gets any sort of meeting, and this is her history.

She was a washerwoman who married an inn-keeper. He became a hotel keeper—an owner of real estate—a speculator in railway shares—and finally *a stiff* (corpse). She had a sister who sang ; war was declared by the aristocracy of N.Y., *i.e* those whose fathers had made the money. But the sister's voice carried the day. Her daughter married an Englishman, and now she is in the odour of sanctity and all New York attends her house on Sabbath evenings.

Another character whom I much affect is Whitelaw Reid, editor of the *Tribune,* who has worked and married his way from the post of long-haired correspondent in Washington to the owner of the *Tribune* and the best house in New York. Jay Gould is on the best of terms with his great and independent journal.

The battle is still raging in the House about the tariff. No one knows which way it will go. A curious feature is that no one reads the speeches or notices them at all. They are mostly rhetorical, about Columbia girded with steam engines and breathing factory smoke. Copyright has a very good chance now. The Fisheries Treaty is practically dished and what comes next, God knows ! "

The next letter is to Ferguson, who had returned after a stay in which he also became an intimate of the American houses where Spring Rice was at home. This visit cemented the friendship to a lifelong durability. Ferguson in this letter becomes as he remained, " My dear Ronald," but he always wrote " Dear Springy." Some of Spring Rice's intimates, notably Roosevelt, used to begin " Dear Cecil " ; but Roosevelt constantly lapsed into " Springy " as the more affectionate address.

[1] Brooks Adams, author of the *Law of Civilization and Decay.*

WASHINGTON,
April 15, 1888.

To FERGUSON.

" . . . The place is full of rumours about Mrs. Cleveland. As she is such a good card for the Democrats to play, the Republicans want to turn it against them and accuse the President of beating his wife. She is said to have fled from Washington in the summer because he became unsupportable and also to have been obliged by him to send away a maid who interfered in her behalf and got a cut on the head with a broomstick.

The fact is that, as anyone can see, they are a most devoted couple and nobody could be more so. But this is a form of politics which in the absence of more important questions, becomes dominant here. The first mutterings of the storm have been heard. Mrs. Fairchild, the most domestic of Cabinet Ladies, was accused in the *World* of having telegraphed to Conkling to institute proceedings for a divorce. The next step will be Whitney, etc., etc.

It is a good discipline for American husbands. I wish you had carried off an opulent American wife, as they certainly seem to make very good ones. My chances, I regret to say, are not much and I daresay it's not a bad thing on the whole. The difficulty with me (apart from the other side of the question) is that I have never been able to fall in love to the smallest extent with any of the ladies. I don't know why, but they don't seem to have the qualities for exciting affection that English girls have, in spite of Chamberlain's opinion. . . .

I take your advice about going home. I hope to be back in May or June to stay in London for good. I don't like diplomatic life at all and I only like this out of pure luxury and wickedness. I shall return to my work and I hope I shan't have lost the habit. . . .

I miss you more than I can say. I wish I had gone back with you.

Your affectionate,
CECIL SPRING RICE."

WASHINGTON,
May 11, 1888.

" I have just come back from my second trip to the South along General Sheridan's track. It was most interesting and I should like nothing better than to go with you there.

We started, five of us, with horses and saddle bags and went along the Potomac through the wild country, with clearings

among the woods and wheat and corn coming up. We stayed
our first night in a very rough inn where we were waited on by an
old slave who had been butler in a Southern family and had run
off to the N. to fight with the enemy. He kept his society
manners and rebuked us for any breach of etiquette. ' The
napkin is to set over your knees, sirr,' he said to me. The next
day we started early and rode along the Canal to a village for
all the world like an English one, where we lunched with a
farmer. He was six feet high—had eleven children, all of whom
were in the neighbourhood. He showed us a darkey whom he
had ' raised ' as a slave, who was passing and saluted him.
Farming, he said, was bad, but one could live. The daughters
told us a good deal about the life of the town. There were the
Pooles, after whom the town was named, and who lived in the
big house. The old man Poole had restored the family fortune
by making carpets in Baltimore. The people were divided into
Episcopalian and dissenters. The former were the nicest to
belong to. One could dance. The Methodists mightn't. On
the table were the Annual Census of the U.S., a Bible, a Tennyson, and a German grammar.

That night, after swimming the horses, we avoided the mists
of the river and took possession of a house of which the owner
was away. He came back while we were routing out his stable
and joined heartily in the work. We had a splendid time with
him and he told us how he had begun with nothing and now was
owner of all the land about. The next day we passed Harper's
Ferry where John Brown[1] began the war. It is a beautiful place,
deep down in the valley of the Potomac, where the Shenandoah
runs in, but the glass was at 89 and riding is hot without proper
hats. Then we entered the famous valley which supported both
armies during the war till Sheridan burnt every barn and killed
every beast, so that as he wrote to headquarters, ' A crow
couldn't fly through it without a haversack.'

We stormed a house in the same way as before and were
received royally. The house was an old plantation house.
The Turners had owned it since the country was settled and all
the land round. The last of them was a hard-drinking old
fellow who, hearing of John Brown's raid, rode down to shoot
him but got shot himself. A Pennsylvanian Quaker took it and
the stables and all the land—a fine fellow, 6 foot 4 inches, with a

---

[1] In Oct. 1859, John Brown, an Abolitionist, seeking to stir up a rising
of the slaves, invaded Virginia from Kansas at the head of a party. He
seized the Government arsenal at Harpersferry, and defended himself
there against troops under Lee; was taken and hanged, and became a
martyr.

growing family. Then we went on through woods covered with blossoms red and white, and fields with very fine stock in them, till we reached Greenway Court where Lord Fairfax entertained Washington. The present owner's grandfather had been a steward to the family and had received a grant of the demesne. He was a great fighter in the war, and told us stories on stories about his cavalry raids into Maryland and Pennyslvania, and his final encounters with Sheridan. He had a ' Life of General Lee ' and a Bible. He loved the Lees and respected Sheridan and his friends the enemy but hated the Republican politicians. He was quite reconciled to his new position. The next person who entertained us was a German who didn't care about the fighting at all but had been impressed when every man in Virginia had to take arms. Then we came to the region where the English live. Loads of them are down there, hunting, shooting, growing vines and raising horses. Those that don't drink do well. The whole country is as fine as any you ever saw. High hills, splendid rivers, beautiful woods and smooth rich valleys. The price of land is going up, but life is absurdly cheap. Our expenses were about 2 dollars a day for man and horse. Which is not very much for strangers.

When I returned I found the good Villiers had done my business and that I was to return by May 31. You see that I have taken your advice and so my fate is fixed. I am glad, as the longer I stay the more loath I shall be to return."

May 12, 1888.

To STEPHEN.

" . . . It is rather unpleasant leaving a place where one has been so long and had such a good time, but it is better not to delay any longer, so everyone, you included, seem to say.

The Senate Committee has reported adversely on the Fisheries Treaty by a purely party vote. The reasons given are addressed not to the Senate but to the more bigoted and disagreeable faction of the Republican party. The time is a hopeless one to have chosen,[1] and every four years politics here become simply the lowest form of personal demagogueism. No one has the time here to understand anything but personal abuse. I don't know what I shall think of English politics after the experiences I have had here. I think I shall be reconciled even to the Irish Members.

I went down South again and saw the great American novelist, Miss Amelie Rives. She is a lady of ancient Southern

[1] " The time " was immediately in advance of the Presidential election, which takes place in November every fourth year.

blood who lives on the ancestral estate in Virginia. She is 23 years old and as beautiful as a lady novelist should be. There is great animosity about her, as her writings are tinged with a passionate flavour which some people attribute to Ouida's novels, and some to her being engaged to four men at once. It is the Eastern *revanche* for Western Mormonism, common in the country. She was what the natives call ' a circus.' She entertained us in a white teagown from 12 till 6 on Sunday afternoon with the most marvellous darkey stories. and exhibited a tame darkey girl six years old who played and sang and recited ' On Linden when the sun was low.' We drove back our seventeen miles *lassati necdum satiati*—one of the party (not me) silent with occasional bursts of enthusiasm. He is moody now.

I shall stay here till my time for going arrives. It does seem odd, I am as much at home here as in London.''

" It does seem odd.'' Spring Rice was by no means cosmopolitan in his sympathies, he had the ordinary Englishman's distaste for foreigners ; and he was not what Americans call a good mixer ; he had none of the talent for being sociable over drinks and cards with the rank and file of American politicians, which he observed to be useful to Sackville-West. Even his gaiety was fastidious. But he delighted always in the society of pretty and well-dressed women, and America offered him this in abundance, on terms of the frankest companionship. He liked ladies to be beautiful and not dangerous, and in return he was ready to give an adoration which would last till they were grandmothers. All his gaiety was at their service ; if they liked gossip, so did he ; he wrote verses to amuse them and himself ; he was a hard-working man who had a fine capacity for the enjoyment of idleness. But his letters show—and the long lasting of his friendships proves—that he gave to his women friends the best of his serious mind as well as of his accomplishment.

With the men, there is no doubt where the link lay. All his American friends were bookish—Roosevelt for all his cowboyishness read and wrote enormously, and he had the passion for political philosophy which was one of the dominations in Spring Rice's mind. Henry Adams had it, too, though his approach to it was the philosopher's and humanist's, while Roosevelt's was that of the furiously active statesman. John Hay, a poet himself, was, like old Mr. Bayard and Senator Lodge, a great lover of pure literature. It is not too much to say that Spring Rice's love and knowledge of English poetry made the most valuable part of his equipment for diplomacy in America. Poetry was to this Wordsworthian the austere expression of high endeavour ; and throughout his life's work he grew more into a sense that the race on both sides of the ocean, under all divergencies of political forms, was held together by its poets—by the noblest utterances of its thoughts and aspirations. With them rank, of course, the most familiar of all his books—the English Bible and the Psalms.

It is curious to note how little this man, whose life for thirty years was one long wandering over the world, busily watching the current movement of thought and action, showed himself affected either by the literature of his day, or by any modern thought that was not English. He spoke French and German without effort, he knew Italian, he learnt to use Russian freely ; but except for a few lines of Dante which are part of Europe's common heritage, there is scarcely a trace in his letters that his mind was influenced by anything that took shape in any of these tongues. He read, as do all men of letters, in two ways, for information and for the pure effect of literature ; and in the latter and deeper sense his mind was moulded by the Greek and Latin classics which had been the best part of his English upbringing. One other literature came to affect him powerfully— the Persian ; but that linked itself back to the mediæval mysticism which reached him in boyhood through Thomas à Kempis.

In Russia he spent three years at the beginning of the twentieth century, when the vogue of Russian novelists was spread through every centre of European culture ; but except for some fairy-tales which he thought would please Roosevelt's children, Russia's literature said nothing to him. It is true that Russia gave him much else than literature to think of. He was, however, unlike most moderns, very little of a novel-reader ; and the stories which he incidentally praises are, as a rule, historical—Stanley Weyman or the like. But in truth for him there was only one novelist who mattered. In this summer he wrote to Ferguson from Washington.

WASHINGTON. (No date.)

" I feel as if I should never be busy again. I am in the habit of undressing in the middle of the day and reading for two or three hours in the heat. The hot weather is delicious. I don't think you know Walter Scott well enough. You try and learn the novels by heart and you won't be sorry—especially if you learn the life, too. Lockhart's Life, especially the end, is magnificent, and an honour to Scotland. I can't tell you what a blessing Scott has been out here. He has always something pleasant to tell one, and every page ought to make a man better."

And again, on September 23, after he had got back to London :

" I have been reading the unveracious Froude in which I revel. He is splendid as a narrator. Especially some passages in Mary Stuart's life. I shall go to Fife [1] with even greater interest. Walter Scott is the real historian though. If I

---

[1] Ferguson's home, Raith, was in Fifeshire.

wanted to be proud of my country as a Scotchman I would
read *Old Mortality*. I have been simply revelling in Scott. I
took up Froude afterwards to get references to State papers
(which he misquotes) and have been immersed in him for the
last fortnight. You don't know how jolly it is to have everything perfectly quiet—work seven hours and then go home to a
solitary undisturbed read—get up early and have a noble two
hours in the morning ; and never a bother or worry except that
the leaves stick when they turn over.

CHAPTER IV

UNITED STATES UNDER PRESIDENT HARRISON

FROM the summer of 1888 Spring Rice was back at the Foreign Office, and until the autumn of 1889 stayed there, living with his brothers and sisters at 113A Queen's Gate. Consequently there are few letters of this time.

He had the chance to make some return for American hospitalities, and Brooks Adams wrote to him on June 23, 1888 :

" There are very few days which, when they are over, I can look back and say that I have enjoyed them from end to end ; but you gave me one at Oxford. Nor was it only the university which delighted me, if you will let me say so ; for to me it was so keen a pleasure to have a sympathetic and appreciative companion. It is so seldom that I meet a man who cares for the sort of thing I care for, or sees in it what absorbs me, that I hope you will forgive me for once setting aside convention and writing you this line."

Again, a few days later :

" My dear fellow, I'm a crank ; very few human beings can endure to have me near them, but I like to be with you, and I suppose I like to be with those who are sympathetic, the more since they are so few."

He paid his debts too by correspondence. John Hay wrote from Cleveland on November 2, 1888 :

" I wonder if I write and ask for it deferentially you will write me another letter so breezy and delightful as your last. Mrs. Hay and I have read it to rags."

Hay then, on the eve of the Presidential election, proceeds to " kick the President about," but apologises for forgetting Spring Rice's " deplorable politics." These—as has been seen—included a sympathy for Cleveland, who was about to be defeated in his candidature for a second term. The letter ends :

" Think of Herbert, engaged—and you still sniffing at our continent, in maiden meditation."

Other letters show that this Washington circle was much bent upon finding an eligible for Spring Rice—though the suggested possibilities and attractions varied from month to month. Another engagement had been duly announced, and its consequences followed. Mr. Chamberlain married Miss Endicott in February 1889. In the autumn of that year Spring Rice, who had been to stay with them at Highbury, wrote to Ferguson :

" He is so domestic now, with Mrs. Mary, that politics sleep at home. I think he is very much improved.
. . . Mrs. Chamberlain has the most wonderful composure I ever saw. She does all the honours and is as gracious a queen as ever Birmingham saw. Jo. is evidently most deeply in love and they are hardly ever separated. The family is very pleased with her to rule it."

The same letter has to do with Ferguson's own marriage, in September 1889 :

" Mrs. Cameron wrote complaining I hadn't written to her on the subject. So I answered and told her in polite language that you had married someone much pleasanter than any American."

He added that Lord Dufferin was said to be complaining that " you had robbed him of his best secretary." Lady Helen Blackwood, the famous ambassador's eldest daughter, as Lady Helen Ferguson and later as Lady Novar, brought a new element into the friendship between the two young men. Henceforward, till death broke it, there was a triple tie.

A couple of other notes from this time seem worth preserving. One, to Stephen, undated, describes a visit to the Tennyson household —old friends of Sir Henry Taylor.

" . . . I have just been to Haslemere. At 8.15, I looked out of window and saw the bard running in the sun. So he is better. Hallam has a bad leg. I am going again. There was a Papist priest who talked theology. He says the bard's mind is wholly set on religious subjects. He read Guinevere in the evening. I heard the priest sigh once or twice at certain passages. . . . "

There is also this impression from the great dock strike which began on August 19, 1889, and paralysed the whole shipping trade of London, till on September 14 the men's demands were conceded. The general public then first became acquainted with the leading figure of the contest—Mr. John Burns, afterwards for many years a Member of Parliament, and a Cabinet Minister from 1906 to 1914.

" I went down to hear Burns. There wasn't much of a crowd nor were they very enthusiastic. We all stood under a

high wall on the top of which a row of men were sitting in the
sun smoking and kicking their heels.   Then a young man got up
and delivered a short and very loud address ; perfectly businesslike, with a little about the civilised world in the style of Mr. G.,
at the end.   Then Mr. Tillett got up : he was elaborately the
working man : a very bad hat and dirty shirt ; but a pretty
sharp tongue.   He didn't seem to stir people much.   I suppose
they had heard it all before ; but it seemed an exciting subject :
100,000 men risen against injustice and determined not to
yield, with ' all the forces of the universe, Cardinal Manning and
the Earl of Dunraven at their back.'   When he had nearly done,
up drove a hansom : out of it got a man in a hurry ; and by
Tillett's side suddenly appeared a man just like the Pirate King
in a Surrey theatre.   He was dressed in nautical blue with a
strap round him from which a bag was hung full of newspapers.
He didn't pay the smallest attention to Tillett, but stood by his
side as much as to show him that he had talked enough.
Tillett didn't much seem to relish this, and only talked louder.
Burns stood before us throwing in observations here and there
and turning over his papers, while all of us in the crowd looked
at him and made our remarks to each other.   He had a dirty
straw hat on[1] but a clean shirt, very deep set eyes and black
hair and beard.

    As soon as he spoke, he showed he had a splendid voice :
he began telling us that he had slept for four hours, put on a
clean shirt (loud applause), and come down to work refreshed.
He went on in the same tone and was good humoured throughout, except when he spoke of the blacklegs.   He boasted of the
absence of intimidation, and said Lord R. Churchill had com-
plimented them on it, which was received with applause.   He
was amusing now and then ; said all the papers from ' the
Times upwards ' were in the dockers' favour, and again, that
if things went worse Mr. Matthews would have to come as
usual and ' preserve a breach of the peace.'   He was H'y and
grammatical except when he addressed Sir D. Currie.   ' We
will make you, Sir Donald, one more stick to beat the *Pachy-
dermatous* skins of the Dock Companies,' which he pronounced
slowly and carefully Patchydermatous.

    I never heard a word of socialism in any of the speeches ; it
was simply a statement of a bargain ; they deserved to win and
were winning.   Nothing about the rich man grinding the poor,
or property being robbery. No intimidation. Burns described how he had intimidated some would-be workers by
marching past the docks with fifty men chanting the ' bloody
and awe-inspiring strains of " We won't go home till morning." '

[1] The Home Secretary.

Altogether it was rather impressive and one couldn't help sympathising. The policemen were lounging about in a contented sort of way, listening to the speeches or talking to the men."

In the autumn of 1889 he was again ordered to Washington, to act as Secretary to an International Marine Conference. Its main purpose was to establish what has since been achieved by wireless telegraphy—an " unspoken language " universally employed by seafaring nations, so as to diminish the dangers of the sea. The conference broke up on December 31, having attained to nothing more than some better agreement for the ensuring of life and property. But after its disbandment Spring Rice was retained at the Legation, having rank now as second secretary.

A Republican administration was now in power, with President Harrison at its head, and Roosevelt, having been appointed Civil Service Commissioner, was now in his office at Washington.   At the Legation, Sir Julian Pauncefote replaced Sir Lionel Sackville-West who had been recalled on the plea that he had interfered in the Presidential election.—A trap had been laid ; a voter, professedly of British origin, wrote asking for advice how to vote ; West replied that the Democratic party were strongly anti-British in sympathy ; and this letter was sent on to the White House.

To FERGUSON.
INTERNATIONAL MARINE CONFERENCE.
WASHINGTON,
Nov. 15, 1889.
" My dear Ronald, this may be a great country, but I am not exactly in a humour to praise it.   I have good reason to suppose that this Conference was got up by the influence of a patent Light company who wished to get the powers to pass a rule for their employment.   One of the delegates of the U.S. appears to have received a brief from this company.   To our astonishment he occupied a whole morning in advocating the cause of this company.   He spent a week before with the agent in lobbying members.   The English and German delegates made the strongest speeches one can imagine.   The proposal was unanimously rejected.   Last night the gentleman gave a dinner.   There were speeches after dinner.   He laid his hand on his heart and said solemnly that the Conference had no object at heart except the good of humanity.   A colleague in proposing his health joked him about the Light company, to the amusement of the other delegates.   No one seemed to think it disgraceful.   Blaine spoke.   He said the U.S. had a ' genius

for friendship.' As neutral ground, they were the best mediators among the conflicting European interests. The Secretary of the Navy made solemn remarks on the sacred function performed by his country. I sat next to a newspaper correspondent. He pointed me out four newspaper men dining. (One of them was dead drunk and embraced Blaine afterwards, which Blaine had to endure smiling.) He showed me the description of the dinner which he had telegraphed to our host's local paper. Also he showed me a candidate for office who was put next to Blaine, a prominent politician down in our host's neighbourhood. He told me how he got information from every official in the navy deparment. How he paid them simply by mentioning their names with praise. He said at the end, ' the whole state is rotten and all we newspaper men here know it.'

Do you know that Harrison, Republican Harrison, has come among the Anglo-maniacs ? He has been publicly convicted of docking his horses' tails. He is said to have lost 60,000 votes by it.

Teddy Roosevelt was appointed Civil Service Commissioner in order *not* to put the rules in force. They chose the wrong man. He obeys the law and enforces it. There is a scream for his removal in consequence. He is having a fine time and going strong."

Jan. 24, 1890.

To STEPHEN.

" The F.O. has made no remarks about me, and Pauncefote wrote a despatch explaining why he had kept me. There is no chance of my going away till someone comes here as the staff are invalided and there is a great deal of work.

There was a great business in the Senate yesterday over the Nigger question in the South. For some time things have been getting worse. There are murders and outrages by blacks every day, and every day reprisals by the whites of the bloodiest character. The criminals in the prisons are taken out and hanged publicly and in some parts the white population is permanently armed and turns out at any alarm, shooting and hanging right and left. The Northern Senators, in whose states there are no blacks, make eloquent appeals to eternal justice and generosity. The Southern Senators say they wish their Northern brothers would change states with them and see how they got on without Winchester rifles and with nothing but generosity. The danger must increase as years pass, and in a short time there will be the devil to pay.

I have a good deal to do and spend my time at work in the mornings, up till about 4, and then go out and ride. As a rule, I dine with Henry Adams who lives with a friend in a house close to me and never goes out. He is a very cultivated man but rather a cynic. There's something rather melancholy about the talk of educated men here. Either they are in politics or out. If the first, they will talk perfectly fairly and honestly about ordinary subjects, but the moment they come to politics they are not only bitter as we are in England, but they make an open profession of partizanship and bitterness, with an open contempt of any of the ordinary considerations of honour or honesty or high feeling. If they are not in politics they speak honestly about everything, politics included. But when they get to talking politics, they have a sort of bitter despair in their minds which is hard to describe and not pleasant to listen to. I daresay the solution is one which was told me the other day. 'There is nothing in politics now—only a sort of scavenging work. Because we employ scavengers to do scavenging work, it doesn't follow that the whole nation is corrupt. It's not corruption, only a sense of fitness.' The New York Harbour Board has just been convicted of paying large sums to a company which dredged in the day time and dumped back its dredgings in the same place at night. A man has just paid a million for a seat in the Senate. No one makes any complaint but thinks him pretty smart. A candidate for the governorship of a state has been shown to have suborned a man by the promise of a state office to forge a letter from prominent opponents, by which they were nearly convicted of bribery. The fraud was discovered just in time. The gentleman is considered ' quite a bright man ' ! Politics is all dullness relieved by rascality. They have never been so bad as now."

" Politics " in the main meant internal affairs. But the Secretary of State, Mr. Blaine, had a serious controversy on foot with Great Britain.

The United States claimed that in acquiring Alaska by purchase from Russia in 1868 they had acquired that dominion over the whole of Behring Sea which Russia had always claimed. In July 1889 three British sealers, having on board skins of seals captured in Behring Sea, were seized by United States revenue cruisers, which put a man on board of each capture, and ordered the captains to take their vessels into a port in Alaska. The order was disregarded and the vessels came to port in British Columbia.

In reply to Mr. Blaine's protests, the British answered that no territorial jurisdiction extended more than three miles from the shore and therefore that British sealers were entitled to fish any where outside the three-mile limit.

The Republican administration had at least the advantage over that of Cleveland that they possessed a majority in both houses, so that a Treaty concluded by the Secretary of State had a fair chance to pass the Senate.

As regards internal politics, questions of currency were dominant, and a strong movement had begun urging the use of silver as well as gold for the basis of currency.

March 25, 1890.

To STEPHEN.

" . . . There is not much going on except an animated debate on trusts in the Senate. It seems a strong measure to bring in a bill making trusts illegal, and its effects will be very far-reaching, or at least would be, if it wasn't for the amazing power of corporations here to avoid laws and their operation. One overgrown president said, ' We very seldom have to spend much money—but, of course, in states where the legislature has declared itself very hostile to us, we are compelled to corrupt their politics in self defence.' The result is either that capital leaves a state for some more favoured scene, or the hostile law is evaded by the action of corrupt officials.

There is an official of the Hong Kong bank down here collecting information on the silver question. The matter is one which, of course, will profoundly affect all our Eastern possessions. It really seems as if the silver men would have it all their own way. The west is for silver, of course,[1] the agriculturalists of the centre for it also on the ground that it will much reduce the weight of their mortgages ; the South is for it, because the Yankees (N.Y. and New England) are against it. The bill, which will probably be passed, will be in the interest of these people and result in a largely increased purchase of silver. Luck for India, isn't it ?

One of the great authorities here says he has sent men all over the world to look for gold and that he is convinced the stock is pretty well exhausted. Is that anything like true : How about the Zambesi ? . . . "

March 28, 1890.

To FERGUSON.

" I like the life here. You see we have several questions of very great interest—the Alaska fisheries and the Eastern

[1] The silver producing states are Western, and the Farmers expected that increased currency would lower values and they could settle their mortgages in a depreciated dollar.

fisheries, which we hope also to settle.　Our relations are on the whole good, but one has to remember that in a happy country like this where politics don't affect great questions, or the happiness of the nation, the people who run them are apt to be a pretty poor lot.　If all you want done is crossing-sweeping, you are apt to get crossing-sweepers employed.　I suppose that there has never been an administration so absolutely unworthy of a great nation as this one.　It is universally acknowledged, but it doesn't affect the happiness of the people.　In fact, the only sensation they derive from it is amusement in the Sunday press.

They have passed some new rules in the house with the help of our friend, Mr. Reed of Maine, that fat, sarcastic man you remember ; the object of them has been, as he tersely put it, to give the minority all the rights which the majority think are good for them.　He has also stated a definition of the Senate—' the place where good Congressmen go when they die.' It would do for the H. of Lords—the place where the good Tories go when they die.　Land is in an awful state here. Values went up and the farms have been mortgaged up to the fancy value.　Then the value has gone down and the mortgage remains.　The result is a growing ' granger ' party. . . . ''

Mr. Reed was the Speaker.　The " Granger " party was officially called the Farmers' Alliance, and advocated free silver, and a tariff with lower charges on articles used by the poor.　It was born of resistance to the sweeping measure of Protection introduced in this Congress by Mr. McKinley.

April 4, 1890.

To STEPHEN.

" . . . I went last night with Theodore Roosevelt to see the President and his wife.　They are both small and fat.　They both said they were very glad to see us, but they neither looked like it.　I talked to the President, who is generally supposed to be the meanest man in the States.　He seemed to me a very clear-headed and pleasant man. . . .

I have been meeting the new Senators from Montana which is to be admitted as a State.　One of them achieved his reputation by hanging three judges and a sheriff to the rafters of the only habitable house of his native village. . . . ''

June 24, 1890.

" . . . Times are troublous here.　The administration has fallen out with the House about the tariff and they are expected to come to blows.　This administration is pretty well discredited. The President has just received a present from a land company who gave him a house by the sea ready furnished, even down to telescopes. A member of the Cabinet is a member of the land company. We are not at all sure that the Cabinet have not been given an interest in the Behring Sea Company which stiffens their attitude. The papers have been considerably interested, too. It's a difficult country for diplomacy.

A Free Coinage bill passed the Senate. The probability is that it will result in a compromise between the administration, the House and the Senate, for the coinage of four and a half million of silver per month. Free Coinage itself will not pass unless feeling alters. Its real meaning is the fearful burden of debt of the South and West, which is mortgaged to the North-East and is naturally anxious for cheap money. The farmers here are in a terribly bad way, worse than in England, because they own their own land and are so heavily mortgaged.

You should have an autocrat like our Speaker here in London. He would clear all difficulties up for you. He is the leader of a party which has the majority. They obey him implicitly ; always yielding after ineffectual attempts to break off. He does what he likes without consulting the administration, which he detests, or his followers whom he seems to despise.

A letter follows which shows how the Republican party when in power ensured that their policy of protection should not be altered even if the Democrat Free Traders came back to office.

HARRISBURG, PA.,
Oct. 27, 1890.

To STEPHEN,

" I am now staying with Senator Cameron at his capital, where I shall be for a few days before I go to Washington. . . .

The Tariff Bill was a piece of political machinery. Cleveland issued a tariff manifesto which severely frightened the manufacturers who raised large sums for the last elections in 1888. These were managed with great skill by a certain Senator Quay of this state, with the desired result. The Republican Govt. performed its part of the bargain, passed new rules in the House of Representatives, by which the bill was hurried through, and admitted four Republican states, by which the Senate was reinforced by eight Republican Senators. The Senate refused to pass rules to govern debate, and had to sacrifice all legislation except the Tariff Bill. That Bill is now passed, and though the Democrats will carry the House of Representatives at this fall's election, the Senate will remain Republican, so that no Free Trade bill can pass for some years, unless the Republican Senators change their minds. It is believed that wages will rise and it is maintained that only the rich will suffer by the Tariff. There is *not* a strong reaction as stated. . . ."

Leaving politics, one may turn to matters more attractive. Spring Rice wrote to Ferguson on May 23, 1890 :

" . . . I am so glad to hear you are so happy. You certainly deserve to be, and so by all accounts does Lady Helen. As for myself, I fear that I have chosen a profession which makes wandering about a necessity and I don't think a wife would have much of a time unless she loved the society of the French and South American colleagues. In that case I shouldn't love her society much. . . . "

He changed his mind about the French—but not till much later.

SALEM, MASS.,
July 17, 1890.

To STEPHEN.

" I moved up here when the heat became intolerable in the south, leaving Congress still sitting ; the Speaker presiding in flannels, canvas shoes, and a large yellow scarf round the waist.

This place is the house which belongs to the Endicotts. A frame house. I go up every day to a place called Manchester, where the Minister is. It is on Massachusetts bay. Opposite the house is a chain of little islands with rocky shores. For miles behind and right down to the sea there is a thick wood. It is really beautiful. Even here the glass is at 95° in the shade. On both sides there are watering places. That means hotels. A summer hotel is a square wooden block with some hundred odd windows all exactly alike ; a wide and deep verandah or piazza which has given a name to a peculiar variety of the sex known as the ' piazza girl.' Opposite are twenty or thirty bathing houses with innumerable women in front of them and around them. Americans don't accompany their wives and daughters on pleasure excursions. There is a general want of men. Those that exist have a good time which they make no concealment about. There is generally a ' stock-ticker " in the hotel office. A man here said it was the only real thing in the place ; and the stock it represented was mostly water.—However, I don't live in a hotel."

July 21, 1890.

" . . . Salem is a curious old place. It was the centre of the commerce of the U.S. at one time and the whole town is dotted with splendid houses once inhabited by the merchants. The

Endicotts' house is one of the few which remain inhabited by the old owners. They are mostly wooden, built in the square style of the eighteenth century; detached, looking out on streets shaded with fine trees. I wonder if you ever heard of the famous witch craze in 1690. Thirty men and women were hanged for witchcraft in this little town after due and fair trial, judged by a very respectable court. They belonged to the best and richest families. The evidence was that of four or five girls who went into convulsions in court and accused the prisoners of being the cause. It seems incredible. The House of the Seven Gables stood next to our street. Its site is shown. The old custom house where the story of *The Scarlet Letter* was found is not far off.

I shall be here for some time to come. We write and play lawn tennis and bathe. Yesterday I met a man who gave me an account of the fight between the ' Chesapeake ' and the ' Shannon.' He was an eye-witness, and saw Lawrence's body carried through the streets.[1] . . . "

Sept. 12, 1890.

To MARGARET.

" . . . I am well, very well ; and still staying by the sea with the Pauncefotes who are not returning to Washington till October. I am alone at present, as the other Secretaries have gone off for a time. I told you I had gone to Newport for a fortnight and seen Brinsley [Fitzgerald], who had made up his mind to enjoy himself and was certainly doing it very thoroughly. The plan there is to attach yourself (called ' to be devoted ') to some young lady who has several other men in the same romantic relation. Her skill, like a circus rider's, is to keep as many in harness at once as possible. Brinsley reversed the process, and managed to ' be devoted ' to all the young ladies of the place at the same time, without their finding it out. I admired the skill he did it with. I can't say that Newport is really a very enjoyable place, except that there was good lawn tennis and a fine beach to ride over with a beautiful grassy point ending in rocks and a superb sea. But the society is, I suppose, the vulgarest in the world ; the refinement of vulgarity. The entertainments are magnificent but not pretentious ; the houses small and cottage-like with wonderful lawns and, of course, double coach-houses.[2] The people beautifully dressed ;

[1] In 1813.

[2] " A cottage with a double coach-house,
        A cottage of gentility."
                    Coleridge, " The Devil's Walk."

their features and figures delicate and refined. They are as hospitable as can be. The sea is splendid—the Atlantic swell rolling in right under the cottage windows. In fact, it is the perfection of watering places ; and I suppose there is no place like it in the world where there are so many means of enjoying oneself, and where people have put themselves to so much trouble and expense to get the means of happiness.

The universal result is boredom. I don't know why. They don't seem to care for anything in the world. They have nothing to talk about, except each other, and nothing to do except to talk. The whole thing is so unreal, that I heard a lady there say that she wondered the water was wet. They are all strugglers in society, some of them succeeding, some of them having succeeded. Those that have succeeded look across the water, sighing for new fields. They count up each others advantages, as money, looks, dress. They say that if Washington is the town to study the American eagle, Newport is the place to study the American mocking bird. The odd thing is, that in society as in politics, the corruptest outside covers a most respectable and religious interior. The people are all good and kind. They are generally the children of virtuous, hard-working parents who attended Methodist chapels in country villages and would have turned green at the thought of an evening dress. I only wonder what the next generation will be. This is engaged in ineffectual attempts to blacken its own character, which everyone knows to be perfectly good.

MAGNOLIA, MASS.,
Sept. 15, 1890.

To STEPHEN,

" . . . I am still here. I hope you are enjoying yourself on the other side of the sea. We have real Irish weather here. Just like Valencia. Warm winds with soft rain—soft and continuous as love should be. I spend the larger part of my time catboat sailing and sculling. The swell is tremendous but not equal to the western shore of the Pacific. There is a good deal of fishing in which I do not excel. The fishermen are a terrible race. We are next door to Gloucester, where all the Yankee fishermen live who fight the Canadians (they call them blue-noses, alluding to the effect of an inclement climate ; the proper colour of a fisherman's nose here is deep vermilion). I am always afraid lest a row should occur in Newfoundland waters and an angry fisherman wreak vengeance on the Briton readiest to hand. Our landlord took an island, but could not obtain possession as it was used as a station for bait fishing. (The

bait, in an advanced state of decay, floats past our windows.)
He applied to a local lawyer, saying that he had paid the price,
that the fishermen paid no rent and that they refused to go.
The local lawyer said he could send an armed force of police to
burn the tackle, etc., of the fishermen. The law would not
prevent him. The fishermen, it is true, would infallibly burn
his house down the next day.

A gentleman tried to preserve game. Some gentlemen from
the neighbouring town came down (uninvited) to shoot his
game. He objected and tried to set his dog at them. They
shot the dog. He tried then to take a man's gun away. They
shot him. The shooter was elected alderman next year as a
proof of the respect in which the community holds independence
of character. You will be surprised to hear that this ancient
state is ruled by our dear Irish. It is ruled and governed and
policed especially the latter, as the Irishman has an incurable
mania for protecting the law for a certain consideration. They
say here, What is an Irishman when he lands at Boston wharf ?
A subject of the Queen ? *Answer*—No.
An American citizen ? *Answer*—Not yet.
What is he then ? *Answer*—A policeman."

Oct. 27, 1890.

To FERGUSON.

" . . . I saw Bryce. He was on his way from British
Columbia to Kentucky. I like his wife. He is an angel and
deserves the Cabinet in this world and Heaven in the next.
Jo. C. is not very confident,[1] but domestically he is absolutely
the most happy man I have seen. Remember that I have not
seen you in that relation.

I do hope Lady Rosebery's illness is taking a good turn. The
worst of being so far away is the uncertainty and delay of all
such news. I don't know anyone who deserves so well of fate
as she does. . . . ''

At the end of this year Spring Rice was recalled to Europe and
despatched to Brussels to act as second Secretary. It would appear
that he received the order in Massachusetts, and made a rapid passage
through Washington to collect his property. John Hay wrote to
Henry Adams (then in Europe) on December 12 :

" Spring Rice has come and gone. He behaved himself very
well here. Threw over a dinner at the Legation where about
thirty people were asked to meet him, and came to dine with

---

[1] About politics. Mr. Chamberlain was in America with his wife's people.

me—telling Sir Julian he would come to him the next day. The Pauncefotes were good-natured and did not seem to bear malice."

This recalls the opinion of a colleague's wife, quoted by Sir Arthur Hardinge in a letter to Spring Rice.

"Mrs. Helyar gave me on the whole a very good account of your behaviour at Washington, but said that you were very eccentric and that one never knew what you would do or say next, which I said was my opinion too."

That was in 1888. But by 1889 Hardinge was writing from Constantinople, a true word spoken in jest :

"You will become quite an American specialist and be consulted on all U.S. matters till the day you become Minister in Washington."

Spring Rice's stay in Brussels was brief, for he was recalled within less than two months and ordered back to Washington. But he saw in January 1891 the disturbances which arose out of a popular agitation for extension of the franchise, then limited to less than 150,000 persons in a population of six millions.

> BRUSSELS,
> Jan. 22, 1891.

To JULIE,

"I have been demonstrating against the constitution of this country, which happened in this way. My illustrious chief, who is most anxious to get full and perfect information for his govt., wanted one of us to go and see a riot which was expected. Being the unmarried one, I went. I wandered about in the streets till it got dark, when suddenly the narrow lane I was in was blocked by a torchlight procession with a band and choir. I naturally joined, as I couldn't go forward and was rather anxious to get home, and so became part of the procession and lifted my voice in the Liberal song. It consisted entirely in repeating the name of the Minister of Justice, to a rhythmic chant, with a repetition of the last syllable. The name is Vandenpeereboom. We passed the cathedral and sang the Marseillaise under Charles V.'s Chapel. It was lighted and I saw H.I.M.'s portrait, which he had put up in the window 300 years ago. Then we went to the Chamber, but as we debouched on the place, we found our way barred by soldiers and police whom we valiantly hissed and invited to join our song. Then I slipped off down a side walk and informed the Minister that I had demonstrated. He said I should be reported to the F.O. I informed him that I was acting under orders."

During his absence from America, the chief of police in New Orleans had been assassinated. Six Italians were tried, and acquitted. On suspicion that the Mafia had bribed or intimidated the jury, armed men, directed by a local lawyer, broke into the prison where other Italian prisoners were confined, shot some, and hanged others from lamp-posts outside.

WASHINGTON,
April 13, 1891.

To STEPHEN.

" . . . The Italian Chargé says he looks at all the ' lamp*en*-posts with tremmoling,' being afraid of lynching. Someone asked the German Minister if he knew a Mrs. Lynch of New York. He answered innocently: ' Do you refer, madam, to the wife of the Chief Justice of this country ? '

I spend what time is left from leaving cards and copying letters, walking up and down the streets under a waterproof in pouring rain. The snow is over and the heat is due—and that very soon. The worst disagreeable thing I have to do is looking through the papers. They are too abjectly bad for words, and like the American skunk, they are twice cursed, they curse him that gives and who receives. I am just starting out for an hour's ride which is a perfect rest : but the roads are a foot deep in mud and I saw a regular typical spectacle yesterday ; a darkey with a mule car bogged in the middle of the road, axle deep ; trying to drag his wagon out. I am just going out to-day to see if he is still there. The mules seemed asleep, the nigger digging in his dreams, and the wagon got deeper every minute.

Free silver was saved by the action of the Speaker refusing to give a day for its discussion. As the next house has a silver majority and the Senate is certainly silver, partly by bargain and partly by conviction, a silver bill will be passed next spring. The President will veto free silver, but he may not have the strength to veto a largely increased coinage bill ; and that would, of course, have a great effect. A new party is coming up which seems to be carrying everything before it."

American politics as well as British were affected by the split in Parnell's party which followed on the O'Shea divorce case.

March 27, 1891.

To FERGUSON.

" The Irish won't get any money at all. The papers say the American people is quite willing to give them money to thump the British but they will *not* supply them with money to thump each other.

There is a great increase of the feeling of annexation here, as Canada presents herself as worth having, and the main difficulties of the formation of the Govt. have been got over at the expense of Canada and the British Govt. I wonder if Canada will take the same view."

The question was naturally prominent, because Canada's claims were clashing with those of the United States on the Pacific seaboard, about the Alaskan seal fisheries, and on the Atlantic over the Newfoundland Banks—though here the French were also involved.

After long diplomatic correspondence a temporary compromise was reached and Commissioners from both parties were appointed to enquire into the question of preventing extermination of the seal herd. At the end of October Spring Rice felt able to tell Cabot Lodge :

" We have practically settled the Behring Sea arrangement (this is between ourselves) and it will redound immensely to the credit of Wharton and the President. They have gained their point, and have behaved throughout with quiet dignity and at the same time have shown their appreciation of the great difficulties of our position."

But in June 1891, when the discussions were only beginning he set out these difficulties and pointed to their ultimate consequences. It is the first remarkable example of the power to forecast events which distinguishes his diplomatic correspondence. He foresaw in 1891 those problems concerning contraband of war with which, as Ambassador from Great Britain to the United States, he was fated to have so grave concern a quarter of a century later.

June 7, 1891.

To FERGUSON.

" I have had on the whole an interesting time, as the Behring Sea business has been anxious. I think it is well worth while getting it settled and out of the way, but our position in all these Western diplomatic affairs is most difficult. The policy of the U.S. is plain and simple. The wrongs inflicted by Canada are done by Gt. Britain, so Gt. Britain is responsible. We make an arrangement. If it is unfavourable to the U.S., this is again an unfriendly act ; if it is acceptable, the newspapers point out to Canada that Great Britain has abandoned her colony, and that the only resource is annexation.—One is naturally anxious to come to a friendly arrangement with the U.S.A., but we are still more anxious not to sacrifice our colony. Then, Canada's position is trying. They have to pay more of the costs of defence. This makes them very violent and out-spoken in their attitude. On the other hand, it is their interests and not ours which we sacrifice in our arrangements, so we are loath to sacrifice them. The upshot is, we argue a cause we don't understand and defend an interest which is not ours. I have never seen it so strongly shown as in these negotiations.

Of course, one might say : What on earth have we to do with the U.S. ? How can their feelings affect us ?

It is a question of supply. We get an enormous proportion of our food supply from the U.S. In case of war in Europe, our enemy will attack our food supply. Under the rule accepted by France, Germany and Russia, the necessaries of life are contraband of war ; this doctrine was protested against by the U.S. and ourselves. So in case of a European naval war in which we are engaged, the U.S. navy is bound to protect our commerce and food supply, which is an important considera-tion. Besides this, our trade with them is six hundred million out of a total of sixteen hundred, and our interests are bound up inextricably.

I must say the country is an odd one and although I don't mind the things that happen so much as I did, I sometimes get rather angry. But suppose we were to swop institutions, I don't know that they would gain so very much."

To FERGUSON.   June 16, 1891.

" . . . All letters are welcome now, as I am pretty well alone with the glass at 95°. Teddy Roosevelt is here and we live together but we are both away all day. The work has been very interesting and quite as hard as it used to be when we were together during the Greek Blockade—only, I see now that there are not many people I am likely to serve under like our chief.[1] I like old Pauncefote, who is kindness itself ; also, in the President we have found an honest man. Perhaps honesty here is like the end of the rainbow, always in the next field ; but I am inclined to hope that on the whole the mass of public opinion is just, and in spite of politicians, newspapers, and diplomatists, that honesty on the whole commends itself and is the main interest of the mass.

You have no idea how great the change of public sentiment is in regard to the Irish question, which seems to have sunk

[1] Lord Rosebery.

altogether into abeyance since Mrs. O'Shea. The chief interest of all Americans at this moment seems to be Baccarat.[1] ' Prince Baccarat ' they call H.R.H. and say, if he had any idea of the eternal fitness of things, Parnell ought to ask H.R.H. to his wedding. There are no end of respectful remarks about the Queen, who is greatly admired.

One of the odd effects of the Tariff here is to increase immensely the pauper emigration from Europe, as a number of industries have been seriously hurt there and the workmen are flocking over. The feeling against immigration is very strong indeed here in the Eastern States, but not so much in the Western who think they want ' building up.'"

To FERGUSON.   July 10, 1891.

" I think this is a grand post for interest, especially in relation to our colonial policy. I have been making a study of the trade relations and sending home long reports, which no soul will ever read and which will in the end enrich the record office. I sometimes feel like setting to work and writing a series of articles, only I should like to bring in confidential things, or more or less confidential things. The Govt. is a good confidante ; like a journal, it's certain not to repeat anything.

What you tell about Rosebery is interesting. It was a strange thing the difference Lady R.'s death made even to me—and I felt it very much in London. It *is* such an important thing (to oneself and everyone else) to have an interest and a real interest in other people, and that she had in a high degree.

I suppose your session will be over soon. If the elections turn in our favour [2] I suppose we must expect a period of chaos for a time, unless we get an enormous majority, and even if we do, till the party gets more consolidated. I should certainly think in a few years it would be pretty strong in personnel and perhaps stronger than the Tories—but at present we have a queer Cabinet. I am not sure about Blaine's liking for England *now*. But he has, like all Americans, a strong feeling against all foreigners ; of course, he hates England, but hates foreigners infinitely more, and his hatred for us is mixed with respect. Indeed, there is too much respect about it, as no one realises how weak our position really is, in spite of Dilke's book.[3] They seem to think us designing tyrants who are doing everything in

---

[1] A libel action arose out of a game of baccarat at Tranby Croft, in which the Prince of Wales, having been one of the players, was called in evidence.

[2] That is, the Liberals'.

[3] *Problems of Europe*, which brought out the fact that Europe, was " an armed camp "—with England less armed than the other nations.

our power to destroy America, from hatred of Republican institutions and love of the Guelph dynasty. It's rather amusing to see their hatred and contempt for the Emperor, and the way they pitch into him for turning up his nose at the Volunteers. They don't allow anyone to abuse us except themselves ; and indeed they use their monopoly.

I suppose there is some awful accusation hidden in Lady Helen's message about ' my character of her to Mrs. Cameron ' ! But I have forgotten what it was, except that I remember very well telling Mrs. Cameron that your family considered her a very dangerously fascinating person (which every woman, I suppose, wants to be)."

To the other of his beautiful friends, Mrs. Lodge, he wrote on July 5 his congratulations because Senator Lodge had carried a Bill concerning copyright, which in Spring Rice's opinion deserved more gratitude in England than the press showed.
"Love to Cabot," the letter ends. "Teddy used to talk about him all day. But Teddy is gone and I am left alone."
In October of that year Spring Rice had to write to Senator Lodge about the announcement of Miss Lodge's engagement.

"Do you remember talking to me on the subject and the young man at Newport, and saying how you liked him. Fortunately I remembered this when I heard the news, which otherwise must have been a great blow. I don't think this is the right form, or quite the right form, in which to write wedding congratulations; but then everyone has not a daughter like yours and I can't congratulate you on losing her out of the house."

The next letter carries on the upside-down compliment :

"As you say, concerning the possibility, it is the best form of a bad job, and although no son-in-law at all may seem now to be better than a good one, yet he is plainly a good one."

These were the arts by which he endeared himself to those Americans whom he liked. But he remained critical of American society.

NEWPORT,
Sept. 1, 1891.

To STEPHEN.
" . . . Newport is an extraordinary place. They say the only doctrine thoroughly realised here is that dollars are worth a hundred times as much as sense, which is intended for a joke but is true. You never hear anything but remarks about

people, dress, dinners and London society, especially the latter, which they talk about much as Scotch ministers talk about heaven, half familiarity and half awe. Every now and then a lady comes back from Europe and is regarded as one risen from the dead, like the gentleman in the *Republic*.

By the way, I read a good deal of the last work in Greek the other day, having nothing else to do, and it is delightful."

WASHINGTON,
Nov. 6, 1891.

To FERGUSON.

"The elections [for the State legislatures] have had the result of ' booming' Cleveland, of depressing free silver, and of demonstrating that the tariff is popular in the West and unpopular in the East. McKinley's election [as Governor of Ohio] was partly owing to his great popularity and partly to the popularity of the tariff, but chiefly to the introduction of a ' free silver plank' in the Democratic platform. The result of the election will be to disgust the Democrats of free silver, which will be an excellent thing for them.

It must be remembered that the tariff is here to stay. With a Republican Senate and Parliament it *can't* be altered till March 1893 at earliest. Even then, the Democratic party would have to *agree* upon a modification of the tariff, and that will be of immense difficulty, as the interests affected are so immense and will be hard to harmonise, as each manufacturer will be ready to depress his neighbour's goods, but not his own. So we must count on the present tariff for a year and a half at least ; and possibly, even probably for much longer. We must reconcile ourselves to it and look for new markets. A serious aspect of it is the reciprocity clause, which drives us out of the W. Indies and S. America.

But it must be remembered that, so far as it means differential duties on American goods, if Americans gain thereby, as they hope, the monopoly of import trade into S. America, the S. American republics will lose the whole of their tariff-revenue. They cannot live on direct taxation. The tariff is a necessity. Therefore the system, if successful, works its own cure, for the reciprocity agreements will become intolerable. Our present danger is in the W. Indies, where the U.S. are holding out the bait of their great market in order to put the colonies in the dilemma of choosing between differential duties against the Empire and commercial ruin. The only way out is annexation. It is a simple game and an answering move is hard to find."

With the beginning of 1892 a transfer came into view which had been announced since the previous June; but Sir Julian Pauncefote had petitioned to have Spring Rice left for some extra months. Now, however, he wrote to Ferguson:

WASHINGTON,
Jan. 22, 1892.

" I am just on the point of leaving this country for Japan. I regret it but I must get into the habit of moving. You have got the habit of staying still now, which is a far better one and happier too, but on the whole mine is the best for me under my circumstances. Life in the outside service is far fuller and more interesting than life in the F.O. because the work is at first hand. I don't know how long I shall stay away; I hope not more than a year and a half or two years, but I can't tell. Unfortunately, I can't afford to take leave from Japan as I should have to pay my passage home.

I am going by Canada. The situation there is the same as ever. The next stage will be an attempted negotiation of a commercial treaty with the U.S. The U.S. will make large offers, coupled with a condition that Canada differentiates against England. Canada under its present regime will make large offers on condition that they are also extended to England. But on both sides the actors look to the gallery. The U.S. expects to bring into relief the choice laid before Canada— to be an appanage of the U.S. and commercially prosperous, or an appanage of Great Britain and poor—the choice, that is, between the dollar and the shilling.

The leader of the Canadian opposition has declared himself in favour of unrestricted reciprocity with a differential tariff against England. The U.S. can afford to wait for that. On our side we have nothing to offer, neither bribe nor threat. We can't differentiate against the U.S., because it would, we think, make food dearer. The most we can promise is not to let our other colonies differentiate against her. I fear unless some commercial concession can still be made that the present situation cannot continue long."

The concluding sentence of this letter and passages of others refer to a crisis which arose just before Spring Rice went to Canada on his way to Japan.

During the Chilean revolution which overthrew President Balmaceda in the summer of 1891, American sailors were attacked. Reparation was demanded from the new Chilean Government, who replied by a note which was regarded as insulting and which demanded the recall of the United States Minister, Mr. Martin Egan. War was threatened till Chile apologised and agreed to pay compensation to the wounded and to the families of the two men killed.

Mr. Egan had been a very prominent person in the extreme wing of the Irish Nationalism. As early as Nov. 1891, Spring Rice wrote to Ferguson, asking him to hint to the *Times* that its opposition to Mr. Blaine on this matter was too pronounced, and seemed to Americans as if England were inciting Chile to war. He thought that the editor was perhaps moved by " spite to their old enemy Egan."

" It is an important matter for us to prevent the *Times* being entirely in the hands of anti-Republicans. There is no measuring the unfairness of one side here except by the unfairness of the other."

So far as Mr. Blaine was concerned, Spring Rice wrote :

Jan. 19, 1892.

To STEPHEN.

" We are on the verge of a war here, which is owing to inconceivable stupidity on our (that is, the American) side and trickery on the other. Blaine's influence is for peace. It is curious, with his reputation, what an anti-Jingo he is. He has done everything he can against war. I hope it may still be avoided, but the President is bent on it."

Again, to Ferguson :

" Blaine has put himself on record as a great peace-lover : he has prevented war with Chile so far, and may do so still ; but the President and the navy are bent on it."

He summed up his commentary in a letter written to Ferguson in April 1892, after he had reached Japan :

" As for Chile, the whole affair was instructive. The President and the Secretary of the Navy wished for war ; one to get re-elected, the other to see his new ships fight, and get votes for more. The naval officers were encouraged in their natural desire for distinction. War was only averted by a very complete apology from Chile. But the moral for us is : what will the U.S. be like when their fleet is more powerful, if the administration acts in a similar manner ? I can't help thinking that serious difficulty may yet spring from the Behring Sea matter, or something else, during this critical year, unless good temper is shown on both sides, which doesn't seem likely. The press on both sides is particularly irritating. The danger is a real one, I think, but I can't say that it seems to be realized at home.

His last letter from Washington is dated Jan. 31, 1892, and reports his decision to apply formally for permanent exchange to the diplomatic side of Foreign Office work. " I'm not keen," he writes to his brother, " but perhaps it is better, as things are in the F.O."

The letter ends with a paragraph which shows how early the drift of works of art across the Atlantic began :

" A friend of mine has just got a Botticelli, a most beautiful one too. It came from Florence and is quite untouched. There are now in Washington about ten Turners ; two or three Botticellis and a number of other pictures, all in private galleries. In New York there are many more. I saw our grandfather's big Turner in the Vanderbilt gallery."

From Tokio he wrote to Ferguson, who like all Members of Parliament was preparing for the General Election, his thoughts on England and America.

TOKIO,
April 25, 1892.

" What a year this will be ! There will be tremendous difficulties and I suppose the next few years will settle what the England is to be that we will die in. I quite agree (and more) in what you say about the U.S. But I feel this. That we can't possibly afford to quarrel, and that if we did, not only would it be an immense disaster, but we couldn't beat them. At bottom the character of the nation isn't bad. The worst faults are on the surface, though I own they are the very faults which are most irritating. It makes me wild to think of the things I saw and heard during my last stay. To have to negotiate a treaty about one of the colonies [1] with a man [2] who had himself been on tour as agent to provoke the colony against its allegiance, and who was writing all the time in the *Tribune* assailing England, putting the worst construction on everything and garbling all his statements—that's the sort of thing I had to see. However, if we come to blows what's to become of us ? Often ' a man's own angry pride is cap and bells to a fool.' I think the policy of Wolsey and Elizabeth towards France is the sort of line we should adopt. To keep friends at almost any cost. Only there is this about the situation : that at bottom the feeling is not so much hatred as jealousy. There is a sort of rude justice, if you go far enough. Our destruction is not desired. And I can't help thinking that our offensive power is vastly overrated. It is quite absurd to see the enormous importance attached to the slightest word of the *Times* or of an English statesman. Americans are still very colonial. But I am sure that peace we

[1] Canada.　　　　[2] Blaine.

must have and our temper we must keep. A break up in our relations now might mean almost any disaster—in the Pacific, on the Atlantic, and in Europe too. . . . "

To this faith he was constant. It is the keynote of his life's work. Blaine's name comes so often controversially into this correspondence that it is well to print here a letter to Spring Rice from Blaine's daughter, Mrs. Harriet Blaine Beale, when she wrote to congratulate him on the news of his engagement

" I had you very much in mind even before Rachel wrote, for about six weeks ago, in an obscure corner of the coal cellar, the furnace man came across a box of old letters and personal treasures which my mother had packed up when she went away from this house nearly ten years ago ; and among them was a beautiful copy of *Marcus Aurelius* with ' For Mrs. Blaine from C.S.R.' in your handwriting. I fell to reading it sitting on the edge of the box and have quietly secreted it from the rest of my family and am keeping it as my own—with your permission. You must have given that to my little mother the year she was so ill, and when you were so kind to her and used to bring in the Dumas books. Do you remember ? I do, and with much affection for you and such gratitude."

CHAPTER V

JAPAN

In 1892, when Spring Rice first went to the East, less than forty years had passed since an American fleet under Commodore Perry warned the Japanese people that they could not continue deliberately to exclude foreigners from all contact, as they had done for more than two centuries. Parties formed in Japan about this issue : there was internal strife, during which the Japanese more than once came into collision with European military armament. Finally, a new epoch, called " the Era of Enlightenment " was inaugurated, under which power was wrested from the Shoguns (Japanese Mayors of the Palace) and transferred back to the old Imperial dynasty, whose representatives had been confined by the Shogunate to a puppet existence at Kyoto. This change was brought when the Satsuma and Choshut clans, most powerful of the great clans which had been dominant in Japanese history, defeated the last of the Shoguns. The Emperor was enthroned at Yeddo, of which, to mark the beginning of the new era, he changed the name to Tokyo. In 1872, a general assembly of the Daimyos, who had formerly held power of life and death and of levying war, voluntarily surrendered their feudal rights. From that onwards, Japan entered on the course of constitutional and administrative advance which, combined with the spread of Western science, was to bring her on a level with the European powers.

Yet even in 1892 Japan still figured to the imagination of Europe much as Gilbert and Sullivan had represented it in *The Mikado*. Not until she went to war with China in 1894 and showed the world how she had combined Western military training with the traditional valour of her race, was Japan taken seriously by all. By that time Spring Rice had been transferred back to Washington. His accounts of the country, left in the form of a diary, show how greatly it had fascinated him. But Japan's picturesque charm has been so often described that it has seemed better to abridge at this point, keeping only those letters which illustrate his interest in the political developments which took place whilst he was there.

He set himself at once to learn the language, as was his practice wherever he was sent : but his stay was not long enough to give him any mastery of it, nor does he seem to have been attracted by Japanese literature.

He learned languages in the fashion of one who has been taught in an English public school, that is to say, by the eye rather than by the ear : beginning by the study of the grammar and pushing on to reading rather than to speaking.   He had not the imitative gift which helps in the acquisition of an accent, and even French and German, of which he had full command, he spoke badly.   But he learned to understand Japanese and use it a little, as later he learned to understand and use Russian freely.   Neither of these languages, however, affected his mental outlook ; on the other hand, Persian became the key to a new world and a new enchantment.

TOKIO,
April 1, 1892.

To FERGUSON.

" Here I am at a sufficient distance from the centre of the world, which I take to be London.   I am living in the Legation compound, a place just opposite the palace, from which it is separated by a moat 100 feet deep; it is surrounded by a brick wall and surmounted by the flag.   It contains the houses of the secretaries and the servants of the Legation and is quite a settlement in itself.   I am living with de Bunsen,[1] who, you may remember did so well for us in Madrid, and he makes a very agreeable companion.   I have a good many books with me and am working pretty hard at various subjects—that is, I read a great deal, but how much I remember I am not quite sure.   Have you read Marbot ?   I am in the middle of him and find him fascinating, but I find it hard to realize the state of things then existing in Europe and the tremendous sufferings inflicted all over the world. Will it happen again ? We have no guaranty that it will not.

The flock of globe trotters is beginning to settle.   Hundreds more are promised and our chief occupation is getting their passports.   They ask intelligent questions about the ' working of constitutional government among a semi-barbarous people,' etc., etc.   In return they and all Europeans are most cordially and heartily hated by the Japanese.   As for the constitutional government, it is now what England may perhaps shortly become.   The party system is not in vogue.   The radical party, so called, desire to institute government by party and that is their main aim.   The so-called Government party simply desire to perpetuate the present state of things, which is that the heads of the powerful clans, whatever their sentiments, coalesce to form a cabinet which advises the Emperor.   This cabinet became unpopular with the House, who refused to vote the

[1] Sir M. de Bunsen, P.C., G.C.M.G., then secretary of Legation; later, Ambassador at Vienna up to 1914.

budget. In consequence, the Mikado has published a decree perpetuating the last budget, and limiting the time of sitting allowed to the House, which will meet, debate, do nothing, and adjourn. The Emperor has great influence as being descended from the sun, a being more important in Japan than in England. But John Stuart Mill and Herbert Spencer are the beings who are next most in vogue, and it will be interesting to see which divinity will prevail. The Government paper has been publishing a series of articles to prove that eclipses of the sun are not caused by the sins of the Emperor, nor the eclipses of the moon by the sins of the Empress, but rather by the luminaries in question being in a line with each other. A serious dispute between the rival journals has been started on this question."

May 16, 1892.

To STEPHEN.

" . . . I am trying to master the Japanese national air : it is really a curious thing ; it has no sort of tune or harmony but has a decided dignity about it ; as it sounds, you can almost hear the Mikado waddle. *Incessu patuit* : he walks with his legs wide apart.[1] As for politics, the session began by the announcement that the Mikado had been graciously pleased to prolong the budget of last year so as to cover this ; the debates accordingly are of a philosophical nature. It is a characteristic view to take of Parliament to give them all power except that of the purse. That was thought quite out of the question. The peers are strongly anti-government ; no parties but clans : each with his hereditary and actual leader and all ' struggling, and rightly struggling to be free ' : generally with effect. But I love Japan as far as I have seen it, and I can forgive false views of political finance."

Meantime there was a parliamentary crisis in England. The Parliament elected in 1886 had run out its full period and a General Election followed, in which Liberals, with the support of most Nationalists, had a small majority and Mr. Gladstone again took office to introduce another Home Rule Bill, which Ulster threatened to resist by force.

Sept. 5, 1892.

" . . . Nobody knows what is happening in politics here. The new Cabinet is formed by the Union of the three of the prominent statesmen who agree not to interfere with one another, or to pay regard to the Chamber. They make no profession of policy and

[1] He is burlesquing Virgil's description of Venus meeting Aeneas when *incessu patuit dea*, the goddess was revealed by her walk. The Mikado's motions in state were prescribed by tradition.

answer no complaint. The Chambers are not sitting, so there is no means of ' drawing ' them at all. The result is a happy and prosperous country—laws and justice seem good, agriculture and commerce respected. Travelling is absolutely safe. The Missionaries say they are barbarous, because they don't wear trousers, and worship their own fathers instead of God's Son. They rather like the missionaries because they teach them English, which is a profitable accomplishment and gets them places in the Tokio stores. . . . "

June 27, 1892.

To STEPHEN.

" . . . Will the election be over when you get this and will there be civil war ? I wonder. It is hard to believe. But it will be extremely disagreeable for English people abroad if things go wrong at home, for they have no resource in the way of voting and abuse. If Home Rule fails now, I hope it will be considered as hopeless ; if it succeeds the matter is settled. So in one way we should be nearer peace by a Liberal gain.

It seems an odd thing that while the monarchical countries are getting in a more unsettled condition, the French republic is steadily gaining politically ; that is, that the government by the chambers seems settling down and becoming more moderate and sedate. Our bad time seems near : and Germany's too. Here Parliament is the Devil, and unsettles everything.

The Frasers go to-day and Bunsen is in charge. He will make a capital chief and I look forward to it. I like my old chief, Fraser, and his wife immensely. He is a perfect gentleman, s'il y en avait jamais, and it's a pleasure to be with him."

TOKIO,
Sept. 18, 1892.

To FERGUSON.

" Is it true that Edward Grey is at the F.O. ? [1] I wish to goodness you were, though he is a good man. What a lot of trouble Ld. Rosebery has crowding on him at once.[2] It is undoubtedly true that Egypt can't be held in wartime and is an endless trouble in time of peace. It is a difficulty hard to face, but if the Liberal govt. abandon Egypt with the character that they have earned in previous years, they would bring a whole host of difficulties on themselves at home

[1] As Under-Secretary for Foreign Affairs in the House of Commons.

[2] The Khedive Tewfik, with whom Lord Cromer had long worked, died in January 1892, and his successor Abbas Hilmi, a youth of seventeen, quarrelled violently with Kitchener and the officers of the British army, claiming full right as an independent autocrat.

and abroad. Turkey would ask for Cyprus. Russia would think, why not the Pamirs? Germany would look for another Heligoland. We are in a position where we can't stay with safety, and which we can't leave with honour. If it was the first time in our history, it might be serious, but it has been almost the normal position of England since the discovery of America. At any rate, I don't see how the Liberal Party can do it. The great advantage of getting a character such as Lord Salisbury got, is that one can surrender Heligoland. We've got to earn the character, in order, if necessary, to be false to it with impunity. But of all characters in the world, this one is the last which attaches to the present Government.

George Curzon is here, full of admiration for Arthur Balfour and Oscar Wilde. He has improved, I think, and has been working hard. He was always a good fellow. I think I shall go with him to Corea, cross the peninsula and perhaps, if I have time, slip into China for a little.

A sketch of that journey was given in Curzon's book, *Problems of the Far East*, published in 1894. But part of Spring Rice's account of the Corean adventure is reproduced here, because its vivid detail gives a picture of what Corea was like before it became the bone of contention between China and Japan, and passed under Japanese control.

To FERGUSON.
" Curzon arrived on September 14 and we had a dinner for him, the Prime Minister, Count Ito, and Mr. Mutsu, the Secretary for Foreign Affairs. Count Ito began life as a little Samurai, or foot soldier : he rose in the wars of the revolution, went over to England (I believe as a stowaway) and came back full of constitutional government. He knows a good deal about that. He is generally described as the father of the constitution. Till lately he watched his child's growth from afar and was known as the black-curtain Minister, because he had all the power without any office. But when the fight between the House and the Cabinet got too bitter, and the Cabinet itself began to split up, he had to enter office, much against his will, and there he is, the most powerful man in Japan with the most powerful colleagues, and no one has the smallest idea what he is going to do, or what is his policy.

Curzon and he were rather amusing, for Curzon asked him the most searching questions on man, on nature and on human life, and as to how long the constitution would last, and was parliamentary government a success in Japan, etc.: to all of which he made the politest and most unsatisfactory answers. The

Foreign Secretary is a tall thin man with a graceful manner and rather wasted appearance. Ito is thick and plump with an energetic healthy face. Mutsu's wasted appearance is due to his having passed six years in a prison, at a time when Japan hadn't adopted our humanitarian ways. I believe he was kept in a box and fed through a hole. The offence was being a Treasury clerk. In that capacity, the money which passed through his hands went to the rebels in Satsuma instead of the Government troops. So they locked him up.

My teacher told me that when the Shogun went to see his dead relations, all the shops in the way used to be shut and no one could venture into the streets. He went followed by the Daimyos and their train in silks and armour. Now Prince Togugawa, the family chief, goes alone, once a year, in a tall hat and frock coat. Close by is a gate full of little round holes. These are made by bullets. When the Shogunate fell, some five or six hundred of the retainers wouldn't go up North with the rest of the party who escaped, carrying with them the Mikado's brother, the High Priest of the Temple. The 600 took refuge under the grove of cryptomerias, to which the temples owe most of their beauty, in the enclosure, not of the memorial temple, but of the great central temple. Here they were attacked by the retainers of the Mikado's Daimyos and almost all killed. My teacher was one of those who escaped. The fighting was pretty bitter—they fought for a time with their guns : then habit was too strong : each side threw guns away and set to work with two-handed swords."

Journal to STEPHEN.

"*Oct*. 4. Sailed from Fusan for Gensan—after a splendid lunch given us by the Japanese Consul to whom we had letters from the Japanese Government. It was a most elaborate European meal in a European room, waited on by European-clothed Japanese. Opposite me was Bjornsen, a young Norwegian in the Chinese Customs Service, the son of the great writer and brother-in-law of Ibsen, and godson of Hans Andersen. A curious place to meet in, wasn't it ? We found at Fusan our guide, a clergyman in the Corean mission, who wished to make the journey and joined us. He understands Corean and looks tough. The voyage along the East Coast of Corea with its mountains and islands on a clear bright day was delightful. The ship was Japanese, the crew mostly Chinese, the captain a Norwegian, a stout old fellow who liked nothing so much as being in command of a sailing ship. The moon was beautiful and I slept on deck till midnight. Next morning the coast was still in sight and the mountains higher. In the afternoon we saw in front of us the opening of Port Lazareff and Gensan. A deep bay runs up, dividing into two harbours like lakes—one of them is Port Lazareff where the men of war of different nations go to watch one another, and the other is Gensan. The Japanese town is a long way off the Corean; here we landed and found our way to a Japanese tea-house. We were rather horrified by an announcement made to us by the inspector of the Customs, to whom we had written about horses; he told us smilingly that there were none.

We were met at the tea-house by about a dozen little Japanese waiting girls who sat round Curzon in amazement at his enormous height. They made an absurd group—Curzon in the middle, the girls all round him squatting on the ground with their bare toes turned up, staring at him. We slept on the floor very comfortably and the next day presented our passports and letters to the Yamen, or Government of the town. These letters gave us the right of demanding horses, but we didn't enforce our right that day, as we had a promise from a gentleman with a face like a patch of putty that he would bring the horses that evening. We fed at our friend Olssen's, of the Customs. He was a Dane talking English beautifully, quite indistinguishable from an Englishman; with him was a German who also seemed half English. The Chinese administer the Corean customs and Sir Robert Hart administers the Chinese. He has a staff of Europeans of all nations and languages, and in every port along the coast you come upon a small European colony.

Evening came and our horses didn't come. The next morning we determined to use our strength, and we called again on the Yamen, explaining that we had been deceived; that we were persons of great consideration, travelling to see the King (Curzon had that aspiration) and that we would make it hot for them if they didn't do what we wanted. They seemed visibly frightened. That is, they laughed uneasily, and in an hour came to call on us at our hotel to inform us that they had put the owner of the horses in prison and threatened a beating and that he had consented to send his animals—which, in fact, arrived in the course of the morning. Ten absurd little ponies, kicking and prancing and neighing, each with an attendant 'Mafu' in white linen, horse-hair hat and enormous white baggy trousers. Then the packing began. Such a business. Everyone wished everyone else's pony to carry the heavy things—and there were about four or five fights in the course of a quarter of an hour. Then came the payment. The owner

demanded an extravagant sum : we refused : he ordered his men
to unpack.   We took him and one or two of the most obstre-
perous mafus to the Yamen.   There was a great festival going
on and a crowd of visitors at the office.   In their presence we
had a violent scene,—we arraigning the horse dealer and he
defending himself.   The Corean interpreter took our side, but
the chief official was manifestly frightened at the mob round and
tried to temporize.   Curzon got very angry, explained that he
was one of the most important people in England, and that it
was a matter of vital importance that he should see the King
that week ; and he threatened beatings and dismissals all round.
Space was kept by an attendant dealing sounding blows with a
paddle on the audience.   Finally the Yamen said they would
confiscate the ponies and lend us mafus of their own to take us
across.

Meanwhile I was down at the tea house seeing that the mafus
didn't unlade the ponies ; they tried to once or twice but after a
time lay down contentedly and slept ; then one of them got up
and began to tell a story with great feeling and gesticulation.
The others squatted down and listened.   The horses would try
and fight every now and then, but after a time the sun had its
effect and they lay down with their loads on their backs.   After
an hour and a half Curzon and the clergyman returned with the
Yamen's mafus.   Immediately all the mafus wished to come
with us at our own terms.   We dismissed the most refractory,
among others one whom we called the village ruffian, with a
most villainous face.   Then the owner had to have his money.
650 cash go to one dollar or three shillings, and we paid him
thirty-two dollars in cash.   The pieces are fastened together in
strings of fifty, but, as you may think, it took some time to count
out the money, and two or three men to carry it.   He gave a
little to the men for their expenses and finally at five o'clock in
the afternoon we started—a long procession of ponies, ten in
all ;   three saddled, the others carrying complicated loads, a
Japanese servant, a Corean, two gentlemen in red-tailed hats
provided by the Yamen for our protection, and ten white-robed
mafus.   The evening was fine ; the first difficulty was to get all
our mafus through the Corean town without losing them, which
cost us and the red-tails a hard tussle ; finally we got clear and
plunged into the mountains.

The sun set about 6, and the moon didn't rise till 8.   The roads
were pretty bad—simply a track through the rice fields or
rocks.   As soon as it got dark the Red-tails ran ahead—the
mafus raised loud shouts of U-sha—U-sha ! and presently we
saw lights coming to meet us along the road.   These were

torches carried by men, boys and little girls—logs of pine,
flaring. We made the torch bearers arrange themselves along
our line and so continued the march. It appears it is the duty
of the householders along the road to provide lights. At the
next village we were met by new torches, and so on from place
to place. The moon rose but the hills were high on each side
and we had to keep to the torches. I remember well the sight
where the whole procession crossed a stream in which the lights
were reflected. At last we reached the town where we were to
branch off from the main road. But here no torches met us.
The red-tails tore about the streets shouting and cursing. No
answer. They seized a post and began to beat down the door
of a house. The owner emerged to expostulate, was immediately banged on the head and knocked down. When he got
up, he enquired the reason and said they had got hold of the
wrong man ; they let him go back to bed again and treated
another house in the same way. We waited, wondering, at the
entrance of the street. A tremendous row appeared to be going
on at the other end of the town. The red-tails came flying back.
They had been repulsed by a crowd of men who were after them.
So we decamped torchless. This didn't matter much as the
moon was up. The poor red-tails were rather knocked about
and we had to go slowly.

About 11 we came to a thick wood and a ravine. The road
got steeper. Before us were the high gates of a temple—three
posts, one laid on the others, two with arrow heads stuck in the
top. The road wound among trees up the hill, past some
graves in a glade till the monastery itself came into sight. The
moon was high and bright and we could see it well as we rode
over a high stone bridge leading to the gate. Here 500 years
ago the founder of the dynasty dreamed that he would be king
of Corea and gathered his followers within the walls and seized
the power. The buildings are of wood on a stone platform built
over the torrent. A high wooded mountain is behind. Our
ten horses and retinue marched in and established themselves
in an outer court. The monks soon came in and made us
welcome. Presently a distinguished old man in a black horse-
hair hat came in. Curzon greeted him warmly with ' Here's
old Abbo.' He answered at once, ' Yes, ole Abbo.' We afterwards found out that ' Yes ' was the only English word he
knew, and I suppose he imagined ' ole Abbo ' a form of greeting,
as he used it frequently afterwards. We went up through two
courts over dilapidated steps to a door which one of the monks
threw wide open. Inside we saw a number of white figures
which rose upon their feet like corpses in their grave-clothes. A

paper lantern was burning on an altar on which was a grim idol
of dusty gilding.   Here we were to sleep ; the corpses removed
themselves, and left us and our luggage. We made our beds on the
floor, which was covered with oil paper and heated from below.
Some fifty spectators, including old Abbo who sat himself on
the dinner chest, watched us boil water, eat and drink and go to
bed.   Finally they departed except one or two whom we
removed with boots.   The next morning early they were back
again.

I can't say I slept well, as at 3 o'clock in the morning the great
bell sounded and prayers were intoned in the court outside.   I
went down and bathed in the stream.   The day was bright and
as the hills were one mass of maples, all crimson and gold, and
the woodwork of the monastery richly painted, the view was
rather surprising.   I had never imagined anything like it.
Old Abbo took us round and showed us all the sights : the
place where the King was to sleep when he came—it was
magnificently painted but open to the air : the great temple with
Buddhas by the thousand—the bell and all the various courts.
When we came back we found the Prior trying on our coats and
hats, while the brothers were regarding him in admiration.
Curzon had an air cushion which delighted old Abbo, who blew
it out, sat down on it and, as it was too full, rolled off on to the
floor.   We gave him some whiskey, which he liked but made
incredible grimaces over—our food he wouldn't touch for fear
of meat.   We wrote our names in his book and at 8.30 left him
with two silver dollars.   I saw him last standing at the gate
with one hand clasping the dollars, at which he took an occasional furtive glance, and with the other ardently pressing
Curzon's.   Dear old Abbo.

.   .   .   .   .   [1]

On the morning of the 17th, after ten days' travel and nine
nights out, we came under a great granite mountain, black and
rugged at the top and with sides absolutely bare of trees or
grass.   At the foot is a plain of white granite sand, with
scattered fields of rice.   On the mountain is the monastery, a
fort guarded by armed monks, where the King takes refuge
when there is a revolution.   From its slope we saw the walls of
Seoul, and we climbed up to its N.E. gate, with considerable
difficulty too, as the road was steep and covered with broken
granite blocks.   Then an hour's ride through the streets, inconceivably dirty streets, brought us to within sight of the Union
Jack, which floated from a rock in the middle of the town with

[1] Several days' travel notes omitted.

its habitual modesty. Hillier the Consul was away, gone to meet his wife after a separation of eighteen months; but his Chinese servant waited on us, soothed us and gave us hot baths and food.

Then came the payment. The coolies and the red-tails and all the ponies gathered round the courtyard of the Legation and we all talked at once for two hours. Finally, we came to terms. I find that the whole expedition cost about £20 or £10 each. So it was not very expensive. I didn't see the sum in cash. I doubt whether Seoul holds so much money !

Oct. 17. Arrived at Seoul, bathed and ate. Then we went round to the mission house and saw Davies'[1] colleague, a young Oxford man—with many Oxford friends and photos. Dined there and talked Oxford, rowing, debating societies, etc., etc. Saw the lodging where six Kilburn sisters, who are on their way here, are to be lodged, also the two rooms where a Revd. Canon is to live with his wife and his furniture : cases on cases filling the courtyard—among other things an evident grand piano. The mission is studying. They attempt no conversions but are learning the language and customs. There are many Americans who come out, it would seem, mainly to be enabled to marry. They get sufficient salaries, with allowances for wife and children—an addition for each child, generally earned. Soon after arrival they dash up country distributing Bibles broadcast and writing reports home. The Catholics, who have endured three persecutions, number 250,000. The preaching is done by native priests educated in the Catholic schools. The missionaries are volunteers not bound by oaths, celibate, living up and down the country, each alone in a Corean house on Corean food.

I saw, too, the missionary doctor, an old man, once Surgeon-General in the army, crusty and decided ; he lost his wife, had a call, and came out here where he lives in a house too low for him to stand upright in, all alone. On the way back from dinner there was a fire. Eight houses were burning. A fire brigade of Chinamen were working hard at it ; pulling the neighbouring houses down, beating out the burning thatch with sticks and working the fire engine, which was supplied with water by a crowd of Coreans from tea cups and saucers and little brass pans. The Chinese marched up and down, knocking the Coreans about and working like fiends. We watched for some time the fight round a house which was half alight. At last the firemen won and the fire was hedged round and subdued.

This town has a very large circuit. A wall is built round the

---

[1] Davies was their missionary companion.

hills which enclose it, the hills are steep, made of bare granite, and some must be some 1000 feet above the town. The wall is about 50 feet high and the work must have been enormous. You can tell the ranks and status of people from their dress. Officials have blue or red dresses. One-third are officials, and do nothing and receive no pay, but have the right to steal. Every now and then a noble passes, riding in a high saddle on a very small pony led by two men, supported by two others and holding on by a rail in front of the saddle. Married men have their hair in a top knot. I saw several married men of ten or twelve. Those who have passed examinations can wear a curly hat without a brim. The people dress in white, which their wives have to wash. All night long one hears the noise of the wooden hammers which give the linen cloth its gloss. The women wear green coats which are pulled over their heads just leaving a space to see through. They mustn't be seen in their houses. An engaged man wears a small straw hat ; a man in mourning for teacher, father or mother, must wear a huge straw roof on his head, sackcloth on his back and a screen in front of his face to keep the spirits off. He must not marry or hold office. The officer-holders are a class by themselves. It is the ambition of every man to become one, as once in office one need do no work and has a right to live at the expense of the low and vulgar. The high offices are held by the original nobles, a hereditary class who must never be guilty of a _mésalliance_ ; below them are innumerable grades of official thieves. Most of the luckiest are the Queen's relatives—she has the court and the country full of them. She is ill and if she dies, it is said, at once all of these gentlemen will have their heads cut off. At present they make hay. The Queen has absolute control over the country ; the King limits himself to squeezing operations. He excited great discontent at the last public examination by selling the fifty principal offices to the highest bidder and then declaring the examination informal and pocketing the money. So much discontent was caused that in future it is believed that examinations will be held on the square, and that all those who pay the requisite sum will pass in the usual manner. The odd thing is that thousands of poor men go up for these examinations all the same, though, having no money, they must know that they can't get in.

I saw the King pass in state to visit his ancestors and worship, and as probably it is one of the few sights of the sort to be seen in the world now, it is worth recording. The booths which fill the streets are taken down—the streets sprinkled along a narrow path in the middle with new gravel. The whole population turns up. Nobles and grandees are carried backwards and forwards in their state robes, and one by one enter the palace. No one knows when the procession is to begin. Suddenly the great door of the palace opens and the royal banner of the winged tiger makes its appearance. The infantry form in line along the street ; they are half German, half Corean, armed with old flintlocks, some without locks, all rusty, most tied up with string. The cavalry are the strangest sight for they are of all ages, are clothed in armour hundreds of years old—leather helmets with the covering dropping off them, old brocade coats and thigh coverings studded with brass knobs, once magnificent but old and faded, enormous felt boots, for all the world like Goose Gibbie at Tillietudlem.[1] After the standard comes a palanquin, which is empty, but is like the King's ; this to deceive the devil, should he take a fancy to carry off His Majesty. Then the bearers of the Royal Palanquin, with red hats and coats, trotting along, bearing the royal burden. He sits under a crimson canopy with gold tassels, looks curiously about. The Minister of War lost three months' salary, by Royal Decree, last procession, because the people came too near the King. The people turn their faces away and bow. Every now and then the ' Board of Silence ' utters a long howl—which means ' keep silence in presence of Majesty.' The King goes past. Then comes an interval and the Crown Prince follows. His litter is carried by men with black hats. The General commanding in chief and Ministers follow, mounted on small ponies on which they are firmly held by two officials each, two more holding the pony's head, several more with His Excellency's spare clothes in a lacquered box. Then some more palanquins, chairs, etc. At the corners of the streets the procession has a race—each man tries to get round it first, the ponies prance and the gilt paper crowns on the nobles' heads bob about suspiciously. They tear round the corner at twenty miles an hour, followed by the rest of the army, who are led by four trumpeters. Nothing like it out of *Alice in Wonderland*.

The return journey with torches is equally curious. All the cavalry are armed with arrows or lances, and at the end of these lanterns are hung which wave about as they move. The procession goes at a run—everyone tears along as fast as they can. As the ponies can't trot, the poor riders have a very hard time of it and are provided with a rail in front of the saddles to hold on by.

We went up the beacon hill to see the town. The hill is very

[1] See Scott's *Old Mortality*.

steep—about 1000 feet, and the whole town with its mountains round it and its walls was visible. Opposite was an extraordinary granite mountain, which I should think must be inaccessible, under which the King takes refuge in a fortified monastery when there is a revolution. The beacon fires were lighted as we went down. Three means ' all safe on the frontier.' Four means ' danger,' and five ' invasion.' We saw the old and new palace. The poor king was besieged in the old palace for some time, and escaped in disguise on the back of a coolie. He built the new palace on his return, and then a snake fell from the roof, and he says he must return to the old palace. Between them half the space inside the walls is taken up. The King is extravagant to a terrible extent, partly in religious missions. When he gets unwell, he sends an expedition to some monastery to pray for him. If he takes a fancy to a wine glass or a mowing machine, he sends fifty men under a high official to Shanghai to buy it. Anyone can get him to invest money in any mad scheme, though he cuts the promoter's head off if it fails. His chief source of revenue now is the adulteration of the coinage, which he declared by decree to be worth five times its face value.

Curzon had asked for an interview with the King. As a preparatory step he had to have one with the President of the F.O., an official of great importance with a salary of rice beans and paper to the annual value of £100. He received us in a small, rather ricketty shed. Hillier, the Consul-General, interpreted into Chinese, and a Corean interpreter from Chinese into Corean, and so back again. Conversation lasted some time at that rate. H. E. asked if Mr. Curzon, being so important a Minister, was not a relation of the Queen's ? Also, if it was not pleasant receiving a large salary ; also how old he was ? The answers must have been satisfactory, for the next day the King sent to say he would give an audience.

Accordingly we put on uniforms and went. We were met at the palace gate by a bottle-green official with a horsehair hat without a brim but with wings like Mercury's, and were escorted through a succession of courts with great double-roofed gates to a small waiting-room, where, to pass the time, Curzon stood the Ministers in a row and Kodaked them, as he said, to give their photos to the Queen. He invited the Home Secretary to England. He said he couldn't go because his father was 90 years old and his mother 85. We discussed each other's uniforms and yawned until we were told that H.M. had woken up. H.M. goes to bed at 6 in the morning and gets up about 2. He begins to transact business at 6 and works all night.—We were led to the door of a wooden shed and the Ministers who led the way fell down on the steps and touched the ground with their heads. H.M. is a little man, about 4 feet high. He stood behind a table covered with a very vulgar Brussels tablecloth—a magnificent Chinese embroidery showing beneath. He had a winged hat rather like a mitre, and scarlet robe with gold tablets on it, and a big belt, gold studded. His officers stood round shading their faces from the glare of royalty. The interpreter crouched by his side in a position of abject servility. A screen was behind him ; to one side of this a crouching figure was visible through a low door. This was the Crown Prince watching. The King was very talkative, whispering in a low voice to the interpreter, who repeated what he said in English—laughing from time to time ; when his Majesty laughed all the courtiers moved their heads simultaneously as if he had pulled their top knots. His Majesty said that he had a great respect for the Queen's character and appearance and he begged Mr. Curzon (whom he appeared to take for the actual Prime Minister of England) to tell Her Majesty—which Curzon promised to do. He said he had always heard England was a fine and large country and that he feared Corea was very dirty. That was strictly true—but Curzon evaded the question.

We were then taken to see the Crown Prince who is an idiot. He gaped behind a table and from time to time barked inarticulately, which the interpreter (rather guiltily, I thought) interpreted to mean assurances of his cordial affection for the Prince of Wales. We got out as soon as we could and inspected the palace buildings. We saw the great audience hall which Curzon has described in a letter to the *Times*—an impressive two-roofed structure, with high pillars said to be made of single logs of wood—vermilion roof, with immense spaces of deep shadow ; and at the back the vast canopy of state—from which His Majesty could look through the wide doors at the long rows of his nobles arranged according to their nine ranks as far as the outer gate.

By the side, a successful candidate at the examination was celebrating his victory. These exams. are held in the open air by the King himself. He opens a classic and reads out a text which is immediately inscribed on a blackboard. Then the candidates arrange themselves in groups on the ground and work away at an essay on the subject proposed. When the King is tired, he gets up and the essays are chucked over a low fence, collected by the secretaries of state and a few days afterward the result is read out ; those candidates who have shown the greatest proficiency and who have given the largest bribes are successful. To encourage the impecunious and to continue the sport, one or two places are given to merit, but this is quite exceptional. Our friend was apparently much delighted with his success, and was celebrating the occasion by dancing about arrayed in a whimsical robe and artificial flowers, dancers were prancing about and a Corean band was playing. A crowd of his friends were round him, kicking, punching and rolling him on the ground. I think we were regarded, in our uniforms, as part of the entertainment and had a huge success.

We had just time to hurry home, change our clothes and make for the Western gate where our ponies awaited us. As we mounted a melancholy and prolonged howl was heard. Then with a clang the gates were closed for the night. We had just got through in time. An Admiral arrived, on his visit to the King, just too late and was hoisted over the wall in a basket."

From the port of Chemulpo, they went to Chefoo, and re-embarked for Tientsin, passing under the guns of the Taku forts.

"These were taken by the English and French. The English bombarded from the sea, the French went round, took them in the rear, and captured them without a struggle. The Chinese explain that forts were made to be attacked in front ; if the French didn't understand, the Chinese were too wise a nation to fight with such ignorant fellows.—Beyond the forts was a landing and railway station. A comfortable train was waiting ; we got in and in the evening arrived at Tientsin, where another blessed Consul met us and treated us royally."

Their purpose was to visit the Viceroy Li-Hung-Chang. Spring Rice's best account of this interview is given in a letter to Ferguson ; but it is preceded by speculations on the international position of Corea. He smelt trouble. In two years it led to war between China and Japan, and in two more, to war between Japan and Russia.

TIENTSIN,
Oct. 24, 1892.

"To FERGUSON,
          I am delighted to hear you are back in the F.O. and I wish I was there too, to see our old Chief at work again and you and Villiers scribbling away at your tables. Does the Hoiker still Hoik ? Does Villiers still have a bottle of Bass every day at 2 ? Is your table still the office-keeper's admiration ?
          I have been travelling about with Curzon, who is an excellent fellow to travel with. I can't help wondering whether all M.P.'s adopt the same attitude in the East. He thinks the Consular service appointed to help him on his journey, feed him

RONALD MUNRO FERGUSON, M.P., 1886

and provide him material for his letters to the *Times*. He is deeply offended if the beds are not soft or the information not complete. He says that they live so out of the world that they must be delighted at seeing anyone who ' freshens them up '—I suppose he is right, but I don't know whether the Foreign Office takes the same view of Consular functions. . . .

" It is amusing to see the usual grouping of the powers in such an out-of-the-way place. Germany and England together : France and Russia together—also backed by America. These last are in favour of Corean autonomy. Japan has the same policy. All these last wish Corea to free herself from China. It is plainly out of the question. The Chinese Resident is supreme ; nothing can be done without his knowledge and consent ! The people too, abhor Japan, despise Europeans, but look to China with affection and respect. The Americans want concessions which China prevents the King giving. The Japanese have no desire to annex anything Corean except trade, and in that they have partially succeeded. Corea is sinking deeper and deeper into debt to Japan, and it is believed that Japan now wishes to annex the customs administration, now in the hands of China. All this seems small and petty and insignificant enough. But it isn't in reality. It is an important branch of the great Pacific question, of which Samoa is part. Vladivostock is frozen for three months. The Siberian line, the rival of the C.P.R., will be ready in, say, seven years (the Russians say three). South of Vladivostock there is Port Lazareff. I have been there. You should see the charts. It could be easily made impregnable. It is one of the finest harbours in the world and it is open all the year. It also happens to belong to Corea. Now, if Russia owns this port, she has a splendid outlet in the Pacific. An excellent terminus for her railway, and a hold over Japan which she could threaten from there—it is only a day and a half to Tsushima. The question is, how is she to be stopped ? Japan, China, Corea and Great Britain acting in concert could stop her. The difficulty is to get China and Japan to act in concert. If we can do that (and common interest should force them to), we can keep off the evil day. But if they quarrel over some Corean question, or excite a Civil War in Corea, then Russia can step in at once. The map will show you what a difference that would make : suppose Canada without Halifax and Vancouver, and you have the position of Siberia at present. That, to my mind, is the great interest of this out-of-the-way corner of the world. The Govt. is sunk to the lowest depths—corrupt, weak and oppressive. The people have all the energy beaten out of them and

the nobles are only ' blind mouths ' as Milton said. The
Chinese Resident, who was a splendid chap, said : ' They can't do
right, but we can prevent them doing wrong.' He is in constant
communication with Li, and when the Admiral went to see Li,
Li told him all the King's private conversation with the
Admiral at Seoul.

I have just come back from a visit to the Viceroy Li, whom
Curzon had wished to see ; as he was going, I thought I would
go too. Brenan took us there. It was a long journey in
chairs through crowded streets, past the ruins of the Catholic
Church destroyed in the Tientsin massacres, to the Viceroy's
residence. We went through a big gate with two huge man-
darins painted on it ; one black and one green. We were met
by the interpreter and conducted through ever so many passages, all more or less seedy, to a room where was an oil painting
of the Viceroy, and two pictures, one of Krupp and one of
Armstrong. Presently the Viceroy appeared, a tall old man
with a grave, kindly face, in deep chocolate coloured coat with
light blue lining showing at his sleeves ; on his head the magic
embossed blue button which means so much. He sat down at
the end of a table, sitting deep into a chair, Curzon on his right,
with the interpreter beyond.

Li asked him what he was in England. Curzon said, Under-
Secretary of State for India. Who was head of the Board ?
It had been Ld. Cross—was now Ld. Kimberley. How did he
manage to be away from his work so long ? Parliament had
adjourned. Brenan here explained that the Government had
changed and Curzon had gone out. Then, said Li, you are a
Conservative ? Curzon said he was. So am I, said Li. (Just
think, Li the champion of progress, railways and a penny
press !) How old was Mr. Gladstone ? Was he likely to be in
long ? What was his policy ? Curzon said Home Rule, and
there followed a little disquisition on that subject. But, said
Li, what would be his foreign policy.—I thought it wise to say
that Ld. Rosebery was Foreign Minister and to quote what
Ld. R. had said about continuity of policy.—Then, said Li, to
Curzon, Gladstone is so busy about Home Rule that he has no
time to look after foreign things, and Lord Rosebery does that ?
Curzon agreed. Li then asked what Lord Salisbury did now.
Curzon explained that he led the House of Lords where he had
a majority. Then, said Li, you have two Prime Ministers and
nothing will be done.—He asked Curzon how old he was.
Curzon said thirty-three. Li smiled. In China old age is much
honoured.—Then, rather abruptly, he said, ' You have been to
Corea.' Curzon said it was true and that he had been much

impressed by the fact that Corea depended for her independence and existence on Chinese support. ' Did you say that to the King when you saw him ? ' said Li.—Now, Curzon hadn't said he had seen the King, and the King had expressed a desire, not at all in that sense, which Curzon had promised to communicate home.—Curzon said that without Chinese support Corea would fall into Russian hands. ' We have an understanding with Russia,' said Li, ' that she leaves Corea alone.' ' But what if she breaks it ? ' Li banged his two hands together and the interpreter observed that ' His Excellency says there will be fighting.' Curzon said, Why didn't he say so to Russia about the Pamirs ? Li asked him if he knew anything about it. Curzon said he was Under-Secretary for India—and gave a short review of the English side of the question ; he then said, without a map, it was difficult to explain. Li sent for a map, and that published by the Geographical Society was brought in. Curzon said he had the Intelligence Dept. map which was much better. Li said he would like to see it.—His manner was changing—at first he was easily indifferent and rather slouching in his chair. He now began to draw himself up, to catch Curzon by the sleeve and to look animated.

Curzon talked of going to Thibet. Li said it was a bad climate for strangers—the Chinese envoy had just died there. When pressed, he said that in two years time he would talk about it. He couldn't give a passport, for if Curzon was killed, he would be responsible."

Pekin was described to " Ferguson as paved, lighted, drained and cleaned with good intentions ; like a city deserted for 100 years, and then re-occupied by swinish strangers."

" The Legation repaired one street running in front of the compound. All Pekin came to drive up and down there, and the street was soon in deep ruts. This excellent government costs more than London or Paris—as much, I believe, as New York. It is supported by an octroi at the gate on all goods brought in, and the post of superintendent which is sold every spring is worth about £30,000 a year. It is really hard to believe that this country will become a first-class power. The same system seems to prevail everywhere.

They (or rather, the Viceroy Li) are building railways, and as soon as the plant is complete will take the Northern railway seriously in hand. But they are mortally afraid of giving any contracts to foreigners and are quite right in that. They objected to telegraphs till the French war [1] showed them their

[1] In Tonquin.

use ; they have adopted them. They see the use for strategical purposes of a railway, but they don't want it to be a means of enriching foreign devils.

I went to a dance last night ! Sir R. Hart got ten people together ; all Europe was represented. The band was Chinese. I asked him what the Chinese thought of our dancing. He said they told him that he was very foolish to dance himself when he could always pay people to dance for him. He told me that the Emperor was learning English. He has two tutors who teach him alternate days. He is very curious to know about Europe and the Europeans ; but last year the audience fell through, as the foreigners wouldn't be received in the ante-hall where the Chinese stand before the Emperor, and he wouldn't receive them in the inner-hall, where all present have to kneel, unless they knelt, too, which they wouldn't do. Jordan says his teachers speak English with difficulty and with a strong American accent, which I hope his Majesty will acquire.

Curzon goes on to French India and Siam ; he intends to travel overland. He is a very careful observer—takes notes and is always at pains to get at the truth. I should think his letters to the *Times* would be very well worth keeping. I haven't read his ' Persia,' but it ought to be good. He never loses a chance of getting information and always does his best to verify it."

Curzon, on his part, wrote in his journal that he had found Spring Rice, " the best, cheeriest, most unselfish, most amusing of travelling companions. For nearly two months we have been together at most hours of the day and night, and have not exchanged one jarring word."[1]

SHIMONESEKI, JAPAN.
Nov. 21, 1892.

To AGNES.

" . . . I have just got back to Japan from my Corean and Chinese trip, and very glad I am to be back.

I stayed a few days at Shanghai, which is the capital of the East and knows it. Shanghai fashions are everything out here and we all look up to a Shanghai gentleman or lady when they visit us. It certainly is rather surprising after a week or two in China to go up the Shanghai river and find a splendid town with wide clean streets and fine houses looking out on an esplanade, crowded with rather elaborately dressed European ladies and gentlemen. The Admiral whom I knew at Tokio offered to take me up the Yangtse to see the famous gorges, but

[1] Ronaldshay : *Life of Lord Curzon.*

I hadn't time and had to make my way back by the first
steamer. It is only two days to Japan. The port one touches
is Nagasaki, and it is difficult to describe the contrasts between
two countries. All about Shanghai are flat mud banks, a
yellow shallow sea, the whole under a misty, cloudy sky.
Nagasaki is like a lake—a deep bay surrounded by mountains
and shut in by rocky islands. All the houses neat and pretty—
temples on the hills and groves of trees. The sea is a clear blue.
It was really delightful to wake up and go on deck to find a
bright sun, clear sky, and the beautiful shore just in front. We
stayed a few hours and I went on shore to see the Consul, who
lives on a hill overlooking the harbour, which has a hundred
little bays in it, each full of junks—one or two ships of war
painted white, with their national flag ; the European settlement and numbers of Japanese villages. We steamed out
through the islets, going quite close to some of them. The
phosphorescence on the waves was magnificent. It is still
quite warm. Last night we steamed up the coast and we are
now taking in coal at Shimoneseki at the entrance of the inland
sea. Thirty years ago it would have been death for any
European to land here, and the forts at the straits fired on
innocent European merchantmen until the combined squadron
came and smashed them up. I hear that a young midshipman
called Boyes led one of the storming parties, carrying the flag ;
everyone round him was shot down, but he ran along ahead of
the column, cheering the men on. I wonder what became of
him. They are building new forts and have mounted a big
gun which fires from time to time over our heads."

TOKIO,
Jan. 16, 1893.

To FERGUSON.

"... There is not very much work here but I find plenty to
do in reading up old despatches and learning the language and
trying to get hold of this Far-Eastern question which is a very
interesting one. The political future of Japan is just a toss up
—both as regards foreign politics and domestic. And, of
course, it is a great matter to us whether Russia will find a
strong Japan opposite her in the Pacific, or whether Russia will
be able to occupy the opposite coast of Asia while Japan is
powerless to prevent it ; and that once done, poor Japan will
not be able to avoid doing what Russia tells her. So all this, as
well as the historical aspect of this and other questions, gives me
plenty to think about, though I suppose I don't lead a particularly useful existence. . . ."

Jan. 18, 1893.

To STEPHEN.

" I have just come back from an interesting trip of three days in the mountains.   I never saw anything like the clearness of Fuji to-day as we were on the railway.   It's a regular spectacle which all the passengers point out to one another on the way from Yokohama to Tokio.   The House is again at a deadlock with Parliament.   The Government propose their budget— Parliament cut it down one-third, without any consideration, or with very little—for instance, one economy was in the oil for lighthouses, on which it was proposed to save fifty per cent. The Government consider the House's objections, and tell them that they are not valid and refuse to accept the budget voted by the House.   So one of two things remains—either that the budget of the preceding year comes into force, or that the Government yields to the House.   The result is not encouraging to those who admire constitutional government in the East. . . ."

Feb. 6, 1893.

" I have at last managed to see the Shogun.   I daresay that you know that the revolution here which turned the Shogun out, took place after the arrival of the foreigners ; so, many people here remember when the Shogun *was* Shogun.   He lived in Yedo, in the castle his ancestors built for him.   When he went out, all the shops were closed and no one dared to look at him— 10,000 men would go with him when he called on the Mikado at Kyoto.   Well, he fought and his troops were beaten.   He returned to his castle, and there his retainers told him that his reign was over and he must die.   They set him the example, because they said they wouldn't bid him do what they were afraid of doing themselves.   However, he preferred to live— and for some years has been living in retirement, riding a tricycle for amusement.   He was the adopted son of his predecessor.   His father was the most truculent enemy of the Shogunate and friend of the Mikado.   In fact, his father (that is, his true father) had the best and most enlightened statesman of the Shogunate murdered just opposite where I am writing. Well, the Shogun's mother, the widow of the old Prince of Mito, the restorer of the Mikado—died, aged ninety.   And the poor Shogun had to come up to Tokyo—the first time since his fall.   The chapel was close by the great temple in which the Shogun's people made their last stand and which was burnt in the fight.   The Emperor gave $500 to the funeral expenses. One of the Emperor's representatives was an old retainer of his own—and he had to take a lower place as being only ' Prince

Tokugau.' I sat just opposite him ; he had a perfectly stolid and immovable face and seemed to take no interest whatever in the funeral ceremony. It's the biggest change I've seen in this world—perhaps President Harrison's will be bigger.[1] . . ."

TOKIO,
March 7, 1893.

To STEPHEN.

" I have just come back from an excursion on Government service to Kobe, which is some way down the Inland Sea. . . .

As I had to wait some time in Kobe for an answer to a request I had made to the local authorities, I made up my mind to go down the coast for the Sunday. The coast is celebrated in Japanese literature for its beauty—and it is very characteristic of Japanese pictures. High mountains go down into the sea, leaving just room for an occasional tea house, or road and a railway. The last so neatly built and banked up that it looks more like an ornamental fence than a railway embankment. All along the road grow crowds of pines contorted in a grotesque way by nature or the wind. Then, under the branches, you see the sea and the islands and the fishing junks—built in the old Dutch model of the seventeenth century with low waists and enormous poops. The sailors mostly naked though it was freezing cold. There is a splendid castle belonging to a young man who has just left Cambridge. He lives in Tokyo, in a place like a ' first-class lodging house in a seaside resort.' His castle is an enormous place with batteries and ramparts and deep ditches, now full of lotus and a big tower in the middle. The tower is now occupied by a tea house and the garden is run wild.

Beyond this castle about forty miles is another—built by a famous hero in 1600. I tried to get in but found it occupied by a regiment. I had a letter to the local police. It was Sunday and the chief was away ; so I was guided to his house and there sat on a mat waiting for him. His wife was at tea with some neighbours and I could hear them discussing me through the paper screens. After a time the chief appeared from some convivial gathering in graceful Japanese dress, a distinguished looking man. He apologised and disappeared. In a moment he appeared again in full European dress—sword and all—an ordinary, rather contemptible looking policeman. He took me with him and got me admittance. I went all over the place and up the tower from which there was a splendid

---

[1] Harrison, defeated in Nov., was about to retire into private life on March 4.

view for miles round the plain. One could see what a point of vantage it was, just at the edge of the mountains. A dark-looking staircase led into a small room in a far corner of the castle. It had a platform on one side. On this the gentle-men condemned to commit suicide cut their stomachs up. The greatest friend stood behind and cut the head off at the same moment. There it was and had been for thirty years.

Some way up the line, there was on that day the festival of a god who brought good luck all the year to anyone who spat at his image on the 16th of February. So all the trains were late. I waited and waited at one junction and finally resolved to walk. So I walked back for five or six miles through the woods, by a splendid moonlight : the sea like a lake, quite calm, and the mountains showing up on the other side. It was perfectly beautiful. The next day there was a violent snowstorm and I only just managed to get through to Kioto, the old capital. I had an order to see the palaces. There are two—one the Mikado's, where he lived before the restoration (or ' honourable-entirely-new-thing ', as it is called in Japanese) which is so absolutely simple that you are reminded of the wooden boxes in which the Japanese keep their curios—and indeed that was the way they regarded him. He was a god and the gods of old Japan—before Buddhism—were worshipped in plain temples thatched with straw without ornament of any kind. And so they treated their Emperor, only sometimes they pushed reverence so far that they didn't give him enough to eat. To the ancestors who lived in this way the Emperor swore to keep the constitution, and recently when he was brought in (as in a Greek tragedy) to make peace in the Diet between the two Houses and the Cabinet, he told his servants that their behaviour ' was not a spectacle to which he wished to call the attention of the spirits of his ancestors.'

Near the Mikado's palace and temple is the house of the Tem-poral Emperor whom we called the Tycoon, and with whom we made our treaties. He had this palace to stay in when he visited the Mikado, to pay his respects to him, or to dethrone him and appoint a baby in his place. It is an enormous place with massive walls and gates which you enter by wooden porticoes, marvellously carved and painted with flowers and birds—all by famous artists of the seventeenth century. The inside is over-powering. The walls and ceiling are black lacquer and gold panels with wonderful paintings—flowers in one room, birds in another, tigers in another. The outline is simple but the colours something splendid, and the metal work is a dream. I stood some time in the great presence hall where the Shogun received the homage of the Daimyos. The guardian—an old soldier of the Mikado's, who had been in his court before the revolution, and had often been in this palace when the Shogun lived there—described the state that was once kept there. I told him how a few days ago I had seen the fallen Shogun at his mother's funeral at Tokyo (his old capital); how no one took any notice of him and how very few people seemed even to know who he was. The old man expressed his surprise, then said something I didn't understand, and then : ' He was the first man in Japan who rode on a European saddle.' He expressed a great deal of contempt for the present Ministers, saying that they were the servants of the servants of the Shogun in old times— and now they were so proud, the Shogun himself would have been ashamed to behave so. . . . ''

The Treaties then in force gave to European subjects in Japan the position which they still (in 1929) hold in China. They were amenable to courts of their own ; on the other hand, their rights of trading were restricted. It was only in 1894 that the British Government (of which Lord Rosebery had become Prime Minister on Mr. Gladstone's retirement) concluded a treaty by which Great Britain regulated its relations with Japan as with an equal Power of the European civilisation. The following letter shows that this concession was based to some extent on the advice of military experts, who had realised the progress made by Japanese forces, before proof of it was given in war—as it was to be in the next year. Spring Rice, however, as the letter also conveys, was not to have an opportunity to observe the progress of these negotiations.

TOKIO,
May 28, 1893.

To FERGUSON.

" Did you hear that I was going to be reappointed to Washington ? I was glad to hear it, though very much surprised. I hope to have time to return via India and China—and if possible to make a journey in some part of the continent— China or Persia. The East is fascinating and quite a new field for me, as I never knew or cared anything about it till I came here. I am very much impressed with Japan as a power, and it will be interesting to see what it turns out to be—bubble or nugget. In England we regard it as a practical joke—and there are a good many arguments in favour of the view, but I shouldn't wonder if it turned out wrong. Perhaps they would look on our parliamentary doings in the same light. On the whole it is more amusing to see parliamentary proceedings in other people's countries. As the American said when he was asked the best place to have a boil : ' On the other fellow.'

Japan wants to revise her treaties and no doubt will begin in

London this summer. If she wishes, she could denounce them, as no European power could afford to go to war with her, and it's not very likely they will go to war jointly. However, Japan is still in a mortal fear of Europe and England, and is especially afraid of the armed occupation of a Japanese Hong Kong. But most of the experts out here think that they are too strong to attack with success. You remember Greece and the blockade,[1] and how the Admiral said he would have to land troops to take forts before the blockade of the Piræus could be really effective. With an army of 70,000 men, well armed and drilled, and undoubtedly brave, Japan needn't be much afraid of an armed descent. And yet, if we refuse to come to an agreement (which we may well be forced to do, by unreasonableness on the part of Japan) this will be the only course left, or an enormous loss of prestige. I hope it will be possible to avoid the alternative. The general feeling in Japan is that England is her natural ally ; not for love of us, but for hatred of Russia."

August 1, 1893.

" . . . The European powers out here are too anxious to extend their European disputes to the East. We get more powerless out here day by day, as China and Japan discover our differences and that the old concerted action is impossible. So the hope among residents out here is on the whole that France and England will be able to come to some permanent understanding. If not, France and Russia will act together to our detriment. Russia still occupies to a certain extent an isolated and exceptional position, menacing China and Japan and in that respect unsupported by Europe and America. What a lot of trouble poor Lord Rosebery is having ! As a Frenchman out here, fresh from the French F.O., told me, it is far easier for the French Government to come to an understanding with a Conservative than a Liberal Government, because public opinion in England would accept at once any agreement between France and Lord Salisbury, but would at once suspect Mr. G. of want of patriotism—while French public opinion is equally suspicious of dealings with the Liberal party. . . "

August 22, 1893.

" . . . I don't think we were wrong to abandon Port Hamilton [2] for several reasons. First, the place would either require a vast

---

[1] In 1886.

[2] Temporarily occupied by British forces in 1875-77 during hostilities between Japan and Corea. The occupation terminated on Feb. 27th, 1877.

sum to fortify or a fleet to defend. We can't spare the fleet and the money is wanted elsewhere. Secondly, we got in exchange for its surrender an assurance from the Russians to the Chinese that if Great Britain took no Corean territory, they, the Russians, would take none. Thirdly, we set the example of non-intervention with Corea. This is a most important point. It is essential to Japan's independence and to China's existence that Corea should not be occupied by Russia for the next few years. One can see that by the map. Its ports give such an admirable vantage ground for striking at either one or the other. . . . "

HONG KONG CLUB,
Oct. 11, 1893.

To JULIE.

" I am really off, you see, and have got as far as Hong Kong. I started on October 2, after a wild week of p.p.c.'s and packing, got to Kobe in the Inland Sea the next day, where I called and found the Consul in the middle of a fierce contest with an American who had insulted him in the Club ; we stayed a day off the shore watching the rain slowly downfalling on us and making everything beastly, then started on the morning of the 4th down the Inland Sea. You go through a series of little islands with green rocks and impossible-looking trees, just like a Japanese screen, then you pass through narrow channels which there seems no way out of ; finally you get to a land-locked bay with two entrances, called Shimoneshi. It is inhabited by almost 20,000 coal miners, also by many butterflies descended from the souls of the Taira ladies, and valiant frogs descended from the Tairo heroes killed about 800 years ago, at that place. Later we bombarded it and destroyed many forts and their defenders for the good of the British merchant.

Then comes two days of sea—such a beastly sea with a heavy swell and the wind from the N.E., the Monsoon. Then we arrived at Shanghai, a low mud flat, the sea yellow with the waters of the Yangtse a hundred miles out. I landed and explored the club and race course and lawn tennis grounds and all the apparatus which makes Englishmen happy. They say they are all ruined. For some unknown reason, every soul in Shanghai invested money in a Mexican silver mine. They have put so much money into it that it ought to be rich. But it isn't and the colony is ruined. But they still drink 100,000 cocktails a year in the Club. All business is transacted at the bar, which runs the whole length of the club. The next morning early we started again—and with a wonderful bright sky and smooth sea and a fine ship, came down in forty-eight hours in sight of peaked mountains, cliffs, innumerable islands, and slipping through a narrow channel, came into Hong-Kong Harbour—full of shipping, sheltered in the hills—most beautiful. A week ago you couldn't stand for the wind, the houses were unroofed, the ships torn from their anchorage. It wasn't much of a typhoon, they said, only a small one and did not last.

There were several amusing people on board. A lady with an illegal Austrian divorce who had just married a British Consul. On our arrival at Shanghai, the previous husband had settled a vexed question by shooting himself. A young lady who had come out to be married. Her lover met her at Hong Kong ; no kisses, I was sorry to see. Two old English residents in Japan, who had been under the Japanese knife, and had rescued the present Prime Minister from death. One kept him three weeks in disguise in his house. A number of merchants cursing British officials. A number of wives returning from the summer to their husbands, each with an attendant and a confidante. Meetings at the ports were amusing, sometimes even astonishing. Everyone is good-natured and lazy in this delicious warm, soft, do-nothing climate. They are not particularly good, but it is really too hot to be energetically bad. I wish I knew whether I shall find England supportable. I fear not. You will be glad when you get rid of me. The East spoils one, it is so pleasant and easy, nothing matters very much (if one's salary is paid in gold and one's boy doesn't drink saki). However, I have said good-bye to it."

SINGAPORE,
Oct. 23, 1893.

To STEPHEN.

" I am now at sea off the coast of Siam, from which country I feel the balmy breezes—a soft, warm wind which makes it impossible to do anything. We are outside the bar (which is rather a bad one) and loading up with rice. I am on a small German steamer with a Sleswig captain. He is a very jolly fellow, very patriotic but civil, with a good deal of the Dane in him as well as the German. The Chinese coolies make the most inconceivable noises, swearing and cursing at one another, but doing a lot of work. All the hard work of Southern Siam is done by Chinese women. The Siamese do nothing but row or paddle about on the river. They say that their heaven is a town where they can go up the left side of a stream with the current, and back along the right side with the current, too. The last day I was in Bangkok the dragon who lives in the

Menam was being propitiated : all the population were out with boats of all sorts and sizes, all decorated with lamps or candles. Thousands of little boats were launched in the stream, one mass of lights—then overturned to propitiate the god with the flames. There was also a fine display of fireworks. The influence of Bangkok is not stimulating. The glass is about 85° to 90°. The air very damp. There is rain and sunshine almost every day. The Legation compound is a fine one but it is flooded every high tide and one side of it is giving, so that it looks as if it might come down at any time. The garden is full of beautiful flowering shrubs and Siamese cats.

Quite close is the French compound. There are the graves of the three men killed on the French warship at Paknam. Little wooden crosses with the names. There is also a menagerie of cats, bears, owls and monkeys. They are good friends and their master loves them. Mr. Pavie is described in the English press as a liar, and in the French as a coward and traitor. He is a small, delicate man, broken down with fever, a great geographer and naturalist. It is no wonder, having given his health and life to the country, he is anxious for his own country to take it. Our own Minister is rather a different man—an old Crimean soldier like Uncle Toby. His view of the French is much what Colonel Newcome's view of Barnes was. There is quite a complete European society at Bangkok. There is a club at which whist is played from 4 to 8, and ladies admitted one evening in the week. The ladies are Portuguese and Danish principally. We had a dinner at the Legation. The German Minister had come from Corea, the Dutch from Persia, the Frenchman was born in Penang. A Japanese Prince was there in native dress. Opposite me was the Belgian adviser—an old Whig, a lawyer and Cabinet Minister, once a rich man but he lost it all in Canada. He is now intent on making a fine new code for Siam. His wife and daughter are coming out soon. We made a merry party. The Belgian played and sang old Flemish airs about William of Orange.

The country is all under water and so I didn't go far beyond the city boundaries. It is endless fun going about in the canals. Every description of boat is there from men-of-war to single canoes with a child of six inside. All the shopping is done on the river and especially the Church-going when the temples are open. The services are in Pali, which nobody can understand, but you ' make merit ' all the same by going. There are 10,000 monks in the place—most of them thieves. They are dressed in yellow, which is the old colour for malefactors in India, and they deserve it. Everyone is a monk for a short time and the King himself became one after he was crowned, and had to be crowned again. I went the round of a good many temples, and have photographs. They are wonderful things——the most striking part are the pagodas—absolutely useless things—2 to 400 feet high—solid, encased in various shades of porcelain—one in gilded glass from top to bottom. I went also to see a Siamese play. There is a certain Prince who keeps a theatre—and you may go into his palace and see it. The entrance is indescribably dirty, through rows of stalls where old women sell betel nuts and cakes and stale fish. Inside it is better. The theatre is large. The stage consists of an oblong space with a canopy at the end, at the back of which is a scene representing an English village with the church spire at the end. On three sides of the central space sit the audience—the women and children below and the men above. The children are mostly naked and climb about the balustrade that defends the stage. On the stage was an army consisting of women in red coats with swords, following two magnificent creatures with swords and spears. The band sat in a corner and played and sang. This was the march of the Siamese army under its princes. I got rather tired of the Siamese army after half an hour. At the end, the music changed and two young persons, a Laos prince and princess, entered. They didn't speak but danced. Dancing means moving every muscle the wrong way. They sat down in the alcove and the prince made love but without success. Suddenly, in a rage, he got up and left. Then the young lady was seriously affected, and, two attendants entering with a tree, she hung herself on it with her scarf. But the Siamese princes appeared and cut her down. In fact, they cut her down three times until that scene was ended. The next was the palace of the young lover. He was asleep and the guards around him. The princes appeared and the guards were drugged. Here came in some clown work which made everyone laugh. When I went away, the Siamese princes were engaged in killing the Laos prince (the lover) in his bed. The dresses are beautiful and fit wonderfully. They are said to be sewn on. They are much more plentiful than in our ballets, as in Siam it is contrary to us and the more clothes you wear the smarter the dress. There is hardly any conversation, the acting is done by the dancing, or rather the contortions. I believe if an actress distinguishes herself very much, the prince marries her, which is the reward of a life-time.

Julie wouldn't be pleased at the position of women here. They do all the work and till a short time ago their husbands could sell them as slaves. If their husbands wish to divorce them, they become Buddhist priests for a month and then marry again. But they are much more cheerful-looking than our women. You don't see the ladies. Probably, as they have nothing to do, they are as melancholy as ours at home. The father generally looks after the baby, and does it very well. There are a lot of missionaries—about twenty-four—Protestants, mostly American. They have made about as many converts. They published a book stating that the first Christian missionary landed in 1815. The Catholics, who nearly ruled this country, and have been here for centuries, don't count. One of these Protestants married a Siamese wife as well as his American spouse. A member of the Mission, a young lady, was so horrified that she took a stick and beat the Siamese and nearly killed her. The American Minister here took special delight in putting the missionaries into prison—he said they were not persecuted enough. The Siamese are tolerant of everybody. Every nation and costume is to be met in the streets and nearly every style of house. The King goes out like Haroun Alraschid and is rather fond of travelling in the electric car. If he is recognised, all the Siamese get under the seat because you *must* be at a lower level than your superior."

On his way back he stopped with Arthur Hardinge in Cairo and wrote to Stephen on December 17, 1893 :

" The most amusing thing by far has been hearing Hardinge's description of Egyptian politics. There is really nothing like it. The whole scene is like an *opéra bouffe* and he does justice to it. I wonder how long it will last ! At present there is an organised conspiracy on the part of French and Egyptians to make the Government of the country impossible, reforms futile, and the finances disordered. It is partly the result of Milner's book and the *Figaro* article which attributed the credit of the good government of Egypt to us. These people are trying to change all that, and it isn't at all impossible that they may succeed in dislocating the government of the country altogether. A curious policy, isn't it ? Cairo itself is the most fascinating city. I can't get tired of walking about in it and looking at the buildings and the people. The buildings of the Saracenic time are especially fine, and it is amusing to see the likeness of some of it to Norman architecture, and to think that Saladin built walls and towers that might have surrounded Caen."

Early in January he was back in London, having seen Lord Dufferin (then Ambassador) in Paris. His health was not good, and he looked forward without enthusiasm to returning to Washington,

"I have no experience of Eastern or Western Europe, and it will soon be too late to acquire it. This, of course, would be the ruin of my professional future, as has been found so often. But nothing is worse than a grumbling diplomatist, and there is always a fair chance of finding a permanent opening in America."

It may be said that he never ceased to play with this idea of leaving diplomacy for something else—probably a literary post—until he had made actual contact with European politics at one of the storm centres. Only then did his task fascinate and absorb him.

As early as August 1893 he had begun to lament over leaving Japan, for one thing because (as he wrote to his sister-in-law) "it is a wonderful country; in every way and every day I like it better"; for another, because he was being moved before he had got enough proficiency in the language to earn the extra £100 a year which he would get if he had passed in it.

But his poignant regret came a year later. In the spring of 1894, rebellion broke out in Korea and Japan sent troops to protect Japanese subjects. When order had been restored, the Japanese troops remained. China sent support to the King of Korea, who sought to be rid of these intruders, and by August China and Japan were at war. Spring Rice wrote from Washington on August 23:

"I am in bad luck just at present. I should have been in charge in Japan, and might have had some interesting work to do. Now, that chance is gone."

He could not foresee that for the rest of his professional career he would habitually fall into places where trouble was on hand.

CHAPTER VI

AMERICA IN CLEVELAND'S SECOND TERM

THE main concern of Spring Rice throughout his diplomatic career was to improve relations between the two great English-speaking powers; and the return of the Democratic party to power, after the elections of 1892, which gave Cleveland a second term of the Presidency, was not at all calculated to forward this object. He wrote to his brother on December 27, 1892.

" I have received several letters from the U.S. about the elections, and my Republican friends seem rather pleased than otherwise at the collapse of their party, because of their hatred for Harrison. I think myself Harrison is far the abler and safer man of the two. For England the Republican administration is the best ; for though unpleasant to the last degree, it was capable and certain under Harrison ; under Cleveland it may be anything—and Cleveland is bound to show that he was *not* elected by British gold, by being as disagreeable to us as possible."

One of the main objects of controversy in America from the beginning of 1893 concerned the island of Hawaii. In January, Queen Liliokalaui was dethroned by a rebellion, and, during the anarchy which followed, the American Minister at Honolulu proclaimed a protectorate of the United States over the island group. President Harrison's Ministry, still in office, proposed to declare formal annexation. The Senate, however, rejected this proposal, and the Democrats after assuming power on March 4, withdrew the protectorate, in spite of clamour from the Republicans that unless America annexed the islands, Great Britain would do so. While anti-English feeling was being whipped up on this plea, friction arose over another matter. The Behring Sea negotiations of 1891-2 had resulted in the appointment of an International Commission of Arbitration, on which France, Italy, Sweden and Norway were represented as well as the United States and Great Britain. In August 1893 the Commission issued its award, which rejected America's claim to treat the whole of Behring Sea as territorial waters. But all sealing was prohibited within a zone of sixty miles round the seals' breeding place on the Pribylov islands, and all sealing in the Behring Sea was prohibited

during the months of May, June and July in each year, which were
made a close season. There was, however, delay in enforcing the
award, and the sealers working from Canada showed a disposition to
disregard it. Spring Rice wrote at once to Ferguson, who was again
acting as parliamentary private secretary to Lord Rosebery.

BRITISH EMBASSY,
WASHINGTON,
March 19, 1894.

"You must be pretty busy now—but excuse me if I trouble
you with a matter which I think rather important.

When Lord Salisbury was at the F.O., he found it necessary
(on a warning) that ' politics ' were getting into the Behring
Sea question, and that the Democratic party were going to make
an issue of it at the Presidential Election)—to insist on the
Canadian Government coming to an agreement. Delay on
delay had occurred, and finally he had to make the agreement for
arbitration and a *modus vivendi* over their heads. It was found
that departmental correspondence between the F.O., the Col.
Office and Canada only resulted in the perpetual discovery of
new difficulties.

Now, it seems to me that rather a similar difficulty has arisen
now. Owing to delays for which Canada is mainly responsible,
we are a long way off an agreement. The sealers in British
Columbia have openly said that they would have another
season in spite of the award. It looks as if they would.

According to the award, the N. Pacific was to be closed from
May to July down to the 37th parallel. We offer an extension
of the old *modus vivendi* over this season. But that would only
cover Behring Sea.

The U.S. Government ask for the area mentioned in the
award. Their reason or main reason is this. The opposition to
Cleveland, based on various grounds, is taking the common form
of opposition about foreign affairs. The old rule—patriotism
the last resort of a politician in distress. Now, the line the
Government wish to take is adherence to the letter of the
award. This puts out of court all discussion as to the exped-
iency of particular measures. It is also an appeal to the honour
of the American people.

If we on our side conform to this situation, the situation
should have no danger. But very naturally Canada objects,
and with Parliament sitting at Ottawa, the Canadian Government can only yield on compulsion. The question is, is it worth
while to incur the risk ? If we do not grant a *modus vivendi* in
terms of the award, the U.S. Government cannot take the line

of ' the award, the whole award and nothing but the award ' in dealing with the opposition in the Senate.   There is also the imputation of delay.   There has been a delay for which our people were responsible and by which they will profit.

Now, as you know, England has steadily gained ground in public estimation here by her integrity.   We did *not* wish to destroy the U.S. sealing interests—nor to annex Hawaii, nor to do any of the crimes imputed to us in the papers.   It is astonishing the difference, for instance, in Lodge's language to what it used to be.   Can we afford to throw this advantage away ?

The matter is one that can't be settled departmentally, and that is evident enough from recent and previous experience. I want you, if you can spare a moment, to hint to Lord Rosebery that it may be the moment for the Prime Minister to intervene as Lord Salisbury did before, and insist on some understanding being reached *soon*.   The season begins May 1.   I daresay the matter may have much less importance than seems to me to be the case.   No harm is done anyhow."

Negotiations on this difficulty were the Embassy's main concern throughout that summer.   A couple of letters sketch the position in America's internal politics :

BRITISH LEGATION,
WASHINGTON, D.C.,
May 25, 1894.

To STEPHEN.

"Things are in an anxious state here and matters will be complicated by the enormous exodus which is now taking place of the propertied classes, who go partly for peace and quiet and partly for economy.   Of course, they take their money with them and swell the sum of foreign liabilities, which is large enough already.   I hear too that railway property is sure to be in a bad way for some time to come.   To begin with, the Electric Tramway system is taking away the local passenger traffic.   Then construction costs very much less now than ten years ago and lines can be duplicated cheaply, cutting the profits of the older lines from under them.   It is expected that something very disagreeable is going to happen in the next few weeks.   Meanwhile Congress can't agree on a tariff bill.   The Senate has decided on a moderate tariff under which the interests of the big trusts are safeguarded.   Naturally the House declares that the Senate has got something out of it. Accusations fly about in all directions.   The temper of the House is so bitter that a compromise will be difficult.   The

South has the whip hand and is forcing all the burden on the northern industries and incomes. The old sectional feeling is growing up again. And meanwhile business people have no idea what will be the new condition of industry, and business is nothing but a gamble in which the Senators know the cards and the public pays the bill. There is a strong feeling against the Senate, which is called the American House of Lords; but the Senate is so strong that it has nothing to fear. One of the Senators is reported to have paid near on a million for his seat. But it must have been a paying speculation, as he is reported to have made more than two millions on the Sugar Trust whose shares have gone up 50 per cent in consequence of the action of the Senate. An investigation is going on now, but nothing will come out of it. You see you are not all alone unhappy. As for silver, they confidently hope here that England will be forced to accept bimetallism at the terms of the Latin Union. Is there the smallest chance of this ? What is the real condition of feeling on the question in London ? What is the best thing to read on the subject ?

June 9, 1894.

" *To* FERGUSON,

The papers here, in view of the Derby, regard Lord Rosebery as Premier for life.[1] As to the influence of parties and politics here on Ireland, the Irish are in disgrace with the Republican party, as it has now been proved that, come what may, they are on the side of the Democrats and for English free trade. As long as a serious defection of the vote was thought possible, the Republicans played with them and the Democrats had to do some tail-twisting to keep them amused. There is, however, no longer much fear of their changing sides, and tail twisting isn't so profitable. Also, it isn't any longer necessary to give money to campaign funds—and besides, there isn't much money to give. The state of depression here is astonishing and there is really small hope of improvement. There are said to be a million of men out of work. The U.S. troops are busy in several states and the railroads are occupied by armed bodies of men. A coal famine is imminent. Most of the railways will soon, people say, be in the hands of receivers. The general explanation is that it is the demonetisation of silver which has caused the trouble ; and naturally the blame is laid at our door. As a matter of fact, as far as I can make out from business men, the real evil is the uncertainty.

[1] Mr. Gladstone had retired from office and been succeeded by Lord Rosebery—whose horse, Ladas, won the Derby, a distinction never before earned for a Prime Minister.

First, as to the tariff.   If the Republicans come in again, as is likely, the tariff will be put up again.   Then as to coinage. The movement for silver is gaining ground so fast that it is thought quite possible that some change will take place next year ; so that no one likes to embark in speculation, to invest money in industrial enterprise or to build a railroad while the conditions are so uncertain.   People expect that values will sink lower still.   I don't know whether you are interested in this question, which is all-absorbing here and which certainly, if the Republican policy in discriminating against gold-using countries is carried out, will intimately affect England.   But it is a question that must soon become the most important for us, and it might be worth while for you to make it up seriously.   If you think that the interest due from this country to England is about £10,000,000 a year, and that if industry continues to decline, England will suffer to that extent, the question appears important enough.   It is the interest of a creditor to get high interest.   But if the payment of the interest ruins the debtor, the creditor will think it worth while to lower the rate of interest rather than to have none at all.   And it looks as if that was our position now.

Scandals as usual are rife.   The Senate, which represents capital, has taken good care of the trusts, and Cabot Lodge moved for an enquiry into the methods pursued by the Trust representatives.   The enquiry naturally ends in smoke.   The New York authorities are being examined, with the result that it is proved that for years past the brothel keepers have been taxed for the benefit of Tammany Hall, which instructs the police to protect them in return for the money paid.

Our relations with this Administration are pretty good ; only the trouble is that the Administration has no particular weight with anyone.   The Republicans are winning all along the line."

Meantime, as the letters show, American hospitality held out open arms to the returned wanderer.

May 18, 1894.

To STEPHEN.

" I have just come back from a visit to the country to the only country house which is still kept up here.   It belongs to an Irish family who emigrated from the North at the end of the seventeenth century under a grant from Lord Baltimore, the Lord Paramount of Maryland.   I saw the original grant. The grandson of the settler was a ' signer,' which is the great distinction here.   The property of 15,000 acres remains still in the family, divided among the different descendants.   Fortunately one of them married a New York banker's daughter who was glad to spend a large amount of money on the place. It is in very good repair. The family portraits are complete. They begin with the settler, a regular or irregular Irish face. The signer has a fine distinguished head, rather like our grandfather Monteagle. His son was a rip, a French Dandy, who quarrelled with his wife. Then the family begins to deteriorate till the New York banker comes in with his firm commercial face, and restores the energy. The present heir is Carroll the yachtsman, an African traveller who spent two years in Mashonaland and afterwards went with a seal-pirate to the Aleutians and carried his wife with him. The tenants on the estate are mostly Irish farmers of recent immigration who pay their rent regularly and make no complaints, partly because there are numerous Swedes and Germans always ready to take up the farms if there is anyone vacant. The old slave quarters are still perfect and inhabited by the descendants of the former slaves, who live very much as they did in the old times. I was rather amused with the conversation of the tutor, a Maine man, descended from an immigrant family of French Huguenots, full of Republican intolerance and Protestantism. Of course, the Carrolls are Catholics and Democrats, and took the wrong side in the war. He comes from a Northern region of rock and mountain and can't feel at home in the South. The country there is very like parts of Kent, wide fields of growing wheat and bits of old wood and rolling hills and a fat contented green everywhere. I rather sympathized with him, of the two parties. They seemed good friends. But it made me realize how this country is divided, and how the North, the South and the West are really different peoples."

HENDERSON HOUSE,
Aug. 15, 1894.

To AGNES,

"How glad I was to get your letter and to hear of the successful wedding.[1] You must be thoroughly happy at Old Church now if the weather is there what it is here. I came here from Long Island for mountain air. It is very high—an old place built on a land grant of George II. All round is the country of the *Last of the Mohicans*, once a huge pathless forest, infested by Indians ; now it is cultivated and fertile. The window looks out over seventy miles of country. The house is 1700 feet above the sea. Here and there are fragments of the old forest left for firewood. The old trees look curiously,

[1] His sister Margaret had married Aubrey Birch Reynardson.

with smug cornfields running up to their sides. The people have been here 100 years—holding their farms from father to son. The farms are mostly 500 acres, the houses of wood, trim and neat with pretty gardens with phlox, hollyhock, roses and all the cottage flowers we know in England. The children are rosy, too. The winters must be tremendous—drifts of ten feet and more and the roads almost impassable. My hostess [1] is an old lady like Aunt Susan. Prayers twice a day and no newspapers on Sundays. Interests herself immensely in the servants. Her one trouble is that they *will* marry, a practice which she regards from Queen Elizabeth's point of view. At meal times we hear a great deal about the food, just like Halsteads. Her son married Miss Roosevelt's sister, a charming woman, full of natural enthusiasm for everything. We read aloud in the evening Stanley Weyman. The old lady reads. I ride and tell ghost stories to the children. They, make a flattering audience. Yesterday being Sunday the old lady brought out some old papers. Seventy years ago there was a young heiress who lived here and made a tour in Europe where she received forty-three offers of marriage. We read some of the love letters aloud. Much in the style of Mr. Collins,[2] we shouted with laughter over them. There was an album in which Scott, Wordsworth, Southey, Lafayette and a host of others had written their names with appropriate sentiments. Wordsworth's letters were quite numerous : one in which he advises her to read more and talk less, and if she reads, to read for the sake of the books and not in order to talk about them. She came back to America and married at forty a man of thirty who quarrelled constantly for five years and then separated. The house is full of relics—pictures, plate and furniture. It is really most interesting."

WASHINGTON,
August 23, 1894.

To MARGARET,

" . . . My life here is the quintessence of quietness. We have just finished our Behring Sea negotiations and are going up north in a day or two to New London, a quiet watering-place by the sea, where there are I hope, pleasant people and not too many of them.

I ride every evening, generally in the woods. I met the other day a man who told me he had fought through the four years war, enlisting at sixteen years old ! He seems to have enjoyed

[1] Mrs. Robinson, whose son Douglas Robinson married Miss Roosevelt.
[2] In Jane Austen's " Pride and Prejudice."

his time very much, ' except when he had a lame horse.' He fought ' on the wrong side ' and found himself ruined at the end of it ; but he is resigned and perfectly happy now. He is anxious to volunteer for the Japano-Chinese war, and was rather disappointed when I told him there was no chance of his being accepted.

Theodore Roosevelt is here, thank goodness, and I had a very pleasant evening with him yesterday. We talked of all manner of things, chiefly politics, which are in a most complicated state, as all parties unite in hating and abusing the President, and yet can't get on without him, for there he is ; firm for two years more. But I have got sick of the papers and their abuse of each other and especially of us."

WASHINGTON,
August 24, 1894.

To MRS. ROOSEVELT.

" I was delighted to receive your charming letter. Charming is a vile word—if I find a better I will write to you to send it. Theodore [1] is looking very well and came here last night much to our delight. He had a killing story about Hell-roaring Bill Jones and the lunatic, which made Sir Julian open his big round eyes and filled Goschen with delight.

I am sorry to say he has a slight cough—nothing to matter, but I hope it will make him careful. It is, I expect, the effect of the climate, which is pleasant now but rather moist. Olney is here and Willie Endicott—otherwise there is a desert in D.C., inhabited chiefly by sir knights in dress clothes with cocked hats and swords and 'ladies.' I am quite surprised at the wonderful beauty of the woods—they have their red leaves beginning—just enough to show the green off and to remind one that everything is mortal. The foliage is extraordinarily thick and the flowers bright. There is little water in Rock Creek. The darkies wander about at their own sweet will ; playing tango, singing and flirting. The town belongs to them. On Sunday the park is full of picnicers who make pretty groups under the trees and envious couples go out buggy riding at sunset. There is something very attractive about Washington now and I sympathise, I really do with you, in not being able to join Theodore here. Mind you get him to write to you about his cough. I wish someone amusing was staying here for him. (Love to the bunnies.)

Yrs.,   C. A. S. R.

I dined with Theodore and did *all* the talking myself."

[1] Roosevelt was still a Civil Service Commissioner and his work kept him in Washington.

(Mrs. Roosevelt's reply suggests that there was some project of making a book out of the story-telling with which Spring Rice amused " the bunnies.")

SAGAMORE HILL,
Sept. 7, 1894.

From MRS. ROOSEVELT.

" It was so good of you to keep a friendly eye upon Theodore while you were in Washington. He came back to me last Saturday, with the Assistant Postmaster-General—looking really ill. I cannot say whether these two facts had any connection, but I comforted him with flagons and started him westward yesterday. I hope he will come home able to defy coughs and colds for the winter. I only wish you were with him, for you never say a word about yourself and I fear such obstinate malaria requires companionship with Sheriff Hell-roaring Bill Jones, and kindred worthies on their native heaths, to exorcise it.

How nice it will be to see ' Frocodile, Frocodile,' as Kermit used to call it—in print, and how particularly nice that poor old Arco-Tiger is to be resurrected. I wish my fingers worked with my mind, for I can see such delightful pictures in the verses."

NAHANT, MASS.,
Oct. 7, 1894.

To FERGUSON.

" It looks as if you would be in office for some time to come. I hope so, if you like it and if it suits you. What a surprise the outcome of this session has been ! I envy you having something definite to do. There is nothing much here going on and I lead an entirely fatuous life. You may imagine how pleasant it is to think that but for an accident I might now be in Japan or China, and have something worth living for, but one must take what comes. I hope to leave this before very long ; and if not, to find work here, literary if possible—only, it's so infer-nally difficult to begin.

I am staying with the Lodges. The Senator is in fine form. I went with him to the Republican convention. It went like smoke. The object was to arrange a platform and to elect candidates for the state officers. The only difficulty was the stalwarts, the ' A.P.A.,' as they are called : ' the American Protective Association,' whose object is to protect native Americans—that is, according to their interpretation, to prevent Catholics, especially Irishmen, from being Republican office-holders. They are mainly old-fashioned Americans and are Orangemen and British—all ardent Republicans. Of course, the leaders want to get all the votes they can, Irish or otherwise, and the stalwarts embarrass them considerably. As they are certain to vote Republican any way, the leaders can handle them as roughly as they choose, and they get nothing. The candidates were agreed on before the Convention met and each name, proposed in a short speech, was carried by acclamation. Nothing could have gone more smoothly. Then Hoar, the old Senator, gave an address—very amusing and full of points which the audience took (after a little hesitation, like the Scotch) with delight—especially where the speaker likened the South to Baillie Nicol Jarvie's description of the Highlanders ; ' they may quarrel among themselves, they may hit each other over the head with claymores—but they will always unite against anyone who has a bawbee in his purse and breeks upon his hinder end.' He also described an educated gentleman who sat for Congress on the Democratic side, and who was not renominated, as having added one point to his vast stock of knowledge —namely, that he didn't like anything his party did and his party didn't like anything he did : a good description of some people in England. The Convention might just as well have been in England—the faces, the quotations, were true English—only I doubt whether such a perfect organisation could easily be got. There were 1500 delegates from the different districts—each had the right of voting for a candidate, but there was not a note of dissension ; everyone was agreed."

WASHINGTON,
Oct. 24, 1894.

To MARGARET.

" I returned to Washington on the 19th and spent all the first day in unpacking and arranging archives. We remove all the papers of two years in a sort of travelling press that packs and unpacks. I took lodgings in a very comfortable place with a nice old Irishwoman from County Cork. She takes quite an interest in my welfare and I supply her with books such as *Trilby*, which she loves. I can get dinner and breakfast there and have room to write and read. Very few people have come back yet and the streets look a little dreary. But all the country is quite lovely. I went out a long scramble with Theodore Roosevelt, up through the Park, which is a very wild bit of wood, river and rock close to the city. I nearly came to grief off a rock but was saved by my trousers. We came back after dark a disgraceful sight for a Sunday afternoon in a great Capital. Think of going out rock-climbing from London. The new Japanese Minister [1] is an old friend of mine and I have met

[1] M. Kurino.

him at dinner.   He takes a very philosophical view of the war. It would, he thinks, have been better if it had not taken place, but now that it has begun, it ought to be finished as soon and as gloriously as possible.

WASHINGTON,
Nov. 8, 1894.

To JULIE.

" . . . You would have liked to have been here during the elections, as the American woman has been in it for all she is worth.   In one of the States where women have the suffrage they downed the populists (a mixture of socialists and madmen) completely and left them not a leg to stand on.   You and I, my dear Julie, no longer belong to the ruling class of New York city, for the Irish organisation has been completely prostrated. Ladies went round the worst quarters in carts—speaking and protesting, calling on honest men to put an end to Tammany, and were listened to with great respect.   They have been successful.   The Tammany government is rather remarkable. It has been shown that the judges appointed under Tammany have systematically practised bribery—that the police have received hush-money from all the illegal establishments and gambling places—that honest citizens have been run in and ill-treated because they wouldn't pay bribes—that business men have had to pay for fear of the police letting burglars into their premises—and that a regular percentage is paid to the central organisation, each judge and policeman paying a specified share.   The amount is supposed to be about three million sterling a year—not to speak of the money taken from contractors and stolen under city grants for street cleaning, etc. So you see how we have governed !   I fear we shall govern no more for some time.   I wonder if Ireland will be ruled some day under Home Rule in the same charming fashion.

The woods have now almost lost their leaves and it is getting cold and miserable—but it suits me to get a little cooled off after all the heat of the summer.   I am still rather giddy and my ears buzz.   I suppose that it is liver.   It is annoying but everyone feels livery after being in the East, and it ought to make me write poems in the prevailing style, or contribute to the Yellow Book.   You haven't mentioned *Trilby*.   I think it perfectly charming.   I have read it several times over and it seems to find the right place, like whisky on a cold day on the top of High Street."

The close of that letter mentions that he had applied for a transfer. " Not that I don't like the people, but it is so stale and useless professionally." Probably he was made restless by the thought of very much more interesting experiences which might have been his.

Nov. 13, 1894.

To STEPHEN.

" I heard from Bunsen that the Japanese intended to make Moukden their winter quarters. What a terrible collapse for the Chinese, and how entirely they deserve it ! You know, in history, China *never* has defended herself. She has always been content with conquering the conqueror. And that she has always done. Mongol, Tartar, Manchu always the same. In fifty years, it is another Chinese dynasty with Chinese officials— only the name is changed."

(A month later).

" I have been seeing a good deal of the Jap Minister, Kurino, who is a good fellow—very civilised—an ex-graduate of Harvard and a great exploiter of the press. Up to all the latest American tricks. The Americans hate that, and like to have the mono-poly. In fact, it is a deadly sin for a diplomatist to contradict in the press a lie emanating from an official of the State Depart-ment. The Chinese Minister goes about his lordly way—quite indifferent. He went to ask about some rumour in the press. The Secretary of State denied its truth. The Minister said, ' Then he lie ' (meaning the newspaper). ' Yes,' said the S. of S. ' Then,' said the Minister, ' he make one much good missionary ' ; an incident which delighted the State Department.—I gather that, as it happened yesterday and I have already heard it twice."

Japan, however, had left him with a bad inheritance of malaria, from which he never completely freed his constitution. He speaks of this in a letter to Ferguson, which has also some interesting observa-tions on the American constitution. Mr. John Burns, who was visiting the States, had been discoursing against the principle of an Upper House.

Dec. 18, 1894.

To FERGUSON.

" I fear I gave a very gloomy picture of myself, owing pro-bably to malaria ; but I have been a fortnight in the north and have been carefully examined, with the result that I have nothing the matter except chronic malaria, which a year in a northern climate will probably cure. If I stay here another summer, it would be a different story, but I have sent the doctor's certificate home, and I'm sure I shan't be kept beyond the spring. If I am, I can always get sick leave.

You will see that our friend Burns has been making himself

rather unpleasant, and if he continues he will find the place rather hot for him. He has been ' blowing ' a good deal since his arrival and is attracting rather more attention than his friends would wish. The single chamber business is rather a shock. Americans can't ' begin to conceive such an idea.' It was tried in some of the States, *e.g.*, Pennsylvania, and the system proved a complete failure. Indeed, the politicians here, though they grumble at the attitude of the Senate, which, of course, entirely defeated the tariff policy of the Government, are really very thankful for it indeed.

When the country, four years ago, by an enormous majority, declared itself against high protection, the new House then elected didn't meet for a year ; and it wasn't for two years that the Administration was changed. Those two years were occupied by very careful consideration of the policy which was demanded in 1890, and as a result, a moderate tariff Bill was presented, which on coming to the Senate became more moderate still. You see, it took four years, for the wish of the country to carry itself out. Now, a tremendous revulsion has taken place. If the new House met at once, with a new President and Senate, the whole financial policy of the country would be changed at a blow. As it is, the next four years will be taken up in the consideration of the question with a view to change. And the result will be a very moderate change—if change at all. Everyone who knows about these matters agrees that the constitution in the last four years of depression and unrest has saved the country from a very great and pressing danger— almost a revolution. This is a commonplace here.

Undated. About Jan. 4, 1895.

To his Sisters.

" I have just been up the Hudson to stay with three young ladies [1] who own a place on the bank. They own it in common, on much the same principle that Old Church is held. The place is pretty old and contains pictures and books collected by several generations. On the way up I talked with a queer old fellow who told me he was the last of his name ; no one was left to succeed him ; ' only women.' His family had lived on the Hudson since the first Dutch settlement. Most of them had been ' Tories ' at the time of the war of independence, and had emigrated to England or been hung in their own country. He himself had lost most of what remained, in the rent wars when the tenants of the old patroons had rebelled and been supported

[1] The Misses Chanler, sisters of Mr. Winthrop Chanler ; see p. 53.

by the state legislature which had practically confiscated the landowners' property. He might as well live in England, he said, for all the protection he got. Then he told me the eventful history of the different properties we passed, how some of the old proprietors had drunk themselves to death and how others had taken to farming, which was more ruinous. A few only had survived; he showed me the place of a lady, from one of the oldest families, who had married the son of her father's gardener, an emigrant to California and mineowner, and had managed to keep her head up in consequence. In fact, she is the leader of the New York dancing society.—I saw the house of the Astors. You remember the Miss Willing who married over here and is become the queen of New York. The Astors are the richest of all the families and date back a hundred years. The founder of the family began life by peddling pianos, and my friend told me he owned one bought by his ancestor from the original Astor. The House had a beautiful view over the river which is nearly a mile wide. Once ' the continient driined down it.' Then the glacial era came and the North-East was covered several thousand feet deep in ice, and the great ravine of the old river very nearly filled up. When the ice retired, the drainage of the North-West went North instead of South and the Hudson is now an estuary without a river. It was frozen over when I was there and I went across on black ice. It was pretty exciting, as the ice was so clear that one could see the tide flowing below, and every now and then a crack would begin a mile and more up stream, and crash under one's feet. Hendrick Hudson's bells, they call it. Just opposite are the Catskills, where Rip van Winkle went to sleep. There was no one but myself, my host and a few niggers on the river. I saw an iceboat slipping along, but there was not enough wind for it. An iceboat can go fifty miles an hour. In the evening the ladies, who have a southern sister-in-law, sang nigger songs with a curious, pathetic turn to them. Also every conceivable song besides. They had good voices and sang in parts. My host and I got hold of two old polo ponies unshod, saddled them and galloped them about over the snow. They had come from the West and delighted in the sight and feel of it. We went to church. It was of wood and rather mean, but the service is never mean. The clergyman's wife told me that there was great difficulty in finding the poor. People would starve almost before they confessed their poverty. It was a large Irish colony that provided most of the entertainment and murderers in the neighbourhood. The native Dutchmen regarded them with horror and fear.—I moved off to Tuxedo, where I was before. There was a lake

two miles long, all black ice. I skated alone at night, the stars
and moon being reflected in the lake. It was like St. Peter
walking on the sea. No one there seemed to care to go out.

Since I have been back here, I have been doing the necessary
calls. It is not a cheerful occupation. Each lady is at home on
a particular day and has her female friends to help her entertain.
That is called ' gracefully pouring tea.' You leave a card on a
tray, are told by four perfect strangers that they are 'pleased and
proud to meet you, Mr. Rice,' and then you gracefully retire and
the duty is performed for a year. The Japanese Minister had a
party in honour of his birthday, to which he invited women
without their husbands and all the young men he could find and
the members of the Cabinet. There was Japanese dancing and
music, which, as it is now the fashion to know all about Japan,
was received with enthusiasm. The President has a reception
at the White House to which the diplomatists go in uniform, and
get inspected rather like wild beasts by a large and appreciative
audience. These act on the assumption that no diplomatist
understands English and make audible comments on our appearance. The Turk was furious because he was described as that
dumpity coloured man with a red bandana round his stomach.
The hustle at going out was wonderful, and as there is no precedence for Ambassadors' carriages, their Excellencies had to
wait, which they did, making vitriolic comments on American
institutions. A number of Americans go to court at foreign
capitals. Half of them make furious complaints about their
own country, and the other half point out how much better
Republican institutions are. I always wait for Americans to
abuse their own country. It shouldn't be done for them. They
don't like it.

I have been to several lunch and supper parties given to
actors and distinguished travellers. They are all much the
same. The guests are of two kinds, the listeners and the story-
tellers. The listeners have generally heard the stories before
but like them just as much. If the story-teller forgets a point,
someone is sure to remind him of the omission. Each has his
turn with his own peculiar story, which is each a work of art in
itself. The stories are long, but the skeleton is short enough.
For instance. At a lunch in New England there was no clergyman present. So the host singled out a pious, solemn-looking
man in a black coat and tie with a religious appearance and
asked him to pronounce a blessing. The gentleman after being
twice addressed, put his hand to his ear and said, ' I see you are
talking to me, sir, but I am so God-damned deaf that if hell
froze over, I couldn't hear the cracking of the ice.'

A southern gentleman described how a broken down slave-owner, coming to the end of his resources, was obliged to become a livery stable keeper to get food for his family. The first job he had was to drive eight niggers to a ball. The night was cold and the ballroom very hot. He sat outside at first, but the cold drove him in. The stove was red hot and there were fifty niggers dancing in a small room and the atmosphere was a trifle savoury. While he was sitting there enjoying it as well as he could, a nigger came up to him and said, ' I must trouble you to move, as the ladies complain of your clothes smelling so strong of horse.'—An Irishman came to complain to the magistrates of his son's conduct. The man's mother had died and he had laid her out and prepared a wake. The son was sent out with five dollars to buy whiskey and came back with three dollars worth of whiskey inside him and set to work to raise Hades in his father's house. He upset everything, including his grand-mother. ' I had laid her out fine with flowers and candles fit for heaven if any woman was, and he treated her so that in two minutes she wasn't fit for hell.'—Another Irishman told how he kept chickens in his cellar and how the water pipes burst and drowned them. He complained to the city authorities, one after the other. They all sympathized and advised him to apply to someone else. At last he went to the mayor. ' And what do you think the spalpeen said to me ? " Kape ducks." '

These stories took each of them about half an hour telling. They were told with action and acting and any amount of detail. As soon as the last was told, the party broke up. The best, to my mind, were the character stories, with no particular point but a funny or pathetic turn.—The northern farmer whose son had been killed in the war and who was heard to swear that as long as he lived he would keep the boy's grave green, even if he had to paint it.—The broken down planter in Virginia who entertains the northern magnate, with the help of an old nigger servant. He orders the Madeira of 1832. The nigger goes down to the cellar and comes up with the statement that the madam had gone out with the key. The party ends with a carouse on the bottle of whiskey which the northerner had brought down with him.

April 1, 1895.

To AGNES.

" I have just come back from a journey to the South. Senator Cameron has bought a house down on an island in S. Carolina. A party went down there and at half an hour's notice I joined them, just catching the train. There was a Boston architect who has made a great reputation out of the

new library at Boston, on which Sargent has been working. He
has been twice married.   His first wife left him and his second
who was a most beautiful and charming person had a strange
illness which resulted in her starving to death in the first year
of their marriage.   He is a bald, dapper man of forty-five, very
enthusiastic and a cheerful traveller.   The others were Mr. and
Mrs. White who were in the American Embassy in London and
have been turned out by this administration.   They were great
social lights in London and she was a queen among the ' Souls.'
He is good nature itself and agrees with everyone in turn
without irritating them as much as one would expect from the
habit.   She is stately, clever and cold, with a very determined
will which makes itself felt, but she generally wishes her friends
to enjoy themselves and carries out her wish.   They made
perfect travelling companions.

On the way we passed Richmond.   As Lincoln said when
someone asked him for a pass to go to Richmond : ' I have given
passes to half a million men to go there and they have not got
there yet.'   It took them four years and it took us four hours.
The country we passed is a battlefield the whole way, but the
trees have grown up and the trenches are filled.   A Northerner
looking out of the window at the red soil said to a Virginian,
' What makes the ground so red ? '   The Virginian said :
' Yankee blood.'

It was snowing at Richmond and it was quite cold when we
were turned out of our berths at a roadside station and were
told that we had three hours to wait.   There were immense
pine woods all round, with pools crowded with duck.   We met a
solitary white man riding.   We asked him whether they went by
Charleston or Washington time ?   He pointed to the sun and
told us that was the only clock they went by in those parts.
We found a nigger shanty with an old woman working in a
garden.   She said she was looking after a family whose mother
had abandoned them.   She showed us a shanty without
furniture and with the light showing through the wall.   The
eldest child was a beautifully made negress of fifteen, as
straight as an arrow.   She was suffering agonies from rheu-
matism.   They had had the coldest winter ever known.   The
other children were lying about on the floor.   The old negress
seemed to think the situation amusing and they all seemed to
enjoy the joke as much as their guardian.

Then we went back and cooked tea and read *Pride and
Prejudice* aloud till the train arrived.   We got out at what was
once a fashionable watering-place but gone entirely to ruin.
The houses with their large verandahs looked as if they had been

fine once. The population were chiefly black. At the wharf
we found a steam yacht waiting and we got on board, and
steamed down a river between flat banks into another river, and
then into another, and so on into an arm of the sea, till at last we
got in sight of the red roof of the house among palmetto and
pine. The roadway and entrance drive is a creek, up which we
steamed almost to the door. On the pier we were met by the
hostess and her guests. One was a young Washington girl
whose face had become quite black with the sun. Another was
the Senator's son, who is a tall, silent man, rather like the
Marshalls. There was also a New York heiress whom everyone
hopes the son will marry. Also a boy of twenty, madly in love
with the black girl, whose proceedings filled us all with delight
all the time we were there. The next day there arrived two
new guests, husband and wife, the wife a very handsome and
perfectly dressed lady with a perpetually moving tongue and
pair of eyes. As she was amusing and pretty, I never got tired
of either. Also relays of young men for the girls. Also a
German lady married to an American, but in a perpetual state
of being shocked.

The country is absolutely flat, and when there was a tornado
two years ago, a number of the inhabitants were drowned.
There are thirty whites and about 10,000 negroes on the Island.
One day we steamed off to a desert island twenty miles off. I
walked through it. In the middle was a wood, chiefly of
palmettos with thick undergrowth and here and there stagnant
ponds of black water. It was full of mocassin water-snakes but
it was too cold for them to come out. The alligators showed
their snouts and sometimes their eyes and there were innumerable water fowl of all sorts. At the end of the island there was
a lighthouse inhabited by a S. Carolinian, an Irishman and a
Swede, with his American wife. They were all fever stricken
and told us they dared not venture into the woods at all in the
summer. We emerged on to an enormous stretch of hard
white sand on which we walked for three miles in a hot sun
which reduced the ladies to tears. Then we lunched and
searched for wood ticks. We all had good sport. The voyage
back was delightful and the sunset splendid over the marshes
and lagoons.

In the evening the negroes came to sing and dance. The
dances are curious. A man stands in the middle and chants in a
low voice : ' Happy day ; Jesus died,' then one by one men and
women take it up, singing in parts. Then they form line and
walk slowly round, singing. Then the leader claps his hands.
Then they all begin to clap and dance a sort of shuffling step,

always getting more rapid.   The leader then improvises to the accompaniment of the refrain, singing and shouting anything that comes into his head.   The dancing gets more and more furious and then, at a sign, suddenly stops.   Then another begins.   A different tune, different words and different steps. Afterwards they sang.   No one knows exactly who composed the songs.   They are very quickly forgotten and it is hard after two years to recover the words or music.   They sing in parts and in perfect time.   Someone begins alone : ' You may break the hearts of many poor little girls (*ter*), but you won't break this little heart of mine. . . . Young man, young man, what have I done that you walk past my door and won't come in, keep awalkin' past my door and won't come in, etc., etc.' Another one was in a minor key : ' Mother, mother, your daughter will condemn you (*ter*) way down in your grave. . . . Liar, liar, your lies will condemn you.   Thunder, thunder, the thunder over yonder,' etc.,   Each verse was sung with more energy than the one before, as they are easily excitable.   The tunes are very effective.   We were all rather excited by them.

We were generally divided into parties ; the kids or lovers, who wandered off in pairs and were under thirty years of age ; and the elders who lived together and sat on the beach or shot or drew.   I did a great number of drawings in brush and ink, all of which, unfortunately, were kept by the hostess.   I think there was never such an idle crowd.   No one read or walked more than half a mile after the first day.   We just summoned up strength to go to church on Sunday.   It was a coloured church and we came in time for the sermon.   The sentences were well turned and delivered with a fine rolling voice.   There was no sort of connection between one sentence and another. We got rather tired and made signals at one another which the preacher immediately noticed.   ' I just about done finished,' he said, and added, ' This is collection Sunday.'   Then a deacon handed round an old battered hat and looked inside with each donation and audibly thanked us.   Then the congregation began to sing, the clergyman reading out each verse. The singing was in parts, very effective, especially from the outside.   We hitched up our team of a horse and mule, and drove home.   In the afternoon the nigger boys came up to sing to us, little fellows of ten to fourteen who sang capitally, quite without training, I suppose.

The next day there was an accident on the lagoon and five men were drowned.   All the shore population turned out ; some sat on the beach and whiled away the time with the help of an accordion, and others went about in boats looking for the bodies. I could not make out why they were so determined to find them but they all told us that the search would never be given up. One of the women said that the men had money on them, but I don't know whether that was the chief reason. On the beach I met a negro telling stories. The story he was telling was Brer Rabbit and the Tar Baby; he told it very well with shouts of laughter from himself and the audience.

The journey back was not exactly pleasant, for the hot weather began with a rush, and the cars were intolerable. Some of our party stopped at Charleston, where there are a number of fine houses. It is rather difficult to penetrate into them as the owners are very poor now and do not like to have strangers come in without offering them the old southern hospitality which is now no longer in their power. One old lady, a Miss Pringle, received them because they had known her nephew in Europe, and showed them all over her beautiful house and battered garden and old silver. All her brothers had perished in the war. There must have been a great deal of stateliness in the old ante-bellum days, but rather on the Irish plan of brag and extravagance and debt.

Since I have been back here, I have visited the old town of Alexandria where Braddock had his headquarters before Fort Duquesne where he was killed. The old house is embedded in a modern hotel, through which you have to pass to reach the portico, still carved with a fine stone staircase. Below it is the remains of a fort built by the early settlers against a possible Indian attack with cellars and an underground passage to the river. The docks are deserted now and nothing remains of the former prosperity of the town. We saw also the church where Washington used to worship and the old pew from which the autograph had been stolen by a tourist a few years ago. A Washington was still one of the church wardens.

I have received no orders, but my successor has been appointed and I suppose I shall hear soon."

It had become plain that the malaria contracted in the East was serious enough to make it unsafe for him to face another summer in the damp heat of Washington, and he wrote as much to his official superiors, who seconded his wish. On March 12 he writes to Villiers:

"I can't thank you enough; Berlin will suit me admirably in every respect, and I am told it ought to cure my complaint in less than a year."

"Every respect" meant that it would also give him a change of scene and new subjects for study. Berlin did that with a vengeance.

But at this moment in his career his feelings about America fluctuated between amusement and disgust.

WASHINGTON,

March 12, 1895.

To his Sisters.

" Rudyard Kipling is here and has been very good company. We took him to see the Zoo. The Zoo here is a valley, with a stream running through it in which the elephants bathe, and rocky banks in which the bears have their caves. Kipling was like a child and roared with laughter at the elephants and bears. There was one little black bear that he loved especially. He said it was just like a lady's muff gone mad. The lions were fed for us. There was one cub of eighteen months which was in such a rage at being kept waiting that he would not eat when his food was given him but sat roaring and growling with indrawn breath and glaring at us. The tiger had just had his claws cut and was lying on his back with his legs in the air and gnashing his teeth at the universe. There is a colony of beavers in a secluded part of the park to which the public are not admitted. They have made clean work of most of the trees, cutting them down as clean as if they had used axes. One only was visible. He had once had a mate who escaped and was killed 100 miles off in Virginia. Others were introduced but the first thing they did was to turn the poor beast out of his home and dam and take it themselves. He was wandering aimlessly round, for ever trying to find a way out and avoiding his old home with the greatest care.

Another sort of beast show was Congress in its last hours. The session closed at midday on Monday, and having wasted the winter Congress was trying to make up time by all-night sittings. I took Kipling to see it. The House was indeed a sight. It is an enormous room without any sort of dignity. Some of the members were lying at full length on sofas at the back of the hall. A great many were smoking. Some were chewing and each was provided with the necessary spittoon. There was a confused noise like a lady's tea party. Every now and then the Speaker pounded his desk—always without effect. If you looked carefully, you would see one man on his legs with a group of five or six men opposite him, standing with their faces towards him and a little man within a yard of him with a roll of papers on which he was writing. The first is the member speaking, the last is the official reporter. You can't hear a word unless the orator is very well known, or unless you are within a foot or two of him. The floor was crowded with members trying to get recognition from the Speaker, newspaper reporters each with a knot of gentlemen round him, and errand boys ; it was also littered with torn papers, cigar ash and other mementoes of members. Kipling resolved that he would not take his wife to see it, as she was an American and wished to respect her country.—I was in the Senate when a Senator accused a new arrival of having fled from Washington as a bank defaulter and forger. A friend said that the attack was inconceivably mean, as the matter had happened so long ago. The first Senator then attacked the defender as having secured his own election and that of his colleague by bribing a judge to make a false decision. The defender was unable to reply to that charge (as the judge in question had been condemned and expelled from the bench) but he answered by a counter attack something to this effect : ' Who is the Senator who is howling his obscene charges on the floor of the Senate as if he had something on his stomach which he wanted to get rid of ? He reminds me of the eloquence of a jackal tearing a dead woman to pieces. But who is he ? We all know that he made his political reputation by falsifying the election returns which would have secured Tilden for our President. He is rewarded by a seat in this honourable body. He ought to be in the States prison.' All the charges are absolutely correct—which being known, the Senate proceeded to discuss the appropriation bill.

Curzon, whom I travelled with in the East, is going to marry a Washingtonian.[1] It is quite a romantic story. They met in London some years ago and I gathered from what he used to say on our journey that he hoped to marry her. But he wanted to go to Cabul first and there was no engagement, but, I suppose, a sort of understanding. As the journey was a very dangerous one, the poor girl was in a very miserable state and as there was no engagement she could give no explanation. At last came a letter and she was radiant. The newspapers take much more interest in international marriages than in Congress, and when Miss Gould married a Frenchman, there were whole sheets of vivid description for days. The illustrations were sufficiently intimate and one paper is now prosecuting another for stealing pictures of the bride's underclothing. Crowds assembled to watch the pair going and coming for more than a week before the wedding.

I hope to be away soon, as Grant Duff is appointed and I shall be able to depart as soon as he comes. There is a great deal to do now with the refuse of Congress on our hands and the papers pouring out floods of abuse every day. I wish I could

---

[1] Miss Mary Leiter.

take a purely humorous view of it, but I own it will be rather a comfort to go to a country where one can read the news without finding in every paper an article accusing one's country of every conceivable crime."

It should be remembered that at this time the Democratic party was fully justifying his forecast of a year earlier that they would show themselves " as disagreeable to us as possible." The occasion was provided by a dispute which had been dragging between Britain and Venezuela concerning the boundaries of a territory which had been British long before the United States became a Commonwealth, or Venezuela a State.

April 12, 1895.

To VILLIERS.

" The papers here are working away at Venezuela. The South Americans are in with all the low press men and every sort of lie is propagated about British aggression. Our best policy is to make a plain and clear statement which would command respect—such, in fact, as we have made. The point left undetermined, and out of which special capital is made, is our refusal to arbitrate as to any territory within the Schomburgk line. With this people, the best plan is to disregard both the official statements of the Secretary of State and the attacks of the press, and to make up our minds to the course which is clearly just and proper, and to adhere to that. In the end, this people will not go to war unless they are clearly in the right, whatever their government or newspapers may say. As there is no point on which the interests of the U.S. and G.B. are diametrically opposed, and neither wishes to take the other's territory, there is no reason whatever why we shouldn't enjoy a sort of peace tempered by newspaper articles. But it isn't the slightest good trying to conciliate the U.S. You might as well conciliate a jackal or, let us say, a tiger. The jealousy of England is so acute that nothing we can do will do the slightest good. Suppose we are civil to their naval officers—still, our ships are larger and more numerous. Suppose we entertain their Ambassador—the English lord on the continent is still a greater personage than the American patriot, etc., etc. Then there is the question of international marriages. It is a most irritating thing for instance, that a beautiful and wealthy girl like Miss Leiter goes abroad to marry. The fact is that as long as we exist and talk English we shall be hated here. No one has a right to exist and talk English who isn't an American. Then we should remember that their feeling for the rest of the world is one of pure and undisguised contempt."

The Venezuelan affair came dangerously to a head in the following December when Spring Rice was in Berlin. President Cleveland sent a message to Congress in which he claimed for the United States the right to intervene as by superior authority and determine the dispute according to their judgment. In this interval, the Liberal party had lost office and the Unionists were once more in power. Lord Salisbury answered without heat, but maintained his ground ; and the United States did not take any action to carry out Cleveland's threat.

In the midst of so much angry satire, bred partly of malaria, it is a delight to come on the quiet inner life of Spring Rice's mind revealed, as so often, to the old man at Eton who loved him like a wise father.

WASHINGTON,
March 18, 1895.

" MY DEAR TUTOR,

I can't tell you what a pleasure it was to get your letter. It shows me that I am right in always referring to you in my thoughts as one of the fixed points in life, to which I can always turn with the certainty of finding it where it was—and what an infinite blessing that is. There are so few, out of oneself, which are certain ; and unless one is worthy of it, not many in oneself.

I agree with you entirely about sickness. It is one of the things which show one the great lesson—that you can't depend on the pleasures of the world for nutriment and support ; and when one realises that, it is so much easier to live, because one hasn't the sense of injustice if things, which ought, one thinks, to make one happy, fail in doing so.

As for myself, I am really all right. All that was the matter with me was chronic malaria which as you know is very distressing and makes one very miserable, but which is really a very common malady and has nothing serious about it. I have received a promise from the F.O. that I shan't have to stay here very long and my next post will be somewhere in Europe. I hope, Germany. Won't you come over to Berlin when I am there if I do go ? Do you remember my trip with you ? How pleasant it was. I know a little more about pictures and music than I did then. What sport we should have together if you came ! Anyhow, I hope to see you shortly. I ought to be back in England in May and the first thing I shall do is to go to Eton. How beautiful it will be then, and your garden will be well again. The trees here haven't begun to bud even, but the crocuses are out at the foot of the bronze warriors in the public squares. Quite close to the town there are wild woods where the feeble spring flowers of this country make their tardy appearance. The prettiest is the blood-root—a delicate white flower with the red juice which is the horror of nurses. Then there is a clustering pink flower, rather like a bog pimpernel, which appears about the same time.   There is a kind of maiden-hair which grows in masses.   The Government, luckily for us, has purchased several thousand acres and turned it into park ; that is, left it wild.   There is a deep ravine with a stream and rocks and a difficult path with plenty of scrambling.   Till lately I had a horse in whose company I went many miles in the woods. Every now and then there is a glimpse of the white dome of the Capitol or the shaft of the Washington monument which catches the light finely.   I have been drawing a little in ink and water with a Japanese brush.   It is a rapid way of working and effective.   Of course, colour is beyond me.   Shall we ever go sketching together ?   Your life is as good as mine, and we might end our days in a Devonshire farm sharing our two pensions.

Yours ever affectionately,

C. S. R."

It is worth while to quote from Professor Mowat's Life of Lord Pauncefote the generous saying of Spring Rice's chief in these years, that " his success at Washington " (in a career lasting from 1889 to 1902) " was due to two of his secretaries, Michael Herbert and Cecil Spring Rice."   Neither of them served under him after 1895 ; but both succeeded him at the Embassy.

CHAPTER VII

GERMANY 1895-96

THE KRUGER TELEGRAM

BERLIN marked a dramatic stage in Cecil Spring Rice's career. Hitherto his study had been mainly of America, which offered huge and shifting problems to the economist, and rich ground in its social and political life for satiric observation. He had felt keenly there an ill-will to his own country, continually quickened by the Irish trouble, but in the main springing from antipathies that were traditional and nourished by education, rather than provoked by any clash of material interest. In spite of American hospitality to individual Englishmen, America's attitude towards England was always quarrelsome. But the America of those days had neither army nor navy and was definitely unmilitary.

Japan had charmed him and had given him his first perception of the East, to whose magic he responded : and he had realised that Japan's effort to equip herself on Western methods was serious and successful. But neither he nor anyone else divined that this new-fledged power, with an army of 70,000 and the beginnings of a modern fleet, would within ten years alter the whole balance of world diplomacy.

He had worked at his profession with the conscientious thoroughness that was part of his family tradition ; but he had worked without enthusiasm or passion. Nothing in his official duties had yet quickened his imagination. But, unlike the mass of men, he had imagination ready to respond ; and long contact with a temperamental hostility in the United States had left his mind jealously sensitive on all that touched the welfare of England. He had as yet seen no grave danger, but all his nature was on the alert to watch for it.

In Germany he first had contact with a power which owed its position in Europe, and even its internal unity of structure, to a vast military success, achieved just one generation before, by the most formidable military machine of which there was record. He discerned at once that its rulers were possessed by ambition to develop the material greatness of Germany much further by the same machinery, sedulously organised and perfected : he recognised also that England everywhere blocked the way to Germany's ambitions, and that Germany's preparation to prevail was unremitting.

178

Thenceforward the thought of this menace never left him ; his life was spent in endeavouring to impress the tokens and the shape of it on those whom he served. It stimulated also in him that fierce love of country which is felt by those whom their profession must expatriate ; and with this went a growing resentment against all that made for unpreparedness.

For the understanding of his life's work, his letters of this time must be given fully ; in them will be found a detailed study of causes which had their full effect in the Great War. It is in the first instance a study of Germany in the days when Wilhelm II. was taking control into his own hands, but it is not a study of Germany only. His apprehension at this period did not point to direct attack by Germany. He feared her as the motive mind in a combination to despoil England, whose striking force must be Russia, and whose point of attack must be British India ; for at this time German armament was not developed at sea. Yet he noted from the first the significance of the Kaiser's naval policy.

But Russia was no less constantly in his mind than Germany ; and for many years to come Russia, not Germany, was the main object of his vigilant anxiety.

Constantly in his mind also was the thought of America, the country which had become to him almost a second home, yet which in its manifestations was so hostile. A conviction that the English-speaking races must act together lay deep in him ; and even at this stage we find him setting himself to instruct those whom he could reach in America on the inner significance of European politics, almost as if he were instructing his own Government. That was the easier because the closest of his American friends, Theodore Roosevelt, was in this period rapidly rising to power. By instinct and by affection, Spring Rice was prompted to seek through the American he knew best a better relationship between the two peoples of the same blood ; and within this period he saw a very great change for the better—largely through Roosevelt's means.

It is noteworthy that although between 1895 and 1898 the " scramble for West Africa " and military enterprises in the Nile basin led to acute friction between France and England, yet in his continuous review of the whole diplomatic chessboard Spring Rice never shows any serious fear of French designs. He had no partiality for France, and was almost curiously devoid of that sympathy for her art, literature and civilisation, which so many who are not Frenchmen feel ; but, as compared with Russia and with Germany, France was to him, like England, a country of freedom. He perceived the danger that she might be drawn by her alliance with Russia into a combination against England ; but his inherent Liberalism made him see the real menace to England in a league of the three European Empires in whose boundaries Liberalism was either suspect or proscribed.

A few facts should be recalled to aid memory. In October 1895, when Spring Rice joined the Embassy staff at Berlin as second secretary, the Kaiser had been seven years on the throne. It was five years since the fall of Bismarck ; the ruler's ascendency was so well established that he had felt able to re-open friendship, or its appearance, with the fallen statesman.—Bismarck's first successor, the Prussian, Caprivi, had in his turn been replaced as Chancellor by the Bavarian, Prince Hohenlöhe.

In England, the defeat of Lord Rosebery's Government (on a question of the supply of cordite) had been followed in July 1895 by a General Election and the rout of the Liberal party. Lord Salisbury as Prime Minister again took charge of the Foreign Office ; the Liberal Unionists were now in active coalition with the Tories, and Mr. Chamberlain as Colonial Secretary gave an immense impetus to forward policy overseas.

In America the Democratic party was in power, but Cleveland's Presidency was due to expire in March 1897. In Berlin Sir Edward Malet was just departing from the Embassy after a long tenure of office : he was too much Bismarck's friend to be acceptable to the Kaiser. Sir Frank Lascelles who replaced him was on the contrary from the first very popular in Berlin. His household included his daughter Florence, who, but not till eight years later, became the wife of Cecil Spring Rice.

In October 1895 all seemed peaceful in the relations between England and Germany. But in the previous February the " naval programme " had been definitely launched by the Kaiser, in a speech which pointed to Japan's success against China as a proof of what naval and military armaments could effect in co-operation. In June, the Kiel Canal was opened, giving Germany exclusive control of a short-cut from the North Sea to the Baltic. And in the same summer Baron Marschall von Bieberstein, Secretary of State for Foreign Affairs, used a significant argument when urging the Reichstag to make provision for four new cruisers. " We desire," he said, " to uphold and protect economic relations with the South African Republic."

Before the year was out, events provided a startling commentary on that aspiration. But during the two months after his arrival in Berlin, Spring Rice was chiefly occupied in sketching light-heartedly the society about him.

BERLIN,
Oct. 5, 1895.

To STEPHEN.

" I am now established in a hotel as I can't get into the rooms I wish to get for some time. The life here is domestic. We dine with the Ambassador [1] nearly every evening and play whist afterwards. It is all regulated carefully. At eight exactly we enter the drawing-room in proper precedence, that

[1] Sir E. Malet. His successor, Sir F. Lascelles, was already nominated.

is by seniority ; we are received by the Ambassadress in turn ;
also in precedence.   Then at eight o'clock and five minutes,
dinner is announced and we go in.   As the same party meets
every night and has met every night for more than a year, the
conversation is not greatly varied.   At nine-thirty we leave the
table, stay ten minutes in the drawing-room with the ambassadress and then file into the smoking-room where we stay till
ten.   At ten precisely we rejoin the ambassadress and drink
tea till ten-thirty, when we play whist till twelve, when we all
go to bed.   This is repeated every day with absolute uniformity
so that there is never any doubt as to when to go and when not
to go.   When I have a house of my own I shall make rules just
as rigid, like dear old Uncle A.[1]   Unfortunately my knowledge
of whist is defective, so I generally sit by and read."

Oct. 19, 1895.

" I have done nothing particular since I last wrote except go
to a great official dinner at the Chancellor's.

The Chancellor's official residence is not far from the Embassy
—a big house with a courtyard.   We waited till our chief had
arrived and then went in after him with opera hats in our hands
—at least I didn't, because I had not got one, a fearful discovery
made at the last moment and too late to be remedied.   The
Chancellor, who stood waiting at the door, is a very small man
with a lively and chirpy manner, who is very warm and kind
and cheerful in his greetings.   There were a few ladies there but
not many.   I was told that they were chosen for their looks ;
the standard in Berlin is, I imagine, rather different to ours.   I
sat between two Germans who were talkative and pleasant ;
one the Eric Barrington [2] of Germany, but as different as
possible—slow, professorish, not too amiable ; the other was
profoundly interested in the dinner and pointed out the beauties
of it to me in detail.   One or two soldiers were there in uniform,
looking very fine, one like Arthur Balfour in a helmet.   Lady
E. Malet said afterwards that the Chancellor had conversed
very gaily with her during dinner.   For instance, he said that
his trouble was that the ducks and hens made such a noise
under his window that he couldn't work.   He was obliged to
throw things at them to make them stop.   His wife thought
that cruel which leads to domestic disputes.   He intends to
retire (when he is worthy of rest) to a house near Nice ; already
Sir E. Malet, the Empress Eugénie, and the Grand Duke

---

[1] Arthur Marshall, of Patterdale.

[2] The Hon. Sir B. Eric Barrington, K.C.B., Private Secretary to three
Tory Ministers for Foreign Affairs.

Constantine of Russia have taken adjoining villas. He talks French with his wife. Altogether he is a contrast to the old Chancellor.[1] We dined in the Conference room, and as I came in my neighbour (who was secretary at the Conference)[2] pointed to a corner and said, ' There lay the Reichshund '— the great dog which Bismarck always took with him."

To STEPHEN.   Oct. 26, 1895.

" . . . If I were to keep a journal there would be very little indeed to put into it. I find the most extraordinary difficulty in getting up in the morning. Why, I can't understand. But so it is and the days get shorter in the morning and the same length in the evening. I read the *Times* regularly and with delight in the morning. What a splendid achievement it is ! I think it the greatest of English achievements.

The Ambassador has just made his last visit to the Chancery. Yesterday he went down to see Prince Bismarck. The house he lives in is almost in the station. I saw it on the way here from Hamburg—quite a small place—very primitive. The Prince was very well and talked English with great heartiness. He was, he said, better than he had been for years and looked it. Dinner was at twelve and lasted till four and there was a multitude of excellent but intoxicating wines. They went out driving together through the woods which were the Emperor's gift to the Prince, and had a farewell of moment to both of them—having known each other forty years and not being very likely to meet again. . . . "

Nov. 2, 1895.

" . . . Our chief has gone away and we have a lull accordingly in business. The life at the end was rather crowded, as we were anxious to show as much respect as possible to the departing. The ceremony at the station was a curious one ; full of formality tempered by kissing. I admire the reserve of both of them ; all sorts of interesting things were going on but neither of them showed it. They were both absolutely impassive. . . .

The German papers are pitching into us strong. We haven't a friend anywhere and it is absurd to talk about obtaining one. We can only acquire one by paying a tremendous price. I doubt whether we could get a friend as long as we are successful and rich. It is curious how detested we are and especially odd to find that in Germany we are hardly ever mentioned without some term of abuse or reproach. I suppose our existence is an

[1] Count Caprivi was Hohenlöhe's predecessor : but the contrast suggested is with Bismarck.
[2] The Conference of Berlin in 1885 on the Niger and the Congo.

offence to everyone and their only consolation is to abuse us. Their present game is to involve us with war with Russia in the East and then to grab S. Africa. They are playing up to the last, through the Transvaal. I sometimes wonder how far England is really strong. It is clear that if we aren't strong, we shall assuredly come down a most prodigious smash, for all the powers are against us. I suppose the navy *is* strong and that we can stand a longer war than most nations—but it isn't unlikely that we shall see soon enough whether we can resist and how far.

I have just been reading Froude's Dizzy. What a curious book ! . . . Everything of Froude's sets one thinking, though possibly in the wrong direction, and sometimes against him. . . "

BERLIN,
Nov. 9, 1895.

To MARGARET.

" . . . The Emperor came out from Potsdam to take the oaths of the recruits. They have been locked up in barracks for a month learning their drill. Then they are marched out into a public square and faced towards each other arranged in several bodies. The Emperor rides round them and each body sever-ally swears allegiance, repeating the words after the adjutant. Then the Emperor makes them a speech and tells them how they have sworn to protect him from men and the devil and enemies outside and inside (meaning the socialists) ; and then they all shout ' hoch ' to him and he rides away. Afterwards the recruits are allowed to walk about the town under the protec-tion of non-commissioned officers and one sees them looking in at all the shop windows and wandering about galleries. A German officer told me that he had whole families in his regi-ment, and that he wrote reports home to the uncle or father who had served in the same regiment before. Sometimes the old soldiers would come up from the country on purpose to see the regiment, so that it was a regular family. It must be a good thing to take poor people just at that age and give them a thoroughly good physical training and teach them to be clean and feed them well. I should think that the nations which do this would have the advantage eventually over our people who to a great extent get no physical training at all. . . ."

Dec. 7.

To STEPHEN.

" . . . Listen to an evening of my life. Went at 2 to see Menzel's pictures—unutterably sad to see, if you like a painter to be pretty, cheerful and kind. A long series of scenes that could never be very interesting but might be brilliant in colour—but aren't ; German crowds, thanksgivings, goings to the war, coronations, Church interiors—the best, some truthful sketches of common men and women. Cleverness in plenty but nothing to charm. Then return to Chancery : go in search of an Asiatic to interview in vain : on the way back along the streets (which were swept by an icy wind and illuminated by lightning) stopped at a colleague's and saw a French lady and her daughter. —French lady married a Talleyrand who is in German service. Hated in France for marrying a Prussian and in Germany for being a Frenchwoman. Two rather jolly girls—neither of them out. Wouldn't ride in Berlin, because it was so *ennuyeux* if one was properly guarded and impossible if one wasn't. Went often to spend a week in *les terres de son père*, where she was to play tennis—with a neighbouring family, etc., etc. Once went out an expedition for four hours ! Evidently thought it something wonderful.

I returned to Embassy and wrote. Then called for Chirol, *Times* correspondent. Found him sending off telegram and sat and waited ; the room covered with maps and fragments of newspapers. We started together for the Concert Haus ; a meeting of a man's glee club ; 100 members in black coats and a usual house orchestra. The conductor passionately interested in the music ; I think the conductor is half the fun and watch him all the time. The song most applauded was a Swedish volks lied, ' Spinn, Mädchen, spinn—Mädchen span, Thräne rann—dies jahr kommt kein Freiersman.' Audience chiefly, as usual in Germany, young ladies. We eat dinner the while in a palatial box—intervals between the music allowing it.

At ten I was taken by Gosselin [1] to a house near the Embassy where the old Princess Radzivill, a Frenchwoman by birth married to a German, lives. A suite of rooms hung in panels of blue silk ; you turn a corner and are greeted by the Princess, an elderly lady, her married daughter, pretty and young, the old fat Prince, who loves to talk English ; his brother, a Russian who talks French ; diplomats (about five) and a nephew or two ; guests sit in a circle ; conversation general mostly and carried on in French. Several young men were there who didn't seem to like it much. The old Prince narrated his experiences in Scotland thirty years ago. And his Russian brother expatiated on the mutual hatred of England and America. At exactly eleven the guests rose to depart, and went thankfully away.

[1] Sir Martin Gosselin, then counsellor (or first secretary) at the Embassy.

This goes on every evening and you are considered very impolite if you don't go rather often. I believe sometimes the conversation is interesting but generally turns on the *Revue des deux Mondes* : a great thing to have a regular standard of conversation !

The acquaintance with Mr. (now Sir) Valentine Chirol which began in the autumn ripened into perhaps the most intimate friendship of Spring Rice's life henceforward : it was the closer because Chirol was much attached to the Lascelles household, and later in England, when he had been appointed (in 1899) foreign editor of the *Times*, became almost part of the Spring Rice home circle, and an initiate of Ullswater and Old Church.

In December Spring Rice went to England on short leave. While he was there, came the first disturbance in the peaceful atmosphere. Cleveland's message concerning Venezuela was published on December 17, and some of Spring Rice's American friends shocked him by their support of its aggressive tone. Meanwhile Sultan Abdul had begun his process of " making Turkey safe for the ruling race," (as Sir Valentine Chirol has expressed it) by killing off the Armenian Christians : protests were raised in England, and the Foreign Office was ordered to furnish a detailed statement of the facts.

THE PRIORY, REIGATE.

(Undated.)

To FERGUSON.

" This is to wish you and Lady Helen a merry Xmas. I came over for a few days from Berlin and am at this moment with Curzon.[1]

What a charming Xmas message of peace and good will comes to us from America ! What do you think of Cabot Lodge ? I suppose he is qualifying for the post of Minister to England.

Well, let them all go and be damned. I can't think of the business with patience. I think Lord R.'s message to the *World* admirable ; only ' sense ' is a quality rather hard to come by. It is like telling a drowning man to keep dry.

The world is in a vile situation. The Armenian papers will be horrible—70,000 killed already by the personal command of the Sultan, who is spending part of the proceeds of the spoils in bribing the European press.

With the New Year came the Jameson Raid.—In the Transvaal, then an independent Republic, with rights defined by the Treaty made with the British in 1884, gold-mining had suddenly raised the population of Johannesburg to 60,000. The Boers, who numbered only some 20,000 voters in the whole Republic, declined to grant

---

[1] Then Under-Secretary of State for Foreign Affairs.

citizenship to aliens except after prolonged residence. The " Uitlanders " resented their unenfranchised position in a country which
their enterprise had transformed to a rich land.—There was a force
of armed men in the territory then ruled by the Chartered Company,
of which the head was Cecil Rhodes, also Premier of Cape Colony.
On January 1 Dr. Jameson with 500 mounted troopers crossed the
border and rode for Johannesburg, expecting that the Uitlanders
would rise to support him ; but the Boer farmer soldiers captured the
entire expedition—which had been denounced by Mr. Chamberlain,
the Colonial Secretary, as soon as news of its departure came through.

On January 3 the German Emperor telegraphed to President
Krüger congratulations on having " safeguarded the independence of
his country without appealing for help to friendly powers."—This
assumed that the Boers had the right to seek such help at their own
choice. But the Convention of 1884 contained a stipulation forbidding this. " The South African Republic will conclude no treaty
or engagement with any state or nation other than the Orange Free
State . . . until the same has been approved by Her Majesty the
Queen." The Kaiser's telegram was taken as a challenge to the
suzerainty thus reserved, and Lord Salisbury's Government at once
mobilised a powerful flying squadron of the fleet and ordered two
regiments to the Cape.

There was a violent explosion of feeling both in Germany and in
England. Spring Rice's immediate reactions are given in two letters
to his brother.—But five years later he wrote to Roosevelt about the
" true patriotism " which will always condemn wrongdoing, even in
the patriot's own country. " This will seem the ordinary English
hypocrisy," he adds, " especially from a person of my profession
who did not at once disapprove of the Jameson raid. But then I
was in Germany at the time."

Here is his letter to Stephen, dated January 9, 1896 :

" I was delighted to get your letter and thoroughly sympathised. I showed it to the Ambassador who takes your view
of the case and I hope many people do over there. It doesn't
do to be wrong oneself because someone else is foolish, and our
case, on the surface at any rate, and as represented by these
damned newspapers, is bad. I am very glad indeed to hear of
Chamberlain's rage against the treachery. There is another side
which I think important. Germany to a large extent lives on
trade in India and British colonies where she would not for one
moment give the same facilities to England, if she were in
possession. And in spite of this fact Germany has been for
some years engaged in thwarting and flouting us in politics and
in insulting us in newspapers. Russia and France they don't
dare mention except in flattering terms, because they think it's
safe to abuse us and not safe to abuse them. They act on the

reasonable principle that it's safe to insult anyone who won't fight. I think it is high time that we show them that whether we wish to fight or not, we are ready. In this case I am sure we won't fight because we are in the wrong so far. But this outburst has come just in time to prevent Germany being in the wrong on her side. In the present temper of England, that last would mean war, and I believe they know it.

That Germany has for years had the design of annexing the Transvaal is perfectly natural, and I believe can be proved. There is no wickedness in that. They are now chiefly interested in preventing us annexing it and that, at any rate, is a gain for us. What a thoroughly beastly mess the whole matter is ! "

Jan. 11, 1896.

To the Same.

" I am almost too tired to write after ploughing through pages and pages of German and ticking at the typewriter. England seems going perfectly mad and is now occupied in insulting her neighbours. I hope they will quiet soon. It's had one good effect. This Government thought we had no kick left in us and that they might insult us as much as they liked. They have done it with a vengeance for the last year or so. We were the only great power whom they thought it safe to bully. Now they have found their mistake and as the lesson has been given, it's just as well to stop howling. I never heard such a noise in my life. Also we are in the wrong technically, and I hope that we shan't go deeper. Patriotism is a fine thing, but I don't believe in being wrong and never will. I think they are whipping the horse up without enquiring where they are going. What beasts newspapers are !

It's quite true. I firmly believe that there is a European plot against us and that we must be prepared on occasion to face the world. It's unfortunate, but it's quite evident that it's everyone's interest to shove off his neighbour's energies on to us. It is less dangerous for Germany if Russia, France, etc., are engaged out of Europe, because Germany has no possessions to speak of out of Europe. England has all the best things, and so naturally everyone says, ' If you want someone's property, go to Asia or Africa. There's a fine property belonging to England which you are welcome to take, and England won't mind.' There is human nature in that and no particular wickedness.

The scheme broke down in this case because it was seen, first, that England would fight, and secondly, that if she did, France would join her. The fact is, Egypt is a splendid bait.

We can always get out of it without any loss to ourselves and win a great deal by doing so. The result of the whole business will be to make Germany more affectionate than ever to Russia, and Russia will be free to do what she likes in the East. But I hope that we shall recognise our real friends and shake hands again with Germany. We hate one another because we are near enough to each other to dislike each other, but it's absurd to suppose that either can assist at the destruction of the other. If the Teutons quarrel now, the world will be Slav, as Bismarck said long ago. I think that on the whole civilisation has made considerable strides, and war is less easy to bring on than it was. I wish a few newspaper editors could be hanged.

Then follows a series of letters to his closest personal friend at the Foreign Office, Villiers, who had asked him for a description of the feeling in Germany.

Jan. 11, 1896.

" My Dear Francis,

With regard to your question : As far as I have been able to make out, the case is this. The Emperor received the news of the invasion with a transport of fury and is reported to have made some remarkable statements, for instance, that he would send back his British uniform, as it was only fit to be worn by robbers, etc., etc. It was quite certain that if he was excited he would do or say something. Accordingly he produced this telegram. He submitted it to the Chancellor, Secretary for Foreign Affairs and one or two Foreign Office officials. It was modified. As to the question of sending it at all—nobody who knows him doubts that it would be no good telling him not to send it. But as to its form. The Foreign Office here is convinced that Lord Derby [1] meant what he said, when he stated that the only restriction in the Transvaal was the requirement to submit Treaties to the Queen, when made. ' Suzerainty,' as defined in the International Law dictionaries, comprises far more extensive rights. Therefore it was believed and maintained that the Transvaal could be addressed as an Independent State. As to the remarks about the attackers, the Foreign Office say that England herself condemned them and had outlawed them.

So it is certain that in its terms the authorities approve of the telegram. As to sending it at all, it is equally certain that the Government here disapproved. There was a rumour that Hohenlöhe had again threatened to resign. Holstein certainly

[1] Secretary of State for the Colonies in 1884, when the Convention with the Transvaal was made.

did not like it and Marschall was also very reluctant.[1] But
they all maintain that although justified in International Law
it was unwise. Its effect on public opinion in Germany was
electric. The Emperor for a time was a hero, and he looked to
public opinion here more than to that in England.

He has fallen into one of his excitable moods. When Princess
Leopold fell into the water, the Empress, her sister, went to see
her. The Princess was much cut about the face and would not
receive her sister. The Emperor heard and rode off to the
Palace in a fury. The servants telegraphed to Prince Leopold
who was in Berlin and returned immediately, after sending a
cheeky telegram : ' I wash my hands in innocency.' He was
ordered at once to the Imperial Palace and then had an explanation with the Emperor. The Emperor asked him why the
Empress had not been received. He answered that no one
could be obliged to render account of what passed in his own
house. The Emperor said that he appeared to forget that he
was the Emperor of Germany. ' And you, Sir, ' said the
Prince, ' to forget that I am husband of my wife.' There is
said to have ensued a sound box on the ear, which was responded
to. Then the Prince was ordered into arrest and the Emperor
himself announced in public that the Prince would attend no
family gathering or festivities this season.[2]

The state of feeling in England is very extraordinary. I am
rather glad it has happened, for it has been a lesson. They have
been kicking us for years, on the assumption that they were
kicking a dead ass. It is a great surprise to see starting up a
live lion. The effect is curious. The Press articles are almost
friendly. But I hope it won't be pushed too far. The Government here firmly believe in the justice of their view that the
Transvaal is independent (a purely technical point), and would
be perfectly ready to acknowledge now that the interest of
England was overwhelming and must be maintained. But if
we now try to prove that the Treaty of 1884 did not abrogate
the Treaty of 1881, preamble and all, we shall, I am sure, offer
the opening which they long for, that is, of proving the Government guilty of dishonesty. It is a fact that we cannot allow
foreign interference, but it is also a fact that we have also
granted the Transvaal certain rights, and that we have no right
to deny it, because it is inconvenient.

I don't think it is possible to deny that a plot of some sort

[1] Holstein was permanent chief of the Foreign Office. Marschall Von
Bieberstein was Minister for Foreign affairs.

[2] Prince Frederic Leopold of Prussia was brother to the Duchess of Connaught. His Princess was daughter to the Duke of Schleswig-Holstein.

existed. When Kruger was in Portugal [1] he received an invitation from Prince Bismarck to come to Berlin and was there given a dinner by the old Emperor, who spoke most kindly to him. The Prince also remonstrated with Lord Ampthill against the despatch of the Bechuanaland expedition [2] and was furious at the annexation. The English ship arrived at St. Lucia Bay only two days before the German, thanks to R. Meade. For the last two years the papers have been full of allusions to the Boer kinsmen and, of course, the Emperor's utterances have been clear enough for some time. Rhodes is continually abused as the enemy of Germany, and ' all he wants is to keep Germany out.' The Official Press have for some time been singing the same hymn in various notes—that Germany has united herself with France and Russia and forms the *trait d'union* between them and the Triple Alliance. All European questions are to be shelved, but the Powers are to be free to carry on their enterprises in the rest of the world—that is, at the expense of England. And where shall Germany's share come in ? Somewhere, evidently. No one who read the German Official Press during the last month could doubt that there was a plot against England on an enormous scale.

If it turned out that Germany discovered that English public opinion, rather than give up the Transvaal, would surrender Egypt, and that France alone would profit by Germany's action, one can quite understand the sudden change. [3] The excitement of the French here passes belief. To get at once Egypt and the alliance of England against Germany ! The Franco-German Alliance falls to the ground as soon as you try to build on it. It is like the Princess who tried to get the Fire God and the Water God to build her house for her. Now remains Russia. The result will evidently be to throw Germany more completely into the arms of Russia. Can Russia hurt us anywhere ? If so, she will have the best European authority for doing so. The next month, I suppose, we shall be well occupied in that quarter.

[1] In 1884 with the Transvaal Deputation.

[2] Sir Charles Warren's expedition set out in October, 1884. The delimitation of Bechuanaland from German S.W. Africa was proclaimed in Sept. 1885. Spring Rice was then at the Foreign Office.

[3] Salisbury informed the French Ambassador that Great Britain desired to destroy Mahdism, and that an expedition to Dongola was under consideration. " Would France agree on condition that there would be no advance beyond Dongola except after consultation with her ?" Gooch, *History of Modern Europe*, 278. This proposal, admitting France to a kind of partnership, was favoured by the French Foreign Office, but the French Ministry rejected it.

But I do wish, and we all do here, that the English burst of feeling against Germany may be modified and that the Government will make some friendly statement.   There is no good in rubbing it in, and the Emperor is a bad customer to insult. Besides such a statement would be looked on with the greatest gratitude here.   The lesson has been given and taken to heart.

I think the moral of it all is that there has been a ' try on ' and that it failed and that we are now as we were—with a difference, as the dog said to the porcupine after he had snapped at him."

The genesis of the Kruger telegram remained the subject of much rumour, as later references will show.   According to Dugdale's " German Diplomatic Documents " (II 387) the draft was made in the Foreign Office and contained the words " have thus been enabled to . . . safeguard the dignity of your government."   This was changed in Marschall's own hand to " safeguard the independence of the country."   The Emperor declared later that the telegram did not spring from his initiative but was " a deeply thought out action of the Foreign Office."

Jan. 17, 1896.

To VILLIERS.

" Chirol is the most ardent advocate of a good understanding with Germany and always has been so.   He has also a great admiration for several members of the present administration. But he is rather a warm-hearted man and takes things seriously. He thinks that the German press has been encouraged for years to answer all our overtures with contempt and that advantage has been taken of the first difficulty to stab us in the back. Naturally he is in a rage and shows it.[1]

It has to be remembered that the articles which we have heard of for so many years have been taken no notice whatever of in England till quite recently, so that the Government has been able to please one section of the population here without offending England.   Of course, an end had to come sooner or later.   Articles, meant for home consumption only, have gone abroad.

There seems absolutely no rudeness anywhere against English people ;   they are particularly kind and cordial here— in the great mercantile circles they know what enormous interests we have in common and how fatal a war would be. The artistic and literary people are practically one with those in England, and, of course, science is a great common interest. The sensitive point is this that the expansion of Germany is barred in Europe, and that out of Europe Germany encounters

[1] In his despatches to the *Times*.

England everywhere. Australia, Africa and America are machines for teaching Germans English. German emigrants are increasing the strength of Anglo-Saxondom every day. Naturally there is a bitter feeling. You can see only one place in the world outside Europe where a dialect of German is still spoken—and there— !

An article in the *Cologne Gazette* to-day says that the circumstances show that England is capable of behaving to weaker powers as she did once to Denmark. If she could, England would inflict on Germany ' a battle of Copenhagen.' Germany never expected that England would stand by her in time of danger, but all the world can now see how England behaves when there is a real conflict of interests, and what view popular opinion takes. Germany should take this lesson to heart, and England too should learn that she is vulnerable, and that she does ill to make an enemy of the power which ' history and nature have made her friend.' ' France and Russia, her natural enemies, can do her infinite harm, and though they are at present combined against Germany, England may soon find herself the chief object of their enmity. The policy of Germany is then clear, if England pursues her policy of blind selfishness. Germany will insist on the independence of the Transvaal, if not now—at any rate at a time when the friendship of Germany is a matter of life and death to England.'

This is continuing the idea, sketched out in the *Nord Deutsche* at the beginning of the year, of the anti-English *dreibund* of Germany, Russia and France. At the beginning of the year, it was described as a *fait accompli*.

It appears that France hates Germany more than England, and it's still to be hoped that Germany hates England less than she does France."

Jan. 18, 1896.

To VILLIERS.

" Up till to-day there is no authoritative statement as to Arthur Balfour's speech,[1] though some days ago there would have been a storm.

Chirol believes that the next step of hostility will be to work through the Sultan or the Mussulman population of India. Chirol is still very sore and rather surprises us by his vehemence.

---

[1] Mr. Balfour at Manchester had affirmed that the Transvaal was subject to the control of Great Britain, which would admit no foreign interference. In regard to the Venezuela dispute, he declared that war between the English-speaking peoples would involve the unnatural horrors of a civil war and ought to be impossible ; and finally that the British Empire had never been a better fighting machine than it then was, though he did not expect it would be put to such a use.

I think that it is the effect of his determined efforts to get the Foreign Office to make some friendly statement towards England. Since he has been here, that has been his chief object. And the result is what you see. He believes in the existence of a determined hostility which takes a brutal and cowardly form. It's quite natural to be offended at the tone of the German press ; but then, read the article in the *Standard* of the 18th. A friendly remark of some kind in the *Times* would cost nothing and go down very well indeed.

The German view (to play *advocatus diaboli*) is :

1. England says she will maintain the treaty of 1884, which gives internal independence and allows the Transvaal to negotiate with Foreign powers ; but,—Balfour says that the internal constitution must be altered, and that Foreign powers have no right to negotiate with the Transvaal.

2. England said that Jameson was an outlaw ; but the Poet Laureate sings his praises as a hero and the whole English press expresses indignation at the idea of his being punished, and says it's an insult if the Kaiser agrees with the English Government !

The whole story as told here is quite in keeping with the character usually assigned to England—even to the moral lectures which we have been lately administering. I really think they are harder to bear than a pile of annexations.

Bismarck's paper, which doesn't mind telling the truth when disagreeable to the Government, says it's no use fighting against nature—meaning that if the English are preponderant in power and numbers, the Transvaal will be English.

Such a solution would leave us our honour and give us the profit too ; but if Chamberlain had faltered a moment in con-demning Jameson, or if any similar attempt is countenanced, we should have the same reputation as Napoleon had after the Spanish incident. Do you remember Talleyrand's remark to him when Napoleon said he had done many unscrupulous things but Talleyrand had not objected—why should he object now ? To which Talleyrand answered : ' Take the case of a soldier. He doesn't pay his debts—you say, it is a pity. He runs after other people's wives—you don't approve of it. *Mais qu'il triche* '—[1]

The Emperor's message is out and nothing in it to offend England ! There is the effect of his Ministers.

One curious thing I have noticed here which is that everyone is most anxious to be amiable to Englishmen, while in a hundred

---

[1] "But suppose he cheats at cards— "

little ways the German contempt for Russia comes out. Even a man in the Foreign Office told me that the army were convinced they would make short work of Russia, but they were afraid of France.

I heard from a banker here that the German banks had agreed to advance a large sum to America, if necessary,[1] although Bleichroeder, at Rothschild's instigation, had refused. Also that Russia had offered the U.S. as much gold as they wanted. That I heard again from a good source in America in the most positive way. It was offered at call, and without interest! I hear also from America that underneath all the jingoism there is a very bad feeling. It is partly from the miserable and unsettled state of the country, just as a man kicks his servant not because the servant has done anything wrong but because something is wrong with his inside. But if the rain falls out of season, it is put down to England. I hope Arthur Balfour's words will bear fruit![2] Such words, spoken of Germany, would probably bear fruit here. It seems the psychological moment. I wonder where the next explosion will be?"

Jan. 18, 1896.

To VILLIERS.

"The remarks in the English press that the German press was calming down have set them all off again and the cursing is as loud as ever. There is, however, nothing in the *Nord Deutsche*, except a very natural denial of the report that the Emperor had written to the Queen apologising. . . .

The organ of Prussian society has a long review of the S. African question which couldn't easily be more violent. . . . But it doesn't offer them German assistance, although it says that the English army and navy are a contemptible factor in any question. For instance, it says that the 1000 men from India 'will seriously weaken the defences of that country.'

This represents what are the feelings of conservative society here although nothing could exceed the courtesy and cordiality shown personally to Englishmen. Marschall said to a colleague that one good point at any rate about the whole difficulty was that it had shown what a good man Lascelles was, and what an excellent man for the post.

If we could see ourselves as others see us, we should behold the following pleasing picture. A company of lords, dukes, etc., with a prince at the head, conspire to steal certain gold mines, the property of a friendly nation. They organize an attack which fails. The Government, which had been bribed with a

---

[1] That is, in case of war against England, over the Venezuelan dispute.
[2] About Venezuela. See above, footnote, p. 192.

share in the spoil, arranged to support the attempt if successful. It failed and England with her hand on her heart protested absolute ignorance and virtuous surprise. The natural delight of the civilised world found expression in the open-hearted greeting of the generous emperor to the successful republic.

England, wild with fury at her failure and stung to madness with a guilty conscience, tries to deaden the cry of indignation from the civilized world and her own better citizens by wild and wanton abuse of the open-hearted greeting above named. The upshot is that the gold mines are saved and England unmasked.

In spite of all this abuse (which it is firmly believed is justified by the violence of the English press) I can't help thinking that there is no deep-rooted hostility to England. We haven't yet attained the dignity of a ' natural enemy.' The abuse would not be so violent, if we had. The German can't believe that we could really ' betray the Teutonic cause,' as they would put it, by joining their enemies."

Jan. 25, 1896.

To VILLIERS.

" It appears that (if rumour is to be trusted) the Emperor *did* fire off his telegram without consulting anyone, except as to details—and that the Foreign Office loyally accepted the responsibility. They are rather appalled at the result.

The Emperor is said to have consulted his Military Cabinet as to the force necessary to reduce the Transvaal and it was decided that England would have to send 60,000 men and that it would take six months. They don't appear to take a serious view of the American difficulty, but all the news I get privately is that it is very serious indeed. The feeling in the country is for war at any cost or on any pretext. The reason is inexplicable, except that they feel they must fight someone and that England is the only country worth fighting. But when the risk of a war comes near enough, and they see what they have to pay for their fun, they may think differently.

Perhaps the Germans are waiting for their chance. Waiting they are. The appeal for the navy falls rather flat and patriotism takes the form of newspaper articles and not of grants-in-aid. Meanwhile Bismarck takes the opportunity of recommending William to mind his own business.

A member of the Reichstag told me that the Emperor was prized most of all in France, next in England, and last in Germany. He judged everything from the outside—and his own military people had a low opinion of him and said that he viewed the army as supers in an opera. But he does attract a good deal of notice and the Berliners stand for hours waiting for him to pass in his carriage. I assure you he looks a good deal of a man riding along the line of his guards in a gold helmet and breastplate.

I'm sure it's correct to say of public opinion here that they regard war between us as impossible. That is the very reason of their violent abuse."

The subject of the Jameson Raid and its echoes may be closed with Spring Rice's comment in a letter to Mrs. Roosevelt—full as usual of messages about her children and family jokes.

" I wonder if Theodore maintains his interest in S. African affairs and which way his sympathies go ? We are all, officially, in transports of indignation over Jameson's proceedings, which certainly look without excuse. But he seems to be just the type of man that Theodore writes about."

The letter of Jan. 25 to Villiers contains a note on affairs of the Far East. Japan's victory over China on land only opened the way to the certainty of a new struggle—unless someone intervened.

I saw Aoki yesterday. He wants to go on to England and see people there. He says regeneration of China is hopeless. It must be done from without. If not done, Russia will be forced to annex all adjacent territories. Japan's army and England's fleet together are a combination quite invincible. Why don't they agree on a settlement of the Asiatic question ? Settlement should be—England, or England and Germany, to advance money sufficient to pay off all debts and charges as security to seize the administration, which they should manage together with the friendly assistance of Japan. If necessary, England to occupy Chusan or Shanghai. Japan would then be safe from the Russian occupation of Corea and the Pechili Gulf. At present with the Russian superiority at sea, and the degeneration of China—Japan had no hope of preventing the inevitable catastrophe. But England ought to take steps soon. —He was very much in earnest. . . .

Armenia now began to engage attention. A joint note from England, France and Russia presented to the Porte had demanded certain reforms ; but on the day when a decree promulgated the Porte's concession of these, European witnesses from a steamer off Trebizond watched a fresh slaughter, which other places emulated. Lord Salisbury promised information to Parliament and Villiers had the task of preparing it.

Feb. 1, 1896.

To VILLIERS.

" How glad you must be that the Armenian Blue Book is out at last. For your benefit, we sent the criticisms of the German press. The argument seems to be : ' So only 700 were killed, inclusive of those who died of starvation ! The English press has been lying all along—as usual. And Chamberlain made a speech in which he quietly ignored these official revelations. Only 700 ! And the Turks might have killed so many more, for they were dreadfully provoked, poor things. What a spectacle of moral depravity ? England got up the massacres herself, and then exaggerated them and then said it was the fault of the Turks, and then tried to get other powers to help her because she hadn't the courage to play her dirty game herself ! Poor, dear Sultan, how badly he has been treated. And how wise the Czar was to join (apparently) with England, in order to watch her closely and stop her if necessary. Good wise man ! And how clever of our Government not to be lured on by those cunning English ! '

It is hard to believe, but it is the actual fact that this is the official view, officially stated in a paper drawn up in the press department of the Foreign Office ! And to a certain extent the view is genuine.—There are other elements that come in, it is true, but this, I think, is what has happened. England refused to join the Dreibund. Very well ; that was taken for granted. But when the Armenian commission was established, it looked very much like England joining the Zweibund.[1] This was insupportable and Germany watched her time. It wasn't very hard to break up the apparent understanding. The German papers pointed out that England had opposed the emancipation of Bulgaria because she had believed it was for the interest of Russia ; when she found it wasn't, she saw that she had made a mistake. And hence her advocacy of the Armenian Christians, for it was plainly easier to make an independent state of Armenia than of Bulgaria where the race sympathies with Russia are so strong. And this was plainly the object of England in crying out ' Atrocities ! '

You are quite right (to judge by common report) that the Sultan has paid a large sum of money to the German press ; but the German Government is also in the business, and the *Nord Deutsche* is just as much the official organ of the Turks as of the Germans.

Things are in a curious state here. The Emperor is said to be very keen about the navy. That indeed is certain. In the

[1] Of Russia and France.

meantime the Ministry are not particularly stable, and the Emperor is again said to be getting restive. ' It's not only his kicking, but he's never kicking the same way twice,' as the groom said. . . . There are as many stories in Berlin as in Rome under Tiberius.

A curious scene took place in one of the big streets. An ' Altesse ' went into a shop and ordered a whip. To try it, he bribed the shop boy to let himself be whipped, so much a cut. He paid in a princely manner. Then a cabman offered his services. He was paid too. As a crowd gathered, the prince was requested to move on. The Socialist paper publishes this under the heading ' Human Dignity.' The Conservative paper publishes a statement by the shop boy and the coachman, saying that they both enjoyed it. Great outcry."

To VILLIERS.   Feb. 22, 1896.

" The papers here are beginning to lose their muzzles and to confess, on the authority of the Ambassadors, that a certain number of murders *have* taken place after all (in Armenia).

The view of the papers and politicians, as far as one can see, is that Russia has only to wait for the ripening of China and Turkey, and that as time works for her, she can afford to do nothing. She would bestir herself only for two purposes—either to prevent any attempt at arresting the ripening process, or else to prevent anyone else stealing the fruit. Imagine, as a man said to me, a bear sitting under a tree waiting for the apples to drop, and you have a picture of Russia now.

According to the Germans, what England tried to do was to arrest the ripening process. How could England expect Russia to join her in saving a portion of Turkey from the decay which is Russia's first interest ? Again in Macedonia : Bulgaria will certainly be prevented from organizing insurrections or instituting reforms. Macedonia, with all the Turkish Empire yet remaining independent, is to be ruled by Turkey until Turkey's misrule makes it necessary for Russia to take her empire over. Every part of Turkey that is at peace and prosperous is so much territory lost to Russia. Look at the difference between Bulgaria and the rest of Turkey, from the Russian point of view. Russia is far less powerful, even now, in Sofia, than at Constantinople. That is what the Russian papers mean when they say that ' Russia has ceased long ago to take a special interest in Bulgaria—her thoughts are cast on larger things.'

We are asking a man to prescribe for an invalid, when he is heir as well as doctor.

This is the view which is accepted by the German Government, on the ground that it implies peace in the East for a certain number of years at any rate. Russia will rule the Turkish Empire through the Sultan and the *status quo* will be maintained. All revolutions will be suppressed if they can't be prevented. No territorial change of any sort will be allowed. It is the most natural line for Russia to take. Every revolution in Turkey has cost Russia hitherto ' blood and treasure ' to begin with, and prestige and power afterwards. She would have done much better not to assist in the disintegration of Turkey ; for she would have been heir to the whole property in the end.

The feeling of this Government for Russia is, of course, very strong. From the time of the negotiations at Vienna in 1815 when Prussia and Russia were united against England, France and Austria, to the time when the old Czar in 1870 promised his support in case of defeat from France, the two Governments have been in reality close friends. Especially if the Socialists get the upper hand, or if a counter revolution is attempted, Russia's help will be all-valuable to the Government. And then, as long as Russia is not actively hostile, Germany feels safe from outside enemies. All this points to inaction and quiet in the East for some time to come ; as to the Far East, the Czar has a personal interest in affairs there which may hurry on events ; and there, there is no Austria to be considered, and Germany will be considered without too much repining. English interests suffer. After all, Germany must be paid somewhere for all she has done, and will probably get something in that quarter of the world.

Society goes on being very kind to us, but the language they use about England, when we are not there, is appalling. The only friend we have is the Socialist, Bebel !

The Emperor swears he will win back all his popularity in England and beat the Prince of Wales with an English-built yacht. But otherwise his temper has been very bad. He wasn't allowed to send Herbette [1] away, and so in order to avoid meeting him, he retired to his hunting-box and absolutely refused to give a ball. The young ladies were all furious and the Ministers were anxious, as when he goes into the country he talks politics with his aides-de-camp and does what they tell him ; as the A.D.C.s are politicians of the Prussian League type, with wine in it, the Ministers are naturally anxious. However he has behaved rather well lately, and people are breathing free again. But for some time it was believed that he would publicly insult Herbette at Court in his own palace.

---

[1] The French Ambassador, whom the Kaiser disliked.

Another Prince is leaving, having had to give up his command for an offence against discipline. I wonder any remain in Berlin."

March 14, 1896.

To VILLIERS.

"The circumstances of the Imperial visit,[1] as far as I saw them, were—that there was a crowd before the Embassy. Three carriages drove rapidly up. Policemen started up from the ground in every direction. The first carriage stopped and a uniformed gentleman stepped out, followed by another, whom I recognised as the Emperor. He was met on the steps by Sir Frank, who escorted him up the stairs, laughing and talking. The crowd observed in stolid silence. Among them I noticed a peculiar-looking Russian who had been for a long time at my hotel, doing I don't know what. He came up and asked all manner of questions. I went to a party and came back. The Emperor was with the ladies. I could hear him talking and laughing away. He talked continually, giving hardly any time to answer—about ' grand mamma ' and Cowes, and Lord Dunraven and his journey in Cumberland. This was about 12.30 and he had come at 10. Then he rose, asked if he could have a cigar and a whisky and soda, and back he went to Sir F.'s room where he talked, walking about rather excitedly, with gesticulations—not waiting for an answer. We waited and waited. No move. At last, at 1.30 a.m. he got up and went.

This is intended to obliterate his conduct to Malet. He maintains that the whole matter [2] has been fictitious—that the expedition was got up by three German Jews who have also bought the *Times*, ' he knows it.' ' I know the men and the money they gave.' He thinks it absurd and dreadful that such influences could sever two countries united by such common interests.

In the meanwhile the fleet-enthusiasts are working away but without much success. Something has been done and the way has been paved for future action. So much good has come out of the Transvaal business for the Government. He is determined to go to Cowes if he can, but his advisers are not sure that it is wise. He gets bad reports still from Hatzfeldt,[3] but is hopeful. A Kammerherr or Court official told me when in a state of semi-intoxication that he expected to have to come here in June or July because the Czar would pay a visit to Berlin then.

[1] To the British Ambassador.   [2] The Jameson Raid.
[3] German Ambassador in London.

The next letter is written after the French Government had rejected Lord Salisbury's proposals for concerted action on the Nile.

March 21, 1896.

To VILLIERS.

" Everything has changed here in a twinkling of an eye. A week ago the French were beaming on us and as happy as larks ; the Germans, on the other hand (to judge by the newspapers) were growling as deep as they dared and longing to bite. Suddenly the French are depressed and angry, and the German newspapers almost friendly. The change is miraculous. I hope that it pleases Her Majesty's Government. From the German point of view, it is easily explained by Lord Cromer's remark that for the next six months we shall have to be on good terms with Germany—for which privilege we shall have as usual to pay. Somebody asked the other day : ' At any rate, if England is not very good friends with Germany, is she still less friends with France ? ' The fear that led to the knuckle-down of Germany was the rumour of the abandonment of Egypt and the *rapprochement* to France. We were, it was supposed, on the point of being absolutely free to do what we liked. And therefore Germany would not be able to take advantage of our weak point to get what she wanted. Now, not only is friendship with France impossible but, as is believed, England is irretrievably engaged ; for they believe that the defeat of fellaheen troops is inevitable, and that British troops will have to be employed. This makes us almost a negligible factor in S. Africa.

The real and deep-seated object of the German Colonial party is to find some part of the world where Germans can emigrate to and live as Germans. They look on South Africa, if ruled by the Dutch element, as such a place, and therefore they all do everything possible to keep up the strength of the Dutch element ; they would gladly surrender all interest in the Nile valley for the sake of the Transvaal.

The other deep and abiding feeling that I think every German has is the fear of the defection of neutral powers to the side of France ; they think England is capable of this, and that she will bring Italy with her. Now, they think themselves secure from this danger, and indeed it looks like it. Now, they can breathe free again. They can give us their support in order to assist us to play their game, and, as they think, exhaust ourselves ; and they can make us pay for it—in Samoa, or Africa— who knows which.

I saw the Emperor yesterday riding back from the park with
a gorgeous staff behind him.   He rides in uniform, looking no
end of a boss and the faithful Berliners stay about for hours
waiting to see him pass.   Indeed, it is a sight worth seeing.
He gave a most cordial smile to Sir F. as he passed.   No wonder.
He has the reputation of persuading us into the Soudan in his
three hours' interview."

The Germans proved to be mistaken about fellaheen troops when
the step which Lord Salisbury had proposed to take in concert with
France was taken without her.

On March 1 the Abyssinians routed an Italian army at Adowa, and
Dervishes immediately threatened Kassala, an Italian outpost.   It
was announced in Parliament on March 16 that troops would advance
from Wady Halfa to Dongola, so as to check this recurrence of war
in the Soudan.

Up to this time, British statesmen had spoken of the withdrawal of
British forces from Egypt as a thing that would be accomplished at
the first moment convenient.   This new forward movement evidently
tended to postpone the evacuation, and France and Russia combined
with Germany to defeat (through their representatives on the international Caisse de la Dette) the proposed allocation of half a million
for Egyptian funds.   England, however, found the money, and after
two successful engagements fellaheen troops under Sir Herbert
Kitchener occupied Dongola.

But Spring Rice did not like the venture.   He had a fear of the
Soudan in his bones since the time when he served under Lord Granville.

March 21, 1896.

To STEPHEN.

" This Egyptian business beats cock-fighting.   It turns us all
upside down here.   No doubt they are justified, but, goodness
me, from our point of view, it is hell.

The Germans have three votes on the Caisse.   Now, as we
are making Egypt bankrupt, Germany has, through Egypt, our
tail between her teeth and can give it a bite whenever we don't
do what she wants.   Also, as we are now hopelessly estranged
from France, there is no longer any fear of our joining the
Zweibund—the German nightmare—the fear which put the
tail of Germany between *our* teeth.

Also, as we are bound, so they think, to employ English
troops, we shall be well and throughly occupied in North Africa
and will have no time to spare for S. Africa—which they value
1000 times more, as Germans can live there.   The Germans,

remember, emigrate and want a healthy place to emigrate to where they will continue speaking German and drinking beer. It looks as if S. Africa were their only chance—under Dutch rule, of course.

Altogether things have gone amazingly well for Germany and I suppose they are only now looking round to see what they are going to make us pay.   I expect Samoa.[1]

And we say in Parliament that it is to help Italy.   Why then at Egypt's expense and with Egyptian men ?   What's Rome to the fellaheen ?   And in Egypt we say it's to protect Egypt. But why not wait till we are attacked ?   The desert is a good friend to have on one's side, and whoever has the desert to cross has the desert against them.   Who has been consulted ? What influence has been brought to bear ?   What is Lord Salisbury !   My goodness, how I love and respect our glorious Government !   Excuse a somewhat excited view of present affairs, but as I was in the private secretary's room at the time of Khartoum I cannot *quite* get it out of my head."

April 18, 1896.
To VILLIERS.

" Everyone here is talking about the Kotze duel.   Poor Emperor !   He seems to be made responsible for everything. The Military Court condemned Kotze for having sued Schroder for libel instead of having challenged him.   The Brigade General who signed the judgment of the Court without consulting the Emperor was dismissed, and he and his wife (Prince and Princess of Hohenzollern) are now travelling in Italy.   The Emperor changed the decision of the Court into a ' warning ' and Kotze had to fight.   He had already fought one of his accusers, who had apologized after having severely wounded him ;   Schroder, however, had persisted in his accusations. So after Easter the duel took place and Schroder is killed after suffering such fearful agonies that his family weren't allowed to go near his room for some time.   The Emperor, as you may remember, imprisoned Kotze on his own responsibility, but liberated and made amends when an enquiry had acquitted him.

It seems true that Austria and Italy are pressing Germany to support us ;   that the Emperor himself is using every means

[1] The Samoan islands at this time had an autonomy guaranteed by England, the United States, and Germany.   There was much friction between the three powers.   In 1899 the islands were divided between Germany and the United States.   Great Britain received the cession of German rights in the Solomons.   This agreement was reached after the outbreak of the South African War.

that presents itself to make signs of friendliness to us. But the influences against an understanding with England are very strong. The entourage of the Emperor, the East Prussians, hate us as representatives of a constitutional monarchy. The underground inspirer of the Foreign Office—Holstein—is using all his influence against us too. Articles like those in the *Morning Post* are instruments in the hands of our enemies here. Of course the Germans are delighted at our being occupied in Egypt and are now directing their attention to South Africa where they hope, at last, to see our influence permanently overthrown.''

April 25, 1896.

To STEPHEN.

'' . . . All Berlin now is occupied with the duel and the Reichstag debate. It is the first time that people in society have shown any interest whatever in the Reichstag and they went there in swarms. The Emperor seems to have done his best to stop the scandal once he had become convinced that he had been mistaken, but it is impossible for him to run counter to military feeling in the country, which is the conviction of an exclusive caste and not to be altered by any influence whatever. The Socialists rejoice in the opportunity of saying disagreeable things. At the end of his speech, Bebel, the Socialist leader, after resuming the various inequalities of the law as affecting rich and poor, said that he did not for a moment intend to complain. ' You are sowing, and we reap.' An appeal to the country is quite out of the question, as there seems no doubt that the socialist vote is growing, and therefore the Government will have to get on as well as it can with its present Reichstag. That is, it will have to be content to see all its Bills defeated one after the other. This is an excellent constitution for doing nothing whatever, and for making the Government reckless and the deputies irresponsible. . . . ''

May 2, 1896.

To VILLIERS.

'' Lord Lonsdale has been here. He came to see the new exhibition and the Emperor's horses. It is rather embarrassing for them. The Emperor asks him what a horse is worth and he tells him his opinion. Then the Emperor repeats what Lord Lonsdale has said to the Master of the Horse who has probably given twice as much. The E. told Ld. L. that he never intended to go to Cowes and will not. He will enter his yacht. He thought of having a crew half German and half English. Ld. L. told him that if he did so they would fight ; if he had a German crew, he wouldn't have a chance of winning ; so he advised him to have an entirely English crew.

There has been for some time a crisis brewing of rather a serious kind. All the Cabinet and the Chamber want the Military Courts reformed. The Emperor's Military Staff and his personal friends are opposed to the reform and now, it is said, have succeeded in shelving it. The moderate Liberal and moderate Conservative papers are furious and breathe vengeance agains the ' unofficial advisers of the Crown.' It is impossible that the Ministers will remain satisfied with a state of things by which an absent Emperor is continually under the influence of a clique of sportsmen and officers.''

Late in that autumn Prince Bismarck's organs published two documents, the first of which, dated 1877, showed that Wilhelm I. had, on Bismarck's advice, decided to support Russia in the Russo-Turkish war by a benevolent neutrality ; and the second stated that a secret treaty between Germany and Russia had existed from 1887 to 1890 but had been allowed to lapse when Caprivi replaced Bismarck as Chancellor. It was also stated that Caprivi had acted under British influence ; and the conclusion was drawn that Russia had been led into alliance with France in consequence of Germany's change of policy. Spring Rice comments on this.

Nov. 7, 1896.

To VILLIERS.

" What an extraordinary business this revelation has been ! Everyone agrees that it was simply the result of spite against the Emperor, to make it appear that he was responsible for the Franco-Russian alliance. The Emperor is quite furious and swore death and murder when he heard it. As soon as he returned he sent for Marschall and Hohenlohe and vented his wrath in their presence. Prince Albert,[1] our informant in Court matters, says the language used was pretty strong. The odd thing is that most people seem to regard the Treaty as rather a smart thing and think that Bismarck could make another of the same sort if he came back to power. Now, one thing about it struck me a good deal. It was made in 1884, and in 1885 the Penjdeh incident occurred.[2] All that time Germany was doing her best to urge both parties to make war—at

[1] Of Schleswig-Holstein.

[2] In April 1885 while preparations for delineating the boundaries of Afghanistan were on foot, Russian forces attacked Afghan troops at Penjdeh. The Amir appealed for, and was promised, British support. Mr. Gladstone proposed a vote of credit for eleven millions, with a view to war. Russia withdrew at the last moment.

least Morier used to say that the Russians told him so ; and I remember well the tone of the Germans at that time, for I used to see Plessen, Bismarck's brother-in-law, constantly. If we had gone to war with Russia, Germany would undoubtedly have helped to keep the Dardanelles shut, as far as influence on the Turks was concerned, and in the state of our relations at that time the alliance was practically one against England. It is certainly so regarded here, and the Emperor is accused of having in 1890 sacrificed the Russian alliance for the chimerical hope of an understanding with England. In private conversation I have often heard people say that the old man was right and that the natural and necessary ally of Germany was Russia.

At the close of the year he wrote to his old Eton tutor :

To MR. LAXMOORE.

" Berlin is not bad. There are splendid concerts and excellent theatres and the way they give Shakespeare is superb. Then they are not afraid of writing modern historical dramas with fine moral sentiments and warlike and patriotic utterances in the good old style—or else fairy stories with polite significance. For instance, our old friend ' the Emperor's new clothes ' comes into a drama which is supposed to reflect on our present august sovereign. The political world is in a highly excitable condition and is almost entirely inspired by envy, hatred, malice and all uncharitableness. When they are tired of abusing each other, they pitch into us. What a chorus of hatred and calumny rises around us like a fountain day and night ! Do we deserve it ? I suppose if we ceased to be successful we should cease to be abused. But as it is, the hatred and abuse is most unquestioned, and we ought to be prepared, and young people ought to know that if they want to enjoy their country long, they must be prepared to suffer for it if needs be. I wish people would learn defensive patriotism—that is to love their own mothers without abusing other people's.

These people are exactly the contrary ; they have a perpetual well of malice springing in their hearts. It doesn't make an Englishman's love for his country less.—On the whole I think Wordsworth's sonnets are the best patriotic utterances we have in our language."

His more generalised thought in this period was given to his American friends ; first to Roosevelt, who was now President of the Board of Police Commissioners in New York (appointed by a reforming Mayor), and endeavouring to put down blackmail.

" MY DEAR THEODORE,

I wish I could see you now and hear you talking politics
with Cabot. What a time you must be having ! I wonder
what will be the end of it. I hope that one end of it will be that
you will get something extremely nice in Washington—if you
wish to go back, and if not, something that will give you a
change in New York. You must have been working yourself
to death. At any rate, you have fought as fine a fight as has
ever been fought in New York—and you were ' ever a fighter.'
Have you time to see the children in the day time ? How long
is it since you climbed trees with them ? Have you been up to
the top of the windmill again with them ? I can shut my eyes
and see every corner of the garden and the glimpses of water and
the ' big Fall river steamers ' and the tree you cut down.
Dear me, when shall I see it again ? What a delightful time
I had then—I wish it had all been turned to better account,
but still it *was* delightful being idle then. I couldn't have
stayed on in Washington. I see Sir Julian is still there,
and I should have been a greenish corpse by now—even the
heat here turns me up. The worst of it is that it makes
it very doubtful whether I can ever make much of my career
now, for, if I can't stand the heat, going to Zanzibar or Egypt
is out of the question—and our best posts are there or in like
places.

Let me tell you what I am about now. It is hard to believe
that this life is tolerable and yet it is. First of all, I have a
respectable home, that is, a lodging with a servant, where I
have breakfast, sleep, read, and as you see, occasionally write.
I have my pictures and books here. I share it with a Colonel,
our military attaché. He is a man of my age, as tough as
nails, has been in six wars and travelled all over the world.
His old colonel and first teacher in the art of war came to stay
here and they yarned away for a week. The Colonel's furniture
is military pictures of the proceedings of his Scotch regiment in
various parts of the world, and of his brother officers ; various
arms, trophies of war, which he won in battle from people who
tried to use them against the Scotch regiment; and one armchair.
In a stable below he keeps a mare and six dogs. He knows
Rudyard Kipling's ballads better than you do, but has a most
hearty contempt for all sorts of literature except military
history. He has a soldier servant whom he discovered looking
at an artillery regiment practising. He was shaking his head
and saying ' Poor chaps, poor chaps.' Grierson asked him what

was the matter. He said, ' They can't ride and they can't dress—and, oh Gawd, did you see their saddles.'

As a matter of fact the soldiers one sees (and regiments go by every day) look splendidly—marching well out, and looking proud and pleased. It must in the long run be good for a nation to take all the young men of a certain age for two years— clean them, feed them, drill them, teach them obedience and patriotism, and train their bodies. The officers are rather different to ours. A prince (and there are numbers of them) has to do exactly what the others do—that is, get up at five and work at his men and his own training till four in the afternoon. Each captain is personally responsible for all the men under him, whom he has to know, and the Government is pitiless to anyone whose men are not up to the scratch. I saw in the papers that an officer who was conducting the gymnasium drill scoffed at one of his men who wouldn't or couldn't do a certain jump. The man made a violent attempt and ruptured himself and was taken away dying. The officer went on parade that day, seemed perfectly indifferent—and shot himself the same afternoon.

The Emperor affords us endless amusement with his goings-on. He was anxious to be civil to us, I mean the English ; so, some admirals coming this way, he invited them to a review of cavalry. There were 4000 or more. He led them himself. Rain had fallen heavily and part of the land they rode over was deep in water. The swell regiment, cuirassiers in white uniform were in the middle and had to charge through—the Emperor at their head. The water got into their high boots ! Many horses went over and swords and helmets were lost. The white uniforms were completely spoilt. Coming back, they charged past the admirals who had to take shelter behind convenient trees as the horses rushed past ; a fat one, who got a small tree, got a smack with a scabbard on the stomach. One of the men fell on a lance of a man in front who had fallen and the lance went slap through his leg. There was no surgeon. The Emperor, of course, helped to bind him up. He doesn't steer his own yacht—but he pulls a rope and says he will steer next year. Wouldn't you like to have 5000 cavalry to gallop about ?

I think the Russians have got China now whenever they like ; when they command and drill the Northern Chinese they will be a pretty big power—such a power as the world has never seen. They are quite conscious of it and mean to wait. They also mean to have a Government and civilization of their own. No suffrage—no liberty of religion or any nonsense of that sort. I wonder if they will succeed. I fear we shan't live to see."

Here is Roosevelt's answer :

POLICE DEPARTMENT OF THE CITY OF NEW YORK,
Aug. 5, 1896.

" DEAR CECIL,

You would have been well repaid for your trouble in writing if you had seen the eagerness with which Mrs. Roosevelt and I read and re-read your letter and repeated parts of it to the children. As you know, we are not fond of many people, and we are very fond of you ; and if you don't come back to America for ten years, yet, whenever you do, you will find us just as anxious to see you as we always were in the old days at Washington. Funnily enough, just about four days prior to the arrival of your letter we were talking you over apropos of Willie Phillips, who was spending a week with us in the house, and were saying that he, Bob Ferguson [1] and perhaps Grant La Farge, were the only people who approached you in our minds as being guests whom we really liked to have stay for no matter how long a time in the house. Mrs. Roosevelt always refers to your last visit as one during which she got steadily to be more and more glad that you were in the house, so that she felt as if one of the family had gone when you left. . . . "

In that autumn Spring Rice went on leave, and from Ullswater he wrote to his friends in America about things which he saw more in perspective when he stood back from them. The United States was already feeling the throes of a Presidential Election in which Harrison for the Republicans was to be opposed by Mr. W. J. Bryan, the eloquent advocate of free silver.—The first is to Henry Adams, once more on his travels ; and by this time Spring Rice had adopted the name given by the young Hays and Lodges to this universal uncle.

OLD CHURCH, ULLSWATER,
Aug. 24, 1896.

" MY DEAR UNCLE HENRY,

Why on earth didn't you write before or visit Germany earlier ? I should have brought you to see the most beautiful places and hear the most lovely music, etc., etc. Everything is pleasant in parts of Germany except the women. But perhaps you are the sort that thinks women only are worth anything—

Since I saw you I have been learning the German language and institutions. You will be glad to hear that the British nation is even more disliked in Germany than it is in America— and the Government papers treat the British Empire in the

---

[1] Younger brother of Ronald Ferguson : he had settled in America.
S.R.L.   O

style of language of the *New York Sun*. I suppose you are
delighted at your year-long prophecies coming true at last, and
America being face to face with Jefferson II. Will they elect
him and see the result ? The race is so pre-eminently sporting
that it seems not improbable, from that point of view. England
and Germany are in a fairly peaceful condition—Germany being
solely occupied with making money. I should think that never
since man began to adorn the universe, was a whole nation so
entirely and exclusively engaged in the occupation of money
making. To call the Americans and the English dollar-wor-
shippers ! An occasional flirtation in face of a constant and
unswerving devotion !

An immense screed to Roosevelt shows the range of interests
common to the two men. After a discussion on America's financial
position, which reads oddly now, some thirty years later, Spring Rice
passes to a sweeping review of Europe, and we see how forces bulked
then in his eyes.—Russia was the Colossus : Japan had not as yet
shown that its feet were of clay. Then, for his American friend,
known to him in the American's home country, he writes of his own
place, his own upbringing, his own people, and their sport.

PATTERDALE HALL, PENRITH,
Sept. 14, 1896.

" MY DEAR THEODORE,

I can't thank you enough for your letter. It was most
welcome and it was splendid of you to have written amid all
your work and worry. What a time you must be having. I
can't help believing in the sense of the American people, and
even if the others are successful now or four years hence, success
will probably convert them into something quite different.
As for the financial question, it appears that owing to the small
amount of interest paid on the foreign debt and the high price
of cotton, gold is going back to America in the ordinary course
of trade. This means that the danger of a depletion is probably
over. In that case the situation will right itself and from the
practical point of view there will be more confidence in the
Government. On the whole, though it is not so pleasant, it is
far safer to be in debt to other people than to live on other
people's debts to you, which is the case in some European
countries. In one case it's one's own work ; in the other
it's other people's and there can be no question which is worse for
national character.

I wonder what you would think of the European situation.
It looks like the gathering of great forces for a struggle, not in
the immediate (that would be better) but in the far future. We

all seem struggling for the honour of kissing the Czar's feet. Germany is as servile as France and (if it weren't so evidently useless) I shouldn't wonder if England would be as servile as Germany. Other European powers are not self-sufficient—live on trade or imported food. Peace is almost a necessity. Absolutely so for Germany, for her navy couldn't protect her commerce, and a good part of her trade is with Russia. But Russia is self-sufficient. She is also practically invulnerable to attack. She is growing and has room to grow. She is also gradually acquiring command over warlike races with which she can carry out a sort of military assimilation, for which her constitution is specially fitted. Owing to Alsace and Lorraine, Europe is hopelessly divided, and it looks as if commercial and colonial jealousies would divide England and Germany in a similar manner. Taking all these things together, it is not at all improbable that Europe may be in a given period at the mercy of a power really barbarous but with a high military organization. Europe is busy providing Russia with the means of perfecting that organisation and the communications to bind the Empire together. And no power will attack Russia —no one can afford to. Russia therefore has simply to bide her time. If America disintegrates, as some Americans maintain is possible—or if it goes mad like Spanish America—the future of the world is not improbably in the hands of the Slavs. No one now can prevent Mongolia passing into their hands and that is one of the best fields for recruiting in the world. I suppose all is for the best in this best possible of worlds, and that nations will be punished deservedly ; however—

I was brought up in this house and in this room I used to have lessons from my governess—whom I know I used to make cry very pitiably. The room is almost in the same situation as it was left by my grandfather, who was a Whig Member of Parliament, and the son of a Whig Member. There is, of course, a portrait of Napoleon. Also an engraving of Johnson's club with the doctor speaking into Reynolds's ear-trumpet. The books are distinctly Whig. I opened one at random and found this interesting passage : Jan. 27, 1806.— "At last ' the extravagant and erring spirit hath hied to his dark confine,' covered with the lavished blood of slaughtered millions and answerable for the anguish of millions surviving to mourn the slain." (In a note)—" Alluding to the death of Mr. Pitt."

I am living generally about six miles off down the lake.[1] We had an old cousin, Aubrey de Vere, staying with us—one of the

---

[1] At Old Church.

few surviving friends of Wordsworth, and for us the only one left of his generation. I went with him over the old places and gardens which he seems to love as much as ever.

Do you remember the possum hunt ? I thought of you this morning (as a fact, I must think of you pretty nearly every day on one occasion or the other). I got up early and went out on the fells. The huntsmen had collected the hounds together (they are boarded out in the summer) and went after a fox which had been worrying sheep. They threw off in a wood near the house—old trees with wide stretches of grass between and steep running streams. They went slowly at first as the scent was bad, making their way up the hill. We followed on foot as well as we could. The huntsman (a man of fifty), their keeper with the two terriers in the leash, and three or four farmer's sons. When we got to the top of the hill we could see the hounds tailing off in a long line along the high fell side, making a beautiful noise which the echoes from the rocks made the most of. Then they disappeared. I followed up a second higher hill. The fox had got into a terribly bad place among the crags and had found his earth, that is, a crevice in the rocks, and the terriers were called into service. Once they found two foxes together and as there were only two terriers and the foxes fought together, one over the other in a narrow crevice, full in view though far below, the dogs had a bad time. The foxes and one of the dogs were killed.

There is a famous old dog called Spearman who acts as whipper in. Of course, the hounds get away from the men at once. Spearman keeps order and is a treasure at a check. He has a habit of going round the farms in the evening and gathering a few hounds together and going for a hunt on his own account. I have heard them at midnight in full cry on the mountains opposite. They come back bloody in the morning. This is quite true. Often they get right away if the fox can't get back to his own mountains and goes straight across the hills. They ran once for nine hours and killed, I don't know how many miles away. The shepherds and farmers along the valleys hear them coming, join in as far as they can—and so one hears news of the fray. The dogs generally come straight home by themselves if not too tired, or ask hospitality of the farmers. I remember one, tired and bloody, running up to an inn where I was staying. He was fed, given a bed, and set off next morning. Once I saw two together on Helvellyn. One was lame ; the other ran on, stopped, came back, nosed his friend, ran on again. I told him he was a good dog, which he received indifferently. He brought news to the huntsmen who were overjoyed. It was one of his best dogs, which had been lost for three days. The others had come back without him. Spearman is the best-known character in the whole valley. He is getting rather old, but you will be glad to hear that he has a son, Codale, who, though ' a bit wild ' (youth is impetuous) has wits in him. But, of course, he will never be up to his father. The huntsman, as I said, is over fifty. He says he is a ' bit puffy,' but you should just see him going up hill. Long thin legs, shuffling gait, no change up or down hill. Three years ago there was a terrible tragedy near Coniston. The fox went over a crag with some of the best dogs after him. All were found dead together. These were not the Patterdale hounds, but John Peel's old pack.

The sun at last ! How are the bunnies ? How I wish I could suddenly turn up and see you all. Have you enjoyed yourself in the West ? You needed it if anyone did. What a fight you have had ! I know, hard as it is, you enjoyed it. Successful or no, you have made a good fight out of it. If you can't show them a good city government, you can show them a brave, honest man. Best love to Mrs. Roosevelt and the bunnies. I wish they were all here. I know they would love this place and the trees and lake and mountains. Though to be sure there is no windmill to climb up. But the rocks are quite high enough to break one's neck. By the way, I find I have lost my mountain head, since I was giddy—which is a bore. How you would hate it.

Yours affectionately,

C. S. R."

During this visit to England, he had made friends with his friend's bride, and henceforward Lady Helen Ferguson was one of his regular correspondents.

BERLIN,
Dec. 26, 1896.

" DEAR LADY HELEN,

Happy New Year ! I hope you will have enjoyed your Xmas. I wonder who was with you. Oh, I forget, a good Scotchman doesn't keep Xmas. Tell me, however, what you did.

Let me see what I have done since I saw you. First of all— never said good-bye ; but after doing that, or not doing that, I don't know that I didn't do, or did do, anything remarkable. I have read a large number of offensive articles in German newspapers and written reports showing how British commerce is being destroyed, etc., etc. One morning I was engaged in that pleasant occupation when a pale servant raced in and said

Seine Majestät der Kaiser was in the Embassy and the Ambassador in bed! I had to go and calm His Majesty whom I found rampaging about with a clattering sword—confidential print lying everywhere about; and he immediately announced his intention of seeing the Ambassador in bed. I rushed up to announce the august visitor and found the Ambassador in pink pyjamas, two horror-stricken servants rushing about his room. He said he would be down at once if the Emperor would wait, but it was a difficult matter to get him to do that; however, he consented and in five minutes an unwashed and strangely apparelled Ambassador shot down the stairs. Shortly after a telegram was demanded, and, of course, it was lost. The delay gave the Emperor huge enjoyment and he asked whether Sir Frank's secretaries were as bad as his own aides-de-camp. Such were the Imperial words which will naturally live for ever in my mind. Shortly afterwards the Emperor visited (owing to a shifting of the scenes) the French and Russians. I wonder whether the lost telegram had anything to do with it. If it wasn't high treason (and you weren't a woman) I would send you a truthful representation of the Emperor waiting for the Ambassador, reading, to pass the time, ' le Grand Napoléon pour de petits enfants,' with a lively representation of the other Kaiser riding through the Brandenburger Gate."

There is much of Spring Rice's characteristic thought in his letters to the Roosevelts concerning a book by their friend Brooks Adams.

" I don't approve of that way of writing history," he wrote to Roosevelt in July 1896. " I'm sick of theories. Everyone has a new prescription for humanity and a new diagnosis. They all begin with the Roman Empire and point out resemblances. The Roman Empire fell because there was no one left to fight for it; as long as we are born and live and are prepared to fight in sufficient numbers, I don't see that the present world is much like the age of the Antonines. At any rate the Roosevelt family are numerous and warlike."

At Christmas he came back to the book, in a letter to Mrs. Roosevelt.

" It is a fascinating book without doubt and one ought to be obliged to anyone who makes political economy interesting. But I don't think it's fair, when one is dealing with facts, to be continually appealing to passion. It would be easy (and has been easy) to write an equally strong book on the other side. For instance—' the imaginative Empire of Spain.' No doubt it was a great act of self-sacrifice and devotion to principle when Philip, knowing that it would be the ruin of his kingdom, condemned the Netherlands to destruction and, with one stroke of the pen, two millions of his subjects to death. The evidence is good that he knew what the result would be, and that without the wealth of the Netherlands he would be unable to make head against his European enemies. He sacrificed that for his religion. But if that was a good act, what are we to take for our criterion of wrong and right? First of all, we are human beings, we are also Protestants and free men, and if we are, for the sake of illustrating an economical thesis, to throw over the traditions to which we owe everything we are, we forfeit our right to profit by the achievements won by those traditions. A happy husband and father of a family has no right, it seems to me, to argue as to the advisability or the validity of the ordinance of marriage. Either his argument is absurd or his life is. I don't think the Ten Commandments are played out, and I don't believe that people who say so are pleasant people to live with. The best master of paradox I ever knew was Oscar Wilde. It will take a long time to beat him and I don't think it is a worthy ambition to be one of his inferior followers. I am probably boring you, but I write to you because I always think that you are one of the people who have fixed ideas, which ideas are also things and actions, and that you don't think these fit subjects for argument.

It is a thing which one should do, if possible, to see the Roman wall—the old limits of the Empire within which everything was prosperity and peace. One can't help asking why it should ever have ended as it did. Gibbon gives a pretty satisfactory answer in his chapter on the Empire as Constantine found it. One of the signs of the decline was the monetary question. But it was only a sign. A man who doesn't exercise will develop some malady in the liver or heart or something: but that is not the real evil."

In May 1897 he was still on the question—Why did Rome fall? All historians in Germany agreed that failure of population—however produced—was the cause. He writes to Roosevelt.

"The question is, how far is our civilisation tending that way? The tendency of the more cultivated classes not to have children has always been the case—as one can see, for instance, by looking at *Burke's Peerage*; a most interesting genealogical collection. As soon as luxury becomes general and wars and pestilences kept in control, children aren't the boon that they were in other times. But as yet there is only one country—France—where the population is going backwards. England and Germany are increasing more slowly and probably will cease to increase at all. Russia has the largest ratio of increase. But as a general statement it would be false to say that the present condition of things was at all like the Roman Empire.

As regards property ; you will see by the income tax returns here and in England that there is an enormous increase of middle fortunes, and a decrease of the number and amount of big fortunes ; the most striking increase is in the sums in safety banks—deposited in small amounts. So that the assumption that a capital class is exploiting the masses is evidently untrue. What is true is that the collections of money belonging to many small holders are directed by a few brains and give great power to small circles ; but the small people are not starved and share in the profits—if they didn't, the pecuniary tendency would be the opposite of what it is. In both Germany and England the weight of taxation falls most heavily —almost exclusively—on the rich and leaves the poor untouched. . . . The fact is, we have to face a diminution of population—an undoubted increase of nervous complaints with their accompaniments—an absolute want of the sentiments, what ever they are, that lead to good literature (and at the same time to good fighting). In all these points we are like Rome. But it can't be true that the cause is a financial one, because you can prove the circumstances different.

It must be remembered that in the first half of 1897 preparations were accumulating for Queen Victoria's Diamond Jubilee. Spring Rice had read too much Greek literature to be free of some apprehension for the fate of the overbearing : he knew already too much of the continental forces arraying themselves to be sure of his own land's security. Rome's history was to him not an incentive but a warning. Meantime he sketched the people among whom he was stationed with a not unfriendly hand.

BERLIN,
Jan. 2, 1897.

To STEPHEN.

" . . . New Year's Day is a great festival. All the Ambassadors go in state coaches to see the Emperor and all the generals and many of the Princes go up to Berlin to pay respects. The place is full of splendid uniforms and gold coaches. In the afternoon the Emperor calls on the Princes and Ambassadors, leaving cards in person ; his coach is bigger and finer than the others.

Needless to say, the Russian coach is the best of the Embassies and looked very fine—a mass of yellow paint and liveries with a tiny old man[1] in a gold coat fast asleep inside. Our Ambassador looks the best. The Austrian[2] is a fine fellow to look at, too, but he looks extremely barbaric in his Hungarian uniform, with a strong, savage-looking face. He is really the best and kindest of men with a strange habit of giving official interviews in the presence of his wife and daughters, who are sitting smoking cigarettes in various parts of the room. The Russians live quite apart and the Frenchman,[3] a dear little professorial-looking man—much like a wizened Lord Salisbury in miniature, if you can imagine such a thing—is evidently only thinking of how he is to get out of a room as soon as possible. . . ."

BERLIN,
March 27, 1897.

" MY DEAR STEPHEN,

. . . Since I have been back here we have had three festivities and the whole place has gone mad. It is quite true that the people had a small share of the show. They provided a good part of it themselves and had to pay for decorations and illuminations, but they weren't provided with much sport by the Kaiser in return and the whole of the Linden was ' gesperrt ' during the parade of the troops, so that no one could see. The avenues leading to the Linden were a mass of struggling people, held back with difficulty by the police. There was an allegorical representation of ' Willehalm ' [4] representing the career of the great one ; Napoleon was rather closely imitated and an improper person in his company was called Lutetia. Fortunately the French Ambassador took the opportunity to depart on leave—and so there was no one there to take offence. The French Embassy was left shut up and no flag displayed. It was on Pariser Platz, occupying half one side, and looked sadly conspicuous. The allegorical play appears to have been of the most portentous dullness. I believe the sight at the unveiling was very impressive. Old Generals weeping at the sight of their old Emperor. He is undoubtedly a sort of patron saint of Berlin. I sometimes wonder whether his particular virtues of quietness, faithfulness to advisers, lack of ostentation, etc., have not been more prized lately than even during his lifetime. . . ."

He wrote also to Mrs. Roosevelt, sending her

" Two books for the children—a French one and a German, the latter a pendant to the Frederick the Great. It will be good

---

[1] Count Osten Sacken.   [2] Count Szögyenyi.   [3] Marquis de Noailles.
[4] An allegorical play about the Hohenzollerns.

for the children's languages and history, besides representing a very real feeling. The good Queen Louise is the idol and saint of Berlin still ; and the wooded glade in the Park where her statue is, is still full of flowers on her birthday, brought there by all the pious little children of the town. There is a very beautiful recumbent statue of her in Charlottenburg, near Berlin, next to her stupid old husband. She is so entirely resting. It's a pleasure to look at her and yet you see people with tears in their eyes by her side."

His dislike of German policy was not allied to any feeling against the German people, whom he thoroughly respected ; and throughout these years he wandered through Germany, noting and observing, sometimes on his own account, sometimes on official errands. For instance he writes to his brother :

" I go to Weimar to-morrow, in consequence of the death of the Grand Duchess—to be present with the Ambassador at the funeral. It is an absurd custom but gives me the opportunity of seeing the place gratis ; the Treasury paying my expenses—yah ! "

" Yah " is addressed by the minion of a spending department to the Treasury official.

CHAPTER VIII

GERMANY 1897-98

THE WAR BETWEEN GREECE AND TURKEY AND THE SPANISH-AMERICAN WAR.

IN the spring of 1897 Europe again became agitated. Turkish proceedings in Armenia had roused a feeling in England against which the traditional British policy of supporting Turkey was powerless to assert itself. Armenia, however, though a part of Christendom, was outside Europe. But in 1897 attacks by Mahommedans on Christians in Crete produced painful disorder and the Cretan insurgents declared for union with Greece, and a Greek force was sent to the island. This elicited a collective protest from England, France, Germany, Austria, Russia and Italy. These Powers sent a joint squadron to establish a blockade of the island and to prevent the union with Greece; but at the same time they declared that, owing to Turkey's failure to protect the Christian population, self-government must be guaranteed to the Cretans, though under Turkish suzerainty.

Meantime the Turks, after demanding recall of the Greek expedition to Crete, and reparation for the act, moved up an army to the Thessalian border. War followed, in which after six weeks Greece had to sue for peace; the indemnity of thirty millions created a fund on which German creditors immediately established claims, which the Kaiser, as Turkey's friend, successfully supported.

It must be remembered that tension in South Africa was still acute, and that England was suspected of a design to annex the Boer Republic; and in Egypt, though England had repeatedly talked of withdrawal, Kitchener's advance to Dongola pointed in quite another direction. Imperial expansion was in the air, and the Kaiser's nature urged him to be well in the fashion. England and France were busy in Africa, but a line of advance lay open to Germany in the Far East, parallel to that of Russia, though far less ambitious, and indeed subserving the aims of what was then the greater Empire.

In 1894 Japan had suddenly and dramatically vanquished China and proceeded to stake out claims which China, unsupported, had no choice but to concede. Formosa was handed over; an indemnity of thirty millions was promised; but in addition the conquering islanders claimed the Liao-tung peninsula, which not only would have given Japan a large holding on the Continent, close to the subservient Korea, but also a position commanding the entrance to the Gulf of Pechili—and so to Pekin.   More important still, this concession handed over to the modernised East the natural railhead for Russia's trans-Siberian railway, which had been begun in 1891.

Hohenlohe's policy, in which his master concurred, was to earn Russia's goodwill when he could ; and this new Oriental power was blocking Russia's path.   Germany therefore in 1895 first warned Japan not to claim territory on the mainland, and then, when China had actually agreed to the surrender of Liao-tung, joined herself with Russia and Russia's ally France to forbid the deal.   China, indeed, formally pledged herself not to cede the restored territory to any other power ; but in 1897 the scramble for territory extended itself to the Pacific coast, and Germany led the way.

On the other hand, in the near East Germany had assumed England's traditional rôle.   Lord Salisbury, when he returned to power in 1895, opened a discussion with the German Ambassador as to Germany's desires in the event of the Ottoman Empire's disruption. When this was reported to the Kaiser, he forbade all further mention of the subject, and declared that the integrity of Turkey must be maintained.

BERLIN,
April 24, 1897.
To VILLIERS.

"Various rather strange things have been done by the Emperor lately, which come out, as no one seems to be able to keep their counsel as to what he says.   In January last year, just before his quarrel with Herbette, he seems to have suggested that Germany and France together should summon an African conference—a sort of bar before which England should be called.   Herbette strongly opposed this in communications to his Government—mainly on the ground that the bad relations between Germany and England would eventually lead to hostilities, and that France should keep clear of it, certainly not take the side of Germany.

To-day appears an article, which is certainly inspired, more venomously abusive than anything which has appeared for a long time, suggesting the advisability of a general combination against England.   The meaning of this is evidently that England is suspected of preparing a coup in Africa under cover of the disturbances which she has brought about by her intrigues in the East.   I can hardly think that that is seriously believed —but, of course, the effect of a war in Eastern Europe is, in the main, to leave England free in other parts of the world ; and, seeing this effect, Germany is naturally inclined to think that it is intended.   I think I have often told you that the ' Grand idea ' as they would say here of German policy, as outlined in

Government speeches and articles is : Peace and, if possible, alliance with Russia—in Europe ; and outside Europe—an understanding with France and Russia to the detriment of England. The Czar used to talk of dividing the inheritance of the sick man ; Germany seems to urge dividing the property of a well man—England. Unfortunately, Europe is more occupied with the sick man ; but Germany is not one of the heirs, and has all her attention elsewhere.

It appears that Germany, while she (as she is always saying) has no interest in the Eastern question, is very much interested in the Levant trade, under present conditions. The alteration of the present state of things would imply higher duties and would be much to the detriment of German trade. Also there is some fear of the competition of Salonica. Hence the very close relations with Turkey. I hear that the Emperor sends private letters to the Sultan by the Ambassador here, and that officers are put at the disposal of the Sultan. From all this one may guess at the sort of language which he used at Vienna, and which will be repeated in St. Petersburg. The Austrians are furious with us (as I can judge by my Austrian colleagues) for changing our policy towards Turkey and refusing to fight any more for Constantinople, and they say openly that we shall suffer for it. So that it looks as if (if anyone can be found to bell the cat) we shall have a lively time this year.

I went to a concert the other day—part of it was the music of a play, *The Ruins of Athens*. No one seemed to notice the appropriateness of the last. It is a mistake, however, to say that there is no sympathy with Greece. There is a good deal which appears in the independent press and also in the Conservative papers, who are strongly Christian, and they believe that the war will not be allowed to lead to blotting out Greece. But the Government papers urge the extinction of the "miserable country—people, dynasty and all."

May 2, 1897.

To STEPHEN.

" I am still in Berlin—but am always thinking of getting leave, only things are so interesting just now. I can't make out what is happening exactly. The impression one gets from the German papers is that the Austrian Emperor has acted the part of German Ambassador to Russia and has executed his instructions to the entire satisfaction of the German Government, so that there is now a sort of cordial understanding between Russia and Germany, which will shortly extend itself to Paris. Of course, with the result that England is left completely isolated. England, on the other hand, is supposed to have acted during the last few years with the sole object of putting the Powers at loggerheads in order to play her own game elsewhere. But, as they note with satisfaction, this cynical policy has completely failed. Isn't it a curious perversion of the facts as they are known to you and me ?

I wish you could tell me what is the real feeling about S. Africa in the city and in political circles. Of course, the army is dying for a war, and naturally there are the usual noisy people who shout for war. And I daresay war may be justified. From the point of view, however, which comes before me, I should say there is even in Germany a strong feeling that the Boers ought to make certain concessions ; there certainly is in France. There is, however, on the other hand a floating mass of public opinion which lives on phrases about English aggression, and everything we do is quoted as an instance. From which I should conclude, that if there is any respect whatever to be shown to public opinion in the world at large, the obvious course from (perhaps) the historic point of view, is to make peaceful professions while being, of course, fully prepared for war, if necessary ; to show a strong disinclination to fight, but if an obvious plain and undeniable infraction of treaty is committed, or an act of aggression—then to wire in with all available strength. The circumstances should be, if possible, of a kind affecting all branches of European capital and industry.

Instead of this course, we have certainly given the impression that the Colonial Office at any rate is war-like, and is going about with a whip on its shoulder."

After the Diamond Jubilee of Queen Victoria.

To STEPHEN. July 7, 1897.

. . . What a time you must have had lately. It will be difficult for you to realise that anyone could be quiet anywhere. But we are absolutely quiet here. We had an English dinner and subsequently a child's entertainment which was a pretty sight—all the little English boys and girls marching along with enormous British flags. They were mostly children of jockeys who belong to the racing establishment near Berlin, and to Yorkshiremen who are employed in big spinning mills near here. They were jolly hearty people and it was very amusing to see them and hear their voices. The Emperor gave a festivity on board his yacht. We all were asked and went down on Sunday morning—six hours' train on a hot day. The country round Kiel is almost exactly like the south of England—woods, hedges and rolling country. Indeed, I suppose our ancestors came from there, but it was queer to see the great likeness to

England there and to think of the great unlikeness to England across the channel.

The Harbour is fine and full of yachts. We were sent for in the usual steam cutter. The Chancellor came down by the same train and had a steamer to himself. The new Foreign Minister [1] came, in ours, and was extremely lively and jolly. On board the ' Hohenzollern ' were numerous statesmen and Admirals and all the boon-companions who are supposed to form the inner Government, and who are the bane of Germany, as the papers say. Also a number of English yachtsmen who looked extremely surprised at the whole performance. Also the King of the Belgians who, in spite of sea-sickness, hired a yacht on purpose to get at the Emperor—no one knows what for. The whole press of the country teems with news about a ministerial crisis. And it was all to be settled at this dinner. I saw it settled. In the conversation, the little Chancellor, who has a queer, small, bird-like face and a stoop which makes him 3 ft. 6 ins. high (he should be 4 ft. 6 ins. by nature) looked up fiercely at the Emperor who gesticulated rather energetically— finally the conversation got less emphatic, and ended in the Emperor patting the Chancellor on the back. It took him five minutes—and the Emperor then turned his attention to the King of the Belgians, but chiefly to the foreign yachtsmen, who each had an audience. Then there was a beer-evening among the boon companions, and at six the next morning the Emperor was off in flannels on board his racing yacht. The crisis, as we saw in the papers next morning, was over. Isn't that an odd way of ruling a country ? . . . "

July 17, 1897.

To FERGUSON.

" Politics are still amusing. The parties abuse one another with so much vehemence that they have only just time for an occasional curse at England. It is the only point of resemblance that I can see between Ireland and Germany.

The Emperor has now at last taken the government into his own hands, and the news having spread through the coach, all the heads are looking out of the window. The confidence shown by the country is not striking.

I heard a sermon yesterday on a dead ' introducteur des Ambassadeurs '—a sort of Ponsonby Fane.[2] The preacher addressed the dead through the coffin and said, ' Oh, you who

---

[1] Count von Bülow had succeeded Baron Marschall von Bieberstein at the end of June, 1897.

[2] The Rt. Hon. Sir S. C. B. Ponsonby Fane, G.C.B., Gentleman Usher to the Queen.

were beckoned by the hand of death from the side of an Imperial Master, the King and Emperor—live in our memories so that we may by our devoted services make up to an august Lord for the loss He has sustained. Let that be our first and our last duty.' This was before an audience mostly—almost entirely of foreigners and in Church. Such is the feeling of certain sections towards the sovereign. I don't think he is at all to be despised. For one thing, he is intensely patriotic—the only thing he really cares for is the greatness on every side and in every direction of his country. This change doesn't mean that he will change the policy of the Ministers ; he tells them to wear their arms, like an old Greek. He doesn't do it very pleasantly. Marschall said in the course of an interview that he hoped if the Emperor wished to dispense with his services he would tell him. The Emperor said nothing. Marschall goes on sick leave and reads in the papers that his successor is appointed—to take charge at the date mentioned by Marschall for the termination of his leave ! And yet the Emperor carries on Marschall's policy and uses even his very phrases !

What a curious master to serve. But it doesn't follow that he is a bad ruler for all that ; and we make a mistake in laughing at him. People here are rather exasperated, however."

July 24, 1897.

To VILLIERS.

" Public opinion is chiefly occupied with political changes inside the Government, which have caused a more violent campaign war than any I have ever seen even in America. Liberal—moderate Liberal—papers call on the country to stand on its defence against the enemies of law and liberty—meaning the Emperor and his friends ; Conservative papers tell the Liberals that they are Jews—swindlers, liars and enemies of their country. The fact is that the changes mean that the Emperor gets rid of the men who stood in his way not from their opinions but from their character ; it wasn't because they were Liberal but because they were independent that they had to go. There is a slight movement to the right—but simply because the right is more absolutist.

The Emperor means to be his own Minister now. His policy has been laid down pretty clearly ; that is, advancement of German trade interests of every kind, agricultural and industrial—in order to pay for a big navy with which to face a possible enemy on the sea. And even the parties most opposed to the Emperor seem to be willing on the whole to support a large increase of the navy. As for foreign policy, it's pretty plain that the tendency is towards a closer understanding with Russia. All the papers which reflect the opinions of the Emperor's entourage are in favour of Russia as against us— partly because of Russia being absolutist, but also because of the great possibilities Russia affords to Germany for investment. Witte told a Frenchman here that he thought that for the next few years Russia would have to look to Germany for commercial and pecuniary support, and already in three months Russia has borrowed ten million pounds in Germany. France seems tired of lending money to Russia and is indeed unloading in Berlin in order to float the French loan which comes out this year. So from dynastic and commercial reasons, we can expect a pretty close *rapprochement* between Germany and Russia for the next few years.

The French Embassy here are convinced that the dearest object of this Government is to come to an understanding with France by any means short of the abandonment of Alsace-Lorraine. The last Ambassador, Herbette, was against taking Germany's side against England in S. Africa, because he believed that England and Germany would go to war within a year or two if France did not interfere on one side or the other ; but what the present French Government will do seems not yet clear. I suppose there has been some sort of agreement for a common programme in connection with West Africa ; [1] but the whole business is kept very carefully secret here.

It is curious to see the anxiety displayed by any paper in connection with the Government to estrange England from France, Italy or Russia—to suggest to Turkey to inspire the Amir against us, etc., etc. There can be no doubt of the wish to be as hostile as they dare, but there can be no thought of war, everyone agrees on that. Their great desire is to be rich and have peace till they have a navy strong enough to cover their supplies. However, it is notorious that every officer has to make a scheme in the staff college for the invasion of England. They firmly believe that it is possible, on the supposition that a sufficient number of English troops are engaged abroad (as in the Sudan), and that the country is threatened by a maritime power in the Mediterranean. Then they would wire in, or get what they wanted by the threat of wiring in. One can't help being alarmist here, especially in view of the Emperor's deep irritation at not being asked to the Jubilee, and the enormous accession to his personal influence (coupled, it is true, with

[1] The ' scramble for West Africa ' was now in full swing, and French and British parties were repeatedly on the edge of collision, at different points from the Niger to Sierra Leone, between 1897 and 1899.

intense unpopularity in certain circles) which is the result of his recent manipulation of his Government."

July 24, 1897.

To STEPHEN.

" Politics here are amusing. At this moment the Prussian lower House is discussing a bill which would give any policeman power to close any meeting which would in his opinion be injurious to the State ! There is a fair chance of the bill being passed—all the gentlemen, courtiers and princes are in its favour. The unseen, unknown influences outside are against it. Which will win ? The entire absence of any representation of Liberalism in the society circles is a striking fact. There seems to be absolute unanimity ; the only feeling is that it is dangerous to trust the entire Government of the country to the Emperor's arbitrary will. There is no doubt he is an able man, although he is vain and exaggerates everything he does or says. But a man doesn't necessarily tell a lie because he talks loud. We may very well undervalue him.

The whole sum of the tendency here is distinctly—organise a continental alliance against England. In the next ten years Germany will build a navy (' we are rich enough,' they say) which will command respect. We shall have to reckon with this. We can hardly afford to build a navy which can face three powers at once. What should we do ?

. . . . I live mostly at Potsdam—going up and down from there to Berlin. Potsdam is a pretty place, all lakes and trees —with a few rococo palaces scattered about and many villas inhabited by Jews. Royalty and Jews ! the acme of our modern civilisation. . . . The worst of the lakes is that they turn green and stink. There is but one lake. Will you go north or not ? I hope to be in Old Church about August 22 or soon after—to stay till end of September. And then to return. . . . "

The " one lake " was Ullswater, of course, for though he loved the beauty of many lands, none ever had the same magic for him as the grey and cloudy landscapes among which his boyhood's holiday time was spent.—The letter to Roosevelt which follows, and the reply to it, show how far ahead the thought of these friends ranged, and how consistently Spring Rice linked questions of strategy to those of diplomacy.—I note that whereas earlier letters began, " My dear Teddie," Teddie was suppressed from 1896 on, because Spring Rice thought it had become " newspaper," as Roosevelt was more and more conspicuous.

To ROOSEVELT.   August 1, 1897.

" This is a very interesting country.   The things that happen
are quite incredible.   I don't think, however, people are quite
on the right track who say, because the august ruler here does
things in a way which would be thought odd in enlightened
circles in London or Wyoming, that therefore the things he
does are wrong as well as the way in which he does them.   Now
I think he has a clear and definite plan and not a bad one.
Germany has lost more than a million of her best citizens in the
last ten years.   Not only has she lost them, but they have gone
to swell the ranks and increase the power of her adversaries.
And not only are these peoples she is feeding opposed to her
commercially, but they are the incarnation of the spirit of
Liberalism which is by far the most dangerous system of all in
the eyes of the ruling classes here.   *Men* can't catch the mange.
Germans can't catch Russian absolutism or South American
anarchy.   But they are extremely liable to catch Anglo-Saxon
Liberalism, especially when imported by their own returned
emigrants.   You see the argument.   At least you can guess at
its working in the official mind.

Well, then, what is the remedy ?   At first the answer was :
Colonies.   After fourteen years the most populous colony they
possess is South-West Africa, with a population of 2000 whites,
of whom more than half are officials or soldiers, and of the rest
more than half English or Dutch.   In the meanwhile emigration
to non-German countries continues.   It is impossible to stop
the stream.   But it can be diverted.   If then Germans cannot be
kept from leaving the country and cannot be induced to go to
German colonies, the only alternative is to induce them if possible to go to those places where, besides making money, they
have a chance of keeping their nationality.   In many places, as
you have seen, there are colonies of Germans living together,
speaking their own language and forming a community apart.
Where this takes place far from the sea in a strong country with
an energetic and efficient administration, such communities
are certain in the end to be absorbed in the general mass.   But
if they can be or are established within reach of the sea, in the
territory of a Government which is neither efficient nor energetic,
the case is very different.   Both South America and South
Africa offer in different ways possibilities of this description.
But suppose such a community existing, with the same sort of
potentialities for Germany as Texas had for the U.S., the thing
to do to carry out this policy of the extension of German
influence is to have a sufficient force to protect these outposts
of Germany in case of need.   So the dream of greater Germany,

which is a worthy and honourable one, having failed in finding a realisation in the extension of the German colonies, is on the brink of finding it here. But the German people are perfectly indifferent to such ideas, in the mass at any rate. The Emperor has set steadily to work to educate his people and to a certain extent has succeeded. He goes a curious way to work, but it's possible he may know his Germans better than we do. He is going to have a good try, and he is acting strongly under the influence of an idea, which in this country is respectable. I find him the most interesting study, and he is truly devoted to his wife who adores him, which is to his credit. So, however, was George III., to whom you have more reason to be grateful than I have.

There's a question which must be interesting to you in your present position [1] and which is more than interesting to us. For Germany and England there are three main sources of grain supply—North and South America and Russia. In case of a war for both England and Germany, the food supply is perhaps the most vital question. If the war lasts any length of time, the question would probably be decisive. Therefore the object of these two would be to cut off the supply. But Germany has no navy sufficiently strong to protect her supply. Most of the continental powers accept the doctrine that the necessaries of life are contraband of war. Therefore food can not be brought in in neutral ships (unless England and the U.S. who dissent from the doctrine fight to maintain their views). The consequence is that Germany is driven to lean on Russia, which is the only alternative. You will see the result of this reasoning pretty clearly if the wise people are not mistaken. However brave people are, they want to have enough to eat, especially Germans. You can apply the argument in another form to England and the United States, and you will draw the conclusion that Russia will probably be much less inclined to be civil to Germany than Germany to Russia.

What do you think of Russia ? The Russians here amuse me and frighten me. I hear them talk, and think of a Hun or a Goth at the court of Constantine. They like and despise our civilisation and firmly believe it will all be theirs in time. They watch the fruits of civilisation growing, intending when they are ripe, to come and take them. They don't make much concealment. When the Czar was crowned, the Governments voted enormous sums ; the foreign representatives vied with one another in display to do the Czar honour and it was like an assemblage of Tribute princes doing homage. There is

[1] At the Navy Board.

absolutely no form of flattery too gross for the German papers to offer to Russia. They contrast Siberia with North America, and say how evident it is that the Russians and only they are the pioneers of true civilisation. The Russians themselves accept it contentedly as their due and without much caring whether it is offered or not. Because, as they believe, the future belongs to them. They don't care for the inventions of our race except as a means to use. They will develop their own form of Government, literature and art. They despise all of us, but none perhaps so much as the Americans, who have, they say, the faults of the old world without its *agréments*. They acknowledge that they are barbarous, but you are barbarians with a past and nothing else, while they are barbarians with a future. I like repeating some of the disagreeable things we hear about you. Do you believe that the Russians are the hope of an effete world ? Anyhow, *they* do.

What are you doing besides your speeches (which I see telegraphed in the *Herald*) and your departmental work, and your navy book, and keeping Cabot from yielding too much to European influences ? You must be quite idle. How did you stand the heat ? Was it as bad as the year we drank the Madeira together ? I am writing to Mrs. Roosevelt to ask her to forgive me that and more recent sins. John Hay seems to be happy and prosperous, doesn't he ! "

Hay had become Ambassador to Great Britain in May 1897 and was being a popular success. The suggestion that Cabot (Senator Lodge) needed this kind of shepherding is, of course, a joke. Nothing, alas ! is known as to the Madeira, but in the summer of 1895 the two were living together in Washington and may have attempted suicide in this fashion. This is Roosevelt's answer :

NAVY DEPARTMENT,
Aug. 13, 1897.

" DEAR CECIL,

. . . You happen to have a mind which is interested in precisely the things which interest me, and which I believe are of more vital consequence than any other to the future of the race and of the world ; so naturally I am delighted to hear from you, and I always want to answer your letters at length. . . .

Before speaking of the Russians and of their attitude towards us, a word about the Germans. I am by no means sure that I heartily respect the little Kaiser, but in his colonial plans I think he is entirely right from the standpoint of the German race. International law, and above all, inter-racial law, are still in a fluid condition, and two nations with violently conflicting interests may each be entirely right from its own standpoint. If I were a German, I should want the German race to expand. I should be glad to see it begin to expand in the only two places left for the ethnic, as distinguished from the political, expansion of the European peoples ; that is, in South Africa and temperate South America. Therefore, as a German, I should be delighted to upset the English in South Africa, and to defy the Americans and their Monroe Doctrine in South America. As an Englishman, I should seize the first opportunity to crush the German Navy and the German commercial marine out of existence, and take possession of both the German and Portuguese possessions in South Africa, leaving the Boers absolutely isolated. As an American I should advocate—and as a matter of fact do advocate—keeping our Navy at a pitch that will enable us to interfere promptly if Germany ventures to touch a foot of American soil. I would not go into the abstract rights or wrongs of it ; I would simply say that we did not intend to have the Germans on this continent, excepting as immigrants, whose children would become Americans of one sort or another, and if Germany intended to extend her empire here, she would have to whip us first. . . .

Now, the reason why I don't think so much of the Kaiser is that it seems to me Germany ought not to try to expand colonially at our expense when she has Russia against her flank and year by year increasing in relative power. Of course, if Germany has definitely adopted the views which some of the Greek States, like the Achaean League, adopted towards Rome after the second Punic War, I have nothing to say. These Greek States made up their mind that Rome had the future and could not be striven against, but they decided to take advantage of whatever breathing space was given them by warring on any power which Rome did not choose to befriend, hoping that Rome might perhaps spare them, and that meanwhile they would stand high, compared to all the States but Rome. If Germany feels this way towards Russia, well and good ; but if she does not feel this way, then every year she waits to strike is just so much against her. . . .

A few years ago Germany could certainly have whipped Russia, even if, in conjunction with Austria and Italy, she had had to master France also. Of course, it would be useless to whip her without trying to make the whipping possibly permanent by building up a great Polish buffer State, making Finland independent or Swedish, taking the Baltic provinces, etc. *This* would have been something worth doing ; but to run about imprisoning private citizens of all ages who do not speak of ' Majesty ' with bated breath seems to me foolish, at this period of the world's progress. That the Germans should dislike and look down upon the Americans is natural. Americans don't dislike the Germans, but so far as they think of them at all they look upon them with humorous contempt. The English-speaking races may or may not be growing *effete*, and may or may not ultimately succumb to the Slav, but whatever may happen in any single war, they will not ultimately succumb to the German, and a century hence he will be of very small consequence compared to them. . . .

Now, about the Russians, who offer a very much more serious problem than the Germans, if not to our generation, at least to the generations which will succeed us. Russia and the United States are friendly, but Russians and Americans, in their individual capacity, have nothing whatever in common.

That they despise Americans in a way is doubtless true. I rather doubt if they despise Europeans. Socially, the upper classes feel themselves akin to the other European upper classes, while they have no one to feel akin to in America. Our political corruption certainly cannot shock them, but our political institutions they doubtless both despise and fear. . . .

During recent years I have seen a great deal of the New York Police Force, which is a very powerful, efficient and corrupt body, and of our Navy, which is a powerful, efficient and honourable body. I have incidentally seen a great deal of the constructors who build the ships, and the public works, of the civil engineers, the dock-builders, the sailors, the workmen in the iron foundries and shipyards. These represent, all told, a very great number of men, and the impression left upon my mind, after intimate association with the hundreds of naval officers, naval constructors, and civil engineers, and the tens of thousands of seamen and mechanics (and policemen) is primarily an impression of abounding force, of energy, resolution and decision. These men are not *effete*, and if you compare the Russians with them (and, of course, exactly the same thing would be true if you compared the Russians with corresponding Englishmen) I think you would become convinced that the analogy of the Goth and the Byzantine is forced. These men would outbuild, out-administer and out-fight any Russians you could find from St. Petersburg to Sebastopol or Vladivostock—if that's the way you spell it. I doubt if our Presidents are as *effete* as the average Czar or Russian minister. I believe our generals and admirals are better, and so, with all their hideous faults, are our public administrators. Of course, both the English and the Americans are less ruthless, and have the disadvantages of civilisation. It may be that we are going the way of France, but just at present I doubt it, and I still think that though the people of the English-speaking races may have to divide the future with the Slav, yet they will get rather more than their fair share."

America also was now beginning to feel the need of reckoning forces in Europe. Insurrection in Cuba had brought about a furious guerilla war which shocked American opinion ; the Cabinet was pressed by the Committee on Foreign Affairs to offer intervention, and the claims of certain insurgents, when captured, to be treated as American subjects increased friction. In 1897 the Senate passed a resolution in favour of recognising the Cubans as belligerents, not rebels. War between Spain and America plainly became probable— and might have ramifications.

BERLIN,
Nov. 3, 1897.

To ROOSEVELT.

" Your letter was of the greatest interest and I showed parts of it to a good many people who were very much struck with what you said. I think we understand one another pretty well now and I hope that we may be able to help one another.

I have been very much interested in watching the view taken here about Cuba. As far as I can judge, the feeling in official circles is much as follows. To begin with, there is the feud that every official German has with America, which is regarded as a huge machine for teaching Germans English and making them Republican. Then there is the economical feud caused by protective measures, and the feeling of helplessness when the U.S. do anything to offend German dignity. All these feelings, which are natural enough, make German comment on American affairs rather bitter. Then there is the sympathy with mon- archical Spain and with the Queen Regent. Another and a stronger factor is the Sugar interest here. If order is restored in Cuba and the normal amount of sugar produced, the sugar growers of Germany will naturally suffer. Chaos is in their interest. The sugar growers, who are mainly in north Germany, are a very influential body because they belong to the old Prussian nobility which has for years been the mainstay of the throne. So the pull they have is considerable.

But with all these strong factors on the side of Spain, I should think it quite out of the question that Germany would move in favour of Spain, although she would be only too delighted if some one else would do it. The prevailing motive underlying German policy is peace and commercial progress. Anything which would endanger their enormous interests on your side, trade, shipping, investments—would be avoided with the most scrupulous care. They dare not go to war and according to the admirable principle which they practise, if they can't go to war they don't pretend that they will. The press is admirably disciplined. Nothing appears in any of the semi-official papers which could be interpreted into a threat against America or an encouragement to Spain. But this, of course, does not mean that there is no interest in the struggle. If the Spanish Government falls, it is certain that it will entail political events of a grave nature in Europe, and this alone would make the question a serious one for this country. To sum up, I think there can be no sort of doubt as to what the Empire would like to see done in Cuba; but I don't think there is the slightest chance of Germany running the risk of being found out doing it. As for a European coalition, I suppose that it would at a stroke settle all your domestic troubles and unite everyone in the same cause. But I don't think there is much chance. Everyone would like some one else to bell the cat. I'm afraid you will have been disappointed in this respect.

If you were here, you would be a good deal interested in politics. I hope it won't bore you to hear a little about them because the questions here are so very different from what they are with us. On the one hand, the monarch with the history of blood and iron and the army of (in theory) absolute slaves. On the other, all the people who are liberal, who read, think, work, make money or books. Now, which would you go with? I am not sure. There is on either side, in France and Russia, a deadly enemy waiting his chance. This time the war will be a war of extermination, which it is hardly likely that the beaten party will survive as a nation. Everything depends on the army and its leaders. . . . [1]

Brooks Adams ought to come here to see the Jew at home and to hear what people who know him well think of him. The odd thing is that this Government which is entirely carried on by the anti-commercial class is the most frankly commercial Government in the world. An article in the organ of the Government boasted the other day, that whereas other Governments were swayed by gusts of feeling and passion, Germany attended strictly to business. The massacres of the Armenians (I am quoting) made England forget her own interest and that of Europe. But Germany stood unmoved. The sympathy for Greece infected England, France and Italy. Germany alone

[1] What is omitted is put more fully in the next letter to Henry Adams.

was able to keep her head and save Europe. When war broke
out between Japan and China, the sympathies of Germany were
on the side of Japan ; but when it was for the interest of
Germany, she changed, and in a moment. As a reward she has
been able to secure the administration of her debt in Greece,
the sympathy of victorious Turkey (which has already resulted
in some valuable concessions) and the friendship of Russia in the
Far East.

The larger part of German diplomacy has to do with commercial matters and the forwarding of trade. The word that is
always in the mouth of German politicians is *real politik*,
the politics of interest. All appeals to passions, except simply
the love of country and the hatred of the foreigner, are eliminated. There is to be no question as to them. There has not
been a ripple of opinion here in favour of the Greeks or the
Armenians. The papers never seem to be stirred either by the
sufferings or the heroism of a foreigner. The question always is :
Is there anything to be made out of it ? I think, if one thinks of
it, the cause may be that the whole nation is now, and has been
for centuries, under the tremendous load of political anxiety
which has crushed out every feeling except an intense desire to
exist. They are like the borderers who were never certain of
their lives nor of their crops or cattle ; naturally they are dour.

But where is the enthusiasm and romance of the borderer ?
There is nothing of it now. The ordinary play or novel is the
recital of mean things, leading to mean conclusions. Good and
wicked are punished alike ; everyone is miserable and chiefly
because they wish to be. Nobody seems to be really angry or
really in love. Life is so thoroughly dull that the natural way
out is suicide. Ask for the real interest here and everyone will
answer—Money ! Probably it is the same in every country
now. But here it is less tempered by other interests and considerations than perhaps anywhere else ; with the important
exception of the army and all that appertains to national
defence. Everything must in the end give way to that. It's
the country of the soldier and the Jew, but between the soldier
and the Jew everyone else is crushed. Which side would you
take ? I would like to see you here for a time and hear your
opinions. I believe you would go on the side of the Soldier and
drink the Kaiser's health with tears in your eyes.

What do you think of Brooks Adams' ' great imaginative
Empire of Spain ? ' I am glad to say that the press of England
at any rate recognises that it is rather hard for people of our
blood to sit quiet with such things going on at the door. I saw
one article in the *Manchester Guardian*, the Liberal paper of the

North, which said that if it were jingoism to object to massacre and robbery, it hoped for the credit of the race and language that all America would go Jingo mad ; it would wipe out some of the stain of Armenia.

What do you think of Mahan's article in *Harper* last March ? I think it extraordinarily true in many respects as far as my own observation goes. I am afraid it will sound the ordinary English hypocrisy and especially from a person of my profession who did not at once disapprove of the Jameson raid ; but then, I was in Germany at the time. What I was going to say was the trite remark that true patriotism ought to be like one's love for one's relations. If they do wrong, it is a personal shame and disgrace to oneself. But that can never justify, except in extreme cases, an abandonment. But I should think that an honourable man should be as much grieved if his brother turned thief as if he had turned bankrupt. One ought to treasure one's country's reputation as one would one's wife's. Probably both our countries have got a reputation for being humbugs by very sincerely professing this doctrine. It has paid. And because it has paid, our enemies say that we cared for the profit and not for the principle. I think if we hadn't believed in the principle we should never have won the profit. I daresay the British part of the common inheritance is going down hill ; all the more reason to look after the other. I don't believe it will prosper unless it keeps up a human heart and noble aims. You are one of the people who can water that particular plant, and God speed you ! By the way, what an amusing time the God of battles must have looking down on our encounters. Each side believes so firmly that God is with him and desires his victory as his own cause ; and really, what the God of battles desires and likes is that people, if they fight at all, should fight bravely."

He wrote also to his brother Stephen at this date :

" What do you think of Chamberlain ? I should like to have someone lay stress on another aspect of patriotism which friend Wordsworth describes so well ; I mean the desire not only that your country should be great but that it should be, as a condition of greatness—good."

BERLIN,
Nov. 7, 1897.

To HENRY ADAMS.

" I promised some time ago to write you something about the struggle going on here between the two great parties representing the interests of land and money, and the subject has come up now into unusual prominence in consequence of the late crisis. I think the best way of making it clear is to quote the words which I have often heard in the mouths of representatives of the two interests. To begin with ; the agrarian. He is generally a soldier, or if not, has been one. He would say, if you asked him what he thought of the course the Government is taking on almost any subject : ' We have one point of view which we have always had and which all the world knows about. Germany has been made by Prussia and Prussia by its king and its army. The army has proved itself better than other armies partly because of its excellent material and partly because of its discipline ; that is the devotion of officers to King and men to officers. Now, our officers are drawn from one class only, the class of landowners. We marry among ourselves. We don't do as the English do, marry a Jew's daughter when the property is in a bad way. We are supported by the land alone. In return for that support we give our lives and ambitions entirely to the service of army and King. And we expect that our means of livelihood will be assured us. Look at the history of Prussia, or of my family if you wish it. There is not a single generation in my house in which one or more has not fallen in battle. When Prussia was at its lowest we sold our property, what we could sell of it, and gave the proceeds to the King. We should do the same again. It is a habit with us to consider ourselves, our property and our lives as at the disposal of the house of Hohenzollern. And we do not expect at this late hour to be abandoned to ruin because other times have come and other men have pushed themselves forward.'—On the other hand you have the manufacturer : he would say : ' What makes the greatness of Germany now ? It is her industrial activity. In a few years the poorest country in Europe has become the rival of the richest. And this is owing to our exertions. And now we are met by this class of poor squires, whom we pay, who live on what our Government gives them, and they insist that the whole fabric of our industry should be shattered if it spoils their view. The Government is abject before them. Though it does not dare ruin us utterly, for its only resource would then be destroyed, it hampers us with every possible impediment and heaps insult on insult. We are treated as thieves and swindlers because we live on our own industry and not on Government pay.' [1] A dispassionate foreigner looking about for the truth comes on certain facts which support both views to some extent.

[1] Another letter to Villiers, describing the position of the middle class, between Social Democrats and the Right, says, " The Conservatives with William at their head are regarded in business circles as the lady in the *Roi des Montagnes* looked on the King's troops—she asked the brigands to send a party with her to guard her from the gendarmes."

Germany is in a peculiarly exposed position from the military point of view, which the years succeeding Jena have brought home to the national consciousness. She may have to fight a war with two fronts and if she does not win she may be absolutely extinguished. How to face the danger ? By a great army which has had to be increased time and again, and also to be fed and armed. For this she has to find men and money. From the agrarian point of view it seems to be true that the agricultural districts in Prussia at any rate supply the best men. There is no doubt whatever that the system by which one class alone supplies officers to many of the regiments is a great thing for the *esprit de corps* among the officers and discipline among the men, especially those that come from the country and are accustomed to look up to the landlord. It is also the fact that the officers' pay is not sufficient to support them and that life is getting more expensive ; and that the burden falls on the landed estates which are thus instrumental in keeping up the army to its present state of efficiency. It is also true that Germany does not provide enough food to feed its population and that in case of war with certain countries, Germany in default of a sufficient navy may run a risk of starvation. From this it should follow that (i) in the interest of the army the landed estates should not be allowed to go into insolvency, and (ii) that every thing ought to be done to prevent the cultivated area going back. I leave out a, no doubt, important factor, the absolute devotion of a whole class to the civil and military service of the state and the danger of doing anything to turn this feeling into bitter disappointment and a sense of undeserved wrong.

Now for the other side. The last time that it was found necessary to increase the army, the new Chancellor, Caprivi, was assailed by a new factor in German political life ; the economist. It was explained to him that the expense necessary could be borne if German industry was assisted, and that this was not to be done by protection properly so called, but by what might be termed promotion ; that is, by providing better conditions. Industry wanted the home market (to be secured by moderate protection) but it wanted also a foreign market for its products, and it also wanted cheap food for its labourers and cheap raw material. The solution was to obtain and secure your foreign market by allowing the foreign nation to give you what you desired to receive ; that is, wanting two things, you use one as a condition to getting the other. It is Cobden's principle sanctioned by treaty. This was the policy which Industry desired and which was accorded. The result was that Agriculture found at once that there was an enormous importation of foreign food and agricultural products while landlords were being ruined in all directions. This came at a time when money had been extremely cheap and when the landlords had been raising money everywhere on mortgages. The effect was a degree of personal exasperation which I suppose, short of civil war, has hardly anywhere been equalled. A ferocious campaign of denunciation and calumny was conducted against the chief promoters of the new policy and now the last of them, Marschall, has been hunted out of service.

What is the ruler of men, a heaven-sent and guided Emperor and King, to do under the circumstances? He is King of Prussia and has been taught history. He knows what his house owes to the Junkers. He is also chief of the army and he knows what is the value of good material and of discipline. But he wants to be able to pay his army and also to build a fleet. How can he do it unless Germany is rich? and Germany can only be rich by manufacturers. He is therefore in a continual dilemma which he generally solves by giving the agrarians everything they want except the essential thing. They hate Caprivi and Marschall; both are got rid of, but their policy is maintained. Every sort of subsidiary legislation is introduced which can appear to assist agriculture—financial facilities, railway rates, agents abroad, etc., etc. If a measure is desired which can gall the dignity of the mercantile classes without doing them much harm, it is probably passed, if not too outrageous. But nothing is done either to save agriculture in the way it desires to be saved, or to inflict irretrievable ruin on industry. Nor is there the slightest chance that anything will be done. But the result is that Industry is furious and Agriculture not satisfied; and that the Government will have to face a general feeling of discontent.

In the meanwhile there is the fourth estate, which has been growing while the others have been fighting. Every year the Socialists have been becoming more numerous and more determined. And they have been faced, not by really repressive measures (for these had to be abandoned), but by insults that did them no harm, and by half measures that Catholics or Liberals in their own defence were obliged to make innocuous. Like the Industrialists, the Socialists have been irritated but not injured. The Government has been always showing its teeth and growling but has hardly ever dared to bite. The Industrial, galled and exasperated, is apt to say, The worst Socialist is the man who has the ear of the Government and wants to take away my property, not the man who preaches a doctrine in meetings and hasn't the smallest chance of carrying it out. This autumn these two were very nearly acting in unison in matters of elections. The Catholics remain. The memory of the Kultur Kampf, Bismarck's confessed blunder, makes them, naturally the conservative element, one of the most determined of the Government's enemies. They can make a bargain, not an alliance.

In the face of all this opposition, what is the Government's strength ? Bismarck had hardly ever a parliamentary majority. This Government has certainly not one. Every one in the country seems to have their grievance. It exists because it *is* the Government, represents union, order, police, money, peace. The Germans seem no less unable to conceive of not accepting the Government as the Government because they object to its policy than a Hindoo would be of not worshipping the Ganges because it had overflowed his crops. Perhaps the reason again is the immense and tremendous pressure from without, which makes a German regard his Government as a sailor does his captain when the ship is in a cyclone.

I have omitted the Jew in this little picture ; and yet this is the city of Jews. What place would you give him ? To begin with, he is socially boycotted, and his activity also is the object of some of the Government's most offensive legislation. And yet Rothschild's agent is admitted into the Foreign Office before ambassadors. The most important object which Germany appears to have been pursuing in recent politics in the East and the Far East seems to have been finance. The press is almost entirely in the hands of Jews and the Government does an enormous amount of its foreign and domestic work through the press. It looks like an alliance between two men who agree to quarrel in public in order to be better able in private to manage those fools, the general public. ' Strike but pay me,' says the Jew. Which uses which ? I know which you think gets most advantage out of the bargain."

16th October, 1897.

" To Villiers,

Nothing is going on as yet, as the Emperor has only just come back. It is really singular how he seems to mesmerise everyone—Nothing can go on without him. The air and the papers are full of him. He came back from his hunting lodge (what he does there is not known), and the Berlin gossips tell all sorts of stories about him. He immediately called a council of Ministers and distributed his orders. To-morrow he will doubtless make a speech—and his speeches are now one more surprising than the other. The army is furious because in

Russia he said in addressing a Russian regiment that he wished
he had a German regiment which would manoeuvre half as
well ! You may imagine the fury of the good faithful Prussian.
In Hungary he praised up the Hungarians to such an extent
that the Germans are angry ; and very open complaints are
made in every quarter. In Bavaria he formed the centre of a
legion of legends. He is reported to have talked incessantly of
' my army ' to the Bavarians, and to have invented the man-
oeuvres as a gigantic advertisement of himself and made a sort
of circus of the whole business. They say if he is deposed he
will make his fortune in reorganising the Circus Busch—which
corresponds to Astley's here."

Nov. 7, 1897.

To STEPHEN.

" There was very nearly a severe crisis, as the Chancellor had
given his word that he would bring in a bill for the reform of the
military courts and the Emperor would not let him keep it.
Consequently, being a gentleman though a Chancellor, he said
he would have to resign. Then the G.D. of Baden came on the
scene, as well as various people interested in the preservation
of internal peace and in the increase of the navy, and told the
Emperor that unless he was prepared to face a general outburst
of discontent he must yield. So he yielded, as Charles II. or
Queen Elizabeth would have yielded, and all goes smooth again.
Whether he is more like Charles II. or Queen Elizabeth I don't
know, but he is quite accustomed to bring on a crisis, to talk big,
and at the last moment to yield. There is certainly a very
general feeling of discontent as expressed in the newspapers, but
how far it goes, it's hard to say. The difficulty is that the
Emperor is not hereditary Emperor of Germany, descending
from the Henrys and Ottos and Fredericks, and yet he behaves
as if he were. The other Princes don't like it ; the Prussians
think he is forgetting Prussia and an enlightened press is rather
inclined to laugh. The fact, however, that, in a matter concerning the relations of the Sovereign and the Army, the
Emperor has yielded to public opinion, shows that this Empire,
however strange its constitution to our notions, still belongs to
the countries governed in the main by public sentiment."

BERLIN,
Nov. 13, 1897.

To VILLIERS.

" Chirol, of the *Times*, is staying and has been going round
among old friends. It is amusing to hear his experiences. He
says the language often used about the Emperor seems sur-

prising, especially with the law as it is which makes it criminal to say anything disrespectful of the ruler.   The fact is that the Emperor has now assumed control as absolutely as Louis XIV. did.   Only Germany of to-day is not France of Louis' time. You can't crack your whip over an engine with much effect. All the men now in power except the Chancellor are creatures of his own, absolutely in his hands.   Bulow is perfectly colourless so far as his own policy is concerned.   And the Chancellor's character is so weakened by age, that, as someone said of him, he can steer well enough if he only had steerage way : but he hasn't—his fall would mean that nothing whatever stood between Germany and the Emperor, and a buffer is badly wanted.   So he was saved—partly at the urgent entreaty of the old house-friend of the Hohenzollern, the Grand Duke of Baden.   But now it is said that Bulow will shortly succeed him with a personal crony and beer-companion of the Emperor—Kiderlin —as Foreign Minister.   Ask them at Copenhagen what they think of him.

In the meanwhile the Emperor must take the initiative in all legislation—must oppose, or sanction or advocate ; nothing in the machine must move unless it is at his personal request. ' He is like the cock who said the sun had risen to hear him crow.'   Naturally the German people, who are engaged in various business and scientific operations, and extremely busy about their own affairs, and quite accustomed for some years past to act the passenger and leave the navigation to the captain, are rather annoyed at the extraordinary antics he thinks fit to play.   The difficulty is ' What is a good sailor or passenger to do when the master of the ship goes mad ? '   That is a question that may have to be decided.

On the other hand, it is always possible that we have a genius at the head of affairs and that when the moment comes he may descend and save us all.   In the meanwhile he is excessively entertaining, and, not being on the ship he navigates, we can watch with keen interest.   I believe myself that though he exaggerates everything he gets hold of the right rope and pulls at it—for instance in the matter of commercial policy.   The French here say he was in the right about Greece, and might have saved all the trouble if his advice of a blockade of the Piræus had been followed for a week." [1]

In the latter part of 1897 a Bill for further increases of the Navy was meeting strong opposition, when there happened one of those minor tragedies which statesmen have often found providential.

[1] Greece, being dependent on sea-borne supplies, could hardly then have gone to war.   The Allies preferred to blockade Cretan ports.

Two German missionaries were murdered on November 4 in the province of Shantung; and on November 14 German cruisers landed marines in the bay of Kiaochow, and declared the territory a German possession. It was a sharp demonstration of the uses of a navy, given to a people whose fast-expanding commerce made the possession of oversea coaling stations a real interest. Germany had no port under her control in the Far East; England, Russia and France were all provided. The town of Tsing-tao soon became an important centre of German trade. But it was plain that this isolated possession could only be maintained by the presence of force in reserve and the Kaiser emphasised this dramatically. Lest China should resist, he despatched at once a naval squadron under the command of his only brother, Prince Henry of Prussia, and in a farewell speech proclaimed that " the German Michael " had taken his stand firmly where the flag was planted. " Should anyone attempt to affront us . . . then strike out with the mailed fist."

China was in no position to resist; Japan waited; Lord Salisbury did not protest. Russia made no sign; but in December the British Minister at Pekin was officially informed that the Russian fleet had received permission to winter in Port Arthur, at the point of the Liao-tung peninsula, which China was pledged not to cede. Japan asked the meaning of this, and was told that the loan of the harbour was only a temporary accommodation. England was told the same; but when two British gunboats were also sent to lie in the port, the Russian Foreign Minister requested and secured their withdrawal. When they were gone, Russia received from the Chinese Government a lease of Port Arthur and Talienwan, with the right to build a railway along the peninsula. She had thus secured the ocean terminus for her Trans-Siberian Railway. Lord Salisbury's answer was to procure from China a lease of Wei-hai-wai, giving a naval station on the opposite side of the entrance to the Gulf. But this concession was calculated to estrange Japan, with whom Lord Rosebery's Government had gained friendship in 1894 by surrendering all extra-territorial rights in the Treaty ports, and by refusing to join the demand that she should surrender the fruits of her victory.

Germany's feeling was expressed by a letter of congratulation from the Kaiser to the Czar, on the execution of this secretly concerted movement. Spring Rice comments :

Dec. 26, 1897.

To VILLIERS,

" The whole history of the last month has been peculiar. Of course, the motive power has been the Imperial will and naturally the Imperial mind does not feel very favourably inclined to England now—and indeed one can hardly wonder at that. But the action has elicited comments which show clearly enough the drift of opinion—which is, quite evidently, that Germany has a great deal to fear from Russia's antipathy,

and very little to fear from England.   As soon as the occupation
of Kiao-Chow was announced, everyone here took the greatest
pains in proving that the action was not directed against
Russia but solely against England, and that is the constant
chorus of their song.   Indeed, the whole incident has been used
as a sort of peg to hang their hatred of England on—which is so
plain and evident that no one who is resident in this part of the
world can doubt it.   But because such a feeling exists, it
doesn't follow that it will find expression in a hostile *act*.   For
this we have as yet ample guarantees.   Of course, after seven
years it is believed that Germany will be quite free from the
danger of an effective blockade, and *may* be so.   In the meanwhile it is plain that the average German at any rate does not
believe in the possibility of a blockade, because they don't believe
England under any circumstances would go to war.   So they
think that unless some evident breach of right is committed,
they will be quite safe from attack, and the Emperor is very
unlikely to commit such an evident breach of right as would
justify a war.

In the meanwhile it would be absurd to deny that both the
Emperor and his people are actuated by feelings of hostility
against England which are only limited by the German regard
for law and by the practical fear of reprisals ; which (as yet)
would be of a very serious nature.

The reason of this is quite simple.   We stand in their way
everywhere—we have most to take—and we are personally
objectionable.   Marschall said openly to the *Times* correspondent that England ought to realise she offered the best booty
and that she had better pay blackmail as soon as she could.

If England is not prepared to pay blackmail, she must be prepared to defend herself—and one knows robbers are not very
particular about the time or manner of attack.

It makes one a little indignant, the respectable-looking
farmer organising a band of bandits to attack his harmless
neighbour ; but it is the policy which is advocated here quite
openly—no secret is being made of it—and it seems to have fair
prospects of success.   You remember the great war song of
Peacock, ' The mountain sheep were sweeter, the valley sheep
were fatter, and so we thought it meeter, to carry off the latter.'
It is the hymn of the ' real ' politician, as he is called here.

In the meantime, the more China is opened up the better for
trade all round—that is abundantly proved by experience ; and
Germany, though filled with hatred for us (which seems to be
returned), produces a class of man, who, as everyone from the
E. will tell you, works admirably with the average Englishman.

He is honest, hardworking, tells the truth, and in general is what the American calls a white man. We ought to be glad that he is established in those parts, and certainly prefer him to the Russian or the Frenchman, with whom the Englishman has far fewer points in common. So far it is a distinct gain. The drawback is that the German is quite conscious of this, and that his nationals have been treated as one of themselves by the English colonists in the East. And this feeling is one of the bitterest possible : the sense of benefits received is, as you know, the most galling sense there is. Germany must now have an establishment of her own without English protection or help, and the rather patronising articles in the English papers were worse than all the abuse of the French or Russians.

I should say that the desire here was to organise a common course of action against us—less perhaps for the sake of Asia, than for Europe, to unite in China what Europe had disunited : to establish themselves in China, to have a *point d'appui* so as no longer to be treated as a negligible quantity by the two allied powers : but at the same time to avoid a direct conflict with us until they are ready—which will certainly not be yet. The way to attack England is Napoleon's—to attack her trade—and this can be done as easily in peace time as in war. If she fails in commerce, she must gradually be extinguished politically, and then the rich inheritance can be divided. And indeed England would richly deserve the fate unless she is prepared to fight. This sounds extravagant and it may be so ; but that it is the common sense of the people and politicians of Berlin no one who reads the papers can deny. An overt action on our part might lead to a retreat on the part of Germany, but it is almost certain to lead to the powers drawing nearer together, and more closely approaching a union against us. An overt action on Germany's part is, as I said, very unlikely. But Germany is arming both with the military and the commercial arm, and there can be no excuse for us not to arm too. When his neighbour keeps cats, the milkman locks the dairy."

Jan. 1, 1898.

To STEPHEN,

"Happy New Year ! I spent the first hour of it in skating, the second, third and fourth in the Chancery : the afternoon in writing my name down on various personages who have to be congratulated (and no one else) on seeing the New Year—and now I am engaged—or ought to be—in making up the bag.

I have done a large financial work, a report on German finance which will, I suppose, be printed in time and will reach you. I shall be curious to see what you think of it. I know nothing of finance but tried from the commonsense point of view to understand something about it. . . .

I went to-day to see the wife of the Minister of Foreign Affairs, Bulow. It was rather amusing—a sort of Italian gipsy, full of fun, hating Berlin and saying so—loving Rome and despising business—surrounded by ancient lovers, and groaning over the misery of being in the wrong place, and hoping it would soon be over. She is a born Italian—was married to a German diplomat who insisted on her (a Sicilian) marketing, keeping books and learning algebra. After two or three years, she preferred the society, first of an artist, then of a statesman, married again and is now queen of this capital of propriety. It will be amusing to watch how it all ends. She is said to have an enormous (mental) attraction for the Emperor. . . .

General impression in the yearly reports that England is going to the dogs. "

This impression prevailed strongly throughout the first half of the year, and was based on the apparent contempt shown for England by the other powers in China. Even in England the seizure of Wei-hai-wai was regarded as a somewhat impotent gesture, whereas there could be no doubt about the importance of what Russia had secured.

In the early autumn Kitchener's success at Omdurman, the recovery of the Soudan, and the enforced submission of France at Fashoda, altered the aspect of affairs.

Jan. 27, 1898.

To STEPHEN,

" . . . I suppose you are as usual rather sanguine about affairs but your letter is very encouraging indeed, and I hope England is really prepared, if need be, to stand up for herself as at the end of last century. I like the remark at the end of the *Times* article that it is true that we are a nation of shopkeepers, but the Austrian writer who made the taunt should remember that the results of English shopkeeping enabled England to prevent the author of the taunt from depriving Europe of her liberties. I think the answer is a fine one—and should be put to the credit of an unknown writer at 2 in the morning ! It is so much better than their infernal German bombast and vituperation. I think, if the gods are just, the wholly selfish and cowardly policy pursued by these peoples must lead to their final overthrow. Only I fear some of our people are just as bad. We must, however, be provided with the powder as well as the God, and we ought to be prepared for every sort of sacrifice for the great name of England.

Do you remember poor Nikias' pathetic appeal : καὶ μέγα ὄνομα τὸ τῶν Ἀθηνῶν. Sad to think of it now. Are we to go under or survive ? I hope at any rate ' valiantly vanquished ', if that is to be, and fighting for a good and just cause. It is certainly refreshing to read an English political speech after a German article : I like the thought of a man facing the vulgar people whose votes he has, and who will have to fight if there is a war, and telling them plainly as man to man what the Empire is for and what they are to fight for. The German writer, a dirty Jew generally, whom his employers are afraid to be seen talking to, gets his ideas from the Foreign Office in a back room ; launches them in secret, is disavowed if necessary ; generally, if successful, is rewarded with some piece of scandal or secret information—and that is the means they have here of making their political opinions known to the world. They are treated as the *Græculus esuriens* in Rome.

' St. Ives ' is delightful ; the characters are so fresh and above board ; it is a pleasure to hear them talk and believe that simple bravery and truth and love-making hasn't altogether vanished from the literary world."

Now comes a series of letters which bring into strong relief Spring Rice's view that the two main English-speaking nations had a common interest, and his determination to use whatever gift he possessed to further this interest. They are addressed to Hay, then Ambassador in London, and Spring Rice no doubt expected that Roosevelt, who was the close friend of them both, would become aware of them. Roosevelt's action in raising the Corps of Rough Riders had made him by this time one of the foremost personalities in America, and the occupation of Manila was attributed to his influence at the Navy Board.

Hawaii was annexed by resolution of the American Legislature on July 7 and the formal transfer of suzerainty took place on August 12, the day on which hostilities between Spain and the United States were officially ended.

BRITISH EMBASSY,
BERLIN,
April 30, 1898.

" MY DEAR AMBASSADOR,

It occurred to me that it might be worth while, with reference to a talk I had with you when I was in London, to write about Hawaii. You see that the official German papers say that Germany will issue no declaration of neutrality ' in order to keep her hands free as she did in the case of the Turco-Greek war and the Japanese war.'

In the case of the Chino-Japanese war, she was able to inter-

fere to prevent Japan reaping the fruit of her victories, and subsequently took to herself a part of the spoils of the conquered
which she had refused to the conqueror.

In the case of the Turco-Greek war, she was able to secure for
herself the satisfaction of her own creditors out of the Greek
revenues, and also to establish a claim for gratitude from the
Turks.   In both cases she spent neither men nor money but
reaped more advantage from the struggle than either combatant.   It is no wonder that such a policy should be thought
the right one.   Now to apply this to the present case.   In
a naval war it must be inevitable that at the end even the
conqueror is worse off than at the beginning of the struggle.
Ships are not built in a day and are destroyed in a minute.
After the struggle is over, America will not be in a position (or
may not be) to resist demands which she would have scouted
before.

What are these demands likely to be ?   I think Samoa, or
some position in the Pacific.

Now, if the U.S. were to annex Hawaii *now*, Germany would
not dare to object.   It is most evident that she is anxious to be
on the sunny side of the affections of the U.S.   But if America
put the step off till the end of the war, Germany would immediately demand compensation—*i.e.* Samoa.   You know how
England is hampered in every part of the world and I needn't
say anything on that subject after the last Blue Book.   So I
think it is worth while (in case this has been lost sight of) to
urge again that it is vitally important, if Hawaii is to be annexed
without compensation, to annex it now."

Hay answered from the American Embassy, London :

May 5, 1898.

" I am extremely obliged to you for your kind letter.   It
jumped so precisely with my own ideas that I sent the substance
of it off to the President (McKinley).   I cannot fathom the
stupidity of those senators, who, preserving the Cleveland
tradition, still fight the annexation, but *gegen die Dummheit*,[1] etc.
Of course, I need not say, I did not give you away."

On May 1st Dewey's squadron arrived off Manila, and this American venture in the Pacific gave her action a new aspect in world
politics.   Spring Rice wrote again, pressing the reasons for prompt
movements in Hawaii.

[1] " Against stupidity " (the gods fight in vain).

To HAY.   May 7, 1898.

" Therefore, as I say again, let us try while we can to secure
what we can for God's language.   Don't let the Americans forget
what happened after the Turco-Russian war, after the Chino-
Japanese war and after the Turco-Greek war.   Those who
profited were not those who fought.

We have just received the glorious news from Manila.
How curious it is—the continuity of history, the struggle that
began 400 years ago of which we are seeing the last chapter.
How the historians criticise Cromwell for siding against Spain !
It was the divine instinct ingrained in the race which has
brought us to where we are."

Again, on May 14th, after details as to the movements of German
ships in the Pacific, and further comments on press utterances :

To HAY.

" As a summary of the present situation here, I should say the
feeling, if national feeling exists at all, is, as always, one of
hostility to the U.S.   You are nearly as much disliked here as
we are, and probably on much the same grounds.   A dog barks
loudest when it is chained.   They can't get at us.   And then
we get such a lot of bones, and in their sight too.   The feeling
in Imperial circles is also one of unqualified hostility, which is
easily intelligible on the part of an Imperial person who doesn't
approve of democracy and whom democracy dares to take not
all too seriously.

On the other hand the commercial classes—who are really the
rulers, for the Empire is now a money-making institution—and
the wise politicians who know that a rising sun is worth a
setting moon—are dead against any unfriendly manifestation
which may lead to unpleasant results.   I repeat, there seems
not the smallest chance of intervention during the war or a
breach of neutrality.   On the other hand it is right to remember
the *curbed* feeling and take it into account.

Another point which will probably come up is Brazil.   A
revolution may break out at any moment.   There is a large
population of Germans in Rio Grande del Sul.   The colonial
papers are already clamouring for a coaling station there *à la*
Kiao-Chow.   They point out that if America makes conquests
outside America the Monroe doctrine has ceased to exist—for
it must be two-sided."

America's war had a double interest for Spring Rice ; the closest
of his American friends was in Cuba, where disease took a heavier

toll than war. In July he was home on leave, and from Old Church he wrote to Mrs. Roosevelt :

> " I think of you every day and I wish every sort of feeling of sympathy could be of comfort to you. I know that Theodore is where he is for the best and brightest motives, and though his energy and power would (as his friends say) do more good to his country at Washington. I don't think that his great self-denial and self-sacrifice and devotion can be thrown away—and yours, too, which is even greater than his. The more I think of Theodore and I think of him constantly—I believe every day of my life—I think that I know in him as pure, high, noble and devoted a character as it is possible to find in our present world. I have found it hard to write and express what I have been thinking all this time."

The Foreign Office had now arranged to transfer Spring Rice to Constantinople ; but before he returned to Berlin, telegrams reported that Congress had decided on the measure which he urged so strongly on Hay. He wrote at once his jubilation to Senator Lodge.

July 8, 1898.

" MY DEAR CABOT,
     I can't tell you with what pleasure I see that Hawaii is at length to be annexed. The pleasure is selfish and has in one sense nothing to do with the real or permanent advantage to America which I believe will result from the step. I think that there can be no doubt that there is an intention (and a natural one) to depose English civilization (I mean yours as much and more than mine) from the Pacific. The new order of things which is to replace it may be better ; but it isn't ours, it is absolutely and wholly different from ours, and we have the right and duty to defend what we most certainly have fairly won on the American, Australian and Chinese coasts. I don't believe that England, the island, is strong enough, or will remain comparatively strong enough to defend English civiliza-tion alone—and I have no sympathy whatever with the people who believe that English institutions, literature, language and greatness are courtiers at the throne of London. I believe they are common possessions, to be defended, as they were won, in common—and to be enjoyed in common too. And I welcome any step which America takes outside her continent because it tends to the increase of the common good.
     I need not say how excited we all are at the very welcome proof you have given that people who talk English can still fight. It seems to be regarded on the continent as an exploded

idea—and you at any rate for your part of the world have proved that it isn't. It's more pleasant than you can have any idea of to hear of the devotion and courage of people who have everything to lose by it and nothing to gain—sons who volunteer and fathers who encourage their sons.

My dear Cabot, you mustn't laugh at me as a ranter—I do really and truly believe what I say, and you must keep a natural sneer to yourself. Please give my best love to Mrs. Lodge with all and every good wish possible."

Lodge replied :

NAHANT, MASS.,
Aug. 12, 1898.

" MY DEAR CECIL,

Very seldom do I receive a letter which has given me as much pleasure as yours of July 8. You need not imagine that I shall think you a ranter when you express thoughts and feelings which have been filling my own mind for a long time. Still less should you think for a moment that I shall sneer at what you say. Sneers have been very far from my lips during the last six months, which have been so crowded with events. The annexation of Hawaii I believe to be a good thing not only for the United States but for the world. I feel as you do about the fate of the civilization of the English-speaking people. . . . The movement which you describe as going on in the East is undoubtedly true, and I cannot but think that our appearance in that quarter of the globe will strengthen England, which of necessity, must always remain the great eastern power. One of the general results of the war has been the coming together of the English-speaking people, and I am optimist enough to believe that it is going to last.

Our own stake in this war has been a very heavy one. Mrs. Lodge's brother has commanded the ' Dixie,' which has been actively engaged on the Southern coast of Cuba, where she was in several small fights, and the other day took the town of Ponce in Porto Rico and received its surrender. Bay is a cadet on the same ship, and has been with them from the beginning. Gardner, my son-in-law, is a captain and assistant adjutant-general on staff of General Wilson, and is now in the heart of Porto Rico engaged in the operations there, which the peace has just brought to an end. The best friend I have in the world has been leading a desperate charge at San Juan, and is coming back now covered with glory,[1] but you know all about Theodore's performance so I need not say more in regard to that. You can imagine, however, what anxious days we have

[1] Lodge's son, a young poet.

had with these lives, which are so very near to us, staked on the result.

I wish you could get transferred to the United States instead of Constantinople, for I should like of all things to see you and talk over these many matters of so much interest."

Before this reply was received, Spring Rice had returned to Berlin and resumed his correspondence with John Hay. Germany had sent ships to the Philippines, and their presence suggested at least possibilities of intervention till Manila was finally taken on August 13.

BERLIN,
July 16, 1898.

" MY DEAR AMBASSADOR,

I came back here on Thursday evening and was lucky enough yesterday to meet Metternich, who is generally with the Emperor on his land journeys as representative of the F.O. I said that the presence of the large German force at the Philippines was plainly regarded in America as a threat, and was likely to lead to unpleasant incidents. Was Germany prepared to face the consequences and had the Government counted the cost ?

He said he quite agreed with the view I took, that it was unfortunate that the ships had been sent, but that it was difficult to withdraw them. It had been necessary to make a display of force to satisfy public opinion at home.

He went on to say that Germany hadn't the remotest idea of engaging in a conflict with America—only of defending German interests. I said that the disparity between the interests and the force sent to protect them was sure to excite remark, especially in view of the published desire of the Germans to get a coaling station. He then began to talk of that question and ask what England would say. I said I hadn't any doubt that the Liberal Party, a section of the Conservative Party, and the great mass of English public opinion, would be opposed to any action on Germany's behalf which would be unpleasant to America. This, I was sure of, and almost equally sure of the Government, though he must know that our Government never liked to lay down a rule for its future policy. Our conversation was, of course, quite private and we ranged over a number of topics. It seemed, however, pretty plain that Germany has no desire whatever to provoke a conflict—rather the contrary— that the Authorities are alarmed at the state of public feeling in America which is attributed wholly to English press intrigues— and that they are anxious to explain the presence of the German ships at Manila. At the same time the desire for a coaling station in those parts remains and whether by a friendly way or by means of threats they probably intend to get it. But personally I don't for the moment imagine that there is the slightest intention of resorting to arms. The battleships of Germany are all in German waters and cannot be sent away—or the German ports would be left open to blockade from France —and without battleships there would be absolutely no use in attempting a naval demonstration."

To HAY.　　　　　　　　　　　　　　　July 23, 1898.

" I have no further news except that it is increasingly evident that the Foreign Office is getting the upper hand over the Navy Department and that it is not improbable that if a friendly way out of the difficulty is found, or a convenient excuse, the ships will be withdrawn. In this country the Emperor intrigues behind the Government and the Government behind the Emperor ; each department responsible to the Emperor alone, intrigues behind the others. But they go in when it rains.

I remember hearing a good German authority say after the Chinese war, ' We are not afraid of the Japanese Navy. The ships have been strained in the engagements, the boilers want renewing, the *guns are fired out.*' Probably this argument was used in reference to Manila.

A member of the staff charged with the American war told me that they were immensely struck with the gallantry of the Americans, especially the volunteers, although they hated Teddy Roosevelt as author of the proposal that the Americans should go to the Philippines."

　　　　　　　　　　　　　　　　　　　　July 16, 1898.

To FERGUSON,

" . . . I see that Theodore has been recommended for a medal for bravery, which is satisfactory. It is an immense comfort that the siege is over and that the troops will get away. Do you see that the Rough Riders have lost half their number ? The whole affair is immensely creditable.

I have just been to the Camerons in the country. The Senator said he was mad with Bob[1] but he added, ' It will do him piles of good in his New York business.' Nothing like being practical !

Last night I saw Metternich, the Kaiser's favourite diplomat. He talked of E. Grey with great admiration as having a real talent for Foreign Affairs. You see that everyone says the

[1] Mr. Ferguson had gone out with the Rough Riders.

same thing, and you and Lady Helen ought to see that he spares a little time from his ducks to learn French." [1]

One other document may be added here. When Spring Rice left the Embassy in Washington, in January 1918, the American historian, Mr. W. R. Thayer, wrote to him :

" Please let me know if you can discover which of your statesmen it was who replied to the Kaiser's secret invitation in 1898 that Britain should join a coalition against the United States—saying that if the British fleet moved at all it would be to stand between the American fleet and the coalition. That seems to me one of the most critical decisions of modern times."

Spring Rice replied :

" The history of the crisis you mention was known chiefly to John Hay. The Kaiser was getting up an anti-American coalition, and he counted on England mainly because of the supposed sympathies of the Tory Party and the Court with Spain. However, it chanced that A. J. Balfour and Joe Chamberlain were in the Cabinet and Lord Cromer the chief adviser to the F.O. Chirol was the chief writer in the *Times*. What I remember about it (or one of the things) is that information reached London (and John Hay) that the Kaiser was on this job ; that J. C., A. J. B. and J. H. all came to an agreement, and I remember going down to Kent (where J. H. was staying with the Camerons at the Derings' place), and telling him, on behalf of J. C., that he would leave the Cabinet if the decision taken was a wrong one : ' Tell him to see if I am still there, and he will know it is all right.' I asked A. J. B. about it here, and he remembered the attitude taken by himself and Chamberlain, but said that there was practically no doubt as to the decision of the Government. It was a great disappointment to the Germans. I was in Berlin during all that time and in correspondence occasionally with J. H."

There has been in this chapter so much of the political student that the affectionate human being, the grave thinker, and the poet, have been lost to sight. But the essence of Cecil Spring Rice's thought on

[1] Like his friend Ferguson, Spring Rice had come to the conclusion that Sir Edward Grey was a wholly exceptional person. But he deplored Grey's extreme attachment to English country life, of which the ducks, native and foreign, for which sanctuary was kept at Fallodon became a sort of symbol. It was " ducks " that prevented this rising statesman from visiting foreign countries—and from learning French. Lamentations on these kindred subjects will be found recurring.

politics, in the sphere where politics mean high human action, is to be found in a letter which he wrote from Berlin on May 30, 1898, to his brother-in-law, the present Lord Farrer.

"Gladstone's funeral must have been a most impressive thing. In a sort of dumb way, as Carlyle would say is the English people's wont, they appear to have hit on the most striking way to do him honour and themselves.   That in Gladstone there lived in a most vivid form ' the substance of things hoped for and the evidence of things unseen ' is undoubted.   Of whom else can it be said with truth ?   He had a fire in him, kindled at a source most people didn't know of.   As for Home Rule, granted a thousand times that the scheme was mistaken and noxious— that it would have had, if successful, an immediate Parliamentary advantage for consequence—yet it is true that at the bottom there was a conviction that it was a message of peace to those at war, and of mercy to the suffering and of pardon to the wrong-doing.   The tributes of Russia and France while we are furiously attacking them are most touching.   From a foreign and hostile country we receive a recognition that England has produced a statesman who can bow his head to a principle greater than nationality,and love his own country without hating others.   Between him and Chamberlain what a difference ! Long may England produce such people.   In people of the same feelings and belief,if such exist, will be the true immortality of Gladstone's soul—purged of dross.   Whatever we say or believe, this is most certain, that the memory of good people whom one has loved is a very loving and breathing force.   A new power is given old words when the lips are still ; we learn from their life how to live, and from its end how to value and estimate our own.   It passes, but the work does truly and absolutely remain.   I remember sending you a sonnet from Japan at the time you were engaged.   Here is another one, written long ago, in which is said something of what I mean."

" True word on word, and deed on dauntless deed,
      So rose the ancient fabric of our state,
      To stand in spite of time and scorn of fate.
   And many an arm must ache and heart must bleed
   Ere all be finished, so has fate decreed,
      Not all unkind—and standing at the gate,
      The spirits of the great dead builders wait,
   And watch the growing pile and cry ' God speed.'

' God speed the eye that sees, the ear that hears ;
   God speed the brain that grasps the mighty plan ;

God speed the heart that knows nor doubts nor fears,
Steadfast and true ; and oh, God speed the man
Who in his soul has sworn, ere all is done,
To carve and lift and lay his corner stone.' "

It would be wrong, however, to give too grave an impression of his nature, which retained its youth far on towards middle age ; and of all his scattered rhyming, nothing has quite so engaging a gaiety as a set of verses that he wrote in the autumn of 1897. He was on leave then, among his own people and the scenery that he loved best of all (" There is only one lake," he wrote to Stephen). They were all staying at Old Church, and the visitor's book there had been much adorned with inscriptions. Miss Daphne Rendel (afterwards Mrs. Dunne), one of the guests, was summoned to make contribution. She passed on the duty to Cecil Spring Rice, a universal provider of verses ; and this is what he wrote against Miss Rendel's name, under date September 7, 1897 :

" I hold a high opinion of the noble genus Rice,
    Its habits are engaging and its character is nice,
    And the species distinguished by the noble name of Spring
    I honour and I cherish above every earthly thing.

    But though I praise the genus Rice, and specially the Spring,
    My ecstasy and rapture conceal a secret sting,
    For, high as my opinion is, I never can forget
    Their own opinion of themselves is even higher yet.

    And therefore, when on leaving I'm expected to express
    My sense of what I owe them in the way of happiness,
    I thought it better on the whole that one of them should sing
    This little song in praise of Rice, and specially of Spring."

CHAPTER IX

CONSTANTINOPLE

EVENTS followed rapidly in other quarters of the world before Spring Rice reached his new post ir the Near East. Chief of them was the victory of Omdurman on September 4, 1898, after which came the confrontation of Marchand's little detachment at Fashoda with an overpowering force sent by Kitchener. There was a prolonged period of tension, as Marchand refused to surrender; and till the fort was evacuated, by order from Paris, on Dec. 11, war seemed probable, between England and France.

In Crete, fighting continued between insurgents and Bashi-bazouks. Germany and Austria had withdrawn from the joint force of the Powers by April 1898 : England, France, Russia and Italy maintained the blockade and decided to take over charge of the island. Candia was in the region assigned to Admiral Noel, who landed a mixed force of infantry, blue-jackets and marines to seize the Customs. The Bashi-bazouks headed a rising of the town on September 6. A British officer and eleven men were killed, after which came a massacre of Christians. Admiral Noel sent a vigorous ultimatum to Edhem Pasha, and by November all Turkish troops were cleared out of Crete.—The question of finding a Governor for the self-governing island under the Turkish flag continued to cause difficulty. Russia, with the support of France, had proposed Prince George of Greece, but Turkey, supported by Austria, refused to accept him. In the end Prince George was put in charge as High Commissioner for the Powers.

In October the German Emperor with his Empress set out on a picturesque expedition to the Holy Land. On his way he visited Constantinople and had interviews with the Sultan, who, '' as a proof of personal friendship,'' bestowed on the Kaiser a plot of ground in Jerusalem, said to be the place of the Virgin Mary's death, to be used for the German Catholic Association of the Holy Land.

It is notable that the correspondence contains no reference to the Tsar's circular letter of August 24 to the Russian Ambassadors at all European Courts, proposing a conference to discuss the reduction of armaments.

A personal change which interested Spring Rice greatly was the promotion of Curzon from Under-Secretary for Foreign Affairs to be

Governor-General of India—with an Irish peerage, as Lord Curzon of Kedleston.

Spring Rice's movement to Constantinople was hastened by the necessity of sending someone to clear up an unpleasant personal incident connected with the Consulate at Smyrna. He went straight there, dealt with the matter, and on returning to Constantinople, learnt that he was destined to a further move, with promotion, as first secretary at Teheran. But he had some months in which to study the extraordinary forces of international intrigue and jealousy on the Bosphorus—made more acute by the friction arising from joint action of the Powers concerning Crete.

Also his journey through Asia Minor and the sight of decaying cities which had once known the height of Greek classic civilisation left a strong mark on his mind. These impressions, as well as his feelings about the great promotion of his former class fellow, were reflected in a letter to his Eton tutor.

October 1898.

To MR. LUXMOORE.

" Here I am in Constantinople. I have seen the three snakes on which the Plataean tripod was, and the wonderful interior of St. Sofia, and in a train I have been through the walls. I have been in Asia Minor and seen the ruins along the shore, and am now engaged in reading Consular reports from Asia. Here was a people civilized, rich, prosperous, but where are they now and their works ? And those who know Greeks and Armenians can only say : No wonder the old civilization perished. The most cruel and brutal of barbarisms has taken its place because it was courageous and strong and in the main truthful. All the science and the gold of the old world availed nothing ; they couldn't be honest and they couldn't fight. It is a terrible feeling, the first time one goes into St. Sofia—really, I think the most marvellous building I know, and on high on the marble walls, over the remains of the wonderful mosaics, the green glaring shield of the prophet. Or, what is almost worse, when you see a fragment of a Greek temple with its pure deep carving and perfect marble, built into a Turkish castle, raised to keep the last Emperor from feeding his people. The judgments of the Lord are true and righteous altogether. But they are indeed terrible. Shall we be wise in time ?

I am always in two minds about Curzon. He has a great deal of industry and courage and also of sterling qualities, but it isn't a fine nature, and I sometimes wonder how much he prizes the thing and how much the show. Is Britain great in order that India may be ruled by G. Curzon ? That sort of dazzling and blatant success doesn't suit my taste very well ; I like a quiet fellow like Noel in Crete who knows exactly what is to be done and does it fearlessly. It has had a wonderful success. Can't they see what a fine thing it is, we and France quarrelling to the verge of war, and yet hand in hand in preserving the oppressed from tyranny ? It is a really beautiful sight, and should be remembered to the credit of both when the reckoning comes.

I fear I don't sympathise with you about America. In spite of all I believe very sincerely in the Americans and hope with all my heart—and almost believe—that we shall one day be cordially together. The enemies of the English race are numerous enough without our putting out our hands to wound ourselves."

He had already written to Villiers, and later wrote to Chirol a more balanced estimate of the new Viceroy, which explains perhaps not only why Spring Rice was always rather on edge against the most successful of his immediate contemporaries, but also why Lord Curzon, for all his ability, rarely got men to follow him with liking.

F.O., Aug. 13, 1898.

To VILLIERS.

" I went to say good-bye to Excellency G. C. Found him in bed with a stiff back, only just in time to avoid a breakdown. Very pleased with the world—not only, I think, to get to India but also to get out of the F.O. Very much annoyed with the *Times*. He said : ' When I last left Calcutta and saw Government House, I said, The next time I shall see it as Governor.' That was eleven years ago. I wonder what he is saying when he goes from the F.O. He talked of the people who disliked him and said, ' At any rate they can't say I'm a sham.' Nor can they, as is true. Also he said that Englishmen had a marvellous knack of working honestly and hard for other people and that he had found that the case in all his offices. I thought he spoke confidently but very manfully. He has an unfortunate habit of making people feel like fools, but he is one of the least *rancunier* people that I know. His wife is radiant but on the point of producing a little Governor. All the American correspondents have come to interview her on the subject of ' A Republican in a Vice-regal Position.'

His note to Chirol (written on December 22, 1898) passes to another person—Bismarck had died on July 30 of that year.

" About G. N. C., I always try and tell myself that he is my own age, started when I did, and is enormously successful. Also that his manner of talking is to make one appear as foolish as he can—and that that comes to him by nature. Therefore, being so to speak my equal and yet my superior, I am jealous of him, and besides that, can never leave his presence without a disagreeable feeling that he has made me appear like a fool. For the double reason, I am angry. But apart from prejudice (which is bound to exist against him in my mind) I have to acknowledge that he has done a great deal, has worked hard, is on the whole honest and plucky, though, of course, quite devoted to his own interest. Many people have been so, as for instance, Wellington. I have no doubt Pitt was also self-seeking. It has been said of Chamberlain. But these people are not our own age and we haven't been at school with them or in St. Ermin's Mansions [1] together. You and I are much too much given to judge people by our likes and dislikes and to like them as they are to us. We will live to be *real-politiker* and *objectiv* some day.

The great apostle of *real politik*,[2] impenetrable to the assaults of affection, allowed himself one luxury of emotion—to hate. On the other hand it is, I suppose, possible to be one 'whose blood and judgment are so well commingled that they are not a stop for fortune's fingers to play what tune she please.' I might go on : ' Something too much of this.' "

On the general position between the Great Powers and Turkey he had written to Ferguson in the early spring (February 12) from Berlin.

" What seems to have happened lately is this :

Russia like a vulture was watching dying Turkey, intending to eat it when it was dead and rotten. It can't eat till the meat is pretty high. But Germany has come in with an antiseptic process, and now Turkey is no longer an edible object. I mean that Germany with her military organisation, etc., has really succeeded in making Turkey capable of self-defence, and also has got the Sultan's ear. Russia sees herself losing the Sultan, losing too her prestige as protector of the Christians in S.E. Europe—and determines to strike a blow, and proposes Prince George with a flourish. Germany says to Turkey, ' Say you would rather fight : Russia won't.' Turkey says so, and Russia yields. The last coup is struck and has failed. What is the reason ? Everything in Russia—finance, railways, army and navy depend on five years peace. Till five years are over she *can't* fight. But she assumes that we can't either. Hence when she is baffled in Turkey she turns to China and plays the same card there which was a trump in the Sultan's hand."

[1] When Chirol was on the *Times* staff and Curzon in the House of Commons both had rooms in their Mansions and saw much of each other.
[2] Bismarck.

Now, from Constantinople, he confirmed this view, and drew his conclusion, for action.

Oct. 3, 1898.

To VILLIERS.

" The Russians are too bad and none feel it more than the French. It is perhaps hard to realise in London the impression caused in this part of the world by the fact that British troops have been fired on in the presence and with the consent of the Turkish regulars,[1] notoriously in obedience to the same orders as were sent before the Armenian massacres ; that a British Vice-Consul was burnt alive amid jeers at the British Government ; and that Lord Salisbury is waiting for the consent of Russia before taking the steps that he has himself declared necessary. The Russian refuses to attend meetings—refuses to telegraph home—refuses to see his colleagues. All the time he is visiting the Porte, and, as we believe, submitting the very terms of the Joint Note with which the palace is now quite familiar. The Russian dragoman openly says the English burnt the town of Candia for their own purposes. The interest of Russia, in view of the Emperor's approaching visit, is clearly not to provoke the Porte but to be on good terms—as good as Germany. It is also the interest of Russia to keep the Cretan question going and to avoid any sort of settlement. It occupies Turkey ; it gives countless opportunities to Russia to be disagreeable or agreeable as occasion offers, it prevents Crete becoming Greek, and leaves inviting possibilities open in case France can be squared. In view of the plain interest of Russia, it is clear that if we wait Russian consent, we wait what will never be given, by those on the spot at any rate—though it may be perhaps as part of *haute politique*. But it is quite plain to everyone here that the *local* Russian consent will never be given to any decisive measure whatever.

But neither of the two friends of Turkey, Russia or Germany, will spend a cartridge to help her. If we have a good cause and popular opinion is roused, we can spend a good many, and at the threat of force all these spider's webs will be blown away. When Russia broke her word to Austria, and proposed Prince George as Governor, the Emperor said (as it turned out, truly) to the Turkish Ambassador, that it didn't matter what the Russians advised or demanded—they could not and would not fight."

[1] At Candia on Sept. 6. The demand for complete evacuation was not accepted by the Porte till Oct. 15.

CONSTANTINOPLE,
Oct. 9, 1898.

To CHIROL.

" I am rather too young here to have impressions. What I gather is more or less this. One power [1] wishes the decay of the country for her own good, while she promises the ruler protection, who sees the ruin of his country complacently if his personal safety is assured. Another [2] is indifferent as to the progress or decay of the country but wishes to get as much out of it as possible before the final smash. These two are the rivals—one wishes ill, the other is indifferent but very determined on its own profit. Italy, France and England are presumably anxious for the real reform of the country ; from the point of view of profit they haven't much to hope. By the force of circumstances they are more or less sincere friends.

It is a curious fact how from every quarter—except the highest—one hears that England is looked to as the real well-wisher. This may be from the opposition, because it *is* opposition. But there is no doubt about it whatever. Germany is perfectly consistent. Her interests are in Central Europe and her friendships *will* consist, *must* consist, in doing nothing. That can be a friendly act, but it can also be an unfriendly act, according to the circumstances. The Germans here complain very bitterly of the Cretan incident coming at this time—just to spoil the effect of the Emperor's visit.[3] We say we can't help it, if it is the time chosen to kill our fellows. They answer in their papers that we got our fellows killed on purpose. The *Times* article about the German papers is quite just. From every quarter—and from many countries, come articles which are quite worthy of Busch and his inspirer. It is a systematic campaign of slander, which sometimes goes into winter quarters, but never makes peace. Whoever does it, there can be no doubt whatever of its existence. Perhaps the old policy is pursued by amateurs. But it has been successful in making every Englishman living in Germany (and every American too) regard the public press of Germany and the public men who inspire the press, as an engine of concentrated and studied malignity which makes one long to give the answer which it deserves. To go to war for newspaper articles ! It sounds absurd ; and yet that is what almost every English resident in Germany must be inclined to wish."

[1] Russia.   [2] Germany.

[3] The German Emperor was received at Constantinople by the Sultan on Oct. 18, 1898.

CONSTANTINOPLE,
Oct. 15, 1898.

To FERGUSON.

" I got a letter in Berlin to tell me to go at once to Smyrna, and as the matter was pressing, off I went. I had under a week in London and that it seems is the last I am to have of London for some time, as I am now appointed to Persia. I rather wish it was China or Japan, but that appeared impossible and getting promotion when I did is an extraordinary piece of luck which I thank Heaven and Villiers for.

When shall I see you again ? I'm sure I don't know. It does seem an appalling way off, but it is part of the game and I've chosen it. There is something rather disagreeable in this part of the world for an Englishman. We are closing up our accounts here—we have bet on the wrong horse and are trying as well as we can to hedge ; and the situation is notorious.

Everyone here seems agreed that things are getting steadily worse ; that not only is the administration getting weaker and poorer but the attitude towards foreigners is getting more defiant. A catastrophe is always possible now, like this of Crete. The circumstances are much the same as those in Armenia. It is known that a hostile attitude to Christians will be well seen at the palace. Both soldiers and governors know this, and in defiance of the official orders they act in deference to what they know is expected of them. They are told, and are sure, that there will be no unpleasant consequences for themselves. And the palace tell them this, because it is convinced that the jealousies of Europe will paralyse European action ; that one great Empire objects to European interference, and another supports the Mahommedans, for value received. So naturally enough the soldiers and authorities act as they are wished to act. It has gone on for four years now, and ended in the assassination of a British official, the murder of British soldiers and a Christian population, under the eye of our ships and officers. If this goes scot free, or unless some striking lesson is administered, there will be very serious trouble in other parts of this country."

A letter to his brother gives indication of his feelings towards the French—whom he came to like the better according as he saw more of Germans and Russians.

CONSTANTINOPLE,
Oct. 30, 1898.

To STEPHEN.

" I hope your health is all right. The main thing for success in life is to be going strong at 55 in nerves and strength ; the other chaps fall behind then. But I daresay you and I will be among the other chaps. But considering the number of good fellows who were at Eton with us and have tumbled into the ditches, we shouldn't complain who still trudge along the road, even if it be with a stick. However, look after yourself.

I have been reading the history of this place and country which becomes more and more extraordinary as I read it—the series of horrors one after the other which Greeks, Persians, Romans, Goths, Slavs and Turks have executed one after the other ! When you come to think of it that the Bosphorus, which has been a highway of commerce for at least 2200 years, has no monument the whole length of it older than the fifteenth century—that is, later than any of our big cathedrals. The Loire looks infinitely more historic and the Rhine more venerable—that is, excepting St. Sofia and the three intertwined dragons of Plataea. The history of the Balkans is quite inconceivably detestable and one can well understand the state of morality which exists in this part of the world. The air is full of lies, robbery and murder, and as Mrs. Poyser [1] says, it's ill living in a hen house if you don't like fleas. I quite agree about France and England. I distinctly dislike the brutal tone of the English papers and the would-be jauntiness of Lord Salisbury. Is an English Lord really the type of courtesy ?

I think our people in England ought to understand that here and (in China too, no doubt) the artificial character of the Russo-French Alliance comes strongly into relief. France sees that she is going against her own interest for the interest of another power, in the hope of being rewarded in another part of the world. That hope has fallen to the ground ; and she still does her duty, a faithful servant, with promises for a reward. You cannot feed capons so. But in this situation is it possible that no change or reaction will take place ? And it would be clearly to our profit. It is right and just that the liberal, enlightened, civilized and idea-ed peoples of Europe should work together instead of against one another. Our struggle would only be to the advantage of the powers of darkness.

I shan't go to Persia before the spring—as the new head of the chancery here doesn't arrive."

A few days later he wrote to Chirol on the same theme, but linking to it his thoughts about Persia, where his work was next to lie.

[1] In *Adam Bede*.

To CHIROL.

" As a good sign of what impressions of people of all sorts are, I quote you Siemens—the head of the Deutsche Bank. He says that every year the Turkish Empire falls lower in every respect. I asked him again and again to be quite sure, and he said again and again that he was convinced that as long as this Sultan lived—and he would have a long life—things should get worse and worse. And when he died there would, he thought, be a revolution. This is the man who is investing so much German capital here. What security have they taken ? He also told me, what seems to be generally believed, that Russia is looking East, not West ; that she has definitely abandoned for a term of years the idea of getting Constantinople into her hands. The King of Roumania, who has just seen Bunsen, told him the same and added : ' She will get to the sea by another route.' That clearly means either Alexandretta, or the Persian Gulf. Now, the former conflicts with Germany and France, besides having an infernal country to cross ; the latter route follows the Euphrates and Tigris, and is the richest district, under a settled government, in the world. I should therefore bet on the Persian Gulf. The state of things in the mountains where the rivers rise will always make it easy for Russia if she wants to interfere ; once she holds the tableland, she can come down into the valley whenever she likes. It is, however, quite out of the question that she should attempt a railway now ; the country is tremendously difficult and she has enough railway building on her hands (*vide* the *Times* article on the Siberian Railway). But I think this Persian Gulf scheme is a distinctly sound one for her, and would offer an excellent basis of agreement with Germany and Austria : ' I leave you alone ; you leave me alone.' The policy of Germany and Russia to divide Europe and Asia between them is getting clearer every day : the basis being that Germany is to help Russia, by keeping her rivals quiet, and by providing the means, while Russia guarantees Germany peace in Europe and a market in Asia.

The possible powers to stand against this combination are now engaged in fighting among themselves. This war,[1] if it takes place, is definitely placing the hegemony of Europe into the hands of the two Empires ; the free peoples will do what free peoples have always done—witness Asia Minor—used their freedom mainly to do each other harm for the benefit of the tyrannies.

[1] Between France and England, over Fashoda.

It is curious to see the manner in which the unnatural nature of the Franco-Russian Alliance is brought into relief here. The French and Russians have no interest in common here—and yet the French have to follow the Russians in everything *because* the Russians have promised them what they intend never to perform. It is so clear that, if we can tide over the few colonial questions left that the natural community of interest of the two nations will have its natural effect. Alas for the folly of the world ! We believe that all is for the best and that the best survives. And yet here is an enormous district where high civilization, philosophy, poetry and religion have flourished more than anywhere else—and it is now a desert inhabited by savages and Greek merchants—the two vilest types I know in their different way. Civilization is neither made nor maintained by accident and by leaving things alone ; it must think and struggle to maintain itself. We seem to be going light-hearted into terrible times. I don't mean for a moment that we shouldn't fight—not fighting might be far worse : I mean that fighting, and fighting France, for the benefit of Germany and Russia, is a damnable necessity.

I sat near Cambon [1] at dinner the other night. He seems very friendly to England and is indeed known as such. He is notoriously anti-Russian here. He is quiet and good-looking and I should think would make a pleasant impression. Of course, as you know, he is personally most in sympathy with our policy with regard to Turkey and this has been growing on him for a long time. His successor will begin by being very Russian—and gradually become like Cambon.

The Emperor did no commercial work, as I gather, only prepared the ground. He appears to have told the Russians he left the concert [2] because he would not be a party to handing over Crete to England. You remember he said to Sir Frank Lascelles that that was the only possible solution and he quite approved of it.—Stead is here fresh from the Czar, on his way to the Pope, and dying to see the Sultan, to whom he has written. (' The Czar is all for peace between France and England.') So is Stead. So we ought to be safe ! ''

The German Emperor's '' preparation of the ground '' consisted in making public declaration of the '' mutual and unalterable friendship '' which existed between Germany and Turkey : and in declaring this at the moment when Turkey stank in the nostrils of civilisation by reason (chiefly) of the Armenian massacres.

[1] M. Paul Cambon went to London as Ambassador in the following January, 1899.

[2] Of the Powers for action in Crete.

CONSTANTINOPLE,
Nov. 24, 1898.

To VILLIERS.

" Constantinople is full of rumours of an impending crisis of a
serious nature. The reason—the real reason—appears to be
a curious one. As you know, the Sultan has gradually sub-
stituted his own government for that of the Porte. He has
practically extinguished the regular Government by sending
orders behind their backs to all his officers which they prefer
to obey. All branches of administration depend on Yildiz. So
if the Sultan is all right and active, the administration goes on in
the appointed path—for instance, Armenian massacres. But
the Sultan has disappeared into the harem. He has taken
again to the pleasures of love and there is absolutely nothing
to be got out of him. But the result is disastrous. He has
destroyed the Porte and now he can't do anything himself.
The Germans haven't even got their concession for a wharf at
the end of their railway.

The effect of the German visit has been, of course, to make
both French and Russian Embassies very anxious to inflict
every sort of humiliation on the ' mutual and unalterable
friendship.' So they are both rubbing in the Servian difficulty
which is bad, very bad, but not much worse than it has been for
years past : only, the atrocities are committed by the Sultan's
dear Albanians, and it is particularly galling to him to have to
do anything against them. Austria and Russia are probably
really sincere in their desire to prevent a row, but they can't
continue indifferent to the facts brought forward by both
Servia and Bulgaria. On the other hand, there seems no doubt
that the Russians are deliberately encouraging the Armenian
revolutionary party ; the information we have on this subject
comes from the Armenian religious authorities.

There are some funny incidents one hears about the Sultan's
reception of the Emperor. He ordered the same wife that the
Empress had seen during her last visit to be brought out of the
honourable retirement in a three pair back where she is living,
and presented anew to the Empress as the mother of the four
children born since Her Majesty's last visit. His mother, or
rather foster-mother, was brought out too, decorated with a
large ribbon and told to behave prettily. The Sultan came to
the audience room in the harem to see how things were looking
before the Empress came in, and found the old lady with her
grand cordon slipped over her capacious bosom. The Sultan
stepped up to her, called her a silly old thing and boxed her
ears, so that she was in tears when the Empress appeared.

The youngest daughter of the Sultan was deputed to give the Empress a beautiful bouquet chiefly consisting of diamonds. The Empress gave the child a gold bracelet. She came back with the present to the harem. The ladies exclaimed on the meanness of the gift, and scolded the child so that she cried. The Sultan, who is fond of the girl, noticed it and asked the reason. When he heard, he went in and made a scene—to which one of the women answered with an energetic speech, saying he was being made a fool of, was cheated himself, like his Empire, by the greedy Giaours, and that in return for jewels worth £10,000 the Empress had given a bracelet worth £2 : ' which I shall put to a worthy use,' said the woman, and clasped it round the arm of a negress, who still wears the Imperial gift.

From every quarter, news comes of very grave discontent, from Sheikhs, common soldiers, professors and statesmen. But they are all in such a state of fear that only the most powerful dare do anything. People are being spirited off every night. They never reappear. The whole place is full of spies, said to cost three-quarters of a million a year. The Palace is full of scoundrels of the deepest dye who are paid by all the scoundrels of the Empire for protection. And the Sultan knows they are scoundrels and prefers it, because, he says, they know that if he went, their day would be over at once."

Dec. 22, 1898.

To CHIROL,

" It appears that a certain gentleman here who was trying to blackmail a friend of the Sultan's was shot and killed in a restaurant yesterday. The same murdered gentleman on one occasion walked into Tokatliari's restaurant when the Armenian cashier was counting out the money, and with a pistol at his head demanded £200, which he got. Another occasion he called on Madame Artemis and tried to rob her nymphs of their jewels. Madame A. jumped out of the window and was caught in the arms of two policemen. The murderer was secretary to the Sultan's go-between, who gets all the bribes and divides them with his Imperial master. As the murdered is an Albanian, there is a hue and cry after the murderer, and the city is in a ferment. The story is a curious commentary on the friends of Yildiz.

As to Macedonia, what I gather is (with all reserve) : The Serbians, Bulgarians and Greeks hate one another more than ever, and would each prefer the Sultan to the others. But the Ottoman Government under the influence of the Albanians (who are, as you know, the bodyguard) connives and does more than connive, at robberies and murders. The two great powers chiefly interested [1] are anxious that no incident should occur, and have agreed together on a programme, should anything occur, and this programme does not include (unless absolutely necessary) annexation.

But the state of misgovernment against which Porte and people protest in vain is growing steadily worse, and murders are steadily increasing. The countries concerned cannot continue to look idly on, and diplomatic intervention has already begun. The palace adopts its usual tactics—sends presents of horses and kind telegrams to powerful monarchs— bribes newspaper correspondents, cajoles dragomen, denies facts—does everything except fulfil the reforms it promises ; and the outrages continue and will continue.

Blood will cry for revenges or for justice, and for that at any rate the palace is prepared : the only steps it takes are to make military preparations, enrol men, mass regiments on the frontier and improve the military roads.

So that if there is a rising, it will be put down with a very strong hand and unless the powers are prepared to intervene with their military strength (which I suppose they are not prepared to do) diplomatic steps will either lead to nothing or to a tremendous calamity. That there will be a peaceable change in Macedonia is out of the question, and there will be no change at all unless Russia and Austria are prepared to intervene by force. As presumably they are not so prepared, they will probably insist on the agitation being kept within bounds. And that depends on whether or no the palace rule becomes absolutely intolerable.

It must be confessed that many people think that this will be the case. Things are going from bad to worse. So much for politics. I am off to bed. Happy Xmas."

Another group of letters to his American friends brings out even more fully the extent of what he had suffered from America's public unfriendliness, and of what he had come to hope from the burst of good-will over a war which first brought the United States into the arena outside their own continent. The first is to Roosevelt, who had just been elected Governor of New York.

Nov. 15, 1898.

I am perfectly delighted you are Governor. I wish you were Senator, but that is to come. What times you and Cabot will have together.

I have *The World* and follow your doings at Carnegie Hall, etc.

[1] Russia and Austria.

Where do you keep the Remington Bronco buster ? I wish I had heard your speech and others. I have them among the few papers I carry about with me. I have been a very bad correspondent. I *cannot* write. But I think of you and the children and Mrs. Theodore very constantly. Not that I suppose that does you any good, except that it is pleasant to know anyone is fond of one, and you may be very sure I am of all of you.

It is perfectly delightful to follow you in what you have been doing, and to hear from you (which was indeed noble of you). I think few people can have such a satisfactory feeling as you must have in realising your own doctrines. I constantly find myself asking what you would think of a certain thing and whether you would approve or not.

It is a relief to see that you have fixed on your policy in the Philippines. We are in difficult times. There can't be any doubt that on the whole the central European Empires hold together, and that they don't much favour the free peoples, especially those that speak English. They look upon the world as their preserve, and it may be said of Europe that it *is* their preserve. But, should the system extend out of Europe ? That is the question which will be decided in the next fifty years. We have very great disadvantages—we free peoples. Our governments are not consecutive, and as a rule we have no trained public servants who are also public masters—for in England it is popular opinion that makes a policy, and not the statesman. Then there is the press. Where governments deal with governments and not peoples with peoples, it is easy enough to get over press articles ; a word of explanation is enough. But between peoples a single newspaper article can create bad blood that will last a year. How can one bring angry peoples together ? So one has no sure reason to be sanguine. The coast of Asia Minor was studded with free cities that quarrelled and were absorbed by a barbarian Empire. But as long as we cultivate (as you teach us) the fighting manly qualities, we are hard to beat ; at any rate, we don't rot to pieces ; and a genuine burst of public sympathy and admiration, such as recently in England for America, ought to make it almost possible, should the object be a great one, to work some day cordially together. I'm not very sanguine, as I know the extraordinary talent of the English to make themselves hateful. When I was last in America, it seemed to me as if I could never go again, as the friends I liked best in the world were chiefly occupied in doing my country mischief ; and I like my country in the same absurd way that you do yours. When this last business happened, I felt as if a nightmare was over. It means possibly that our race and civilisation is safe. You laugh perhaps, but when one lives in Europe, one realises that at any moment a combination may be created that will be irresistible. I believe we should make a game fight of it. I only hope so—but it may possibly end very badly. In that case, the fall of England itself will not mean the destruction, or anything like it, of the work of England—provided that the different branches of the race have not got divided by irreconcilable hatreds. For whether the British Empire goes or not, the English people throughout the world will make such a power as can never be destroyed. I don't care for black millions and red maps; what I care for, which I learned from you, is a brave manly and honest people; the people who speak English throughout the world. What I hope is that they will never be permanently divided by mutual hatred. And I really believed that was going to happen—only three years ago.[1]

This is an extraordinary country. The ruling class, the Turks, have all the rudimentary virtues; brave, devoted and manly; but absolutely no governing power, and the moment that any of them are in a position of authority they break down altogether. The rest of the population are clever, educated, businesslike, but they lie, cheat and funk. So you have bravery without any sort of leadership or government, and on the other side, intellect devoid of any manly qualities. It is the most instructive of countries, for it shows in the most evident way the faults of the two extremes of character. The Hamadiyeh cavalry in Anatolia are the most attractive people in the world—honest, brave, hospitable, dignified; and *they* did the Armenian massacres. The Greeks are the ablest and cleverest people that exist, and their history speaks for itself.

I am going to Persia. I wish to goodness it were Japan, for then I should have a chance of seeing you. But chance has arranged differently. I am not in a very up-in-the-air condition. I haven't had the energy to write, and have had no opportunity of doing responsible work, and the time is past, rather with the result of making my mind rotten before it is ripe. But the great thing is to retain the power of being fond of people and that I have done, and most especially of you. I wish I could do something to show it.

He had evidently telegraphed his congratulations as well, for Roosevelt wrote before the letter could have arrived and, it will be seen, expressed in substance the same thought.

[1] He refers to Venezuela and Cleveland's message.

" Of course, I was delighted to get your cable, and I knew you would be pleased with my success. I have played it in bull luck this summer. First, to get into the war ; and then to get out of it ; then to get elected. I have worked hard all my life and have never been particularly lucky, but this summer I *was* lucky, and I am enjoying it to the full. I know perfectly well that the luck will not continue, and it is not necessary that it should. I am more than contented to be Governor of New York, and shall not care if I never hold another office ; and I am very proud of my regiment, which was really a noteworthy volunteer organisation.

Isn't it nice to think how closely our two nations have come together this year ? We must make every effort to see that they stay together. Do you recollect a letter I wrote you last year about Germany and especially Russia ?. . . . "

The next letter gives a good idea of what the talk was which made his company so valued in these homes. He never, it seems, talked of himself or his own affairs ; but he was a born teacher, and loved giving instruction.

CONSTANTINOPLE,
Dec. 22, 1898.

" DEAR MRS. ROOSEVELT,

I think the children might be interested in the enclosed cards ; one represents St. Sophia with Greek dome (built by an angel and a Greek emperor in the sixth century and the minarets put in by the Turks). In the middle of it is the mark of a hand, said to be where Mahmoud the Conqueror, standing on Christian corpses, set his hand against the wall to take possession, and the half obliterated Christian frescoes are still on the walls.

Then there is the obelisque brought from Egypt by a Greek Emperor, recording the conquests of Egyptian kings. Then there is the brazen pedestal of the Golden Tripod which the Greeks dedicated to the God at Delphi after the battle of Plataea, with the names of the conquering Greek cities engraved on it.—And this is the old hippodrome where the Greeks spent all their time watching horse races, while province after province was swept away.

The next picture is the inside of St. Sophia. The four great green pillars were taken from the temple of Diana of Ephesus, the pillar at the back is red granite from the temple of the Sun at Heliopolis. Below are the Mahomedan pulpits where the priest preaches with a drawn sword in his hand, as is the case when a Mahomedan service is read in a former Christian church. Beneath are a group of students learning the Koran, and a German tourist. The next picture is the wall that was defended by only 4500 Greeks and 3000 foreigners of different nations; the 4500 were all that could be induced to fight for their homes—which was all that was left of the Great Roman Empire. It is an amazing story altogether, and not without its lessons, which Theodore will sympathise with. The Christian religion as practised in this part of the world condemned fighting, and the Greeks fell, having maintained themselves by their wealth of cunning so many hundred years.

I wish you could see St. Sophia—I think it is the finest building I have every been in, and its associations are overpowering. I can quite imagine how it acts as a magnet to the whole Slavic world, drawing them down to Constantinople to purify a great church of its desecration.

I should be so glad to hear how you are getting on and how the children are. I did so long to get appointed to Japan to stop on the way and see you all. It is a misfortune to be so fond of people I can't see and a country that isn't mine. But some day or other these friendships will come home to roost.

Dec. 22, 1898.

" MY DEAR MRS. LODGE,

Won't you write and give me a little news of yourself? I don't deserve it, but if you knew how I hate writing! and what could it interest you to know that Constantinople is a city on the lake of Marmora, inhabited by Mahomedans, and the residence of the Sultan?

That gentleman (whom my country has helped to keep on his august throne) is now engaged, according to report, in killing his wives, whom he suspects of wishing to murder him (which is a natural wish). Strange rumours float about. Two Turkish workmen disappeared. They had been employed in the palace. On inquiry, such disappearances turn out to be common. The Sultan is making secret passages and the workmen employed always disappear. The yacht is seen to have her steam up very often, and a carriage is often noticed waiting in the evening inside the palace gates. The poor man is afraid.—Then we are told of a diver who a year ago was sent down to examine the foundations of a new quay. He came up horrified and refused to go down again. The bottom of the harbour was covered with corpses, some tied by the leg to a chain and waving backwards and forwards in the current.—A school will be suddenly raided, and half the students put on board ship for Africa. But they never arrive. Spies are everywhere and overhear everything. East and West there is plundering and murder ; the Powers complain ; the Sultan promises redress—and orders more murders and increases his Army. It is now in Macedonia that the storm is growing blacker. I heard an old Turk with tears in his eyes say that the end had come, and God had sent the Moslem world this plague for their sins. ' What is other's good is evil to him ; he knows no other rule.' He is surrounded by the worst cut-throats and blackguards. He knows they are so ; and keeps them because he knows that they know that his power is all that keeps the country from destroying them. He can trust them because they will fall together. And all the time he is afraid. He is shivering morning and evening, so that everyone can see it ; he only dares to go outside the palace once a week, and that to go to the mosque. He is haunted by the fear of deposition and death, which is about him night and day, yet I believe there is no human being in the world upon whom so many human souls depend for guidance, implicitly and fearing nothing but him—the bravest people in the world. And he knows the sort of man he is, and says so openly, and he knows that the foreign powers and the Christian German Emperor, who make love to him and calumniate each other to him—know what he is too. What an idea he must have of the world and of grandeur and of professions ! He is very fond of his little children, however, and teaches them to play the piano, and when he had to drive to Saint Sofia and thought the people would assassinate him, he held his little boy on his knee all the time— to intercept a bullet or a sword !

Now I can imagine how bored you are but what can I do ? I have nothing else to tell you except that I think of you all very often indeed and hope some day to hear from you."

He wrote again to this adored lady on Jan. 31, 1899, with thanks for a Christmas present, and enquiries after members of the circle— especially her son, Bay Lodge, and Mrs. Cameron.

" Are you happier or sadder than when I saw you ? Does one get sadder ? You live with a few people you are very fond of indeed ; that's the way I would like to live, and can't. I am now among complete strangers, only I like them well enough. Children have a sort of familiar look but the little girls don't take to me much, being, I fear, too old and ugly. It is a horrible habit of children to begin making distinctions so young. I am just come back from a Greek children's dancing party and have been dashing about. One of them was born in Pekin when I was there, as I found out on inquiry. I could write about myself for hours, only it can't be interesting to you, whereas I know everyone of your friends, I think, and every corner of your room downstairs. What a jolly room it is ! Since I left Washington it seems to me extraordinary that I submit with equanimity to this sort of life I live now, in comparison with those days. But then, it had then the terrible disadvantage of the genuine feeling against England, which in friends is simply heart-breaking, and so I was glad to go ; but I hope that is changed now. But, now I think of it, I have never enjoyed myself so much as in Washington and Nahant, or in a way which I like to look back on so much. And how much of that I owe to you ! It makes me sad enough to think—and here there is nothing to make one sad, if one doesn't think, if one keeps the door resolutely shut on the people outside.

This isn't after all getting much forward. Since I have been here, I have been out on long rides over a wild country with glimpses of the sea—the Black Sea, or the Bosphorus—and the domes and minarets ; such views ! And then the history is so tremendous. I wander about to a certain extent in old Stamboul and read and work a good deal. And I am now packing up. There are practically no great friends ; I like my colleagues but, of course, there is none I feel quite at home and intimate with : in fact, all that part of one dies miserably away, and leaves a stump more or less well trimmed."

The end of the last letter had a touch of pre-vision. Marriage was still to come ; but henceforward he made no great and lasting friendship. The latest of his life-long intimacies had been formed in Berlin, and this friend was in trouble when Spring Rice wrote in the New Year a letter which passes from personal concerns to those smouldering fires out of which, within fifteen years, the European conflagration blazed up.

Jan. 18, 1899.

" MY DEAR CHIROL,

I feel an endless beast for not answering before. I felt so sorry for you and didn't know how to express it. This sort of calamity falls on one and one has to bear it alone, only I know it is a great comfort to know that other people are feeling for you—and I am sure I am. I have often, very often, thought of you sitting in your room with your wretched thoughts and no one to talk to. I wish I were over there to have a good long talk—even though the fog is dark outside, and things not particularly light within. The calamities that fall on one have one good thing at any rate—they bring a sort of feeling of courage and independence. Let the world do its worst : I will still exist and do what I was meant to do. We are apples on a tree, we watch others ripen and fall, or fall before they are ripe, till our turn comes too. This is not writing to console, and there *is* no consolation except time and memory—the golden haze that makes earthly things so divine when they show through—being, I suppose, a heavenly thing itself.

Here the condition of things is, I think, as follows :

The Sultan continues his military preparations ; the three European Army Corps are being strengthened and are prepared to march in four days. The Vali of Salonica has been changed for another one—a palace tool. The reason for the former Vali's leaving was that he could not stand the exactions for military services which swamped all administrative expenditure.

No attempt of any kind is being made to reform the Government of Monastir and Kossovo, and the Porte justifies the action of the local authorities.

There can be no doubt about the intensity of the evil of misgovernment, but there *is* doubt as to whether it is much worse than it has been on the average for years.

The [revolutionary] committees are hard at work, with funds supplied to them from various sources, sending in arms, pamphlets, etc.

Servia and Bulgaria both urging the Porte to grant reforms but not agreed between themselves as to the course to be advocated ; Bulgaria desiring a large autonomous province and Servia objecting to that solution.

Russia imperiously says *no* to all suggestions that the Sultan should be appealed to ; Russia will not join in such representations and will not permit France to do so. Austria is also within Russia's influence, and for some reason does what Russia does. The Bulgarians and Servians are being threatened and cajoled to keep quiet ; they growl and growl, but as yet obey.

Feeling in Turkey is strongly against the Sultan ; all the high officials are clamouring for reforms ; only the Albanian Palace gang object.

One is forced to the conclusion that on the Russian programme—the integrity but disorganization of Turkey—the Sultan plays the first part as most important of Russian agents : and therefore Russia will not allow any step to be taken which might lead to the Sultan's deposition. Their programme might be, perhaps is : Prevent any part of Turkey being reformed, either by Turkey itself, or by separation from the Turkish Empire : prevent any power from meddling in Russia's preserve, and above all, prevent the extension of Bulgaria.

Such is the programme in which we shall have to play our part. On the other hand :

If we say, ' These murders, etc., can be endured no longer in Europe : you, Sultan, stop them ', he will order the massacre of thousands, as he did in Armenia—*unless* he is threatened with force, dethronement and death. Are we prepared, in face of Russia, to do that ? If we and Italy are—then let us go ahead. If not, do nothing, but *make it quite plain why*. We promised help to Armenia, the Sultan ordered the destruction of the people, and Russia told us she would not permit the employment of force to prevent that destruction.

Therefore, do not let us promise help to Macedonia unless we are sure that either Russia will help us to prevent the *certain* destruction of the people, which is probably already ordered, if there are representations ; or unless we are prepared to help the Macedonians, in spite of Russia, against Turkey.

But let it be clearly understood that we do nothing for these Christians, because Russia—or Europe, if you will—said on the last occasion—' We will not allow you to help the people you said you would help ' ; and that we don't intend to commit the same crime again."

These comments to the *Times* correspondent are expanded in a letter to his other friend, who could act through Parliament. It was by such means that Spring Rice, over and above his duty, always laboured for " the Idea."

March 10, 1899.

To FERGUSON,

" I am starting to-morrow for England via Athens and Rome, and will stay there a short time on my way to Persia—rather an out-of-the-way route but I have got to get an outfit, also I want to see my friends before diving into the wilderness.

Things seem to be going fairly well in politics. How is C. B.[1] doing ? I suppose that is rather a hard question to answer. Edward Grey seems to have done extremely well. Fashoda has done us a lot of good but I hope we won't rub in the pepper too much. Our interests can hardly be to drive France into an anti-English alliance with Germany.

With regard to Macedonia I sincerely hope that nothing will be done by the Liberals to encourage the revolutionary committees. The position is certainly a dangerous one. But it is worth while to consider the elements seriously and it is certainly our duty, if it is the case that words on

[1] Sir Henry Campbell Bannermann was now leader in the House of Commons.

the part of our public men make a serious difference in the situation.

The Sultan is most anxious to avoid a row, as he knows that if one does take place, followed by a massacre, the results will be serious. But he is afraid of the Albanians in whom he trusts for his personal safety (in his bodyguard) and who are ready enough to revolt at any moment. In order to conciliate them, he works on their devotion to the Caliph as Moslems. Of course, this has another side to it, the good Moslem hates the Christian as well as he loves the Caliph. This creates the danger of the situation ; the Sultan has stirred up religious feeling with the result that a massacre might happen at a small provocation. But he appears to be taking every precaution (in the way of instructions to governors, military measures, bribery and cajolery of Albanian chiefs) to prevent a disturbance and on the whole with considerable success.

The Christians are divided into three camps mutually antagonistic, indeed, the Bulgarians are accused of forming societies to murder prominent Greeks and Armenians : they are cowed and unwarlike and by themselves they can do nothing.

Servia and Bulgaria could do a great deal, and if they pleased could no doubt bring the question to its final decision. But they, especially Bulgaria, have no money and without the help of Austria and Germany can get none. Meanwhile Russia has been using the most violent language to both to induce them to keep the peace and it is certain that Russia's advice has had the greatest effect both on the Christian powers and on the Sultan.

But government is no better—murders and outrages exist as before, and all the powers are able to do is to prevent the outbreak of a horrible catastrophe.

From this point it might seem that acquiescence is a crime. But if we were to preach revolt or encourage the Christian population—at a moment when the powers principally concerned are not themselves willing to act—it would be a great act of folly on our part, and if our words were not followed by actions to protect those whom we had roused to rebel—it would be a great crime."

CHAPTER X

PERSIA 1899-1901

SPRING RICE's first stay in Persia—the only country except the United States to which he was more than once accredited—was to bring him novel experience. Hitherto, wherever his work had lain, he had found himself the representative of an England whose power seemed steadily rising. In Persia, he knew for the first time a sense of powerlessness ; and this came to him when he had his first experience of responsible charge. Since the extension of the Trans-Caspian railway Russia absolutely dominated the Persian situation. Spring Rice's nature was never optimistic ; but even had it been, he could not have deceived himself as to the facts ; and they were bitter to him. Then, while he was at this unsupported outpost of British influence—for it was a principle of British policy that Persia should be maintained in independence as a buffer state between Russia's Asiatic dominions and British India—there came to pass a series of black disasters to the British power, in the region where it had been most arrogantly proclaimed by the chorus which surrounded Cecil Rhodes. Vehement love of country, nourished by years spent in America and in Germany where, in different fashions, England was the object of jealous hate, had bred in Spring Rice a temper that shrank from the boastfulness of the second Jubilee, and he was always apprehensive lest in some hour of trial what was so proud should fail ignominiously. Now, in a war which to all the world outside England seemed a war of aggression, prompted by financiers against a small freedom-loving people, England's bulk winced under blow after blow ; and when these reverses came, Spring Rice was the representative of England, surrounded by foreigners, cut off as he had never been before, from communication with his friends.

There had been little solitude in his life ; he had lived always, by choice and by the nature of his profession, much in society. But in Persia there were at any time few Europeans for him to associate with on such terms as he had always known ; and now this torment threw him in upon himself, to escape the mocking faces that surrounded him. He had always lived much in books ; now, in the long hours and days he had recourse to the more complete absorption of writing. By far the greater part of what he wrote and published comes from the years he spent at this post ; and much of it bears the stamp of the East. Persian literature which, though Eastern, some-

278

how touches hands with European mysticism, charmed him from the first, as it has charmed so many.

The country itself, the open-air life on horseback, appealed to all in him that was fed by poetry and music, and he described his life in scores of letters, from which a selection has been made to show, from the beginning, its impact on his sensibility.

LENCORAN,
June 1, 1899.

To STEPHEN.

" I am here just on the confines of Persia and begin land journey to-morrow. There is no difficulty about it, as there is a coach road all the way now. At least we are told so—though everything in this part of the world requires verifying.

The journey has been most fascinating. From Constantinople we went along the N. Coast of Asia Minor which is most beautiful—high mountain ranges going down to the sea with small towns in quiet bays. Trebizond has enormous walls and a very fine church on a point outside the town, with a campanile and wall paintings. I saw a coin of the later Comneni, of quite appalling workmanship, giving one an awful idea of what the Roman world came to. The only thing they could do at last was build walls and cower behind them.

In Transcaucasia we had a terrible time with our luggage, which resulted in our having about eight days to spare. We spent them in visiting the old Georgian cities and churches which were most interesting. One city was carved out of the rock with churches, palaces, etc., made out of glorified caves. We have also seen the oil wells at Baku which are a most extraordinary sight. I just missed a spouter, which came on the day we arrived. Baku is inconceivable. There is an old Persian town with mosques etc., and then the black town of distilleries which is just like Manchester. Beyond is a waterless prairie with camels stalking along dusty tracks."

GULHEK,
June 27, 1899.

" I arrived here in a fine condition of dirt—that is, I arrived at Teheran where I changed and drove on here, which is only about seven or eight miles off across a dusty plain. Gulhek is one of many villages which are created by the water given by the mountain. The streams are artificial and underground—the underground channels being dug by a race of men peculiar to this part of the world who go about in little squads, digging enormously deep holes with tunnels in between them. First a well is dug at the foot of the mountain, sometimes 300 or 400 feet deep. When water is struck, the object is to lead it to its destination, and the channel is then dug upwards from the house to which the water is to be led. At intervals of 100 yards a breathing hole for the digger is made and his food is let down to him with a windlass. When he gets near the fountain head the danger is great, for if the water bursts through he is lost. So he digs himself a refuge just below the main well ; he drives his axe through the partition into the water and then flies to his refuge, where he sits till the water has run down a little. It is an amazing system and I suppose was invented shortly after the Flood.

The fields exist where water can be led to them, and you see on the bare plain the little colonies of trees that mean a garden or village—everything else bare sand and stones. Our garden has two beautiful running streams in it with three ponds, in one of which we bathe. There are masses of trees with nightingales which, as the roses are over, are mostly gone south. But I have heard one or two. There are plenty of hoopoes, which are very friendly and come and sit on the window sill. Each secretary, etc., has a house except me—mine is taken for the Chancery, but the Minister [1] shelters me. The houses are made of mud, and if it rains they are apt to split and dissolve into their element."

TEHERAN,

June 27, 1899.

To VILLIERS.

" This place is quite the queerest I have come across yet in my experience. Since I have come here, the Legation in Teheran has been twice attacked by burglars. Our guard, a set of bare-legged ragamuffins (who in default of pay live on the fruit of Lady Durand's kitchen garden) let off their rifles under our windows, I suppose, to show they are awake ; the Russian bank has been robbed of all its ready money and the robber tied up into a bundle and buried alive ; an old gentleman whose three wives were plotting to kill him took refuge in the Legation and stayed there for some days on the roof until we interceded with his family and got him to retire. He showed his gratitude by presenting us with a turkey. Plague has broken out at Bushire and the Persian Government took the ingenious line of denying its existence mainly because they didn't want to spend any money. This place is a green garden watered by a stream which runs to us from the mountains in an underground passage : where there is water there are trees and field, but failing water nothing but stones. The colleagues are somewhat arid too, even

[1] Sir Mortimer Durand, of whom much will be heard.

including the dentist, who is the most brilliant member of our society. A good many are divorced, most of them suffering from fever. They spend a good time in bed, whether alone or by twos, I can't quite make out.

We get on very well in our garden. We play various games on horseback which fill me with alarm. The last is to jump over a hurdle with an enormous spear in one's hand and then to spike a tent peg. I hear the Amir uses the heads of his buried subjects for the purpose! I can imagine that adding zest. Whose head would you use?

The old residents here all say that Persia is getting worse every day, that unless a loan is granted by some confiding person there will be trouble. In the meantime the Cossack Colonel [1] wants the bank to advance him £50,000 a year to pay his regiment. As long as they are paid, we are safe from revolution in the North, and the Colonel much prefers to be paid by our bank as they don't ask questions like the Russian bank. This, however, will not secure the South. The Russians have an energetic man at Ispahan. He arrived and took up his quarters, not in the Armenian city like other Europeans, but right in the middle of the Mahomedans and hoisted his flag as the Muezzin was calling to prayer. He then proceeded to make the Mullahs pay for a road to the Consulate through the city. As he has a body of Cossacks he can do what he likes.

The Germans and the Russians hate one another here more even than in Constantinople, and the Russians have recently put a stopper on a German scheme for a railway into Persia from the East. The Germans complain that they can't get hold of any information as to what the Russians are doing here— mainly because they work entirely through Mahomedans. They have the Sadrazam [2] in their pay as is generally believed. They are very friendly with us, but our best allies are the Germans who are very good fellows. The Persians are extremely polite but not very willing to do what we want."

The last sentence in the letter is " Stamps for Miss Ex-curly head." Spring Rice had been a guest in the Villiers household, and wherever he had been, he never forgot the children. This young lady comes in many times, at the end of long dissertations on high politics.

                                                        TEHERAN,
To MRS. LODGE.   June 31, 1899.
    " . . . All the circumstances here are delightful. It is hot but not at all trying, although it is up to 100°. But it is dry and

[1] Of a force recruited in Persia, but officered by Russian Cossacks.
[2] Prime Minister.

the nights are cold. Opposite is the mountain range. It has
patches of snow, deep valleys full of running water, rocks and
scented shrubs that burst out their smells at you as you walk
through them, a wealth of flowers, zone after zone in different
worlds with each zone its own butterflies. There are also
beasts which interest the hunter (Bay, for instance) ; and on
the other side a different world altogether, rain and cloud, vast
forests sloping into swamps and so down to the sea.

On our side is the partially watered desert and the diplomatic
circle, also partially watered. My chief (Durand) thinks
Teddy R. the greatest man in the world and has treated me with
immense respect since I let on that I correspond with Teddy.
I tell him stories and he listens open-mouthed.—I like him
immensely. He is a former Indian civil servant and wishes he
had been a soldier ; as a civilian he has been in three wars and
has twice seen Tommy Atkins in a rout. ' It seems to me, sir,
that the British Force is demoralised,' said one of them to him as
his companions were taking headers down a neighbouring
ravine into mimosa bushes. He is full of stories about his
former term in India (he wishes he was there). So does his
wife : she talks about Simla and ladies and their doings. . . .

There is a quiet little bearded Consul, who has studied art in
Japan and Florence and read about everything that is to be read.
He does the accounts. Such is the dispensation of Providence.
Then there is a Colonel whose wife is away. He has been six
years here. He doesn't seem to mind but talks of applying
for another post nearer home. He is a keen soldier and tells one
a lot. I suppose there is a European society. I have called and
they have called. But I can't tell you much about them and
I don't think you would read much more if I began. . . ."

GULHEK,
July 22, 1899.

To STEPHEN.

" This is written in the Indian Durbar tent in the garden here,
with a pond in the middle of it and a bubbling stream running
by the side. It is thirty yards long by fifteen wide, is
carpeted and furnished and the whole thing cost under £250 !
We dine there every night which is rather sumptuous and
oriental. The heat is considerable. A man who goes to town
told me he found it getting rather hot in his room, looked at the
glass and saw that it was 115°. In the sun it is about 160°.
Here it doesn't go up so high, though one morning I noticed that
it was 90° at 3 a.m. out of doors which is pretty good for the
coolest part of the day. Women suffer more than men. It

doesn't last very long.   I went up to the hills—forty miles off, for a few days.   Tremendous limestone cliffs leading up to Demavend—a great cone which rises high above everything. I long to go up it, but find my breath come with difficulty above 12,000 feet.   Our camp was about 9000 feet and we think nothing of that.

The harvest is in, but the price of bread keeps up and the outlook is very bad.   We are buying our supplies for the winter and this is what most rich people do : some of them hoard to sell.   The people are getting exasperated and talk of looting the Imperial bank to attract the attention of the Government.   A new Governor was appointed and his first official act was to cut off the ears of three bakers, which reduced the price of bread for a short time.   It has gone up since. Then they have taken to persecuting the Jews, but that has also proved inefficacious.   Between Persia and revolution is the Cossack regiment, officered by Russians, but they are not paid and there is no money to pay them with.   In the meanwhile the Shah is in the mountains, having just managed to borrow enough money from the merchants in the bazaars and the Russians."

GULHEK,
22 July, 1899.

To MARGARET.

" Where are you spending the summer ?   I can't answer your letters, as the post comes in just after ours has gone out.   It is a great event.   Once a month the dusty messenger comes riding in with his postbags which he deposits on the floor.   Then we open them and separate their contents and distribute them. It is a great disappointment sometimes, or a great delight.   Now and then but not often, letters come by the Persian or Russian post, generally in the evening.   There is never any apology for opening letters or papers but we fall upon them at once.

I think I have told you of my life here—it is quite monotonous but filled up.   In the morning I wake, stretch out my hand and pull back the curtains.   I am lying in a window opening on a garden, flowers enough but no grass, plenty of trees ; bright green above but with many dry branches and the leaves withering below as if it was autumn.   Always a bright sun and the hum of insects.   No birds any more now.   Then after, as it were, lying in the flower beds for a time, I get up and run across the road in pyjamas to a deep pond with a blue-tiled bottom, in which I have a short and very sweet swim.   A water wagtail is always there but nobody else.   Then I have tea.   It is now eight.   Then to the Chancery where my Mirza or teacher waits me. I talk or write with him. He reads Persian stories aloud. I write them down and then translate them and parse the words. It is rather a fascinating occupation and I have really got to like it. We are now occupied in talking astronomy and philosophy, so you see we are getting on. He tells me the world is getting old and wants to die. That is why things are going so badly. The world thinks if the creator sees how badly things are going, he will kill it out of anger or compassion. Food is three times the ordinary price and people are in despair. The harvest is in but it seems to make no difference and the prospect for the winter is very bad indeed.

Well, when my Mirza is gone I go to the typewriter and do official business till 1, and then lunch. Then I see the Minister, then Chancery again till 5, when it gets cool enough to ride or play lawn tennis. Dinner in a great tent, with a tank of cool water in it and a running stream paved with blue tiles and carpets from Sultanabad on the floor. That is very pleasant. But in the daytime it is pretty hot."

To VILLIERS.   Aug. 23, 1899.

" I went two days ago with Durand to the Foreign Office here. It is not very like a visit to Downing Street. We started in the morning on horseback and rode for an hour across the dust and stones till we came to a garden gate ; that is, a hole in a mud wall, by the side of which some unkempt soldiers and half a dozen maimed and diseased beggars were standing. Inside the gate was a garden, that is a grove of trees with irrigation channels about their roots. A one-storied mud house was in the middle and we were shown into a room where there was a sofa, one or two chairs, a table and the Foreign Minister, a nice old man in a black lamb's wool cap and a dressing gown, who gave us weak tea and cigarettes. Sir Mortimer and he sat down on the sofa and began to talk in Persian which I can understand to some extent now. The Persian began at once with a solemn voice to say how sorry he was that the old friendship between Persia and England was waning and that the Sadrazam was no longer on such intimate terms as he used to be with the British Minister. Sir Mortimer said if it was true he was indeed sorry, but what, for instance, could be done ? The Persian said that Persia wanted money above all things ; England was great and rich and if the British Minister wished it, he could persuade the Government to give the money. It was plain he was no friend to Persia or things would be different. And so it went on. Durand said that England *had* offered a million. The Persian said, ' But we want two ; can you expect us to be grateful for so little ? ' When Sir Mortimer said it was English capitalists and not the English Government that could provide the money and that security was needed, the Persian said that such a rich country as England could not really want security : and he suggested that a letter should be written by the English Government saying what reforms were required to advance Persia economically. ' They will be begun at once, if you promise to lend us money.' And finally he hinted that Persia would be obliged to look elsewhere.

His manner throughout was of sad remonstrance, very like an Eton Master who is telling a boy why he will have to be whipped next morning. He appeared to take it for granted that England, by saying a word, could provide Persia with as much money as was needed.

They certainly do want money very badly indeed and what will happen next winter if money is not obtained is a problem. The soldiers won't be paid, and as there is terrible scarcity, there will be riots of some kind and I don't see how the army can be expected to exert itself to put them down. If things get very bad the Russians will have to send troops in, but it will cost them less to make small money advances, enough to keep the soldiers quiet. At present, I am told that they refuse to make any large advance without the security of control of the northern ports,[1] but if they *do* give money they may very well make some sort of arrangement, in addition, about the southern ports—not for control ; but for eventual cession of some port or other. The wants of the Persian Government are such that we could probably get a promise of first choice if a port in the south is ceded to a foreign power ; or an agreement not to cede any gulf-port, or rights in any gulf-port to any other power. The second ought to be easy enough.

There seems to be a general belief in England that England and Russia might come to an agreement for the establishment of spheres of interest in Persia. The residents here and the natives laugh at the idea. It is quite true that Russia doesn't appear to wish to take any part of Persia ; she has enough to do elsewhere and quite enough territory at present. But if she wants anything she wants the whole. Persia is the route by which she intends to reach the sea, and one end of a road is not much use without the other. Everyone here says, ' Russia wants the whole and not the part, and you can never come to an agreement with her to stop anywhere.' She has been sending agents south and pressing her influence for all it is worth, and wherever there is an enemy of British power or commerce, the

[1] On the Caspian.

agent of Russia is sure to be in communication. But that Russia is not in a hurry is plain. Indeed, till the roads are more opened up, an advance would be very expensive. But cavalry and artillery can reach Teheran by the new Russian road in five or six days from the Caspian, and both Meshed and Tabreez can be taken whenever the Russians wish. It is simply a question of whether Russia wants to or not. Probably she doesn't, because if she did, it would be undertaking new and heavy responsibilities and because she thinks we would seize the gulf ports, so that while she opened one door we locked the other. Her best policy is gradually to prepare the ground, to disintegrate Persia, and prevent Persia improving. To wait an opportunity when England is engaged somewhere and to make a pounce. Does this all sound very remote ? It may be remote but it may also be near enough. We have no treaty right to prevent the absorption of the Persian Gulf ports by a foreign power, and no authoritative *recent* declaration like E. Grey's about the upper Nile."

Aug. 23, 1899.

To STEPHEN.

" I am getting on with Persian and have been ten days without speaking anything else. It is very easy and I am just in the exciting stage when to speak and understand seems a great feat of dexterity."

Sept. 1, 1899.

To CHIROL.

" I have been wandering a good deal since I have been here, in mental and physical way. Durand takes in books and I get a good deal of modern reading. Also there is a Dante, at whom I am having another go, and certain poets in English. Then there is Persian to learn which is absorbing. Then there is travelling. That here is really delightful. I have been a good deal in the hills which are just above Gulhek, as you may remember. Have you forgotten the way one travels ? The caravan goes off in the morning. One starts in the afternoon on pony back, and in the evening, comes under the sudden shade of trees with a noise of falling water. Here is a little tent and dinner, the mules wandering hungrily round, the ponies tied up for fear of fighting, the stars coming out one by one. The early bed, on a most comfortable traveller's contrivance ; before sunrise one gets up, breakfasts in the dark and starts while the stars are still bright—the sword of Orion remaining as long as any. Then on the top of the hill, if possible, before the sun gets hot, the burst of the golden light on the rocky tops and at last the view of the other side ; hill after hill with Demavend behind. Then the awful descent, the poor pony struggling behind, looking appealingly at you as you try and pull him down some particularly bad drop, and his sad grunt as he steps down all four feet at once. Then the valley and a long delicious canter between the rocky sides till the river begins to grow and springs appear and the green patch in the distance means the camping ground. Then a bathe in the river and a long drink at the spring into which one plunges as much as one can. Don't you remember it, how jolly it was ? The hot mornings and afternoons in which one does nothing but read and then the start again in the cool of the evening, and late return to camp. I make my headquarters by a good spring, fish or wander about the hills—then after a day or two move on. Perfectly aimlessly, except so far as lazy enjoyment and health is an object. The Persian servants are wonderful in camp—good-humoured and energetic ; within the limits one gets to learn, perfectly willing. One mustn't ask them to be clean or quiet or to take a mule more than twenty-five miles ; or not to break the dishes ; or above all, to wash. Fishing isn't a bad occupation and I have been rather bitten by it. There is a place near Demavend where the river runs out of one huge ravine and wanders about a little before plunging into another. Enormous mountains with Demavend as the biggest stand all round. The water is clear and lively with the familiar voice, and the world is at some considerable distance. I like it almost as well if I catch no fish, but it is difficult not to catch some.

I got so tired of seeing Demavend look down at me from wherever I was that at last I persuaded a servant to go up with me. I spent two nights on the mountain with him and two guides and got up without any difficulty except getting very giddy from the thin air. I was rather proud of the achievement till John Ford,[1] learning of it, went up too, and the taste of glory has turned sour. Everyone here wants to do a record and asks one always, ' How long did you take on such and such a journey ? ' I have come to the conclusion that the only way is to travel alone with some good books, trustworthy servants and to leave everything to them, becoming simply a baggage."

A letter to his Eton tutor, recounting this climb, lets one see how it touched his imagination.

" Demavend is about 19,000 feet high, stands quite alone and is visible 200 miles off. Darius passed beneath it, with Alexander on his trail ; the Saracens swept from the South to

[1] An attaché.

its feet, and the Mongols from the East. Now one sees the
Caspian from its top, and there is Russia. What a place Asia
is ! I wonder how many sites of great cities I saw, each one the
scene of an appalling disaster. No wonder that the Asiatic,
after all these experiences, looks with a quiet eye on our restless
emotions."

The next letter introduces a modernised Asiatic :

Sept. 10, 1899.
To VILLIERS.
" I think I told you about a Balliol man (an ex-U.P.) whom I
found here. We used to call him Kasim Khan, or Curs'im for
short. He is now called the Nasr-ul-Mulk, which means the
Victoriousness of Empire. When I knew him, he was one of
Jowett's oriental pets, a good historian, immensely hardworking,
and an eloquent opponent of Curzon's in our debating society.
He is now an ex-adherent of the late Sadrazam's, who made
him his Minister of Finance ; he is not a great friend of the
present Prime Minister, partly because he hoped, but in vain, to
be Foreign Minister. He is too independent. He is not very
popular, as when in office he took no bribes, which was thought
foolish, and gave none, which was thought wicked. But he is
very well informed, very patriotic and a good friend of ours.
You would hate him because his beard is always two days old,
but we believe him to have as many of the moral virtues as any
of his nation."

Abu'l Kasim Khan died in December 1927. He had attended
the then reigning Shah on a journey to Europe in 1889.

Sept. 15, 1899.
To CHIROL.
" About politics here. The general impression I have is
something like this. The Shah is an excellent soul, kind and
well-meaning, but very weak. He is surrounded by Turks
from Turkey, savage, avaricious and very ignorant. At their
head, his body physician, a good strong man, with good intentions but without support in the country. The present Sadrazam, who has been put in by the Court party because they
thought he would be useful, is no business man ; he is ambitious,
resolved to be the only power, has filled the offices with insignificant creatures and allows the finances to run to ruin, in order
himself to get support from those he allows to peculate. The
governors, who are not afraid of the central government, send

in no money whatever.   The only financial resource which is to
be depended on is the customs.   A Belgian official has been
employed for some time to set them in order, but he is not
given a free hand, and less money comes in than before.   Besides,
more than half a million—more like three-quarters—owed to
the Russian and English banks, the Government owes large
arrears to the army and civil service.   To set them on their
legs again, they require a large sum—they say two million.
But the state of disorganisation is so complete that it is certain
that the greater part of this, if obtained, will be wasted and in
two years the condition of affairs be worse than ever.   But the
Sadrazam, to save himself, must have money, and he has turned
in vain to us and to the French.   Both asked for terms which he
could not, he said, give ; we asked for immediate control of the
Gulf customs, and the French for about all there was in
Persia.   There remains the resort to Russia.   The Sadrazam
is notoriously Russian in his sympathies, and will be, if there is a
Russian loan, absolutely in their hands.   The Shah objects and
so does his entourage, who look to us for help, but we can give
none.   If the Russians advance money, it will be in consideration of such terms, political and commercial, as will virtually
destroy the independence of Persia.

There isn't much left.   The only disciplined force here is the
1000 Cossacks, armed and officered by Russians.   The Russians
can take Tabreez in one day, Meshed in two, Teheran in six.
Should the Persians do anything the Russians dislike, the
Russians can move their troops forward.   We can only operate
on the Gulf ports which affects them far less than the threat to
the capital.

We may thus be on the brink of important events and I
wonder how far our Government realises this and what
measures will be taken or what plans are being matured.   It is
quite plain that the Russians can make themselves masters of
all Persia. . . .   Meanwhile they will, of course, be dead
against any scheme for the improvement of Persia ; they don't
want a revolution, but they won't have reform ; like a lady's
doctor, they don't want the patient either to die or to recover.
It is, of course, the same policy as the one we are so familiar
with in China and Turkey.   They are determined that Germany
shan't renovate Persia as she has done Turkey, and warn her
off in the most unceremonious way.   The German Government
replies when the Minister objects—' that a concession in Persia
is not worth a quarrel with Russia.'

Sept. 15, 1899.

To STEPHEN.

"There is nothing new happening, only this poor country goes deeper and deeper into ruin.   The Shah is a most excellent kind-hearted, and well-meaning man, but the people aren't afraid of him and the rich men grind the faces of the poor without having their own ground.   Money doesn't come in and the Government is in a desperate case.   In five days they have to pay our bank certain sums which they say they can't pay, and the soldiers and civil servants get no wages.   The people have great difficulty in getting wheat which is stored by the rich men and they are getting discontented.   But they are curiously quiet and resigned and seem to make no very loud complaints. It is said there is plenty of money in the country, but none of it is forthcoming for the Government.   I don't imagine that the poor here are quite so miserable as ours, indeed, they are moderately happy and contented.   The sun is always there ; if they don't get food, they beg or steal it ; and stealing food is not considered a very serious offence, if the thief is really hungry. One sees how an Eastern despotism works.   If this Shah were a cruel man and robbed the rich, giving part of what he robbed to the poor, the people would be happier.   They complain that he is too just, and that if he were unjust the country would be better off.   There are in every department enormous numbers of useless employees who are not paid but who have a share in all the stealing.   In this way they live ; only the soldiers who have no opportunities have to suffer for it, and the poor Shah can't travel for want of funds. . . .

Sir M. Durand is going for two months and a half to the South to inspect a new road—so I shall be left in charge—not as chargé d'affaires, but to look after business.   There isn't much business to look after of a satisfactory kind—and the slackness of oriental ways is falling on me—as it does on everyone.   I read a good deal.   In fact, I have never had so much time for reading before, and it is a great pleasure."

Oct. 16, 1899.

To MARGARET,

"The deaths of Lord Farrer and Augusta [1] mean, I suppose, a great deal to you—although you have filled up some of the breaches.   I don't myself quite like to think of such things, as my reserve is a limited one and the gaps are appalling.   I think one is justified in talking of death from the entirely selfish view ;

[1] Augusta Butcher had married Mr. Charles Crawley and was drowned with him while boating.   Lord Farrer was father-in-law of Eva Spring Rice.

for the persons themselves it is indifferent; only it makes it infinitely important how they live while they can live. I think these two were very perfect lives, and when I remember meeting them, it seems as if there was always something definitely gained, something to be borne in mind afterwards and refreshing and strengthening. I am sure it was so the more I think of it. And it is now gone so utterly : that is, the possibility of having that feeling again. And yet what has been gained is part of oneself and remains so for ever. So one becomes numbed outside, unwilling and unable to receive new impressions, but I hope even within, living on past strength. Does one ? I sometimes wonder. I remember your saying you were losing your sense of beauty. It is so with me too in a way, but when it does come, it does come with such force and tremendous go. The other day I got wet at last. I was tired and hungry, but the good rain came down from these thirsty skies and spoke in such clear words of old days ; the old familiar patter coming before the growl, which one thinks at first is only the wind ; then the rush of wind, thunder and rain together.—Sometimes, too, riding on the plains here alone, or watching the evening making way for the stars—and, of course, books move one more and more. But about nature I don't know. I can't do without it, but it's like fresh air. A whiff does one no good, one must live in it and open one's mouth.

A different side to his preoccupations shows in the correspondence with his American friends. Roosevelt had been elected Governor of New York, on the strength of the popularity which he had gained during the war in Cuba ; and he wrote on hearing of Spring Rice's transfer, before it actually took place, dwelling specially on the change of feeling towards England which had grown out of England's cordial support during the Spanish-American conflict.

ALBANY, Feb. 14, 1899.

" DEAR CECIL,

I am very glad you are in Persia, because I know it is interesting but I do wish there was some chance of getting you over here while I am Governor. The chances, of course, are very small that I shall again hold any important position, for New York politics, as you know, are of a very kaleidoscopic nature, and now during my hour of triumph, I should like very much to have around me the few people for whom I really care.

By the way, the change of tone in this country may perhaps be illustrated by a letter I have this morning received from an applicant for appointment, who bases his claims partly upon the fact that in a public speech he answered Burke Cochran's attack upon England and explained the debt the world owes to England and the way that the English and American should work hand in hand! Of course, there will be differences between the nations and the present fervour of feeling will probably cool off, a little, but I do not believe it will ever cool off entirely. I do not believe that we shall ever go back to the old unfortunate ways. A curious thing is that I think those Americans who were Anglo-Saxon by adoption, as it were, are quite as strong about the unity of the two peoples as any others. The applicant before spoken of is like your humble servant, of Holland ancestry. The third generation of Germans feel far more akin to England as a rule than they do to Germany. . . .

About the straightest man I knew in the legislature, Kruse, was a German, and I have been trying in vain to have him elected Judge. About the best executive officer in Samson's fleet was Haesler of the 'Texas.' He has charge of the 'Texas' big guns, and he remarked to me, patting them lovingly after the war was ended, that he had hoped before peace came to turn them on Von Diederich's fleet. Our Admiral at Samoa, Kautz, is of German parentage, and he is the especial bugbear of the Germans, next to Captain Coghlan, who is of Irish blood. (The delightful Coghlan was out here to lunch the other day and was great fun.) The navy is a unit in wanting to smash Germany. The professional Irishman is losing his grip and the bulk of the Irish are becoming Americans. The feeling of hostility to England is continually softening. One of our best Captains in the navy, for whom I got a ship in the war, is Delahunty, Senator Murphy's brother-in-law. He casually mentioned to me the other day that until a year and a half ago he always hated England, but that now he was for England and expected to remain so. Laffan of *The Sun* said the same thing to me. The feeling here in favour of England is deeper than you would think. The other day I addressed thirteen thousand Methodists at Asbury Park, and the programme included a song by two girls, descendants of Carroll of Carrollton, in which one carried an American and the other a British flag, the first singing 'Columbia' and the other 'Rule Britannia,' and then crossing the flags. The taste of the manifestation might possibly be criticised, but the sentiment it stood for was excellent, and the audience boiled with enthusiasm and demanded two encores. This could not have occurred a couple of years ago. Again, take what the Canadians have recently been doing. As you know, the Canadians do not like the United States. I do not know whether you have studied the Alaska boundary question. Without going into the technicalities of the case, it is perhaps sufficient to point out that the Canadian maps until less than twenty years ago gave the same boundaries that ours did, and that American towns have grown up in the disputed territory and have for years been administered under the American flag. Because of the hitch in the negotiations over this, the Canadian Prime Minister and other prominent Canadians of the Opposition and the Government both recently indulged in public threats, in which they used the word war, as being one of the alternatives.   Two years ago this would have provoked frantic retaliatory denunciation on our part and action in the State legislatures and Congress, which really might have endangered the peace. Now it is for the most part dismissed by our papers and by all of our public officers with the good-humoured remark that there is to be no interruption of the friendship between England and America.

Now, all of this may not last, and it probably won't last quite in its present good shape, but I am greatly mistaken if we ever slide back into the old condition of bickering and angry distrust, and there will always be at least a good chance that in a great emergency, the nation of the two which vitally needs it may get more than moral aid from the other."

Spring Rice's reply to this is missing—but Roosevelt's next letter suggests its trend.

Aug. 11, 1899.

" DEAR CECIL,

. . . Do not misunderstand me ; do not think me a mere optimist. I do not pretend to be able to see into the future. I feel so perfectly healthy myself and the Americans and English for whom I care, with whom I have been thrown, seem so healthy, so vigorous, and on the whole so decent, that I rather incline to the view of my beloved friend Lt. Parker of the Gatlings, whom I overheard telling the Russian Naval Attaché at Santiago that the two branches of the Anglo-Saxon race had come together, " and together we can whip the world, Prince, we can whip the world " ! But it may be that in the future, disaster may overcome you in Asia and most certainly there are evil forces at work among us in America.   The diminishing birth rate among the old native American stock, especially in the north-east, with all that that implies, I should consider the worst. But we have also tremendous problems in the way of relations of labour and capital to solve. . . .

All of which, old man, when condensed, amounts to saying that while the future is dim and uncertain, there is no more reason for saying that it is black than for saying that it is all light ; and in any event we have all of us got to face it, and do the best we can with conditions as they actually are.

Give my warm regards to your chief. I wish I could meet him. Everyone here sends you warm love. Col. Lee, the British Military Attaché,[1] who is a trump, has been visiting us and will visit us again this fall, and so will beloved Speck." [2]

A letter from Spring Rice must have crossed this on its way.

Aug. 27, 1899.

" MY DEAR MRS. ROOSEVELT,

Mrs. Cameron, from whom I heard yesterday, described her meeting with Theodore and the enthusiasm of the populace. She says you are becoming absurdly young-looking in spite of your necessary queenliness. I wish I could see you at an official reception. Perhaps I may live to kiss your hand at the White House.

How you would hate it here ! except that there is no chance of a warlike ending to a stay in Persia. I am living in a garden watered by an underground channel from the hills ; not by rain, which never falls. The stream runs through the grounds and makes a few trees and flowers flourish ; there are several pools paved with green tiles ; a mud house with enormously thick walls ; innumerable wasps, grass hoppers, frogs and praying mantis's ; the nightingales are long silent. All round is a glaring white desert ; behind us the plain in which Tehran is and in front a great mountain wall, 8000 feet above us. There are innumerable mountain sheep and goats, and Theodore would enjoy himself. I have been out a good deal ; but I find that my head is completely gone and that I am no good whatever at climbing. I suppose the effect of giddiness at Washington. Then east of us is the great cone of Demavend, 20,000 feet above the sea. I went with mules, horses and servants against the mountain and after a struggle got to his top and looked down over the world for the space of half an hour. Travelling here is absurdly luxurious. The Persian servants love it—one camps with every comfort. No rain and little wind—only the sun is terrific in the day time. I am generally off by starlight and one has strange moments on horseback alone in the hour before sunrise. Theodore will know the feeling well. I like being alone with the Persian servants and speaking no English ; with very few books and those solid. I take the Bible and Dante and try and pretend I have

[1] Now Viscount Lee of Fareham.

[2] Speck von Stenberg, formerly at the German Embassy in Washington, and a great friend of both Roosevelt and Spring Rice.

never read them. I wonder if you teach your children the Bible—I suppose that is a question one shouldn't ask.

I said you would hate it here because you would have no friends and yet I'm not sure. How quiet it was at Oyster Bay and how quite perfectly delightful. I'm not sure that even on Ullswater (excuse the exception) I ever enjoyed myself so much. Will it come again or shall we all be too much changed? I suppose, having had no opportunities, or being too lazy, I shall get steadily stupider, but I shall try and be as fond of people as ever, and more; and that after all is more important.

Nov. 29, 1899.

"Dear Mrs. Lodge,

Allow me to introduce to you Mr. C. Spring Rice who says he met you in Washington, but doesn't expect you to remember him. I am rather glad to be able to reproach you. I don't see why you shouldn't neglect people just as much as I ... What are you about? Where will you be? I suppose in Washington, as Nahant would be a little East-windy at this time of year and might affect your nose and the Senator's liver. Will you have Constance and the grandbaby and the boys with you for the New Year? I wish I could suddenly turn up and begin exactly where I left off, as I do believe I should. I am glad to be able to assure you that you are quite as good company as ever : when I see you, or rather hear you, which is quite often, it seems to me that your spirits are just as high and your laugh just as wicked as ever. It is odd how clearly one sees absent people (dating from a certain time) when one is in this sort of place. And you would be surprised, being a modest person, if you knew the huge amount of pleasure you give. I have hung up here those dissipated yellow dragons that you once housed. They used to be at the back of the library, behind the raised place at the back, and had the pleasure of looking at the Senator playing patience for a considerable number of nights. Now they see me having Persian lessons. They began life by assisting at Buddhist orgies in a monastery in China. Where will they go next? ...

In the evenings, I pass the time pleasantly enough. I dine in an enormous bedroom, waited on by two silent Persians who hate one another but tell me all their troubles and insist on my directing them. They are quite wonderful on a journey; in the house they are about as dirty and forgetful as man can be. So am I, and so we get on well. After dinner I sit by the fire and read. I wish I had Cabot to read aloud. I can't swallow novels. I read history and poetry and biographies—also letters, which I like a good deal, but how sad they are apt to be ! Fitzgerald's, for instance—and an old Eton tutor of mine [1] whose journals and letters have been privately printed ; we called him ' Blind Billy Johnson,' and he turns out to have been a man made of passion and tenderness and intense unselfish ambition and infinite regrets for what life had denied him : and such delight in the little life could give."

Nov. 30, 1899.

To HENRY ADAMS.

" I wonder where you are, and if you will be unhappy enough on New Year's Day to thoroughly enjoy yourself. I have just written to Mrs. Hay and it amuses me to think of this letter going side by side with the other one and arriving next door after a month's journey. I wonder if you hate receiving letters from dull people several thousand miles off. But I know you do every day of your life things that you hate (that is if there is the smallest chance of anyone being the happier for what you do) and so here goes. This is a country which would suit all your ideals. The ruler is a kind good gentleman who hates hurting anyone. But since his father tried to poison him (he was saved just in time by a course of violent emetics which even now make his face awry) he thinks it probable some one will put an end to him ; he lives in fear, pistol in hand, and fear has possessed his brain so that he can neither think nor act. Also he can't sleep, and lives night after night in a room lighted by brilliant electric lights in coloured shades, starting up from bad dreams and falling back into short dozes. In the daytime he kills beasts in the mountains, and his great joy is to sleep under canvas, wandering from place to place with a tribe of camels, soldiers, women and courtiers at his heels.

He brought up to Teheran with him from Tabreez, where he lived as heir apparent, a whole tribe of hungry courtiers, who insisted, when he became king, on his giving them property ; and he parted with most of the crown lands to them, so that he is absolutely indigent and has to beg money when he wants to go on a journey. The consequence is that the wheat grown on the former crown lands is garnered and stored by the courtiers, who corner it too for the rise. Now, after a fair harvest, bread is twice what it was the year before and three times what it was two years before. The high officials are ordered to provide the town with bread, but as they are all speculating themselves, what they do is to use their power to prevent grain from coming into the town and sell their own

[1] Cory, the poet.

stores at famine prices. The people sell everything to buy bread; the bakers mix all sorts of filth with the bread they bake—mud out of the streets, straw and stones—and diseases are rife, especially among the children. People meet and look at one another and groan and talk of a riot, but their only leaders are the Mullahs, who themselves are speculating in grain. The roads are fallen into hopeless disrepair and the beasts of burden are starving. The other day there was a sort of a riot. A number of women met the Shah as he returned from shooting and cursed him. The result was a new Governor who is worse than the old one.

The Prime Minister is an old man, half Armenian, whose only idea is to stay in office—naturally enough, as if he is turned out he will probably be murdered. In order to stay on, his business is to cajole and flatter everyone with promises and most of all with a promise of a loan in Europe—which would be immediately divided among the courtiers and the Shah. Bread and money are the two things which they all talk about—money, if possible, from Europe. Nothing is being done to earn money in the country; the Governors pay no taxes though they collect them from their districts. They buy the office, and reimburse themselves after a year or two—then retire to a garden in Teheran —buy a property and store the grain for speculating. Industries have been started from time to time by foreign companies. The Persians have always succeeded in destroying them, but they will do nothing for themselves. In the meanwhile the Russians are pressing on their borders. Roads are being built to the Persian frontiers, manufactures started, law and order introduced, robbers suppressed. There is no interference with Persian independence, but the Governors know that the whole thing exists only on sufferance and that they mustn't do anything their neighbours dislike. The only stable element in the whole country is the Russian regiment of Persian Cossacks, trained and commanded by Russian officers—at their head a great giant of a Russian, kindly, honest and energetic, on whom everybody will depend if there is a crisis. The Sadrazam is now quite lame and leans upon the Russian Government as his only support—mindful of the new road which could bring in the Russian army at ten days notice and of the Russian banks which (at 18 per cent) will lend him money if only money can save him. The whole country waits contentedly for this end—knowing that it won't be worse than what is now; that after all the Russians too are Asiatics, and that Persia has been conquered since history began at least once in two centuries.

And all the while the poor, harried and robbed as they are,

are not unhappy. There is the sun and charity, no one starves
and life is passably amusing. And for the rich, if this world is
too harassing, one can become a Dervish, exchange one's robe
of honour for a rag, buy a filthy tent and a brass bowl and live
happily ever after, begging and thinking of the Infinite.

As for religion—the leaders, the mullahs, are the worst
robbers in the state. Being administrators of the law, they are
gradually acquiring vast landed property, swamping village
after village. Money will buy them all, but they are still the
only gathering point and focus of popular feeling, and the
Sadrazam knows it and pays for their support. In the meanwhile the Babis, half-way between Christian and Mahomedan—
without fixed doctrine or any sort of bigotry—make steady
progress. They live for their own souls, despising the corrupt
Government and the ignorant priesthood, and look to Russia as
the hope of the country, under whose rule they will be able to
philosophise tranquilly. This is all dull, but you should come
here to study the ways of the land. It won't last much longer
and you will see something even more satisfying to your corrupt
tastes than the decadence of England.

Now I have poured all this out for you. Do something for me.
Tell me how you are—what you are doing—whom you have
seen—what our friends are doing—whether you have found a
new baby, helpless and ungrateful, to whom you can give yourself without any foolish expectation of return. I have often
thought of your saying in that respect, that the most satisfactory friendship is one entirely give-and-no-take nor hope of
taking. Why should it be otherwise ? You don't draw a
mountain because the mountain likes it ; why should one look
at people to please them ? As one grows older, one learns this,
with other lessons which are useful but not always agreeable.
Anyhow, whatever you may think of people, tell me about them.

But mostly about yourself. How are you feeling ? What are
you enjoying ? I am enjoying quiet and books and a certain
not too distant contemplation of our kind. Darius passed this
way with Alexander on his track and his lost empire behind him.
Beyond is Khorasan, where the great cities were which Jenghis
Khan so utterly destroyed. Opposite is the door of Sefarati
Roumi—Legation of Rome, meaning Turkey—heir of Constantinople, who was heir of Rome. And not so far to the North is
the young man[1] who in his turn will step into this caravanserai,
to sleep his turn, till he too receives the summons and mounts
the white horse to ride away into space. I wonder if that is
why Russian music is so sad—because they know that they are
the *last* attempt of nature in this poor continent."

[1] The Czar.

Nov. 29, 1899.

" DEAR MRS. ROOSEVELT,

This is to wish you a Happy New Year—you deserve it if anyone does. I wish I knew how you would spend New Year's day and where, and that I could suddenly drop in and see. But in this lonely life which I lead now, people whom I know and liked as I do you and Theodore and your children, become actually present, and it really seems as if I see you and talk to you—and remember so clearly and vividly all sorts of little circumstances that happened long ago, which gives a very real and living after life to friendship. Only I hope and believe I shall see you again, and I am sure however grand you are you will be just as nice. I fear I shall be rather dull and stupid, but as you get older, you won't mind that so much in people who are really fond of you, as I am. I have had some delightful letters from Theodore, which is immensely kind of him, considering all the work he has to do. I hope you will write and tell me all about what you are doing and how the children are, and what they are like ; and how Theodore spends his evenings and what new friends he has. I have had the most *immense* pleasure out of his *Rough Riders* [1]—so have we all. I only wish we had a man like him—but that is difficult in any country.

I haven't much to tell you about myself. I live in a large empty house with a few rooms scantily furnished. I chiefly spend my time in a large bedroom (where I dine) and small adjoining sitting-room where my books are. I read a good deal—history and memoirs and poetry. The evenings which I spend alone are really delightful—the absolute quiet and independence and the good company of the men in the books, and a great deal of rather pleasant idle thought, looking at the fire. There is the daily horror of telegrams which you are familiar with—and sometimes when I wake at night unpleasant spaces of anxiety and regret. But on the whole the life is pleasant.

Every morning I have a mirza come to teach me Persian and read with me. I have got to take a pleasure in the old Persian mystic poets, which I see through a glass darkly. These people only belong half to the world. They can escape from it into another world of their own at any moment, and so it doesn't much matter to them if things go badly. We are altogether of this world and we make this place which is our one dwelling place as happy as we can ; but the other plan has its advantages too.

[1] The book describing the experiences of Roosevelt's regiment in Cuba.

I know you will feel for our war anxieties though yours were
so much greater ; but there is this added grief of a very doubtful
issue and tremendous consequences ; and *doubts* of all kinds
which are most horrible.   I wish for one hour I could have a
good talk with Theodore."

It will be seen that to the Roosevelt household he mentioned that
on which he kept silence even to Adams and Mrs. Lodge—his heart-
burnings about the Boer War.   To his own people, he had already
written his heart out.

These war anxieties had accumulated swiftly.   The despatch from
the Transvaal Government which was considered an ultimatum was
dated October 9 ; the first engagement took place on October 12, and
before the end of the month the Boers were investing Ladysmith,
Mafeking and Kimberley, all in British territory.   A series of minor
reverses followed.

Nov. 14, 1899.

To STEPHEN.

" What news will you have when you get this ?   This uncertainty of suspense is awful.   I think a war to be a good war
should be one when one would be happy in it (in a way) even
when unsuccessful.   Is this one only to be justified by success—
and then not successful ?   On the whole though, as I think
about it—it seems inevitable.   There was really no way out—
but I wish that public utterances had been a little more satisfactory and that the British Beast had not been so blatant.
There will be a tremendous reaction against Imperialism before
we are done.   We shall see now what sort of stuff our people are
really made of—how much stay they have and whether they
stand beating as well as they used to.   I only hope so.   If not
we must give up our present occupation and take to tailoring.

Stephen Spring Rice was a civilian to the bone, and an old-fashioned
Liberal ; so Munro Ferguson, the ex-Guardsman, was the friend to
whom Spring Rice constantly imparted his constantly growing feeling
that general military service was the only way to security for England.
He thought the spectacle of a people monopolising all the best
possessions in the world outside of Europe, and yet unarmed in a
world when all other nations were arming, was a temptation to an
invader ; he thought also that it demoralised a people to rely for
its defence on what could be bought with money.

Nov. 14, 1899.

To FERGUSON.

" I entirely agree with your letter.   I couldn't follow the
correspondence and hated to read the speeches—just as now I
dread and hate the telegrams that come daily.   We live in bad

days. But, thinking it all over, I come to the same conclusion. If the Boers aimed, as they did, at driving the English out—used their independence to arm when no one else armed in S. Africa, used the money of the foreigners to buy guns with, and were looked on by all the Dutch in S. Africa as the nucleus of the new state which was to succeed the old—I don't see how war could be avoided ; and it has come—whether on one pretext or the other, doesn't matter much. The two couldn't ride on the same horse without one being in front of the other. We couldn't retire without a fight now, and we should have had to, the moment we got into a tight place elsewhere. We are in a tight place now and I wonder whether we realise it and are waking up ? We are surrounded in the world by a depth and intensity of hatred which is really astonishing. If we fall we shall have a hundred fangs in our throat. Do we know that ? Imperialism is not so bad a thing if you pay for it in your own blood, but spending 3 per cent out of your stock-exchange gains to buy people to fight for you in picturesque places, in order to provide you with interesting illustrated papers (or new investments) is a different thing.

I hate the screaming despatches as much as you do. I have avoided them of late as much as possible and read the proceedings of the British Association instead and Roosevelt's *Rough Riders* and *The Life of Peel*.[1] Did you read that ? Don't you think it was splendid and didn't it make you feel proud ? Also I liked the *Rough Riders* ; if we can get such sort of people by the thousand among our fellows, we shall do well. But I rather doubt it. I wonder what Bob[2] thinks. Bob has done his turn. Don't let him go again. There I go—willing everyone else should go, but objecting to anyone I am fond of going. And yet, if the war were the right thing, one should wish everyone to go and be ashamed of anyone who didn't.

I am not sure. But I shall be sure, if I see a great danger threatening and a great trouble, and if England stands firm without boasting or flinching, sure of her rights and of herself, determined to go on as long as she can stand, and in the end nobly victorious—or if defeated, the wonder of the world. Have we that sort of make in us ? Or are we like a man who dreams of being a great admiral and goes on shore at once because he is sea sick.

I wish we hadn't boasted and shouted so much and spoilt our own game and turned the whole thing into a burglar's prowl. What news will have arrived when this comes ? You will

[1] Lord Rosebery's.

[2] Ferguson's brother served with the Rough Riders.

write to me occasionally, I hope. As I am of your way of thinking, it is a comfort to hear from you. I hope you are trying to organise a rifle range at Raith."

He lived to see such a danger threaten England, and he, like the rest, had the chance to prove himself in service. There was no such trouble in his mind then.

He wrote to Villiers on November 15, with a pen sharpened by anger, a description of the environment in which he lived.

" Here there is a universal desire for our ruin—even among the Persians in whose interest it would seem to be that we should prosper. But the whole foreign population of Teheran is unanimous in wishing for our destruction.

I see a lot of the German Minister here who is an amusing old boy who got into disgrace with Holstein in the German F.O. for not taking his side against his own chief at St. Petersburg, that being one of the pleasing duties of German secretaries, occasionally. Consequently he takes a very outside view of diplomacy, in which he can't hope to succeed very well. He just loathes the Russians here and so do all the Germans. I really think they hate one another more than they do us. I think in that case the hatred has a personal spite, as one hates one's own wife ; whereas they hate us as they hate the devil.

I like the Minister for Foreign Affairs and the Sadrazam immensely. They are most amusing and very friendly, and they look upon politics in the light of a joke, as they look upon my Persian. They are both body and soul in the possession of the Russians and repeat to the Russian legation pretty nearly everything that is said to them, and they both take bribes pretty freely—especially now that they know that their rule may come to an end. The Shah's doctor said to Adcock (the English doctor) when the latter warned him that the Shah might die—' Well, I have done pretty well for myself as long as it lasted ! ' In fact he has, and is one of the rich men in Teheran, having arrived quite poor three years ago. This is the Shah's principal friend. The Shah himself thinks he is going to be assassinated. A man ran after him with a petition. H.M. nearly died of fright and had the man bastinadoed. He is now away in the country. He always has a pistol ready and he is one of the best and quickest pistol shots imaginable. So the assassins will have a hot time of it. He is never alone. Even at night he has three or four women always about him, and a Eunuch to tell Persian (bawdy) stories, and two little boys to continually spank him, without which he can't sleep. This I had from a doctor who once had to spend the night in the next room—a terrible time he had of it. The man of greatest influence in the palace is a mullah who says prayers to him during a thunderstorm. The private secretary used to forge, steal, falsify documents and get the Shah's signature to documents he had never seen. He was finally found out and removed by the influence of one of the wives whom he had robbed.

The Sadrazam has a queer life. At his big dinner and feast, the supper was stolen while we were dining, and he had to send up the remains of our dinner for the supper. The servants, enraged at being despoiled of their perquisites, threatened to strike, and the service had to be done by soldiers. On his way to the palace every day he has to distribute alms ; a crowd of beggars half a mile long are waiting every day. If he is angry with the Shah he resigns. Sometimes he goes to bed for two days. The Shah always relents and sends for him. Last time the Shah had to go himself.

He has a low opinion of his master. When I said ' The present Shah is different to his predecessors ' (in his views about telegraphs) he made a sort of grimace and said, ' I should rather think he was.' He openly, I believe, says he is incapable and ought to be deposed. He is now with his Imperial Master and I wonder how they are getting on."

December brought news that left Spring Rice no heart for such pasquinading. In ' Black Week ' the reverse at Stormberg was followed by one more serious on the Modder River, and that by the final disaster of Colenso, when more than a thousand lives were lost, and eleven guns, and not an inch gained.

Dec. 20, 1899.

To CHIROL.

" Your letter was indeed delightful and letters are a great boon, though nothing makes up for a good long talk. What wouldn't I give for one now ! These are most terrible times, only they prove us what we are and we shall know whether we are willing to pay the price for the thing we have been boasting of so long. I hope at any rate we shall learn. The great fault has been in the intelligence department, or at any rate, in the attention which is paid to it by the governing persons. This ought to teach us that we can't separate our politics from knowledge of the military conditions. The intimate connection of the two departments has been one of the main causes of Germany's success. They learnt in a hard school and we shall have to learn too. Life is a prolonged nightmare now. The daily telegrams are a horror, and waking in the morning or late at night is a terrible thing ; one lies alone with a living and growing fear staring one in the face. But after all, I have some faith left in the strength and determination and courage of the people and the colonies. And the fellow feeling of America is a real and constant delight. The only person here whom it is a real pleasure to talk to is the American Minister, he is so honest, sincere and kind. I hope we shall never forget it. I don't think we will. In this you have borne a good and noble part. Who knows how great a one? It must be a real satisfaction to you to remember. After all, it isn't in easy victories that a nation grows but in facing a great danger bravely, in being constant in good and evil times. And sorrow binds together—classes and peoples— We have much to gain. But, oh, the present horror of it— and out here with vindictive and sneering faces—and the utter helplessness.

I really haven't the heart to write though I could talk to you for hours. Only, through it all I think that we shall be the better for it; we were perhaps too fat and prosperous, and now the chastisement has come. How will we take it? I hardly dare read the papers; I try not to think, I try to build a wall against the door which is always flying open.

Write again, if you have time—if you can find it. I hear you have been suffering from overwork again. Is it true? Let me know. Take care of yourself and let me find you lean, strong, and lusty when I come back. What shall we talk about? You must let me hear—just a line if nothing more. Your letter was in the nick of time. I see clearly that all this was inevitable and must have come sooner or later and that we can't help it. All other things are swallowed up in this. A war for existence or the fair and equal rights we grant to everyone ourselves—surely this isn't an unjust war.

I won't write about Persia now, as you won't have ears for it, and I couldn't if I wished. Everything depends on one thing now."

Dec. 20, 1899.

To Mr. Luxmoore.

" We are going through the fire now and we shall see what metal we are made of. It is curious here—like an inlet far away inland, where the water retreats because there is a tide ebbing in the great sea. We are ebbing and all the faces are looking at us in a mocking way—wondering what we are saying and thinking. In spite of the present miseries, we have faith on the whole in the perseverance and grit of the race; this is a sharp lesson but we have a good deal to learn. I hope we shall learn it. At any rate, if we fail now we become something different to what we have been ; we begin over again, perhaps well, perhaps ill. For our generation it is hard to change. The Americans stood worse things in 1862, and prevailed in the end because they believed in themselves and their cause. The *Life of Lincoln* is the best of lessons for us now, as old Cory long ago pointed out. How curiously appropriate some of his letters are now. I have your copy—also a *Golden Treasury*, also a Shakespeare—all given at Eton and constant companions in Japan, Germany, Teheran. Where will they go next ? It will be dreadful to face the world next year unless we show we can be as firm and dauntless in evil days as we were blatant in the good. The Psalms are not exactly pleasant reading now. I shut the Book in shame. ' Put not thy trust. . . . ' But if one takes one's punishment well and nobly the sin becomes a virtue or the means of virtue. I hope this generation will learn. . . . ''

These cries of passion should be remembered when the reader thinks of the part which Spring Rice had to play in a war when not merely England's prestige but her very existence was at stake.

Roosevelt's comment on the same events written a few days later shows no perception of what his friend's feelings would be ; but it was calculated to be a good tonic after depression.

ALBANY, Dec. 2, 1899.

" DEAR CECIL,

. . . I wish you could be here during my brief moment of greatness, for it is certain soon to pass, of course. What I should really most like to do would be to be Governor-General of the Philippines, but I do not suppose I could leave New York, and in any event, it would not occur to the President to appoint me.

I have been absorbed in interest in the Boer War. The Boers are belated Cromwellians, with many fine traits. They deeply and earnestly believe in their cause, and they attract the sympathy which always goes to the small nation, even though the physical obstacles in the way may be such as to put the two contestants far more nearly on a par than at first sight seems to be the case. But it would be for the advantage of mankind to have English spoken south of the Zambesi just as in New York ; and as I told one of my fellow Knickerbockers the other day, as we let the Uitlanders of old in here, I do not see why the same rule is not good enough in the Transvaal. The Boers are marvellous fighters, and the change in the conditions of warfare during the past forty years has been such as to give

S.R.L.   U

peculiar play to their qualities. Mere pluck in advancing shoulder to shoulder no longer counts for as much as skill in open order fighting, in taking cover and in the use of the rifle, or as power of acting on individual initiative. A brave peasant, and still more, a brave man who has been bred in the garret of a tenement house, needs years of training before he can be put on a par with the big game hunter accustomed to life in the open. In our congested city life of to-day the military qualities cannot flourish as in a mounted pastoral population, where every male is accustomed to bearing arms, and, what is quite as important, is accustomed from his youth up to act under a rough but effective military organisation. My regiment was composed of men much like the Boers, but who had not had their military organisation, though this had been partially offset by the experience of many of them as deputy sheriffs and deputy marshals. Such a regiment was at the outset worth any three from our big cities, or even from our purely peaceful farming districts, although there was no difference of race. The same thing is true of the Boers ; and the fighting will be hard and bloody beyond a doubt. But the end is inevitable. I am amused at the cordial hatred felt by France toward both England and America.

In the Philippines, where we have blundered for a year in a way that would have cost us dearly had we been matched against Boers instead of Tagals, we at last seem to have things pretty well in hand, and I guess there will be no trouble of any serious kind save in administering the islands hereafter.

My own business goes on fairly. At any rate, for this year I have had an absolutely honest administration from top to bottom in this State, and an absolutely efficient one too.

To-day is the thirteenth anniversary of my marriage, and I have just given Mrs. Roosevelt a really handsome little watch. Having a good many children, and not being in any remunerative business, this is the first year when I felt that I really could afford to give her something handsome, and I grasped the opportunity !

What a wreck Gengis Khan and the Tartars made, from China to Muscovy, and south to the Persian Gulf. They were able to make the wreck because they struck people who could not fight as well as they could, and the feelings inspired in them by getting the upper hand made them irresistible. The idiot peace-at-any-price individuals, if they were capable of reasoning at all, might learn something from this. The experience of the Greeks with the Turks, of the Italians with the Abyssinians, and of the Spaniards in Morocco, proves perfectly clearly that if the northern races were not still fighting races, the Mahdists would have over-run the Mediterranean littoral as their lightly skinned Arab kinsmen overran it twelve centuries ago. I believe in the expansion of great nations. India has done an incalculable amount for the English character. If we do our work well in the Philippines and the West Indies, it will do a great deal for our character. In the long run I suppose all nations pass away, and then the great thing is to have left the record of the nation that counts—the record left by the Romans —the record that will be left by the English-speaking peoples."

In this dark time Spring Rice turned willingly to anything that could distract him from brooding on misfortunes which he could not help. He was, throughout life, almost morbidly secretive concerning any writing in which he expressed intimate feeling. But in the letter of December 20 to his tutor, he had enclosed " the record of a sort of pilgrimage." These were his sonnets—sixty-six of them— strictly for Mr. Luxmoore's own eyes.

Three months later, when the post had brought the reply from Eton, and much news as well, he wrote again, a letter revealing much of the influences that had formed him, and of the mysticism that underlay all the surface activity of his thought.

March 29, 1900.

" I can't write a long letter as I have had a small sort of breakdown. The Minister suddenly going,[1] things left anyhow, and general disorganisation with politics, entertainments, and Persian to be learnt and spoken, and not much help. I am all right now. I wish I was less nervous, but in a week or so things will settle down. You write very kindly, and your letter, eagerly looked forward to, was very welcome. I would give a great deal to see you in your garden now with the stone pinnacles of the chapel as sanctifying background. I remember on the top of the chapel roof (where I climbed surreptitiously) trying to climb one. It was made of crumbling oolite, since restored. Somehow those pinnacles have often hung in my eye. They had such a queer history—made of wrecks of sea shells and then put up there.

TO WAYNEFLETE

A million living things have given
Their bones that you might build,
Sowing the fields that know not heaven—
The fields that none have tilled.

[1] Sir Mortimer Durand had been recalled and Spring Rice became chargé d'affaires—for a year, as it proved.

And well the deep his secret kept,
　　And many a billow rude
Went roaring o'er them where they slept,
　　The silent multitude.

And now they greet the rosy day
　　Above the sleeping plain,
The stones the cunning hands did lay,
　　That did not build in vain.

The stones thy dear dead master planned,
　　Oh loyal heart and true !
And sure God's hand was with thy hand,
　　And sure He builded too.

—A later day complication of geology, architecture, and Dryasdustery, such as the modern muse mixes in her drink ! But don't we build our national life of dead bones, sunk in silence, welded in long secrecy, but in a strange sort of way giving their strength to a living edifice ?　A pinnacle red in the morning, over a place of prayer ?

As for my sonnets, I am indeed ashamed, as nothing is so beastly as a manuscript work, or irritating as a friend's poems, or less enticing than sonnets.　But as you say, it was a mark of friendship—that is, of your friendship.　There is no idea of publication in their present form.　Nor is there much idea of poetry or style.　They were gradually worked up during many years, the sediment of a good deal of thought, and the barkings of one of Lucretius' pack.　The idea is : (I) : The Platonic (sediment of pupil room) ; the visible beauty, a form of the invisible ; sensible love, the contact of the soul with the invisible by the artifice of sense and the particular object.

That is, I learn to love God by loving my neighbour.　If this is so, it is loving, and not enjoying, which is the good.　It is a pure action of the soul, the accidental accompaniments of which may or may not be satisfaction of subsidiary kinds, the feeling, not the result.　Does Job fear God for naught ?

And also, by loving one thing one learns love for all things : love is a door into the temple.

And the mere perception of beauty or truth is not enough, it is an outside thing ; for union the welding fire is needed, so that faith is knowledge on fire.

I said ' to love God because one loves one's neighbour.'　To the platonist the ideal grows more and more real, and the individual object sinks into nothing.　Therefore, in Part II., enter the Bible.—The real has revealed the ideal, the particular, the universal. But the ideal sanctifies the so-called real ; the universal is in the particular and makes it sacred. From the mountain the soul comes back again with the tables in its hand. And having begun by loving one's neighbour as oneself, and finding that is not enough, one turns to that which satisfies ; for, once loving, one must go on, and so one learns to love God by loving one's neighbour. And the ideal is, not to stop there ; for when one comes to the God we are taught about now, and says, ' I have forgotten Thy creatures for Thee,' He answers, ' But I died for them.' And one should end by loving one's neighbour because one loves God. It is all in St. Bernard, as you taught us long ago—also in pupil room. Do you recognise St. Augustine—an old remark of yours in the year '75 ? He came up again here in Persia in 1900."

It should be said that a reader might well spend hours over these sonnets—which are included among the hundred and twenty published in Bernard Holland's edition of the poems—without suspecting that they were in praise of any but mortal love, though of a love high and supersensuous. Again and again by their fluency, their open cadences, and something in them tempered " to trampling horse's feet more oft than to a chamber melody," they recall those of Philip Sidney. For instance, this :

> What is your lady that you praise her so ?
> Is she not even as other women are ?
> In all the heavens is there one only star
> Which you have eyes to see or heart to know ?
>
> .   .   .   .
>
> Oh, you that ask me, have you never loved ? "

Some (like the one which has already been quoted in reference to the death of Gladstone) suggests a discipleship (like that of his elder kinsman, Aubrey de Vere) to Wordsworth, who was the poet *par excellence* for that whole kin and clan. Nowhere is there a strongly marked individual style, but everywhere they have personality of thought. How many were written before he came to Persia, or how long before, we can only guess ; two or three show by their subjects that they were made during his stay in Japan. But his early Persian time was of all periods in his life the most prolific in poetry—the only years, indeed, when he may be said to have worked continuously as a poet. The second of the two books which he published while he lived is really a series of love poems in prose, translated and adapted from a Persian manuscript which he studied with his teacher ; and in them there is the same fusion of human love with love mystical that this letter adumbrates.

The Sonnets, though he added to them in the course of years and often played with the idea of publication, remained in manuscript till after his death, shown to very few.   Up to this date, except in the letter to Farrer from Berlin, there is no mention in his correspondence of any serious writing, though the lighter verse was scattered about him at all times and places.   But now during this distant stay he took another friend into his confidence on a different production, which could not be taken for a personal expression.   He wrote to Chirol on June 26, 1900 :

> " I want you as a very great kindness to send the accompanying typewritten documents to some publisher.   The expense will be paid by me for an edition of say 200 or 300 copies, to be published in the ordinary way. . . . Also, Don't breathe to a soul anything about my having written or translated the things, as it would be for some reasons extremely awkward.   Don't tell my people either.   The idea is to have someone who can write dramatic music to set the things and then, oh, to hear someone who can sing dramatically sing them ! "

On November 12 he wrote to his sister Margaret, congratulating her on her firstborn.

> " Many, many congratulations again.   I am so delighted to think of you and your child and how happy you and Aubrey must be.   It is wonderful and really the most wonderful thing in the world.   By which, in fact, we know in some fashion that the world is not the place we thought it was.
>
> In a sort of way I have had a child too.   If you see a booklet called *Songs from the Book of Jaffir*, published by Macmillan, you might read it as a sort of nephew.   But don't give me away as it would be very awkward.   As you will see, it consists of the skeletons of pieces of music, and until the flesh and skin is put on by some kind hands, skeletons they will remain.   I wonder if the kind hand will ever come. . . . "

He wrote again to Chirol, November 15, 1900 :

> " I am ashamed of all the trouble you took about my libellum.   It is, I suppose, a slight and rather ridiculous thing ; but has given me infinite amusement for some years, all condensed in fifty pages which I am the only person in the world who will ever understand, I suppose.   That is probably the case with every book, which is 1000 times more blessed to him that gives than to him that receives."

If " some years " be accurate, it means that before ever thinking of work in Persia he had been studying Persian literature.   *Songs from the Book of Jaffir* is said to be " Adapted from the Persian translation of Jamshid of Yezd, the Gueber."   There are three sections, each with an introduction in prose (modelled on the Old Testament), each

SIR VALENTINE CHIROL

From a portrait by the Hon. John Collier

telling of an eastern king and his triumph and his love, and his overthrowing ; in each section a series of dramatic songs illustrates the crucial moments of the story.   Moore would have liked them, and they show a talent like Moore's for catching the picturesque features of an alien legend.

But in the meantime he had other literary work of greater interest in hand.   On February 8, 1900, he wrote to his sister :

" I am now busy translating a book which I have just bought. It is the history of a gentleman who was in love with a beautiful cousin, married to an Afghan a hundred years ago.   The book is the author's own copy with his annotations and extracts from the lady's own letters and her precious seal, under which is written in the poet's hand :

> ' The seal of Hadiji of the tribe of Saghar in Dagesten, queen by the grace of God of the Kingdom of Beauty and Chastity.'

All about are scattered little verses in Arabic, Persian and Turkish, telling of the love which none of the famous lovers of history have ever equalled—calling on the hearers to hear a story more wonderful—praying that he may be spared to sing a little longer the praise of Hadiji, and also, because at his death, Hadiji may drop a tear !   After this comes the invocation to Allah, then to Mahomed, then to the prophet Ali, then to Love, then the introduction, and having done fifty pages, I have just got to the first meeting of the lovers ! . . . "

August 20, 1900.

To STEPHEN.

" Every morning, my solemn Mirza comes, eager for the book which we are translating together.   It is nearly finished now. I have found that the author died in India two years after the book was finished and sent to his beloved.   After fourteen years separation, he has just written a letter to her which I am now beginning.   After that, he has a dream and then the book ends.   Unfortunately the lady's relations or the lady to whom the book was sent have rubbed out some of the final lines, but they can be made out in the sun.   It is a curious idea to write a unique book, have it copied in the best possible handwriting with illuminations—and then send it as a memorial. There is no story in it—only two cousins in love with one another and not allowed to marry and then one of them is sent away to India and dies there after sixteen years at Delhi.   During those sixteen years he must have seen the sack of Delhi by Nadir Shah and the practical downfall of the Moguls.   The spirit of the book is curiously religious and pure minded and would make the translation dull reading. Still, *sunt lacrymae rerum et mentem mortalia tangunt. . . ."*

To Mr. Luxmoore he wrote later, in 1903, just before it was published :

" As to the book, it is a real translation—almost literal, and I will show you the book. All the words written down were actually said, or as nearly as possible, and are slightly adapted from the notes of my lectures and lessons. Read it carefully and you will see that it is really intensely interesting—quite consecutive and reasoned out, and to all appearance both outwardly and inwardly a true history. The Eastern idea—that knowledge is really a revelation only possible through love as we call it, and not by any means possible by logic alone or reasoning, which is only, as Ruskin would say, the horse which carries one to the gate—this idea is worked out so naturally, and from so many new points of view, that it seems to me a very curious and interesting phenomenon. The book itself is quite beautiful and I intended to deposit it in the Eton Library. It is now in London. . . ."

It is necessary now to turn back to the political side of his correspondence. The Shah's health was very precarious, and a journey to Europe had been advised for him, which actually took place in June 1900, the great exhibition at Paris being the chief attraction.

Further, the whole situation was affected by the fact that all available British resources had to be directed to South Africa. There was obviously a chance for Russia to advance in the East ; and it was taken in Persia. Nothing was done that openly encroached on British claims ; but Spring Rice was fully convinced that no resistance could be offered to encroachment, and from March 1900 onward he was left in charge of British interests.

In June 1900, anxiety spread all through the East, because China's resentment against the European annexations of coastal territories had produced the anti-foreign Boxer movement, which got secret encouragement from the Empress-Dowager. Murder of Europeans through the country was multiplied, and finally in June the European Legations in Pekin was attacked. The whole foreign community, shut up in the British Legation, stood a siege for eight weeks till the relief expedition despatched by Japan and the European Powers fought its way in.

Under these discouraging conditions Spring Rice had his first experience of representing his country, and it will be seen that he was discouraged. A whiff of danger reached him and that was exhilarating. But—perhaps because his sympathies were always with the Liberals—he was much discontented with the British administration.

Jan. 19, 1900.

To VILLIERS.

" All the business about the Shah's journey has been very amusing. The Russian Legation, naturally enough, wished him to go to Russia first ; the German Legation didn't want in the least to interfere with that arrangement (as Germany considers Persia within the Russian sphere). No one considered the Shah's health till a personal appeal was made to the Czar, who immediately sent a most kind telegram telling him to do exactly what suited him best. As to the visit to England, the Shah talks as if he would like to go, but the officials are anxious he shouldn't, and have told us that the Shah is too much afraid of the sea to cross the channel. Austria, Germany, France, Russia and Belgium have been approached with a view to invitations, but nothing has been said to us, except through Dr. Odling incidentally. The object is probably to make us appear churlish. These are the daily incidents of life here, and the desire to trip us up and humiliate us is universal among foreigners and Persians alike, with a few exceptions who lament in a melancholy tone the decline of our influence ' which on the whole worked for good.'

We must certainly soon fix on a definite policy for this country. But I hope it will not be fixed without consulting the military and naval authorities first—an omission which appears to have been made in a recent case. Are we prepared to break the eggs to make the omelette, and how many eggs have we to break ? The question seems to me almost purely military. If we are not inclined to send troops up into the Gulf in great numbers—which I bet we are not—we must resign ourselves to the inevitable consequence of this Government being absolutely in the hands of a great military power which wishes for an outlet on the sea. But I see that we will make magnificent pretensions, and warlike speeches, and will one fine day find Russia on the Gulf, and raise no more dangerous objection than newspaper articles.

The people here who study the situation say that the sand-dam which kept Russia from the sea southward has been turned into stone at its west end in Turkey (by the Germans), at its east in Afghanistan (by the English), and that there remains Persia in the middle, where the sand is still sand and crumbling. And they say this part will soon give way. They don't care very much. The Government here is so bad and corrupt and hopelessly disorganised that the people would almost welcome a foreign ruler—at any rate at first.

If there is a crisis owing to the Shah's death, there is a fair chance of a big row, the troops not being paid. In that case we shall depend for our protection, either on ourselves, or on the Russian Colonel and his Cossacks. As we have given away all our guns as presents, we are absolutely without protection, but nobody knows that here, fortunately."

Feb. 5, 1900.

" These are dark days. No one comes near us now, everyone delights in our misfortunes, and it is almost impossible to get any information whatever. With regard to communications to the Persian Government, Schneider knows no more Persian than I do and our conversation must have a surprising effect on the Minister's mind, though he conceals his feelings like a man. It is an extraordinary system, that which prevails here, leaving the Legation at a moment's notice without any trained specialist. But I suppose it is not more surprising than many other parts of our administration. *E.g.*, have we an agent at Baku? Nothing would be easier, as there is a considerable English population and numbers of Armenians who would give regular reports for money. We have no idea how many troops are actually passing. Sorry to be grumbling in such a sorrowful time.

Excuse my haste, I have been about since 7 in the morning and it is now 7.15—doing nothing but see people and talk in all the languages I can master. They all agree in the same opinion that England is gracefully bowed out. The Minister for Foreign Affairs asked what I thought of it. I said it seemed to me that Russia had become the husband of Persia and England could at best be the lover. To which he wisely answered that it was generally the lover who gave the money."

Feb. 15, 1900.

To FERGUSON.

" . . . I have often talked to you about what struck me after Berlin as our radical fault. That is, in the entire absorption of the departments (except finance) in the daily departmental duties. There are two sides to this. One is that no question is regarded in its entirety, as a whole ; that is, in its history and development—the momentary phase of it being the only one regarded ; and secondly, that no question is regarded in its fundamental relations, as the Germans would say—that is, as it affects, and is affected by, numerous other questions. For instance, in Berlin no political question can be considered without giving due weight to military considerations—for which purpose an immense department exists for amassing military information, and for applying the results experimentally and theoretically.   I remember well the Emperor saying to our Military Attaché (who denied it) that at least 80,000 men were necessary for the present war—which was before the Boers' purchases of arms were completed.   Every political question is there first considered on its military merits—which is the *ultima ratio*.   For instance, when we screamed about Armenia, the thing to be considered was—could we act alone? if so, how? and if we could not act alone, with whom should we act, and what were the infallible securities for common action ?   Nothing of this sort was done.   In Germany the question first considered is—can Germany act in this matter with advantage ? If she cannot, she does nothing and says nothing; if she can, she both does things and says them.   Our plan is to say what we want or don't want, and at the last moment (at best) to find out whether we can or cannot do the thing in question."

March 6, 1900.

To CHIROL.

" . . . I wish I had been in London when you heard that Ladysmith was relieved.   It must have been a great moment. The news was given me by an Armenian who had heard it from the telegraph office.   I didn't believe him and rushed off to find the news true.   The ' fall of Ladysmith ' has been announced here every day for two months.   The Persians are all delighted, naturally enough, at any news of our misfortunes, though the wiser ones know that it is serious enough for them.

I shall be in charge to-morrow and a nice charge it will be. The Sadrazam is now entirely Russian and actively hostile to us on every possible opportunity.   The Shah is ignorant and lazy and though excellent in disposition is absolutely useless for purposes of government.

We must take for granted that Persia is lost to us, unless the Shah in Europe wakes up and realises the position into which his Minister has brought him for personal ends.   I suppose the people here will trip me up if they can and I shall have to look out for squalls.

I don't see that the war could have been avoided, but it is unfortunate that the military preponderance of the Transvaal, which could have been a just cause of asking for explanations of the continual armaments, was mixed up with the franchise question.   At the same time, turn it as one will, the same conclusion is arrived at.   The military force was owing to the possession of gold mines, worked by people who had no votes for the benefit of a military class. The only way of putting an end to a situation which put S. Africa at their mercy was either to make war and destroy them, or to get votes for our people who provided the money. It is as well perhaps that the question has come up now. But in case of a long war, foreign intervention is not improbable. Say, in the shape of a demand for compensation from France, Russia, Spain and Germany. But the struggle is inevitable and must be faced. Our insular position has emboldened us to face the nightmare which threatened Bismarck—the ' nightmare of combinations,' and now we are in a measureable distance of them. Yet as we do no one any real injury—our empire being on the whole of great benefit to the commercial world—there is a fair chance of no one caring to run the risk of attacking us for the benefit of the party which is at peace.

This is a long story written in an armchair late at night, in the enjoyment of a warm fire with violets growing outside and making the air sweet. What a different evening some other Englishmen are having ! This is a breathing time after months of terrible and haunting anxiety—the like of which I have never had in my life before. Shall we have it again ? . . . "

American friends did not withhold their comfort. Henry Adams as usual was not easily pinned down to any precise meaning, but the sympathy under his queer irony was plain.

WASHINGTON,
Feb. 1, 1900.

" MY GENTLE DIPLOMATE,
. . . I would I could have an hour's talk with you to-day, for in truth, my son, I am weary and oppressed by the stupidity of your class, and am desperate at finding in this waste of imbeciles not one poor wretch who can tell me why I consent to talk with him. The entire diplomatic class has, in my forty years of acquaintance with them, supplied me with just two interesting specimens, and you are one. I pay you that compliment free of charge. Don't grow fat on it ! For it is wrung from me in bitterness of soul.

I have thought much of you and your position of late, and I doubt whether you have yourself been so anxious as I about your welfare. I have had much nightmare these three months past, as you, who know my previous incarnations, can easily imagine. . . . Suddenly, out of the clear sky, comes the devil on a broomstick in the shape of a mob of howling Jews who upset my world, send all my friends to heaven before me, and bedevil man and beast beyond recognition. And the worst of it is that my poor world can't help itself. Stupid it is, and was, and will be,—stupidity is dear to the Gods and their best gift to man—and if the diplomate were not stupid, how could he serve ? Nature did not make you stupid, and consequently my sympathies are acutely for you until habit shall have accomplished what nature denied. . . .

Ever your attaché,

HENRY ADAMS."

Roosevelt as usual was explicit enough—a sententious, but alive, enjoying, strenuous and friendly man.

STATE OF NEW YORK EXECUTIVE CHAMBER,

March 12, 1900.

" DEAR CECIL,

. . . I am sure the change in the news has made you feel happier. I sympathise very deeply with the way you felt. It has been a sad war, although glorious from the valour of the combatants ; and the frenzy of England's continental critics has to my mind furnished a measure of the disaster which it would be to the civilised world and the progress of mankind if the British Empire were to lose its strength.

Although your letters are sad, they give us great pleasure. You have lost none of your old charm of description and we can see the life you lead before our eyes. What a strange life it is ? Even in their ultimate decay, which must inevitably come to all nations, the peoples of the West will differ from the hoary eastern nations. Well, nobody can tell when or how soon disaster will come. Death is always and under all circumstances a tragedy, for if it is not, then it means that life itself has become one. But it is well to live bravely and joyously, and to face the inevitable end without flinching when we go to join the men and the tribes of immemorial eld. Death is the one thing certain for the nation as for the man, though from the loins of the one as from the loins of the other descendants may spring to carry on through the ages the work done by the dead. I hope and believe that for our peoples the end is yet many centuries distant, and though there are signs of senility here and there, or of gross vice and moral weakness which is worse, yet I think all this is purely local and that as a whole we are still in the flush of our mighty manhood. Nevertheless, be this as it may, our duty is the same, to strive toward the light as it is given us to see the right, and take with iron front whatever fate befalls. . . "

April 2, 1900.

To STEPHEN.

" I am, as you must be often, very tired. When Durand went away, he was hardly on speaking terms with the Ministers here, and owing to his wife's illness had not had anyone inside the Legation for six months. I had to get things together for entertaining—to run round and see everyone, to have endless dinners and to be my own interpreter. Can you think of a worse piece of management in a place like this where we have so many interests—that there should be *no* oriental staff whatever : —simply a couple of Indian officers, one of whom knows no Persian, and the other gone ? It *must* be reorganised with a regular oriental staff, like China or Japan, and the office of works business—two big legations and gardens—ought to be done by a professional. But I am only in charge and can't do anything. It nearly ended in a breakdown, but fortunately the doctor here got hold of me and shut me up for two days.

I had to give the Sadrazam a dinner—thirty Persians and band and I don't know what. The result will probably be a severe financial crisis but if I am left in charge for a few months I shall recoup.

Things here are as bad as they can be—finance, of course. The customs have been reorganised, but nothing else, and I don't see that anything will be left of the Russian loan money in two years. In that case Persia will have her hands tied, as she can raise no more money whatever and will have mortgaged her revenues. We must face this eventuality and shape our policy. I hope nobody will say anything to pledge us to a forward policy in S. Persia without carefully considering the military conditions. The Transvaal ought to have been a lesson to us in this respect. I think our policy should be to interest other nations in the Southern trade and the Persian Gulf ; to be prepared for the Russians seizing a port and to consider what steps we should then take to neutralise the advantage gained. The Russian railway from N. to S. might be made, but it is improbable—would cost six million and bring in nothing, unless it was free to foreign trade from the South, and that would ruin Russian trade. Besides, a port on the Gulf would be a convenient object for us to attack if necessary. If this war were only over—! "

This lack of equipment, to which he returns in other letters, so vexed him that he took the step, very bold in a subordinate, of writing to Lord Salisbury, and, as he told his brother, urging that the Persian service should be " put on a business footing, and not organised like a circus."

May 3, 1900.

To STEPHEN.

" I missed the bag and shall try the Persian Post. The last one was robbed by robbers ' disguised as Cossacks ' as the post described them—which made us laugh.

Here things go their usual way. Minister after Minister is leaving and we are entering the reign of *chargés d'affaires*. The old Turk left to-day, a dear old man, very kind and good, a philosopher and a devotee but not at all anti-Christian. He is kind to beggars and to young diplomatists and never, I believe, does a stroke of work. Our French colleague goes soon. He has just been furiously attacked in a Vienna paper. What a curious institution the press seems to be. A man came here who was a rogue. He wanted the French Minister to do something for him which he refused to do. The man goes back and spends some time raking up the ' record ' of the French Minister and his wife, and then publishes it in a Vienna newspaper, which, of course, is sent over here and creates no end of a fuss. At the same time a Persian Calcutta newspaper publishes a libel on our German minister here, who is as good a man as ever stepped. Isn't it curious, the role played by newspapers ? And now their business is to libel whole nations. . . . Fortunately a great storm of rain came to-day and that may bring plenty this year, and if there is plenty we shall have no riots or revolutions; so much depends on two or three hours water from the sky. I am got quite Persian in tastes. I hear with delight the distant hum of the rain approaching and the near patter when it is really come, and count the puddles in the road by the house and ask anxiously if the rain has been all over the neighbourhood. What a difference from Cumberland. . . . "

May 28, 1900.

To FERGUSON.

" I fear I shan't improve my not too shining reputation here. There is nothing that can be done, and I am not going in for sham successes which may do me good but will certainly do us harm. When the predominance of one power over the other is so marked as that of Russia over England here, it is best to acknowledge it. This doesn't suit newspapers or perhaps Foreign Offices, but it is safer to stick to facts. Order is kept in this town by a Russian colonel and his Russian drilled troops, by the guns which the Czar gave and by the advice which the Russians are giving. Finances have been for a time set in order by a Russian loan. Corn is brought into the starving city by a Russian road. We have done nothing and given nothing and we cannot expect to get anything. Will Lord Salisbury insist on English officers being employed in the Persian Army ? Will Parliament lend Persia two million, or vote another million for a road from the sea to the north. No, because it won't pay. If it won't pay to invest money, it is plain it won't pay to invest prestige, which is what we do when we offer to help people and don't help when the time comes. Therefore I intend to try for no diplomatic victories, even if I could get them. ' I,' ' I,' ' I '—how ridiculous it all is. Curzon is the type of it all, and he has the great advantage of being industrious and honest, which many of the ' I ' talkers aren't. I fear, however, his affection for his own glory makes it rather difficult for the ' Council ' to walk with him contentedly. This will make government more and more difficult. I expect a man of the Elgin type is really the sort we want.

I am delighted Durand got his G.C.M.G. and I hope and believe that the kindly hand of your noble old father-in-law [1] was there. The more I hear of him and his doings, the more I respect him. I wish I could have a talk through the telephone with him from here."

GULHEK,
June 27, 1900.

To STEPHEN.

" Here we are at the end of June. It is just a little warm—enough to make a sleep in the middle of the day very pleasant, and we dine in the tent provided by the O. of W.—a glorious dream of particoloured canvas with Persian carpets 87 feet by 25 feet—rather magnificent for four men to dine—with a tank in the middle and a stream running down the side. No mosquitoes. I sleep under an open window and will soon sleep out of doors. There isn't much time to spare as I am busy with—bread. The Government is engaged in a wheat corner, in which the Commander-in-chief, the Governor and the Chief Priest are the principal shareholders. The result is rather unpleasant to the people who live on bread and have a mixture of straw and earth given to them at exorbitant prices. H.M. village of Gulhek [2] was a sufferer. They refused to give us bread without an order from the Governor. I applied for one and got no answer. Result—starvation. So I sent a man to the Minister for Foreign Affairs to tell him I should telegraph to the Shah and ask whether it was by his orders that we were being starved,

[1] Lord Dufferin.

[2] The village about the Legation residence was under British authority and rule, and gholams, (gendarmes) were provided to act as orderlies for the Legation.

and went down myself to the town.   I went with two gholams
into the market-place.   No wheat.   I asked where it was and
was told it was stored in the Governor's serai.   I went in there
and asked for the chief person.   He was away (in fact he was in
prison for stealing without the Governor's permission).   I
demanded the second in command.   He came in a long green
robe followed by a curious crowd.   I was on horseback under
an arch, the sun being something intolerable, and he had to come
up to my stirrup.   I asked him for wheat.   He said he couldn't
give it without the order of the Governor.   I said he must write
that under his seal.   Then the gholam made an impassioned
speech, saying I had come from Gulhek with the majesty of
Britain on my shoulders to ask for bread for the people whom the
Shah had put under my protection.   Could he dare refuse ?   He
relented and said he would give a day's supply—no more.   I
said he must write that.   He sent for his secretary who took his
portable inkpot out of his pocket and wrote.   The officer affixed
his seal and handed me the paper in two hands.   ' Then,' said I,
' We will go to the Governor,' and rode off to the office which
three days before had been sacked by the mob and a woman
killed or wounded there.   There was a crowd in the Governor's
office who all vanished, standing at the door and pretending not
to look in.   The Governor, who is an old acquaintance of mine,
was cordial but embarrassed.   Why didn't I come to his house
to see him ?   Because I came not for the pleasure of an interview with my friend the Assaf ed Dowleh but to ask the
Governor of Teheran why my request for wheat for Gulhek was
not complied with.   ' But it has been granted a week ago.'
Then why hadn't I been informed ?   ' That must have been the
fault of the Foreign Office' (the Foreign Minister told the attaché
that he hadn't answered because the Governor had sent him no
reply).   I said, as the Government had shown such scant
courtesy and as ' a hungry man has no religion,' I had come to
Teheran for food.   He said he had no wheat to dispose of.   I
said so powerful a Governor could make wheat grow out of the
ground.   He sent for his secretary who said, Yes, we could have
half a khalvar—1 khalvar—2 khalvars; and so with compliments I departed to bring the good news to the village, who
immediately set to work to get up an intrigue between the two
rival bakers—one half saying all the wheat should be given to
one baker and the other half taking the side of the other.   The
fight is still going on.

   Yesterday we were told the Europeans were to be attacked
and the town destroyed.   It didn't take place, but is put off
till Friday next.   I don't believe much in these reports, but

there is always a chance that the people may go mad with hunger and be turned by the Government on to the foreigners. But we have created a holy funk in the minds of the Foreign Minister and his friends—and I expect there is no danger, but the bazaar is full of talk about China.

Love to Dom, Molly and Julie. I hope Brinsley was not among the yeomanry taken—though I see they are recovered."

Dom and Molly were Stephen's children. Brinsley Fitzgerald was Julie Spring Rice's brother.

July 23, 1900.

" These are troublous days, though it is hard to believe that anything is really happening in the world. What is thought, I wonder, in England of the massacre at Pekin ? Here it gives the Persians keen pleasure, and I rather hope for the sake of Europeans in the East that the punishment inflicted is a severe one. Though I daresay the murderers had a good deal to say for themselves. We have, of course, for some time been discussing the course to be followed here in case of a row, but the difference here is that the Persians only get dangerous when one of them is killed, and the chief object at first is to avoid this. When a row once begins, we should be done for in a few days. But it is most extremely unlikely that a row will take place of a serious kind, even if the Shah dies. We have our programme more or less made out. It is odd that when Durand went away I had a long talk with him about it. So did we in Pekin, I remember : so also in Constantinople—laughing at ourselves the while. I sometimes think it would be rather a pleasure once in one's life to have to confront a crisis ; it would at any rate be curious to see one's own behaviour and that of other people. In a sense, all one's life has been a system of training for one moment—and the moment is come. One would then judge oneself once for all. What a curious discovery it would be to some of us ! "

Aug. 15, 1900.

To CHIROL.

" . . . Of course, you know that there is a great deal of excitement in Mahomedan countries about the news from China and that it is very necessary to put a speedy and emphatic end to these disorders, if this can be done. If it can't, the position of all Christians in Mahomedan countries—certainly here and Turkey—will be compromised. Also, I fear that it is the general feeling that the Russian Government is too apt to separate itself from the rest of Europe. The Russians are in a manner distinguished here from other nations—but in the case of a general upheaval they would not be. We are all equally unclean. The mistake made in Petersburg is that, because Russia has an Asiatic origin and destiny, she is looked on as radically different from other nations in Asiatic countries. This isn't the case, and the result of believing that it is the case is disastrous to both Europeans and Russians.

The rôle and destiny of Russia—as viewed by Russians—is to be the arbiters and *natives* of Asia. But to Asiatics they are as much outsiders as ourselves, though when once conquered by the Russians they probably feel more sympathy with the Russians than with us. But certainly I don't think it's true, either here or in China or Turkey, that a conquest by Russians is more acceptable than a conquest by France or Germany. This rather noble dream haunts the Russian mind—that the tired Asiatic will turn to his kindred Russian for help and refuge from his own detestable government, as the Greeks did to Alexander. I see little sign of the *fact* here, though much of the belief. The Russians are a great imaginative people, moved by ideas which they don't think but feel, and profoundly moved. They are children of destiny and have no need to hurry the years, who are their friends and move as fast as God wills, and bring the good things fated. They laugh at us—each generation snatching at the good within reach, because we have no faith in eternity, nor in our own race.

Things here are so bad and the misery and misgovernment so atrocious that I can hardly think foreign government would be objected to by the people, but only by the spoilers of widows and orphans and grinders of the faces of the poor."

At the end of this letter comes the announcement of a new step in his career, which looked like a step out of it.

" I have been offered to go to Egypt as Commr. of the Caisse. I think this would be better than loafing about much longer as secretary of Legation and will probably accept. This means good-bye to a good many things. What do you think ? I care damned little, but am sick of the aimless and pretentious trifling here."

Sir Arthur Hardinge, his contemporary at Eton and Oxford, had meantime been appointed Minister to Persia. Spring Rice wrote again to Chirol :

Aug. 20, 1900.

" I don't know when A. Hardinge will come here. I am quite delighted at the appointment and would like to stay with him.

Poor man, he little thinks what is in store for him. The position is an absurd one—to be accredited to a so-called independent power and to know all the time that there is no question of independence and that the Ministers are simply the creatures of a foreign power. That is what the French must feel in Egypt. But here it has cost the Russians so little, and has cost us a good deal in Egypt. The farce is played every week with a serious face. I go and see the Minister and discourse of the great benefits which Persia derives from his high wisdom, etc., etc., after which preface I take some tea and ask him to settle a little bill for £25.—Thank you. Good-bye.—So it begins again and again. Poor Hardinge. I hope you will say good words for him. He is our best man, I should think, and a most lovable character. If you see him give him my blessing. . . ."

Sept. 20, 1900.

To STEPHEN.

" It's an odd feeling that I may be chucked out of the diplomatic service after spending about sixteen years of my life in learning the business, and set to work at something quite new. But to tell you the truth, with the present management I had almost rather leave the service of the F.O. altogether, or indeed of the Government—and I am glad to get a chance of serving under Lord Cromer, who seems to be a man who knows his mind. . . . This place, delightful as it is, has sickened me officially, and I will turn my back on this country of gibbering liars with complacency. The country is splendid in its facilities for enjoying oneself outside one's business. But the business is simply disgusting, and when I think that it has to be carried on with the three highest paid officials absent (the Minister, the Oriental Secretary, and the Consul at Ispahan) and that my life is spent in struggling with servants who steal, foreign secretaries who lie, a staff which quarrels and colleagues who trip one up if they can—and with nothing in sight—neither useful work to be achieved here, nor of course the slightest encouragement or help from the F.O.—it sometimes makes me a little bitter. But I suppose it is good practice. It trains oneself, and that is better than any result or any gratitude, for one carries it about with one in one's pocket.

Well, here's a growl. And poor Brinsley's up to his knees in dust in a burning sun and doesn't complain—and I am sitting whining in a £500 tent with a dinner waiting. I ought to be ashamed. But I have a feeling that we are badly governed ; the spirit is gone out of us. The leaders are too tired, or too old, or too busy to think ; there is no proper organisation and

we are like Swift, dying at the top.   If only some young, strong
man would come and clear it all up !   Grey is the only man I
can think of, and I suppose he is feeding ducks.[1]   I have had
this feeling growing since first I came back from Japan through
India and China, and came back to find Lord Rosebery and
Reggie Brett talking about Ladas.   It wasn't that, but the
whole impression, as well as the end of the journey, was that there
is something wrong, wholly wrong about the working of the
machine.   Since I went to Germany the feeling has grown
stronger.   We must reform or perish, and I don't want to be an
Englishman without England.   The proper Imperialism isn't
to conquer abroad—but at home, where the real seal of Empire
is.   *Non quod regnas sed quod regnare mereris*, as the gent said of
Rome.   I am a little Englander now ;   I should lop off a good
many branches to save the trunk.   But I have just been reading
Mommsen.   As long as there was an Italian people who could
fight, it didn't much matter if the Romans were beaten by
Mithridates or the pirates.   They were always sure to come
right in the end.   But when there was no Roman people left—
the best generals and organisation couldn't help the Greeks,
they were bound to go down—in spite of Narses and Heraclian
and all of them.   I think our *gents* are right, but our manufacturing classes are not.   I want to see compulsory military
service as the only means of saving us physically, and also
of preventing us from lightly going into little or big wars.
The people would think twice about them if they all had
to fight."

Sept. 1900.

"We are in hopes of a reorganisation.   I don't see why it
shouldn't be possible, but the resistance on various sides is
considerable.   I suppose Durand was not really a business man
and relied on his own knowledge of affairs and the East ; for the
rest, rather liked show than business.   Certainly he had a very
strong liking and sympathy for soldiers and a strong contempt
for civilians.   The plan worked while he and Picot—both able
men and good Persian scholars—were here ; after their departure
there was nothing left.   Our object should be to create a
system which doesn't depend on one or two men, but will work
of itself.   This is the case in China and Japan and Turkey, and
with all other Legations here except only ours.   There are
two things to be guarded against.   First : against the too long
continuance of the same man in the same post—so that he
makes his own likes and dislikes and gets steeped too deeply in

1 See above p. 253.

local colour: and secondly, against perpetual change—man succeeding man too quickly for local experience to be acquired, or for the following out of a tradition. It has been rather unfortunate for me to have to attack (as I had to do) the Minister and his policy. The real reason, however, for the failure of the system was his own knowledge of the country and language. This is not to be counted on in the ordinary Minister, and some different system must be followed in consequence. I hope I shall never again have to go through such an experience as I have had. It is useless to complain, however, and the worst is long over. As for any credit, that is, of course, out of the question, and if I acquired any, it wouldn't be of much service now. . . ."

Meantime he neither forgot nor was forgotten by his American friends. Mrs. Roosevelt wrote :

                              EXECUTIVE MANSION, ALBANY,
                                    Dec. 15, 1899.
" DEAR MR. SPRING RICE,
        I wish you knew how often we speak of you and how much we want to see you. We have never been happier in our lives than we are now, but I cannot describe the feeling with which I look back to those years in Washington when we were all young. It is one thing to look young and another, quite another, to be young. Do you remember the year that little Ted was so ill, and you used to ride up to the steps of the tiny Jefferson Place house with your pocket full of wild flowers for him. I can see him and Alice now making a baby garden by sticking the flowers in the seat of a cane chair. I can see you and Theodore too running up and down the sandbanks along the shore at Sagamore. Please come back before we all are too staid and middle-aged. Alice is taller than I am. Do you remember how you used to tell us ghost stories all dinner time at Sagamore. It is lovelier than ever there. . . ."

She wrote again on March 25, 1900.

        " . . . It seems a long time since we saw you and a whole lifetime has been compressed into the last year. Do you remember how we used to call Theodore the Chilean volunteer and tease him about his dream of leading a cavalry charge? Remington (the painter) has done the San Juan charge now."

                                        Sept. 25, 1900.
To MRS. LODGE.
        " . . . If nothing unexpected happens I shall be in Egypt for keeps in the early winter. Is there any chance of your coming

over to Europe ? I will show you around. You won't think much of me. I am bald, fat and stupid. However, though you can never be bald, fat or stupid, you have many friends who are, and whom you pardon on account of their affectionate hearts. If you want to know what I am doing, I am giving virtuous advice to dissipated old Persians, talking of the duty of patriotism, etc., and recommending the Devil to bathe in holy water. When I'm not doing this, I am asking them to pay money to various British thieves who want it on various pretexts.

The ways of diplomacy are devious. I live in a really delightful garden—a mass of flowers under the window, a murmuring stream and branching trees inhabited by hoopoes and fly-catchers and little brown owls. The hoopoe, that is the ancestor of all hoopoes, brought King Solomon news of the Queen of Sheba. That is why he was given his crown. At first it was made of gold, but the Jews killed the bird for his crown, and so they petitioned King Solomon to make the crown of feathers. One of them hopped about just in front of me and looked round with a knowing eye. I wonder if he wanted to tell *me* of a Queen ? I expect he wanted bread-crumbs, but it would have been pleasant if he had observed that he has just arrived from Nahant where the weather was very fine, thank you, and the bread of a superior quality."

Again, after the elections which had made Lodge a Senator again, and Roosevelt Vice-President :

Nov. 21, 1900.

To MR. LODGE.

" A New Year's wishes ! You don't deserve any recognition from me and you wouldn't have it, if I thought you would care a Boston imprecation.

... I am so delighted at the election (*now* I can say so) and wish to goodness I could have been in Washington then. I would give anything to be in your library again and hear the Senator talk and listen to your silvery chuckle. Do you chuckle still ? I wonder if anyone chews the Senator's cigars as I used to, and he bore it for years."

Undated—Winter of 1900-1.

To MRS. ROOSEVELT.

" Every afternoon I go out a long walk over the snow alone, coming back during the sunset. In front is the huge range of hills, snow-covered, looking small enough except for Demavend, which always manages to look a certain height. The plain slopes gradually up, covered now with snow, under the snow stone and earth, not a blade of grass nor a flower. Here and there a mud wall with trees behind it, watered by an underground canal carefully guarded. A colleague of mine fell with his horse 20 feet into one, had to be hauled out with a rope ; the horse was shot. He was an hour in the cold water and in the dark. Another colleague noticed that the plaster was cracking in his bedroom, got up and left : in half an hour the whole house subsided into mud—being built of that material hardened in the sun. I came back overnight and found what I thought a large dog in my path ; it moved slowly off and sat in the moon, or at least in the cloudy light of one. I couldn't make out what it was but thought it a jackal. It turns out to be a wolf which has made several visits. This is in the town of Teheran ! A leopard was seen the other day, but some way off. It is very different to Washington and those beautiful woods and the rows on the Potomac—and the jungle. It is impossible to tell the difference and how great it is. But it is something to learn to do without things. I think this might be done positively ; I mean by teaching people to love and enjoy what no one has given, and what no one can take away. We learn this by loving what is outside us, in the proper way—for what is really lovable and good in it : and then, having been at school and learnt our lesson well, we can face the world bravely, knowing that one has something in one which is indestructible. Having, both you and Theodore, been very happy, you may not realise easily how many lives there are which are not blessed in the same way, yet which are truly blessed ; and one of your children perhaps may not be possessed of the means of happiness which you have, and may complain, thinking the world has a spite against him. I have seen in my own home, as a boy, so much misery and grief, that what I have seen since hasn't surprised me. I was at school early. But your children, thank heaven, have seen nothing but happiness. Taken the right way, that ought to help them afterwards, as people coming from a warm climate can best stand the cold of Canada. This is an unwarranted sermon ! born of solitude and other things."

The next is after the " Khaki " General Election, which put Unionists in by a huge majority :

To FERGUSON.   Dec. 6, 1900.

    " Merry Xmas to you and Lady Helen ! Your prophecy has come exactly true that there would be a dandy Cabinet of the husbands of ladies related to or befriended by Arthur Balfour. . . .

    Dear me, here is the old ship, on her beam ends, engines out of order and compass gone wrong and she goes into port—to receive a set of officers in kid gloves and a new suit of white paint !

Anyhow, I am quitting ; I don't know for how long, but I suppose I shall stay in Egypt for some years.

Please give Lady Helen my best love and believe that I think a great deal about you and long to have a good talk. Keep Edward Grey up to the mark and shoot his damned ducks for him."

He himself, as chargé d'affaires, was obliged to entertain and had a Christmas dinner of forty persons and a ball.

" My head servant has just retired to bed ; he is a martyr to delirium tremens, and I tremble for my guests," he wrote to Villiers on December 6, 1900.

"I am doing nothing here, not because there is nothing to do but because there is no means of doing it. Things are no better than they were, and the Persians have only returned (from the Shah's tour in Europe) with new clothes and decorations ; inside, they are just the same, but far more conceited. We shall have to stop playing the game of pretending that this is an intelligent or civilised or independent power. I hope to get some more claims settled but that is the most possible. We shall have to be ready for defending our commercial interests in the South in case of serious disorder brought about by the culpable negligence of the central government."

His mood was altogether one of disgust, when he wrote on February 7, 1901 :

To FARRER.

" I hate and loathe our present system of life and government and am only anxious to get out of it in some decent way. I wish I was a carpenter. A word of advice to a father. Teach your son a manual trade early, like carpentry or metal-work or gardening. If the world goes smash, it will come in useful. I wish I had a mechanical trade (*not* art) to fall back on. Morris hit the right nail on the head.

I am surrounded with furniture for which you (with forty millions of fellow subscribers) have paid ; palatial rooms with plaster work from S. Kensington, carpets of divers colours ; a vast garden with running water ; twelve scarlet servants on twelve horses, in whose company I ride out to see the King of Kings—and the whole doesn't amount to ½d. worth of advantage to H.M. Government and people. However, it is very grand and I thank God it is nearly over, and I shall return to one room and a scrubby servant. These people are the liars of liars.

The Cretans, I think, must have emigrated here shortly after St. Paul's visit."

In February came the joyful news that Sir Arthur Hardinge was coming out as Minister. " I wonder what he will be like as chief and overlord," Spring Rice wrote to his brother. " It will be amusing to see his gravity; also to hear him laugh, if he can still laugh." But there came also the news of Queen Victoria's passing. He wrote to his sister-in-law on February 7, 1901 :

" MY DEAR JULIE,

I am still here waiting for Hardinge to come. I shall meet him outside the town in uniform with eight men in red and all on brown horses, and the Shah will send his Master of Ceremonies and half his available army, and we will all fall down and worship our little quicksilver image. It will be difficult to preserve becoming gravity although I have served under Sir Mortimer Durand, who took these things seriously and was born to manage a circus.

I have been occupied with our poor Queen. What a terrible change ! The way the event was represented here took away half the sorrow and made it boredom. There was a memorial service in the American church. We got black stuff and palms and draped the chancel : then there were the invitations. How many Persians ? Where were they to sit ? They absolutely refused to come unless they were in the front row, so in the first row they were put, and sat struggling for the best places and sitting on each others laps. The foreign Ministers were much in the same style and I had some difficulty in getting a place at all for myself and the staff. When we were all settled down, our eight scarlet gholams walked in and took up their places and the choir sang ' Rock of Ages.' Then the American missionary read the funeral service and then we sang in unison ' Oh God our help in ages past.' It was all very simple indeed and I thought most impressive. But then, I understood, which most people didn't. The Armenian Bishop requested to come, and sat in the chancel in full canonicals. The next week I spent rushing about the town paying visits. It is a horrible business here. The gholams ride two in front and three behind. I ride in the middle with anyone who goes with me. We have to go a good pace and the streets clear like magic. Then a man gallops ahead and announces our coming. We find a number of seedy-looking servants waiting for us and are ushered through various courts till we arrive at the room of honour, generally furnished in appalling colours with a large number of glass chandeliers with coloured shades. We exchange compliments and drink, first tea, then coffee, then smoke cigarettes. Then I rise and say, ' You have taken too much trouble,' and depart as I came. This exciting business lasted about a week. Thank Heaven, it is at last over."

He wrote also to his Eton tutor :

" To think of England without her Queen ! The Persians believe she was the good angel who saved us from destruction and that our glory is gone with her. I feel half as if this were the case. Arise, let us go hence. Do you hear the music under the home Park, as Hercules, our guardian, leaves us ? "

He was eager to be off—partly from simple desire of a holiday and change—back to the familiar. " I am rather longing to pay visits in the civilised hansom—like you," he wrote to his sister-in-law. Also, the work had been depressing :

To JULIE.

" I have been here in a time of unexampled decay of British influence which I have accepted with as good a grace as I could manage. But it has not been pleasant, and the F.O., of course, has done nothing to help. How could it ? Only, I think, something might have been done to reform the personnel. But it is over now, and diplomacy, I think, is over too for me, for which I am not very sorry."

He departed at the end of February, on the rather laborious journey to Batoum, " riding for the last time on my beloved Arab." There is no sign in his writings of any special love for dogs, cats or any other indoor animal friends ; but in Persia and in Egypt the companionship of horses was a delight to him. This Arab of which he speaks would ' when it was in good humour '—follow him like a dog.

It is only right to put in here two letters of remonstrance which Spring Rice received about this period, from two men who had nothing in common but their friendship for him. The first is from Roosevelt.

ALBANY.
Nov. 19, 1900.

" DEAR CECIL,

I received your last very pessimistic epistle while in the middle of my campaign for Vice-President. You recited in the most gloomy manner how England helped the United States against Germany and how now Germany was going to use the United States to ruin England. About five days afterwards came the news of the Anglo-German agreement, which is as near an alliance as England could wish for, it seems to me, and which certainly shows that at the moment Germany is to be counted as a great factor in favour of and not against England

—primarily in China, but, of course, secondarily elsewhere. I happen to know from the inside that one of the factors in bringing about this agreement was the conduct, public and private, of the American Peace Commissioners at The Hague. As you doubtless remember, they supported England's attitude throughout, and one of their number who is by parentage a German, but a thoroughly Americanised German (who, for instance, has gone further than I have gone in backing up England against the Boers) was able to bring about a wholly informal and unofficial conference or correspondence between Balfour and the German Foreign Office, or certain officials of it, which laid the foundation for the present Anglo-German agreement. Last spring this man told me that he was certain there would be such an agreement during the course of the summer, basing his belief upon the information which had come to him because of the relations he had thus succeeded in establishing.

You say it is rather funny to think of McKinley and myself being quoted as Anglomaniacs. I am not an Anglomaniac any more than I am an Anglophobe; I do not believe in ' slopping over '; but I am keenly alive to the friendly countenance England gave us in 1898, and throughout the campaign I have made hearty acknowledgements of this, as contrasted with the attitude of the continental European powers. I did this, for instance, in a book of essays which appeared on the 1st of October.

I have been very uncomfortable about the Boer war, and notably in reference to certain details of the way it was brought on ; but I have far too lively a knowledge of our national short-comings to wish to say anything publicly that would hamper or excite feeling against a friendly nation for which I have a hearty admiration and respect. I do not think you will find any utterance of mine during the last campaign, or for the preceding three years, which was unkind toward Great Britain, or which in any way excited, or sanctioned the excitement of, any hostile feeling toward her. I think we should dwell in peace and friendship with all nations, but especially with yours.

For some reason or other a portion of the English press has objected to our attitude in China. I have not made a close study of the matter, but most emphatically our policy has been anti-Russian rather than anti-English, while Secretary Hay's friendship for England is well known. Indeed, I am inclined to think that our attitude has been essentially the proper attitude to take. Don't you think you were a little bit jaundiced when you wrote ? ''

The second, which cuts much deeper, came from Mr. Luxmoore:

ETON,
March 17, 1901.

" DEAR CECIL,

... I have, I believe, kept your letter till last, so then I shall have done arrears, save to the family. They can wait.

Is it a compliment to keep you till last or the reverse ? Obviously the former, and please take it so. But I want to scold you a bit, too.   You are quite right in saying that faith in loving is stronger than in the *opus operatum*. But you need not be so despondent about the last, and I don't like you starting off for new work—which is a great compliment—with a sigh of distrust.   I was talking to a F.O. clerk of good sense the other day, and he said his chief thought a lot of you, but he, for his part, though he liked reading your despatches, held that you were too ready to acquiesce in the disagreeable. You accepted the inevitable and went out to meet it and he believed that more tenacity with a narrow view would make a more valuable public servant.   It struck me that this was true and especially true in the East, where your largeness of sympathy put you in touch with the oriental submission to fate and the philosophic indifference to the petty objects about which such a dust is raised in society and in politics ; but in going to Egypt there will be less of this : for good or evil the die is cast there, and Egypt is to be deorientalised whether we like it or not.   To be quite honest, I confess I would think of Persia as happier in some ways under Persians than under us.   But in Egypt where at all events twenty blades of grass are being put for one, etc., justice is driving out gross forms of oppression, and you ought to begin work with more elation than your ' cabhorse entering a new stable ' ; and, in your power of sympathy with the best and not merely the material objects, you may be of great use in raising what is peddling ultra-English in the men who at all events are setting right some wrongs.   No, there is no sighing Hercules[1] here, but plantings of young trees and spring rushing into bud. As for that good woman and great queen, she redeems the ideal of England—for she was utterly English with all its bourgeois and Philistine limitations, and yet how admirable and useful ! She shall be ' genius of the shore ' and ' good to all that wander on the perilous flood ' as long as we have a fleet afloat.   I am afraid that the mixture of two civilisations is apt to spoil each, but still there are great things doing, and irrigation is a blessing east or west, isn't it ? ... "

[1] See p. 331.

No one loved Spring Rice better than the writer of this rebuke ; and it was true that he too easily lapsed into the humour of a melancholy Jaques, and thought the world unkind to him. But he had been through a severe emotional strain, followed by heavy and disheartening work, with the handicap of physical delicacy which never left him. Nothing, however, had sapped his will-power or his disposition to work ; and what he really needed most was the call to act where action could be effective. He had to wait for this, but when it came, he was equal to it.

CHAPTER XI

CAIRO

SPRING RICE's stay at Cairo, which lasted two years, was an episode detached from the main course of his life. This Egyptian bondage was anything but laborious ; it offered fleshpots, for he was probably better off then than at any other period of his life ; the income of a Commissioner was very ample for a man of forty-two, to all appearance settling down into confirmed bachelorhood. There was much to interest him ; his letters tell of meeting with, for instance, Rhodes and Jameson ; if he had been lonely in Persia, here was wealth of gay society ; if he had felt himself at Teheran the upholder of a steadily-losing cause, in Egypt under Lord Cromer a Briton had plenty to be proud of. He came into contact with men of his race working as engineers, as soldiers, and as administrators, with a passion for their work, and his heart went out, as always, to men of action. Perhaps it was the contrast in his own department that made him uneasy.

The Caisse de la Dette, a representation of the European bond-holders, was originally established in 1876. France, Italy and Austria at the outset nominated commissioners ; Sir Evelyn Baring (Lord Cromer) became the first British Commissioner in 1877 ; in 1885, after reorganisation under the British occupation, Germany and Russia also appointed Commissioners.

The Commissioners had under their control the annual proceeds of certain revenues earmarked for the service of the debt ; they paid the bondholders, and administered the surplus ; and they were entitled to a voice in general administration, since no fresh loan could be raised without their consent. Lord Cromer in his *Modern Egypt* says that, after the British occupation " the inutility of the Commission became more and more apparent," and in 1904, the year after Spring Rice left, its functions were radically transformed, and the Commissioners became merely receivers on the part of the bond-holders, and could not interfere with administrative action.

Cecil Spring Rice was acutely aware that he was part of a compli-cated and highly paid organisation, all of whose essential duties could have been discharged by one man with a staff of clerks ; and he dis-liked the feeling. Also, he was in the atmosphere of international finance and he breathed it with distaste. Already in Constantinople he had misliked the reputation left by prominent English financiers,

335

and he did not find it congenial in Cairo to be associated officially with the stockjobbers and servants of stockjobbers—not with the hardbitten men whose tents were pitched wherever rebellious tribes had to be subdued or rebellious water to be harnessed.

So, after a while, he rose out of it, but not before an intense personal crisis had passed in his life.

No attempt has been made here to illustrate his official work, which did not seriously engage him ; but many of the letters of this time are very characteristic.

It should be added that during this period he was completing his second translation from the Persian, *The Story of Valeh and Hadijeh.*

CAISSE DE LA DETTE PUBLIQUE,
CAIRO, Mar. 21, 1901.

To STEPHEN.

" I found your letter to-day, I having arrived about four days ago. I was delighted to hear of you and I hope to be in London shortly. I am to have leave at once in order that my seniors may take leave during the hot weather. I have been taking lessons in finance, little I know about it ! But my duties are mainly semi-diplomatic. I get coached by Lord Cromer and Gorst and hope to know my business in a few months. The main occupation at present is leaving cards and looking for a house. The latter is really a difficult job and I don't know when I shall get installed. I am at present in an hotel full of vast shifting swarms of Americans and travelling English, mostly ladies on the look-out for husbands and lovers. They amuse themselves after their watering-place kind. . . .

Thanks to Lord Cromer things are going well here. It is really an infinite pleasure to be under him. I liked my former chiefs but they are not men like him. In spite of all his work and worry he doesn't seem in the least over-tired or fagged or anxious, which is, I suppose, the mark of a good man. It is a contrast to Persia where nothing is being done by anyone. . . . "

le 21 Mar., 1901.

To VILLIERS.

" Here I am at last. Very glad to have arrived but bothered to death with house-hunting and visits. How are you ? You have been a perfect angel to me all the time I was in Persia— and, oh heavens, how glad I am it is all over ! I hope Hardinge will be successful ; and he began by making everyone like him very much indeed. He was quite well too, which was satisfactory, and full of energy. His ideas were quite different to mine, so it was very lucky my suggestions as to staff, etc., were not adopted. Lord Cromer seems to regret a good deal that the oriental school at Constantinople was done away with and I think we ought to have some means of recruiting trained men regularly into the Persian service. However, this is not my business now. Lord Cromer has been most extraordinarily kind to me and it's difficult to describe the encouraging effect he makes ; I hear the same from many of the younger men here. But he will be hell and Tommy if anything is done wrong. Gorst is also very pleasant and easy to get on with and I expect that so far as they are concerned my position will be delightful so long as I give satisfaction. I like my colleagues too, who are very friendly indeed, though they regard me as improperly *young* ! That is a new sensation indeed."

Henry Adams had written, as usual, cryptically.

WASHINGTON,
Feb. 8, 1901.

" MY AFFECTIONATE NEPHEW,

I am the original Conservative Christian Anarchist. If you are to come into the party you must confess and obtain absolution. What road to Damascus have you travelled since it has not led you to Cairo ?

How can a C.C.A. go to Boston to live ? Obviously not. I forbid it. Washington or Paris I permit, because I am there. Especially Paris, because it is nice and nasty and rotten and free from cant, humbug and hypocrisy. Even Washington is very trying to a serious C.C.A."

And so he proceeds in good set terms to descant on the world's deformity, amongst other phrases calling Russia a " giant dwarf." Spring Rice replied in the humour of the game :

SHEPHERD'S HOTEL,
LE CAIRE, le 14 Mars, 1901.

" DEAR UNCLE HENRY,

I have just received your cheerful and invigorating letter here. I ought to have told you (as chief of my sect) what has happened to me.—I was appointed Commissioner of the Caisse and ought to have come here some six months ago. But I was in charge of what remains of British interests in Persia and wasn't allowed to go. The charge was not inspiring and I made some vain attempts to get off. But the Persian Government was afraid that if I went, leaving a junior secretary in charge, it would be said that England had given up the game and left them to Russia—and protested. So I stayed until my Minister arrived, Arthur Hardinge, a young favourite of fortune, full of

enthusiasm and beans, who came at last and sent me packing.
He was an old friend of mine who used to advocate the strong
old Tory line in our college debating societies. He has been
engaged for the last six years in founding a new British Empire
in E. Africa (for which I and some silent and talkative millions
are now paying) and is sent by Lord Salisbury to restore the
tottering balance in Persia. I developed my ideas (those of the
C.C.S.) with the result that he told me I was mad and sent off
various telegrams without consulting me, so one sunny morning
at six I mounted my beloved Arab for the last time and galloped
off into the desert, preceded by my luggage. That was three
weeks ago and since then I have been travelling as hard as I
could. As for the giant dwarf, I passed through part of his
dominions, a crumb in his loaf called the Caucasus. Do you
want sensations ? Go to the Caucasus. First Baku, an
enormous town in a desert, breeding petroleum ; once the home
and temple of fire worshippers—now mostly owned by the
Rothschilds. There are no Russian entrepreneurs there, or
next to none. Those that do business or have made fortunes are
Germans, English and Tartars, the latter worth millions and
living on 5000 dollars a year. The Russian provides the police
and levies taxes on the foreigners. But I don't think there will
be an Uitlander war for Baku. One travels through a desert
which a little irrigation from the Kura will make into an
enormous cotton garden. Then one reaches Tiflis, once the
capital of a Persian province. The Persians punished the
Georgians for uniting with Russia by a war of extermination,
which resulted finally in Russian intervention, but not till the
Georgians were not in a position to do anything but pray.
This is quoted by the Russians as a great stroke of policy, for
if they had interfered before, the Georgians might have become
dangerous like the Bulgarians. Don't save a snake until his
fangs have been drawn. The Georgians are intensely discontented ; have lost their ancient power and will lose their
language. The shrine of their saint who converted them eight
hundred years before the Russians, is *not* very highly venerated
by the conqueror. Then there are the Armenians, who too,
have had their lesson and know that it is dangerous to speak too
loud. They are not massacred, but their schools have been
abolished, their churches are ruins and they are told if they
complain they will be sent to Turkey. Then there are the
Tartars ; they and the other Moslems, Lesghars, Persians, and
so on, are treated with perfect tolerance and contempt and are
fairly happy. The Russians have made a military railway
through the heart of the country—the old trade route from the

East ; one can see the ruins of the rich towns through which the caravans once passed. But transit is forbidden ; European trade is not to use the route, which is solely for Russian commerce. Along the line there are evidences of enormous possibilities, riches of every kind. Minerals, vegetables, and all, but foreign capital is shy and there are no subsidiary roads and the Russian official looks askance, whatever the Minister of Finance says. The Governor General hates a foreigner and shows it, and yet every scrap of industrial energy shown is foreign. Along the stations are every sort of people in every sort of national costume, and all policed by the Cossack who stalks about among them, conscious of his present and his future. At Batoum a great port is being built which could be the port of ingress and egress of all Central Asia, and *is* merely a Russian port on the Black Sea. Stories are going about among the business men of a State in financial difficulties, enormous manufacturing interests in peril, and State help needed but impossible. Witte encouraged foreign capital to start metallurgic works with promise of Government business, but railway industry is slack and the works are idle and capital clamouring for help. Where can it come from ? It is difficult to avoid a great financial crisis ; but the enormous riches of the country are there, whatever happens, and in the end no doubt the country will right itself. But in the meantime there are difficult times ahead, and the Giant has alienated the Finns, oppresses the Jews and the Germans, hates the Poles, bullies Georgians and Armenians, and looks to Tartars and Chinese for sympathy ; is coalescing with the inferior elements of its Empire turning instinctively to the new savage blood. What will be the end ? Evidently a new civilisation, disdainful of the old, the successor of Tamerlane. I travelled with pilgrims from Bokhara. They talked Persian and told me of the glories of Russian rule, how the soil was being irrigated and silk and cotton produced and money in abundance flowing into every village. A Tartar from the Crimea, in Russian dress, talked to them in their own language—one of Tamerlane's men. I asked them about Tamerlane and on the Black Sea coast pointed out where his great victory was won over the Turks. They knew about it. ' Amir Timour, *our* Amir Timour.'

Here I am among crowds of Americans, mostly women spending their husbands' money, the proceeds of your great boom. *They* are not despondent and flaunt their jewels and I suppose cheerfully dream of duties.

And I have been, in a fortnight, past what immense records of destruction ! The ruins of Moket in Georgia ; Trebizond with its vast walls standing still and as useless as they were, and then Constantinople. What a place the Hippodrome is ! There were all the most glorious statues of Greece, melted down by the Crusaders ; there is still the bronze serpent of Plataea, and the unutterable glories of St. Sofia. Did you ever make a careful study of that glorious building ? Still the centre of the religion of all Russia, and the proudest trophy of Mahomedanism, the shell still perfect, all its treasures gutted—mainly by Christians themselves—just as Justinian's laws are still in the main the laws of the Latin world. And there, in the middle of the Hippodrome, the Emperor William's new fountain erected in memory of his Imperial friendship for the Sultan ! What enormous and colossal jokes Providence does play with us ! It is past all laughing at, if one hasn't the jaws of Behemoth.

One of the many amusing pranks played by Provvy is the Chinese question. Li Hung Chang seems to have offered magnificent promises of boundless concessions to the Americans in return for which they are perfectly willing to go in with him hot and strong. As for the Germans, they make a bargain with England, which they say means that what is England's is theirs and what is theirs is their own. In secret they tell Russia to come in as she likes. And you see the result. She will stay, the others will have to go after some ineffectual protests, and Russia will take another part of that continent which God (in her view) has set apart for her.

I have by this post a letter from you, not too cheerful ; a letter from a philosopher who has been commissioning in the Transvaal and a young savage who has been fighting there ; a letter from a correspondent who went out to study the Chinese question for the third time ; all in the same cheerful spirit. And then I have a letter from my sister who has recently had a baby on whom she lavishes stores of affection in the vain hopes of winning its gratitude, and is perfectly happy and full of wonder for the goodness of the Lord and thankfulness. So the world goes on. There were mothers in Rome in the fourth century. I saw to-day the fellaheen working in the fields with the same ploughs which you can see in the tombs of the fortieth century B.C. Nothing has changed their lives. Is all politics the fringe of the *real* reality, the ripple on the deep ? And the curse of men and women (which is also their blessing) as written in Genesis—the real thing ! A question for the C.C.A. to decide. I am full of all sorts of vague feelings, chasing each other like ghosts in a haunted house ; and I don't know their language and I have no idea what they are at. I'll shut this

door and go out again into the street where there are living
people, mostly Jews, hurrying to business.

Good-bye, beloved Uncle and Chief—I perceive we shall end
in the same madhouse."

21 Mar, 1901.

To MRS. LODGE.

" I wish I were in America, but here I am for an indefinite
period and I don't know when I shall be able to cross the
Atlantic. I am very lucky to get this place—which gives me
little work and for me an immense income of 10,000 dollars, but
I feel very depressed, perhaps because the Khamsin is blowing,
perhaps for other reasons. I am looking for lodgings, or rather
a house, and am living in a hotel. In a short time I shall be
going to England for a rest and then back here for the hot
months. Those will be rather dreadful—worse than Washington—and I am not sure whether I shall find many friends. I
can't make new ones now and those I have are dead or across
the seas. At any rate *you* haven't that to complain of.

You can have no idea what a queer society this is. First there
are the travellers who swarm all over the place, largely consisting
of smart ladies and their lovers. The Americans have certainly
the advantage of looks, and they are better behaved. The
really smart English ladies make one tired. They go from
morning till night ; they are mostly nervous and on the point
of collapse. They don't seem to care for anything except
spending money and making love. Of course, there are exceptions but they don't show. I dined last night at a house
furnished and designed in Arab fashion with beautiful gardens,
etc. ; the guests were like Mrs. Townsend's in Washington, and
the conversation as brilliant. I felt inclined to get up and
curse—and longed for the hour of departure. I found myself
next to a British officer who told me he had been sent there
because he had done well in upper Egypt, and had been a year
in Cairo doing accounts. He had lived in the desert for two or
three years and was now dining out seven nights a week. He
was almightily sick of it and longed to be back. There was an
artist there with whom I talked too, who told me he had known
Egypt for twenty years and went every winter to sell his
pictures. He inveighed (I think honestly) against the money-
grubbing of the time, and said it was visibly growing. His real
pleasure was in his painting and he had eight hours of it every
day. Every evening he had to go into the world to make great
people's acquaintance in order to sell his pictures. Lord
Cromer is a real man and it is a pleasure to know him. He is a

stalwart, high-coloured man with white hair and clean-shaven face and a quick, kindly way of talking which is unlike that of most diplomatists that I have ever met. He has lost his wife, an enormous irreparable grief, but he has the pleasure of good work well done. Everything centres in him and he looks as if he knew it and liked it. No sign of worry or anxiety but confidence which inspires confidence. A little man, younger than me, who looks after finance, is another man who is pleasant to look at, like a locomotive on the point of starting, with steam up. My colleagues here are kind old retired diplomatists who look on me as a boy—*me*—and are most kind and agreeable, but I shall have to fight the old ideas for all I am worth. They look at me a little askance and wonder what I am here for. This doesn't interest you very much but it is what is uppermost in my mind at present and so I unload on you. Oh for an hour of quiet talk with you—not in a beastly hotel but in Mass. Ave. ! Is the room just as it used to be ! I long for a pleasant house and beautiful things and people, but I can't afford the price and if I could it would be against what I now think right to indulge. A vile priggish sentiment and not very sincere. I like Bay's behaviour and think of him as perfectly happy and enviable. Don't encourage him to make money but to like things which make bought pleasures unpalatable. Tell me more about John who must be happy too in his music.''

He went on leave to England in March and wrote to Henry Adams from the house of his brother-in-law—now Lord Farrer :

ABINGER HALL, DORKING,
April 1, 1901.

'' DEAR UNCLE HENRY,

Here I am in a place you know of. Spring comes reluctantly in with showers of rain and blasts of wind, but is beautiful all the same, and hasn't forgotten its violets and primroses and daffodils. It's a wonderful thing after the East so unlovely in its details, to see the extraordinary beauty of every nook and cranny. The little villages have a hundred points of view, all beautiful, and there isn't a hedgerow which one can't stand and study with pleasure. However, you know it all. I was amused as I came to the station to see two fine carriages waiting ; out of the train came a lady with a violet bonnet and a little squab, hook-nosed, whiskered German Jew with the airs of a master, who, amid the respect of the station, swaggered into his carriage and drove off. This is the new element and the supreme master of villages, violets, daffodils and all. I suppose this is to be seen in all our prettiest places, the spreading blight of London. As for the condition of things here, we are waiting for the Budget, before which I suppose we shall have the announcement of another great victory—like the Spanish victories in Cuba—a likeness even more striking. There is no good talking or thinking about these things. I content myself with enjoying the still uncorrupted beauty of this wonderful country. It is worth while being away so long to enjoy the return and to feel one's feet on the chalk turf and see the fields and woods fading into mist under the branches of the beeches on the top of the downs. In Persia I had a beautiful garden full of roses and nightingales, but outside was the desert and the grim peaks of snow and black rock showing through the trees. Here beauty is as wide and general as the casing air, and it is free to everyone and fills every inch of the ground. Also there are my two little nieces who are quite delightful. They can't move without dancing or speak without a sort of rippling laugh. There are plenty of things in the world to make one contented and happy, and why should one mind the Jews and the newspapers? The Jews hurt us because we care for money, and the newspapers because we must have excitement. Don't care for money and scorn excitement and their coin doesn't pass current in one's mind. If we have our own currency the devil may offer his bribes as much as he likes: with the best will in the world we can't take them, we live in a country where his coin is not recognized. I can't bribe a porter at Gomshall Station with a Persian kran or a Japanese yen. What are you doing? I went to Rome to see the Chanlers: they were away but Miss Laura received me and entertained me and showed me the sights. We went out into the country and hunted for a lark's nest: in the evening we thrilled and throbbed over the Grail music not badly sung by a choir of Italians. Then I went to Paris. On the way I met a soldier just returning from famine duty in India. He organized droves of children who went in squads to table; he taught them at beginning and end of their meals to thank the Queen and pray for her. Also a squire from Hereford with two buxom daughters; he laughed at talk of decadence and said that he didn't see much of that in Herefordshire. He hadn't been in London to stay for twenty years. At Paris I asked for Mrs. Cameron. Gone to the S. of France, of course; Bay not to be found, though I enquired of all the grocers in the Rue du Bac. So I went to the Louvre and saw the pictures and then on by train to London. I found nobody at home but a letter from Tom Farrer and came on here to find all my people collected here, including an old Etonian friend from Queensland and my brother, a stalwart farmer from Western Canada, and many babies. I have spent a week drinking in long-day blessed idleness, and getting religiously wet every morning and afternoon and reading Scott and St. Simon. The last is interesting reading in a queer way and gives one much food for thought. How is the Secretary of State ? [1] Let me hear from you at 1 Bryanston Place, W.—I am just off to see J. W. Mackail, of whom you have never heard, the finest scholar we ever had at Balliol, and a Conservative Christian Socialist preacher."

Roosevelt also had a word to say about decadence.

March 16, 1901.

" DEAR CECIL,

. . . In spite of all the unhealthy signs in this country, I still see ample evidence of abounding vigour. There is certainly such vigour in Australia. In South Africa I earnestly hope that, when the present dreadful muddle is ended, a process of amalgamation may go on which will build up a great English-speaking commonwealth south of the Zambesi. I also earnestly hope that England will continue her supremacy in southern and partly in Eastern Asia and throughout Africa as a whole. But remember that the loss of supremacy there, or the loss of American supremacy in the Philippines, though a serious thing, to the great bulk of the race, would not be by any means a fatal blow. Neither Germany or Russia can ever stand to the civilised world as for a brief period the Macedonian, and for many centuries the Roman stood. Holland and Sweden have had a couple of centuries of perfectly healthy life since their greatness vanished. The loss of the greatness was a real and terrible loss, but yet a good deal remained. The same would be true of England. This may seem a rather gloomy kind of comfort. Remember that personally I do not think our greatness is vanishing. France has gone down relatively to England. The Russian growth—the growth of the Slav—is slow. At the same time that the German Empire has been built up, the German race in Austria has gone back relatively to both the Magyar and the Slav. If ever we see German-Austria united with the German Empire, the Catholic and reactionary forces within the latter will exercise a force so nearly controlling as to make it impossible to foretell what course the new Empire would take. In any event, I do not think it possible that in the long run Germany, which has to face the Slav on land and the English-

[1] John Hay, Adams's closest friend.

speaking peoples on the sea, can take the first place. Russia's day is yet afar off. I think the twentieth century will still be the century of the men who speak English."

Spring Rice's English leave extended itself to a visit to Berlin where he was the guest of his former chief, Sir Frank Lascelles. During the years since 1898 he had written regularly to Miss Lascelles, though with no suggestion of courtship. But from this period on, till he married Miss Lascelles, all roads appeared to lead through Berlin.

He wrote his political observations from that capital to Villiers. A docket shows that the letter was submitted to Lord Lansdowne, then Foreign Secretary, by Sir T. H. Sanderson. The precise words are, " The enclosed from Spring Rice to F. Villiers is entertaining and in some ways instructive." Lord Sanderson (as he became) on retiring from permanent headship of the Foreign Office) was among the officials who thought Spring Rice more entertaining than was quite suitable for a diplomat. He figures through the correspondence as " Lamps " (short for Giglamps, which was Lord Salisbury's name for him) and was evidently regarded by his juniors much as schoolboys regard their schoolmaster—though certainly in Spring Rice's case not without affection.

BERLIN,
June 15, 1901.

To VILLIERS.

" It has been very interesting here and I have seen a lot of old friends. The Germans seem very keen about Persia and hope naturally enough we shall make a row if the Russians advance. This probably is in hopes of occupying the Russians and our- selves ; but there seems a general impression abroad here that England has been uncomfortably weakened in the last two years and that with Austria and Italy doubtful quantities, the position of Germany is becoming more and more uncertain ! brave it out as they may. But Lord ! How they do hate us ; the feeling is general and has spread very far and deep, the common people are as much affected as the army. Only the Emperor and a few thinking men at the top are getting per- turbed and look on the difficulties of Austria and England as affecting Germany as well as the principal parties.

The Emperor is furious at the continuance of the South African War and I have no doubt would do a good deal to put a stop to it. He had quite a scene with Waters [1] about the with- drawal of the seasoned troops and almost lost his temper. I suppose we shall have some talk of an alliance soon, but the military people say England must reorganise not only the army

[1] The military attaché.

but the whole system before she can enter on alliances on equal terms. Lascelles is immensely popular here."

By July he was back in Egypt.

CAIRO,
July 31, 1901.

To STEPHEN.

" . . . We have a great difficulty with that hero of freedom, Wilfred Blunt. He appears to have very autocratic views about the right of property and has been in the habit of falling on trespassers and incarcerating and beating them. His Arab servants follow his example. It appears that a few British officers were out hunting the fox and trespassed on to Blunt's property. They were fallen on by W. B.'s servants and severely handled. The servants were prosecuted and punished with considerable imprisonment. W. Blunt telegraphs that he is responsible, which is true. In defence the servants urged that they had seen their master ' beat trespassers till the blood ran down their backs ' ! Isn't this rather a queer aspect of the bird of freedom ? I wonder what exactly he will say for himself. . ."

Mr. Blunt—poet and breeder of Arab horses—had been very prominent as a champion of Irish evicted tenants. Spring Rice as a counter-demonstration took a gun and walked up and down in front of Blunt's house as if in pursuit of game—but was unmolested. Another letter in the papers refers to this quest.

" DEAR SPRING RICE,

(1) Arma virumque cano.

(2) αλλ' ευτυχοίης νοστιμον δ' έλθοις ποδα

Please excuse accents.

Yours,

P. W. MACHELL.

If you have a report to make to the police, I recommend you to make it to the Commandant Cairo City Police, Paterson."

Then came the sudden news of President McKinley's assassination in Buffalo by a Polish anarchist on September 6 ; Roosevelt who was Vice-President went to the White House.

Sept. 15, 1901.

To STEPHEN.

" . . . I wonder if the Americans will take any step about anarchists now ! It is extraordinary to think of Theodore Roosevelt as President. He will make things hum. I don't suppose there will be a war but there will be plenty of amusement. The U.S. is awfully lucky to get the best man possible by a fluke."

What Spring Rice wrote to Roosevelt—if he wrote—is not extant ; there are only these two notes—from which it would appear that he did not write.

EXECUTIVE MANSION,

WASHINGTON,

Oct. 1, 1901.

" DEAR CECIL,

Just a line to say how much I have thought of you. I do wish you would come over now and be my guest at the White House. Is there any chance of it ?

Ever yours,

THEODORE ROOSEVELT."

WHITE HOUSE,

WASHINGTON,

Nov. 7, 1901.

" DEAR CECIL,

Can you get over to America ? I am really very anxious to see you. Now that, contrary to what any human being could reasonably have expected, I am in the White House, I wish you could be over here and see for yourself how I manage things.

Not only Mrs. Roosevelt and I, but all the children, would be delighted if you could only come.

Ever yours,

THEODORE ROOSEVELT."

Dec. 28, 1901.

To STEPHEN.

" . . . Rhodes is here for his health. He seems to have done no business and is now gone. Went to-day with Jameson. He is in a bad condition ; heart weak, excitable and fretful ; he said the best and only chance for us in S. Africa is organised emigration. He likes Milner more than Kitchener. It appears from what we hear here that there is a great deal of friction in S. Africa between the civil and military. There would be here if the civil weren't represented by Lord Cromer, who don't allow anyone else, military or divine, to have much of a show. It works well enough. I don't know what would happen if Lord C. were to go. He doesn't intend to at present ; that's clear enough. He will be here for another nine years. I hope so. I don't know how long it will be worth my while to stay. . . . "

Letters to Ferguson and Lady Helen deal with the English political situation. Lord Rosebery was still one of the foremost men in

England but he had detached himself from his party, and showed no disposition to work with them or for them.

Jan. 10, 1902.

To FERGUSON.

" I can't help thinking that what is more important than wit and cleverness and suggestive speeches is—especially in England —character ; and Lord Rosebery's character is still an enigma. I don't mean in a narrow sense, but as regards unselfish belief in an ideal and unflinching courage in carrying it into practice. Such a man is followed of necessity and makes a party by force of his nature and not by political combinations. Practically he seems the only possible head ; but having become a head, will he be a leader ? A party, like a locomotive, is a thing that has to move, and till it is on the move one can't judge it. Probably it isn't only Lord Rosebery who is in fault but the materials and the circumstances. If I were a member of the party, I should give him a fair and honest trial, follow him and obey him till he was able to show himself what he really is. If he is continually hampered by contradictory demands, he can't be blamed for being a trifle uncertain. He never had a fair chance. I should say give him one, and the way to give him one is to do what he orders, once the general lines of policy are accepted. It may be the fact that Parliament is going down in the world and that the party system is breaking down. But if we take for granted that this is so, we only make the ruin fall faster. If Lord Rosebery has his faults as a leader, aren't they rather the consequence of the faults of the party ? Something must be done to restore the efficiency of Government and give life to the Government service. Something, too, must be done to rebuild or create a party capable of taking the place of the present rulers. I don't see that there is any alternative except to accept Lord Rosebery's leadership and do one's very best to make it a success. He is not only the best man but the only possible one at present. If we persist as we have been doing, it isn't only the party which will suffer, but the whole nation and the business of the nation throughout the world. One can't base a Government on bands of banditti. And the business before us is plainly to make a Government. It is plain enough that if in a short space of time a Liberal Party isn't formed and disciplined under the old lines, a series of short, unstable Governments will follow this one—composed at first of fragments of the old school men ; but afterwards when these are disgusted, of new school men on the French type, from which the Lord deliver us. When will you come out here. I think I shall go to the U.S. to have a look at the President."

Jan. 16, 1902.

"DEAR LADY HELEN,

It is rather amusing to compare what you say about
Lord R. and what Villiers said just before he became
Prime Minister. At that time Villiers described the universal
consensus of opinion that he was the only possible leader—
everyone of every rank said so and he ' was bound to yield to
the general pressure in spite of his reluctance.' A few months
afterwards, there was an equal consensus of opinion, but not so
favourable to him. He seems to excel in raising hopes and con-
ciliating sympathies, but he doesn't seem to be skilled in the
difference between to have and to hold. He rather reminds me
of a child which catches hold of a ball with eagerness but can't
keep hold—or hasn't perhaps learnt the force of gravity—and
cries when the thing falls out of his hand and gets broken.
What a queer character ! I don't believe in separating one's
life ; a man isn't really different from his associates and his
favourite occupations. The Tories who maintain the existing
state of things can get on with a lively respect for what is, and
don't need much more. But we want to change and reform.
For what ? For an idea, an image of something better in our
own minds ; not for fear of other people or to bribe other
people to put us in power. The man with the idea who believes
in it is our natural ruler. I am not sure that Lord Rosebery has
the idea, or much belief in it, if he has it ; but what must we
do ? We must have an alternative Government. Otherwise
when this one sickens the country and sloughs off, we shall be
under the influence of the discomfort and discontent engendered
by the war and its burdens, which feelings will be exploited by a
set of men without unity or coherence, or experience in business ;
they will succeeed each other in incoherent groups, and we shall
fall into the French and German parliamentary systems and it's
worse for us than for them. Germany has its rigid bureaucracy
and its crown. France its highly organised centralisation—
both have a Parliament as a luxury and not as a necessity. Ours
is a head, not a hat. Where shall we be if that goes wrong ?
Therefore I should hope and pray that Lord R. has his
chance : that he is accepted and followed and that we use this
hut whatever its peculiarities as a shelter to run into out of the
rain. All the same I agree with Haldane : I'd like to have a
good seat on the Judgement Day when Lord R's case comes
up. But I fear we shall have to leave our seats in the middle of
the trial and be called as witnesses. ' Whose fault was it ? '
we may be asked. And we shall all be damned together.

I am doing nothing here, mainly by my own fault ; there is plenty to be done of one sort and another here but I can't choose without compulsion. I like Lady Cromer and it is refreshing to go and see her, she is so much herself and one is as sure of her as a rock in the sea. Do you know Lady Edward Cecil ?[1] What do you think of her ? She is clever enough for ten : also extremely nice to look at, and eminently alive.''

When Spring Rice went on leave in 1902 he carried out the intention which he had expressed to Ferguson : the desire to see Roosevelt in his new glory was irresistible. Mrs. Roosevelt also had written :

> WHITE HOUSE,
> WASHINGTON,
> Jan. 27.

" MY DEAR MR. SPRING RICE,

It was good to hear from you and it will be still better to see you. Last night the Lodges and Mr. Adams and Austin Wadsworth and his wife were here and we talked of you and of the empty place which you have left. I count on long, misty moonlight evenings on the White House porch. Theodore in his rocking chair, you and Cabot settling world affairs over your cigars. While Mrs. Lodge and I meekly listen, as becomes our sex and position. Being the centre of things is very interesting, yet the same proportions remain. . . . ''

Incidentally, on his visit to England, the traveller met Miss Lascelles who was staying with her English relatives. He wrote to her before sailing. She, unlike her father, shared the feelings which the German Government inspired in Spring Rice—and in their common friend, Chirol.

> QUEENSTOWN,
> April 17, 1902.

" DEAR MISS LASCELLES,

. . . You would be interested to see the effect created in England by the German treatment of us. The change is extraordinary. Everyone in the office and out talk as if we had but one enemy in the world, and that Germany. It is no manner of good trying to assure us unofficially or officially that they are really our friends. No one believes it now and the only effect is to disgust. The change in Chamberlain's mind is most remarkable. The last time I saw him he was a mad philogerman, and now ! . . . ''

---

[1] Afterwards Lady Milner. She was a daughter of George Meredith's friend Admiral Maxse (the original of his Beauchamp) and sister of Leo Maxse, editor of the *National Review*, with whom Spring Rice corresponded much on the German menace.

Mr. Chamberlain, at the close of 1899, had been at all events philo-German to the point of being anti-French, and the Kaiser on a visit to Windsor exploited this propensity by suggesting to Mr. Chamberlain, who was also a guest there, that some steps to a *rapprochement* between England and Germany should be taken.   At a hurried interview with von Bülow, held by the Kaiser's wish, it was settled that Mr. Chamberlain should give a lead to which von Bülow would respond cordially in the Reichstag.   Lord Salisbury was consulted and consented to the experiment, but warned his colleague that he risked his personal reputation if Germany disappointed him—as Lord Salisbury thought would happen.   The outcome was Mr. Chamberlain's speech at Leicester, in which after a violent attack on France he went so far as to speak of " the natural alliance between ourselves and the great German Empire."   This utterance had a bad press in England and was fiercely denounced in Germany, and Count von Bülow in the Reichstag derided the overture.

In October 1901 Mr. Chamberlain, replying to attacks on British military measures in South Africa, used language which was regarded in Germany as an insult to the German army.

All this had produced the change of feeling described in the letter.

When Spring Rice returned from his visit to America, he had more about Germany to tell Miss Lascelles.   Prince Henry of Prussia had been in the United States, nominally to see the launching of the ' Meteor, the Kaiser's American-built yacht ; really, of course, on a general diplomatic errand.

OLD CHURCH, ULLSWATER,
June 2, 1902.

" It is extraordinary how our German friends are pursuing the customary game there.   Holleben[1] has a regular press bureau and distributes anti-English calumnies among his compatriots.   The Germans make representations to Congress on the subject of the purchases of mules[2] and say the administration will lose a million German votes if they don't do as they are told.   This is rather a serious threat but it probably defeats its own end by alarming those who are not Germans and don't want to have their policy dictated to them by foreigners. Prince Henry was very popular and did his business extremely well.   He was not abusive of us but only said that Germany wouldn't like to be second to England in the hearts of the American people.   The visit was made use of to organise still more the German vote, and the work is being continued by the Pan-Germans under the same influences as the work in Austria. Only, though they may possibly influence the administration to do unfriendly things to England (by which they won't profit in the least) they will never for one moment be able to induce the

[1] Ambassador at Washington.   [2] For the South African War.

American Government to be favourable to Germany at the expense of America. They may spite us but they won't help themselves. I wonder at the German Government which pretends friendliness to us allowing its representatives abroad like Holleben and Metternich, to take openly and visibly and audibly a line hostile to the last and bitterest degree to us. How can they think for a moment that we are deceived ? No one is, in America, and they are regarded there as the natural enemies of England. America won't take sides but will profit by the disunion of Europe and get what she can out of the scramble. It is absurd to suppose that princely visits and gifts of royal statues will alter the policy of the most practical people on earth. All these French and German flatteries have no other effect but simply just to amuse and then bore them. They know that if they had failed in the last war, all Europe would have been on the top of them, and if all Europe flatters them now they know it is only because they have won. America is not in the least like France, to be won over by social attentions."

Of his own experiences on the visit, he wrote :

" It was great fun there. I saw a good deal of a number of old friends."

Letters to Mrs. Lodge convey the extraordinary warmth of his feeling for these transatlantic people with whom he was so happily at home.—He puts it, as so often, in a whimsical inverted compliment.

" It was more pleasant than I can tell, being with you and Cabot—of course, in a way it is unwise to build up another home where I don't properly belong. If I could forget you both or find someone like you—I would drop you like a shot, but I can't and so—"

He wrote to Mrs. Lodge again on Aug. 5, 1902 :

" I have just been up the river. It was so hot that two of the employees at the dam-works died of heat : one had remarked a day or two before that he had been all over the world but had never found a nicer climate. Where had he been ! I slept in the open air under a mosquito net with nothing on whatever, and yet it was too hot to sleep ; I watched the buildings of Philae change in colour under moon, stars, and finally sunrise, and then got up for breakfast. It wasn't bad fun—only rather exhausting. Then I went to Assiut, further down the Nile, and saw a village where cholera was raging, under the care of an

English doctor (who had to build a hospital, dig wells, make a cemetery and form a sanitary staff in two days). The native doctors except one had bolted and all the local police. He was just married and his wife (an American) was coming out to see him ! If she could have seen him in the hospital tent struggling with a soldier just attacked with cramps, or driving the natives away from the infected wells ! I never saw anything like the rows of stolid faces against the walls of the streets waiting for death. It comes pretty quick—about one to four hours. The captain in charge had just come from S. Africa with fifteen bullet wounds in him. He said cheerfully it was the finest place to raise a thirst in he had ever known. It was 120° in the shade and a hot wind. This is the sort of thing your soldiers in the Philippines have to go through.

I am translating the story of the Persian Lover. It is no end of nonsense. Shall I describe it to you ? "

In the meantime there were changes in the British Government. Lord Salisbury retired, passing on the succession in the Premiership to his nephew, Mr. Balfour ; and Sir Michael Hicks Beach resigned the Chancellorship of the Exchequer. Spring Rice was no admirer of Lord Salisbury, and, though he liked and admired Mr. Chamberlain, he had been horrified by the overtures to Germany.

ALEXANDRIA,
July 17, 1902.

To JULIE.

" . . . What is the effect of Hicks Beach's resignation ? Does it make much difference ? I wonder why he resigned. I am very sorry, it seems the end of the old order. What will happen next ? Will Austen Chamberlain succeed and the Chamberlain dynasty confront the Cecils ? Cranbourne seems to have been putting his foot in it a good deal lately and to be a worthy son of his father. . . ."

Lord Cranbourne, then Under-Secretary for Foreign Affairs, replying to a complaint that the alliance with Japan, just concluded by Lord Lansdowne, might have been secured earlier, had said : " It is not for us to seek treaties, we grant them."

TURF CLUB, CAIRO,
July 28, 1902.

To LADY HELEN FERGUSON.

" I don't know why you shouldn't write to me—you or Ronald. I have just come back from Upper Egypt where it was 120° in the shade. There is now cholera here (infection is not carried by paper, so you needn't be afraid). The people

behave pretty well ; they are really afraid of cholera because
it is so sudden and don't mind a certain amount of police supervision.   But it is impossible to prevent all the female friends
and relations from coming into the room where the dead is
lying and accompanying the corpse to the grave.   So we allow
them to do this, but insist that according to Mahomedan custom
the body should *first* be washed and for this we use water and
corrosive sublimate which is colourless and scentless, and so they
are disinfected without knowing it.   My clerks are some of them
in a terrible state and say so, which is amusing ; one of them
came and said he was afraid, he couldn't be alone, would I
send someone to him ?

I want to quit Egypt which I dislike ; it is living on its
reputation of past years, and it is now nothing but an entirely
dull and ordinary place in which everyone is pretentious and
idle and inclined to be smart, except the workers, whose salaries
are low and who don't count.   Use your influence to get me
something less highly paid and more interesting.

I rather like it at this time of year, for all the bosses are away
and the little people are not so overshadowed ; besides there
are no ladies.   I don't like the Cairo lady much.   I wish I had
seen you after coming back from America.   I had a great time
there although I didn't see Mrs. Cameron—nor any lady under
50."

Cholera was a spreading menace, made worse by an exceptionally
low Nile ; but Stephen Spring Rice's health was a graver trouble to his
brother than the cholera.   Long and persistent overwork had produced a complete breakdown ; the first project was that he should
come to Egypt.

CAIRO,
Aug. 18, 1902.

" MY DEAR STEPHEN,

I was more delighted than words can say to get your
letter.   Keep up and rest and don't bother and you will have a
great time in Egypt—don't come before December.   The
cholera is most interesting but a great nuisance.   It is just like
a vegetable which uses up the soil it lives in.   It came weak and
feeble from Mecca, where it had been raging and had reached
the end of its tether.   Then it was, so to speak, fostered and
cultivated in a noisome pool at a place called Moucha and by
degrees became virulent.   Its existence was concealed by the
Omdeh (chief of the village) because the sick people were at first
in his own family.   So it grew and prospered and then spread
over the whole of Egypt like wet mud over the ground.   The

carelessness of one quarantine doctor and one Omdeh has brought on the whole business. If we could prohibit the pilgrimage we could probably keep Egypt clear of the cholera. . . ."

For a fortnight after that Spring Rice sent off a succession of letters rejoicing in the prospect of a meeting, and filling them with the detail most likely to content a born statistician. He wrote in this vein even on September 6.

" MY DEAR STEPHEN,
    . . . In the irrigation department there is a great chart with the rise and fall of the Nile at Assouan, marked in curves of different colours representing the years since 1877. This year is far the worst we have ever had, and in Upper Egypt the water level hasn't reached the canals at all, so that a large district will be desert. Opposite the pyramids on the other side of the Nile where there used to be beautiful fields and gardens, all will be dry for miles and miles.
    Middle Egypt and the Fayoum have been saved by an extraordinary act of courage. The irrigation department built a great dam at Assioul, half-way between Cairo and Assouan, where the old canal into the Fayoum, mentioned by Herodotus, called the Bahr Yusef, or Joseph's Canal, takes its departure from the Nile. The dam is built on a great table, or platform of concrete, floated on the mud with steel apron at either end of it. The concrete takes some time to set and the dam was not supposed to be ready before next year. Also it was only intended to shut it after the flood was passed, so as to avoid the scour. However, it was shut while the tide was rising, with the result that the whole of the Nile rushes over the sluice gates and throws itself on the concrete platform below—a very dangerous experiment ; however, nothing has happened yet ; it stands without any appearance of weakness and by thus raising the level of the river, the requisite amount of water is thrown into the canal. The man who did all this is a quiet, undemonstrative Indian officer. I think the dam is the apple of his eye ; he showed me over it and I could see by the way he talked of it that it was his own beloved child. . . ."

But that same day he wrote to Miss Lascelles :

    " My elder brother (in the Treasury) has broken down in health, which is a dreadful thing, and is seriously ill. His little son had to have an operation for appendicitis. It is dreadfully sad. This state of perpetual exile is rather sickening."

Two days later, a telegram told him that his brother was dead.

CAIRO,
Sept. 8, 1902.

To MARGARET.

" This is the end of many things and I don't know what it all means, or what to think. I can't realise it at all.

Anyhow, a death like this, from refusal to abandon a post, and then from a blow to the tenderest affection, is a very noble death, and we should be thankful that, if it had to come, it came like this. May my last end be the same. Duty and affection, which were really Stephen's predominant feelings in life, have been the cause of his death.

I feel it bitterly that I couldn't have gone back, and can't go back yet, but I must stay on here.

Let me know how Dominick and Molly and Julie are."

The reason which kept him was that, by statute, two of the six Commissioners were bound to be in Egypt ; but five of his colleagues were away, and some were overdue for return—in this season of pestilence. He wrote on Sept. 12th to his sister-in-law : " I can't hurry them, as they would think I wanted to bolt."

He was still alone on September 27. " But the cholera has begun to go down now, so I hope to be free," he wrote to Ferguson.

Sept. 19, 1902.

To JULIE.

" I think I understand. It was a great and utterly devoted love—in the same way as it was a great sense of duty to the state—both natural and sincere and perfect, and now it is all gone. Bernard Holland wrote quoting the Psalm, ' the zeal of thy house hath even consumed me '; and it is true of his devotion to the state ; it was a noble death, like dying in the battlefield, and so single-hearted a love and sense of duty would be hard to find anywhere. I have never seen its like. However, we must let the dead bury their dead, we must live for the living, and therefore I say again, you must take care.

You will, of course, let me know about plans. In the meanwhile, dear Julie, *don't* worry, shut that door altogether and don't put your hand on the lock. Trust Dominick to the doctors and remember how absolutely necessary it is to him not only that you are alive but that you are well. Remember the time when he and Molly will be growing up and what a burden you will be on their lives if you aren't well and strong."

To FERGUSON.

" I am most grateful. As a matter of fact, my brother was automatically a servant of the state, and naturally gave the best he had to give, because he couldn't help it. That was practically what killed him. I hope the quality is not rare. At any rate it is most valuable to the nation.

Men like you appreciate it—partly because you knew Lord Dufferin so well and felt the influences which shape that sort of man. I suppose it is a sort of instinctive religion of a kind. It isn't till one is outside England, and in a place where such feelings don't exist, that one feels the want of it. I have observed in our own service certain characters which are very different; they soon get marked down by their fellows, though many of them perhaps succeed almost the better for it.

The loss to me is, of course, something which I can't realise yet—but will realise more as time goes on, but which I know to be frightful. He and I have been at school together, brought up together and in the same service. We differed in every single point but never vitally.

My dear Ronald, I am very deeply touched by your letter, more than I can say, or write. The worst of it is, as time goes on, one feels that while the worth of life so greatly depends on friendship, friends are not to be made after the bark has greatly thickened; and the friends one has made go off one by one. That is a reason for not letting go those that remain."

It is plain that this loss made him terribly lonely and therefore restless.

CAIRO, Dec. 1, 1902.

To MARGARET.

" I can't say I like this job. There is a feeling all the time of being out of it all because the real work is in the hands of a few, a very few persons, who naturally don't try and participate. However, the pay is good, the climate pleasant, there are some very nice people, and it won't last for ever. But as I have said, I have the Mopygrowls to some extent.

" How is Cassel ? Have you seen him ? Did he go to the Finance Ministry ? What did he say about the railways ? Isn't Maguire the man who was in the know with Rhodes and made such a fine pile ? What is he after ? Oh, possibly buying new Dairas. I am sure new Dairas is the thing—and how about the light railways ? Oh, I heard Cassel say," etc., etc.

This goes on all day, so that there is a pervading sense of the Hebraic which makes us all agog. I keep out of it, more from inability to get in than anything else, and order ham for lunch contentedly. I don't think one can praise the absolute purity and disinterestedness of the Egyptian official: as a matter of fact, most people here get orientalised. *Not* Lord Cromer, who is too hard a stone to take much moss on him; but he accepts the inevitable and makes the most out of it. . . ."

He wrote to Villiers about the opening of the Assouan dam.

Dec. 13, 1902.

" The Kaiser's sudden telegram was rather a disturbance, as his personal representative was a difficult person to manage. It was finally arranged that he should be given a chair, like the Imperial personages, but should, of his supreme courtesy, not sit down on it. Then the Italian came forward as another special ambassador. For a brief moment it was feared that a row of gold chairs would have to be provided, but fortunately the zeal of the sovereigns of Europe came to an end. Cassel is the real hero of the occasion and the whole place reeks with him."

It is not surprising to find that his mind was at search for a way out; and America attracted him the more because Herbert, the new Ambassador, was a close friend.

Dec. 16, 1902.

To MRS. LODGE.

" My brother's loss is really, as you say, the fall of a tower of strength. But as he had used up his power and could hardly hope to work any more, it was far better that he should go and rest. He had the most enviable capacity of loving. I never knew anyone who, when he loved, loved more deeply; and also he had the quality of unselfish and devoted work—as I could see in the numberless letters from the men whom he had helped. As it was, he broke down suddenly in the middle of his work and as soon as he could work no more, died, so that no death could be less regrettable, for himself. I have talked with some hospital nurses returned from South Africa and they all agreed that death itself is so natural and easy that anyone who has seen much of it (even in these awful and sudden forms) cannot regard it as a proper object of terror or pity. There is the question of the survivors and their great loss, and there is the great reluctance inbred by nature for her own obvious purposes. These are the facts around which we have built up these huge structures of mystery and terror. I expect the best and truest word is 'Nor love thy life nor hate, but what thou livest, live well.' I wonder if I shall see you soon—I am hoping (but don't repeat this) to get to Washington—as I am not keen on staying on here, where I have nothing to do but conciliate old women of both sexes and draw my salary. If Cabot will kindly use his influence in the British diplomatic service and appoint a secretary as he has appointed an ambassador, I shall be grateful, and promise to write a letter in favour of his appointment on the next occasion he wants political assistance."

Jan. 11, 1903.

" DEAR MRS. ROOSEVELT,

I see in the telegrams that you are going to have Specky [1] again. What fun. Especially a married Specky. I hear nothing of whether I go or not from here and where I go to. I should like, of course, to go to Washington, but as I should like to, I suppose I won't get there ; I think I shall try Japan and teach Ted junior Ju-jitsu. Will you send him ? I am delighted with the books : they are delightfully got up and what is perhaps more important (though I speak with diffidence) are worth reading. I like particularly *Corrymeela* and the *Hills of Ruel*.[2]

I am off to the Soudan to-day and shall be some weeks away. I heard a curious Soudan ghost story which might interest Ted junior. The 9th Soudanese, a black regiment, made a charge at Abu Hamed and lost two officers, Sydney and Fitz-Clarence. This to them was like losing a gun to a battery. Their women, when they came to camp, wouldn't speak to them ; the other black regiments jeered. One of the black sergeants, badly wounded, was dying in camp. The doctor was looking after him. He asked to see the senior sergeant in the regiment who came to see him. He told him to tell the women and the regiment that it was all right about the ' Beys,' because he would look after them. The next fight was at the Atbara river. The Ninth charged with Mason, their colonel, at their head. When you command a Soudanese regiment, you have to run very fast indeed to keep ahead of them and they don't obey you much unless you do. Mason, who was a very big man with long legs, rushed along with his men behind him. But they caught him up, took hold of him by the arms and legs, crowded round him, he shouting and cursing, and so carried him bodily into the lines. They lost 30 per cent. of their number but did most terrible execution. Mason, however, never saw a Dervish ;

[1] See above, p. 294, footnote.

[2] Evidently Mrs. Roosevelt had sent him Moira O'Neill's ' Songs of the Glens of Antrim.'

he was the centre of a thick mass of his own men who made a shield all round him. Some time afterwards an engineer officer called Metcalfe arrived at Abu Hamed to look after the stores. His Berberi servant (the Berberis are cowards) wouldn't stay with him, he said he was afraid of the ' Black soldiers.' One night Metcalfe was walking about near the station when he heard a challenge, ' Who are you ? ' He answered mechanically, ' Amin,' (Friend), and heard the clatter of arms at the salute and the guard called out, in the darkness. He went on home and then remembered that there were no troops there. The next morning he went to the same place and saw the two white crosses where Sydney and Fitzclarence were buried. The black sergeant and the blacks of the 9th who were killed at Abu Hamed had been on guard. This is universally believed."

Spring Rice had now definitely settled on giving up the Caisse. In August 1902 he had told Miss Lascelles that he was " still in a fatuous way balancing the advantages and disadvantages of staying on. It looks, however, as if something would be going on in the next year or two, but I am rather tempted to kick up my heels and go."

In December he was determined not to leave unless for a secretaryship of Embassy—and he had in mind the possibility that Sir Frank Lascelles might be transferred to Rome, where he would evidently have tried to be on the staff. For it was plain that his plans were shaping themselves with reference to Miss Lascelles. By February it was settled. The news of his appointment to be first secretary at St. Petersburg reached him at Khartoum, where, he writes:

" I slept on the roof of the house. Mason of the Egyptian Army, Hall, and a lioness shared my room. The lioness was very affectionate but deprived me of the power of riding by tearing my breeches to pieces."

Feb. 20, 1903.

To FERGUSON.

" I had to give up my job here—tho' it paid well—as there was nothing to do and no prospects. So I put a bold face on it and have now cut loose. It will be an interesting job to be in Russia and learn something about it. Herbert wanted me to go to the U.S. and I should have liked it better in many ways—but on the other hand there is the fact that I have never been in Russia, which is the missing link in my experience of the world. This is enough about myself. I have been to Khartoum and have been very much impressed by the keenness with which the Soudan is managed : the whole place reeks with work and enthusiasm, new buildings are springing up everywhere and some of them quite impressive, and the officials, mostly soldiers,

can do nothing and talk nothing but business. And most of
them have had, or have or will have fever, and the cruel summer
is growing nearer every day. One wonders if it is worth the
tremendous sacrifice of health and happiness. But one hears
nothing of that. They are all willing and anxious enough to
serve in any climate they may be sent to, live alone and forgotten, ruling districts as large as France, living in mud houses,
eaten by mosquitoes and racked by fever."

The last word is a letter to Miss Lascelles, who had invited him to
stay at the Embassy in Berlin on his way to Russia.

OLD CHURCH, ULLSWATER,
April 14, 1903.

" DEAR MISS LASCELLES,
    . . . I shall certainly come (if you don't think better of it)
and stay as long as you will have me. I came back here from
Cairo, lamenting greatly, as I liked it much more than I had at
first. All the same, I was, I am sure, right to go away, as there
was no prospect of having anything to do, and that ruins one,
and I can't afford to use up my capital, such as it is. Lord
Cromer is most kind, but naturally he doesn't particularly
relish people who busy themselves about other people's business,
and that was the only business I could do, if I wanted to do any.
And there was really no prospect of any other job in Egypt.
So you see there was nothing for it but to go. At the end,
however, I rather shuddered at the thought of the arctic
winters and the towny summers and the close rooms, after so
many years in the open air. However, there it is, and I am very
lucky in getting it. . . ."

CHAPTER XII

RUSSIA 1903

FROM February to the middle of June 1903 Spring Rice was in England, on leave but preparing for his new post at St. Petersburg. Of its importance there could be no question. The Ambassador was Sir Charles Scott ; but this veteran diplomatist had somewhat lost the confidence of his Government.

Russia at this moment appeared the power from which British interests had most to fear. In January 1902 Lord Lansdowne (Foreign Secretary since 1900) had concluded an alliance with Japan ; and apart from the menace to British trade (for Russia, where her sway extended, shut out all commerce but her own) it was plain that England's ally must be threatened by the rapid transformation of Manchuria into a Russian dependency. The Siberian railway now controlled this region throughout ; Japan had protested, but the promised withdrawal of troops had resolved itself into their concentration in a series of towns along the line which were simply military centres.

This was only one branch of Russia's forward movement in Asia. New roads to assist trade penetration, and if necessary, the passage of troops, were being actively constructed into Persia. The Ameer of Afghanistan was faced with a demand to admit Russian caravans on routes leading through Herat to Kabul. Germany's project for carrying the Bagdad railway through to the Persian Gulf, with the assistance of British and French capital, which in the spring of 1903 Mr. Balfour and Lord Lansdowne inclined to support, was resolutely opposed by the Czar's government, whose aims embraced all Asia : and the British Government withdrew from the project, feeling that their co-operation had been asked in order to screen German designs from the menace of Russian hostility. In Tibet, which was nominally under China's suzerainty, Dorjieff, a Siberian, Buddhist by religion, had been busy with the Dalai Lama ; and after his intervention the Indian Government could get no replies from Lhassa to its communications. Lord Curzon, a most enterprising Viceroy, was unwilling to submit to disrespect, and in the spring of 1903 Colonel Younghusband was despatched to meet representatives from China and from Tibet at Khamba Jong, within Tibetan territory. Younghusband's mission, having a military escort, threatened to cause friction.

Also on May 5, 1903, Lord Lansdowne made an emphatic declaration that Great Britain claimed prior rights over the region of the Persian Gulf, and would resist by all means any attempt of any other power to establish a naval base or fortified port there. Lord Curzon (after receiving the report of this utterance) wrote from Simla :

"I am glad that you have come back to the Foreign Office instead of counting shekels in Egypt. Do write to me sometimes from St. Petersburg and tell me what they are after. Lansdowne is at last reported to have spoken out valiantly about Persia. What a struggle it has been to get them to say anything. Best luck.

Yours ever, C."

A Viceroy of this temper was not likely to be placable when his messenger to Tibet was left waiting for an indefinite period at the trysting place, without even an apology. Thus at the time when Russia heard herself warned off the Persian Gulf, her nearest way to Southern waters, she was aware that the Dalai Lama, trusting in the Czar's friendship, was disregarding England's pretensions.

In short, there were many angry contacts between the two great powers whom a popular simile likened to the whale and the elephant.

Meanwhile internally Russia was full of revolutionary symptoms : strikes with rioting, mutiny among the army recruits, and assassinations of officials. In this movement Jews led ; and the answer was given by anti-Semitic outbreaks, of which the chief was at Kishineff. Spring Rice was going to a country in which no one knew what would come next, and where it was plain that anything might happen.

Also, in his own country, Government itself was singularly disorganised. Since the "Khaki" Election of 1900, Unionists had a huge majority in the Commons ; but Mr. Chamberlain's plunge into a Protectionist policy had split the Unionist party. Mr. Balfour's balancing attitude left it uncertain who was really in power ; but from this summer onward, Mr. Chamberlain was out of office, and preaching Tariff Reform.

On June 16 Spring Rice wrote a leave-taking letter to Ferguson, and it is full of his outcry against this new Protectionist campaign. He applauded the Duke of Devonshire's plea for setting off against the interest of the large and more articulate industries that mass of smaller industries which were not organised.

"What is everyone's business is nobody's business. If a company manufactures air and creates an air trust, it will have advocates enough ; the men who breathe will have no special representation. . . . What a blessing it is to have at last an issue. I only wish there was a certain leader. I am going to the most protectionist country in the world, which is also the country nearest to revolution. It will be interesting to see what happens there."—It was indeed.

In St. Petersburg he settled down at once to his work of noting and reporting, with his usual responsiveness to new contacts : and before long came a letter dated September 10, 1903, from Colonel Young-husband at his waiting-post on the Tibetan border. Spring Rice had written comments on the situation, as it affected India, to Lady Curzon, who had forwarded them to the head of the mission.

" There is no doubt the Russians have got a great hold in Tibet through their Buriat Lamas from Mongolia and Siberia," Younghusband wrote. " Darjieff certainly got hold of the Grand Lama."

But the real voice rested with the monks of the great monasteries at Lhassa in their Assembly. From them Younghusband looked for resistance to the advance of the mission.

" They think that with their magic power they are quite equal to us, but that if the worst comes to the worst they can always fall back upon the support of the Mongols and Russians. The Chinese they do not care twopence about."

He asked for any definite information about Russians in Tibet that might be gathered in St. Petersburg.

In short, there was a stirring all round the tentacles of the huge sprawling organism to which Spring Rice was accredited.—After Central Asia came the Near East. Macedonia was in revolt against Turkish rule, the Grand Vizier complained of bands despatched by revolutionary committees in Bulgaria, and desperate reprisals were inflicted by the Turkish troops (largely Albanian Bashi-Bazouks) on the Bulgarians in Macedonia. The Macedonian Revolutionary Committee appealed to the European powers for international inter-vention ; and in what concerned the Balkan States, Russia had a traditional leadership. But Russia now definitely demanded that the Bulgarian Government should arrest the leader of the revolutionary committees ; and although the Czar and the Emperor of Austria jointly forced the Sultan to accept a scheme of administrative reforms, no practical result followed ; whereas the Czar issued a general warning to the smaller Balkan States (" which," he reminded them, " had been called into existence by the sacrifices of Russia,") that no further sacrifice, however small, would be made for their sake if they resolved to use " revolutionary and violent methods."

Spring Rice's comment on this is found in a letter to Villiers :

ST. PETERSBURG, Sept. 17, 1903.

" What do you think of the events in S.E. Europe ? Here they do all they can to suppress news, but it filters through, not in telegrams, which are stopped, but in letters and the papers are getting rather excited. But considering what happened after the last war with Turkey, it isn't surprising that the Government moves rather warily. Are we going to lay our money on the wrong horse again ?[1] If not, Germany and Austria will have to face Russia alone, and Germany is not likely to act openly against Russia, while poor Austria isn't much of a factor in any case. So I suppose Russia has more to fear from Bulgaria than from Europe ; for if Bulgaria fights successfully, she will have the whole of the Balkans, and Russia is dished. Russia's best plan would be to let Turks and Bulgarians thoroughly weaken each other, and then to step in when the ground is thoroughly prepared, as heaven-sent liberator. Of course, the Government are convinced that the Macedonian bands are very dangerous to an absolute Czar. They may find imitators, and in any case it doesn't do for an Imperial Government to ally itself with frank revolutionaries.

At present Russia is only prepared to fight to prevent other people interfering ; certainly not to help Bulgaria to the position in the Balkans which Russia wants for herself. So the atrocities will continue for a time. What a curious thing diplomacy is ! I hope, however, we won't interfere, or say we will, and then not interfere. We can't do anything. Russia is the only power which can, and *she* won't."

In that same month Ferguson paid a flying visit to his friend, found him in unhealthy lodgings and suffering from chronic catarrh. Fierce mandates for reform were issued, to which Spring Rice submitted, as this letter shows ; as also that with characteristic untidiness he had bungled the arrangements for his friend's departure. The letter continues the conversations which the two had held on politics, national and international.

Oct. 1, 1903.

" MY DEAR RONALD,

It was awfully nice having you and I felt rather low in my mind when you left. But you must really come again. I am having the drains seen to and am irrigating my nose. I still can't smell. I feel more and more ashamed about the passport the more I think of it. That damned ass seems to have arranged with the porter who arranged with the police who arranged all wrong. Next time you will find it all right.

Your prophecy came true. What do you think will happen now ? It is rather new in politics that we should have a Prime Minister who openly says he has no convictions until he has found out whether it pays or not.[2] Of the two I prefer Chamber-

---

[1] An allusion to Lord Salisbury's *obiter dictum* that in Lord Beaconsfield's day, by supporting the Turkish interests, we had " put our money on the wrong horse."

[2] Mr. Balfour declined to commit himself for or against Tariff Reform.

lain. He seems to have some idea at any rate of fighting his battle. What chances are there of a change ? I suppose it is wrong for a civil servant to be such a partisan as I am growing, but I do so hate the present system. Do you notice that all the vulgar people have now left the Cabinet and that practically none are left except those who move in the best society ? How long will it last ? I fear the reaction, as Lord Rosebery long ago prophesied, will be a tremendous one, and that after ten years of silks and velvets we shall have twenty of fustian. So I daresay the Smarties are quite justified in making the most of the few sunny days left. But they are spoiling the time of the great middle class. I doubt whether the middle-class will have a look-in now. . . .

This government, the Russian, has rather cynically decided, as it can't afford to fight itself, to prevent anyone else fighting for the Christians. The only thing we can do is to appeal strongly to the powers interested and throw all the responsibility on them. We shouldn't mince matters. Without Russia's support the Sultan couldn't go on as he is going on now. Let Europe tell Austria and Russia : ' We gave you a free hand ; put a stop to this by the only possible means, that is, by coercing the Sultan.' Unfortunately Russia believes, naturally enough, that she is to be enticed into a war and then, when she has liberated the Christians, will have them turned like the Bulgarians into her deadly enemies. This was Lord Salisbury's policy and I fear Lord Rosebery's also. And we and the Christians are reaping the rewards of it. If we could make Russia and Austria believe that we didn't wish to get anything out of a turmoil, or to bring on a war, we might hope that our advice will be followed. . . . ''

One reason for British reluctance to press Russia hard was that at this time tentative negotiations were on foot between the Foreign Office and the Russian Government for an agreement to respect the general *status quo* in Asia. On October 26 Louis Mallet [1] wrote :

" Your telegram to-day (or yesterday) saying that Russia seems more anxious to treat is interesting. We certainly have shown compliance with their wishes in the Balkans—even to the extent of suggesting reforms which will give them a foot-hold in the Balkans. H.M.G. are therefore committed to a certain extent to a policy of not opposing Russia's advance to Constantinople. At least, I read it in that light, though I dare-say they would scoff at the idea of a consistent policy in the Near

[1] Sir Louis Mallet, K.C.B. ; then précis writer to Lord Lansdowne.

East. That being so, however, does it not seem to you that we might get a *quid pro quo*. I suppose we should not get a withdrawal of the Russian claim to direct frontier dealings with the Ameer ? What should we be likely to get ?. . . . It's a chance Russia will never get again of buying off our opposition to their advance to Constantinople. If they meet us half-way now, it will be an immense encouragement and would certainly be taken up by a Liberal Government."

Sir Charles Hardinge[1] and Lord Lansdowne pushed the matter hard with the Russian Ambassador, but before any conclusion could be reached, the outbreak of war with Japan embittered Russian feeling hopelessly against Japan's ally.

At this time, things happened which made it seem for a moment as if Spring Rice would be at once whisked away to another destination. In September, 1903, Sir Michael Herbert, Ambassador to the United States, died at Davos, aged only forty-six ; his career in diplomacy had been extraordinarily successful. When Spring Rice was attaché at Washington, " Mungo " Herbert, as his friends called him, was Counsellor to the Embassy. Only a few weeks before the news of his death came, Lady Curzon wrote to Spring Rice from India recalling old memories of days when she was Mary Leiter.

" What fun it will be if we all meet again in Washington some day. Think of the President and John Hay and Henry Adams and Speck and Sir Mungo and Belle[2] and you and I, all gathered together again—at Mr. Adams' breakfast table. What varied courses our lives have run since '90 (when was it ?) when we were all there together ? "

Herbert's friends were Spring Rice's friends ; and even in the shock of that great loss it was natural that some of them should see an opening for Spring Rice. Those in America at once took advantage of an occasion which offered itself.

The boundary between Canada and the United States had long been left uncertain ; but the discovery of gold in the Klondyke gave the matter a very different importance, and a joint High Commission was appointed under M'Kinley to settle the contested claims between the neighbour countries. This body failed to reach agreement ; and Roosevelt, after succeeding to the Presidency, insisted that a new Commission should be appointed which would decide the issue ; and he named as Commissioners for America Senators Lodge, Root, and Turner.

The Commissioners left America at the end of October. It seems that Spring Rice applied to be secretary to the Commission, but was

[1] Lord Hardinge of Penshurst, G.C.B. ; then Assistant Under-Secretary for Foreign Affairs.

[2] Lady Herbert ; see above, p. 74.

forestalled ; yet his mind was turning to Washington, and an opening seemed to offer.

Sir Mortimer Durand, Spring Rice's chief in Persia, succeeded Herbert, and his total lack of acquaintance with America made it seem more desirable to have Spring Rice on his staff.   Mr. Gerald Balfour moved in the matter ; but the most energetic push came from Senator Lodge, backed on behalf of Roosevelt by Mr. White, then Counsellor at the American Embassy.   Allusions to this project run through the correspondence till the close of the year.

Nov. 25, 1903.

To MRS. ROOSEVELT.

" I wish I had a chance of seeing you soon, but I hear nothing at all from London and I can't say anything there, as for one or two good reasons, I am not much in favour.   Yesterday I woke up ; the guns from S.S. Peter and Paul (where they hang political prisoners and bury the Czars) were booming every few minutes.   The wind was howling.   I found when I got up that the Neva was over the parapet and that the streets were swimming.   A large part of the population lives underground and the guns are fired to warn them to get out.   Some of them don't and there are some destitutes the less.

The palace was on an island ; the river running high with great waves, and a terrific blizzard tearing at one as one walked. To-day it is beautiful—and the river is behaving like a good child.   I live in the Chancery and occasionally sally out for exercise or to see someone.   The Empress has a bad ear, the Emperor won't attend to business and no one can do anything at all.   What becomes of the U.S. when your ear aches ?   How I wish I could see you all.   Though, I do confess, I should much prefer you *not* to be Presidents.   Do you ever see Henry Adams ?   I have translated a Persian book which I will send you.[1]   It is very inefficient and rather irritating but quite unlike anything European and so perhaps worth reading as it only takes two hours.   It will make the President sick.

There is not the least reason to believe the statement in this letter that he was out of favour with his chiefs at home ; his habitual pessimism constantly led him to form such suspicions, which his friends constantly reproved.   A hint of the same obsession comes in a letter to his sister.

Nov. 24, 1903.

" MY DEAR MARGARET,

I have been going through a period of silence—finding it very unpleasant to use a pen except for official documents. You mustn't think I forget you for all that.

[1] *The Story of Valeh and Hadijeh*, of which more will be said later on.

What you say about affection makes me think a great deal. Stephen had the gift and so had Evelyn and so has Gerald. We don't seem to be so much gifted. I hope it is because we have other gifts instead—but what gift is worth as much? It is quite priceless. At any rate let us stick to one another as much as we can and *learn* how to love one another, if, even if nature hasn't taught us as much as other people. I should have thought, however, that *you* were not wanting. I know I am in some ways though not in other ways. I *do* get very fond of people but am hide-bound in restraint. I turn more and more to my own people, though I don't show it perhaps.

. . . I have been thinking a good deal since I came here— whether it is really worth while going on in this wandering and most un-loving and un-friendly life. It is, of course, very interesting—most absorbing and fascinating at times, with moments of intense disgust and annoyance. And now that politics are what they are at home I feel more and more disgusted. I can't help believing that our Government (with the consent of the people) is becoming more and more the Government of interested people, with the trail of finance over them all, bound together by the narrow feelings of a set, without much sense of honour or duty—and worst of all, without any qualms whatever as to their being the best people in the world. I think they are a ' set ' and not a good ' set,' and that their virtues are fidelity to each other and to the ideals of their class which I don't think are good ideals. And when people have the ' treasure of their hearts ' wrong, there is no doing anything with them. I don't think the opposition are any better; the most able, Asquith and Rosebery, are in fact exactly the same. I rather want to be ruled by a good man, who, ' knows what he fights for and loves what he knows,' like Cromwell's simple men in brown. I feel half inclined, if I had the courage, to cut and run. But don't be alarmed, I won't.

I don't know how you heard I wrote good despatches. As a matter of fact I don't think I do. Nor does the governing spirit in the F.O. think I do. Not that that matters materially.

How is Baby Evelyn? This is the country of toys and the Government helps the peasants to sell them, establishing a selling place in St. Petersburg at which one can get things. I send you a doll for Evelyn. Open it and you will find many little dolls inside—quite a family of them—made, I suppose, by some poor peasant in a perfectly horrible and inconceivable house. The people here are so accustomed to misery that what we should think abominable, they don't mind in the very least. I can understand the intense mournfulness of Russian literature.

Their history is so sombre, and their country is so ugly and their climate so intolerable, they must be marked out by nature to bear and inflict suffering. But they are undoubtedly liable to ideas, and the popular religion and patriotism and devotion to their Czar are wonderful. Only it is all instinctive; there is nothing reasoned about it, like some women's virtuousness; and therefore, as Tolstoi says, it is more admirable. . . . "

About the same date he wrote to Mrs. Lodge :

" Happy Xmas! I send you (if you look inside the Russian pamphlet) a photo of the famous missal of Mary Queen of Scots. You will see that she spent her time during church writing amatory verses in the margin. The missal is in St. Petersburg, where nobody looks at it; but an itinerant Scotchman, Ronald Ferguson, was beside himself for joy. I daresay it will bore you. So should I myself, although, as I adore you as you know, I wish I could have the opportunity. I haven't heard as to my being transported from this happy kingdom. . . .

I am going to Germany for a time to change the air. It is the nearest civilised country to this. That sounds severe. I like this on the whole very well. It isn't dull. You may always be blown up, or revoluted, or drowned and the people are really quite delightful—the best and most charming imaginable. The women are not pretty but they are very nice. At least two are : isn't that enough ?—I have got to love Frenchmen. . . . "

As to his " transportation," Roosevelt wrote on November 9 :

" Cabot has told me that he endeavoured by every means to get you sent over to this side, and Harry White writes that you may be sent. I don't know whether there is any chance of your coming, and still less whether you would be willing to come, but for selfish reasons I so eagerly hope that you may come that I must just send you a line to say so."

Definite information about this matter was conveyed by Villiers from the Foreign Office on December 2, in a letter which incidentally disposed of the view that he was " out of favour."

FOREIGN OFFICE, Dec. 2, 1903.

" MY DEAR SPRINGY,

. . . I want to let you know that when Mr. Senator Lodge was here for the Alaska Boundary business, he urged both with Lord Lansdowne and Mr. Balfour that you should be transferred to Washington as Secretary of Embassy. He has since written to Lord Lansdowne, saying that the President approved his recommendation and abounded in the same sense. Lord L., looking at the matter from a purely service point of view, was unable to entertain the idea because he could not spare you from St. Petersburg. So you have scored heavily all round, much to my satisfaction.

Mallet asked me whether from the private point of view, you would have liked the transfer. I said I thought not. I did not imagine you wanted to go back to Washington officially, and besides you were very greatly interested in your present work. Was I right ? Your despatches are very interesting and that is the general opinion."

Spring Rice answered on December 9 :

" . . . As a matter of fact I should be in a hole if I were moved out of this just now, as I have taken a house for a season and this is rather an expensive place. If I am wanted, of course, I go off at once. I daresay Roosevelt and Hay might want someone they knew well there, considering how complicated matters sometimes get and I should, of course, enjoy it.

How are you ? I hope you are all right and not overworked. One advantage of being abroad is that one doesn't sit in an office. I am moving about all day, collecting information from all sorts of persons, like a lobbyist in the House of Commons. But the appalling side of life here is the official dinner-going. It's awful—intolerable—and one hates it worse and worse. Here, there isn't a pretty woman in the whole place, except one, and she is a French lady kept by a Jew. You have no idea how one misses it. Sometimes I go and see people in the evening. Always the same story : frights 1 They are very nice however—as jolly and kind as possible. I wonder whether you will come to Finland ? I think it wouldn't be a bad place, a sea voyage via Sweden, plenty of rowing and fresh air—not so nice as Egypt, but then not so hot. I am rather sorry I left Egypt, but this is certainly a most interesting place. I don't think there will be a revolution because the people are too stupid and the army too faithful; but they will have to stop annexing the whole world, or they will find themselves pumped dry inside. There is fearful disorganisation in all the central provinces—no police and a great amount of misery. So that if a rising does come, it will be rather a serious thing. But it won't come while you're in Finland—unless there is a war— and then anything may happen. . . .

It's such an odd thing to talk about, but it seems to me that most Russians when they meet discuss how long it will be before the revolution comes. Just as in Japan we always talked earthquakes."

Another letter of the same date, however, makes it plain that the idea of returning to Washington was always present in his wishes. It is addressed to Mrs. Roosevelt, but manifestly was meant to inform the President. He probably felt some scruple about writing on politics to the head of a Government that was not his own.

ST. PETERSBURG, Dec. 9, 1903.

" DEAR MRS. ROOSEVELT,

I have just received a delightful letter from the President which is just like him. Of course, there is nothing I should like so much as to come over permanently. But if they won't do it for Cabot and White, they certainly won't do it for me. It is no good whatever my asking, I have simply said I would go as soon as I received orders, but I imagine there is some reason against it—I daresay a good one. . . .

Would you like a disquisition on politics here ? ?

Taxation seems to have reached its limit and the worst of it is that it is all *national* taxation, so to speak ; that is, it is not spent on the districts where it is raised but in Petersburg or on the frontier, so that the central regions are continually getting poorer, and the population really has not enough to eat. The Government will be obliged to spend money on the agricultural population, and they cannot go on as they are doing now without a series of loans, the interest on which will be too heavy for the country to bear. So I think either they will go in for an enterprise which will distract attention, and may end in a revolution, or they will try and pacify everyone all round, make separate arrangements with everyone and start reforming. But to do this a strong man is wanted. There is only one in the Government, that is Plehve, the Minister of the Interior, and he is an enemy of all reform. Witte is a strong man too and might be a reformer, but he is responsible for the excessive taxation and the misery of the country districts ; and besides, the Emperor has a very strong feeling of dislike towards him. So there seems no strong man at hand to inaugurate the required reform ; and meanwhile everyone agrees that the Emperor, while he is not getting stronger in will, is daily getting more autocratic in policy. So we have here a condition of things which necessitates reform, and an autocrat who has no power of decision. Perhaps it is fortunate. Louis XVI. was weak and half a sympathiser with the revolution ; Nicholas is weak but has no spark of sympathy with the Liberals. There appears to be no sign of revolution. The peasants are quiet enough ;

the workpeople not as discontented as they are in America or England; but the question is, how long can the present state of things go on without an economical crisis ? Russia's finances are all right; the danger lies in the money being in the State bank and not in the peasant's houses—so that our general view is not correct. It isn't State bankruptcy which is the main danger, but the inpoverishment of the people.

Where does this all lead ? It seems to me that Russia must keep the peace, and that if she doesn't there will be inevitably a crisis; perhaps a tremendous crisis.

If she does keep the peace (but the weakness of the Emperor is such that there is no security that she will) and if she turns her attention to reorganising her internal taxes and administration, she may be all right in ten years or so; and then she will be indeed formidable. I feel I understand Russia much better from having been in Asia. The whole view is Asiatic. For instance, Japan asks for an answer. She is told, the Emperor is taking a holiday. Then, that the Empress is ill; finally, that the Viceroy must be consulted. There is no sign that Russia imagines for a moment that Japan would be justified in pressing for an answer, even if the Empress were ill. Everything must wait for that. I could give you a hundred instances of slights to foreign nations, some intentional and some unintentional. At any rate it is clear that this court and Government regard with sovereign contempt all democratic nations; and that all the courts in the world look on this court as the ideal and the model of what a Government should be, if it were only possible.

One of their chief characteristics is that no Russian Government will make a treaty if it can possibly help it. They give *assurances*. How can an Emperor bind his successor ? and an assurance is good only so long as the Emperor is pleased to call it good. When in his supreme wisdom he sees that circumstances change, his assurance is also changed. If he was a vulgar person one would say, 'his word is not as good as his bond.' I am sure the feeling here is that no one but Russia has a right to be in Asia; it is the natural destiny of the Russian people to live supreme and solitary in Asia. It is the instinct of the mass of the people and of the most cultivated too. And ultimately they will obtain the control they desire—for really there is no possible obstacle; and when they do, the empire which will succeed to the empire of China will as usual be governed by Chinese ideas.

I must say I rather sympathise with them; there has been nothing like it for grandiosity since Tamurlane. The whole of Asia and half Europe! and all *Russian*; no divergent opinion allowed. All one language and religion. This is where the weak point is, because in their former history they were able to get over the language and religion question much more easily than they will be able to do in Asia; and the Mahomedans are rather hard to swallow. The Buddhists could perfectly well receive the Christian gods into their temples and there is a great deal of sympathy between them already. The Czar is thought to be a fourth incarnation.

All this is rather dull for you, but it is amusing to me, however dull it is to hear about. I am glad I belong to a free nation. The odd thing about the Russian is that he is glad he does *not* belong to a free nation; he rejoices in his Government though he pretends to grumble at part of it. He will never receive liberal institutions second hand. He will work out his own salvation in his own way and he will pay the smallest possible amount of attention to other people's feelings. In fact, Russia is a sort of huge beast and the national emblem ought to be the mammoth."

A further note as to the suggested transfer came from the Foreign Office on December 15. Mallet wrote:

" DEAR SPRINGY,[1]

There is a general consensus of opinion highly favourable to you, and Charles Hardinge was only saying yesterday how excellently well you were doing. Indeed that is the reason why Lord Lansdowne did not respond at once to the request of Lodge that you should go to Washington. That request was made and repeated before Durand's appointment when they were nervous about a new Ambassador and thought that your presence as Secretary of Embassy would help to smooth matters. It was most carefully considered and Lord Lansdowne eventually said that he would bear the suggestion in mind in case of being able to comply with it at a later date.

His ground was, as I have said, that you could ill be spared from Petersburg at this moment—when a change of Ambassadors is contemplated[2]; and that you were doing so well. You might give the former as the reason of noncompliance with the American request, if you answer Roosevelt's letter."

---

[1] He was " Springy " to all these people, though Villiers and Mallet were " Francis " and " Louis " to him.

[2] Sir Charles Scott was shortly after retired.

The discussion was wound up by a letter from Roosevelt on January 18, 1904 :

"Well, I am very, very sorry, as we all of us are, that you are not coming here.   All along I had a feeling that it was too good to be true.   I have a strong desire during the period when I was ' up ' to have the people I am fond of around me, just as there are quite a number of people I should like to have visit me here in the White House—Morley, Trevelyan, and Edward North Buxton, for instance."

A new change, however, had by this time put other matters in the shadow.   That Christmas was spent by Spring Rice with his former chief, Sir Frank Lascelles ; and it settled the future shape of his life, for he became engaged to Miss Lascelles.

His method of announcing the fact to Ronald Ferguson was entirely characteristic.   Nobody could be more tongue-tied than this most fluent talker and correspondent.   This letter is given textually.

ST. PETERSBURG, Jan. 15, 1904.

" MY DEAR RONALD,

Very many thanks for the paper with your speech which I thought admirable.   What a fearful business ' heckling ' must be !   It makes me tremble to think of it.

I see now that every time a business fails in England because it is badly conducted or carried on under unfavourable conditions, the owner will apply for protection instead of doing better or putting his capital elsewhere.   This is a nice prospect ! You don't make your army more effective by getting waggons for the dead-beats.

I have just been in Germany.   I heard from a man sent by the Government to report on our education that the well-educated Englishman was the most effective instrument in the world, but that the majority of the people were not educated at all, and also that in the technical schools we began to build the house from the top, which was a great fault.   We ought, he thought, to aim at *grounding* and not the showy part of it—the high-grade technicalities.   He said strongly that our great fault was want of education.   Now, if we tell people that they needn't educate and needn't take the trouble because J. Chamberlain will see to them, then we shall have no chance of curing our faults.   The cure for a first attack of gout is abstinence and exercise and not colchicum.   The other terrible objection to J. C. seems to me (after my experience of Germany and America) the *vile* results in politics.   The Chambers become mere lobbying halls for interested groups.   Protection has ruined German party life, and has made corruption a recognised part of American politics. This is, of course, stale but I have seen so much of it that I am really horrified at the thought of England too going that d—d way under the influence of this fatal pied piper.

Turning to personal matters, I am engaged to be married to Miss Florence Lascelles. I hope you are glad. I am tremendously.

Yours,

C. S. R."

To Mrs. Roosevelt he was a trifle less reticent; but he naturally went on to discuss the prospect of war, which looked daily nearer, for Japan had virtually sent an ultimatum.

Jan. 20, 1904.

" DEAR MRS. ROOSEVELT,

I am engaged to be married! Isn't it extraordinary! I hope you are glad. I am much surprised—and at my age it is rather absurd. The name of the brave young person is Florence Lascelles. As I have known her for eight years there is a certain amount of safeness about it—if one can say that about anything of the kind. I am rather accustomed mentally to ask about a contemplated action, ' What would T. R.[1] think of it ? ' and of a contemplated *person* ' What would E. R. think of it ? ' The answer in this case was satisfactory. I am quite sure you would like her if you knew her.

The papers are abusing America like anything. You will soon be hated here as much as the English—no, that is an exaggeration. But I never see the paper without seeing something against the President, who really seems to be feared here as much as Napoleon was. I expect to see him worshipped, like N., by the peasants.

Your Ambassador [2] here is a very nice man ; he is very fond of this country—which is a good thing for an Ambassador to be —and like most diplomats, the slave of the smile of royalty. I have never recovered my stay in America. For me the best monarch in the world is—never *you* mind who. Anyhow, I am rather amused to see the newspapers here saying that peace is certain because the Emperor says there must be peace. I remember a fat boy at school saying he didn't wish to hit anyone. A little boy observed, ' You needn't, if you give me that apple ? ' Little Ted, I understand, was brought up on a different principle.

The idea of war is immensely unpopular here because no one knows what is being fought about. But I have no doubt the

---

[1] ' R ' for Roosevelt, of course, in each case.   [2] Mr. M'Cormick.

Russians would go on fighting all the same, bearing with cheerful minds disaster after disaster like the stupid British, but without so much shouting and with fewer surrenders. They are nearer the ground. I do respect them and so would you. But their heads are too big for their hats and the *only* argument they understand is the fighting argument. After all that is the main thing. If you want to understand (which may not be the case) the difference between nations, look at the Canadian and Indian frontiers respectively, and at the history of the Clayton-Bulwer Convention[1] and the various agreements between Russia and England. When inconvenient to Russia she simply cancels them ; because, as she says, can you expect to bind the will of our great Emperor or to criticise his actions ? The Empire is above law as well as morality, and I am sure this most estimable Monarch here thinks so. The conclusion to my mind is—Make up your mind what you are going to fight for, and take for granted that you will get that much, but not a penny more, however much it may be promised. As a man here said, Russia is not a government, it is a growing organism (of rather a rudimentary kind), and you can't get an organism to promise not to grow, though you can, if you like, cut off its extremities.

Here is lots of politics for you. Don't forget I am going to be married. Isn't it most extraordinary ? "

When a popular bachelor who has reached the age of forty-five announces his engagement, there is a sensation; and cheers came from all parts of the globe. President Roosevelt's may stand for an example of the cordial affectionate greetings.

WHITE HOUSE, WASHINGTON, Feb. 2, 1904.
" DEAR CECIL,

No other two friends could be more pleased at the news, old fellow, than we are. Give my love to Miss Lascelles. Can't you both take in the White House on your bridal trip ? Come to America *some time* before March 5, 1905,[2] anyhow—you and your wife—and stay at the White House with us. You know I do not think that any man can ever be really happy unless he is married to a woman whom he loves.

I always agree with what you say of the Russians. I have a strong liking and respect for them ; but unless they change in some marked way they contain the chance of menace to the higher life of the world. I knew they now disliked the United

---

[1] About the Panama Canal, which the United States respected against strong temptation to override its terms.

[2] When his tenure of the Presidency would have expired.

States ; I did not know that they singled out me. In one way they are right. Our people have become suspicious of Russia and I personally share this view. Probably our interests are not at the moment so great as to make it possible for us to be drawn into war with them ; I shall certainly not fight unless we have ample reasons, and *unless I can show our people that we have such cause.* Remote though the chance is, it does exist, if the Russians push us improperly and too evidently. ' Peace, if possible ; but in any event, Justice ! '

Yours ever,
THEODORE ROOSEVELT."

In general, Spring Rice's friends were left to find out the news for themselves. Senator Lodge wrote :

March 13, 1904.

" DEAR SPRINGY,

. . . On the whole your letter of Feb. 19 was the most characteristic I ever received from you and for this reason. When I wrote, I did not know you were engaged. Soon after I had written, I heard the news, but not from you. Then comes your long letter, and although you undoubtedly know of your own engagement, you never mention it anywhere. Such oversight you may explain to Miss Lascelles as best you may. I forgive you, such is my softheartedness, for not telling me because I am so glad to know of aught that makes for your happiness, and if report speaks true, and for once I have every reason to believe in ' rumour painted full of tongues,' you have every reason for happiness and are greatly to be congratulated. Will you also congratulate Miss Lascelles for me ? Here I speak not from report but from a somewhat intimate knowledge, when I say that I am sure Miss Lascelles is to be congratulated and very sincerely too, for you are, my dear Springy, a man who I should be glad to know was about to marry any one whom I loved. This last sentence is I think a little mixed, but the sentiment is not and is as genuine as it is possible for it to be.

I wish you would marry and come here. We should rejoice to see you both and try to make you happy. . . . So why not come ? You have as many old and attached friends here as in England, I really believe, and you ought to be here while Theodore is in the White House. He is going to be re-nominated and I believe overwhelmingly re-elected. You would enjoy life here under his reign. We shall rejoice to have you and, alas, the years are ever going past and the night cometh and we ought not to make separations too long."

Even Mr. Luxmoore was left to hear of it by chance, but rejoiced none the less.

ETON COLLEGE.

" DEAR CECIL,

Seldom has a line of newspaper made me gladder than what Willy Leigh has just read out. *Hoc erat in votis* ; always have I been hoping of late years that you would complete your life and find that other half that somewhere must be. You of all people seemed to me to need it for full achievement and for comfort, hope, efficiency, happiness. You are one for whom it is good to be happy, and you will do much more so with your great powers and possible opportunities. But I think you a traitor to me for not having told me. No doubt this is why your letters have ceased since the Russian move. Never mind. I willingly stand back in such a cause. I was expecting to hear about the Russ country and the Russ cause, and then your book came out and it was only by a chance sight of an advertisement that I saw that.

Well, I absolutely and entirely forgive you all silence, past and future, in my happiness at the news. May God bless you and her."

But to this friend Cecil Spring Rice was not so entirely reticent. He said that the marriage seemed to him a rash venture, because of the seventeen years between—but, he said, breaking into complete surrender of his reserve, " I couldn't help it."

Mr. Luxmoore answered him gladly.

Jan. 25, 1904.

" DEAR CECIL,

. . . Your letter is quite right ; if you couldn't help it, it is perfect and I have heard good things from other quarters. No one cares much more for your happiness, and the completion of your activities and usefulness than your old tutor and friend, and it has long been a pain to me to see you lonely. The Persian is right and love is an education and a philosophy and a large part of Christian religion.

Always yours affectionately,

F. H. LUXMOORE."

" The Persian " is the author of the mystical love-story which Spring Rice had translated ; and in many of the letters which concern his engagement, the two themes are entangled ; for Duckworth had published the book in the last weeks of 1903. The work had been long meditated ; there is mention of it in a letter to Miss Lascelles, written from Egypt on September 19, 1902 :

" I have finished my Persian translation. It is a mystical love story with an allegorical philosophical under-meaning and will probably read very dull. It has greatly interested me and served to pass the time here. I will send you a copy if published; but I shan't use my own name as it is so ridiculous—I mean, the translation.''

What he does mean is that here, in prose (though in a prose that has the rhythm of poetry) he was the mouthpiece of lofty words concerning love and religion. On these two subjects there is scarcely to be found any utterance in all this mass of his correspondence. For his thought and emotion on this plane, one must turn to his Sonnets and his serious poetry. Beyond doubt also, the passionate mysticism that pervades the Persian tale expresses a side of his nature which he did not show to the world.

This shyness as to the signature, however, was got over and the book appeared as '' Translated from the Persian by Mirza Mahomed and C. Spring Rice.'' Yet few at first believed in the existence of this collaboration ; even Mr. Luxmoore with his fine instinct inclined to think that the whole was spun out of a Western brain, enamoured of the East. Only one real Orientalist instantly recognised the truth. Miss Gertrude Bell, writing that the happiness of her cousin Florence Lascelles '' lay very near her heart,'' and that she '' did not think it could be put into better hands,'' added this postscript :

'' I have just been reading your book which has given me a real breath of the East. You have given Persia from the inside—and filled me with a Sehnsucht for my Persian friends.''

And in a further letter :

'' I knew it was a real book. It seemed to me impossible that you should have invented what was so intimately Persian in every page. I will turn to my St. Bernard. You know, of course, the poems of St. Francis of Assisi which are almost literal translations of some of the Odes of Hafiz. I don't really understand any of these people, but the point is, as you say, that thesis is also a way of thinking, and it cannot be ruled out. You can think that way too, I believe, and that is what interested me in your book and in your letter.''

She was quite right ; in truth there was far more of the Eastern mysticism in his mind than in hers, though not a tithe of her Oriental learning. Spring Rice entered into the soul of the East through that familiarity with Christian mysticism which dated from his early schoolboy love and study of Thomas à Kempis.—In another letter, written a year later, to another real student, he had more common ground to go on ; for Henry Adams was a transcendentalist as well as a humorous philosopher. Spring Rice sent his Mirza in exchange for Adams' famous book on Mont St. Michel and Chartres, and this letter went with it :

R.M.S. " TEUTONIC,"
Feb. 17, 1905.

" DEAR UNCLE,

I wish I had acquired another sex, in which case I would
have been your niece and more worthy of your attention.

The book has been of the greatest comfort, and as I have read
most of it twice over since I saw you, I can speak with conviction.   Also I can hail you poet the next time I wish to irritate
you, and call Thibaut as witness.   Why do you omit Bernard ?
I wish you would explain.   You quote a terrible remark of
Peter's ' That he could do the difficult but not the easy duties
of religion—he couldn't love ' and a shorter and more decisive
remark of Eloise which squelches him wholly.   But I should
like to know why.   This, however, is a detail of curiosity.   The
book is wholly delightful and as my mind was quite uninter-
rupted I could understand parts of it.   Martha [1] told me you
printed nothing which you hadn't first ascertained she could
understand perfectly.   Was the Sermon on the Mount first read
aloud to the little ones—before the Pharisees failed to understand it ?   Nicolette is thoroughly Eastern.   If you read
Magnum and Leili and the hundred other love stories of the
sort you will see the counterpart.   As this is Arab, Nicolette
may well have come back with the crusades, especially if the
' Caitiff ' writer had learned Arabic.   ' This leads me ' to the
remark which you will have heard before, to wit, that Petrarch
and the sonneteers represent the direct succession of the Persian
poets and gazellists.   The Persian poet aims at representing
the infinite to the finite in a sensual form ; the simplest way to
do this is to represent the atom of dust, floating in space, called
man, in the ray of passion—the emanation of the immortal and
resplendent sun.   The mote of dust becomes, in the darkness of
our life, to those who can never see the sun, as the image and
similitude of the sun himself to those other motes on whom the
sun doesn't shine.   That is, the man who loves, or is angry, or is
drunk—especially the first—becomes luminant, and for those
to whom reality can never be revealed, is an image of reality—
but not for the mote's sake but for the sun's.

Love, however, being of earth, is selfish and asks a wage ; if
it were pure, the delight would be not in being loved but in
loving ; and so to be a true similitude, love must be represented
as quite unselfish (*vide* Thibaut *e.g.*).   Then the sonnet sequences
are usually (this was the convention) devoted to an unhappy or

---

[1] Mrs. Cameron's daughter, one of the young women who, as Henry
Adams said, flew in and out of his house in Washington like pigeons.

unselfish love, and Shakespeare's to the love of man for man—
the most unselfish of all. But the world seems to have felt for
some time that this passion, and woman as the representative of
it, was the window by which light entered our dormitory. Was
this Eastern, or was it concomitant in West and East? I shall
send you my translation (which is, however, of the eighteenth
century, though a rechauffé) and shall like to hear what you
think. I had a sharp attack of fever and was in bed for some
time. I also read the 'Antiquary' where there is indeed a
twelfth century death scene. Were you thinking of that one?
Altogether, between you and Scott I had a pleasant voyage.
I forgot to thank you for Washington! Although I should be
too old now to be ungrateful. When shall we meet again?

C. S. R."

That letter was written after a flying visit to Washington in
January 1905 where Spring Rice was the guest of Adams under circumstances about which much will have to be said in the next
chapter. But his first letters about the book were addressed to much
more normally typical Westerns, whose attitude was perhaps best
put by Theodore Roosevelt :

" Both Mrs. Roosevelt and I were delighted with your
Persian book: Mrs. Roosevelt more, perhaps, than I was, with
the actual Persian story itself, because I have what we will
euphemistically, and in a vein of strained compliment, call a
robustly Occidental type of mind. But I read what you yourself wrote for the the foreword and the epilogue again and again,
and I could see Persia before my eyes as I read, and the endless,
shadowy perspective of its strange and mighty past stretched
backward through the ages that have gone.

Their thoughts are not our thoughts! Nothing could be
truer ; but I am not sure of the reason. It is not merely that
they are an Oriental people, or a non-Aryan race. The Finns
and Hungarians, although, of course, much mixed with our own
blood, are perhaps less akin to us and certainly far less by
speech, than the Persians ; yet they do not differ from us a bit
more than the Slavonians and Croats do. There have been
moments during the past two years when I have felt that the
non-Christian and non-Aryan, Far-Eastern, Japanese were in
some essentials closer to us than their chief opponents ; and I
am certain that there is an immense amount we could learn
from the Japanese with extreme advantage to us as a nation.
Certainly they are less alien to us than, for instance, the Balkan
Slavs who have become Mohammedans. Their orientalism is
utterly different from that of the Persians. I never know

whether to be more astonished at the complete divergence between portions of the same race which have adopted antagonistic creeds and cults, or at the complete change which creed and cult suffer when adopted by a different race."

Spring Rice replied, to Mrs. Roosevelt :

" Thank you so much for what you say about the book which I sent you. It is quite incomprehensible to the Occidental mind and I wonder you got through it. But it has a curious parallel in St. Bernard—with the important difference that St. B. was one of the most practical men who ever lived."

A letter to Lodge explains a good deal more of the book's genesis.

Feb. 19, 1904.

" MY DEAR CABOT.

I fear you are much too kind but you are very encouraging. The Persian story made me sick for boredom while I was translating. Then I cut out three-quarters. Then I suddenly chanced on an American book about St. Bernard (do you know it?) and it struck me that *here* in the East was the same idea expressed in Bernard's sermons—which after all is a strong proof of the fact that such an idea has some importance. The notion is, of course, the *passionate* nature of true knowledge, and the denial of the possibility of real knowledge without fire as well as light. The classical and most ancient image is the moth and the candle, the knower becoming consumed by the object of knowledge and becoming unified with it by fire. It sounds nonsense written down, but I do believe that the idea existed to a great extent all over the world ; and I also suspect that it may have some truth and that we may have, as they say, to go, as a race, occasionally to the East to be vaccinated. It was rather a shock to find, as I began to examine the question, that a large number of people actually do and did hold a belief quite inconsistent with our manner of thought. To them the effort of knowledge (science, etc.) is really nothing, and the means of arriving at knowledge (observation, etc.) mere idolatry. The result is that we always drank dirty water at Teheran, because the servants didn't care for filters."

The framework of the book which was thus described consists of prologue and epilogue, between which are set passages of the direct translation. In the prologue, Spring Rice and the Mirza are sitting on one of the bare hills which look down on Teheran, contemplating the wide prospect so often described in his letters. They had been talking politics and the European pointed to the long line of iron telegraph poles, "Yes," said the Mirza. "Once in Persia the lightnings and the fire were our Gods. And you have made the lightnings your courier and the fire we worshipped at the hill of the winds above Baku is your baggage mule to carry your merchandise." Then he looked up at the far-off cone of Demavend and down upon the plain below, and began to review all the powers that had passed, and triumphed and passed away : down to the greatest of all, the Amir Timour. What enemy did Tamerlane not destroy ? and what remained now of his empire that stretched from China to the Grecian Sea ? "

And the Mirza repeated, half to himself, the Persian verses :

> " Hail to you who after me will come and will go :
> Sweet may your days be in this place of no abiding."

Then the two went down into the Legations garden, and still the Mirza discoursed of history ; how, less than two hundred years before, the native Persian rulers were driven out by an Afghan robber, with a few thousand ragged men, and the Turks on the West, and the Russians on the North, came in : and yet in less than twenty years, Nadir coming from the Mountains of the North had rebuilt the Empire of Persia, till it reached from the Caucasus to Delhi.

" He drew out a book from the bosom of his dress. The binding was lacquered, the lacquer covering rich flower-paintings, the colour dimly showing through the golden film. The leaves were of fine vellum ; each letter of the text was lovingly and carefully finished by a skilful penman ; and the margin was illuminated with delicate tracery-work in gold. But the peculiarity of it was that here and there verses were written in the margin in a careless hurried handwriting, and that round these verses the delicate gold tracery was lovingly drawn so as to make a rich framework for them.

The title-page was covered with writing in red and black, written in every direction ; also there were the impressions of seals large and small, and when I looked closely I saw that thin pieces of paper with writing on them had been pasted into the page. Only one of these remained ; there had been two others, which had vanished. And all round the seals and the writing, in every available place, the illuminator had drawn with minute and loving care his curves and flowers and branching lines, in gold, red, blue and yellow.

' What is the book ? ' I asked. ' Tell me its history.'

' It was written,' he said, ' by a poet called Fakrir, who lived in India two centuries ago. It is the history of the love of a friend of his, who called himself Valeh. And he wrote it to please his friend. His friend had been in Ispahan when the Afghans took it, and went to Delhi, where he lived when Delhi was taken and sacked by Nadir. The book was the history of Valeh's love—and he wrote verses of his own in it, and he fastened into it fragments from the letters of his beloved, who lived in Ispahan, and when he died it was sent to his beloved, and it remained in her family, till one of them sold it, and here it is.'

The Mirza opened the book at the first page and said, ' Here you see Valeh's writing, here he bids the reader listen to him.' And then he read from the manuscript the verses :

' We have all read the stories of hapless lovers, but no story tells of a sorrow greater than mine, the story of Majnun and his Leila is old and out-worn ; read the story of me ; waste not your days reading old stories, listen to mine.'

' You see,' said the Mirza, ' he wants an attentive listener. Now hear what comes next,' and he proceeded :

' In my heart may the sorrow of the world become the sorrow of my beloved, even as new wine ripens in the vat.'

' Do you understand,' said the Mirza.

I confessed that I did not.

' Perhaps you will understand before you have finished. But have you seen the vine-picking ? If the grapes are not picked, they fall to the ground and no one is the better. But the earth does not grow them to be picked. Yet you may pick them if you will. And then we put them together in the vat, and in a month we have wine, and in ten years good wine. And so is the sorrow and the joy of the world, even as the grapes of the earth. Make them your own, through love, and store them in your own soul, and you will have the excellent wine which we call by many names.'

The Mirza turned the page. The next page was elaborately illuminated. In the centre was a medallion. Written on it in white on gold was an Arab inscription. ' This,' said the Mirza, ' is the verse of the Koran with which the story of Joseph begins. Now I will tell a story better than all the stories of the world. And here is the title of the book, *The Tale of Valeh, King of Words, Lord of Knowledge, the Dervish of Delhi*. And above and below are the seals of Valeh and of his lady Hadijeh Sultan. And here along the sides are written verses in Valeh's handwriting.' And the Mirza read : ' Save my beloved, let me have no friend ; save her, let me know no refuge.'

' Here he has added in the Arabic language : " Oh, my friend, thou art my God, and, save thine, I know no worship." '

' And here, you see, down the side, he has written some more lines : " I am the wine in the cup of Hadijeh, the lips of Hadijeh are wet with me. Oh death, I fear thee! for Hadijeh would mourn for me, Hadijeh would weep. Alas for the nightingale who mourned outside the garden, so weep I, parted from Hadijeh." And then you see the impress of the seal he made for Hadijeh : "Hadijeh, daughter of Hassan, the glory of Daghestan, and by the Grace of God Queen of the Kingdom of Purity." And now look at these two blank spaces. Once there were fastened there fragments of Hadijeh's letters, as you see by what Valeh has written beside them. "These three fragments of her letters bear witness how my heart was broken in three pieces when I read her words, the preface of the book of my life. I was drunken with love. Lost to me, far from me, she wrote them, and I have fastened her written words to this page, that they may abide there as a blessing and good omen, living and present. I have lost her, but her words are there. Ali Ghuli Valeh, may Allah make great his love." '

'But as you see, the paper has dropped off, or been removed. Only one of the fragments remains. You see it there. That is the writing of Hadijeh. It is good writing for a woman. It is a quotation from Hafiz : "Oh friend, if one said to thee, ' Enquire not after her welfare,' let him be a stranger to thee, cursed be his name." And here you see Valeh has written beside it, "This also is from her letters." ' '

'We will read the book together,' I said.

'Yes,' he answered, ' but you must remember when we read that our language is not yours, and that your thoughts are not like our thoughts.'

.   .   .   .

The next day, an hour after sunrise, I found the Mirza pacing slowly along the garden. He had the book in his hand. We sat down and he read, and as he read he explained the meaning of the lines, and I wrote it down in English."

After this comes the translation of the story, in twenty-eight short chapters, making just over a hundred pages ; and then comes the Epilogue, which is here abridged.

" We had finished our work and went out into the garden, the Mirza and I. The long rainless summer was over. The last few days there had been clouds on the mountains ; this morning there had been a strange smell of freshness in the air—and now the first drops were falling. The whole garden seemed to wake up and to be busy drinking. We stood bare-headed in the rain for the pleasure of being wet.

'And so,' I said, ' the book was sent to Hadijeh as we see it now. Do you suppose she understood it ? '

As usual the answer was a parable.   ' You understand where
this rain comes from, and how the sun sucked up the water from
the sea and how the wind brought it.   That flower does not
understand, but the rain is its life.'

I asked him if he could explain the meaning of the book, for
I found it very difficult.

' I told you,' he said, ' that our thoughts were not your
thoughts.   But I will try and explain it as my master, who is
dead, would have explained it.'

' I have been a schoolmaster, and have taught boys to write
and count.   I have a big black board, and I wrote on it letters
and numbers.   And the boys learn them. . . .

Now the world is Allah's school, and Allah has many school-
masters ; and they have many names ; and the name of one
is Love.

And lovers are his scholars.   And he holds out to them his
rewards and punishments ;   the pleasure of meeting and the
pain of parting ; but the rewards and punishments are not the
learning.

And my master said that those whom the world calls lovers
are often but love's hirelings and not his scholars.   They have
received their wage, the joy of beauty, the delight of home and
riches and the blessing of children.   Yet they have not learnt
his lesson.   But if you can show me one that loves and continues to love without hope of reward or the joy of meeting ;
one, in fine, who does his work and asks no wages, and learns
his lessons and demands no reward, then, indeed, you have
found a true scholar of love who has truly learnt the lesson which
love was sent on earth to teach.' ''

An echo of these words will be found in the last and best poem
which Spring Rice wrote and which utters the praise of a love strange
perhaps to Orientals—his love of country.   In considering this man,
the mystic in him should never be forgotten ; and in all his ceaseless
political thought about his country, and its destiny, his hopes and
fears for it, and about the lessons to be gathered for it from the
facts of life in other countries, recorded in the past or noted in the
present, one idea always dominated—the necessity of self-sacrifice.
The only effectual fusion between the minds of East and West is
through the religion which, coming from the East, took its hold most
strongly on the West ; and when Eastern imagination touched the
spirit of this European islander, it wakened in him, not the luxuriant
delight of beauty, but an asceticism, which, transmitted through the
saints of the Middle Ages, had come down to his hardy race through
the Puritan strain.

CHAPTER XIII

THE RUSSO-JAPANESE WAR

On Jan. 13, 1904, the Japanese Government addressed to the Russian a series of demands concerning the position in Manchuria. The message by its form needed a prompt answer. None was given. On February 5 their Ambassador at St. Petersburg announced the severance of diplomatic relations. On the 6th the Japanese fleet put to sea, along with a number of transports.

The main Russian fleet was at Port Arthur but a squadron was at Vladivostok and a few vessels were at Chemulpo, the Corean port. The Japanese transports with a covering squadron were sent to Chemulpo where the Russian vessels put out to face them, were beaten back and sank themselves in shallow water—a British warship, the " Talbot," taking an active part in saving the crews. The transports then landed a military force which marched to Seoul and soon completed the occupation of Korea.

Meantime the Japanese fleet approached Port Arthur and in the night of February 8-9 attacked with torpedo boats the Russian fleet in harbour, crippled several battleships, then engaged the fleet and forts with gunfire, and endeavoured to block in the entire fleet by sinking vessels across the entrance.

On April 30 Admiral Makaroff made his way out of Port Arthur, but his flagship, the " Petropavlovski," struck a mine and was lost with all hands. The fleet put back. A month later, the Japanese, using Korea as a base, fought their way into Manchuria at the battle of the Yalu River, and drove back the Russian forces so far that they were able to cut the railway which ran along the Liaotong peninsula, and then invest Port Arthur at its terminus. This fortress, however, with its huge garrison had been made almost impregnable, and a great proportion of the Japanese forces was detained before it, thus weakening their army for its thrust through Manchuria along the Siberian railway. On the other hand Russia could only bring up such portion of her masses from the West as the long constricted line was able to carry. She had immensely more resources in armed men than could be brought to bear at that point of her huge circumference.

Russian feeling, galled by the reverses which a despised enemy inflicted, was furious against England. She, Japan's ally, was pledged

to intervene if a second power—China, for instance—should join on
the Russian side.   On the other hand, English anger was aroused
by Russia's declaration in regard to contraband.   An Imperial order
of February 29 classed as liable to seizure all articles adapted for
war on land or sea, and also provisions, beasts of burden and other
things capable of serving a warlike purpose, if consigned to the
enemy.   An extended list on March 18 added forage and parts of
machinery for the manufacture of guns.   To these were added on
May 9 naphtha, alcohol and coal.   Yet at the Berlin Conference on
West Africa in 1884 Russia had declared that coal must not be
treated as contraband of war.

On July 13 the " Malacca," a British vessel, was seized in the Red
Sea by two cruisers of the Russian Volunteer Fleet, which had passed
the Dardanelles as merchantmen but, once through the Suez Canal,
had hoisted naval colours.   In the Pacific on July 16 the Vladivostock
squadron, which had still freedom of movement, sank off Port Arthur
the British " Hopsang " and on July 24 the " Knight Commander,"
which was carrying railway material.   German vessels also were
sunk or captured and their cargo confiscated ; but that did not lessen
the tension in England.

Throughout the whole of this period there was grave apprehension
that war might break out between Russia and England.   English
relations with France were good ; the informal *entente* of 1903 had
been followed by formal negotiations for agreement on the main points
at issue between the countries.   This agreement was diplomatically
concluded in April 1904, and left—broadly speaking—a free hand to
England in Egypt, and to France in Morocco, while French claims were
satisfied in regard to the rights of French fishermen on the Newfoundland shore.   Ratification, however, was still to be obtained.   Moreover,
France was definitely Russia's ally ; and Germany, Russia's friend, was
no friend to England.   Serious peril might arise if the ill-will felt to
England in Russia should lead to embroilment somewhere in Central
Asia, and if England should be committed to another war overseas.

At this moment an expedition had been despatched against Tibet
from India, owing to the prolonged refusal of the Tibetans to admit a
British mission ; and it was known that formidable Russian forces
were being mustered in Turkestan.

The maximum of danger that war would spread from Asia into
Europe came in the autumn from an accident.   By October, Russia
had accumulated some 350,000 men in Manchuria, and Kuropatkin,
who had taken over the supreme command from Admiral Alexeieff,
" Viceroy of the Far East," declared that the time had come when
Russia would move forward to victory.   Port Arthur still held out,
and drained Japan of blood; and on October 13 the Baltic fleet
left Libau for the Pacific.   They entered the North Sea on the night
of October 20-21, and, having been nervous of attack by mines or
torpedoes in Danish waters, probably had further apprehensions of
a raid from the Dutch coast.   At all events, they were sixty miles off

their direct course for the Straits of Dover when they found themselves by night in the middle of many vessels. These were the Hull fishing fleet on the Dogger Bank; but the Russians opened fire at once, sinking one trawler, damaging others, and killing and wounding several fishermen. On October 24 a deputation of the fishermen came to London to make their complaint, and the Russian Ambassador Count Benckendorff was hooted in the streets. The British squadrons at Cromarty, at Gibraltar and at Pola received orders to be ready to put to sea and there was every appearance that a British naval force would pursue Admiral Rozhdestvensky. But on October 27 the Russian Admiral telegraphed from Vigo [1] his explanation of the Dogger Bank incident. He declared that his fleet had been approached by two torpedo boats with lights out, under cover of the trawlers, and that his fire had been directed on these. It also became known that before leaving the North Sea the Russian ships, in their apprehensiveness, had fired at Swedish, Norse and German vessels. On October 28 Mr. Balfour at Southampton explained that Russia had expressed regret, and that officers of the Russian fleet would be landed at Vigo to be brought before an International Tribunal of Enquiry at The Hague.

So war was averted; but the situation remained perilous, all the more because of the political conditions in both countries. In England the Unionists were in power by a huge majority since 1900; but Mr. Chamberlain's advocacy of protection had split the Unionist party; the Duke of Devonshire's resignation of office in October 1903, was only the chief of many defections. There was always the fear that war might be the less carefully avoided because it would probably consolidate what had been disrupted, and might lead to a new " Khaki " election.

In Russia, discontent bordered on revolution. Throughout 1903 there had been a widespread demand for some kind of representative institutions; this was reinforced not only by assassinations but by strikes, used as a political weapon. When war began, it was denounced by leaders of Liberal opinion; and the Minister of the Interior, Plehve, suppressed these manifestations of discontent by the usual method of banishment to Siberia. Agitation was fierce in Finland, which had recently been deprived of its limited autonomy; and on June 17, 1904, the Governor of Finland, Bobrikoff, was assassinated. On July 28, Plehve was blown to pieces by a bomb. In both cases the slayers were arrested, and both were educated young men of good position and family.

The long-hoped-for birth of a Tsarevitch on August 28 occasioned a return to clemency. Plehve's successor, Prince Sviatopolk Mirski, declared himself an advocate of the greatest possible liberty of conscience, and of decentralisation. The press was loud in approval; but nothing was done to make good the pledges. In November a conference of delegates of the Zemstvos protested against the delay,

---

[1] Wireless telegraphy was not then in general use.

and demanded a share in legislation for representatives of the people, and freedom for all from arbitrary punishment.   Meanwhile reservists for the army mutinied in many centres and there was outcry against the war.

No victory came to turn the tide.   On January 1, 1905, Port Arthur surrendered.   Next, in the battle of Mukden, lasting three weeks up to the middle of March, the Russians were driven back from Mukden after terrible slaughter on both sides.   On May 27 the Baltic fleet ended its long cruise in the action at Tsushima, when the Japanese all but annihilated it.

Meanwhile internal confusion spread.   In January a monster demonstration of strikers, led by Father Gapon to the Winter Palace, was deluged with rifle fire.   Trepow, formerly Minister of Police in Moscow, was appointed Governor of St. Petersburg, and reaction had full sway.   Yet manifestations continued ;   the Czar vacillated between promises and threats ;   anarchy broke loose everywhere, especially in the naval centres ;   there was much Jew-baiting, and though in July President Roosevelt's intervention brought Japan and Russia to negotiations which led to peace in August, the country was dreadfully torn and mangled ;   till, finally in sheer weariness, the Czar made firm his promises of a Duma.

The letters which follow give many details of this history from week to week ;   and they help us to reconstruct that amazing drama.   But they cannot fully reproduce the mood of the time.

It is difficult now to realise, or even for those who were then in middle life to recall, with what incredulity ordinary opinion received the suggestion that Japan, the dwarf, should attack the giant Russia. She had, it was true, recently overthrown another giant ; but China had persistently despised war.   This Colossus was armed to the teeth and had kept Europe in terror.

On November 4, 1903, the most official of his official superiors wrote to Spring Rice from the Foreign Office :

" Your letter is interesting, but strikes one, if you will pardon me for saying so, as somewhat imaginative.   The Japanese have not, as far as I can see, any intention of going to war in order to turn the Russians out of Manchuria."

On Dec. 29, 1903, another correspondent, this time Sir Charles Hardinge, " could hardly believe that Russia would risk a reverse in the East where time is all on their side " ;   but he agreed with the view which Spring Rice had expressed—that an arrangement enabling Russia to feel secure about the Baltic had been secretly reached with Germany, since the Russian Baltic fleet had gone almost *en masse* to Chinese waters.   But by Jan. 5, 1904, Hardinge was of opinion that the Japanese would force an issue within a week or two, and that if Russia refused to give any definite assurances respecting the integrity of China and Treaty rights in Manchuria, " it would be a wicked war without justification, whether the Japanese were or were not technically the first to begin it." If war came, he went on to say, all hope of agreement between Russia and England must be abandoned, and pinpricks and petty aggression on British interests must be expected.

Even Sir Ernest Satow, writing from Pekin on January 11, said he was " engaged in altering anticipations of the event from day to day." One thing, however, was clear to him " that war would be popular throughout Japan, but in Russia not so." " China," he wrote, " means to remain neutral, and this at the request of Japan." In his opinion the Russians had blundered badly in taking things out of the hands of their Minister in Pekin, " the wily and supple Lessar," to put them in those of the " bluff and hearty Admiral Alexeieff," to gratify whose ambition (" and that of a few more "), they had been spending a huge amount of money. He agreed with an opinion which Spring Rice had put to him—that Russia's action at Lhassa was aimed at securing influence in Mongolia through the religious authority of Tibet.

But meanwhile Spring Rice, gathering from all his far-flung correspondence what he could about the intentions of Russia, was even more concerned with Germany's part in the whole affair. The German aim everywhere, as he saw it, was to be the *tertius gaudens*, picking up cheaply the results of conflicts in which she took no active hand. He wrote on February 4, 1904, to Ferguson, who had congratulated him on his engagement :

" I do thank you most heartily and sincerely for your good wishes. I know how real they are. May we always remain such good friends—and I think that we shall now be even better.

I fear things look badly now. The Czar wishes peace, but he refused to realise how serious matters were until his constant delay had irritated the Japanese to exasperation, and now it is too late to retire. The view of Russians is that their Emperor is above all the world, as he is above Russia itself, and that the mission of Russia is to conquer Asia. So what can be done ? It is the sacred duty of all other powers to yield. This makes it rather difficult to argue. It is like trying to discuss theology with the Almighty on the judgment throne.

The result may very well be that we shall be dragged into some tremendous complication in the Far East and have to send a big fleet out, leaving our seas exposed to a flank attack— so that Germany may be in a position to get any terms out of us which she wishes. I fear she will have to be bought off. It isn't a pleasant look-out and I think that a new Government, if it comes in, will have very seriously to reconsider our position. We *must* play up to the alliance with Japan, or else we lose our position entirely ; but we can't afford to have rows with Russia and Germany at once, *unless* and only unless we are absolutely safe from invasion at home ; which a fleet cannot make us."

In the same way, his replies to congratulations from the Roosevelt household were only a preface to a picture of the huge drama which he now had to watch and study.

Feb. 11, 1904.

" MY DEAR MRS. ROOSEVELT.

I am so grateful for your kind letter which is just like you.
I am in doubt still as to my destination—but still hope, though complications here are serious.   What a dreadful business this is !   It is a real case of drifting into war, both ships gradually drawing together till the collision comes.   The people here are extraordinarily quiet and self-restrained.   The first day the streets were full of officers hurrying to the Palace where a religious service was held in all solemnity in the Emperor's presence.   Everyone volunteers, but the officers are not allowed to leave their regiments.   There was a general movement in the streets but no demonstration.   The National Anthem is called for wherever there is a band and listened to standing.   One's driver turns round on his seat and asks for news, and says he would like to go and fight ' the yellow men,' but would like to look them in the eyes and not fire guns at a distance.   I have known Kurino [1] for a long time—you remember him at Washington and the dinner in which he told the President all about the battle of the Yalu.   He has done all he could to bring about an understanding, as that was the policy of his master Ito.   It was a great blow to him.   I went yesterday to see him off.   It was a curious sight.   The station was full of people, most of them with the special edition of a newspaper in their hands, announcing a great naval victory of the Russians.   The crowd stared at the carriage containing the Japanese but made no sign of approval or disapproval.   The train moved off.   When it was well out of hearing a very slight sound of whistling was audible and a slight cheer.   Then the crowd went off quite quietly.   There weren't more then two or three hundred.   I thought their behaviour very creditable. There is not a word of news to-day and the town is quite quiet —apparently having forgotten about the whole matter.   When the news first came of the Japanese attack [2] there was a good deal of indignation expressed—but only one policeman at the Japanese Legation, and no crowd.   The next day the news of

[1] The Japanese Minister at St. Petersburg.   The battle referred to was in the Chino-Japanese war of 1894.
[2] On the fleet in Port Arthur.

the Russian victory set the girls shaking hands in the streets—
otherwise nothing noticeable. Extra editions of newspapers
with news from the seat of war are not allowed, so that we say
or believe what we choose. It is such a curious sensation."

A few details were added in a letter to Mrs. Lodge.

" On the arrival of the news of the outbreak of hostilities
(which reached the Emperor as he came back from the opera
where he had been cheered and cheered again) a religious
service was ordered, and all the officers in turn went to it and a
great silent concourse of people stood outside the palace to
watch. The Empress went to see the little cadets (on whose
grounds we played lawn tennis and who used to cheer the
Ambassador's pretty daughter) and they ran after her sleigh,
200 of them, all the way to the palace, yelling and shouting.
Then they had tea and promotion."

In writing to the President, he dealt rather with the large issues
which lay behind these happenings.

" DEAR THEODORE,
    I can't tell you how delightful it is to get such a letter
from you and how glad I am to have such a friend. The world
is not in a very satisfactory condition and it is one firm pleasure
at any rate to see a real man in the proper place for him, and to
know that I know him.
    I can't help thinking we are on the verge of great changes.
What has happened here seems to be that the Emperor believed
Japan was bluffing—was assured so by interested parties—was
encouraged by the war party and found it too late to retract.
He absolutely refused to listen to his official councillor Lamsdorff and very often did not even tell him what had occurred.
    Russia had been successful for many years in Asia in the
policy of peaceful penetration—especially with England, who
raised some ineffectual howls, and ran ; Japan had no question
but one, that is Asia—and did not run. We spoiled Russia and
she has to take the consequence. It is the firm conviction of
Russia that the ' Russian God ' (an official expression) wills that
Russia should occupy the whole of Asia ; other nations are
tresspassers from overseas and have no rights. Treaties and
engagements are temporary concessions to the weakness of the
flesh, and must be got rid of when convenient. The point of
view is that of a moral and religious right, supported by a feeling
of innate conviction, and it is difficult to change. Japan was a
mere trespasser in Corea, to be tolerated for a time and then
removed. Treaty rights of foreigners were a temporary phase

in the development of Asia which must disappear before the light of dawning Russia. This is no exaggeration, it is the general and universally received opinion. It is Russia's strength that this conviction exists and is acted on with all the force of the national conscience.

That Japan should have dared resist is inconceivable ; that she attacked when Russia was not ready, was monstrous. The explanation is—England and America. These friends of Japan incited here against holy and just Russia ; and they must be punished. America is far off and rather tough. England has the juicy and succulent morsel (India) within reach. So England can be made to pay and must pay. If this were all, it wouldn't be a very serious matter. I quite agree with what you always said : England is where Englishwomen can breed English children—not where millions of black men, sweltering in the sun, admire, prostrate, an Imperial Viceroy. I could support the loss of India with equanimity, if it did not mean the loss of a great free market, as well as the destruction, and hopeless destruction, of the work of two centuries. But what is that in the East ?

What is serious from a wider point of view is what one can't help seeing ; that is, the sure and steady movement towards common action of the two great military despotisms—Germany and Russia—on the common ground of spoliation. There are so many signs and tokens. The Emperor of the West turns his back on the Emperor of the East, and lays his hands on the little peoples of the West, while his brother is free to gobble the East. They have common enemies at home—the Liberals : and common enemies abroad—the free nations. And the temptation for France to play jackal is so great. There is so much to offer her. The dream here, clearly, is, common action against England (America being wicked and succulent, but unfortunately distant). Could England be engaged in a distant war in the East, a sudden attack on her flank, at home, against her vitals, might be successful ; and then comes the division of the carcass, which affords much rich eating.

I really don't think this is so very impossible. I must say I feel a sort of excitement, not quite disagreeable, at the thought of such a conspiracy. It would be so grand to face it—even without success, and it would do our fat millionaired and belorded land a lot of good. I should gaze with complacency at the ruined and smoking remnants of Hyde Park Corner. ' Here burning Nathan dined unhung.'

I hope that England will prepare herself and take care that the attack, if it does come, will be an unprovoked attack, and that it will not find her unready. There are many signs that an attack is being prepared, and would be immensely popular. Indeed, many people say it is the only thing which can save the autocracy. People say that never has the autocracy been in such a dangerous position. Discontent is universal and must lead to something. A popular war would divert attention but, of course, only for a time. The danger to us of such an attack is not very great, as it would take some time to work through Afghanistan, but it would probably dislocate the Indian Government for a time at any rate. There would certainly be many disorders. And then the work of sending reinforcements is immensely dangerous with a doubtful France, and Germany on the flank. Germany has for years been preparing popular opinion at home for a war with England. It is really her only true policy if she is to extend, and she must extend. I don't see how the war can be avoided. The two countries hate one another so much that an ' incident ' can lead to much. For the present Germany is not ready, and England will be flattered and courted, as France was in '68 and '69. The next move will very probably be Holland. The postal answer is expected shortly : [1] afterwards comes the customs union. By cutting a canal from the Rhine to the Ems Germany can divert all the Rhine traffic from Holland and this would be a fearful blow, as Holland largely lives on the entrepôt trade. This Holland knows, and the pocket is not a bad argument for daily use. Denmark is gradually falling into the orbit ; and this is natural, for Denmark's interest is the neutrality of the Baltic and a German army and fleet is the best guarantee that no ships shall pass through the Sound. So I think Germany has a good game to play in the immediate future, for Russia and England are now hopelessly hostile and this is Germany's chance either to take England's possessions by force, or by the threat of force and a peaceable arrangement. At any rate, it would be impossible for England to object successfully to the annexation of Holland. And this, of course, would be the price Germany would get for supporting Russia in the war.

This sounds all fancy ! but I really don't think it is. It is possible—perhaps almost probable. And the result is that Europe and Asia are likely to see the history of Napoleon and Alexander all over again, but on a much more formidable scale.

This is the time when an Englishman thinks with some satisfaction that whatever happens to the old establishment there is a new branch on a larger scale, which no Emperor,

[1] To proposals for a postal union between Germany and the Netherlands.

however splendid, can do any harm to, and which is now ruled as it ought to be.

I don't think there is the smallest good in taking action in China, except possibly to keep a port open if it is illegally closed. This is only a small part of a very great question and I think our part is to wait until the question developes, and then, if one must, to strike with the whole nation and its conscience at one's back. To take military action now, or under these circumstances, is wantonly to provoke the great question which must come soon unless the two great aggressive empires change their policy. And I hope, if it does come, it will not come at our seeking."

This is Roosevelt's reply :

March 19, 1904.

" Your letter about the Russian situation was most interesting. I have been rather surprised at the unexpectedly hysterical side of the Russian nature, which the Japanese success, and the supposed hostility of this country, seem to have brought in evidence. There is much about the Russians which I admire, and I believe in the future of the Slavs if they can only take the right turn. But I do not believe in the future of any race *while it is under a crushing despotism.* The Japanese are non-Aryan and non-Christian, but they are under the weight of no such despotism as the Russians ; and so, although the Russians are fundamentally nearer to us, or rather would be if a chance were given them, they are not in actual fact nearer to us at present. People who feel as we do would be happier to-day living in Japan than living in Russia.

I am entirely sincere in my purpose to keep this Government neutral in the war. And I am no less sincere in my hope that the area of the war will be as limited as possible, and that it will be brought to a close with as little loss to either combatant as is possible. But this country as a whole tends to sympathise with Russia ; while the Jews are as violent in their anti-Russian feeling as the Irish in their pro-Russian feeling. I do not think that the country looks forward to, or concerns itself about, the immense possibilities which the war holds for the future. I suppose democracies will always be short-sighted about anything that is not brought roughly home to them. Still, when I feel exasperated by the limitations upon preparedness and forethought which are imposed by democratic conditions, I can comfort myself by the extraordinary example of these very limitations which the autocratic government of Russia has itself furnished in this crisis.

From all I can gather, Russia is as angry with America as with England. The Slav is a great and growing race. But if the Japanese win out, not only the Slav, but all of us will have to reckon with a great new force in eastern Asia. The victory will make Japan by itself a formidable power in the Orient, because all the other powers having interests there will have divided interests, divided cares, double burdens, whereas Japan will have but one care, one interest, one burden. If, moreover, Japan seriously starts in to reorganise China and makes any headway, there will result a real shifting of the centre of equilibrium as far as the white races are concerned. Personally I believe that Japan will develop herself, and seek to develop China, along paths which will make the first, and possibly the second, great civilized powers ; but the civilisation must, of course, be of a different type from our civilisations. I do not mean that the mere race taken by itself would cause such a tremendous difference. I have met Japanese, and even Chinese, educated in our ways, who in all their emotions and ways of thought were well-nigh identical with us. But the weight of their own ancestral civilization will press upon them, and will prevent their ever coming into exactly our mould. However, all of this is mere speculation. It may be that the two powers will fight until both are fairly well exhausted, and that then peace will come on terms which will not mean the creation of either a yellow peril or a Slav peril. At any rate all that any of us can do is to try to make our several nations fit themselves by the handling of their own affairs, external and internal, so as to be ready for whatever the future may hold. If new nations come to power, if old nations grow to greater power, the attitude of us who speak English should be one of ready recognition of the rights of the newcomers, of desire to avoid giving them just offence, and at the same time of preparedness in body and in mind to hold our own if our interests are menaced.

I cannot believe that there will be such a continental coalition against England as that of which you speak. Undoubtedly England is in some immediate, and America in some remote danger, because each is unmilitary judged by the standard of continental Europe, and yet both rich and aggressive. Each tends to think itself secure by its own position from the danger of attack at home. We are not so spread out as you are. We are farther away from Europe ; therefore, our danger is for the time-being less. But we have to a greater degree than you have, although you have it too, the spirit of mere materialism and short-sighted vanity and folly at work for mischief among us. A society of which a bloated trust magnate is accepted quite simply as the ideal is in a rotten condition ; and yet this is exactly the condition of no inconsiderable portion of our society. Many people of property admire such a man ; many people of no property envy him ; and both the admiration and the envy are tributes to which he is not in the least entitled.

However, I cannot write all that I feel. You must come over. Can't you bring Mrs. Spring Rice here as soon as you are married? It will be such fun to have you at the White House."

Meantime the human side of what he was witnessing comes out in letters to the sister who was closest to him in age and comradeship.

ST. PETERSBURG, Feb. 16, 1904.
" DEAR MARGARET,

Oh, my goodness, what times we live in ! Oh for a little peace ! But after all, there was peace in Egypt and I thought it, dull. We had peace in England, and for very love of excitement started a tariff war-cry. We are overwrought and cannot possess our souls in silence. I wonder if anyone understands the point of view of the oriental as so eloquently described in my book ? I hear it is supposed to be an invention. It isn't, as a matter of fact, but no matter. I had such nice letters from unexpected sources—mostly alas—unanswered.

Now, do tell me how you are, dear Daisy, don't get ill. I feel horribly selfish in saying this for your being well makes a very personal difference to me—but I daresay I think of you and Aubrey too. We are selfish all of us and I am fearfully so by nature. Did you see the case of the Russian captain who blew himself up with his ship to prevent it getting into the hands of the Japs ! Isn't it splendid ? I wonder if one should have done this ? It seems a terribly fierce war and the indignation here is deep and bitter—mainly against us and the Americans. Life here will not be very pleasant for some time to come."

March 3, 1904.
To the Same.

" How are you ? You have now abandoned me. Have you seen Florence ? [1] I hope she has been giving satisfaction. She is quite delighted with all of you. That is a good beginning. Aubrey is, I hope, making my will and providing for her second marriage. She is 28 and I am 45. She seems to me very foolish to marry under such circumstances. However, it is her look-out.

I am to have a chief about my own age—a little older— Charles Hardinge who was with Stephen at Cambridge. He is

[1] Miss Lascelles was in England.

very keen, determined and successful. He has a charming and
fascinating wife who has the Queen in one pocket and the King
in another. Hardinge himself is no courtier but he is a good
business man and perfectly fearless and decided. I shall get
rather bullied—although he has always been very kind to me.
Florence will catch it, but she is accustomed to brilliant ladies
sitting on her and won't mind much.

I don't know when I am going to be married and should
rather like to know. Nor do I know where I am to go when I
am married. Nor how long I am to stay here. I suppose I
ought to take measures to find out—but don't see how I can.
In the meantime, life is fairly interesting and certainly nothing
could be more exciting than the present position. The autocracy here is on its last trial—so everyone says—and now they
are all pitching into the poor Emperor—who looks so mild and
harmless too all the time! Everyone expects a big row if the
Russians are beaten—or even if they are successful. The best
solution for them is a war with us, as this would be popular—
whereas the war with Japan is odious to them—for they don't
know where Japan is for the most part. They are as odd as
we were about our war. A month ago it was ' those absurd
little Japs; ' and now they talk of the capture of Port Arthur as
certain. I went to see Countess Benckendorff yesterday and her
son came in who is leaving for the front to-day—in a fine Cossack
uniform—as pleased as can be. All is charity and collections
now for the war—although very few have been killed as yet.

This won't be the end of wars for some time."

March 17, 1904.

To MARGARET.

" The ladies of the British Colony are all upstairs working for
the Russian sick and wounded. We have to give money too,
which the Russians take gladly, though they curse us as they
take it. Poor things—I suppose they are rather sore. What
a terrible history this last month has been for them! God
shall strike thee, thou proud mouth. It struck us that way too,
and we are catching it still. I wonder how long this imperialism
will go on, which exalts some splendid Milner or Curzon or
Alexeieff, makes the fortune of some hundreds of Jews—and
brings mourning to many poor families and poverty and ruin
to a nation! Here is a fine sermon and yet it *is* odd that two
nations, so different as we two, Russian and English, should
have a war so strikingly alike in its causes and its beginning—
perhaps also in its end. At any rate both countries are fighting
not for their own country but somebody else's, so perhaps they
don't deserve so much sympathy."

It had been settled that his married life should begin in a house in Finland.

To MARGARET. March 24, 1904.

" I wish I could come over and see Abinger and the spring and all delights. This is beautiful in its way too. I went to Finland—saw forests with deep untravelled snow—the lake a mass of white—a level plain with paths along it. The air very bright and clear—so still that I could sit in the sun and enjoy it. The house was all locked up and the windows had shutters drawn in front of them—in the form of boards nailed against them. The other day I went out a long walk on the sea. It is, of course, frozen and covered with snow—masses and masses of it—thawed at the top and really only passable where roads have been worn by the carts which pass from island to island. The sun was low and it was a curious sight to see the white plain—perfectly flat, with a vanishing sledge galloping off to the horizon and one or two barges frozen in—and the low banks with dwarf forests, two people in sight and the capital of Russia within three miles of us ! It must be a terrible thing to be lost, as must sometimes happen in a fog ; or to be caught by a storm which breaks up the ice and carries great pieces off into the Baltic. The ice is still on the Neva, but there are wide gaps with running water, black on the white, and we are expecting the break.

Yesterday I went to the gallery and found happy Mr. Menpes hard at work copying Rembrandts. He does about two pictures a day, and thinks of nothing else. He does them wonderfully well for his reproductions in colour which he organizes himself. I asked him about a picture of a child reading the Bible to its grandmother, the child thinking of the spelling of the words and the G.M. of the meaning : all so simply told and as clear as daylight. And a descent from the Cross, as it might be in Holland. Just as real as could be. He said, ' Oh, the literary picture ? ' and explained that he only cared for the surface of colour—that was all he thought of. I liked the confession. It was genuine and true. Anyhow he is quite happy. There is nothing ' going on ' now except charity concerts for the wounded Russians. They are quite hospitable in asking us to subscribe and to come."

To the Same. March 30, 1904.

" War, War, War ! I wonder when it will stop. I suppose when people cease to covet other people's goods. This is pure aggression on both sides, only Japan absolutely must have an outlet for her trade and Russia has about enough territory already. It looks better, so far as we are concerned, but who knows what may happen! Fancy our defence depending on Arnold Forster! Although he is about the best man—and fancy his being the best man! I should rather like to spend some time thinking of other things than politics and to do some other sort of work. I might have done this in Egypt, but I was strung up continually by the pretence of work and having none. Here I have little—but I observe and collect information and watch the great drama which is being played out. How curious it all is! Now the war has become popular. The *mujik* really believes that Holy Russia has been insulted and that the insult must be avenged. The Emperor really believes that he is the chosen of God to fulfil his great work in Asia, and to accomplish the historic mission of Russia. I wonder what God thinks of it all—and the curious mixture of prayers that come up, all together to the throne!"

High politics came back in his letters to friends who were politicians —both in England and in America.

To FERGUSON.

March 2, 1904.

"Pretty interesting times! What you say is quite right. We have to be very careful. From all I hear the general situation appears to be this:

The Emperor never believed in the possibility of war— mainly because he was told that the Japs were not in earnest but bluffing. On the other hand the military party wanted war in the spring. The two influences together led to the result that the negotiations were being prolonged and delayed with a view to a campaign, if necessary, in the spring; but it was believed that by that time Russia would be so strong that Japan would not be able to fight, and would not dare. Japan saw through the game, and as soon as she was ready, struck, having as she thought a clear case against Russia, who consented to negotiate about Corea, but not about Manchuria— the essence of the Japanese case being that Corea and China were to be treated on the same footing—which indeed was reasonable.

The outbreak of war found the military party which had brought it on unprepared, and the Emperor almost incredulous. The headmaster of ceremonies, when Japan broke off relations, asked the Empress if the court balls should go on or not. She consulted the Emperor, and said yes. The same night he was called up from bed and shown the telegram announcing the torpedo attack on Port Arthur and was told to countermand the balls. Everyone agrees that even after the breaking off of

relations there was no idea of the possibility of an open attack
in the Emperor's mind.

In order to justify the false information which had been
sedulously instilled into his mind, the advisers then set to work
to prove to him that the impudence of the yellow man could
only be explained by the promises of support made by England
and America. At the same time came from all parts of the
country news of the profound discontent of all classes of the
Russian people, who hated the war and regarded the monarchy
as responsible. It was plain that in order to justify the Government and to popularise the war, it was necessary to lay the
blame on the old and well-known enemy England. This was
done. Countless protestations of loyalty came in from all
quarters, assuring the Emperor of popular support against
'Japan and her secret instigators.'

Should a new disaster happen—as is not unlikely—this
movement must grow in strength. It is so evident a card to
play—if the dignity of Russia and the reputation of the monarchy is to be saved. A war against Japan has no glory in it.
It is very different with a war against England.

Of course, it would be difficult for the peace-loving Emperor
to declare an unprovoked war on England. But occasions can
be found and you see what a series of perfectly unfounded
accusations have been made. It is no good making contradictions. The speeches and answers in the House only arrive here
in the form of telegraphic abstracts, mangled in Berlin. The
text is never printed. The Government—that is Lamsdorff—
inserts formal official contradictions. The next day the newspapers return to the charge. The evidence as to the kind
treatment of Russian sailors at Vladivostock by the 'Talbot'
is suppressed. Admiral Avlen telegraphs his thanks to the
French and Italians but not to us. He justified this by saying
'there is no Admiral at the head of the English navy.' The
work of inciting public opinion against England goes gaily on.
It is, of course, immensely assisted by Germany, as all the
Russian news comes through Berlin, where it is edited in a
sense hostile to England.

The result of this campaign is evident here in a general and
systematic boycott of our Embassy by Russian society—although
many families have practically lived at the British Embassy
who now will not even speak to any member of it. The English
governesses are insulted and ill-treated in the houses of high
Court officials. Lamsdorff himself admits that if he were to
take open measures against this campaign of falsehood, his
position would suffer seriously and he would do no good.

Naturally one would ask : Why should Russia having a dangerous war on hand, wish to have another one ?

The answer seems to be : (1) that she doesn't believe the war will be localised—she has a strong hope of eventual German support. She believes that Germany, Denmark and Scandinavia will close the Baltic—and make her safe from that side, while the Dardanelles protect her in the South ; (2) and this is the most important point—she would be able to use her army. Along a single line of rail, it is doubtful if 100,000 men can be fed and supplied. She needs 400,000. She cannot move more than 1000 a day. She has still 200,000 to bring up and Kuropatkin does not intend to go to the front till the force is collected with which he will take the offensive. But this force has its limits. Therefore it is likely enough that Russia will be in the miserable position of possessing vast forces which she is not able to use—like a man paralysed by a magic charm and only able to use one arm or one finger. Then the obvious cry of all the military men will be—use the rest. By the autumn the Orenburg-Tashkend line will be finished, giving Russia a second line of attack on the Afghan frontier and 200,000 men can easily be massed and fed. This would make the capture of Herat a matter of no difficulty and even the successful invasion of Afghanistan highly probable. The expense will not be great. The men must be paid and fed, and why not in Central Asia as well as in the Caucasus ? The railways are State property and money payments on a large scale will not have to be made.

It is impossible not to admit that such an issue is possible, even probable, and we must provide against it partly by proving to the pacific Czar himself, his French ally and the whole world, that we are *not* the aggressors—and partly by a strong and sure arm. . . . But whatever policy is adopted, it must be by the consent and with the knowledge of the naval and military experts ; Parliament must have no right to dictate what policy is to be adopted unless a secret committee pledged to secrecy is informed of the reasons. The question is now what is England to do in the presence of one of the greatest dangers which has ever threatened her—that is, the possible combination of Spain, France, Germany and Russia—a combination which I hear on very good authority was actually being organised by Lobanoff at the time of his death. . . .

England stands for liberty of thought and government and for the free exercise of foreign enterprise throughout her empire. Russia is the personification of autocracy and the exclusion of foreign trade. Her refusal to negotiate with Japan

about China was due simply and solely to her intention ultimately to exclude foreign trade and suppress treaty rights.   On
the other hand, England in India and Egypt admits the right
of all foreigners to trade without restriction.   Would Europe
join in a crusade against England in favour of the power which,
if successful, will substitute Russian exclusion for English free
trade ?   What would French Egypt or Russian India mean
to the trading world ?   If such a coalition takes place, we at any
rate have at once the sympathies of all neutral powers, and
especially of America—indeed these sympathies will be so
strong, in view of the terrific dangers which would then menace
the world, that it is hard to believe that the rest of the world
will stand aloof.   But if the blow struck is a sudden one and our
resistance is paralysed at once, these sympathies will have no
opportunity to show themselves.   We must be prepared for a
long and desperate resistance which will no doubt result in our
ultimate success—for such a coalition would inevitably break up.
But we must be prepared for a possible struggle—the most
desperate one of our history—and not improbably for a descent
in England itself, for if our fleet is occupied elsewhere, or struck
a heavy blow, a landing force may attack Lancashire or London.
. . .   This is long and no doubt you will see it all in the
newspapers, but I hope you will listen to what I say, not as a
trustworthy prophecy of future events, but as the statement of a
possibility which must be provided against.   And after all, I
have seen this Government which had every reason to wish for
peace—which was warned by Witte and Plehve and Kuropatkin that war would be useless and dangerous—plunged
suddenly into a wholly preventible war, by the action of a few
interested and irresponsible people and the invincible ignorance
and conceit of the Directing power.   And what has happened
before may happen again.

And you must remember too that the advice of Germany here
is the advice which has most weight—not only in the Government but through the press on public opinion, and the first and
greatest interest of Germany is and must be a war between
Russia and England in which Germany is neutral—until the
end, when Germany, who has nothing to get from Russia and
everything from England—will receive her compensation.

But what I wish to insist on is this, that if war does come it
ought to come in the form of an entirely unjustifiable aggression
against us, and also should find us fully prepared in every
respect.   And if war comes in the form of an overwhelming
coalition, I hope we shall put up such a fight as will bring in all
the sympathies and resources of America on our side.   I'm not

sure that a pretty severe trial won't do us a good deal of good. I should look with equanimity on the smoking ruins of Hyde Park Corner ! "

Senator Lodge's letter of congratulations, which has been printed already, had ended with an interesting picture of American feeling— Swedes, Finns, Poles, Jews, all those whom Russia had wronged, now " finding their hour of revenge." Spring Rice shows always something of a proselytiser's tenderness for this friend who had originally been no way inclined to think that the interests of Britain and the United States ran in harmony ; and he is dexterous in stating the situation to Lodge, though there was never the least doubt of his own sincere belief that those who " speak God's language " ought to act together.

St. Petersburg,
March 25, 1904.

" My Dear Cabot,

. . . I know I was a pig not to write about my engagement, but I did write to Mrs. Lodge, and not having been engaged before I didn't know how to do justice to the subject. You write very kindly about it, but I have lived so long in such a very self-centred way that I own I feel terribly afraid. I fear I shall prove intolerable. But my lady is fortunately tolerant and so I hope for the best. But I told her I thought her a fool, in which opinion I still persist.

Things are interesting here. What you tell me about America is very interesting, though I see there is a change of opinion which is made a great deal of here. The *fact* is that both in Germany and here, in Government circles, the hatred of America is intense. You are a standing reproach to their systems of government. You deny their first principle—and you have the impudence to exist ! Even to prosper !

Judging by the talk in the town and the newspapers the Russian Government intends to irritate the Chinese into biting and then to take their territory—North China, with Manchuria, Pekin and Mongolia, and to occupy it and administer the revenues, either excluding foreign (maritime) trade, or raising heavy duties. As Russia has very strict laws for coasting trade, which gives immense facilities to Russian shipping, foreign ships would be at a disadvantage in Chinese ports, even if they were admitted. And the one object of Russia now (and this will be intensified with the expenses of occupation) is to gain revenue. So the question must arise in a violent form some time or other, for neither England nor America can afford to lose such an immense free market as that of China. I rather suspect Germany of being ready to exchange Shantung for a free hand in Europe as regards Holland and Austria, and that the two Emperors have the idea of one taking the Atlantic and the other the Pacific. There is no doubt about this Emperor's views as to war; for by an accident a telegram which he addressed to the Viceroy on Kuropatkin's appointment to command has just been published, and in this he says : That the war is for the command of the shores of the Pacific. If the Kaiser plays on this string, he will be successful. If Japan is wiped out, we, the trading nations, have no base to fight from to keep the ports open.

Of course, all this may blow over, and the war remain localized, and end in a compromise; but if it ends in a complete victory for Russia, as Russia believes, the results will be very serious, and if other powers are drawn in, the end may be to revolutionize the present balance of power. England is an artificial institution and the British Empire may perhaps be destroyed by a succession of well-directed blows. The Islands would remain, with a large population, but dependent altogether on foreign markets and supplies and not capable of taking independent action for fear of losing them. Perhaps that would be better for her and the world. But for an Englishman it is not a pleasant prospect. I believe the U.S. to be the real fortress of our race and it is an infinite satisfaction to see its prosperity and power. Also it is a satisfaction to think that the President is the President. May he remain ! "

Americans did not stint their praise for his labour in keeping them informed. Roosevelt wrote :

" I was speaking to John Hay about your letters the other day and he was so interested in them that I sent them to him. He returned them with the enclosed note, which I thought you might like to see."

DEPARTMENT OF STATE, WASHINGTON,
March 21, 1904.

" MY DEAR THEODORE,

I return Spring-Rice's letter, which I have read with great interest.

I know no one in any diplomatic service who could write anything so vivid and convincing. He knows his trade better than any of them. What a pity he will have to wait till he is an old man before he can be an Ambassador.

Yours faithfully,
JOHN HAY."

For the purposes of his work as observer, he moved a good deal through the country and a letter renders one salient impression.

To MARGARET.
April 15, 1904.

" I went to Moscow and accumulated all sorts of experiences. It is certainly a wonderful place. The view is quite what it is cracked up to be—a mass of golden and coloured roofs and fanciful walls with impossible fairy tale sort of towers. Not old—sixteenth century, and built by Italians and English, but to suit the Russian fancy. Nothing is quite like it that I have ever seen and there it is altogether—like the Acropolis. That is far the best thing. Every city ought to have its holy place where it does its very best, and then an *enceinte* and a hideous, commercial city outside if it is wanted. I wish we had an enclosure in London—Westminster, for instance—into which no one was allowed to intrude for commercial purposes.

The evening service is very fine. I chiefly remember the sombre singing and the sombre-gorgeous effect of the wax candles reflected on the gold of the walls and pillars—it is all gold.

It is the place of relics. Long processions of poor and rich form line and take their turn in kissing the faces and hands of the sacred images—with fervour and rapture. I saw the image and tomb of the little Prince Dmitri, son of Ivan the Terrible, the last of the line of Ruric. He was made a saint —I suppose because he was too young to have done any harm—and he is very much honoured by the people.

It seems to me that Ivan the Terrible is the hero of Moscow, as Pericles is of Athens. What one reads of him is too awful. It explains so much in the Russian character and literature. Unless they had a tyrant like Ivan they were sure to be ill-treated by the Tartars, or subject to fierce civil wars, and the domestic tyrant was far better. Tyranny made the Empire and maintains it, and its prestige is enormous. But the people are beginning to be rather inquisitive now and to want rather better administration. This last blow [1] is a terrible one and it came immediately after a great period of elation. Now they are down in the deep, poor things."

From April 26 to May 16, in the period between Sir Charles Scott's departure and Sir Charles Hardinge's arrival, Spring Rice was in charge of the Embassy ; and a draft among his papers shows that he had to report to Lord Lansdowne upon an interview with the French Ambassador, who had noted improvement in the feeling towards

[1] The Japanese attacks on the Russian fleet in Port Arthur.

England in Government circles. This he attributed to the influence of King Edward, " as to whose great services to the cause of peace the Ambassador spoke with enthusiasm." But there had been suggestion of arbitration. The Ambassador said :

" Russia would not hear of it. And the worst was that many people believed that England and France were plotting to force Russia to make peace, the one in order to save her ally, the other that she might save her pocket." [1]

Further, in regard to England's action, the Frenchman thought the Russians specially uneasy about the question of Tibet.

The mission from India had assumed the character of a military expedition. Since no representative came to meet Colonel Young-husband where he waited on the border, Lord Curzon's Government had decided that its representatives must go to Lhassa itself ; and on March 31, 1904, a column under General MacDonald escorting Colonel Younghusband advanced towards the border fort, and met with resistance which was easily overcome. Anxiety as to what this step might mean was heightened by a speech of Lord Curzon's, to the effect that the safety of India needed a " glacis " beyond its mountain barrier ; this, it seemed to the Russians, might justify a claim for control over all countries in the neighbourhood of India.

Spring Rice's view, written to Ferguson, was that England should have been content to exercise influence in Tibet through gifts and through native Lamas, there being a colony of some 3000 Cashmiris and Nepalis in the country. But Curzon had preferred a more resounding method. " To win now we have to use a great amount of force and make Russia the protector of Tibet against the foreign aggressor."

His uneasiness was gravely increased by letters from Lord Kitchener, whom he had come to know in Egypt, and who wrote to him with great frankness, about military as well as political affairs. The Russians, Kitchener said, had an army corps in Turkestan and were pushing on their railway communications to that region fast. He was anxious to have all information that could be procured about the abilities and dispositions of certain officers who were then in Turkestan.

Meanwhile society in Russia was showing its feelings plainly. On May 25, just before he left St. Petersburg for Berlin to get married, Spring Rice wrote to Mrs. Roosevelt :

" People here are rather depressed about the war and don't like seeing foreigners—especially English and Americans. Indeed they don't see us at all. Mrs. McCormick [2] had some ' evenings at home ' and asked the Russians whom she knew to come. Only two came. A lady and a man—of all her acquaint-

[1] France had provided a loan of 32 millions.
[2] Wife of the American Ambassador.

ances. The rest of the company were the foreign dips. The same thing happened to my Ambassadress ; she was boycotted with determination and success. This is a curious contrast to American manners. It seems to me a silly business to treat the McCormicks in this way because they have been particularly friendly to the Russians—indeed some of us thought, too friendly—and certainly McCormick sympathized more with the Russians than the Japanese, and did all he could to influence public feeling in America in favour of the Russians. I was talking the other day to a painted lady who owns the house now occupied by the McCormicks. She said she had written to him asking him to give up the house, as it seemed a disgrace to her family that it should be occupied by the representative of Japan for the time being. She was much hurt at McCormick's refusal. It appears also that McCormick once wrote a letter to ' My Dear Grand Duke ', which was thought an unheard of atrocity. Also that he pressed the Emperor's hand with too much effusion on one occasion. The fact is that the feeling against the English and Americans in court circles is about as bitter as can be and that any excuse is good enough. I wonder how the Cassinis [1] are treated at Washington ? The absurd thing is that a word from the Emperor could make the whole of society polite ; but this word is never spoken. Unfortunately a diplomat is rather prone to accept any snub from princes and emperors, and I think both the American and English embassies were somewhat undignified in making any attempt at all to be civil to people who certainly don't mean to be civil. But as we are democratic countries, society here (mainly descended from the lovers of former Empresses) thinks itself justified in snubbing us as much as it wishes ! This will interest you from the social point of view. It is rather odd.

I am going to be married in a week (if I can get a ticket to go to Berlin). Do you remember your wedding in St. George's ? Best wishes. Hurrah, for R. . . . ."

It will be remembered that Spring Rice had acted as best man when the Roosevelts were married. " R. . . . .," of course, means Roosevelt, whose candidature for a second term of the Presidency was now approaching. The suppression is to indicate some show of conformity to the rule forbidding representatives of a foreign power to express any desires concerning an election in the United States. The punishment meted out to Sackville West in 1888 was not forgotten.

Hardinge's arrival made the way clear for Spring Rice to be married ; but his mind was none the less full of anxious thought. He was having his first near view of war, and his nature recoiled sensi-

[1] Count Cassini was the Russian Ambassador.

tively from the suffering ; and his fears for his own country were redoubled—all the more because the governing class at that time seemed to lack force to lead. He wrote :

May 25, 1904.

To FERGUSON.

" I fear that as you say the opposition aren't able to find a man with a sufficiently strong following to take the place of the present Government and impose themselves on the country. I can't help thinking that the fault is that you are fighting like with like—that your Asquiths and so on are much like your Balfours and Chamberlains, only not quite so clever. You must fight with new weapons and new men, and till you get fire into you, as there was in Mr. G., you will never burn up this dry tinder. I wonder why he and his like have so thoroughly disappeared ? What a curious new age it is. I half believe that there will be a big movement from below which will turn you all out together, and roll you flat and plant you with potatoes.—I am not a revolutionary myself, as I get a fixed salary for obeying the powers that be, which I earn regularly ; besides, I am going to be a married man, which is a pledge of respectability.

When shall I see you ? Don't you think another voyage out here will do you good ? It would be worth while to see this country now as it is with revolution in the air and war on the frontier. This is the ideal of all the snobs, and all the Imperialists and all the protectionists of Europe. The Emperor, the idol of the snobs, is in daily terror of his life ; his policy is the laughing stock of his people ; he is surrounded by charlatans and incapables. The Imperialism of his policy means that, for a district in the Far East which can only be inhabited by Chinamen, he is sacrificing all the future of his race on the Bosphorus and the welfare of the native population of Russia. As for protection, it has resulted in a more widespread and complete ruin of industry than has ever been observed anywhere."

Cecil Spring Rice was married to Florence Lascelles on June 1 in Berlin—the Imperial Guard forming an escort. The duties of his post did not permit him to take a long holiday. A letter to his sister tells of the honeymoon—and of the strange world he came back to.

St. PETERSBURG,
June 22, 1904.

" DEAR DAISY,
It was so nice seeing you all in Berlin and it was angelic of you coming. I wish I could go over to England now, but

it is intensely interesting here and I feel rather attached—not perhaps to the country—but to the work—the spectacle.

We went to Stettin. Thence straight by sea to St. Petersburg. Florence was not much inclined to travel about Denmark and Sweden, and was bent on getting to Finland in order to have a real rest. It was very jolly arriving there. The house looked charming. It is in a wood by a lake and has lots of woods all round it and very few neighbours. We work and read all day—have a nice old lady to give us lessons in Russian ; she is very strict and has a marked predilection for Florence and thinks (with justice) that I am very stupid. I read the Russian papers which arrive in the afternoon. Always something exciting—too exciting. This week we had the battle north of Port Arthur—the sinking of the ships, and then of a sudden the murder of our Governor [1], quite close to where we are living. It was supposed that in a few weeks a new Chamber would have met under the Governor's supervision, and abolished all that remains of the Finnish constitution. The young man who committed the murder will be honoured as a martyr. It is a curious state of things. In the year that I have been here there has been a Governor killed in Finland, an attempt to murder the Governor of the Caucasus, and a man blown up, as it was thought, in bringing a bomb to blow up the Minister of the Interior.

Things seem quiet enough all the same. You wouldn't think by the look of the streets that anything peculiar was happening.

Life is very pleasant in Finland—quite delightful and there is lots to do. But we had to come up here to St. Petersburg in order to look after our house and also to do our duty by our chief. I like the new Ambassador and his wife. They are the picture of success. She is also pretty and charming. I hope and believe that Florence and she will get on well. Florence and I get on splendidly as we seem to like exactly the same things—and fortunately she is so terrifically capable that I hardly dare to make a suggestion of the practical sort. It spoils me too much I fear. She really enjoys being here—and doesn't in the least mind our savage and lonely life in Finland. Indeed, it seems to suit her thoroughly. It suits me down to the ground. I fear we are naturally all rather of a savage disposition. *You* are. Whom do you like seeing but your nearest relations ? Florence is a tremendous walker and we go out a tramp three hours every afternoon. The afternoons here end at 10.30 p.m.—one can still read. Then there is a long

[1] Bobrikoff, Governor of Finland, killed June 17, by the son of a Finnish Senator.

twilight night with a yellow glow on the lake. It is very fascinating and so pleasant that I feel quite ashamed of being so happy. . . . ''

ST. PETERSBURG, June 23, 1904.
'' MY DEAR TUTOR,

It was a dreadful shock to hear that you might have come. I didn't ask you because of the long journey and the useless waste of time. No one from England was asked but if I had thought you would have come, who else would have been asked if not you ? My wife is most deeply touched by your letter. You will see you have gained and not lost a friend.

At present I am rather crowded with event after event. It is all so bewildering. The Russians are calmly confident. They swear at the Government but say, of course, they are beaten at first because they wished peace and meant to have peace, and so were not prepared, but in the end, the Russian colossus is certain to crush the Japanese pigmy. Has the colossus a secret sickness that will sap its strength ? Nobody can tell. At any rate the mass of the people, ill treated, over-taxed, over-worked, have the enormous strength of patience and passive endurance, and perfect faith in the mission of their Empire and the authority of their Czar. They breed and eat and sleep, and pay taxes and fight when called upon, and don't think. It is the broad base on which the Empire is founded, and it seems a safe one. There is no sign of grave discontent in the army, though there is the usual difficulty about mobilisation, and the usual suffering and sacrifices called for by war. Poland and Finland and the Caucasus are discontented and impatient, and the working classes in the new factories talk socialism, but all this seems like the parasites which run about on the back of the Moujik, to which he is accustomed, which may wake him up occasionally, but which don't destroy his strength. Reading the history of former years here it is hard to believe that the present state of things is worse than has often existed before. But the bucket goes many times to the well.

Perhaps as I write a great calamity or a great triumph has happened. Who knows here ! There is an absolute absence of all news whatever. The papers are bare.

I am living in a small house in Finland on the side of a black lake with woods all round—crowded with mosses and very few flowers. Violets, anemones and a sort of everlasting which we don't seem to have in England. Shall I send you a specimen ? What fun it will be to take my wife to see you at Eton. By Jove, what fun ! ''

These were notes on the immediate situation. But Spring Rice's mind always ranged far, and his anxiety was so great that he even urged on the Foreign Office in these days to attempt some agreement with Germany. Louis Mallet chaffed him with turning Teutophil, and added that the Anglo-French agreement was still unsettled ; signed in April, it could not receive ratification till the autumn ; and to coquet with Germany would jeopardise this advance—which indeed had notably cleared the ground. It prevented disputes for the future between England and France about three regions, Egypt, Morocco and Siam, all of which had caused grave apprehensions ; and it disposed of an old question by defining French fishermen's rights on the Newfoundland shore. But there was still, in Spring Rice's view, imminent danger of a clash with Russia, which might have unforeseen consequences ; and Lord Kitchener continued to warn him that Central Asia was like a tinder box.

Also there was the menace arising from Russia's regulations as to contraband. These affected American interests as well as British ; and it was Spring Rice's desire to keep the two English-speaking governments as far as possible together in this matter, and his chiefs in Downing Street cordially endorsed the aim. Accordingly he sent information concerning the whole bearing of forces as he saw it, to John Hay, then Roosevelt's Secretary of State.

ST. PETERSBURG, June 1904.

" Germany is certainly making progress here. She has many advantages.

(1) The help of the German police is essential to the Russian Minister of the Interior. (2) Germany can keep the western frontier tranquil while Russia is engaged in the East. (3) Germany can make the Sultan keep the peace in the Balkans. (4) Germany is able and willing to sell ships.

Consequently Germany will certainly be able to draw closer to Russia in consequence of the war, and if Russia consents to turn and keep her attention to the Far East, Germany could perhaps let her have the use of Kiao-Chau which would be most important to her. But this, of course, would only be as the price of an alliance.

Neither Germany nor Russia is much inclined to an alliance. There is a strong suspicion here that Germany would thereby obtain complete control over the foreign and internal policy of Russia. In Germany on the other hand an alliance with Russia would mean a commitment of the Government to a reactionary policy. This would possibly bring about serious opposition in the Reichstag. But the German Government itself and the Conservatives would certainly welcome a return to the policy of the Holy Alliance.

France is undoubtedly losing ground here. She is irreligious
and the Czar is more and more under religious influences. But
as Russia wants to borrow and France to lend, or rather to
secure the payment of Russian interest—the two countries are
still bound together very closely.

Austria seems to be regarded as an unknown quantity
in the future. For the present it is believed that her policy
in the Balkans is loyal to Russia and the cause of peace.
But if a change happens in Austrian politics, anything may
happen. For this purpose it is almost indispensable that
Germany and Russia should agree beforehand as to what is
to be done if the Emperor [1] dies and a break up is threatened.
This great danger ahead makes it all the more desirable
for both Germany and Russia to come to a general
agreement.

England, as the corollary of the French agreement, wishes to
settle all outstanding difficulties with Russia. It is very unlikely that Russia will ever make a treaty about the most
important question—Persia and Afghanistan—for as long as
Russia is free to frighten England on the Indian frontier, she
has the power of making her do what she pleases in other parts
of the world. The wolf will consent to anything as long as the
sheep fold is left open. England however, hopes to modify the
bitter feeling which now exists between the two peoples.
Russia will not object to this as long as she retains her general
liberty of action. Both nations are profoundly convinced of
the innate faithlessness of the other.

The feelings of the Emperor (who must wish to finish the war
successfully) and the interests of Germany both point the same
way, *i.e.* that the whole energies of Russia should be turned
East. This may be one of the causes of the intense bitterness
felt against America as a trespasser in the Pacific and a possible
rival to Russian development. If the war is at all successful it
is very probable that some pretext will be found for occupying
Pekin, as this would be a morsel worth having. Corea is *not*
worth a great war. In that case the whole of North China
would come under Russian influence and Germany would be
geographically bound to act with her, as owning what would be
the best port in N. China. The explanation of the Russian
feeling about Thibet is that it is feared that the occupant of
Lhassa would be in a position to influence the Buddhists of
Mongolia and North China, as these Llamas come from
Lhassa. There can be no doubt of the desires of Russia
towards annexing North China or getting it under her

[1] The aged Francis Joseph of Austria.

influence. A combination with Germany would make these two powers practically supreme in politics and trade, as soon as Japan was eliminated.

Neither England nor America is in a position to fight for the maintenance of commercial rights, as the peoples would probably not think the enterprise worth the money.

It is quite impossible to get Germany to act with anyone against Russia. It has been tried several times without success. The danger on the Polish frontier is too great. The most that can be hoped is that Germany will not actually co-operate with Russia in closing the market of N. China against the rest of the world.

However that may be, the prevailing tendency of the present time is towards a close agreement between Germany and Russia on the ground of common action against socialism, in external affairs in the near and far East. As soon as the new treaty of commerce between the two countries is agreed on, it is very probable that further steps will be taken for a more general agreement. The nature of it will, of course, depend on the continued existence of Japan as a factor in the question, for if she refuses to come into the agreement and is still powerful, quite another line of policy would have to be followed. For then Japan becomes the natural ally of Germany, as France was the natural ally of Russia—because she can always threaten the other front of the enemy. Thus it is hardly to be expected that Germany will make up her mind till the war and its issue are clearer than at present."

Meantime Roosevelt himself wrote with extraordinary fullness and freedom, marking his letter " Personal.   Be very careful that no one gets a chance to see this."

> WHITE HOUSE, WASHINGTON,
> June 13, 1904.

" DEAR CECIL,

Like everyone else I, of course, continue to be immensely interested in the war in the East.   Do you recollect some of the letters I have written you in the past about Russia ?   I never anticipated in the least such a rise as this of Japan's, but I have never been able to make myself afraid of Russia in the present. I like the Russian people and believe in them.   I earnestly hope that after the fiery ordeal through which they are now passing they will come forth faced in the right way for doing well in the future.   But I see nothing of permanent good that can come to Russia, either for herself or for the rest of the world, until her people begin to tread the path of orderly freedom, of civil liberty, and of a measurement of self-government. . . .

The other day the Japanese Minister here and Baron Kaneko, a Harvard graduate, lunched with me and we had a most interesting talk. I told them that I thought their chief danger was lest Japan might get the ' big head ' and enter into a general career of insolence and aggression ; that such a career would undoubtedly be temporarily very unpleasant to the rest of the world, but that it would in the end be still more unpleasant for Japan. I added that though I felt there was a possibility of this happening, I did not think it probable, because I was a firm believer in the Japanese people, and that I most earnestly hoped as well as believed that Japan would simply take her place from now on among the great civilised nations—with, like each of these nations, something to teach others as well as something to learn from them ; with, of course, a paramount interest in what surrounds the Yellow Sea, just as the United States has a paramount interest in what surrounds the Caribbean ; but with, I hoped, no more desire for conquest of the weak than we had shown ourselves to have in the case of Cuba, and no more desire for a truculent attitude towards the strong than we had shown with reference to the English and French West Indies. Both of them, I found, took exactly my view, excepting that they did not believe there was any danger of Japan's becoming intoxicated with the victory, because they were convinced that the upper and influential class would not let them, and would show the same caution and decision which has made them so formidable in this war. They then both proceeded to inveigh, evidently with much feeling, against the talk about the Yellow Terror, explaining that in the thirteenth century they had had to dread the Yellow Terror of the Mongolians as much as Europe itself, and that as their aspirations were in every way to become part of the circle of civilised mankind, a place to which they were entitled by over two thousand years of civilisation of their own, they did not see why they should be classed as barbarians. I told them that I entirely agreed with them ; that without question some of my own ancestors in the tenth century had been part of the ' white terror ' of the Northmen, a terror to which we now look back with romantic satisfaction, but which represented everything hideous and abhorrent and unspeakably dreadful to the people of Ireland, England and France at that time . . . Of course, they earnestly assured me that all talk of Japan's even thinking of the Philippines was nonsense. I told them that I was quite sure this was true. . . . I then said that as far as I was concerned

I hoped to see China kept together and would gladly welcome any part played by Japan which would tend to bring China forward along the road which Japan trod, because I thought it for the interest of all the world that each part of the world should be prosperous and well policed ; I added that unless everybody was mistaken in the Chinese character I thought they would have their hands full mastering it—at which they grinned, and said that they were quite aware of the difficulty they were going to have even in Korea and were satisfied with that job.   They then began to discuss with me the outcome of the war, if they were successful in taking Port Arthur and definitely establishing the upper hand in Manchuria over the Russians.   They said that they were afraid the Russians would not keep any promises they made, in view of what I was obliged to admit, namely : the fact that the Russians have for the last three years been following out a consistent career of stupendous mendacity, not only with Japan but with ourselves, as regards Manchuria.   It was evident from what the Minister said that their hope is to get the Russians completely out of Manchuria and to turn it over to the Chinese, but that he was not sure whether the Chinese would be strong enough to support themselves.   I said that of course if we could get a Chinese Viceroy able to keep definite order under the guarantee of the Powers in Manchuria, that would be the best outcome ; but that I did not know whether this was possible, or whether the Powers would even consider such an idea.   The Minister was evidently very anxious that there should be a general international agreement to guarantee the autonomy of China in Manchuria. Some of the things he said I do not wish to put down on paper— which may astonish you in view of what I fear diplomats would regard as the frankness of this letter anyhow.

Well, my troubles will be domestic for the next few months. By the end of this month I shall probably be nominated for President by the Republican Convention. How the election will come out I do not know, but in any event I shall feel that I have had a most enjoyable three years and a half in the White House, and that I have accomplished a certain amount of permanent work for the nation.

P.S.—Don't understand from the above that I was laying the ground for any kind of interference by this Government in the Far East. The Japanese themselves spoke purely hypothetically as to whether circumstances would arise to warrant such interference, even to the extent of the offer of good services to both parties, and I explained that I could not say that so much as this offer could be made.   I was immensely interested to find out the way in which their minds were working. . . .

The Japs interest me and I like them. I am perfectly well aware that if they win out it may possibly mean a struggle between them and us in the future; but I hope and believe not. . . . I am not much affected by the statement that the Japanese are of an utterly different race from ourselves and that the Russians are of the same race. . . . The Turks are ethnically closer to us than the Japanese, but they are impossible members of our international society, while I think the Japs may be desirable additions. . . ."

To this letter, from which some passages of extended speculation have been omitted, Spring Rice replied :

" I have just received your most interesting letter.

I share your admiration for the Russians and I am at the same time absolutely convinced of the truth of what you say that as long as the present constitution exists the character of the Russian people, however worthy of praise in many respects, makes it almost impossible for a free people to have dealings with them on a footing of equality. England has a long experience. I give a few instances.

As part of a bargain at the time of the Berlin Treaty, Russia promised not to fortify Batoum and to keep it an open port. Twelve years later Russia closed the port, (instituted customs), fortified it, and prohibited transit trade to Persia and the East through the Caucasus. She justified the proceeding by saying that since the promise was made, ' circumstances had changed.'

She promised not to have relations of any sort with Afghanistan ; at the time of the Boer War, she repudiated this promise and said that she intended to open up the northern frontier of Afghanistan for the same reason—circumstances had changed. The Amir's opposition alone defeated this attempt.

She held out hopes to England of a general understanding, part of which should be the acquiescence of England in Russia's having a port on the China Sea. England agreed provisionally, on the understanding that the port in question should be a commercial port. England withdrew her fleet from Port Arthur as an earnest of her friendly intentions. Russia occupied the port, proceeded to fortify it and then said that she had no further desire to negotiate.

No doubt exists (I quote the best Russian authority) that Russia never intended to evacuate Manchuria ; but allowed her representatives in Europe to make declarations to that effect with a view to quieting, for a time, European opinion. Her experience with England (in the three instances above mentioned) made her sure that Europe would acquiesce. Europe would have acquiesced. Japan, however, having, unlike Europe, no other question except just the Corean and Manchurian question—determined to resist, and has resisted.

The reason she did resist was that from authentic sources Japan had learnt that it was the intention of Russia to strengthen her position in the Far East gradually, and when it was firmly established, to repudiate her engagements. This was openly professed by Russian officials, who also were convinced that Japan like England was only 'bluffing' in pretending to object and would, like England—accept the *fait accompli*.

The action of Russia, which seems to our ideas cynically immoral—when so openly professed—is no doubt due to the conviction that it is the right and duty of Russia to fulfil her destiny, and that it is also the duty of all Russians to obey the Emperor—who alone has the responsibility before God and man for the action of Russia ; and is the appointed instrument for carrying out the will of heaven—which has ordained the supremacy of Russia over the whole of Asia—the 'Russian God' as the people call Providence.

With such a point of view it is no good to struggle, using such weapons as treaties, professions, assurances, etc. Like the Templars with the Saracens, the pious Russian has the duty of breaking faith with the Infidel. And, it must be remembered—only the orthodox is regarded by the people as being really a Christian.

Therefore, unless the arrangement (if we desire an arrangement) is made direct with the Emperor—it is of no avail : one department (*e.g.* the Foreign Office) cannot bind another (*e.g.* the War Office) : the Emperor alone has the power to bind the country, and the Emperor's will and word is always subject (1) to his death and the succession of a new Emperor with new ideas ; (2) to the will of providence, as he conceives it.

Against such a government only one argument can prevail and that is *force* : the argument now being used by the Japanese.

With regard to the issue of the War. We have it from the highest authority here that if the war is quickly successful for Russia, the demands made by Russia will be excessive—and amount to the practical annexation of all N.E. China and Corea, and amount also to putting Pekin in tutelage—with the gradual absorption of the whole of the Chinese Government in Russian hands. By the extension of the railways in nominally Belgian hands, this power will be extended to the Yangtse and Tientsin.

Should the war, as is more probable, be long and difficult, but end in the practical victory of Russia, the demands of Russia will be : (1) Manchuria in Russian hands, with all the country except Newchang under Russian control ; all enterprises, trade, transport and local government in Russian hands ; (2) a fortified port on the Yalu ; (3) another in S.E. Corea ; (4) prohibition to Japan to have a fleet ; (5) her exclusion from the Corean and Manchurian markets.

There is no doubt that the plain between Kharbin and Moukden is very rich and that Manchuria can support a very large army. The Russians intend to station permanently in N.E. China a force of 200,000 men, which will be supported on the country.

Thus their military position will be so good that no power will be able to expel them. Their idea is that their naval position must be rendered unassailable by the maintenance of a fleet of overpowering strength and the prohibition to Japan of possessing one at all.

Using this unassailable military and naval predominance, they intend to acquire and maintain an exclusive commercial position at first in N. China, and subsequently in the whole of China.

They are sure of the support of Germany and France because Germany is unable to maintain a strong military force in the Far East, and intends to keep her fleet for use elsewhere, according to the plan proposed by the German Emperor, when he gave the signal, ' The Admiral of the Atlantic greets the Admiral of the Pacific.' France is, of course, obliged to do everything that Russia tells her.

To carry out this plan, of course, it is necessary to ' render Japan helpless.' That is the programme. Russia doesn't believe that England or America will have the power or the will to interfere. Once this is done, the published programme of the Emperor will be fulfilled ; that is, the supremacy over the Northern Pacific will be assured for Russia.

Two side observations. 1. England is as little likely as America to interfere, for the simple reason that we have not the military force. We can't do as the Russians do—take peasants from their farms and force them into trains, with the women and children clinging to the locomotive and policemen beating the weeping relations off—and send them to fight in distant countries which they have never heard of and in which they have no interest. The English people won't send an expedition of 200,000 men to the Far East to maintain the integrity of China. And as for the fleet. The action of Germany has the effect of paralysing our fleet for work in distant parts of the world. Germany has built up an enormous fleet which is kept for service in the North Sea and Atlantic, a permanent menace on our flank.

Another one. As to the ' yellow peril.' In Helsingfors you may see in the streets the Cossack garrison—Cossacks from the Ural, Asiatic savages in appearance and manner, who are quartered in every district which shows signs of disaffection. Ivan the Terrible destroyed Novgorod with Tartar troops, because it showed leanings to the Hansa league, and devastated, with horrible atrocities, the plains of Lithuania, again with Tartars brought up from the S.E. Poland is held by similar troops—to a good extent of Mongol blood. Why should not Russia use Mongolian or Chinese troops as she has used her Tartars—to coerce the Teutons, and Europeans ? Her history shows that she has done much the same in past years. To this day the larger part of the Imperial guard, who watch round the Palace, are not Christians but Tartars. They are less amenable to ' revolutionary ideas.'

We see the yellow danger which is at our doors more clearly than that 6000 miles away.

It is a commonplace among Russians that Russia is Asiatic—and that she is returning whence she came, to acquire new force and strength in order to turn the new force, when necessary, against the used-up continent of Europe. This, repeated again and again, cannot be ignored.

As the Russian people become permeated with liberal European ideas, they become less amenable to the despotic government established by God. Then, to whom to turn ? To the peoples which are not affected by such ideas—to the ignorant savages of the South and East who only know that they must obey orders. It is the inevitable fate of despotism that it must look for its defence to the worst and most ignorant elements among the governed. And these are the savages who have been last to accept the government of this central power.

We are trying our best to come to some sort of understanding with Russia (when the war is over)—so as to put an end to the continued régime of panic in India, Persia, etc. The reason we are doing so is that with the establishment of a strong German navy on our flanks we can't afford to have a life and death struggle in Asia and the Far East. Germany is rapidly acquiring a very strong position in Russia. The occupation of Kiao-Chao and the Polish frontier, make it essential for Germany to be on good terms with Russia, and Russia hopes to get money from Germany, to use her police to suppress Russian Liberals in Germany, and eventually to use her help in the Far East against the Chinese, English, etc. In any case, if we were at war with Russia, Germany would either take Russia's side, or exact very hard terms from us for her neutrality. The German fleet has really revolutionized politics. I hope to goodness we shan't be such fools as to be dragged into a war, our experience of war makes us extremely anxious to keep the peace with everyone, but we must be ready for all emergencies.

Anyhow I see no prospect of Germany joining Europe and America in guaranteeing the independence and integrity of China against Russia; and England can't take action on a large scale in Chinese waters unless she is assured of the friendly neutrality of Germany. This is a craven policy, isn't it? Unfortunately the crux of the situation is—neither America nor England will consent to compulsory military and naval service. That being so, we can't compete with ' million ' armies.

Good luck—the best of luck be with you."

Then follows a significant postscript—indicating the one chance which actually altered relations between England and Russia.

" In writing this, I have taken no account of the possibility of the country, exhausted by a long and profitless war, insisting on a change in the autocratic government and on the abandonment of the policy of aggression which is a necessity of the autocracy. But such a change (which is not immediately probable) would, of course, alter the whole situation."

On July 25, after the first exchanges had passed concerning the capture of the " Malacca " by vessels which had passed out from the Black Sea under a commercial flag, Spring Rice wrote to Ferguson:

" Things are humming just at present. I intended to write by last messenger but hadn't time. The situation has been very critical indeed, and though I hope the danger is over for the present the danger will certainly be increased if there is any doubt as to the unanimity of feeling in England. I suppose there is no doubt of that.

War would be a terrible calamity to both England and Russia and we should be incurring a great responsibility if we allowed misunderstandings to exist here as to the determination of England to take up a decided line. If on the other hand England does not intend to take up a decided line she should have said so before—which she has certainly not done. We hope for the best here and indeed matters at present have a more satisfactory look. C. Hardinge is profoundly anxious for peace, for every reason, and is doing his utmost to ensure it."

These letters make an introduction to a series of despatches to the American Secretary of State. Of course, we read after the event, in which Russia virtually lost; whereas Spring Rice was concerned with what would happen if Russia won—as even then seemed probable to most onlookers. For German opinion, nothing was decisive till after Russia was defeated decisively on land. Then, Germany saw that the whole balance of power was altered. Spring Rice's letters teach us indirectly the importance of Japan's achievement.

St. Petersburg,
August 31, 1904.

" My Dear Mr. Hay,

We heard that the ship ' Malacca ' was seized by a ship which had passed through the Dardanelles and the Suez Canal and which had evidently hoisted the war flag at sea after leaving the canal. As Russia is bound not to send warships through the Dardanelles, we protested. Lamsdorff at once said he knew nothing about it—the Minister of Marine knew nothing about it. It must be a mistake. In that case, we say, the ship must be given up. Of course it will, says Lamsdorff. The next day Lamsdorff says he spoke not as Foreign Minister but as friend— he hopes satisfactory orders will be given but he is not sure— the Grand Dukes and the Emperor are much opposed to any change in the status of their ships. The same day (by an accident) the British Mediterranean squadron arrives in Alexandria ; the British Ambassador hands in in writing a statement that H.M. Government to its great regret will be compelled to take the necessary measures to defend their interests; and the Grand Dukes at Council are compelled to yield. That night Lamsdorff arrives and says he speaks as Foreign Secretary and not only as friend.

However, we hear soon afterwards that one of the ships is still operating as a man-of-war. At the christening festivities [1] Hardinge calls Lamsdorff's attention to this fact. Lamsdorff is very sorry ; couldn't H.M. Government lend one of their ships to convey the order of the Russian Government to the Russian ships ? The Admiralty had no idea how to reach them. The next day a prince (Louis of Battenberg) had an interview with the Emperor, in which H.M. said he couldn't understand why the order hadn't been given ; the ships had a defined programme with fixed dates and rendezvous, etc., and it should be quite easy to give them orders. Hardinge writes to Lamsdorff to suggest that he should ask the Admiralty for the necessary information. Lamsdorff writes back that he doesn't consider

[1] Of the Czarevitch.

it necessary to communicate the programme of the ships, as the orders will be ' delivered immediately.'

In talking over the matter with his brother-in-law, Prince Louis, who is also an English sea captain, the Emperor said he wondered why the English papers made such a fuss. Did they think he had broken his word ? Prince Louis confessed that some papers did hint as much, which caused the Emperor painful surprise.

You will see that this country has no real Government ; each Minister acts on his own, doing as much damage as possible to the other Ministers. Alexander, son of Michael, the Emperor's brother-in-law, is the most able of the Ministers and has complete control of the Emperor's mind, so far as he has any mind at all. It is generally full of religious fancies of some kind or another ; lately, with the ardent hope of an heir through the help of St. Seraphim (whose chief title to sanctity appears to have been his great success in relieving cases of sterility). He thinks that God has appointed him to suppress radicalism in Europe and the heathen out of Europe and that anyone who opposes him, opposes Him that sent him. It is impossible to describe the contempt which he has for Liberals or Liberal nations. The Italians dared—some of them—to say that he would be treated with disrespect as a tyrant if he came to Italy : he refused to return the King's visit. He likes the English King but he has a hearty contempt for the English nation— although it has the privilege of being ruled by a Conservative Government. America hasn't even this qualifying virtue of a constitutional King. You are altogether damned.

It is a curious state of things. There is the Emperor, a religious madman almost—without a statesman, or even a council—surrounded by a legion of Grand Dukes—thirty-five of them and not one of them at the war at this moment, with a few priests and priestly women behind them. No middle class ; an aristocracy ruined and absolutely without influence, an underpaid bureaucracy living, of necessity, on corruption. Beneath this, about 100 million of people absolutely devoted to their Emperor, absolutely ignorant, kept ignorant for fear of the consequences of knowledge (by an elaborate conspiracy between Church and State), gradually becoming poorer and poorer as they bear all the burden of taxation ; drafted into the Army in thousands—which they enjoy, as they fare far better than they do at home. This army, devoted, brave, enduring, religious, will do everything which their Czar tells them. Poles keep Caucasians down, Caucasians garrison Poland ; both fight side by side for Russia in the Far East or Central Asia, for the glory of the Czar. What a magnificent instrument to wield! Here is all the fanaticism and endurance of the East with something of the organization of the West, just as these German sovereigns are putting Occidental uniforms on the despotism of the Tartars and the Byzantines. There never was, I am sure, since this world began, such a tremendous engine in one man's hand; not in Napoleon's—because his army depended on his success, but the Russian army is faithful to the Czar, successful or unsuccessful. And the Tsar's two objects are to suppress the heathen and to suppress the Liberal, and he is convinced that the Lord is with him. How long will it last? Of course, the system has the obvious objection that the peasants will ultimately find out how they are being treated—in one way, by actual starvation. But short of that it seems that nothing affects them very much.

It is certainly a wonderful country. It is the paradise of snobs and the Emperor is, I suppose, the snob's ideal. I don't think I should care to be his subject. But of one thing I am quite sure that he and his brother Emperors are going to have a good try at suppressing ' Liberal influences,' not only at home but also in Asia and America. If Japan is badly broken—as seems very possible now—autocracy will have taken a large step in advance. Manchuria, it appears, is about the richest place in the globe. Russia will support easily 200,000 men there. With them she will control China, which will give her the industrial qualities she has not yet. The Russian and the Chinaman together are the two most malleable instruments of despotism which it is possible to find on this degenerate earth. I think this is the real yellow peril. When I see a party of Cossacks from the Ural sent out to terrorize a Finn electoral district, I think too that the Asiatic peril has already reached Europe.

Well, here is a tirade against absolute monarchy. I used to laugh when I heard it talked of in America as a danger and a crime, and really I don't wonder now. I wish I were in a Republican country again with all my heart. But I can't run away from here because it is disagreeable."

The British Foreign Office at this time decided to act on the same lines as America in the matter of claiming rights for neutral trade. Their protests against blockade restrictions and seizures were modelled on those made by Roosevelt's Government—through John Hay's pen. The American Minister in St. Petersburg communicated these to his British colleagues.

Sept. 29, 1904.

" DEAR MR. HAY,

I can't say how I admire the despatches which I have seen lately about a certain interesting subject. I am proud to be the vehicle through which an imitation of them goes into the Russian Government. It is a delightful turn of fortune that after all you have turned out to be my chief.

As far as we can make out about the German agreement [1] the history seems to be as follows. Last year there was great bitterness here against the Germans in connection with the Macedonian troubles and the murder of the Russian Consul. Germany's support of the Turk was odious to the Russians. Then the Emperor went to Germany. There it was explained to him that the Balkanites were after all socialists rebelling against their lawful lord; that if they succeeded the contagion would spread to Russia; in fact, the Panslavists were painted *red*. At the same time the French began their quarrel with religion,[2] and the Italians couldn't promise that the Czar shouldn't be hissed in Rome. Also Plehve, who was all powerful, explained that without the support of the German police it would be impossible to suppress the revolutionary movement. At the same time the Japanese question became more and more urgent. Altogether it was easy to impress the Czar that he and the Kaiser had two enemies in common, internal and external— the perils yellow and red. Then came the meeting over the billiard table. Probably only a few words passed, but it appears that, since the meeting, the Germans were convinced that Russia would accept the German Treaty of commerce as drafted in Berlin, although Witte had always maintained that Russia would never accept.

It is a bitter pill for Russia to have to swallow, as wheat and rye are the chief exports and the German duty will hit them hard. On the other hand the whole structure of German commercial policy is built on the adherence of Russia—and with the commercial policy Bülow and his master are closely bound up.

(Did Germany promise to discriminate against U.S. wheat in favour of Russia ?)

When the war broke out, it was soon evident that Russia would have to rely on Germany for many warlike supplies— for possible assistance at Kiao-Chao and above all for a guarantee that neither in Poland nor Constantinople would Germany

[1] The commercial treaty which Germany and Russia signed July 28, 1905.
[2] The repressive policy of M. Combes against the religious orders.

take advantage of Russia being occupied in the East. There was also the question of escaped reservists and of a possible loan. Under the pressure of the war, the Emperor yielded and sent Witte to conclude a treaty with Germany on the German terms. It was understood at the same time that Russia could safely denude her Western provinces of troops and had nothing to fear at Constantinople. It doesn't necessarily follow that any express terms were drawn up and embodied in the ' Treaty.' This was never the case between the former sovereigns, who made the agreements under which Prussia was left free to annex Holstein, to conquer Austria and organize North Germany, to destroy France, and under which Russia was continually assisted in Poland, assisted to clear away the Black Sea Treaty, assisted, and indeed almost forced, to free Bulgaria. (For the Berlin Treaty exactly followed the terms of an agreement arrived at long before the war.) The policy of fifty years was broken by Alexander III., who hated Germany and the Germans—and it has been the main object of Germany to restore the old relations. A year ago it seemed as if this was hopeless—and as if Russia, England and France would act cordially together. Now it is doubtful how far, if at all, this French alliance is more binding than a formal alliance which only leads to a divorce.

But as I said, events have led to a renewal of the old understanding which is based on community of monarchical instincts —on aggression abroad and repression at home. And I do firmly believe that this agreement will not end in what the Germans are doing now. I hear from a quite certain source that it relates to common action after the war is over. My informant said (not to me) ' Unless England and America are prepared to fight a combination of European powers they will have to yield and accept our decisions.'

I think it quite likely that Germany will *not* seek compensations for herself at the peace negotiations. They will come afterwards in the West—in Holland and Austria. This is certainly the common impression here.

It seems to be also believed that England and America are getting sick of Japan—especially if the U.S. Government and the British Government are both changed at the next elections. In that case Japan will be induced (it is hoped) to submit to the inevitable, and come into the Russian system as a faithful ally of the great protector of Asiatics and as a faithful sharer of the spoil.

We live in interesting times. I don't think that I could ever have felt so strongly about a system of Government as I feel about this one. I can understand now the phrases that one was taught in the schools, and was taught afterwards to laugh at as outworn commonplaces. I mean the sort of commonplaces which lie at the foundation of the American constitution. Here at any rate the old commonplaces become a new fact. One can't laugh about the ' rights of man ' here."

It appears to have been decided that these unofficial despatches ought not to be addressed to a member of another Government, and a precedent was established which was followed later in regard to Roosevelt. The messages when addressed to Mrs. Hay became even less official in tone.

Sept. 13, 1904.

" MY DEAR MRS. HAY,

We are quite overcome with your kindness and can't thank you enough. The worst of it is you will receive a constant stream of letters from us which will make you sorry you ever gave me an inkpot.

I refrain from any observations on the subject [1] nearest my heart, remembering my former chief, Lord Sackville. I am not acquainted with Mr. Parker or I would write him an encouraging letter, poor man. We have such a nice ruler here who hasn't been chosen by vulgar caucuses but by the special nomination of Providence, on a plank of His own making. He (the ruler) has seen the plank and tells us what it is. And we all believe him.

Whatever it is, life in this country is particularly interesting. Since I have been here, two Governors and a Minister of State have been assassinated and an army of 200,000 men has been sent off to fight in a war of which every single one of them—and more so their families—cordially disapproved. Many of them have been killed—but this doesn't matter much as many of them were Jews and Poles, and were much better dead. The other day the Ruler went down to a review. He brought images with him with which he blessed the kneeling troops. The newspapers say many of the people had fasted all night in order to be worthy to look on the holy features of their God-anointed sovereign. I hear from someone who was there that the proceedings were marred by a stupid old woman who burst through the guard and fell before the feet of the ruler, praying him to stop the war ' before we are all widows.' I heard various odd things in Finland—at an out of the way place where I was staying. The Parliament is to be called in December, and as most of the leading men have been exiled and the Cossacks are to be quartered in any district electing unpleasant persons—it is

[1] The U.S. Presidential elections. Mr. Parker was Roosevelt's opponent.

probable that the Diet will do what it is told. I am told that it is expected that after the diet the Russian laws will be introduced, with the result that there will be no more good roads, cheap education and sober villages, but that ' the country will be as wretched as Russia.' It was in order to prevent the summons of the Diet that a young man of good family stabbed the Governor on the steps of the Senate House. He told his friends at supper the night before, that he was going on a long journey. He was so gay that everyone said he was going to be married. The next morning he killed the Governor (who died in great agony because he was wearing a coat of mail), and shot himself. No one was in his secret. Nice young gentlemen of Northern blood, with good prospects, don't behave like that for nothing. We were, it seems, on the edge of another revolution. The Minister of the Interior Plehve was about to issue a scheme by which every province, and every factory would be under the immediate control of an official responsible only to the Emperor, a sort of organized tyranny which has never, I expect, existed in so perfect a form anywhere. Plehve was condemned to death, and the sentence executed in a sort of inevitable way—which showed that there was no help for him even if he had escaped. The murderer, in spite of torture and persecution, kept silence and nothing is known, or was known till lately of his history. Everyone was perfectly delighted, but not at all surprised, to hear of Plehve's death. A common man said the other day to a friend of mine that ' women were throwing their children into the river' because their husbands were being sent to the war, and they would have to starve. This is believed, whether true or not. A lady said to me that her two nephews had volunteered. ' But what is the war for ? Nobody knows, what is it for ? ' This is what they all say. Kuropatkin went to the Far East, and came back saying that the Japanese were a formidable nation and were ready, and that all the money sent by Russia had been wasted or had not got further than Moscow. The Grand Dukes and Imperial favourites, who wanted war, explained that such a man should not remain War Minister, and he wished to buy a property in Finland and resign and fish quietly all the rest of his life. But when the war came, he begged to go out and the Army insisted on his going. And so there he is.

We are having interesting times with contraband and captured vessels. At our Embassy we beg copies of the American notes and send in similar ones so that I have the advantage of copying Mr. Hay's instructions. I must say they are in a more direct and satisfactory form than our own and I am very glad to have the advantage of serving under Mr. Hay.

We have been having such a funny time lately. We have made our (your) protest about contraband. The Foreign Minister says, 'Very good—we have done all you wish, but don't, for God's sake, say I said so.' The Foreign Office tells all the English and American correspondents that a satisfactory answer is sent—is being signed—has been sent. But it has never arrived. As a matter of fact the Grand Dukes who rule the country are absolutely determined to have their own way, and the only way to stop them is to interpose the thing called by vulgar people a fact between them and their prize money—in the shape of a man-of-war. Vulgar radical nations who don't own an army are not worth consideration—when they talk; but when they kick, the hobnailed boot is quite as painful a weapon as the patent leather pump. I can't help thinking that Kaiser Bill is giving good advice—I mean good from the point of view of the friend of autocracy; and he is certain to be listened to—especially as, if food is contraband of war, England is much more easily starved out in case of war. Do you tremble at all these marine speeches? They are meant for you and for us. The new German Empress [1] that is to be is the niece of our great enemy in Russia, the Grand Duke Alexander, and of our great enemy in Germany, the late Regent of Mecklenburg.

Somebody told me that the mother of the two fighting Grand Dukes, Boris and Cyril, was complaining that the other Grand Dukes (thirty-five in number)—none of whom have been to the war, or have any intention of going—tell all sorts of stories about her two sons. It is true that Boris left Liao Yang just before the battle began, and Cyril has not gone back after his accident on board ship; also that Boris is said to have instituted regular orgies at his house at Liao Yang with certain male boon companions and Red Cross ladies; and he also defied Kuropatkin. He arrived here to bring news of the delight of the Army at the birth of the Emperor's heir : the day he arrived, a French lady friend of his arrived at Petersburg from Paris and they have since seen a good deal of one another. The place teems with stories of every possible description. In fact, as I was saying, life is quite interesting, only it can't be said to be altogether pleasant.—Spencer Eddy is not enjoying himself vastly as he is a sort of social pariah, not because he is wicked, but because of the war and America. We are all social pariahs but I rather prefer it. My deep respect to the S. of S. and your family (if they are with you). How is the White Angel?"

There was, no doubt, at this time, and at all times, a tendency to discount Spring Rice's counsel as that of an alarmist. Lord

[1] The Crown Princess.

Kitchener did not share it. On September 6, 1904, he wrote from Simla :

" Many thanks for your letter. I hope you rub it in to the people at home that we ought to be ready without delay. I am doing my best here, but it is not easy to get people at home to move or allow others to do so."

In October the crisis came, with the Dogger Bank incident. Louis Mallet wrote on October 29 :

" One line to catch the bag. What an awful week, but thank heaven the worst is over. The light-heartedness with which everyone (not H.M. Government) seems to contemplate war is really astonishing and it makes one tremble at the possibility of a new incident."

Spring Rice himself wrote to Ferguson after things had settled down. The letter raises questions concerning contraband of war, to which ten years later Spring Rice himself had to find answers.

Nov. 10, 1904.

" You may imagine that we have been busy. Hardinge has done very well—kept his head and his temper and been as firm with his own government as with the Russians. It would undoubtedly be a very good thing to get him back at the F.O. But though he is willing to go if asked—he is not willing to present himself as a candidate. The pecuniary loss is very considerable. . . . As you say, it is absolutely essential that someone who has experience abroad and the courage of his opinions should be there and he is undoubtedly the best man for the place. If you come into office, he would relieve the Government of many anxieties, for you could be pretty sure that the new Secretary of State was well advised. Nobody could be more moderate and safe than Hardinge. It would be very undesirable that a new Minister with a new Under-Secretary should go to the F.O. without a competent staff to advise him. I should strongly recommend that Louis Mallet (a convinced Free Trader) should be kept on as précis writer. It is a very important point and if you get an opportunity to suggest this, do. He is one of the few men there who is in the habit of thinking and he has any amount of courage.

As to the U.S. Above all things, make Grey go, and go yourself. It is most important that we should have some cordial co-operation between persons—if not governments—in the Far Eastern Question. It is a curious fact that the U.S. Embassy in London doesn't seem to be consulted by Lansdowne, and our Embassy in Washington reports nothing from

Roosevelt. And yet I know that both Roosevelt and Hay would like—not joint, but parallel action—and would be ready to co-operate in spirit if not in deed. The Pacific Coast which once divided us is now a great bond of union. Our interests are identical, and we should pursue them side by side.

Take an instance—*e.g.* cotton. Russia, in order to cripple Japan's cotton industry, declares that raw cotton is contraband of war on the ground that some raw cotton may be turned into gun cotton. But Japan imports eight millions sterling of it, half from America, half from India. All our Imperialists who in the case of Tibet have been so anxious about Indian trade are silent. The subject (if it hadn't been for Hardinge) would hardly have been mentioned. And yet if this doctrine were enforced against us, in time of war, where would Lancashire be ? But America stands up manfully. Why don't we too ?

It seems (again) somewhat strange that whereas Lord Granville, in the time of the Chino-French War, at once declared that England would never accept the doctrine that the necessaries of life were contraband of war, England has in the present case allowed months to pass without speech. Hence much of her trouble. Russia thought England did *not* intend to protest. The fact is our Government is so much occupied with tariff questions and its own existence that it has had no real interest in the interests of the nation—until some open and evident scandal affects public opinion and makes the Government tremble for itself.

As to this extraordinary business [1]—we could not go to war because we weren't *sure* of the facts ; that is, it was such an inconceivable action that it *must* have been by accident, or from panic, or from some occasion, and not from design. The only remedy was to arrive at the facts. And as we couldn't (in the face of Europe) accept and insist on a purely English decision, we had to appeal to an international court. Once we had accepted this, we should have stopped our abuse.

You must remember that, incredible as it seems to us, the Russians devoutly believe in the Russian naval story about torpedo boats and are certainly sincere in their belief.

I have a strong impression that Germany got up the whole affair but has covered up her tracks." [2]

Spring Rice was convinced that warning of a probable attack by torpedo boats was sent from the German authorities to the Russians

[1] The Dogger Bank incident.

[2] See Dugdale Vol. III. under date Oct. 13, 1904. Metternich from London asked the German Foreign Office to warn Russia, but Berlin, it is said, declined to pass on the message.

and that this caused the extraordinary nervousness. It is, at all events, now known that the Kaiser was at this time—as Spring Rice divined—in correspondence with the Tsar to bring about a Russo-German alliance, aimed specially at England, which Russia would constrain France to join. In pursuance of this policy, he telegraphed to the Czar that Hull fishermen acknowledged having seen foreign steamcraft among the fishing fleet to which these vessels did not belong " so there has been foul play." Under the impulse of all the circumstances, the Czar consented to the draft of a Russo-German treaty, to be personally and secretly concluded between the sovereigns.

A sudden event in this autumn was of great moment in Spring Rice's career. The British Ambassador to the United States, Sir Michael Herbert—known to his friends as "Mungo"—died at Davos on September 30th. He was only one year older than Spring Rice and they were close friends, since the time when Herbert was Counsellor and Spring Rice second Secretary in Washington. Herbert's very rapid rise in the service had been largely due to his personal success in America, and it was natural that a possibility should suggest itself both to Spring Rice and others. He wrote on October 2 to his sister :

" I am afraid the idea is quite impossible, though, of course, it would be very magnificent. Perhaps if I had stayed in Egypt it might have been but I don't think there is any prospect. Nothing that anyone in England could do for me would be of the slightest good, so don't think of it. . . . "

Yet in fact the loss of Herbert created a gap, which could only be filled by a man with similar qualifications. On Nov. 9, 1904, came the presidential election and Roosevelt's victory. He wrote on the 9th :

" DEAR CECIL,

I was delighted to get your telegram. It has been a great triumph. Great Heavens, how I wish you were Ambassador here ! There are fifty matters that come up that I would like to discuss with you, notably about affairs in the Far East, and you could be of great service to your own country as well as to this country."

Such wishes find an echo and on November 20, J. C. O'Laughlin, editor of the *Chicago Tribune*, wrote from Washington :

Nov. 28, 1904.

" Both the President and Secretary Hay were delighted to get the statement you so kindly gave me for them. Both said almost identically the same thing : that the views of a diplomat so keen and intelligent and broad, as yourself, were of the highest value, and that they would be of use in enabling them to deal with the situation.

There have been rumours, which have reached the State Department, that you were coming here, and I know that nothing could be more gratifying to Mr. Roosevelt and Mr. Hay. As you know, Sternburg [1] has made a strong impression by his personal relations with Mr. Roosevelt, and I should think your Government would want to play the same card. But of far greater importance is your knowledge of American questions and particularly your acquaintance with the foibles of Americans.''

Sir Mortimer Durand, who had been Spring Rice's chief in Persia, was now appointed to succeed Herbert ; and though Spring Rice knew him to be a keen personal admirer of Roosevelt's, he knew also that the ex-Indian civil servant had no acquaintance with America. But the President and his friend were in constant communication. Here is Spring Rice's exultation over Roosevelt's election to the Presidency—mixed with comments on the Dogger Bank:

" This is the very best news I have heard for ages. I heard it early yesterday morning by telephone, and Eddy and I wired our delight. It is simply grand.

Now you are safe, thank goodness, for the four years at least, and even *our* good wishes can't do you any harm. I suppose you are sick of good wishes and congratulations, but as I don't expect to be a postmaster even under civil service rules, you can read my ecstacies without a qualm.

They are so glad here you are elected ; so glad that gladness approaches sorrow. Lamsdorff told someone the other day your real name was Rosenfeld and that you were a Jew from S. Germany and that was why you were so keen on the Jews in Russia. I didn't know this side of your ancestry. Did you ? I think you have somewhat disappointed them here by your majority although they had discounted the victory before hand. Things look rather serious, with mobilisation riots and threatened constitutional revolutions, etc., etc. But the Emperor and the war go on. They are a wonderful people, accepting everything that comes and putting a brave face on it. It is fearful to think of what this people must have suffered in past ages to bring them to this pitch. They endure anything and everything with the same calm and heroic bravery—not of an aggressive kind, but patient, enduring with a real solid foundation of fighting pluck behind it all. I can't help respecting them though their predominant characteristic at present is to hate England. But many people (including my own)[2] have done that.

The North Sea incident is rather like the joke on Bill Jones. Do you remember it ? And how ' they put the nigger in a

---

[1] The German Ambassador.   [2] The Irish.

barn—I disremember what happened to the nigger.' The fact
is someone told the Russians we were going to lay for them and
so they started in a state of nerves that made them attack
anything they saw.

I don't believe that unless we had made our naval preparations that the Russian Admiralty would have moved a finger
to get a report from their Admiral. It was just like the
'Malacca' over again. They don't and won't understand any
diplomatic request whatever unless it is backed by force. There
force don't make a diplomatic request *unless* and until you are
ready with the big stick after the soft word.

As to the future here it is hard to make a forecast. Emperor
William has got the ear of the Emperor here; he has his
adjutant always bringing him messages and making all manner
of suggestions. I don't think it follows Germany will seek for
compensation after peace is concluded—in the Far East.
Judging by analogy, the compensation will be in the West and
in Europe. Russia allowed Holstein, the Austrian war, the
French war—and then got her compensations (rather thin ones)
in the Near East. I think that William will get his nearer
home. However that may be, it is plain that Germany
naturally enough wants to see Russia have a free hand in Asia,
and hopes in exchange to have one in Europe; that if England
could be engaged in a war with Russia which would require her
fleet to be absent in the East—the German fleet, especially if
France would come in, would have a good chance for a sudden
descent on England. It is a mobilisation fleet, made for quick
action and quick repair and for action of a particular nature in a
particular place.

Oh, how glad I am!"

By the same mail went a letter of introduction to Roosevelt, on
behalf of his other friend, Valentine Chirol. It stressed the support
given by the *Times* to the United States in the Spanish-American
War—when there had been some fear of another attitude.

"Chirol fought like a demon. I saw a good deal of him at the
time and can assure you of it at first hand; and there was never
any doubt as to which side the *Times* took. I don't mean that
this did *you* any good. I mean and hope that it will do him good.
Since then (and before too) he has been a great traveller, has
written the best small book on China, and the best large or small
one on Persia. He is the best informed man on European
questions, especially German questions (he lived in Berlin for
some years), whom I know. His influence is supreme in the
Times, when the *Times* has time to think. He is as intimate in

the Foreign Office as anyone can be, and absolutely trusted. He would certainly be the best person to convey to that thick-headed institution his impressions of America; and as he can always apply to the Government the argument of *fear*, he is sure to be listened to. No one there wants to have the *Times* on his back. I don't think anyone by experience or position could be a better tube to speak through, either to the Government or to the country. Also, as I am very particularly fond of him I should like him to know the man who occupied the first position in the world and is the best suited for it. You see, flattery haunts the steps of thrones, but mine is of old standing."

It has to be admitted that this bringing together was not wholly a success, and Chirol wrote his disappointment. He had not been able to fix Roosevelt continuously in discussion. Spring Rice replied :

" If you took an impetuous small boy on to a beech strewn with a great many exciting pebbles, you would not expect him to remain interested for long in one pebble. You must always remember that the President is about six."

On Dec. 6, 1904, he wrote to Mrs. Roosevelt :

" Happy New Year and many of them. This is a glorious year and I wish I could see you during it. Here, life is as dis-agreeable as man and weather can make it, but it is all business, and must be gone through with. I am going to Berlin for Xmas to see my father-in-law and study the Germans. Then I shall go to London for a time—a few weeks only and return here. I wonder what you would say if you were English and not American. I fear you would say your Government had a very big voice and a very small stick. I wonder if we are getting soft and cowardly ? I think sometimes we must be, when I read about the Japs and the Russians and how they fight. We have just heard that the Russian Government has organized a raid upon your Legation with a view to stealing the cypher : they have already got the letter book and photoed it. The organizer of this pretty game is an officer in the Army who drinks champagne with the Chancery servant. They have got our man and pay him. He has got an impression of our key and we are dancing round the safe all day. . . . The other night after dinner we caught a man in the Embassy. He was half-killed by the English servants and kicked out into the snow. The fun is that we have full information of all that goes on in the ' office,' as it is called, where these raids on the Embassies are planned. I wonder when I shall be in a white country again."

Next day followed a despatch to the President.

To ROOSEVELT.

Dec. 7, 1904.

" I am so immensely grateful for your letter which was received with acclamation at our house. I am still chortling with delight at the results of the election. I wish I were there to see. At present I am tied here, as we can't have any change just at present while things are in this condition.

The situation is odd. It is quite plain that the policy of Russia is to frighten or beat Japan into accepting a peace—which will be not a very hard one ; but the object is to get Japan to turn her back on America and England and the feelings and policy which they represent. To accept Russia's hegemony, and, like China, enter into her system—Asia for the Asiatics under Russia's leadership.

The object is (1) to weaken or even crush Japan—and especially by a blockade and a wide extension of the doctrine of contraband to ruin her trade ; (2) to point out to her that the help of England is feeble, and America's merely platonic ; (3) to offer her the friendship of Russia the brave and terrible foe, instead of that of England the faithless and the impotent friend. Russia will then, in agreement with Japan, be able to dispose of and partition the good things of the East. The French Ambassador has just come over here on a hurried visit. His language makes it clear that he is anxious above all things that Germany should not supplant France in the affections of Russia ; and France seems convinced that Germany has made very liberal offers. He thinks that England will necessarily find herself isolated. The Continental Powers will be forced to act together ; Germany with an eye to the destruction of the dual Alliance and France with an eye to its maintenance. These two powers will not mediate, but they will facilitate a settlement by friendly action in Tokio and Petersburg and will acquiesce in any agreement arrived at between the two. England and America will not be consulted. If they object to the settlement they will be confronted by a Continental Alliance of overwhelming strength. England will be isolated and hopelessly isolated and America will be forced (not having a striking army) to accept the *fait accompli.*

This is the programme the weak point of which is that neither Germany nor France [1] is prepared to give much more than moral support to Russia ; although, of course, in case of war

---

[1] The Dual Alliance between Russia and France did not extend to action in the Far East.

between England and Russia, Germany's 'neutrality' will be friendly to the latter, and her fleet, mobilized on our flank, will keep a large part of the English fleet inactive. Germany will also do policeman in the Balkans and on the Polish frontier so that Russia will be able to direct all her attention to Asia, India and China.

But a more serious point—because it is practical—is contraband. Russia, by her rules, has practically declared all Japan under an effective blockade—for every ship trading with Japan will contain ' unconditional contraband.' The cotton trade of America is at least twenty million dollars raw cotton exported to Japan and the Indian export is the same.   To declare all this liable to seizure (if it could be enforced) would be to ruin the main industry of Japan.   And here Germany and France can render signal services to Russia, for they can accept the Russian view and in return receive special facilities.   Here seems a common interest of the trading nations of the greatest magnitude ; and it is quite clear that no international conference can settle this question, which is already settled in advance by a tacit agreement.   There is no argument which can be effectively used except force."

He recapitulates the details of the " Malacca " incident and the Dogger Bank, then concludes :

" I could multiply instances.   The result is that nothing is of any avail whatever except the determination and the readiness to use force ; force need not be employed, for this proud and imperial Government yields to threats as America in her poorest days would never have thought of doing.   The point of honour is different.

The Kaiser has enormous influence here and has through the Russian and German military attachés direct access to the Emperor's ear—which he uses. . . .   They say here ' Berlin is the capital of Russia.'   Of course, the policy of Kaiser Wilhelm is a secret to nobody now.   It is to have the hegemony of Western Europe and leave the East to Russia.   At home he is to crush the Socialists and Liberals with the sympathy and support of Russia whom in turn he is to help to crush her own internal enemies.   He is to be the central telephone office in which all wires meet and which have no cross connections and everything that passes is to pass through him.

He has won an almost phenomenal success here.   In a year he has absolutely put an end to the national opposition of the Slavs to the Germans and the personal dislike of the Emperor to himself.   He is now and is likely to remain for some time, the arbiter of the fate of Russia.   He can now afford to turn his attention to England and America.   But, of course, he would prefer France.   The triple alliance of France, Germany and Russia with Germany supreme (as she was with Austria and Italy) is the ideal.   And the Far Eastern question gives him his chance.   For a purely local agreement may well extend itself further—a far Eastern agreement may become a world agreement.   And therefore I think that there are few sacrifices which he would not give to attain that end.   A Chinese province is worth less than a world empire.

I wish you had a really good Ambassador here.   Our man here is a very good one.   Strong and independent."

CHAPTER XIII

PRESIDENT ROOSEVELT'S INTERVENTION IN THE RUSSO-JAPANESE WAR

THE long chapter which opens now could not be restricted, because it concerns the turning-point of international policy during Spring Rice's observation of it. Throughout 1903, as from 1896 onwards, his attention was focussed upon Germany ; but the question to him then was what Germany might do in a Europe overshadowed by the military ascendancy of Russia. Germany's action could be fatal to Great Britain, if combined with that of Russia.

Russia then wielded, with more absolute power than any other state, much the greatest and most docile mass of human material ; she seemed irresistible. In 1904, that semblance was challenged ; within less than a year and a half, nothing was left of it. Changes followed in Russia itself—which had seemed unchangeable. The whole European outlook had to be reconstructed.

On Dec. 27, 1904, Roosevelt replied to Spring Rice's letter of December 7. He wrote at great length ; but the document is so important that most of it must be given.

The opening concerned his election. He claimed to have broken up in his candidature for the Presidency whatever undue allegiance the Republican Party owed to the plutocracy, and to have drawn his personal strength from among the " plain people " and especially the younger men. Then he passed into the wider speculations to which both he and Spring Rice were addicted ; but in the midst of these came a definite proposal for personal communication :

" . . . While I feel that these popular contests are not only inevitable in great free nations, but must be recognised as in effect indispensable so long as the nations are really free, I do not at all agree with the view of those amiable closet philosophers who hold that they are the only important things in the life of a free people. It is just as true now as ever it was in the old days that every free people must face the very difficult problem of combining liberal institutions and wide opportunities for happiness and well-being at home, with the power to make head against foreign foes. I do not suppose this problem ever will be perfectly solved, and if the solution is too imperfect the nation will eventually go down. Liberal institutions mean of necessity government by elected representatives, who must have a multitude of immediate and pressing personal interests, both of their own and of their constituents, to distract them from the considerations of great and far-reaching policies—especially foreign policies. Moreover, liberal institutions of necessity tend to invite factionalism and such absorption in party contests that the successful party leader, the successful parliamentary manager, the victor in struggles at the ballot box, usurp an altogether improper place in popular estimation when compared with the military administrator, with the man who is preparing the resources of the nation for the event of war, and who is watching the course of other nations and the trend of developments in international affairs. Opportunities for individual happiness and wellbeing also tend to mean a certain softness and luxury—a condition of mind and body in which long-continued hardship becomes intolerable ; a condition in which the stay-at-home people become fickle and hysterical under pressure of a formidable foe, while they shrink from the grim necessities of war, a condition in which there is danger lest a soldier may be developed who will not show the necessary brutal heroism in attack and defence, shown to-day by the Japanese and Russians, as it was shown by the English under Wellington, and by the Americans when they had fought for two years under Grant and Sherman and Farragut.

All this is by way of preface, so that you may see how interested I am in what you tell me. Largely because of what you set forth, I shall probably send George Meyer to St. Petersburg. He is a close friend of mine, and I have told him that an Englishman (I did not mention your name) would speak to him and tell him that he had been in communication with me, and by my request was to keep in full touch with him. You can show him this letter, if you feel it safe to take this letter with you[1] to St. Petersburg.

It is always possible that Japan and Russia may come to terms of agreement, as I suppose Count Ito truly wished them to do so some few years ago. I have reason to believe that the Japanese were disappointed and unfavourably impressed by the English vehemence of speech and exceeding moderation of action in the Hull fishing fleet affair. Personally I appreciate to the full the difficulty of committing oneself to a course of action in reliance upon the proposed action of any free people which is not accustomed to carrying out with iron will a long-continued course of foreign policy. It would be well nigh impossible, even if it were not highly undesirable, for this country to engage with another to carry out any policy, save one which

[1] Spring Rice was then in London.

had become part of the inherited tradition of the country, like
the Monroe Doctrine.   Not merely could I, for instance, only
make such an engagement for four years, but I would have to
reckon with a possible overthrow in Congress, with the temper
of the people, with many different conditions.[1]   In consequence,
my policy must of necessity be somewhat opportunist ; although
as a matter of fact I have very definitely concluded what I
intend to do if circumstances permit, so far as this Far Eastern
question is concerned.   I do not like to write my conclusions
even to you ; and unfortunately there is no one in your Embassy
here to whom I can speak with even reasonable fullness.[2]   I wish
to Heaven you could come over, if only for a week or two and
I think it would be very important for your Government that
you should come over.

For similar reasons I would hesitate in counting upon the
support of your Government and your people.   I am not quite
sure of their tenacity of purpose, of their fixity of conviction, of
their willingness to take necessary risks and at need to endure
heavy losses for a given end.   Both your Government and ours
must reckon with the possible clamour of the great business
interests, who regard anything that will tend to ' unsettle
values,' as they call it, with unaffected horror, as being worse
than any possible future national loss or even disgrace ; and we
also have to reckon with a fundamentally sound, but often
temporarily unstable or mistaken, public opinion.   Moreover,
in large parts of both of our countries there is undoubtedly too
much softness.   The amiable peace-at-any-price people who in
our country have been prancing about as anti-imperialists for
the last few years are, not invariably but generally, men weak
in body or mind, men who could not be soldiers because they
lack physical hardihood or courage ; and though in their extreme
form these people are not very numerous, there are undoubtedly
large sections of the population whose men, if drafted into the
ranks, would need long training before they would become
effective fighters against formidable foes; and those stay-at-
homes, moreover, simply because they are unused to it, would
become utterly appalled by slaughter in the field.   In the
Spanish War, for instance, and in the Boer War, our generals
and yours, our public leaders and yours, had to grapple with a
public sentiment which screamed with anguish over the loss of
a couple of thousand men in the field ; a sentiment of pre-

[1] It will be seen that Spring Rice in after years had not forgotten this
principle of American policy.

[2] Dugdale III. under date Sept. 27, 1904.   Spack von Sternburg reports
a conversation with Roosevelt who said—" How am I to deal with this
Ambassador ?   If I had Spring Rice here, things might be different."

posterous and unreasoning mawkishness, as is instanced by the fact that the actual mortality in the two wars, taken in the aggregate, did not equal the aggregate mortality in the two countries, during the same number of years, of the women who died in childbirth ; nor, as regards my own country, of the men who were killed in private quarrel.

Russia for a number of years has treated the United States as badly as she has treated England, and almost as badly as she has treated Japan. Her diplomatists lied to us with brazen and contemptuous effrontery, and showed with cynical indifference their intention to organise China against our interests. Russia could, of course, under no circumstances make any attack upon the United States ; not even upon the outlying possessions of the United States, in the Philippines. I should have liked to be friendly with her ; but she simply would not permit it, and those responsible for managing her foreign policy betrayed a brutality and ignorance, an arrogance and shortsightedness, which are not often combined.

The Japanese, as a government, treated us well, and what they contended for was what all civilised powers in the East were contending for. But I wish I were certain that the Japanese down at bottom did not lump Russians, English, Americans, Germans, all of us, simply as white devils inferior to themselves not only in what they regard as the essentials of civilisation, but in courage and forethought, and to be treated politely only so long as would enable the Japanese to take advantage of our various national jealousies, and beat us in turn. . . .[1]

It is only ten years since foreign nations ceased to treat Japan with official contempt in the matter of consular courts and the like, and I think, Springy, you and I will both admit that our travelling countrymen, not to speak of the inhabitants of Continental Europe, are not always ingratiating in their manners towards the races which they regard as their inferiors. If the circumstances were reversed, and if English or Americans had been lorded over by one yellow race for a long term of years, and then had won some striking victories over another yellow race, I doubt whether the victorious soldiers would have shown any great courtesy or consideration towards men of the first yellow race. I yet have hopes that this is only a passing phase and that when Japan settles down, she will feel a desire to enter

---

[1] He added that the American military attachés with the Japanese army, though originally pro-Japanese, thought them insolent in their victory. It appeared to them that America " had thwarted Japan's hopes in regard not merely to the Philippines but to Hawaii."

more and more into the circle of the great civilised nations as one of their number. There are many individual Japanese for whom I have a sincere liking and there is much in their civilisation from which we can with advantage learn.

But all this is aside from the main point, which is that in international affairs, as things are in this very human world, each nation, while striving to act fairly by other nations, must rely for its own safety only upon its own forethought and industrial efficiency and fighting edge. Unless it has this fighting edge and this forethought it will go down. Whether Russia wins or Japan wins, the victor will in the long run only yield either to England or to the United States substantially the respect which England or the United States is enabled to exact by power actual or potential. Moreover, looked at from the standpoint of a long course of years, no nation can depend upon the mere friendship of any other, even though that friendship is genuine, unless it has itself such strength as to make its own friendship of value in return. When affairs come to the time of settlement in the Far East (even if previous to the peace no other nation gets embroiled beyond the present pair of combatants) we shall have to look sharply lest our interests be sacrificed. If it were not for the attitude of England and the United States, I think that Germany and France would probably have already interfered on Russia's side. But, of course, this does not necessarily mean that all four powers may not form a friendly agreement in the end ; even an agreement as against us. But I hardly believe this. Japan has shown herself to be astute and farsighted, and she must know that if Russia made peace with her now, with the purpose of joint hostile action against some other power, it would only be with the further purpose of eating her up a generation or so hence. So long as Japan takes an interest in Korea, in Manchuria, in China, it is Russia which is her natural enemy. Of course, if Japan were content to abandon all hope of influence upon the continent of Asia and to try to become a great maritime power, she might ally herself with Russia to menace the American, the Dutch, or perhaps the English possessions in the Pacific. But in any such alliance between Russia and Japan, do not forget what surely the Japanese would think of : viz., whereas the sea-powers could do little damage to Russia, they could do enormous damage to Japan, and might well destroy the Japanese navy and blockade the Japanese islands. In such an alliance the entire risk would be run by Japan, and an altogether disproportionate share of the advantage would come to Russia. I hardly believe that Japan would fail to see this.

But the summing up of the whole matter is that we must trust in the Lord and keep our powder dry and our eyes open. What turn military or diplomatic affairs will take, I have no idea but so far as possible I intend, as your people should intend, to be vigilant and reasonably ready to adopt whatever course is called for.

Give my love to Mrs. Springy. I do wish that both of you could come over here. I think it is really important that I should see you and have a little talk with you so that you could tell your people just what I think of things.

Faithfully yours,

THEODORE ROOSEVELT.

This important communication was received by Spring Rice in London and was handed by him to his superiors at the Foreign Office.

A few days before Christmas, he and his wife had left St. Petersburg for her father's house in Berlin—glad to escape from a city of dreadful night which was also seething with revolution. He wrote on Dec. 23, 1904 :

" DEAR MARGARET AND AUBREY,

. . . I am much impressed with Berlin's order and pleasant arrangements after the land without any order, where day is even as night, in which I have been living. Florence tumbled out of the railway carriage in order to ' walk in the sun.' It wasn't much of a sun, it was lean and watery with a sort of German-silver brightness and it shone on a wooden railway station and a brick platform, but it *was* the real sun and we hadn't seen it for a month. Think : dark every day about 3, and then electric light, or paddling in muddy streets with the remains of ice and snow, and a thick white mist so that you couldn't see across the Neva. The bridge ended in clouds, like the bridge in Thingummy, and the river was snow-covered ice in hummocks with black patches of water between, with here and there (like Port Arthur), the hulks wrecked when the ice came down, which are slowly being pounded to pieces. There are the war telegrams plastered at the corners of the streets, not many people reading them and not cheerful reading either. The one point of animation is the office of the Liberal newspaper ; crowds of men of all ranks running to subscribe—officers and workmen shaking hands—several girls and ladies in furs ; all bent on liberty and constitution ; now it is closed. Poor Russia—what will happen next ? I must say people don't seem to mind very much. Florence and I went a drive on Sunday and saw the main street full of police on horseback parading up and down. Half an hour before, students and studentesses had been walking about with red flags, and the police had ridden them down with swords, cutting and slashing. One student was kicked to death. No defence was made. They just waved the red flags and got knocked down and arrested. The same thing happened at Moscow. It is a dumb protest, in the hope that some day the police may refuse to act and the people join. There was no sign whatever of that. In fact the people as a whole seem to accept the Government as it does the climate—something that comes from God or the Devil but in any case can't be changed by cursing. We are hated just as much as ever and the newspapers are a sight."

After Christmas, leaving his wife with her father, he went on to London—where on January 1 the news came that Port Arthur had surrendered. At this moment Ronald Ferguson was in Washington, and wrote on January 7 to Spring Rice to say that the Embassy was ill-served and should be strengthened.

" There is absolutely no one here to help Durand, and he is not a professional diplomat. We are, therefore, greatly handicapped compared with France, Germany and Austria, all of whose Embassies are well equipped. Durand, for whom I have the warmest regard, talked to me quite openly of his difficulties."

Ferguson did not contemplate the possibility suggested by Roosevelt. But the Foreign Office, to whom also Ferguson had written, decided to act, and by January 14 it was roughly settled that Spring Rice should go out. Yet the whole affair was so informal, so delicate and so full of awkward possibilities, that a letter from Villiers shows Spring Rice to have been sensitive and irritable when it was mentioned.

" If it is the initial step," Villiers wrote, " in an attempt of which I have since heard something to effect a new and most important combination, I quite understand your services being required. We have no one else on such good and intimate terms with the right people.

As for our friends on the other side, we know what they want and we cannot blame them for trying to secure their friend.

So in every way a great compliment is being paid to you."

Detail is given in a letter to his wife, written from his sister's home at 30 Norfolk Crescent :

" Here is my story. When I came back I received a letter from Harry White [1] asking me to call at once, which I did. He gave me a letter from the President setting out at length his

[1] Counsellor at the American Embassy : afterwards Ambassador in Paris.

desire to talk with me about Eastern matters and especially as
to the policy of H.M.G.   H. White had received a letter from
the P., telling him that he was to suggest to Lord L. that I
should be sent over with a message and saying that he could
not get on with Durand.   H. W. told me that Lord L. had
replied that, as Durand was the recognised Ambassador, he
could not commission me to act behind his back, but that I
could go off on a private visit, if I wished.   I saw L. Mallet,
who told me that these were Lord L.'s opinions, and that if I
called the next day he would talk about it.   So I called and had
a long talk about the general situation.   I said to him that being
on leave I could do what I wished.   And that I should not
consider myself as being under his orders—so that he need not
consider that Durand's position was in any way affected.   He
agreed—and said I should see him before I started.   As yet I
have not seen him, but have received a letter from G. Balfour
which I enclose for you to keep. . . . I think I am right to go and
I am sure you will approve."

Manifestly this unofficial go-between was being put into a difficult
relation towards the Ambassador, his former chief, whom he greatly
respected and liked.   But Ferguson wrote from Canada, where he
had gone to visit his brother.

Jan. 17, 1905.

"... Durand is really a saint.   The way he accepted the
suggestion to invite you ; made another that, if the President
were determined he couldn't do business with him, he should
clear the way ; the little history he gave of his long-felt aspirations for mutual good will between Britain and U.S.A. ; all was
as honest, as touching, as clear sighted an exposition of a really
fine mind and character as one man could make another hear.
It put him among my half dozen of friends. . . .

As to the Ambassador himself and the State Department—
he is not nimble enough and the others are too nimble.   They
do not sufficiently recognise that a proposal from our F.O.
commits the more vulnerable empire to every consequence,
whilst that of the most autocratic President commits his
country to nothing.

On the other hand, our people have not yet grasped the full
significance of this President's status.

Durand's weakness I guess to lie in the lack of any definite
British Far East policy.   There was none for nine years past
and I have no reason to apprehend that there is any now.   If
that's so, what wonder if the President and Durand don't
get forwarder, though they, and Hay, were made to co-operate.

I'll do all I can to help, and it was necessary I should be in England by the last of the month.   I hadn't enough time with Durand ; you and he would be the best possible combination if only for a week.   The President should see that either he must trust Durand or state his reasons against doing so, if any open channel is to be kept.

There has been nothing like the President and his Government before in America.   (Has there on the other hand ever been anything in Britain quite like ours ?)   I felt under some disadvantage in being so rusty in Foreign affairs (and will brush up) and also in being alone.

Had E. Grey or N. [1] been over, more could have been done, for they have the best judgments I know on the simple facts on which policies should be based.

What I was not quite sure of was of how *completely* our policy runs on lines parallel with U.S.A.   All I knew was that I could detect no divergencies.

However, one of the opposition cannot intervene, confidentially, in the affairs of a Department of his Government, so that don't much matter.   I had one very interesting talk with the President walking, when he told me all I could wish to know on his Far East policy.   Also I heard him talk a good deal and get others to talk.   Really, Germany and America are the only two states with effective executives. . . .

God bless you and keep Durand, for no good man ever struggled with greater adversity."

On January 17 Mr. Gerald Balfour wrote to Spring Rice.

" The Prime Minister asks me to tell you that he thought the President's letter extraordinarily delightful and characteristic."

It seemed " to suggest a proposal for joint action at the end of the war in connection with possible terms of peace"; and since Mr. Gerald Balfour was of opinion that the interests of England and of the United States in the Far East were identical, and that they harmonised with the professed aims of Japan, the way appeared to him clear.

Concealment of the visit was, of course, impossible ; and since Spring Rice with Durand called at the White House on the evening of February 5, all the world was agog on the 6th.   The official denial of any " political purpose or result " was duly published, and as much believed as such denials are.   Two days later, on February 8, a telegram from New York reached Mr. Roosevelt at the White House : " Good-bye to all.   Cecil."

[1] Lady Helen Ferguson.

It had indeed been a flying visit, and for form's sake, to keep up the appearance of his unofficial character, Spring Rice avoided the Embassy and stayed as the guest of Henry Adams at 1603 H Street.

Brief though his stay had been, it gave him the welcome chance to renew intimacies with his circle of friends.

R.M.S. " TEUTONIC," Feb. 14, 1905.
" DEAR MRS. LODGE,

It was delightful to get your telegram which the steward gave me half way across the Atlantic. But it isn't *quite* as satisfactory as seeing you all. What fun it was ! I still think, and shall go on thinking, of coming through the curtain and finding you in the old place and just the same.

I saw Wint, Mrs. Wint, and Wintina [1] who seems to me to have great possibilities of mischief in her—I trust more to others than herself. I liked her very much. Wint, I fear, is growing virtuous but he is in some respects the same. For instance, having harried his wife out of Rome and driven her to Newport, where he said he was going to nail her to the mast, he now says sunny Italy is the place for him, and off they are going. He, of course, will not do much of the packing. *What* do you think of it ? Mrs. Wint is to perform the woman's mission which is as you know. In the East they walk behind their husbands (who ride the donkey), carrying the baby and other family luggage till they drop. In the West they housekeep and pack. This is what I explain to my wife, quoting your example, and she is exasperatingly servile. Don't do it any more, it is very hard on you and bad for us. Make the beasts look after you ! I don't mean Cabot, who is, I perceive, angelic, but the whole crowd. I wish I could do something nice and disagreeable for you—only it wouldn't be disagreeable—for you. What are you doing now ? I departed with a cold and it developed into fever, which I enjoyed on ship in bed with the *Antiquary* and Uncle Henry's book.[2] They really didn't go badly together which is good for Uncle Henry. It is a fine production—I fancy, a little bit like the monument at Rock Creek, in memoriam.[3] There is the real voice of passion so that the very stones cry out.

I saw Lady Herbert and talked for a long time about Mungo. She had a very living love for him and it was a great satisfaction to give her comfort by telling her the absolute and living truth. One can't always do that. A clergyman here told me how a friend of his was consoling a gent who had just lost his wife, by

[1] Mr., Mrs. and Miss Winthrop Chanler.
[2] Adams' book on Mont St. Michel and Chartres.
[3] Erected by Henry Adams in memory of his wife.

enumerating her good qualities.   The gent said : ' That's all very true, but I didn't like her.' "

He wrote also on board ship to Mrs. Roosevelt :

" I can't tell you how delightful it was to see you all again (though I do say from the purely selfish point of view that it will be much nicer to see you in Oyster Bay).   However, I did see a good deal of you.   The President I thought looking extremely well and in greater form than ever, and it was splendid to see him where he was—As you know, I want to see him (as he will) play an even bigger part on an even bigger stage and it seems to me this time is coming on apace."

The letter went on to transmit some rumours as to the Russian sortie from Port Arthur and the naval action—which proved to be ill-founded.   Roosevelt replied disputing the rumour, and pointing out the disadvantages which offset Admiral Rozhdestvensky's immense superiority.   Then he ends :

" I am having my own troubles here and there are several eminent statesmen at the other end of Pennsylvania Avenue whom I would gladly lend to the Russian Government, if they cared to expend them as bodyguards for Grand Dukes wherever there was a likelihood of dynamite bombs being exploded."

When Spring Rice landed, Mr. H. White, then Counsellor at the United States Embassy, wrote to say that he was about to sail for America and that the King had sent for him in order to make him the bearer of a special and cordial message " which is all that you or I could desire."   He was also instructed to convey that the King meant to write to the President on the occasion of his inauguration. Mr. White added that, in conversation with Lord Knollys, the King's private secretary—" I rubbed into him, in all sincerity, the great work you have done in bringing the President and Durand together, which doubtless was duly transmitted to the Sovereign and certainly gave Knollys much pleasure."

This brought Spring Rice to personal interviews, first with Lord Knollys and then with King Edward.   It would appear also, from a draft in his writing, that he was asked to suggest the lines of such a letter as would be suitable to an occasion outside the usual ceremonious etiquette ;   for it was not in accordance with precedent that the King should address a personal and official congratulation to a President of the United States on his inauguration.

It is at all events quite certain that King Edward consulted Spring Rice as to a personal memento which should accompany the letter, and that the happy thought was Spring Rice's, which suggested sending a miniature of Hampden from the collection at Windsor.

The story was told long after in a letter which has already been published but cannot be omitted here.

May 7, 1910.

" MY DEAR THEODORE,

I think I ought to tell you something about our King who died last night.   When I came back from seeing you in Washington after you were President, he sent for me and talked a long time about you.   I told him what I thought you stood for, quite frankly and fully though, if popular impression at that time had been quite justified, he would not have sympathized much with what I told him.   But he did listen very sympathetically. He said he wanted to get into personal relations with you, not as King and President, so much as two men with certain aims in common.   He mentioned what his father had done on his death-bed for good relations, and wished to do something himself.

He told me he intended to write to you himself, and his first intention was to send quite an informal letter.   He also wanted to send you some quite unofficial memento and asked me what I thought you would like as a personal sign of good-will—not as a formal presentation.   I thought of something I had seen in his collection which was of great historical value—but not at all the sort of thing a King of England might be expected to give to an American President, because it was the picture of a man who had led a successful rebellion against the Royal cause. But that was the reason he jumped at the idea at once, because, as he said, you were a man who could understand why he like you (and you like himself) should join in admiration of a great Englishman.   His Librarian and other people objected strongly, but he insisted.

I am quite sure that if you had seen him, you would have understood some things which seem rather difficult to understand—that is, why he did as a fact exert a great influence, and how very thoroughly and sincerely he desired certain things and did do a great deal to promote their accomplishment.   I am very sorry you didn't see him, but I daresay you won't forget what I tell you now—quite privately and for yourself.

Yours ever,

CECIL SPRING RICE."

At the time he wrote of this matter to Mrs. Roosevelt when he got back to St. Petersburg (in a letter the bulk of which will be found further on).

March 13, 1905.

" I saw Lord Lansdowne at once when I returned and found him very much delighted at the messages which had reached him from the President. He for his part is quite determined to play up. The difficulty lies with the Liberal Party; but Lord Rosebery, Grey and Haldane were all ready to continue the alliance with Japan, and, as you see, they have all made speeches to that effect. In England, of course, as Chamberlain told me very earnestly, every thinking man is convinced of the absolute necessity for England of a good understanding with America— but they know, most of them—that they had better not say so. The King as much as anyone. He sent for me and asked me again and again what the President had said—what he was like —he expressed (rather to my surprise) especial admiration for his bravery; ' such a brave man too,' ' fought like a tiger.' He insisted on writing, rather against the wish of the Government, who were afraid it would embarrass you; but he would do it, and wanted to say much more than he did. I hope you liked the miniature. There will be an awful row in the Librarian's department in Windsor about it because there is no duplicate. But the King *would* send it. He thought it would be the most appropriate and convenient form of souvenir. The Queen (Victoria) was especially interested in it, although the Librarian had some doubts as to her liking for a gentleman who wasn't in all respects a friend of monarchy.

They determined to reorganize the Embassy staff at once. I hope you will approve the changes.

My wife was *furious* with me for not bringing her and we had our first quarrel about it. She said I ought to have wired and that she would have come. If I had, I should have had the devil to pay with her father—so I was in a hole either way. She swears I shan't be allowed again to get within reach of America without her. She sends her respects.

I wish I had seen more of you and had a good talk. The fact is that I am such an official that I am not at my ease with a sovereign, and heartily pray for the time when you descend from the throne.

The last word on this matter is a despatch from Sir Mortimer Durand, of which a copy was sent to Spring Rice.

BRITISH EMBASSY, WASHINGTON,
March 10, 1905.

" MY DEAR LORD LANSDOWNE,

On the 2nd March I received the special bag containing the King's letter for the President, together with your letter of the

22nd February.   On the morning of the 3rd I called at the
White House and saw the President.   He was in his office, and
asked me to sit down and look at a book on African sport while
he signed some papers sent up by Congress.   It was the day
before the Inauguration, and I thought he would be very busy,
but he soon cleared off his work.   I then gave him the King's
letter, which he read with evident pleasure.   As I telegraphed
to you, he asked me to express his cordial thanks.   He said he
should value the miniature very highly and considered it a
singularly appropriate gift.   He spoke warmly about the tone
of the letter, which he said differed in that respect from any
letter he had ever received from a reigning sovereign.   He is
sending his answer by Henry White, who will tell you how
sincerely pleased he was.   There can be no doubt about this.
The letter will, I feel sure, have an excellent effect.   Regarding
the miniature, he said he would speak to Hay, as he was not sure
what course to adopt.   ' I mean to stick to it,' he said, ' whatever happens, but I think I had better say nothing about it,
or Congress might refuse permission'; and he asked me to take
the greatest care that no one got to know anything.   He
seemed really anxious on this point, which on the eve of his
triumphal inauguration struck me as rather pathetic.

After talking about the King's letter he went on to assure
me of his firm resolve to stand in with us.   He said with a
laugh, ' I know Springy thinks I am inclined to fall under the
influence of the German Emperor, but he is quite wrong.   I
like the Emperor very much in a way, but I don't trust him, and
am not in the least affected by the ridiculous messages he makes
Specky bring me.'   (Specky is the German Ambassador.)
' I have told Specky that his fears of an attack by England are
utter nonsense, and Specky is half ashamed of them himself.
You need never be the least afraid that I shall take the Kaiser
seriously.'

I tried to assure him that Spring Rice did not take the view
he supposed, but it is never easy to get in a word when he is
started.

He said a good deal more on the same subject.   He told me
the Emperor had been gravely alarmed at the idea of a Franco-
Russo-Anglo-Japanese Alliance against him, also that the
Emperor wished him to believe that the French and Russians
had vainly tried to bring Germany into a coalition against
England.   He hinted that England attached too much importance to the German naval preparations, and said he would like
to see Germany more friendly towards us, but that she was not
so unfriendly as we imagined.   He also said he had told Specky

that Germany had only herself to thank for any hostility on our part, as her behaviour to us in the Boer War was unpardonable.

As we parted he said, " So far as my descent goes I suppose I am hardly an Anglo-Saxon, but I firmly believe that our two countries must stand together.'

That same evening he had dining with him a man called Morgan, who has lately come from China.   He showed Morgan the miniature and talked freely about it.   On Sunday Morgan called on us and at once began about the President's great pleasure at receiving it.   ' Specky's ' wife was having tea with us, and though I turned the conversation she doubtless heard. I told Hay yesterday, and he laughed and said, ' The President can no more help talking about anything that pleases him than he can help breathing.   You may be certain he has talked about it freely to half a dozen people.'   Hay told me the letter had been a great pleasure to the President, and was most happily worded.

While I was with the President, I took one of the very rare chances which he gave me, to tell him the King had been much pleased at the language he had used in his former interviews with me.   I also told him what you had said about the tele-grams being kept strictly secret.   He said ' Ah, that's right— that's right.   As long as they stick to that I shall feel quite comfortable.   Whatever you do, don't let anything get round to Germany.' "

The letter to Mrs. Roosevelt (already quoted in part), written after the President had been formally inaugurated, resumes the story of Russian affairs.   The decisive land battle had been fought and lost at Mukden, where after three weeks' fighting the Russians retreated under cover of a dust storm on March 9.

ST. PETERSBURG,
March 13, 1905.

" The great day is passed.[1]   I read the accounts—you may guess with what interest.   I think the inaugural splendid and am reminded of the litany, ' *In all time of our tribulation, in all time of our wealth, Good Lord deliver us.*'   America has to prove not only in her tribulation but in her prosperity that the great experiment of Government by the people is not a failure. I have always thought Theodore's special mission was to form character, and to make history that way—not so much by making the law as by forming the man behind the law.

[1] That of Roosevelt's inauguration for his term of the Presidency.

About the same time we have read the manifesto of the Czar in which he tells us he is determined to maintain the contrary principle to free Government, and to take his stand on that. We shall see with what results. He too is on trial. This manifesto [1] was his own heartfelt expression of conviction. The Ministers were in despair. They had not been consulted and read it in the train as they went down to the Council at Tsarskoe. One after another they made their speeches. The Minister of the Interior said he had such news from the country that unless the Czar consented to issue the rescript promising a constitution —prepared already for several days—he would have to resign. The Finance Minister said he could not place a loan in France without the promise of a constitution, and would also have to resign. At last the Emperor yielded and signed. But it is generally understood that nothing will be done for months. In the meanwhile the manifesto is read in all the Churches by order of the Holy Synod, and *without* the rescript. Appeal is made to ' the people ' against the reformers—who are repre- sented as traitors to Russia and the Holy Czar. The peasant movement against the proprietors is due to the operations of the police, who have told the peasants that the landlords want to restore serfdom. The police are organizing bands of hooligans in the principal towns to terrorize the reformers and there is a strong party among the workmen against reform and in favour of the Czar. At a council held yesterday it was resolved to continue the war, and more reservists will be called up. This means war to the knife with Reform.

It cannot be said that the cause of reform, advocated by about one million out of a people of 140 millions, has much chance of success. But what is certain is that the whole fabric of society is falling, and that disorders are increasing and that the only hope of the Government now lies in allying itself with the ignorant masses against the thinking element—which is not an element which can organise or act. The only people who are capable of action are the bombists, and the future lies with them.

What this country is now, you may gather from a lunch I had the other day. The hostess had lost her brother, Count Keller, killed in a Russian defeat. Her nephew was on the way to Mukden. She had no notion what had happened there, though

[1] Two documents were published on March 3. The earlier was a manifesto which exhorted the people to co-operate with the autocratic might of the Czar . . . " in the great and sacred task of overcoming the foreign foe and of eradicating revolt at home.'' The second was a rescript which announced that the Czar would '' convene the best men, possessing the confidence of the people, and elected by them to take part in the elaboration and consider- ation of legislative measures.''

Mukden had already fallen.   She did not know whether she was
ruined.   Armed bands of peasants, headed by priests with
eikons, had burned the houses of two of her country neighbours.
A lady working in one of the military hospitals said that some of
her cured patients were hanging about penniless, as the Government had not given them permission to return to their homes
and gave them no money.   One of the guests had seen from his
window an officer pursuing a woman and cutting her down with
his sword.   A mill owner told me that in case of difficulty he
had no one to whom to apply.   The chief of police referred him
to the Minister of the Interior, and he to the Minister of Finance.
Crowds of carriages, with women come to ask for news of their
husbands, were round the office of the General Staff on Friday
and Saturday.   People were told the ' Office was shut because
of the Carnival.'   It was shut for three days while the battle
was at its hottest.   On Saturday, the last day of the Carnival,
all the restaurants were full of officers with their female friends
—many of them drunk.   The theatres are full as usual.   People
don't even buy the papers in the streets.   There is no news in
them.   On Friday the papers appeared with the headings,
' No telegrams from Mukden,' and there was literally no
news whatever.   The Emperor had not given permission to
publish.

In the spring the misery of the people will be at its height
because they have had to sell all their foodstuffs to pay taxes
and the new crops will not be gathered.   There are thousands of
women and children without support.   The men are at the war.
No news comes as to whether the men are alive or dead.   Even
as to officers, nothing is known for weeks and weeks.   Everyone
has stories of frightful peculation.   The officers are accused of
robbing the men and the railway officials of robbing the trains.
Whole trains are simply lost and a commission has been sent
along the line to try and find the missing pieces of a submarine.
Even a battery of artillery *disappeared* and was only found
after some time—hidden away in a siding.

A poor lady I was talking to the other day burst into tears
and said that she could not bear to think of her country.   Her
daughter was in a country district menaced with a jacquerie and
her son had disappeared in Manchuria.   And in the whole of
Russia, except perhaps Witte—there is not a single *man* ; and
Witte is merely a self-seeker and is believed by everyone to be
merely waiting his chance.   It is not like the French Revolution—a struggle for an idea : there is no dominant idea and no
one except the assassins is prepared to sacrifice anything for an
idea.   And politics are now reduced to a war between the

Assassins and the Autocracy, which still disposes of vast forces in the country and an army perfectly willing to fire on women and children.

As to the terrible Sunday,[1] the *mot d'ordre* of courtiers and diplomats is that it was ' inevitable and a very good lesson.' The streets were ' quite quiet ' an hour afterwards. That may be, but for four days it was known that a demonstration would take place and nothing was done to prevent it. The police were told to do nothing. Notices were posted at the last moment—which few people could read. The crowds were permitted to assemble. They believed they would see the Czar. In one or two cases the soldiers, commanded by sensible officers, dispersed the crowd in a harmless way by threatening them with bayonets and treading on their toes—or a squadron riding slowly drove the crowd before them. The firing *may* have been necessary, but the Government had no right to allow the people to collect. It looked so much as if they really intended to ' give them a lesson.' There is absolutely no proof that the people were armed ; and why did so many bring their wives and children ?

But it is quite true that before long a ' lesson ' will be indeed necessary, for there is every sign of the outbreak of disorders of a fearful description—a general breakdown of all order throughout the country. The Government for centuries has lived by the poverty and ignorance of the masses ; and the country and especially the educated people will have to pay for it. In the meanwhile the Emperor lives quietly, a prisoner like the Sultan at Yildiz, in his palace garden ; and plays with his baby and will hear nothing but baby talk. If you come with disagreeable truths, he listens and says nothing. His ideas, if he has any, are to maintain the autocracy undiminished and to continue the war until he has gained the ' mastery of the Pacific.' Doesn't the expression sound odd ? Where is America ? Has she no interest in the Pacific ? Or is she to confine her interests to Russia's care ? It is really stupendous.

In the meanwhile all the talk is of a palace revolution, and of worse.

I saw Meyer [2] at Berlin. I liked him very much. He is sure of a good reception here, as the Kaiser has written about him, and the Grand Duke Vladimir has seen and admired Mrs. Meyer at Homburg. He evidently has a good head and won't be in anyone's pocket. It is difficult, however, to resist a

---

[1] January 31, 1905, when the procession of strikers (headed by Father Gapon) to the Winter Palace was riddled with rifle-fire.

[2] Successor to McCormick as American Ambassador at St. Petersburg.

Grand Duke in Petersburg.   I don't know any, so I am free from temptation."

It is necessary now to indicate the formidable European complications which developed from the change in Russia's position.

The battle of Mukden made it plain that Russia could not win ; but it was by no means certain that Japan could force her to accept defeat, for the change of positions shortened the Russian line of communications appreciably, while Japan lost much of her original advantage in fighting near her base.   Russia might prolong the struggle almost indefinitely.   But while she did, her resources were not available for contest with any continental power.   She might engage England in a Central Asian conflict, where only small forces could be employed ; and such a war would be less remote from her centre than it would be from England's.   Yet while she could injure England, she could not help her ally, France ; and the German Emperor saw his opportunity to bid for the dictatorship of Europe.

Morocco was at this period, owing to internal dissensions, a country practically without any effective government.   By the Anglo-French agreement of April 1904, it was recognised that France had special interests in Morocco, since disturbances there spread to her Algerian territory ; and Britain agreed that France should be free to intervene to maintain order and to assist the Sultan in carrying out reforms. The claims of Spain in the north of the country were recognised by both parties to the agreement—which was ratified by the French Chambers in November 1904.   M. Delcassé, the Foreign Minister, was reputed to be the chief author of the *entente*, from which had issued this agreement.

In 1904 Germany had made no protest.   But when the defeat at Mukden made it finally clear that Russia was at least temporarily crippled, an obedient German press rang with denunciations of the French mission to Fez in March 1905, which proposed to assist in framing a scheme of border police and of economic reforms.   There was undoubtedly strong resentment among the Moors, who naturally regarded France as a menace to their unchartered freedom.   The German Emperor announced his intention to visit Morocco, and landed at Tangier on March 31, 1905.   He was received as a protector of Moorish interests, and the German Minister at Tangier was sent on a mission to Fez.   On May 28 the Sultan rejected the proposed French scheme of reforms, and proposed a Conference of the powers to discuss the affairs of Morocco.   Germany at once accepted ; England declined.   Delcassé was disposed to refuse, but by this time the chancelleries were full of rumours ; and on June 6 Delcassé tendered his resignation, which was accepted, because it was understood that he was a *persona ingrata* to Germany.   Yet, soon after this public submission, threats were still used by the German Chancellor, who was then in Paris ; and on July 10 it was announced that France consented to take part in the Conference.   It was, no doubt, hoped that France would reflect that her *entente* with England was a poor defence against the might of Germany.

The Kaiser had succeeded in inflicting humiliation on the French, but he had roused bitter hostility in England. Queen Alexandra, then on a visit to Spain, emphasised her feelings by leaving Gibraltar two or three hours before the German Imperial party were due to come there. King Edward on his part refused to send any nearer relative than Prince Arthur of Connaught to the Crown Prince's wedding in June.

Meanwhile, word was current already of approaching separation between Sweden and Norway—countries whose integrity had been guaranteed by England and France in 1855. Intrigues were said to be afoot to put a German on the Norwegian throne.

But for Germany, as for England, the immediate problem concerned future relations with the new power that had so dramatically asserted itself. Germany was said to aim at a Japanese alliance—and also to entertain the idea of coming in as mediator between the combatants. England, on the other hand, had to consider whether her existing alliance should be renewed or modified. Beyond question it had served Japan in this war; but the very effect of Japan's victory in the Far East might tend to create danger for England in Central Asia. Even after the news of the Baltic fleet's destruction at Tsushima, Lord Kitchener wrote to Spring Rice that there were moves in Seistan which looked as if a forward adventurous policy were in the ascendant; and that guns and strong reinforcements had been sent to the eastern frontier of Bokhara. Under her Treaty with England, Japan need not move a finger to support England in Central Asia, so long as the assailant was a single power. In such a case, her benevolent neutrality would not be of much value.

According to Spring Rice, not only British but German opinion counted with certainty on Japan's victory from March onwards; and as early as March, rumours spread that President Roosevelt had been asked to mediate and had expressed his willingness to do so. But no definite step towards intervention was taken till Russia's last hope of an effective counterblow disappeared when Rozhdestvensky's fleet was annihilated on May 27, 1905, at Tsushima.

Yet even then Russia's military lines of communication remained intact; the Russian army though defeated was not destroyed, and many in Russia believed that victory was still possible.

Spring Rice's letters to Roosevelt's Secretary of State describe the events of this time.

ST. PETERSBURG, March 15, 1905.

" DEAR MR. HAY,

The Russian Government thinks it informs the public sufficiently to-day as to the events at Mukden by announcing that a German General has fallen from his horse, and that no news of further fighting has reached headquarters. This does not entirely allay anxiety.   There was a war counsel at Tsar-skoe the day before yesterday.   A member who was present said immediately afterwards that ' all he could say was that there was no hope of peace.'   The French bankers here say, ' If this is so, ruin is certain.'   The obvious course is for France to refuse a new loan, which would bring the war to an end.   Without at least 50 million sterling at once, the war cannot be continued for another year, and a whole year is necessary if, as is now intended, a new army is to be mobilized and sent to the East.   This, of course, is from the monetary point of view.   From the internal political point of view, a new mobilization would almost certainly be disastrous.

It appears that the reform party are not sanguine.   There are few men and there is no organization.   The labourers will get sick of political strikes.   They have got practically all they wanted from the employers whom they informed yesterday they intended to remain quiet till after Easter when they would be called out again to ' make political demands.'   In the meantime the police will inform them that they are being made fools of—which is true.   A desperate minority may arm themselves with bombs and fight.   But this can hardly lead to a constitutional reform.   In the country districts, disorder grows apace.   But this is not a reform movement.   The evidence tends to prove that it was started by the police to punish the landlords for opposing autocracy.   The proclamations circulated among the peasants are disowned by the reformers.   They say the Government agents themselves are issuing them.   In the Caucasus, the Government actually armed the Mussulmans and turned them against the Armenians, whom they were allowed to murder.   In every town the blackguards are being organized and paid by the police to persecute the ' intelligence,' *i.e.* students, doctors and other sorts of reformers.   The same is true of the Baltic provinces of Finland.   The Government is with ' the people ' against the ' traitors,' *i.e.* the reformers. . . .   Tolstoi himself does not expect that the reform movement will succeed.   Indeed, how can it, in a country where less than one out of a hundred understands what reform means ?   Putting all this together, we have the likelihood of an enormous jacquerie, led by the Government, in which perhaps all Government and order will be swallowed up.   The result will not be anything like the French revolution but something more resembling the Boxer movement in China.   This is the danger for Europe, although not for years.   You will remain in peaceful enjoyment of a very well-deserved happiness.   Germany is very nearly concerned.   The Kaiser sent a letter to the Czar by the Prince of Prussia, urging him to make peace and look after his own country. The Czar returned a categorical negative, and the Kaiser so informed the General Staff. The popular movement in Russia is economically and politically dangerous to Germany, who will be obliged to find some other support than Russia. With this the influence of Germany here will be compromised and probably the sympathy of the German Government lost. When I was in Berlin two things were evident ; the Kaiser's violent love-making to Tower [1] and Meyer ; and the conviction of the Japanese Minister that Germany was really and in truth the friend of Japan. Thus there is every appearance of a radical change in Germany's policy, and that she will join herself for the time at any rate to America's point of view. You are sure of her vote for the present. The change probably took place when the General Staff had reported that Russia could not win, and when Prince Frederick Leopold brought back the answer that Russia would not make peace (a month ago). France will probably be cured of her sympathies with Russia, and there will be a new era—perhaps the era of the Russian revolution. What an enormous and portentous change wrought by Japan—a nation which did not exist forty years ago.

I repeat it ; most people here seem to think that in the spring there will be here—not reform, but a violent convulsion, anti-law, anti-order, anti-foreign. They think it will be terrible. This Government has for years exploited the ignorance of the people and has now to take the consequences."

In regard to what follows, it must be recalled that while the interests of Great Britain and of the United States lay in the same direction, the United States had much greater freedom of initiative than Great Britain, Japan's ally.

"In London I found Lord Lansdowne intensely interested at what he heard [2] and very much rejoiced. Chamberlain spoke with the greatest earnestness—indeed his language was very striking. He regarded a good and complete understanding with America as the corner-stone of English policy. Odd from him. Lord Lansdowne was nervous as to outward manifestations· which he was anxious to avoid. But he had absolute confidence in you, as to the diplomatic side of the question. The King was (as you know) anxious and more than anxious to do everything in his power, and in fact his enthusiasm had to be damped by constitutional reminders. I should think you

[1] American Ambassador in Berlin.
[2] As to Roosevelt's attitude.

could be certain that we will follow your lead and that you will find us ready and anxious to take any action which you suggest beforehand. I should recommend suggesting beforehand. Meyer will find a most sympathetic colleague in Hardinge here ; Hardinge has many good sources of information, long knowledge of Russia, and would be very useful.

Things move so fast here that we are really ignorant of what the next week will bring. There is likely to be a prairie fire and we shall have to begin ploughing fireguards round our farm. It is not impossible that there will be a palace revolution. Egalité's is a part attributed to the Grand Duke Alexander Michaelovitch, son of a Jew of the name of Meyer who had the good graces of a Grand Duchess, and intelligent in consequence. He hates the Vladimirs. The Vladimirs are out of it, as he is old and broken and the Czar doesn't consult him. Boris and Cyril are loathed, also they are incompetent. Witte is in disgrace—universally distrusted, by Autocrats and Liberals alike—but the only strong man. What is wanted is a man. And Witte appears to be the only one. If a man does not come forward, the results may be sufficiently surprising.

The next post brought the bad news of Hay's breakdown in health and migration to a water cure in Germany. Spring Rice wrote :

March 29, 1905.

" I only hope the voyage will do you lots of good. But your departure from Washington just now is a universal calamity and it is a great blow to all right-thinking people, as you had all the strings in your hand ; and, as we are in the coach, it is rather an anxious moment. By the time you get this, we shall, of course, have moved a good many steps further. At present all that is known is that the Emperor is not disinclined to peace, and that he is only hesitating as to how he is to express his high decision. But war came because peace came to an end, and I suppose peace will come because war will come to an end. The Government doesn't take decisions, and it is no wonder when one sees what the Government is. The Foreign Minister hasn't talked politics with anyone (except about Bulgaria) for weeks. He says the East is not his province—it is still the Viceroy Alexeieff's. The Government has just issued regulations for the preservation of forests in the peninsula of Dalny, so we may suppose the war is to proceed until Dalny is retaken. Witte, ex-Finance Minister, wrote and spoke to all and sundry in favour of peace—but everyone answers that it must depend on the Emperor's orders. As the Emperor lives surrounded by courtiers and generals and his troops in his palace at Tsarskoe, and only sees Ministers once a week, there isn't much to be done with him.   However, we hope that facts will reach home at last.

The general talk is that there will be a sort of voluntary congress of reformers here in the spring, and that if this is opposed by the Government, resort will then be had to bombs. Meanwhile anarchy is increasing everywhere.   The odd thing is that the police seem to be taking part with the strikers and peasants—anything to punish the reformers, who are mostly the rich and educated.   This country rather reminds me of what Lord Chesterfield said about himself and Lord Lyttelton— ' We have both been dead for some years, but we don't want to have it known.'   It *is* getting known now, however, by the smell.   Poor people !   The workmen are striking, the students are striking, the Ministers struck when the Emperor published his manifesto—and now all that remains is that the Emperor should strike too.   It looks rather as if he had.   The Bourse struck to-day, and forced the funds down 5 points.   This is to continue till the Government yields."

Hay replied to these letters from Nervi on April 12, 1905.

" MY DEAR SPRING RICE,
    . . . After a month of silence on board the steamer and a fort-night of groping in the twilight of Italian and French papers, it was a great comfort to receive so clear and intelligent an exposition of affairs as your letters contained.

The greatest surprise I have had in years was on arriving in Genoa to find that nothing important had happened while we were at sea.   If this check in acceleration continues a while, I may get back to Washington before the end of the world. . . .

I shall go to Nauheim in a few days for a cure of a month, and then expect to be able to return to my amusing task of pouring water into my sieve.

Adams, the angel, came with us and has not yet deserted us.

Mrs. Hay and he send their love, and I am more grateful than you can imagine for your letters, which are worth their weight in diamonds. . . . "

At Nauheim Hay received another letter from Spring Rice, which unluckily is not in the correspondence, and to this he replied on May 1, 1905 :

" I received from Jack Carter your letter about the debacle of the ice in the Neva and kindred matters, and was, as usual, much edified and correspondingly grateful.

I believe you are already aware of our views about the Moroccan question, which are the same as yours—but the inferences you draw as to the final outcome of the present discussion, derived from the diminished quotation of the Alliance Russe, are very interesting. What a cold-blooded calculator this seemingly reckless orator is ![1] When you reflect that but for the encouragement he gave his unhappy cousin, there would probably have been no war, it must be maddening to Tsarkoe Selo to see his present attitude of detachment, and his prowl on the battlefield for spoils. . . . "

The German waters proving of no avail, Hay took his passage home in June, passing through England. Spring Rice was then there, having been summoned by the Foreign Office for consultation, since the event of Roosevelt's intervention to make peace was foreseen. They met and, as will be seen later, arranged for freer consultation between the British and American Ambassadors at St. Petersburg. Hay's last note was written on board ship :

R.M.S. BALTIC, June 8, 1905.

" Your telegram reached us at Liverpool. We thank you for your kind remembrance. I am glad that through the gloom of my furtive flitting through London there pierced the cheery ray of my meeting with you. . . . "

Less than a month later came the news of his death. So passes out of this record one of the most sympathetic and charming among Spring Rice's friends. He had begun public life in 1860—the year after Spring Rice was born—as private secretary to Lincoln, when it was still a question whether the United States would remain united. He ended it as Roosevelt's Secretary of State, when America, already an imperial nation, was beginning to act as arbitress between the great powers of the modern world. There needs no apology for stressing the value set by such a man on the help given to him and to his chief by the English diplomat who was the friend of both.

Spring Rice continued to keep the President in touch with the Russian situation as he saw it, in all its bearings. His despatches, as before, were not personally addressed to the President.

March 29, 1905.

" DEAR MRS. ROOSEVELT,

Here things go their course, which is a sad one. It is quite true that anarchy is growing and incidents abound. It would be difficult to give an idea of the disintegration which is taking place. It is like a great animal dead and rotting, with jackals tugging at its tough hide. The peasants are going round in

[1] The Kaiser Wilhelm.

bands destroying and sometimes killing. " I can't let my wife go to the country this year "—one hears on all sides. The German landlords [1] characteristically have armed themselves and their servants and say composedly, ' Come on if you like,' and the peasants *don't* come on, after the first time. In South Russia the landlords fly to the towns or call for the police who hide themselves. Then comes a regiment and the peasant movement disappears—to reappear elsewhere. It is all done with system. A bonfire is lighted to call the peasants together. They systematically loot everything and go away.

As for the police, they are trying to persuade the workmen and peasants that the Autocracy is their real friend.

Autocracy has lived by *fear* and seems to have destroyed every other feeling—now, it is by fear that Autocracy is being attacked. Nobody seems to be able to appeal effectively to respect for law or to a sense of duty. The most ardent reformers acknowledge this. It is a return to primitive anarchy which seems to be going on now and the only possible issue is a new, but reformed, Autocracy.

Everyone seems to expect a great row in the spring. Perhaps it won't take place. But what is to be done ? Not one single reform has been carried out yet. The police do exactly what they like. Indeed, since Plehve's death they seem to be more out of hand and more outrageous . The schools and universities are shut up. The mill hands won't work. The Ministers themselves are resigning every day—and the Tsar won't accept their resignations. The centre of Government and source of power is hidden in his palace surrounded by his soldiers and spies— and no one can get at him to tell him the truth.

Witte, who is a strong man and in earnest, thought the matter out and wrote him a letter in which he described the state of things in the country in the most forcible language, and said that the only hope for the country was peace ; and that the Emperor alone could make peace. Witte used such language that, as he said—the Emperor must either take his advice or dismiss him. He did neither—but a sort of indirect message arrived from the Palace—that the Emperor was thinking it over. Witte comes to us and entreats the Embassy to tell the King that a slight push might bring the Emperor over to the peace side of the fence. Our Ambassador gives the message, with all reserve. Now we are told that there are peace rumours in the air and that something has happened in the highest circles. The Emperor is inclined to peace and peace will be made. The soldiers and

[1] In Lithuania and that region most of the landowners were German, though Russian subjects.

courtiers and the War Office and Admiralty all deny that Russia can ever so demean herself as to ask for peace from the yellow dwarf—without a signal victory of her arms.   But there are persistent rumours all the same.   You will know the truth by the time you get this letter.

The policy which finds most favour here is to make an alliance with Japan on the basis of an understanding in Northern China.   This would give Japan the needed guarantee for a permanent peace.   Otherwise peace would mean a truce, to be spent by Russia in acquiring an enormous and overpowering navy with which she could get command of the sea.   In that case, all Japan's acquisitions on the mainland would become absolutely valueless.   On the other hand, if Russia could persuade Japan to enter into a friendly understanding with her for the division of spheres of interest and the common exploitation of China, Japan might look on this as a sufficient guarantee. Japan has the choice between this policy and a policy of an alliance with England to secure her naval communications. As a return, she would promise assistance by land if India was attacked.   The basis of the understanding would be the maintenance of the *status quo*, or present situation—that is, the open door and the integrity of China.   But America wouldn't make such a Treaty, and the new Government in England [1] might be unwilling to make one either, for fear of 'foreign entanglements.' So Japan will either have to lean on the support of Russia's promises, or to content herself with the hope that the English Navy will, in the end, not allow the Japanese Navy to be destroyed.   Whether this will content her or not is another question.

I hear the President thinks I fear he will fall under the Kaiser's influence.   I don't, but I have every reason to know how overpowering the Kaiser's influence is.   The great struggle which the Tsar has always made has been to resist it ; and he has finally fallen under it, or did, to a great extent.   The Kaiser has so many overpowering qualities and I can't help admiring him immensely.   If you saw him riding through Berlin with his staff, in uniform, you would see what a personality he is ; in talking, he is quite irresistible.   Perhaps in writing too.   He is a man of great ideas too, but as I believe wrong ideas, because they are based on pure selfishness, or a patriotism which is enlarged selfishness.   You know that I don't think *your* patriotism enlarged selfishness, because the base of it is—to make one's own nation play that part in the world's work which it

---

[1] A General Election was impending and a Liberal victory was already regarded on both sides as sure.

was made for, and to do it well—and to help other nations to do theirs—and to promote good feeling and the happiness of nations. But this was not Bismarck's policy, perhaps because of the fearful dangers of the situation of Germany. His policy was to set other people by the ears, and to think Germany's, advantage was the rule of right and wrong. And I profoundly distrust and dislike the monarchical feeling which is at the bottom of the Kaiser's temperament—the profound contempt for common persons except so far as they contribute to the monarch's glory and comfort. The Germans are having their doubts. I asked a very clever man in Berlin if the Germans weren't very proud of their Kaiser. He said, ' His reputation is chiefly *European*,' and smiled.

He has been making up to the French lately, and without success. The result was that he published a threatening article in the official paper, and is going to Morocco to show the French that they must reckon with him. I should think he would like to head a sort of European coalition against something or other. He is always finding a new something. Once it was the yellow peril. Then it was the American peril. Then it was England. I think the next will be the social peril from Russia—and here he is entirely in the right. The danger of a Russian revolution is not to be sneezed at, and the army of Germany is a priceless bulwark for Europe. The object of us all should be to have no deadly quarrel in Western Europe which should make it impossible to unite if we were really seriously threatened.

I like to think, turning to the other side of the world, that the forces of civilisation and freedom and equal dealing are likely to be marshalled together under the guidance and inspiration of the American President. Lord, what a happy person I shall be when I see it.

The reform party seem to have given up hope of serious reforms on the part of the Government. They will hold a meeting of *their own* in St. Petersburg and if the Government disperse it by force they will appeal to force. These are brave words. At the back of them are *bombs*, which is not a nice prospect."

April 26, 1905.

" DEAR MRS. ROOSEVELT,

We are to be murdered on Easter Monday, sure. I hear it from the best and highest authority. I wish I had learnt a little more Ju-jitsu. In the meantime things are interesting. I don't believe in a revolution but there seems to be a general breakdown.

The main interest here is, of course, the Admiral.[1]   Everything depends on his proceedings—reform, peace, the Emperor's life.   Poor man, what a position!   The Germans have taken advantage of the Russians being taken up to fall on the French.[2] It is rather hard.   I see that they are asking your President to join in a Conference which will bring the French to order.   I hope he won't.   The break up of Russia is having a tremendous effect in Europe.   It is just like the departure of a big bully from a school.   The other bullies have such a good time and kick the little boys.   Did you realise that France really is a little boy in comparison with Germany, simply from not having children enough?   She can't fight, and England and Italy her new friends have such small armies that we can't protect her.   So Germany can do pretty much what she pleases, unless she is ashamed.   It makes it look as if times would be very interesting in Europe in the next ten years.

I spoke with a Chilian just back from Mukden.   He said the military attachés thought the Russians were to the Japanese as four to two.   The fault was the *moral*.   They didn't like attacking, and men and officers had no heart in it.   The Japs were wonderful.   He said the only difference between the false and the true attack was that the false attack was made with an insufficient number of troops.   The fervour and ferocity was the same.   He said war was an awful and cruel thing and that such a war as this, if one saw it near, made one think everyone who began a war a criminal.   And yet. . . .

C. S. R."

Roosevelt replied in person:

WHITE HOUSE, May 13, 1905.

" DEAR CECIL,

Of course, in a way I suppose it is natural that my English friends generally, from the King down, should think I was under the influence of the Kaiser, but you ought to know better, old man.   There is much that I admire about the Kaiser and there is more that I admire about the German people.   But the German people are too completely under his rule for me to be able to disassociate them from him; and he himself is altogether too jumpy, too volatile in his policies, too lacking in the power of continuous and sustained thought and action for me to feel that he is in any way such a man as, for instance, Taft or Root. You might as well talk of my being under the influence of Bryan.   I very sincerely wish I could get England and Germany

[1] Rozhdestvensky, with the Fleet, then approaching Japanese waters.
[2] In Morocco.

into friendly relations. While my business is to look primarily after the interests of my own country, I feel that I help this country instead of hurting it when I try to benefit other countries. I do not intend for a moment to be improperly meek about it. I have steadfastly preached a big navy, and I have with equal steadfastness seen that our navy is practised until I have reason to believe that, ship for ship, it is as efficient as any. I do not believe that, as things are now in the world, any nation can rely upon inoffensiveness for safety. Neither do I believe that it can rely upon alliance with any other nation for safety. My object is to keep America in trim, so that fighting her shall be too expensive and dangerous a task to likely be undertaken by anybody ; and I shall try at the same time to make her act in a spirit of such justice and good-will toward others as will prevent anyone taking such a risk lightly, and will, if possible, help a little toward a general attitude of peacefulness and righteousness in the world at large. I have tried to behave in this way toward England primarily, and also toward France and Germany and toward Japan. As for Russia, I like the Russian people and earnestly hope for their future welfare, but I agree with all you say as to the Russian system of government ; I loathe it.

Now, in treating with the Kaiser I have simply applied in his special case my general rules. In one of your last letters you speak of the German army as being a bulwark for civilisation against disorder in view of the break-up in Russian affairs. I doubt if I really have as strong a feeling for Germany as this that you thus by implication express. I wish her well. I wish the Kaiser well. I should never dream of counting on his friendship for this country. He respects us because he thinks that for a sufficient object and on our own terms we would fight, and that we have a pretty good navy with which to fight. I shall hope that on these terms I can keep the respect not merely of Berlin, but of St. Petersburg and Tokio both. I know that except on these terms the respect of any one of the three cannot be kept. But by combining a real friendliness of attitude with ability to hold our own in the event of trouble coming, I shall hope to keep on good terms with all, and to lend some assistance to Japan in the present war, in which I think she is right. The Kaiser has so far acted with me in the Far East. I do not for one moment believe that he has any long-settled and well-thought out plans of attack upon England, such as Bismarck developed, first as regards Austria, and then as regards France. He is, and I think your people ought to be able to see it, altogether too jumpy and too erratic to think out

and carry out any such policy.   If England ever has trouble
with Germany, I think it will come from some unreasoning
panic which will inspire each to attack the other for fear of
being attacked itself.   I get exasperated with the Kaiser
because of his sudden vagaries like this Morocco policy, or like
his speech about the yellow peril the other day—a speech
worthy of any fool congressman ; and I cannot, of course, follow
or take too seriously a man whose policy is one of such violent
and often wholly irrational zigzags.   But I don't see why you
should be afraid of him.   You have told me that he would like
to make a continental coalition against England.   He may now
and then have dreamed of such a coalition ; and only last
December your people were fully convinced he intended to
make immediate war on them.   But it is perfectly obvious that
he had no such thought, or he would never have mortally
insulted France by his attitude about Morocco.   If the Kaiser
ever causes trouble, it will be from jumpiness and not because
of long-thought out and deliberate purpose.   In other words he
is much more apt to be an exasperating and unpleasant than a
dangerous neighbour.   I have been reading de La Gorce's
Histoire du Second Empire, and I can imagine no greater contrast
than that offered by Bismarck's policy from '63 to '71, with that
of the Kaiser during the last eight years, the only ones in which
I have watched him closely.

To turn to matters of more immediate importance, I am, of
course, watching to see what the Russian and Japanese fleets
will do in eastern waters.   France has obligingly given the
Russians a base, but she may have to take it away from them.
The Russian fleet is materially somewhat stronger than the
Japanese.   My own belief is that the Japanese superiority in
morals and training will more than offset this.   But I am not
sure, and I wish that peace would come.   Personally I wish
that Japan had made peace on the conditions she originally
thought of after Mukden was fought ; as I pointed out to her
Government, a few months extra war would eat up all the
indemnity she could possibly expect Russia to pay.   Just at
the moment, Russia is riding a high horse and will not talk
peace."

Another letter from the President was dated May 25.   It was
chiefly concerned with a report (through the German Embassy) that
Spring Rice was quoted as alleging the existence of a Russo-German
alliance directed against Japan and against England.   " I told him I
doubted if you had ever made any such statement," Roosevelt wrote.
The conclusion of the letter shows him to be marking time till the
approaching naval battle should be decided.

THE WHITE HOUSE, May 26, 1905.

" From over here it would look as if the Russian internal situation had temporarily quieted down.   The Russians still feel fairly confident that Rozhdestvensky's fleet is so superior to Togo's in material that they will win ; and the Japanese have certainly not done as well on sea as on land.   Nevertheless I think that Togo's fleet will possess a superiority in personnel which will offset their disadvantage in physical strength.   Undoubtedly, however, there is reason for great uncertainty on both sides as to the outcome of the conflict."

After Togo's victory President Roosevelt was approached by the Japanese Ambassador. On June 8, 1905, he issued invitations to Russia and Japan in identical terms, proposing a conference in America between representatives of the belligerents. He wrote his reflections to Spring Rice on June 16.

THE WHITE HOUSE, June 16, 1905.

" DEAR SPRINGY,

Well, it seems to me that the Russian bubble has been pretty thoroughly pricked. I thought the Japanese would defeat Rozhdestvensky ; but I had no conception, and no one else had any conception, save possibly Admiral Evans and Lord Charles Beresford, that there would be a slaughter rather than a fight, and that the Russians would really make no adequate resistance whatever. I have never been able to persuade myself that Russia was going to conquer the world at any time near enough for us to be justified in considering it, and I suppose this particular fear is now at an end everywhere.

What wonderful people the Japanese are ! They are quite as remarkable industrially as in warfare. In a dozen years the English, Americans and Germans, who now dread one another as rivals in the trade of the Pacific, will have each to dread the Japanese more than they do any other nation. In the middle of this war they have actually steadily increased their exports to China, and are proceeding in the establishment of new lines of steamers in new points of Japanese trade expansion throughout the Pacific. Their lines of steamers are not allowed to compete with one another, but each competes with some foreign line, and usually the competition is to the advantage of the Japanese. The industrial growth of the nation is as marvellous as its military growth. It is now a great power and will be a greater power. As I have always said, I cannot pretend to prophesy what the results, as they affect the United States,

Australia, and the European Powers with interests in the Pacific, will ultimately be. I believe that Japan will take its place as a great civilised power of a formidable type, and with motives and ways of thought which are not quite those of the powers of our race. My own policy is perfectly simple, though I have not the slightest idea whether I can get my country to follow it. I wish to see the United States treat the Japanese in a spirit of all possible courtesy, and with generosity and justice. At the same time I wish to see our navy constantly built up, and each ship kept at the highest possible point of efficiency as a fighting unit. If we follow this course we shall have no trouble with the Japanese or any one else. But if we bluster ; if we behave rather badly to other nations ; if we show that we regard the Japanese as an inferior and alien race, and try to treat them as we have treated the Chinese ; and if at the same time we fail to keep our navy at the highest point of efficiency and size—then we shall invite disaster.

You, of course, have seen all that I have had on hand in the matter of the peace negotiations. It has been rather worse than getting a treaty through the United States Senate. Each side has been so suspicious, and often so unreasonable, and so foolish. I am bound to say that the Kaiser has behaved admirably and has really helped me. I hope that your people are sincerely desirous of peace and will use their influence at the proper time to prevent the Japanese from asking impossible terms.

In this particular case I think that peace will be in the interest of all mankind, including both combatants. If the war goes on for a year Japan will drive Russia out of East Asia. But in such a case she will get no indemnity ; she will have the terrific strain of an extra year's loss of blood and money ; and she will have acquired a territory which will be of no use to her. On the other hand, Russia will have been pushed out of East Asia and will have suffered a humiliating loss which a century could not repair. If they now make peace, Russia giving up Saghalin and paying a reasonable indemnity—these being the two chief features of the peace, together with Japan retaining control of what she has already obtained—then we shall have Russia with the territory she possessed in East Asia a dozen years ago still practically intact, so that no unbearable humiliation and loss will have been inflicted upon her. Japan will have gained enormously by the war. At the same time each power will be in a sense the guarantor of the other's good conduct. As I told you, I do not need any such guarantee as far as the United States is concerned. In the first place, I do not believe that Japan would menace the United States in any military way ; and in the next place, if the menace comes, I believe we could be saved only by our own efforts and not by an alliance with anyone else. And I believe that the peace I am trying to get will not be only a good thing temporarily, but will be a good thing permanently. I earnestly hope that your people take the same view, and that they will not permit any feeling that they would like to see both combatants exhausted to prevent them doing all they can to bring about peace. Germany and France should make their influence felt by making Russia willing to yield what she ought to yield ; and England should make her influence felt in making the Japanese terms not so severe that Russia, instead of granting them, would prefer to continue the war."

Spring Rice replied to Roosevelt's Secretary of State—writing from London, where he was retained for consultation.

Memorandum.   July 10, 1905.
    " The President's letter of June 16, received July 9, seemed to me of such importance that I thought better to communicate it at once to Lord Lansdowne. I saw him the same day (July 9). He will see Whitelaw Reid [1] on the 12th and explain his views fully.
    In the meantime I write down what he said to me. The day before he had made a speech at the Independence Day Banquet, in which he said that the President in promoting peace was rendering the very greatest possible service to the cause of humanity. These words were spoken from his heart and represented the feeling of his own Government and, as he was convinced, of the country. English interests (apart from the general interests of humanity) suffered from the war. The object of England was to see peace established and above all a durable peace—a peace which would be satisfactory to both Russia and Japan and create a state of things in Asia which would preclude the outbreak of another war whether in the East, the South, or the West. The sooner peace is established the better for us—provided that the peace in question has the guarantees of stability—i.e. leaves no intolerable wrong behind it, demanding revenge. Lord Lansdowne read out your words, ' I hope that the English people are sincerely desirous of peace and will use their influence at the proper time to prevent the Japanese from asking impossible terms—and that they will not permit any feeling that they would like to see both combatants exhausted to prevent them doing all they can to bring about

---

[1] American Ambassador.

peace, and that England should make her influence felt in making the Japanese terms not so severe that Russia, instead of granting them, would prefer to continue the war.' He said these words exactly expressed his own sentiments and those of the King and Cabinet. These words represent his policy—but the question arises—how to bring it about ?

Our treaty with Japan, which is now in force and remains in force as long as the war lasts, binds England not to allow a hostile combination against Japan. England must not only observe the letter but the spirit of this treaty. Whatever our momentary or practical interests, our duty (and with our duty our chief and main interest) is to be absolutely and resolutely true to our plighted word. Suppose Japan to be convinced that this or that condition is essential to her safety. We cannot exercise pressure on her—even if it were our interest to do so— to waive that condition because other powers desire her to waive it. We are not in the position of an impartial friend : we are sworn allies. Whatever our personal opinion, or interests may be, we are absolutely bound to her, so long as the Treaty lasts, in the same way as one is bound to one's own country— so far as the limited territory is concerned which is in the purview of the Treaty.

France is bound to Russia by a limited Treaty which does not comprise the Far East. She can offer advice to Russia in quite a different way to that in which we can offer advice to Japan.

Germany and the United States are bound to no one and can offer impartial and friendly advice to both parties in the struggle.

You probably don't realise the immense personal prestige and power which you exercise over here. But you may be quite sure that your action in promoting peace meets with the most cordial appreciation in England, and that no grain of suspicion of your motives has ever for a moment entered into that appreciation. But you yourself will be the first to recognise the claims of honour as the first interest of nations ; and honour commands us to abstain from putting any pressure whatever on Japan to abstain even from actions which may eventually entail very severe sacrifices from us under the Treaty. But Lord Lansdowne in reading your words repeated the phrase, ' I hope the English people will use their influence *at the proper time* to prevent the Japanese from asking impossible terms which make peace impossible.' He thinks that the ' proper time ' may come if and *when* it is apparent that Japan is asking ' impossible terms which make peace impossible.' Up to the present moment, he has no information which points to this. The moment may come. When it does, he hopes the American

Government may communicate with him with absolute frankness. They can be quite sure that their opinion will receive the fullest and friendliest consideration. In speaking in general terms of our relations with Japan, he pointed out that from the very first our political interest had been to prevent the war, which must not only expose us to great dangers and to loss in Asia itself, but must seriously imperil our good understanding with France, which is the most popular event in modern times in England. But the English Government, while kept fully informed, abstained from offering advice or exercising pressure on Japan; for we did not think ourselves justified in trying to make Japan abandon what she thought were her interests in Asia because they conflicted with ours in other parts of the world. Great pressure was brought to bear on us in this direction; but, like your Government, we thought that Japan must be left to judge of her own vital interests and defend them as best she could, relying, as to other powers, upon the plighted word of England. As a result, we all but lost our agreement with France; but it would have been worse if we had broken our word, on which the value of any agreement with England depended. As the war went on, we were in constant danger of complications with Russia or of difficulties with France at a time when, owing to the losses of the South African War, peace and recuperation were of vital necessity to us; and the financial situation became more and more alarming. At the present moment, interests of every sort and description urge us to do all in our power to promote peace. If Russia is excluded from the Pacific, she must seek an exit for her energies elsewhere—in Persia, Afghanistan, or the Near East. And besides this it is a very narrow policy which sees in the ruin of Russia the interest of England. We do most sincerely desire to see the lot of the European Christians of Turkey improved; and the downfall of Russia has had the effect of encouraging the Turks till they became more than ever impossible to deal with. But the most serious aspect of the question is the general balance of power in Europe. Since 1870 the military party in Germany has twice (1875, 1887) done its best to bring on a war with France, with a view to bleed her to death, and so end once for all the cry for revenge. On both occasions the sovereigns of Russia and England appealed directly to the good old Emperor to urge him not to permit such a crime—and their appeals were backed by an immense naval and military force. On both occasions the appeals were successful. But now, the Russian army does not exist for Europe. And the English fleet cannot prevent the invasion of France. The German Government, after publicly stating that their interests in Morocco were not affected, and after a year's interval, during which occurred the crash of Russia, suddenly proclaimed that their interests were vitally threatened and must be defended, even at the risk of war.   The French people, who had no very great interest in Morocco or in the diplomatic triumphs of French Foreign Ministers, refused to incur the risk of a terrible war on account of a political scheme to which they were indifferent.   They had to yield.   As a result, it is plainly evident to the whole world, by this tremendous object lesson, that, as soon as the military power of Russia is broken by an external enemy, and that of Austria by internal dissensions, Germany is perfectly willing and able to threaten France with a war of 60 against 40 millions.   England cannot allow France to be annihilated or turned into a province of Germany, to be directed as a subservient ally against herself. In case of such an act of aggression, England, in self-defence, will have to fight, and the war will, if it does break out, be a terrible one and will mean that we must organize an immense land army to assist France against her enemy.   All this is due to the upsetting of the balance of power in Europe, which leaves France practically alone as a continental power against an enemy who has an immense numerical superiority.   It is most probable that Germany will pursue her advantage, and that in the Morocco conference it will be made evident to the world and to the French people that France must yield, or incur the immense risk of a war with the support of a power which has not an equal stake in the struggle.   So far as the small interests immediately concerned are affected, we cannot complain. Germany may think them worth fighting about and France not ; in which case France would have to yield.   But if the negotiations result in the virtual surrender of French independence and the dictation by Germany of French policy, we are of course face to face with a very great danger.   For my part, I shouldn't be sorry to see the English people convinced of the necessity of enduring the greatest sacrifices in a good cause.   We shall, I hope, take to heart your own words to your people that ' We can only be saved by our own efforts and not by an alliance with anyone else.'   At the same time, we do have a great confidence that in addition to the physical force which we provide ourselves, we shall have the moral force of believing that we are in the right, and that we retain the sympathy of men like you, whom we understand and believe in, and who, we hope, understand us.

Of course, this is written on the supposition (which we trust is false) that the policy of Germany will be guided by pure aggression.   German diplomatists at Rome and Madrid and

German financiers in Paris have definitely stated (perhaps in bluff) what German policy will be ; and there is a general feeling of alarm in Europe, much like that excited by Louis XIV. And this feeling is based on very serious grounds. Nothing, however, will persuade the English and French people to be aggressive in order to anticipate possible German aggression. That is out of the question. The danger is that their peoples, which do profoundly detest the thought of war, may be suddenly confronted with a danger which can only be met by courage, resolution, and *acts*. And here comes in the great inferiority of a free commercial people in preparedness and military organisation. Their strength is in staying power—the strength of a monarchy in striking power; and in modern warfare the first blow counts for almost everything. Herein lies the ground for our anxiety."

The reply came to Spring Rice from the President.

WHITE HOUSE, July 24, 1905.

" . . . Don't you think you go a little needlessly into heroics when you say that ' claims of honour must be recognised as the first interest of nations and that honour commands England to abstain from putting any pressure whatever upon Japan to abstain from action which may eventually entail severe sacrifices on England's part ' ? When I speak of bringing pressure to bear on Japan, I mean just such pressure as Emperor William and the French Government have sought to bring to bear upon the Czar. It either is, or ought to be, unnecessary for me to state that I should put the honourable carrying out of plighted faith as above all other considerations, national or personal. I most cordially approve of your position in stating that England must prevent anything like a hostile combination against Japan. As soon as this war broke out, I notified Germany and France in the most polite and discreet fashion that in the event of a combination against Japan to try to do what Russia, Germany and France did to her in 1894, I should promptly side with Japan and proceed to whatever length was necessary on her behalf. I, of course, knew that your Government would act in the same way, and thought it best that I should have no consultation with your people before announcing my own purpose. But I wholly fail to understand the difference in position which makes it proper for France, the ally of Russia, to urge Russia in her own interest (that is, in Russia's interest) to make peace, and which yet makes it improper for England, the ally of Japan, to urge Japan in her own interest (that is, in

Japan's interest) to make peace.   My feeling is that it is not to Japan's real interest to spend another year of bloody and costly war in securing eastern Siberia, which her people assure me she does not want, and then to find that she either has to keep it and get no money indemnity, or else exchange it for a money indemnity which, however large, would probably not more than pay for the extra year's expenditure and loss of life.   If Japan felt that she wanted East Siberia and wanted to drive the Russians west of Lake Baikal, the position would be different, and I would say that it was foolish to try for peace ; but the Japanese Government have assured me most positively that this is not what they want, and that practically the only territorial cession they wish from Russia is Saghalin, to which in my judgment they are absolutely entitled.   I think that Lansdowne and Balfour (not Chamberlain—his ideals and mine are different) ought to know (what however they must keep absolutely secret namely) that I undertook this move to bring about peace negotiations only at the request in writing of Japan, made immediately after Togo's victory.   Up to that time, I had continually advised the Russians to make peace, on the ground that it was their interest to accept defeat rather than to persist in turning defeat into overwhelming disaster.   But I took no move toward bringing about peace negotiations until I was requested to do so by Japan ; and while I purposely refused to try and find out the exact terms that Japan wanted, I received their explicit assurances that they did not want East Siberia as a whole or the acquisition of Russian territory aside from Saghalin.   I do not know what they wish about the dismantling of Vladivostock, or the surrender of the various interned Russian vessels.   Of course, they expect to succeed to Russia's rights and possessions in Manchuria and to have Korea come within their sphere of influence.

However, most of this talk of what England ought to do is academic, because I think the Japanese have probably made up their minds just what they will accept and what they won't. . . .

In my own line I am having small but irritating experiences in carrying out a wise foreign policy.   The last time I saw poor John Hay, I told him that the more I saw of the Czar and the Kaiser, the better I liked the United States Senate ; to which he was evidently inclined to respond that he drew no fine distinctions between them.   It is evident that the Senate is a very poor body to have as part of the treaty-making power.   But, of course, the business of an active politician is not to complain of defects which cannot be changed, but to do the best he can in spite of them.   Some of the people on the Pacific coast, under

the lead of the San Francisco labour unions, apparently think
this a good time to insult the Japanese.   They will not do one
thing against them while I am President—I won't let them—but
they may create an ugly feeling of distrust ; and, of course, they
are of exactly the type which positively refuses to prepare for
the trouble which they are willing to bring about.   I am having
my hands full also in endeavouring to make our people act on a
rational interpretation of the Monroe Doctrine.   No such
policy as that of the Monroe Doctrine can remain fossilized
while the nation grows.   Either it must be abandoned or it
must be modified to meet the changing needs of national life.
I believe with all my heart in the Monroe Doctrine and have, for
instance, formally notified Germany to that effect.   But I also
believe that we must make it evident on the one hand that we
do not intend to use the Monroe Doctrine as a pretence for self-
aggrandisement at the expense of the Latin-American republics,
and on the other hand that we do not intend it to be used as a
warrant for letting any of these republics remain as small bandit-
nests of a wicked and inefficient type. . . .

John Hay's death was a severe personal loss to me, entirely aside
from his position as a public man.   But after all, Springy, it is
a good thing to die in the harness at the zenith of one's fame,
with the consciousness of having lived a long, honourable and
useful life.   After we are dead, it will make not the slightest
difference whether men speak well or ill of us.   But in the days
or hours before dying, it must be pleasant to feel that you have
done your part as a man and have not yet been thrown aside as
useless, and that your children and children's children, in short
all those that are dearest to you, have just cause for pride in
your actions.

In Elihu Root I think I have the very best man in this country
for Secretary of State."

This letter disturbed Spring Rice, who forwarded it to Lord
Lansdowne with this comment, on August 6 :

" He evidently has not yet grasped the point of view that
our alliance is a specific one relating to the Far East, while
France's alliance with Russia is of a more general character
and does not include the Far East at all.   But in view of the
Kaiser's success in persuading the President that he has always
been in favour of peace, (which it was quite easy for the Kaiser
to do, since knowing the disposition of the Czar he could safely
insist on peace) it might possibly be advisable to explain in a
clear and authoritative way, to be put on record, our strong and
earnest desire for peace.   Japan herself could not object to our

telling the President that his efforts have our sincere sympathy, although, of course, Japan is the best judge of her own interests, and though, if we do offer her friendly advice, it is always with the proviso that we acknowledge her full right to refuse it if she considers it incompatible with her interests."

The negotiations at Portsmouth, New Hampshire, dragged on, the plenipotentiaries being, for Japan, Baron Komura and M. Takahira ; for Russia, Count Witte and Baron von Rosen. Dr. Dillon, the well-known British publicist who had gone from Russia to America to be present on the scene, returned to London and thence to St. Petersburg. He was always in close touch with Spring Rice, who, however, regarded him with the excessive suspicion which was one of his characteristics, except where he had given his entire confidence. In any case, it was clear that Dr. Dillon was intimate with the chief Russian negotiator, Witte—whose own position was no way assured.

On July 29 Spring Rice, then in England, wrote to Mr. Gerald Balfour, his only personal friend in the Government.

ROUNTON GRANGE, NORTHALLERTON,
July 29, 1905.

" MY DEAR BALFOUR,

I am very glad indeed you spared the time to see Dillon and I think it will be very useful that you have seen him. He has written to me privately that he does not think that peace will be arranged without an alliance, as Witte will not be able to accept the terms that Japan will think acceptable. If an alliance is out of the question, the chances of peace are slim. It would be a very satisfactory solution if Russia could be induced to enter into a compact giving Treaty sanction to existing conditions in the Continent of Asia—but if she refuses to do this, the only safe course for us is to be in such a position that Russia cannot without great risk attempt to alter those conditions to her own advantage. This is what the military arrangements and agreements of Austria secured for her in S.E. Europe, where Russia has on the whole acted correctly, not so much because she wanted to but because she had to. I saw Witte shortly before he left and his views, which he expressed quite frankly, were that, with or without intention, Germany's action had greatly contributed to the war, and that the result had been that Russia had been forced to accept Germany's terms in the Treaty of commerce, and politically, to abdicate her position in Europe. He spoke strongly, with deep feeling, no doubt accentuated by the fact that he believes the Kaiser personally hostile to himself—which I believe to be the case. The Kaiser is no doubt aware of this, and knows that Witte's mission to the United States will not in any way accord with his own policy there, and that his language to American statesmen will not be favourable to Germany. This was probably one of the reasons of the Kaiser's insisting on an interview with the Czar.[1] His information is probably the same as ours—that a peace is unlikely and an alliance (between Russia and Japan) almost out of the question. He can therefore with safety urge peace on Russia and Japan, and no doubt is doing so and informing the President of his proceedings. He will, of course, add that England is responsible for Japan's excessive demands in her desire to see hostilities prolonged. It is most important that no doubt should be allowed to remain in the American mind that we do desire peace most ardently, but that we are bound in honour not to put pressure on Japan to make such a peace as she herself considers disadvantageous. With regard to an alliance with Japan, it might well be pointed out that India is, after China, the most important export and import market for Japan, and that our free trade policy, which Russia would reverse if she succeeded us in India, is necessary to Japan economically. From this point of view, it is only fair that Japan should under certain circumstances join us in sharing the burden of defence of what after all is a possession of England, and not English soil. This aspect of the question is useful for us, should we be accused (as we shall be) of asking a yellow race to bear the burden of defending our interests—an accusation which is calculated to do us harm abroad and especially in America. You may be sure that the Kaiser will use it. His main line of attack will, however, be that the interests of the world in general are that both Russia and Japan should be allowed spheres of development in Eastern Asia, acting as counterpoises to one another : and that England by her alliance with Japan is doing all she can to exclude Russia altogether from Eastern Asia, leaving Japan sole mistress. He would say to America and France that it is quite clear that England is acting contrary to the real interests of the rest of the world, and that the only answer to her selfish policy (which she bases on fear for her Indian possessions and the desire to see them protected by a Japanese force) is a moral combination of the peaceful and disinterested nations. Russian folly is practically unlimited in its possibilities ; but experience has shown that it is quite possible by suggestion to control the most important of the many engines of government—namely the Court ; and the Kaiser probably thinks that the action of both Witte and Lamsdorff will be disregarded by the Czar, if his mind

[1] It took place on July 23, 1905, on the island of Björkö. See below, pp. 485 and 489.

can be occupied with some fixed idea instilled into him by an Imperial brother. Everything points to the fact that the internal situation is regarded by the Czar as more important than the external : and if so, then the natural friend of an autocrat is an Emperor and not a Republic. The growing influence of the young Empress—now wholly autocratic in her views—will strengthen this tendency, and we must reckon with it for the present as a serious possibility. The Russian Foreign Office is alive to the danger—very much alive, but it fights against it in vain. So should we. Unfortunately there are signs that Roosevelt, especially now that Hay is gone, may in spite of his independent mind be more and more inclined to listen to the Kaiser, so that those two important sovereign powers are likely to be under influences absolutely hostile to us. With the Czar we can do nothing, but with the President it would be very desirable, and not difficult, to keep in touch by personal intercourse between him and English visitors of sense and perseverance, and also through his friends who pass through England. I am glad to see that this has been done through Lodge and Loomis. I shall see Lodge before he leaves and it will be interesting to see the impression in his mind."

A letter to Mrs. Roosevelt from Raith, where Spring Rice was staying with Ferguson, carries on the story.

Aug. 10, 1905.

" DEAR MRS. ROOSEVELT,
    I saw the Lodges in London. The King, Arthur Balfour and Lord Lansdowne and as many of the Liberal leaders as were in London, saw him as the President's friend, and unfolded their minds to him. They all seem to have had very satisfactory interviews with him. I daresay he will have told you of his interview with Rouvier who said a very remarkable thing. Talking of the possibility that Germany might in the end force France into a war, by adopting a persistently provocative attitude he said, ' If this is the case and a war is forced upon us, as it so nearly was in 1875 and 1887, we place reliance in the sympathy of America and especially of your President who is the greatest moral influence of the age.' This is a splendid thing to have said about one, and personally I regard it as the fulfilment of an old wish of mine ; and that is to see the President acting the part of a practical and disinterested preacher and example, in the world at large as well as in America—a living influence and force for all good things.

    Here in England, we don't at all know what to make of the present position of affairs in Europe. Two of the great powers have practically disappeared so far as active intervention in European affairs is concerned, Russia and Austria. Germany is by far the most powerful of the remaining powers, and she has an old feud to settle with France. If France is attacked, there is no Russia to help her and the English Army is at present practically negligible for a continental campaign. If France is forced to accept German hegemony, England remains the only independent great power, and we are in much the same position as during the Napoleonic wars. We consider it therefore our duty to prepare for contingencies. The people won't accept compulsory military service, and without it France would have to fight alone against the German Army.

All this may be pure supposition and it is incredible that the Kaiser should deliberately bring on a war of pure aggression. But there is a strong party in Germany which desires it and there is also a strong party in France which is quite inclined to come to an arrangement with Germany rather than fight her; and the only possible arrangement which will satisfy Germany is a promise of (at least) friendly neutrality in case of a German attack on England. Of course, nobody here, except the small body of hot-heads who exist everywhere, desires to attack Germany. Our interest in peace is supreme and in fact perhaps too dominant. But we all have an uncomfortable feeling that always and everywhere we encounter the fixed and determined hostility of Germany, and that, when opportunity offers, this hostility will take an active form.

It is satisfactory that the Kaiser is showing such anxiety for peace. But he is far better informed as to the movements of the Emperor's mind than anyone else. If he believes that the Emperor will not consent to peace on certain conditions, he knows that all efforts for peace are useless unless Japan grants these conditions. For Germany it is a very serious danger if Russia is excluded from the Pacific; for then she must seek an outlet for her energies elsewhere, possibly in Europe. Germany has the same interest as we have in Russia, getting a fair field for her energies in the Far East. And the spread of revolutionary feeling in Russia is undoubtedly a danger to Germany, who has nothing to gain in Poland, where Germany is more hated than Russia. There are evident and obvious reasons for Germany to desire that Russia, who is now sufficiently weakened not to be a dangerous enemy for some time to come, should now be able to come to terms with Japan. If on the other hand she refuses to come to terms, Germany has played the honourable part as peacemaker, and stands to win in Europe, where for some time to come she will be able to play her own

game without fear of Russian interference.   It would be interesting to know the exact language held by the Emperor to the
Kaiser and vice versa.[1]   All we know is that the Emperor
returned in very good spirits and that the court people spoke
very enthusiastically of the Kaiser, and that the Emperor
immediately after published a statement showing that ' he
would never consent to dishonourable terms,' *i.e.* that he would
not consent to be excluded from the Pacific.   This certainly
looks as if the Kaiser had expressed his desire for peace, but not
such a peace as Russia would object to signing.   How interesting it would be to have a general diplomatic clearing-house where
all secrets would be revealed !   At any rate the President has
nothing to fear from such a clearing-house, as his policy is the
same to everyone.

I hope you like O'Beirne.[2]   The King and Government here
wanted to send as good a staff as possible.   He was supposed
to be our best junior.   Lindsay[3] goes too, who is one of the best
fellows I know, manly, straightforward, and as good a specimen
as we could send.   Rennie,[4] who goes soon, is a real good fellow,
as I knew in Persia where I went long expeditions with him.
The King wanted him to go as he has a high opinion of him and
also he is a friend of Durand's.   I think I ought to have been
sent and I believe it would have been a good thing for us as well
as myself.   But it is quite impossible for me to press for it
because Petersburg is so notoriously unpleasant that it is like
running away from a disagreeable post.   Besides Lord Lansdowne, who likes Durand, would look on it (perhaps) as a slight
on him.   I hope to be in Russia again in a month and to see
your Ambassador there.   How I wish it was America and not
Russia that I was going to !   But I hope some day before we are
all dead that I shall have a chance.   I enclose a memorandum
for the President which may interest you.   I wonder if he has
seen Dillon and if he has liked him ?   I think him a very
remarkable man, though I never know exactly what to make
of him.

C. A. SPRING RICE."

The enclosed Memorandum enphasised the secrecy observed in
regard to these letters.   " Nobody knows about them except the two
Balfours and Lord Lansdowne."   A reply from Lord Lansdowne

[1] After the meeting at Björkö—see supra, p. 482.

[2] H. J. O'Beirne, C.B., appointed Counsellor at the Embassy in St.
Petersburg : drowned in the Hampshire, accompanying Lord Kitchener.

[3] Sir Ronald Lindsay, K.C.B., now Permanent Under-Secretary at the
Foreign Office.

[4] E. H. Rennie became First Secretary at Washington.

commenting on Roosevelt's letter was dated Aug. 7; it merely reaffirmed the position which Spring Rice had outlined. England had every desire to see peace proclaimed, but saw no reason to hold that Japan's demands were excessive.

"I cordially concur with the President when he says that it is not to Japan's real interest to spend another year of bloody and costly war in securing Eastern Siberia. I do not for an instant believe that that is her desire, and the interesting fact mentioned by the President that she made overtures to him immediately after Togo's victory seems to me to show conclusively that she holds this view.

I shall watch the events of the next few days with intense interest, and with an earnest hope that I may be able, before I am much older, to offer to the President my best congratulations upon the conclusion of a peace which, if it is concluded, will be so largely due to his fearless efforts.

LANSDOWNE."

Peace was still uncertain when Spring Rice set out again for St. Petersburg in September, but it came. Russia recognised Japan as holding the paramount interest in Corea ; the lease of Port Arthur and its dependencies, with the railway in the Liaotong peninsula, were transferred to the victors, who retained also half the island of Saghalin which had been seized by them on July 31, 1905.

Both powers agreed to evacuate Manchuria and restore sovereignty there to China.

Public opinion in Japan had expected more from this victory over the most arrogant European power. There was rioting in Tokyo instead of rejoicing. But the publication of a new Anglo-Japanese Treaty of a closer character, by which each power bound itself to assist the other in case of an aggression on either, helped to reconcile the Japanese.

The inner story of the negotiations was now told to Spring Rice by Roosevelt who had presided over them.

Sept. 1, 1905.

" DEAR CECIL,

After the plenipotentiaries of Russia and Japan got together it became perfectly evident that they could not make peace if they did not receive outside assistance. The Russians took the ground positively that they would not surrender a foot of Saghalin or pay a cent of indemnity. The Japanese insisted that they must have both. My judgement was that the Japanese were entitled to all of Saghalin, but that they could get a small sum if they were willing to return the northern half, and that it was absurd for them to try for a heavy indemnity to

which they were not entitled.   I became convinced that I
could get at the Czar only when I sent Meyer[1] to see him ; and
this was perfectly true, for it was only after the greatest difficulty
and after a long conversation that Meyer succeeded in showing
him that he had to give up the southern half of Saghalin, the
part which the Japanese absolutely insisted upon having.   I
sent three personal cables to the Czar, but he would go no
further than this.   Meanwhile I had written to the Japanese the
following two letters :

OYSTER BAY, N.Y.,
Aug. 22, 1905.

'MY DEAR BARON KANEKO,
        I think I ought to tell you that I hear on all sides a good deal
of complaint expressed among the friends of Japan as to the
possibility of Japan's continuing the war for a large indemnity.
A prominent member of the Senate Committee on Foreign
Relations, a strong pro-Japanese man, has just written me :

> " It does not seem to me as if Japan could possibly afford
> to continue the war merely for a money indemnity.   I should
> not blame her if she broke off on the issue of obtaining the
> island of Saghalin.   But if she renews the fighting merely
> to get money, she will not get the money and she will turn
> sympathy from her in this country and elsewhere very rapidly.
> I am bound to say I do not think her case for indemnity a
> good one.   She holds no Russian territory except Saghalin,
> and that she wants to keep."

I think your Government ought to understand that there will
be at least a very considerable sentiment in America among men
who have hitherto been favourable to the Japanese, along these
lines.   The willingness to retrocede the northern half of Saghalin gives a chance to get some money, in addition to that
which is justly due for the Russian prisoners ; but I do not
think that anything like the amount advanced by Japan as
what she wants—that is, six hundred millions—should be
asked or could possibly be obtained.   You know how strongly
I have advised the Russians to make peace.   I equally strongly
advise Japan not to continue the fight for a money indemnity.
If she does, then I believe that there will be a considerable
shifting of public opinion against her.   I do not believe that
this public opinion will have any very tangible effect, but still
it should not be entirely disregarded.   Moreover, I do not
believe that the Japanese nation would achieve its ends if it

[1] Ambassador at St. Petersburg.

continued the war simply on the question of the indemnity. I think that Russia will refuse to pay and that the general sentiment of the civilised world will back her in refusing to pay the great amount asked, or anything like such an amount. Of course, if she will pay, then I have nothing to say. But if she will not pay, then you will find that after making war for another year, even though you were successful in obtaining East Siberia, you would have spent four or five hundred million dollars additional to what has already been spent, you would have spilled an immense amount of blood; and though you would have obtained East Siberia, you would have obtained something which you do not want, and Russia would be in no condition to give you any money at all. She certainly could not give you enough money to make up for the extra amount you would have spent. Of course, my judgement may be at fault in the matter ; but this is my judgment, speaking conscientiously from the standpoint of the interest of Japan as I see it. Moreover, I feel of course that every interest of civilization and humanity forbids the continuance of this war merely for a large indemnity.

This letter is, of course, strictly confidential ; but I should be glad to have you cable it to your home Government, and hope you can do so. If cabled at all, it should be done at once.

Sincerely yours,

THEODORE ROOSEVELT.'

Aug. 23, 1905.

' MY DEAR BARON KANEKO,

In supplement to what I wrote you yesterday, for the consideration of His Majesty the Japanese Emperor's envoys, let me add this.

It seems to me that it is to the interest of the great empire of Nippon now to make peace, for two reasons ; (1) self interest ; (2) the interest of the world, to which she owes a certain duty. Remember, I do not speak of continuing the war rather than give up Saghalin, which I think would be right ; but of continuing the war in order to get a great sum of money from Russia, which I think would be wrong. Of course, you may succeed in getting it ; but in my judgement even this success would be too dearly paid for ; and if you failed to get the money, no additional humiliations and losses inflicted on Russia, would repay Japan for the additional expenditure in blood, in money, in national exhaustion.

1. It is Japan's interest now to close the war. She has won the control of Corea and Manchuria ; she has doubled her own

fleet in destroying that of Russia ; she has Port Arthur, Dalny, the Manchurian railroad ; she has Saghalin. It is not worth her while to continue the war for money, when so to continue it would probably eat up more money than she could at the end get back from Russia. She will be wise now to close the war in triumph, and to take her seat as a leading member at the council of the nations.

2. Ethically it seems to me that Japan owes a duty to the world at this crisis. The civilised world looks to her to make peace ; the nations believe in her ; let her show her leadership in matters ethical no less than in matters military. The appeal is made to her in the name of all that is lofty and noble ; and to this appeal I hope she will not be deaf.

With profound regard, sincerely yours,
THEODORE ROOSEVELT.'

Whether these letters had any effect or not I can not say, but apparently they did, for at the last moment the Japanese accepted my views. Unless some unexpected hitch arises peace will now follow, and upon terms which I consider just about straight. I think the Japanese gave up more than they need to have given up when they returned the northern half of Saghalin, which I am confident I could have obtained for them— or at least which I think I could have made Russia redeem for a small sum of money. But on the whole it is all right, and I think the peace is just to Russia and Japan, and also good for England and the United States.

In my letters to you I have sometimes spoken sharply of the Kaiser. I want to say now that in these peace negotiations he has acted like a trump. He has done everything that he could to make the Czar yield and has backed me up in every way, and I thoroughly appreciate how he has behaved.

Give my love to Mrs. Springy.

Ever yours,
THEODORE ROOSEVELT."

During the months while Spring Rice was in London, events had moved rapidly towards a *rapprochement* between Russia and Germany and on July 23 Kaiser and Czar, at the Kaiser's suggestion, met at the island of Björkö. On July 24 a Treaty of Alliance was signed, to come in force on the conclusion of war with Japan. Russia pledged herself to invite France to enter the alliance. The Kaiser wrote to the Czar : " The moment the news of the new grouping becomes known, Holland, Denmark, Sweden and Norway will all be attracted to the new centre of gravity. They will revolve in the orbit of the great block of European powers—Russia, Germany, France, Austria and

Italy." Again on September 26 : " The ' Continental Combine '
flanked by America is the sole manner effectively to block the way
to the world becoming John Bull's private property." [1]

These negotiations were so secret that even the Russian Foreign
Minister was not apprised of them. When he was, he pointed out
what proved to be the fact : that France would regard the compact
with Germany as a breach of the Alliance with her. So the whole
fabric crumbled as soon as even a ray of daylight was let in. But it
will be found that Spring Rice had guessed accurately what was the
Kaiser's intention.

He wrote a chronicle of the episode, as seen from the other end, to
Mrs. Roosevelt, for the President.

ST. PETERSBURG. Sept. 26, 1905.

" I have just received here a most interesting letter from the
President which came by messenger from London. It just
missed me there, so I am sending a copy privately for A. B. and
Lord L., and for them only. You will have seen Meyer and
heard all he has to say, which will be more than I am able to tell
you. The whole history of the negotiations is astonishing and
only one man comes out of it with an absolutely clean and
straight record as chief engineer.[2]

You know that Witte was Lamsdorff's candidate for peace-
negotiator and that the Emperor strongly objected to him. So
first an old ambassador [3] in feeble health was proposed, who
refused because he wouldn't leave Paris. Then an able and
jealous diplomatist, anxious to be well at Court. Lamsdorff drew
up for him instructions, which made negotiations practically
impossible; and knowing he was poor and rather avaricious, gave
him an extremely shabby allowance. Then this man refused
and Witte became necessary as the only possible negotiator. On
his way he spread everywhere the impression that peace was
impossible—that the Emperor would never yield. He did this
in England by a series of confidential messages to the effect that
his instructions made peace out of the question. These impressions were naturally conveyed both to the Japanese and to his
own Government. The Japanese saw and believed that the
Czar meant war, and the Russian Court party were reassured
and believed peace to be impossible. The deadlock, as was
expected, came, but not till a number of ' lesser ' points had
been settled—these in reality being of great importance. The
result, however, was clear to everyone. Neither Japan nor
Russia would give way on the vital points.

[1] See Gooch's *Modern Europe*, p. 380.

[2] Roosevelt himself is meant.

[3] Mouravieff is named in other letters.

Then came the letters from the President, and the telegram [1] to Meyer telling him to demand an audience. It was impossible to refuse, as it was the Ambassador's right to have one. When once the Emperor was face to face with a man who, conciliatory and friendly as he was, knew his own mind and expressed it firmly, it was difficult—almost impossible—to meet his request with an absolute refusal. So his categorical ' No ' was tempered with the condition of half Saghalin ; and he himself, knowing his environment, asked the Ambassador to put down his words in writing, then and there, and sent instructions to Lamsdorff, to state in writing that the Ambassador's memorandum correctly represented what had been said. There it was in writing—an Imperial pledge which could not be violated without dishonour. And then the Japanese accepted the ultimatum. It was impossible to go back on the written promise, and peace was assured.

The blow was a heavy one because the Court firmly believed in the imminent victory of Russia. The forces in North Manchuria were supposed to be in splendid order, and dying to be allowed to fight. And a memorandum drawn up by a clever French financier, just home from Japan, showed clearly that Japan could not continue the war for financial reasons, as her stock of gold was exhausted. That of Russia was larger than at the beginning of the war. So Russia, on the point of victory, is compelled to make peace and that after a war in which she has gained not one single redeeming success. The autocracy, whose justification before the eyes of the people is its military efficiency, has failed even in that. And now the autocracy has to face the people.

When I returned here, I came by ship. I didn't know what had happened, and when we arrived at Cronstadt, we asked the pilot who came on board whether there was peace. He said, Yes—the Japanese had yielded everything. We asked a Customs official who said, No, the Emperor would never make peace till Japan was well beaten ; fighting was going on still. We asked a sailor who was put on guard and he didn't know— or seem to care—whether there was peace or war. As we drove through the streets, there was no excitement ; here and there a group of two or three people reading a printed proclamation, posted at the street corners, containing the Emperor's message to his army—The Japanese (having been refused all their demands) had ' begged for ' half Saghalin, which had been theirs but a few years before. The Emperor did not think it worth while to fight for such a small matter, and so he had ordered his army to stop fighting just when they were ready for a crush-

[1] From President Roosevelt.

ing blow against their redoubtable enemy.—Shortly afterwards
a communiqué appeared in the official press stating that Meyer
had made certain formal proposals which the Emperor had
definitely refused, but that His Majesty had agreed out of love
of peace, etc., to cede half Saghalin, all other demands having
been rejected.

There was no sign of enthusiasm and the police have not
' invited ' illuminations ; no one would have imagined that
any important event had occurred here.

You see that so far as regards Russia, peace was simply the
result of one interview—the second—between Meyer and the
Emperor, in which the Emperor was induced to formulate his
ultimatum from which it was impossible to recede. Having
yielded to the other demands in order not to appear obstinately
warlike, and thinking that they were of no account, as an agreement on the main demands was impossible—the Emperor was
unable to retrace his steps; and the Japanese undoubtedly (as
far as can be seen from here) did the right thing in at once accepting. The danger, of course, is the internal situation. The old
rule in Japan was that if a Minister made an unpopular treaty
he was killed. And in this case it isn't yet certain whether their
Emperor's authority may be able to override the popular will
and whether the young Japanese will submit. We shall see.
Anyhow we are living through very dangerous days and I shall
be prepared for any development there. I remember Ito
telling me before the Chinese war that it was better not to have
war ; but if war must come, he would rather the Japanese
fought an enemy abroad than each other at home. And he said
that if the people weren't allowed to fight there might very well
be another insurrection.

But, looking at the matter impartially and from without—
there seems to be no doubt that Japan acted for the best. She
ought to be secure from further fear of aggression by her
alliance with England, which gives her command of the sea and,
with the security of India, a sure source of supply from the
Continent of Asia. She would never have got the indemnity
she demanded and she would have lost the sympathies of the
world in fighting for money.

Of course we don't know what the Kaiser did in the matter
except that (as both you and the Tsar have said) he has used all
his influence for peace. The Tsar is most grateful to him—not
for urging peace, but for his tactful manner.

As far as I know, neither England nor France ventured on any
active steps. The French, like ourselves, doubted the exped-
iency, although the gain to them like ourselves by peace was

colossal. But they thought that Russia would resent their advice and that it would do no good. As you know, we thought that there were strong reasons against our formally using pressure in Tokio—though the Japanese knew perfectly well how desirous England was to see the war come to an end. I don't think, for various reasons, that the Kaiser's telegrams to the Czar had any practical effect. The practical effect was undoubtedly due to the direct influence of the President here and the language of the American Ambassador in his interviews.

The Emperor is peculiarly sensitive to personal impressions and is very suspicious. Fortunately Meyer at once impressed him favourably and the President's motives were beyond all suspicion. As I said, it seems to me, and to all of us here, that the peace is directly and solely due to the President's personal intervention.

You will have heard the news from Paris. The French are still dreadfully nervous about the probable fall of their alliance, and of Germany's taking their place. Germany is quite willing that France should be admitted as third to a partnership of the two Emperors. She thinks, however, that in that case Paris will hold the same position as regards Germany, as Vienna or Rome did—that is, that Berlin will be the real capital and the French Foreign Office be directed from Potsdam. This is a sore thought. But the alternative (says the German press) is invasion. So opinion still hangs in the balance. What Witte will do when he gets back, nobody seems to know. The Foreign Office here undoubtedly desires to be independent of Germany and to resume the old place taken by Russia in Europe before the war. But a strong party want a closer understanding with Germany and a gradual cooling off of the French alliance; or a tripartite alliance in the Far East to frustrate the aims of the Anglo-Japanese alliance. The Liberal papers want an *entente* with France and England; the reactionary press is all for Germany. The Emperor is at present very much under the influence of the Kaiser's charm and the young Empress is said to be entirely for Germany and the preservation of autocracy. As you know, the Prussian traditions are purely autocratic, and the two courts of Prussia and Russia have always kept each other up to the true autocratic doctrine. Poland, the common danger, has been the bond of union. Two men holding the same wolf by the ear can't afford to quarrel.

There is no good prophecying, as from day to day the situation may alter; but at present it looks as if Germany were gaining influence both here and in France, although in both countries there is a great deal of jealousy and suspicion of

German aims.   In both there is more *fear*—real *fear* than either
would like to confess.

In England it is believed most confidently that Germany is
making an anti-English combination ; the Germans are convinced that the English are making or trying to make a combination of France, Russia and England in order to annihilate
Germany.   The two courts are on the worst terms, and at a
recent election a man with whom Bülow must have been in
personal relations spoke violently against England.   I suppose
there will soon be anti-German speeches in England—and so the
game goes on.   The practical aspect of the matter is that France
doesn't want to fight, as is clear : that Russia *can't* fight, which
is also clear : that England could probably damage German
trade for a time but could do no vital harm to Germany.   On
the other hand, Germany with her big army could do for England
at any time, the moment her fleet is as big as the English—
which is not yet ; and also she could certainly do for the French
or inflict a very severe blow on them—now.   Nor could Russia
interfere.   If, however, France is forced by fear of Germany to
enter into her orbit, *i.e.* to join in an attack on England, that
attack could be made with some hope of success, after some
years—or even now if the English fleet could be divided, part
of it being on a distant station, and a sudden attack delivered
with tremendous force.   It would, of course, be risky, and the
more immediate danger to England lies in the fact that Germany
could even now do pretty well what she wants in Europe
without asking England's leave.   I mean that it would be a
tremendously dangerous and costly proceeding for England to
make war on Germany.   This in itself is an excellent thing for
peace ; but suppose Germany wished to do certain things in
Europe which would entirely alter the balance of power—the
situation would be serious.   This is a terrible long history and
I oughtn't to write to you at such an awful length.

I am watching Miss Alice's progress with the greatest interest.
It is reported here by telegraph day by day.   What a time you
must have had at Oyster Bay during these days.[1]   Do you
remember the very quiet summer I passed there with you ?
How delightful it was !   Very different to this.   I wonder if it
will ever be quiet again.   I feel a selfish wish—an entirely
selfish wish—to see it quiet again some day or other—I wonder
if you do too.   Still, the world is not a place to be lazy in, and
you haven't married the man who wishes to be lazy."

[1] Miss Roosevelt had just come out.   During the peace negotiations
Roosevelt was at his home in Oyster Bay, to be near at hand.

" DEAR MRS. ROOSEVELT,

I saw Dillon who was very deeply impressed by his interviews with the President.   He gave me some interesting information which I daresay is known to you, but all the same it is worth while repeating, especially as we have some very good reasons from other sources for believing that his information is correct.   The story is now fairly complete and there can be no sort of doubt as to who was responsible for the peace.

When Meyer extracted the ultimatum from the Emperor, which as you know, was approved in writing (by the Emperor's orders) by Count Lamsdorff, he at once informed the President, who at once informed Witte.   But that communication from the President arrived before the official telegram from the Russian Foreign Office, if such was ever sent at all.   When it was received, Witte at once saw that there was a possibility of coming to an agreement, but he disbelieved in it himself.   On Monday night a telegram was received by Witte from the Emperor ordering him to ' finish the negotiations and come home at once.'   He and Rosen discussed this telegram at 8 the next morning, and Rosen maintained that Witte had no right to attend the conference at all that day, as the Emperor had ordered the negotiations to be broken off.   But Witte maintained that, as it was certain that the Japanese would refuse the terms offered, it was better that the odium of breaking off negotiations should rest with them.   So he went to the meeting, but in his hand he carried a formal ultimatum in the name of the Tsar and his people.   He prepared the communications to the press and a telegram to the Tsar, *in English*, stating the reason of the rupture of negotiations.   But to his intense astonishment the Japanese gave way.   I need not repeat the circumstances as you know them already.—What follows is absolutely secret, and please don't tell anyone but the President.   After the Japanese had agreed to the ultimatum, several days elapsed before the signature.   In the course of this interval tremendous pressure was brought to bear on the Czar, and as a result a telegram was sent to Witte, the only meaning of which could be that a pretext should be found for breaking off the negotiations on some subsidiary point, and so preventing the final signature.   Witte however, clearly saw that such a proceeding would forfeit definitely the sympathy of the President and the American people as well as of the whole world, and went on in the face of his instructions, as in fact he had done throughout.

Several people whom I know have seen the Czar and the Empress in the last few days. They one and all say that the Emperor described himself as having been tricked into the peace. To one he said, ' If I had only known that the Japanese were willing to yield on the indemnity, I should never have consented to give half Saghalin.' The Empress also expressed bitter regret at the conclusion of peace. They both say that it was entirely Kouropatkin's fault that the Russian army was not victorious and that everything was ready for a crowning victory. They speak bitterly of all who had a hand in bringing on the peace which they say was a disgrace to Russia.

So you see that it is a fact beyond any question that the President single-handed effected the peace, against the wishes of the Japanese people and the Russian Government. Had Meyer not had his interview, the Emperor would never have consented to part with half Saghalin. Had the Emperor not made that concession, the Japanese would never have been able to agree to peace, and without the President's letters as to the effect on public opinion of a continuance of the war for the sake of an indemnity, and the fatuity of such a policy, it is extremely doubtful that the Japanese would ever have given in. Our information was quite definite. We were solemnly assured by the Japanese that they would not and could not yield on the question of the indemnity, and it seemed that all representations were absolutely useless. And what is now quite certain is that the Emperor from the very beginning was personally opposed to peace, and that it was the open and courageous language of the President that made it impossible for him to refuse to treat ; and, once the negotiations were begun, it was impossible for him to withdraw. But as it turned out, if the Japanese had delayed their answer one day, there would have been no peace at all. On what does the life of thousands of men so often depend !

You asked about Witte. I have not seen him since his return but I can tell you a good deal about him. When in America, he was inclined to make an agreement with England and America as part of the arrangement with Japan, and he sent to offer Hayashi in London an alliance with Japan as part of the price of peace. He added that he would have no objection to asking England to join. Hayashi gave an evasive answer. A friend of mine saw Witte the other day. He exclaimed against the Anglo-Japanese alliance[1] and said it was an insult to Russia. He said that under no circumstances could England now hope to come to an agreement with Russia. He was in favour of joint action with France and Germany, and, if possible, America,

---

[1] The new and extended Treaty, signed August 12, 1905.

in order to form a counter combination.   He spoke with intense gratitude to the Kaiser for his reception of him.   ' When I came to Cherbourg, I was put into the third class room of a fourth class hotel.   In Germany I was treated like a prince. Nothing could have been more charming than my reception by the Kaiser.' [1]   He pointed to the Kaiser's portrait on his mantelpiece with as much adoration as if it were an eikon.   He was asked if the Kaiser had spoken to him about England. He said, No, only about the necessity of bringing France and Germany together and the common danger which threatened Europe.   It was the Chancellor who had pointed out the immense dangers entailed by the Anglo-Japanese alliance.   He is now determined to use all his influence to bring about a *rapprochement* between France and Russia on the basis of Far Eastern affairs.   The French Ambassador is greatly alarmed and has postponed his leave.   If Russia insists on asking France to enter such a compact, it will be very difficult for France to refuse, and it will very materially increase the difficulties of the situation, as if she enters into an anti-English combination it must weaken the present *entente* with us, on which the equilibrium in Europe depends.   The French are also very nervous as to the attitude of the United States.   It is being said here that the U.S. are inclined to enter into a combination or an understanding hostile to England and Japan, which would make it even more difficult for the French to stand out.   The French will enter into no hostile combination against anyone, (Germany included) ; but an attack on England by Germany, or an attack on France by Germany, would, if successful, make untenable the position of the country not attacked.   We are therefore obliged to stand together in self-preservation.   It is most regrettable that both in England and in France, and in Germany too, people seem convinced that there will be soon an outbreak of war ;   each country believes that the other intends to attack her.   This is out of the question as far as England is concerned, and even more out of the question as far as France is concerned.   However, feeling in Germany seems to be that England does intend to attack her.   The King and Emperor have again had a row about the refusal of the Crown Prince to go to Windsor and there is a fine rumpus.   It is most regrettable.

This letter will be much too long but there is so much to say. We had hoped that we should have been able to get the Russians first, and other nations afterwards, to come to a general arrangement about Asia, which would have settled the Asiatic question

[1] He was received at Rominten and the general project of a Russo-Germo-French alliance was explained to him.

for a considerable time. The great difficulty for us has always been the fact that the Russian army was numerically larger than the British, and that the strategic railways built by Russia put her within striking distance of India. Now, we thought, by the insurance policy of an alliance with Japan we can confront Russia with such a display of force, of the Japanese and English army and navy, that no one in Russia would advocate the invasion of India; and that we could therefore come to an agreement, the more so as we have long ago repented of our advocacy of the unspeakable Turk. But this beautiful policy of peace is all out of the question for some time to come, and all that we can do here is patiently to try and remove the different causes of disagreement as they occur. This is rather a difficult matter as the Russians begin to demand everything as soon as they are offered one thing.

The unfortunate quarrel with Germany grows from bad to worse, and though I do not believe in war until the German navy is increased or until Germany has a strong naval ally, yet the indications are most threatening.

Witte has not yet been offered the Premiership but the Emperor told him he is thinking of making the offer. Some of his friends say he had better not accept. If he does accept, he will be regarded by the Liberals as the organ of autocracy and they will hate him. As he has already quarrelled with the Emperor and been turned out of office, he may well be so again; and he would be wise, say his friends, in not putting his faith in princes. But he will probably take office all the same, as the opportunity will not recur. If he does, it will be an excellent thing for the Germans and I suppose the English will howl. So perhaps will the French as they always suspected him of being German at heart."

ST. PETERSBURG,
Oct. 10, 1905.

" DEAR MRS. ROOSEVELT,

Lord Lansdowne writes that he is most grateful for the letter of September 1. He adds: ' I think we may assume that the letters to Kaneko did have the desired effect, or at any rate that they were a most potent factor in determining the Japs to give way. There were also probably others. Hayashi says that after all they could not be quite sure of winning the next battle, and that after their unbroken series of successes a reverse or an indecisive conflict might have seriously prejudiced their position. He also said that the latest levies had swept into the military net an immense proportion of youths belonging to the educated and business classes, and that a big butcher's bill might have had a very serious effect upon the position of the country.   There may have been other reasons which we can only guess at.   But the President may fairly be assigned the credit of having done a big thing, and I for one take off my hat to him.'

We are the gainers by this peace, as well as the world at large; for, as soon as peace was declared, the long protracted negotiations with France about Morocco came to a sudden end, to the immense relief of both France and England, as neither of them want to have a war forced on them, and as long as this unfortunate question is left open, a war is always possible. It is quite certain that France won't fight if she can possibly help it ; but the French are still very jumpy.   They think that the alternative is either to fight, with the extremely insufficient backing of an English army, or to yield and allow their foreign policy to be dictated to them from Berlin, which hasn't proved a good arrangement for Austria or Italy.   The English appear to think that they can improve the situation by howling against Germany.   Those who are most convinced of the danger are the least inclined to howl.   I don't myself believe that any country can go to war now-a-days without some perfectly overwhelming reason, and I think that it is no longer possible to force a war on another power which is perfectly pacific.

As to your friend Witte, he has been offered, or thinks he will be shortly, the position of Prime Minister.   He will appear to the country as the Emperor's man.   But the Liberal Party, as such, will refuse to accept him and will reject his overtures. So he will have an extremely stormy time between the Court which hates but uses him, and the parliamentarians who will have nothing to do with him at all.   He is foolish to take the job ; but he fears if he doesn't the chance may not recur.   His reputation is that of an able and energetic man, but he is of the angels who ' were not for God or God's enemies, but fought for themselves alone.'

I have just this moment had a letter from Tokio dated August 31.   ' I simply *can't* understand it (the peace).   The President's message had great effect on them, and the money became damned as filthy lucre.   Of that there is little doubt. But fancy sharing an island [1] with a convict establishment ! —and if they meant to drop out all these things, why didn't they get the full glory of their moderation and start very low ?   We never expected anything like it, but we do expect one thing, and that is that a few statesmen's lives are in danger of coming to an abrupt conclusion.'

[1] Saghalin.

So you see that perhaps your little Jap friends may be going back to their death, like Regulus, of whom we used to read. It is all part of the game.

Witte is still raging against England for her treaty with Japan—although there would have been no peace without the treaty. But he is so much engrossed in domestic affairs that he lets foreign affairs pretty well alone. But it is quite possible that we shall suddenly hear of a Russo-German declaration or understanding. I hardly believe it, as Russia wants badly to bring out a loan and France and England are powerful in the money market. How I pester you with politics ! But you are quite a politician now, aren't you, and so I treat you.

We are all to be killed on Saturday. This our servants firmly believe. I can't make out why. It appears that we are to be slain as a protest of the Russian people at the inadequate representation of the intelligent classes in the Duma. Finland is gradually getting full of Russian troops and the Chambers are not going to be called, so the taxes will all be illegal. However, what can two million people do against the Russian Empire ! The oil fields in Baku are giving us a good deal of trouble.[1] The English have lost four million dollars at least, probably much more and they say it is the fault of the Government. The Russian Government say that may be so ; but they don't intend to pay : there is no Russian law which provides for payment and they would have to pay too much if they once began paying. We are invited to prosecute the police. I am amused to think what a storm we made in Washington over the Lendinara hangings[2] and how the Italian fleet was coming. No one in Europe talks of sending a fleet to the Black Sea. You see the disadvantage of being reckoned a civilized country.

To-day's news from Moscow,[3] not published but rumoured in the streets is creating much remark. It is thought that the Liberals have altogether lost control of the extremists and that almost anything may happen. You never heard such talk. An official said to me, ' We bureaucrats know nothing of the country, but I don't believe it will last much longer as it is. Each day it gets worse, and we do nothing.' The restaurants, the hotels, etc., do a thriving business and the return of Madame Transfiguration to the ballet is noted as a great event.

[1] In the general disorder, Tartars at war with their Armenian neighbours had set fire to the oil wells.

[2] See above, p. iii.

[3] Strikes, collisions between working men and troops, and assassinations of police officers.

Kondratenko[1] arrived here yesterday. His old hat and his horse were with him, and his brother walked alone as chief mourner, though at first he was so much overwhelmed by the presence of six grand dukes that he couldn't be found. Neither Stoessel nor Alexeiev were present. 'Society' was also absent (except the grand dukes) and the Emperor was detained at Peterhof for police reasons. The crowd was large and very respectful. The papers say, 'We have one hero at any rate : he is dead.'"

ST. PETERSBURG,
Oct. 15, 1905.

" DEAR MRS. ROOSEVELT,
I congratulate you 1000 times on the signature [2] which puts a seal on a great achievement. Your doings are matters of great interest here. When the Anglo-Japanese agreement was first published, the attitude of the Government here was rather friendly than otherwise, although reserved. Our Ambassador asked the Foreign Minister, Lamsdorff, if he had any answer to give to the explanatory despatch which Lord Lansdowne sent with the Treaty,[3] pointing out that it had no aggressive character and only came into force if anyone attacked Japanese or English territory or took such action as could only be explained by a desire or by preparations to make an attack. Lamsdorff replied that he could give no answer of a definite character, but, speaking privately, he could say that the Treaty had had a very bad effect and had left an unpleasant impression upon the mind of the Emperor, and he would recommend our Ambassador, as a friend, not to press for an answer as it might be a disagreeable one, nor to open negotiations as to a definite treaty between England and Russia as to their interests in Asia.

All this somewhat disappointed us, and the French too, who had hoped to see a definite end put to the perpetual squabbles between England and Russia in Central Asia, which, among other things, made the French holdings in Russian stock a precarious investment. Besides which they did not like being offered the alternative of joining their ally Russia against their friend England, or of refusing to do so and seeing their place taken by Germany, which might have the effect of leaving them

[1] General Kondratenko, the hero of the defence of Port Arthur, was killed by a shell a few days before the place was surrendered. After peace was concluded, his remains, escorted by representatives of the garrison, were brought to St. Petersburg, receiving military honours along the whole route.

[2] The Treaty of Portsmouth between Russia and Japan was ratified on October 14.

[3] The Anglo-Japanese Treaty of August 1905.

alone in Europe. Nor did they like the idea of joining a continental coalition of which Germany would be the centre and hostility to England the probable object.

However, nothing new occurred for some time. The newspapers and the general public were not at all averse to the idea of a general and peaceful understanding with England, provided Russia gave away none of her established rights, and England gave adequate securities against an aggressive policy on the part of England and Japan. Japan is most anxious for peace in order to repair the ravages of war and would be most happy to see a stable state of things established in Central Asia. But yesterday the French Ambassador had an interview with Lamsdorff in which L. used very violent language against England and said that a continental coalition was the right and proper answer to the Anglo-Japanese alliance. England, he said, had insulted civilization in her South African War and now again in her East Asiatic alliance. ' Il faut mettre fin à tout ça.' He added that if France refused to join she would be left alone. The United States were in favour of this course, as the American Government was hostile to the Anglo-Japanese arrangement as they thought it a menace to their own interests.

The French Ambassador left for Paris last night in a state of perturbation. He is very anxious to know whether it is true that America is favourable to the proposed combination and, if so, in what manner the American Government has made it known here.

Witte is holding language in the same sense only even stronger. And there is no doubt whatever that the language of Witte and Lamsdorff is also the language of the Court.

If all this is true we are on the eve of new and surprising developments.

What do you think of the Delcassé ' revelations ' ? [1] The facts as regards ourselves are simple enough. We cannot allow France to be attacked without joining in and this is well-known. But we cannot offer military aid which could be of immediate service in repelling invasion, and therefore it is the interest of France not to invoke our aid, and our clear and evident duty not to encourage France to go to war—which indeed she is unwilling to do except on a vital question affecting her existence or her honour. In 1875 and 1887, when it was believed that an

---

[1] On Oct. 10 a statement appeared that, although M. Delcassé's retirement was demanded by the German Emperor, and this demand took effect in June, 1905, he had been already asked to retire by his own colleagues on April 22 of that year, and would have been forced to go but for a strong protest from King Edward.

invasion of France was probable, Russia and England (through their sovereigns) intervened, and it was then known to the German Government that an attack on France would ultimately lead to war with other countries besides France, simply because a further diminution of the power of France would upset the balance of power and render the remaining countries of Europe comparatively helpless against Germany. It is, of course, quite out of the question that either France, Germany, Russia, or England will really be guilty of unprovoked aggression against anyone, because it is incredible that any country would run the tremendous risks of war without an absolutely convincing case. After all, public opinion does exist and can't be outraged with impunity. Each country, however, is trying to prove (and no doubt believes) that other countries *do* intend an act of unprovoked aggression : and the result is this very disagreeable chorus of newspaper howls. America, which is serenely indifferent, can speak a quieting word and I sincerely hope that she will, as a continuance of the present irritation is intolerable."

The chapter may conclude with a message from Mr. Gerald Balfour, to whom Spring Rice had been writing in the same sense as he wrote to Mr. Roosevelt.

Oct. 25, 1905.

" My Dear Spring Rice,

Your last three letters have been most interesting. I have shown them all to the P.M. and one of them—that which relates the conversation between Witte and Dillon—to Lansdowne also.

Since you wrote the situation seems to have changed again— at least so I gather from a F.O. telegram from St. Petersburg. Has Witte himself abandoned all idea of a Russo-Franco-German combination to counterbalance that of England and Japan ? Or has he been over-ruled ? In either case what is the immediate cause ? I take it France has had a finger in the pie —another proof of the value of the *entente*.

I am glad you have written privately to the President as to the alleged readiness of America to fall in with an anti-English continental League. I do not believe a word of this, and feel sure he approves the Anglo-Japanese treaty. All the same, there are signs that the Emperor W.'s constant assiduities are not without their effect. We hear indirectly that the President is much annoyed with us for refusing to bring pressure to bear on the Japanese to moderate their terms, and contrasts our attitude very unfavourably with that of the Emperor W., who has managed to persuade him that it was *he* who brought the Czar to listen to reason.   In view of what you have told me about the Czar's real sentiments I am disposed to think that the Emperor W. has been playing a double game, not for the first time.

I wish to Heaven you were our representative at Washington.

Yours ever,

G. W. BALFOUR."